CRISIS AND CONFLICT IN NIGERIA

VOLUME II

JULY 1967–JANUARY 1970

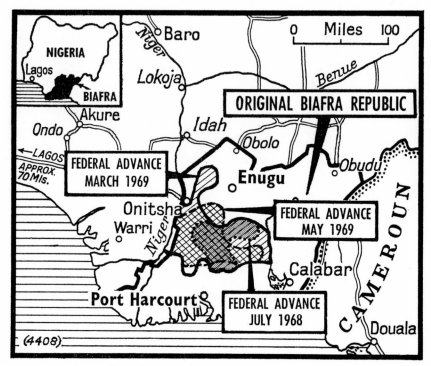

Reproduced by kind permission of *The Times*

CRISIS AND CONFLICT
IN NIGERIA

A Documentary Sourcebook 1966-1970

VOLUME II
JULY 1967–JANUARY 1970

A. H. M. KIRK-GREENE

Senior Research Fellow in African Studies
St. Antony's College, Oxford

LONDON
OXFORD UNIVERSITY PRESS
NEW YORK   IBADAN
1971

Oxford University Press, Ely House, London W.1

GLASGOW NEW YORK TORONTO MELBOURNE WELLINGTON
CAPE TOWN SALISBURY IBADAN NAIROBI DAR ES SALAAM LUSAKA ADDIS ABABA
BOMBAY CALCUTTA MADRAS KARACHI LAHORE DACCA
KUALA LUMPUR SINGAPORE HONG KONG TOKYO

SBN 0 19 215642 X

Printed in Great Britain
by R. & R. Clark Ltd., Edinburgh

PREFATORY NOTE

WITH the outbreak of hostilities on 6 July, the verifiability of the statements included in the documentation of these four years of crisis assumes added complexity. The commonplace that when war comes the first casualty is truth is here compounded by the flood of partisan literature whose quality is by no means commensurate with its quantity, by the total absence of official casualty figures, by the general reluctance to allow war correspondents to fulfil their conventional role, and by the sometimes Bond-like cloaked and covert moves from foreign diplomats, international organizations, oil companies, public relations agencies, roving emissaries, mercenaries, arms-dealers, and blockade-busters as well as by the controversial humanitarian and Church bodies that figured so prominently in one headlined context or another over these thirty months. All conjure up J. P. Clark's imagery in his 'Casualties 1966/68' of

> Caucuses at night, caucuses by day,
> With envoys, alien and local,
> Coming and going, in and out
> Of the strongroom. What briefs
> In their cases?

The detailed ebb and flow of the military campaign is barely touched on in this essentially politically-focused narrative. Those who are looking for a carefully chronicled record of the fighting will not find it here.

The materials on which the text is based and from which the documentation has been drawn are necessarily but a fraction of those collected in several years' active researching, and this in turn is but a proportion of that consulted. Much of its origin is identified in the textual footnotes and in the bibliographical notice included in this volume. There are three points on sources that need to be made in addition to the guidelines set out in the Preface to Volume I. Firstly, whereas the grave absence of Nigerian newspapers in British universities and research libraries for the period from January 1966 to July 1967 may endow citations from that primary source with an enhanced value in this country, their growing availability in the U.K. from August 1967 onwards has allowed Volume II to devote greater attention to the well-preserved, readily accessible, and often indexed files of the leading British newspapers and journals. In the event, the handling of the civil war by Fleet Street was to result in something like a subordinate war in its own right; but this is not a premiss to develop here. Secondly, while many of Ojukwu's speeches have subsequently been published in book form, they are reproduced here as they were publicized at the time. Thirdly, by and large, Biafran propaganda documentation in Nigerian libraries and archival repositories has not yet reached the scale of holdings in Europe and America, so that cross-references to such sources in this volume are additionally justified.

Because of the internationalizing scale of the civil war and of the escalating level of propaganda, above all in its forum of publicized peace talks and the disputatious context of humanitarian intervention, the amount of documentation available to the researcher working in the period covered by Volume II is considerably greater than that to hand for the period of Volume I. The selection of materials for inclusion has thus been a far harder task. The narrative, too, spread over a much longer time span, has perforce been a matter of closer compression. Once more, political speeches broadcast over the radio have retained a high degree of documentary importance, especially where they have not subsequently appeared in print (e.g., the Mid-West in August and September 1967). And once again, for a day-by-day diary of events, there are few better sources than the pages of *Africa Research Bulletin* and *West Africa*.

St. Antony's College
Oxford   A.H.M.K-G.

CONTENTS

WAR AND PEACE

1967 (JULY)

WITHIN seventy-two hours of war being declared on 6 July, the resources of Radio Nigeria's external programme were geared to issuing strong warnings against any African state daring to support Biafra and thus 'promoting its own future disintegration':[1]

A friend in need is a friend indeed. A more suitable adage can hardly be found for measuring the depth of the perfidy of some of Nigeria's so-called friends in the current situation. Foremost on the list of those who want Nigeria divided is the new clique led by Ojukwu. It is clear that without a group of misguided fellow travellers encouraging him, the rebel leader alone could not have singlehandedly embarked upon his hopeless gamble. . . . But justice will soon catch up with them. So much for these internal enemies of Nigeria.

But now external forces, some of them old friends of Nigeria, are not only deserting and playing the double game, some have even jumped on the bandwagon of the rebel Ojukwu. High on the list of such external enemies of Nigeria are some commercial interests. A number of them are within our gates. They were allowed to exploit the natural and other resources of the land for their benefit and that of all the peoples of Nigeria. . . . Like their new-found friend in Enugu, these enemies of a strong Nigerian economy have adopted some questionable actions lately. They have pleaded duress for their abuse of trust. But their move in paying royalties to Ojukwu and his gang was deliberately premature by at least 21 days. There has not been a scrap of evidence, physical or otherwise, that they have been forced to take such a step. . . . Nigeria, however, knows how the minds of these economic exploiters are working. . . .

Gradually, African nations have come to realize that where international economic conspiracy emerges, diplomatic intimidation follows. This pattern is repeating itself in the Nigerian crisis. . . .

The press also mounted an urgent internal campaign to explain to the people the righteousness of Lagos's decision to go to war.[2] It warned of the perilous lessons to be learned from involvement with the international currency of 'black gold' and emphasized the validity in international law of the challenged oil blockade.[3]

Military success came to the Federal troops rapidly enough to encourage General Gowon's definition of the fighting as 'a surgical police action and not civil war'.[4] Ogoja was captured on 12 July, and Nsukka fell to the Federal troops three days later. Its capture was accompanied by a spate of radio denials and counter-rebuttals[5] that were to set a bewildering precedent for the months ahead. Further bomb outrages in Lagos[6] resulted in the issuing of a decree carrying the death penalty by

[1] B.B.C. ME/2514/B3.
[2] *Morning Post*, 10 July 1967.
[3] *Morning Post*, 11 July 1967.
[4] In a television interview quoted in *Daily Times*, 13 July 1967.
[5] Radio Enugu, 20 July, and *New Nigerian*, 22 July 1967.
[6] *Daily Times*, 20 and 21 July 1967.

a firing squad for anyone found in unlawful possession of explosives[1]
and in the imposition of stricter security measures by the Inspector-
General of Police. In a broadcast he called for civilian co-operation:[2]

> May I also appeal to you to be extra vigilant during this period of emer-
> gency. Without necessarily reverting to witch-hunting, all peace-loving
> Nigerians must constantly be on the look-out for subversive elements,
> saboteurs and other agents of destruction no matter who they may be, and
> report their movements to the police. . . . Do not shelter, assist or protect
> any subversive elements. Report all suspicious persons, movements, activi-
> ties or strange objects to the nearest police station. Do not assist in spreading
> false and dangerous rumours. Report all pedlars of such rumours and all acts
> of intimidation and threats to the police at once.

Abroad, Chief Enahoro appealed to a press conference in London,
taking the theme of Nigeria's 'Struggle for Survival' [DOC 120].[3] At
home the radio crackled busily in the last half of July with uncompromising talks[4] and a whipping-up of public opinion along the lines
of:[5]

> Every inch of Biafran soil desecrated by the filthy invaders from Nigeria
> must act as another gallon of fuel to the spirit and determination of every
> Biafran citizen. The enemy has dealt you fatal injuries in the last one year.
> The same enemy is now rubbing salt into the wounds. It has never happened
> in history; it is a taboo in African tradition; it is a cruel travesty of natural
> justice; it is against the law of God. Here is a ruthless and implacable enemy
> who chased you out from the village square and your commonly owned
> stream. The enemy pursued you along all the by-paths and followed you right
> into your father's compound. The enemy wants to murder you right inside
> your father's courtyard and your mother's bedroom. It has never happened
> anywhere.
>
> Your family god is watching out from his shrine to give divine assistance
> to your resistance and fight. The skies will turn blood red, and God will in
> anger send armies of cherubims to your side. Your ancestral fathers will
> jump out of their graves to help you defend the honour of the family tree.
> Africans believe that no injured child is ever defeated in an unjust war
> carried into his own father's compound. An African proverb says: 'It is only
> when you say yes that your guardian angel says yes; if you say no, your
> guardian angel says no.' The guardian angel of every Biafran has shouted
> 'no' because every Biafran has said 'no' to the unprovoked aggression of a
> feudal vandal. Every Biafran should hold a quiet communion and conference
> with himself or herself and ask: How can I run away from my ancestral
> home? How can I run away from my father's compound? Where do I run
> to? . . . To these questions every Biafran answers: It has never happened,

---

[1] Gazetted on 28 July 1967.

[2] Broadcast over Lagos Radio, 20 July 1967 (B.B.C. ME/2523/B7).

[3] Cf. the Biafran skit on this press conference in *African Weekly Review*, vol. 1, no. 4,
pp. 8–9.

[4] e.g., 'The Inhumanity of the Rebel High Command', by Muhammed Sani and
'Nigeria's Final Rejection of Ibo Domination', by Edet Jackson.

[5] Broadcast by the Voice of Biafra, 16 July 1967 (B.B.C. ME/2519/B1).

and it will never happen. If it were to happen, every Biafran would for ever remain the laughing-stock of the world; if it were to happen, your ancestral fathers would curse you for life, and withdraw their blessings from you. . . .

The flames of freedom are inextinguishable. The same tide of history is shaping the spirit of every Biafran to greater determination and defiance in the face of an enemy who has chased us right into our family compound. After massacring 30,000 of our people, the enemy has dared to penetrate into our borders to drink more blood. Every Biafran is determined that every pint of blood drunk by these vandals, either now or before, has to be vomited out and repaid with 10 pints of the enemy's blood. This war will be a long, long tournament. It will go the full 15 rounds. It is only the first round that has ended.

Vivid visions of the war were described by Ojukwu [DOC 121] and Sir Francis Ibiam, who spoke of genocide.[1] Ejoor still advocated a policy of non-involvement and warned Ojukwu against violating the Mid-West's territory.[2] The British Government continued to come under attack from the radio stations of both combatants, but while Kaduna accused it of bolstering the Ojukwu régime, Enugu launched the first of many tirades of virulence and venom against the British High Commissioner in Lagos and his 'uncivilized utterances of a noble savage'.[3] Sir David Hunt's cold comfort may have been that he was soon joined in this competitive exercise in vilification by the fellow-martyrdom of the B.B.C.[4] Another stick for beating Britain with came to hand in the British Government's delayed decision—accompanied by the first of what was to become a series of three years' major parliamentary debates on the Nigerian war—not to forbid the export of arms already ordered, and paid for, by Lagos.[5] This permission was quickly followed by publicity given to the search for no less than forty charter aircraft to ferry the arms to Nigeria, leading to an outraged public advertisement by the activist Biafra Union of the United Kingdom [DOC 122]. In Britain, too, the Church committed itself on this issue [DOC 123]. The Nigerian High Commissioner in the U.K. challenged their externally 'inspired' call to refuse arms [DOC 124], and Biafra exploited the church leaders' hint of a religious struggle by accusing the Sudan of supplying arms as part of a Pan-Moslem jihad.[6] In the event, it was Russia that became the first major arms supplier,[7] a move that caused Biafra to accuse Lagos of selling out to Communism.[8] She kept up this

---

[1] Broadcast from Enugu, 21 July 1967.

[2] *International Herald Tribune*, 13 July 1967.

[3] Talk over Enugu Radio, 1 August 1967 (B.B.C. ME/2533/B6).

[4] In the event, the B.B.C. was to have a 'bad' war, incurring the odium of both Biafra and Nigeria.

[5] See *Financial Times*, 10 August 1967. The same newspaper carried an important survey of the arms position in its issue of 18 August 1967.

[6] Enugu Radio, quoted in B.B.C. ME/2556.

[7] For part of the war, the Russian MIG fighters bought by the Nigerian air force were piloted by Egyptians.

[8] *The Russians Now Hasten to Grab Nigeria* (Enugu, 1967).

B

allegation throughout the coming months as the U.S.S.R. progressively consolidated her new-found entry into the attractive Nigerian scene.[1]

The fighting hit the headlines again on 9 August when, after a sustained radio campaign of incitement of the Ika-Ibo people of the Mid-West to join their Ibo kin across the Niger in their struggle against an alleged Hausa/Fulani domination[2] (of which the authorities had been amply aware since at least May[3]), a partial insurrection took place. This mutiny of an Ibo-led section of the Mid-Western army made it easier for Biafran forces to swarm across the undefended Niger bridge at Asaba and, linking up with the mutineers, seize Benin. Brigadier Ejoor was lucky to escape: he was to give an interesting account of the Mid-West coup when he came out of hiding six weeks later.[4] The citizens of Benin learned by radio on the afternoon of 9 August that they had apparently been 'saved from the dark shadows of Fulani-Hausa domination'.[5] Anxious Lagos took a different interpretation of this invasion than did jubilant Enugu.[6] The next day the new Commander, Brigadier Victor Banjo, congratulated the people of the Mid-West on their *soi-disant* 'liberation':

Fellow citizens of Mid-Western Nigeria, this is Brigadier Victor Adebukunola Banjo, Commander of the Liberation Army from Biafra, speaking to you. Some time in the early hours of yesterday morning, some of you might have woken up to the sounds of some minor firing in the capital city of Benin as well as in some other areas of Mid-Western Nigeria. In consequence of this, some of you have fled your homes and places of work under the misunderstanding that Mid-Western Nigeria was in the process of being invaded by Northern troops. I am happy to reassure you that you have not been invaded by hostile troops. As some of you have found out within the last forty-eight hours, the soldiers amongst you are disciplined troops of the Liberation Army from Biafra, which I command, acting in close co-operation with troops of Mid-Western Nigeria to ensure that the territory of the Mid-West is adequately protected from invasion by Northern troops. This action

[1] e.g., *Nigeria: a communist beach-head in Africa* (Enugu, 1968); Biafran Radio talks on 'Russian Imperialist Manoeuvres,' 21 August 1967, and 'The Implications of Russian Revisionism in Nigeria', 9 and 27 November 1967.

[2] e.g., Biafran Radio talk quoted in B.B.C. ME/2539/B1, following up the propaganda directed at them as far back as September 1966 by Enugu E.N.B.S. reports of 'Mid-Western Ibos desire to join East' (B.B.C. ME/2277/B2).

[3] e.g., Radio Kaduna warning against Mid-Western Ibos as 'saboteurs', 19 May 1967: 'What are their objectives? Merely to win power and abuse it with reckless abundance. Paradoxically, these are the people who shout loudest that they are being pushed out of the Federation. They are those who have sworn on their part that Nigeria can only survive on their own terms or be destroyed. Sometimes one is tempted to ask why not let these people go and stew in their own juice, for what good riddance it would be.' (B.B.C. ME/2472/B1).

[4] Press conference of 25 September; *New Nigerian* and *Daily Sketch* (Ibadan), 26 September 1967.

[5] Special announcement over Benin Radio on 9 August 1967.

[6] Special announcement broadcast over Enugu Radio on the night of 9 August and on the following morning (B.B.C. ME/2540/B7).

is consistent with the desired intention of Biafra to assist in the liberation of the people of Nigeria from domination by the Fulani-Hausa feudal state.

I would also like to reassure the people of Mid-Western Nigeria that this is neither an invasion nor a violation of the integrity of the Mid-West. This action of the troops under my command, in close co-operation with their Mid-Western counterparts, is designed to insulate the people of the Mid-West from the coercive threats of Northern military presence in neighbouring areas and occasionally in the Mid-West, which has for long prevented the Mid-West from declaring its true stand in the Nigerian crisis of the last 18 months. It is my hope that by our presence, the people of the Mid-West will, in complete freedom from any restraint direct or implied, be able to seek their rejection of the fiction that peace in Nigeria is only possible under the conditions that the entire people of Nigeria should be dominated by the Fulani Hausa feudal clique. . . .[1]

For the next forty-eight hours the radio network poured out communiqués and orders from the Region's new military administration.[2]

By now Ojukwu was in a position to announce to the Biafrans the success of this first stage in his 'crusade of liberation' [DOC 125]. He even felt himself strong enough to deliver a formal note of protest to the U.K. High Commission's representative in Biafra against Britain's involvement in the war.[3] Ojukwu's choice of a Yoruba, Banjo (a radical and politically-minded officer, who had been detained for allegedly trying to kill Ironsi during the unsettled week of the army's coming to power in 1966), for this new Benin command was not without longer-range significance. In a press conference,[4] and then again in a very important broadcast, Banjo, besides throwing new light on his role in the January 1966 coup, outlined his plans for an interim administration [DOC 126]. Instrumental in its success would be an uprising in the uncertain West. Hence the series of appeals, such as the following to the Yoruba troops to defect and join in the fight against the alleged Northern-inspired aggression of Gowon's government, made by Banjo:

Brig. Banjo called on all Mid-Westerners to rise for the defence of their own survival. This also goes to all Yoruba people of the West and the Yoruba areas of the previous Northern Nigeria to rise in arms. They should remember their grandfathers who fought relentlessly to halt the march of the Northern hordes. The Yoruba people have at this period been humiliated enough. He said that today the territories of the Yoruba people have become occupied areas for the prosecution of a war in which they have refused to take part. The leaders of the Yoruba people are being forced under threat to their lives to identify themselves with a war they have refused to join.

Brig. Banjo continued: 'As an act of crowning insult, Yoruba troops have been shabbily thrown into this war against their will, merely to further commit them into a war in which they would rather fight on the Biafran side.

[1] Broadcast over Benin Radio on the evening of 10 August 1967 (B.B.C. ME/2541/B1).
[2] The fullest collection of all these announcements and directives is to be found in the B.B.C. monitored reports ME/2541 and 2542.
[3] Government of the Republic of Biafra, World Press Briefing Document No. 5.
[4] B.B.C. ME/2542/B2.

Henceforth, every Yoruba man, woman and child must rise to arms to fight on the side of the liberation army in order to restore the pride and integrity of our people.' Brig. Banjo appealed to all officers and soldiers of Yoruba origin to join his command with all their weapons as his army moves forward. All Yoruba troops who are at present too far away to join should stand still until the assistance of the liberation army reaches them and all Yoruba people should stand prepared to use every means possible to render Yorubaland untenable to Northern troops. 'This shame to our people,' he stated, 'must not be allowed to go unchallenged in our lifetime. The pride and integrity of our people must be restored and sustained.'[1]

Now that the tribal, and hence in Nigeria often political, line-up had changed, Lagos reacted to the Benin invasion by a declaration of 'total war' against the rebels, for this was the very depth of black treachery:

From now on, the forces of the Federal Military Government will reply with heavier blows to every act committed by the rebels and will pursue them in an all-out drive until the rebellion is completely stamped out. . . . No mercy will be shown to the rebels' clique and their collaborators anywhere. . . . Nigeria must be saved at all costs.[2]

This resolve was welcomed in a special announcement by Colonel Hassan Katsina in Kaduna.[3]

It was a moment for decision by the long-divisive, often indecisive Yoruba politicians. If they were to heed Biafra's insistent calls to throw in their lot with the Ibos in a common struggle to rid the South of supposed Northern domination, it would mean the immediate collapse of the government in Lagos. Could the acknowledged 'Leader of the Yorubas' justify his novel title? Chief Awolowo did not equivocate this time. Despite his earlier endorsement of 'secession for one, secession for all',[4] he now came unambiguously forward on 12 August and joined the West's Military Governor in calling on the Yoruba to ignore Biafran appeals for co-operation and to support the Federal Government.[5] Ojukwu was thus prevented from effecting by force of arms what the apparently ill-matched temperaments of the great political figures of 'Zik' and 'Awo' and their respective peoples had in their heyday failed to do by mutual reconciliation when an equal opportunity to coalesce

[1] Report of broadcast by Brigadier Banjo from Benin on 11 September 1967 (B.B.C. ME/2568/B1).

[2] Special statement issued in Lagos, 11 August 1967.

[3] Released on 11 August 1967. He spoke of 'a full-scale war on the rebels . . . to bring a quick end to Ojukwu's rebellion and crush him and his rebel soldiers and civilian advisers without further delay.'

[4] See Vol. I, p. 93. He himself referred to doubts about his stand, as reported by Lagos Radio on 12 August 1967 (B.B.C. ME/2543/B3).

[5] Text in *New Nigerian*, 14 August. Ibadan Radio carried important statements from these two leaders on 16 August 1967.

the Ibo and the Yoruba into one alliance had come their way:[1] the unification of the 'South' against the 'North' as an insurance (if nothing more) against any temptation for the North's constitutional majority to ride roughshod over parliamentary opposition. Had either union taken place, in 1959 or 1967, how different could have been the story of Nigeria. But now, at any rate, Lagos was saved from a sentence of death. Nigeria, too, was spared from immediate disintegration.

But was this just a postponement of the end? Regrouping in Benin, the Biafran forces headed for Lagos and the West: in the politically and psychologically motivated idiom of Radio Enugu, they continued their 'onward march to liberate Western Nigeria from Hausa-Fulani domination'. A dusk-to-dawn curfew was imposed in Ibadan, a Home Guard was raised in Lagos, the Western State was now invaded, and Northern towns like Okene and Lokoja had their first taste of war. Writing in the *New York Times*,[2] Albert Friendly likened the Nigerian war at this confused and critical stage to Matthew Arnold's

> darkling plain swept
> With confused alarms of struggle and flight,
> Where ignorant armies clash by night.

The battle of Ore, where a Biafran mobile column was held only 100 odd miles away from Lagos and a dashing canoe-carried commando all but penetrated the shorter creek approaches from Okitipupa, must rank as the most crucial engagement of the war. Those who like to speculate on the 'ifs' of military history may one day add the hypothesized reversal of the Mid-West blitzkrieg of August 1967 to their repertoire of what might have been had Ojukwu's forces not paused in Benin but thrust straight towards undefended Lagos a few days earlier than they did. For Biafra, this loss of momentum was to spell the loss of the campaign and, in the long run, of the war. For Lagos, it meant salvation. By the end of August, the thrust from Ore and Okitipupa had been contained and the Biafrans were retreating to Benin. Lagos could breathe again; and, consolidating its determination to wage an all-out war after the frightening threat posed by the Benin coup, it now set up on 26 August a War Cabinet.[3] The curious refusal of the Federal spokesman to give names or clarify the position of General Gowon therein ('The names of members will be released later.') unfortunately encouraged malicious speculation in the press about a split in the Federal leadership consequent on the setback suffered in the Mid-West.[4]

[1] See the mutually recriminatory statements issued by Azikiwe and Awolowo immediately after the formation of the N.P.C./N.C.N.C. coalition government in December 1959, summed up in the publicized premiss that 'The N.C.N.C. is as different to the A.G. as light is to darkness.'

[2] *New York Times*, 20 August 1967.

[3] Radio Lagos, 26 August 1967.

[4] *The Times*, 29 August 1967.

In Benin city itself, there had been a sudden change in command when Ojukwu, broadcasting direct to the people of the Mid-West,[1] appointed Major Okonkwo as Military Administrator in succession to Brigadier Banjo's 'mayfly week of power'.[2] He, in his turn, broadcast over Radio Benin (momentarily known as Radio Liberation) a long address to the people of the Mid-West on their new independence [DOC 127] and gave a press conference,[3] in both of which he castigated the 'brutality and vandalism' of the Hausa troops in violating the Region's neutrality. The Mid-West's next shock (her last, and her most agonizing shock, was to be the atrocities that accompanied the terrible tide of Biafran withdrawal before Nigerian reoccupation; so ironic considering her refusal to become a battleground by allowing either side to move troops through her territory) came, in one of those out-of-the-blue broadcasts now no surprise to the peoples of Nigeria, namely the dramatic proclamation by Major Okonkwo of the independent Republic of Benin on 20 September [DOC 128]. Okonkwo listed eight reasons for this abrupt step:

1. The Mid-West's earlier proposals for the preservation of Nigerian unity had all been frustrated.
2. The State's leaders of thought had favoured a loose form of association.
3. At least 10,000 Mid-Westerners had been 'slaughtered or maimed by the people of Northern Nigeria'.
4. No apology or compensation had been forthcoming from 'the perpetrators of this heinous misdeed'.
5. Neither Lagos nor Kaduna had honoured the agreement reached at Aburi.
6. The Federal and Northern governments had sought forcibly to impose on the Mid-West 'an unacceptable type of government'.
7. It was Lagos and the North that had declared war on the Mid-West as well as on Biafra.
8. The State's 'innocent citizens' had felt the brunt of the fighting.

In a would-be rationalization of these curious arguments, Okonkwo assured the people that the Oba of Benin had given him 'unequivocal support'.[4]

But it was a short-lived sovereignty, for within a matter of hours Federal troops, brilliantly led by Lt.-Col. Murtala Mohammed, had recaptured the city. Instructions were at once issued to the citizens:

All Mid-Westerners in Benin City should go about their normal business quietly and they should not harbour enemies. Anyone doing so will be treated as an enemy.

Looting on all fronts must stop immediately. Anyone found looting will be shot.

[1] Text in Biafran Office (New York) press release dated 21 August 1967.
[2] The phrase was used in *Sunday Times*, 20 August 1967.
[3] Reported by Benin Radio on 21 August 1967.
[4] Benin Radio report, 20 September 1967, quoted in *Africa Research Bulletin*, p. 865.

Civil servants and Corporation staff should return to work immediately.

Officers and men of the Nigerian Army should report at the Army head-quarters in Benin City immediately.

Posters were displayed ordering an end to looting:

The military Administrator of the Midwest State of Nigeria, Lt.-Col. S. O. Ogbemudia has ordered that all civilians in possession of Army uniforms and arms should return them to the nearest Police Station not later than today. After which any person found with army uniform, and or weapons will be shot.

No houses occupied by persons who have fled should be occupied. Persons found occupying them will be severely punished. ALL looted property should be deposited in the nearest Police Station at once. Houses will be searched for looted property.

ALL escaped prisoners should give themselves up or when captured will be severely dealt with.

and citizens were warned to:

Stop looting at once, anyone found looting will be shot.

Stop pointing to innocent Midwesterners and non-Mid-Westerners.

Report suspects to the police.

Molestation of anyone is an offence and will be dealt with as such.

Civil servants should report for duty forthwith.

Don't use soldiers to perform duties not authorized by a competent authority.

The officer commanding the relief column, Lt.-Col. Murtala Mohammed, made a broadcast [DOC 129] and Lt.-Col. Ogbemudia was appointed Administrator. He announced over the radio his policy for the State's recovery.[1] This turned out to be a slow, bitter process, and the evidence painstakingly collected by the Omo-Eboh Rebel Atrocity Committee set up by the Administrator is, despite its overflowing gruesomeness, only part of the story of the rape of the territory by rampageous soldiery from both armies. Scarred Benin, like Belgium a generation earlier, was to pay the appalling price for unrealistic neutrality.

In Biafra, too, the repercussions were to be swift and severe. Ojukwu found his Mid-West military plot now played on himself. As he had done earlier over the loss of Nsukka,[2] he blamed the fall of Benin on the

---

[1] Broadcast from Benin on 21 September 1967 (B.B.C. ME/2576/B3).

[2] Cf. the special broadcast by the Biafran Army P.R.O. and Commissar (*sic*) from Enugu on 15 July 1967 (B.B.C. ME/2518/B5): '. . . The monster head of internal reaction without our young nation has struck a blow seriously threatening the integrity of our young republic. There is strong evidence to show that traitors of Biafran origin, not necessarily from the so-called minority areas, have been revealing the inner structure of our basic military plans for prosecution of the war and that quite recently our plans for each battle have either been disclosed to the enemy or sabotaged by mysterious orders to our field commanders, supposedly given from the Military Headquarters in Enugu, addressed to our field commanders, and aimed at preventing our forward troops from launching certain attacks which would have completely liquidated enemy troops. Yesterday, a special attack which would have completely sealed the doom of enemy troops in the Nsukka sector of the northern front was ruthlessly sabotaged by a myster-

treachery of his own staff who had ordered the withdrawal of tactical headquarters to Agbor without his consent.[1] He had four persons executed by a firing squad for plotting to overthrow his government.[2] One of these, it may be noted, was Major Ifeajuna, who had been among the five Ibo officers responsible for the implementation of the January 1966 coup and who now joined Major Nzeogwu (killed in action within weeks of the declaration of war) as a casualty of the civil war.[3] Ojukwu's stern action brought no further challenge to his leadership, and the *Biafra Sun* greeted this 'Operation Ferret' with acclaim.[4]

Before this momentary split in the Biafran leadership, however, there had been important developments at the political level. Following up his statement of 21 August that recognition of Biafra's sovereignty was the sole prerequisite to peace,[5] presumably generated by his military triumph of the opening days of his strategically successful Benin campaign, Ojukwu released on 29 August a White Paper defining the possible areas of future association between Biafra and the rest of Nigeria [DOC 130]. Gowon, however, was now in a strong position. He was victorious in the Mid-West, he had been reassured of Britain's support by a renewed pledge from the High Commissioner, as well as by a personal letter from the Prime Minister, and he had an increasing flow of arms[6] (in particular the hope of launching a telling air-strike force with Russian MIG fighters). This, in addition to half of Biafra being occupied within six weeks, enabled Gowon in his dawn broadcast from Lagos on 2 September to counter Ojukwu's proposal and dictate the Federal Government's own three conditions for peace [DOC 131]. These included the refusal to accept Ojukwu as a negotiator. Although Biafra indirectly turned down the Nigerian offer by an attack on its contents and on Gowon himself over the radio, followed by Sir Francis Ibiam and thirty-seven other leaders publicly renouncing their British

---

ious order from the Army high command, obviously aimed at confusing our valiant commanders in the front. As a result of this wicked betrayal our valiant troops in that sector were treacherously exposed to the enemy flanks and had to be retreated as a temporary measure. The local collaborators of the Northern vandals and invaders are now either through ignorance or deliberate treachery jubilating over this obviously temporary situation. But the revolutionary wing of the Biafra Army backed by the entire working people will soon prove how hopelessly wrong they are. . . .' For the Lagos reply, see B.B.C. ME/2523/B7.

[1] 'All this happened without reference to me as the Commander-in-chief. . . . Without the unhealthy influences of these disloyal elements we would by now have been seeing the end of the war'—broadcast from Enugu, 21 September 1967 (B.B.C. ME/2576/B2).

[2] They were Victor Banjo and Emmanuel Ifeajuna from the army, and Samuel Agbam and John Alele, both civilians. See also Biafra Radio, 24 September 1967, and *West Africa* (1967), p. 1285.

[3] *New Nigerian*, 2 and 3 August and *Financial Times*, 2 August 1967. Christopher Okigbo's death in action was commented on in the *Guardian*, 4 October 1967.

[4] Editorial 'We shall vanquish,' *Biafra Sun*, 23 September 1967.

[5] Ojukwu's address to a delegation of staff from Aba hospital, 21 August 1967.

[6] *The Times*, 31 August; *West Africa* (1967), p. 1093.

honours,[1] the Biafran Chief Justice, Sir Louis Mbanefo, in London on his way to present the Biafran memorandum on joint services to the U.N., made a flexible enough statement to show that mediation was uppermost in the minds of many.[2] The peace offensive had now started in earnest.

Nor was it confined to internal negotiations. In England, Lord Brockway had, in his capacity as leader of the Movement for Colonial Freedom, written to all heads of African States urging on them the need for a goodwill mission to be quickly sent to Nigeria and Biafra. More important still, the fourth session of the O.A.U.'s assembly of heads of state opened in Kinshasa on 11 September. In view of Biafra's conspicuous failure to secure any recognition of its claim to sovereignty, it was imperative for her envoys to secure the opportunities for lobbying afforded by this meeting. Dr. Okpara, the former Premier of the Eastern Region, flew in from Kenya and, with much literature and many words-in-the-ear, made effective use of the corridors of influence outside the debating chamber, particularly swaying a number of the anglophone East and Central African leaders known to incline towards positive mediation.[3] A closely reasoned presentation of Biafra's case against Nigeria was privately circulated to member states represented at Kinshasa [DOC 132]. Publicly, parallels with Hitler's extermination of the Jews and modern Israel's defiance of the Arabs were drawn [DOC 133]. Despite Nigeria's initial objection to having the civil war debated,[4] an allusion by the leader of Nigeria's delegation in his post-script speech in condemnation of all secession allowed nine states to take the reference in the Emperor of Ethiopia's opening address[5] a step further and introduce a resolution which resulted in the appointment of a top-level mission of six heads of state[6] to go to Lagos and press for an end to the fighting [DOC 134]. Lagos courageously met the challenge of this potential diplomatic setback.[7] Admittedly, thanks to

---

[1] 'In the circumstances, I no longer wish to wear the garb of the British Knighthood. British fairplay and justice and the Englishman's word of honour, which Biafrans loved so much and cherished, have become meaningless to Biafrans. . . . Christian Britain has shamelessly let down Christian Biafra'—quoted in press release issued by the Special Representative of the Republic of Biafra, New York, 8 September 1967.

[2] In an exclusive interview with the *Financial Times* (11 September 1967) Sir Louis was quoted as saying that recognition of Biafra was not a cease-fire pre-condition. See also *West Africa* (1967), pp. 1125 and 1250.

[3] See, for instance, the Tanzanian press over this period and the editorial in the *Standard*, 8 October 1967; also *Financial Times*, 15 July 1967.

[4] *African Research Bulletin* (1967), p. 856. Cf. Dr. Arikpo's explanation (DOC 151).

[5] See *Ethiopian Herald*, 12 September 1967.

[6] These were the Emperor of Ethiopia, as Chairman of the Consultative Committee, the Presidents of Liberia, Niger, Cameroun, and Congo (Kinshasa), and the Chairman of the National Liberation Council of Ghana.

[7] *Sunday Times*, 24 September 1967. The *Guardian* (15 September) described the visit as being forced on Lagos against its will. Cervenka describes Gowon's agreement to receive the mission as 'reluctant'—*The Organisation of African Unity and Its Charter* (London, 1969), p. 197. For Nigeria's initial hesitation see also R. Nagel and R. Rathbone, 'The O.A.U. at Kinshasa', *World Today*, November 1967, p. 481.

consultation with the leader of the Nigerian delegation in Kinshasa and his telephoned clearance from General Gowon,[1] the wording of the resolution did endorse the Federal Government's point about this being an internal matter and an issue fought to prevent the contagious malady of secession; and so, despite reservations in the local press, Gowon agreed to meet the mission which he tried to see as one simply of solidarity.[2] However, despite the intention of the mission's leader, Emperor Haile Selassie, to arrive in Lagos on 21 September, it was two months and several postponements later (the Federal Government had to issue a denial that it was resorting to stalling tactics so as to enable it to present the mission with a military *fait accompli*,[3] and the press carried repeated reports of the deep anxiety caused by such post-ponements[4]) before a quorum of the O.A.U. mission—its value now debased in the opinion of both the Biafran and Nigerian information media—finally gathered in Lagos on 22 November. They were wel-comed by General Gowon, who firmly set the framework for the mission's discussions:

Despite the doubts expressed abroad about the value of your Mission, the Federal Military Government is convinced that our friends in Africa can be of assistance in our determination to maintain the integrity of Nigeria. We have, however, always insisted that our friends are only those who are firmly committed to the maintenance of the territorial integrity and unity of Nigeria. Our true friends are those who publicly and genuinely condemn the attempted secession by a few who have imposed their will on the former Eastern Region of Nigeria. The Kinshasa Resolution of the O.A.U. Summit on the Nigerian situation proves that all African States are true friends of Nigeria. I wish to take this opportunity to express formally our appreciation of the brotherly spirit of the O.A.U. Summit in recognizing the need for Nigeria to be preserved as one country.

It is in the interest of all Africa that Nigeria remains one political and economic entity. The O.A.U. has rightly seen our problem as a purely domes-tic affair and in accordance with the O.A.U. resolution, *your Mission is not here to mediate.*[5]

The Emperor replied shortly, advising the mission that 'as you are all familiar with the details of the present Nigerian crisis, we deem it un-necessary to delve into them.' He concluded:

We feel that the fratricidal war that is going on in the country will only weaken the sister State of Nigeria by depleting her valuable human and material resources and by denying her a climate of peace and co-operation which is so essential for nation building. In view of this we believe that a solution needs to be urgently sought—a solution which will accommodate the

---

[1] *West Africa* (1967), p. 1223.

[2] *International Herald Tribune*, 24 November 1967.

[3] Statement issued in Lagos on 21 October 1967.

[4] e.g., *New York Times*, 14 October, and *Sunday Times*, 15 October 1967.

[5] *Nigeria and the O.A.U. Mission* (Lagos, 1967), pp. 4-7 (italics added).

varying interests in Nigeria but specific enough to ensure the steady development of the Nigerian State.[1]

Without visiting Ojukwu (a prospect of dubious value, given Biafra's
pre-rejection of the O.A.U.'s competence,[2] the mission left the next day,
leaving the Federal Government to issue a brief and emollient communiqué [DOC 135]. (President Ahidjo was later to add a personal sidelight
in a radio interview.[3]) And that was that. Little came of General
Ankrah's 'hot line' to Ojukwu, and it was another eight months before
the O.A.U., whose support was so crucial to Nigeria, showed a sufficiently
strong hand to resume the peace initiative from non-African bodies;
by that time, its respect in Biafra was nil, and the military situation
was very different.

This consideration of the O.A.U.'s unproductive first move to repair
the injury done to Africa's standing in world opinion has taken us
beyond our calendar. Deliberately choosing the grim anniversary date
of 29 September, Ojukwu broadcast a midnight message to his people in
which he categorically ruled out the possibility of surrender [DOC 136]
and restated his case against Gowon who, twenty-four hours earlier had
appealed to 'all the people of the East-Central State' to overthrow their
leader: 'Throw Ojukwu out—lay down your arms, not your lives.'[4]
General Gowon, equally alert to the magic of anniversary dates, now
delivered a Nigeria in 'retrospect and prospect' broadcast on National
Day [DOC 137], praising the achievements of the Federal troops and
concluding that 'the sacrifices will be heavy, but the cause is worthy
and just'. Indeed, with Ogoja, Nsukka, and Bonny in Federal hands,
and Enugu about to fall, it did not seem too early to be thinking ahead
to the weighty problems of post-war reconciliation and reconstruction.[5]
Such was the theme around which Awolowo, in his capacity as Commissioner for Finance and Deputy Chairman of the Federal Executive
Council, built his seven-point programme for rehabilitation and the
consequent austerity measures now introduced in a broadcast to the
nation on 19 October [DOC 138]. His estimate of the war costing £50m.
to date was simultaneously doubled to £100m. and 50,000 lives since
January 1966 by the Federal Permanent Secretary to the Ministry of
Finance,[6] and then raised at the end of the year to £100m. in Biafra
alone by Dr. Okigbo, the former Nigerian Economic Adviser now in the
Biafran camp;[7] by mid-1968 it had risen to an estimated £300m. and
two million casualties.[8]

[1] ibid., pp. 8–10.
[2] There is room to reflect on the Biafran *volte-face* in its attitudes towards the O.A.U.
between April and October 1967.
[3] Interview reported in B.B.C. ME/2701/B2.
[4] Statement issued in Lagos, 28 September 1967.
[5] See special articles in *West Africa* (1967), pp. 1475–7 and 1509–11.
[6] *West Africa* (1967), p. 1317.
[7] In a paper read to a meeting of Commonwealth finance experts: *The Times*, 10
October 1967; *Financial Times*, 9 January 1968.   [8] *West Africa* (1968), p. 1317.

Abroad, the fall of Enugu on 4 October (despite typical contradictory news reports) was accompanied by reassuring statements from Nigeria's embassies on the future of the Ibos.[1] At a press conference in New York, Arikpo was able to promise no 'hunting down of the Ibos',[2] glossing over Enahoro's sterner hint that there was little future for the guilty Ibos and that 'it would be idle to pretend they could reoccupy abandoned positions—their posts had been filled and opportunities taken by local people'.[3] At home, this success in seizing Enugu—perhaps of even greater psychological than military value, for unlike the capture of most capital cities the fall of Enugu was not to lead to a rapid end to the war —was exploited to the full in one of the Federal Government's too rarely effective propaganda gestures, when it ferried scores of the foreign journalists to the 'ghost town'[4] and allowed them to interview officers and prisoners. It arranged special conferences, the hand-out of a new presentation of its case,[5] and a victory broadcast by the Commander of the impressive First Division, Colonel Mohammad Shuwa, in which he sought to disabuse the Ibos of the evil effects of Ojukwu's disproved propaganda lies.[6] Finally, the Federal Government released the facsimile record of top-secret minutes, seized in Enugu, by Biafran army commanders purporting to reveal plans for an Ojukwu-ruled Nigeria.[7] But by and large correspondents complained that they were not welcomed at the front and that they had to be content with campaign briefings from Federal spokesmen back in Lagos and undiscussable hand-outs at the Commissioner for Information's weekly press conferences.

Faced by the fall of his capital, Ojukwu summoned his Consultative Assembly to Umuahia on 11 October and reported to them on the state of Biafra after three months of war [DOC 139]. They responded with a further vote of confidence in his leadership, promoted him to the rank of full general in the People's Army of Biafra, and, in an allusion to Gowon's condition of refusing to accept Ojukwu as a negotiator for Biafra, 'strongly condemned and rejected any attempt from any quarter to impose any [other] leader on the people of Biafra'.[8] A public relations windfall came to Biafra in the press conferences and several articles by the influential scholar Dr. Conor Cruise O'Brien who, after a week's

[1] *New Nigerian*, 7 October 1967, commenting on a press conference held in London on 6 October and on a release from the Nigerian Embassy in Brussels. See also the remarks of the Chairman of the Federal Public Service Commission quoted in *Daily Times*, 10 October 1967: 'All will be on merit only.'

[2] *West Africa* (1967), p. 1289.

[3] Quoted in *Financial Times*, 18 October 1967.

[4] *The Times*, 23 October 1967.

[5] *The Struggle for One Nigeria.*

[6] B.B.C. ME/2602/B1.

[7] *Nigeria: the dream empire of a rebel?* (Lagos, 1967).

[8] The nine resolutions passed are contained in the release issued by the Biafran Representative's office in New York, dated 16 October 1967.

visit to Biafra, came out unequivocally on its side, emphasizing that while this was not another Katanga it was essential for the U.N. to arrange a cease-fire in order to prevent 'mass murder on a scale unparalleled as yet in Africa'.[1] Militarily, too, the fall of Calabar on 19 October after heavy fighting was offset by Biafra's morale-booster in the severe losses incurred by the Federal troops in their fruitless efforts to storm Onitsha from the river.

Less cause for Biafran rejoicing attached to the purchase of Soviet aircraft that was the tangible expression of the letter of personal good wishes from Kosygin to Gowon, in which he spoke of how: 'The Soviet people fully understand the desire of the Nigerian Federal government to preserve the unity and territorial integrity of the Nigerian state and to prevent the country from being dismembered,' and how 'We proceed from the fact that attempts to dismember the Federal Republic of Nigeria run counter to the national interests of the Nigerian people, and specifically in the conditions of the increased activity of the imperialist and colonialist forces on the African continent.'[2] Lagos, however, was equally vexed at the growing involvement of Portugal. Here Biafra had opened a mission, which was destined to prove highly effective in organizing a dangerous milk-run of arms supplies. General Gowon took the opportunity of an exclusive interview with an American journalist[3] to follow up his attack on the Portuguese role included in his speech on United Nations Day.[4]

With so much of Biafra now firmly in Federal hands, Gowon took the bold decision to appoint a civilian administrator for Enugu and the recaptured areas of the East-Central State. The man who courageously accepted the post on 28 October was Dr. Ukpabi Asika, one of the few Ibo lecturers who had not fled Ibadan University in late 1966. His subsequent explanation of his personal dilemma and decision—'you are in a real sense the Federal case'[5]—makes valuable reading, and contrasts with the concurrent pro-Biafran sentiments of other Ibo and non-Ibo intellectuals.[6] Asika appealed to Ibos to come out of hiding, and in the first of a number of notable public speeches he urged his fellow-countrymen to lay down their arms [DOC 140].

Mid-November was notable, too (discounting the speculation caused by the Emir of Kano's visit to London, for medical reasons, that he

---

[1] 'A Critical Analysis of the Nigerian Crisis', *Pan African Journal* (New York), 1, 1968. This is the same article as his 'A Condemned People', which appeared in *New York Times Review of Books*, 21 December 1967.

[2] *Soviet News*, 7 November 1967.

[3] Reproduced in *The Times*, 31 October 1967.

[4] B.B.C. ME/2607.

[5] 'Why I am a Federalist', *Insight* (Lagos), 22, 1968, pp. 7–14. See also his personal views set out in two interviews (with *Drum* and *Transition*) reprinted in the first volume of his speeches (Lagos, 1968), pp. 55–72.

[6] For example, the interviews with Chinua Achebe and with Peter Enahoro, 'Why I left Nigeria', in *Transition* (Kampala), 36, 1968.

might draw on his ambassadorial experience to act as a mediator),[1] for several public statements. One was a detailed and important reply by Dr. Azikiwe[2] to a report published in *The Times* of London[3] which had developed a suggestion, attributed to Enahoro in Nairobi, that the ex-President might still have a part to play in resolving the crisis and speculated on his capacity to provide the alternative Ibo leadership that General Gowon was insisting on. After answering points raised, Dr. Azikiwe went on to give an important description, within the limitations of his delicate position living in a Biafra at war, of his own feelings:

> ...It is crystal clear from all available evidence, judging from what is disseminated regularly in the Nigerian mass-media of information, that the Ibo is not wanted anywhere in Nigeria. It is only in Biafra that they and other Easterners have found a place of refuge. In fact, the word 'Ibo' has become anathema almost everywhere in Nigeria.
>
> The logical conclusion is to face the facts of contemporary Nigerian history and recognize the natural and inalienable right of the Ibo and fellow Easterners to self-determination and autonomous existence as a free sovereign and independent nation, christened the Republic of Biafra. That is the straightforward way to resolve honourably the problem of future peace in Nigeria. In which case, I should be happy to co-operate in any reasonable manner. To do otherwise, is to turn a blind eye to an unjustifiable pogrom and inexcusable genocide of eight million Ibo-speaking peoples with six million non-Ibo speaking peoples, contrary to the international convention on genocide and the internationally accepted standards of civilized life.

Mr. Udo-Affia, Biafran Commissioner for Health, with Dr. Dike also on the platform, was invited to put the Biafran case to a press conference in the House of Commons sponsored by the Movement for Colonial Freedom [DOC 141]. Enahoro held a press conference in Benin at which he reminded the Mid-West of the importance of accommodating its own Ibo peoples.[4] Lastly, Ojukwu recorded a long message urging international recognition of Biafra's right to separate existence. This was specially prepared for Biafra's active and articulate student supporters in the United States, where it was later converted into an item for fund raising and played on an amplifier at public 'support Biafra' rallies on a number of campuses.[5]

More importantly, General Gowon, taking advantage of his position as Visitor to the University of Ibadan to speak at the installation of the

---

[1] *Financial Times*, 1 November 1967.

[2] *The Times*, 16 November 1967. The letter was date-lined 'Zungeru Haven, Onitsha'. See also the disapproving editorial in *West African Pilot*, 2 December 1967, 'Let us reason together.'

[3] *The Times*, 17 October 1967: 'Problems of Future Peace in Nigeria: Lagos Looks to Dr. Azikiwe.'

[4] *West Africa* (1967), p. 1583; B.B.C. ME/2622/B6.

[5] For obvious reasons, the Michigan State University campus became the scene of a lot of factional in-fighting between Nigerians and Biafrans, students and staff alike. See the various issues of the M.S.U. *Collage*. Other campuses also had their ginger groups.

new Chancellor, launched a scathing attack on the machinations of the Ibo intellectuals at the University of Nsukka, abetted by those who had withdrawn from Ibadan to Nsukka, for plotting the East's secession there. Rubbing in this charge of secession hatched at Nsukka, Gowon went on angrily to declare: 'It is an unforgivable crime for a learned man with all his privileges and opportunities for a wider vision to limit his horizon to his personal aspiration and those of his own ethnic group and no more.'[1]

This speech may permit us to refer in passing to related statements on the role of the Nigerian intellectual in his alleged part as 'the tribalist *par excellence*'. These include the strictures of Dr. Dike when he castigated the Convocation assembly at Ibadan in July 1966 on how 'it must be said to our shame that the Nigerian intellectual, far from being an influence for national integration, is the greatest exploiter of parochial, clannish sentiment . . . educated advocates of tribal division and strife, and worshippers of tribal gods;'[2] of Sir Francis (or, as he now preferred, Dr. Akanu) Ibiam himself blaming the war on the intellectuals;[3] and of contributors to the monthly magazine of Nigeria's most respected national intellectual group, who were 'struck by the notoriety, by the opportunism, the parochialism and the negativity of their [intellectuals'] activity,'[4] which led them to conclude that 'their role in terms of consolidating national consciousness has been negative.'[5] When, in the middle of 1968, Biafran territory was rapidly overrun and yet no middle-class or upper-class people (the 'urbanized Ibo')[6] were among those who gave themselves up, arguments were again advanced that this was in truth a war waged by the Ibo intellectuals fearful of losing the economic rewards they expected from Nigerian society. To some, such remarks echoed the complaint heard during the American Civil War that it was a rich man's war but a poor man's fight.

The year ended with, as a close observer of the situation pointed out,[7] no substantial progress and little more than sporadic fighting since the Federals' initial victories had been dissipated by their spectacular setback in attempts to storm Onitsha across the river. Thus it is on the traditional Christmas messages from the various leaders that our attention is best focused for a break in the lull on the war-front. At Umuahia Dr. Ibiam, in reply to a welcoming address by Dr. Okpara, reminded the new Biafra Peoples' Mutual Understanding Association in a lengthy speech of their motto that 'United we stand—we are one in Biafra' and gave an unusual insight into inner Biafra:

[1] Foundation Day Address, University of Ibadan, 17 November 1967.
[2] Convocation Address, University of Ibadan, July 1966.
[3] B.B.C ME/2468.
[4] *Nigerian Opinion*, 1 December 1966, p. 141.
[5] ibid., January 1967, p. 152.
[6] *The Times*, 5 October 1968.
[7] Walter Schwarz, *Guardian*, 7 December 1967.

Before concluding this address, I would like to bring to your close attention certain observations which are disturbing and disagreeable to my way of thinking. This is a time for serious reflection and a period of great national emergency. Biafra is at war and you are all aware that war is a matter of life and death. As I move around, however, I see Biafrans indulging themselves in certain sports, like soccer (Association Football) and Lawn Tennis. In some areas Biafrans masquerade and fleet around, evidently in glee, and cause unpleasantness. In this connection, I get the unhappy impression that some Biafrans could [not] care less whether Biafra burns to ashes or not.[1] How can we go about rejoicing and making merry while our bitterest foe, Nigeria, is moving heaven and earth to exterminate us or make us slaves, and our generations of Biafrans to come? Because of the war, the normal and due process of education for the youths of Biafra has had to stop; but only temporarily, I hope. Our soldiers are valiantly facing the bullets of the enemy. Now and again there are air raids here and there and the enemy sends down lethal metal to do its worst. Enemy infiltrators are busy looking for loopholes to break our defences. Some evil and greedy Biafrans who have been bitten hard by the bug of inordinate ambition are underground seeking ways and means to collaborate with the enemy to help him strike at us and betray our fatherland for a mess of pottage and filthy lucre. And true Biafrans find time to make merry!

Fellow Biafrans, I ask you: Is this being vigilant? Is the war over and finished with a victory right here with us? Is it?[2]

In Dar es Salaam, Dr. Okpara reiterated to a news conference that 'we have reached a point of no return. . . . It is a question of win or perish.'[3] In a special order of the day, Ojukwu congratulated his troops, and also broadcast a 'we shall vanquish' message to the 'fourteen million virile and dynamic people of Biafra'. Like most charismatic leaders, he dreamed his visions aloud:

. . . The initiative for ending this war must come from those who unleashed it. Let those who started the war stop it. Born out of the gruesome murders and vandalism of yesterday, Biafra has come to stay as a historical reality. . . . I see the birth of a new Biafran society out of the carnage and wreckage of the war. I see a new breed of men and women, with new moral and spiritual values, building a new society—a renascent and strong Biafra. . . .[4]

From Enugu, Asika issued another appeal to his fellow-Ibos to renounce secession. Quoting Ojukwu with approval, and speaking as an Ibo, he agreed that 'the entire world has praised our courage' and added that 'with this sacrifice we have expiated our bitterness. We have proved, beyond all doubts, our valour and our manhood.' This point granted, he went on to ask:

[1] Visitors to wartime Lagos also questioned how serious the war effort was as they noted the merry-go-round of cocktail parties. The banning-of-drumming order assumed a farcical degree in the opinion of some.

[2] *United We Stand* (Enugu, 1968).

[3] Quoted in the *Nationalist* (Dar es Salaam), 12 December 1967.

[4] Biafra Office (London) Press Release No. 66/1967.

We fought to prove that we are equal to other Nigerians. To seek to secede is to do away with and confound our claim and our right to that equality. To secede, to run away, is to make nonsense of our fight and of our sacrifice. It is also equally bad, useless, and stupid to even now continue fighting. As I have said, as the world has known, we have made our point. No one ever again will dare to take the Ibos for granted. All Nigerians now know that this is so. What are we still fighting for? Are we fighting so that we can run away? Are we still fighting in order to show our bravery? Surely no, one fights to show something that all the world can see. Indeed the fight, now, is a hopeless one. Because in the present situation of things, as Ojukwu himself has said repeatedly, you are now 'fighting against overwhelming forces'. To continue such a fight is madness, not bravery. It is suicide, not courage. It is blindness, not wisdom. Are we fighting to show that we can die? Even a goat knows how to die.

A year ago our bitterness was coloured with despair. We despaired at the prospect of our ever achieving full equality, as Nigerians, so long as the former Northern Region remained as it was, so big, so powerful, so very different from us. It was because of this that in years past, we placed our faith and our hopes in a strong Central Government. Today, because of the very agonies of the past year, the former Northern Region has withered away. The Alkali courts have been abolished. In the six new States in the former Northern Region a new leadership has emerged: youthful and unafraid, progressive and nationalistic in outlook and as committed to and as anxious, as we used to be, for a strong Central Government. Thus this new year, we can truly say that we have achieved, even by indirection, the major goal of several generations of our leaders. That is, that we have achieved the institutional and constitutional conditions for the full equality of all Nigerians.[1]

It was General Gowon who dramatically caught the outside world's waning attention in the so-far 'forgotten war'. First, in his Christmas message he spelled out the Federal stand in terms for all to understand:

... The objectives of the current operation to crush the rebellion of Ojukwu and those whom he has blackmailed and misled are: firstly, that the territorial integrity of this promising country is preserved for now and for posterity; secondly, that we ensure equality of each and every ethnic group in this country and equal status and opportunity for all our citizens; thirdly, that we establish and strengthen the new administrative structure so that no State can dominate the country; fourthly, to create the internal condition of stability and freedom of movement for persons and goods necessary for the most rapid economic and social development of the country; and fifthly, to win the respect of the outside world for ourselves and for the African and his capacity to order his own affairs. These are the great goals for which we are fighting.

Our detractors have tried to confuse the issues. Some of them have suggested that we are fighting a religious war of Federal Muslims against Christian rebels. This is nonsense. All the world should know by now that more than sixty per cent of the officers and men of the Nigerian Armed Forces

---

[1] Speech made 31 December 1967.

C

are Christian and not Muslim. Others have suggested that if the rebels surrender the Ibos will be annihilated. This wicked lie has been exposed by the fact that Ibo-speaking parts of the Mid-West are fast recovering from the ravages of the rebel incursion. Nigerians there have resumed their normal life and are co-operating loyally with Federal Forces. Indeed, hundreds of Ibos are today serving in the Nigerian Army; many more are in the Nigerian police and on normal duties in Lagos and elsewhere. Civil servants and employees of commercial firms who are Ibos number scores of thousands in Lagos, the Western State, and elsewhere. The Administrator of Enugu has himself confirmed the absence of rancour and the eager welcome awaiting our compatriots from the East-Central State once the evil of secession is removed.

Let the malicious propaganda among our detractors cease, let the rebels stop pushing innocent Ibo youths and others in their thousands to a senseless and untimely death. I and my Government guarantee the Ibos a future of absolute equality with all the other ethnic groups in this country.

We must have the conditions for lasting peace. This is why the Federal Military Government reiterates its conditions for the cessation of military operations: first, the rebels must renounce secession; second, the rebel regime should accept the present administrative structure of a federal union of Nigeria comprising twelve States; third, a body of men should come forward from the East-Central State, willing to work for national reconciliation, peace, and reconstruction.

The existing constitution confers on the States the power and functions and the autonomy of the former regions. . . . Those functions can only be reversed in a forum in which all the twelve States are properly represented. . . . As soon as possible an independent revenue allocation commission will be established to review this. Each State will continue to have its own public service. The East-Central State is thus offered the same concrete deal as each of the other eleven States.

There is therefore no question of treating Ibos as second-class citizens, let alone exterminating them. It is now for the people of the East-Central State to save themselves from the falsehood and madness of the rebels. . . .[1]

Then, in a special New Year message to the Chairman of the Northern States Interim Administration and the field commanders on the war fronts, General Gowon set a date by which the war must be won: 'I am resolved this crisis won't continue for long. Let's all put our shoulders to the wheel and end it by 31 March 1968.'[2]

[1] Released in Lagos, 23 December 1967. See also B.B.C. ME/2654/B2.
[2] Official text quoted in *Morning Post*, 2 January 1968.

1968

IF 1967 had opened in a mood of optimism engendered by the news that the young colonels had agreed to get together round a table in Accra and discuss their differences, 1968 broke no less hopefully. The arrival in Lagos of two papal envoys, coinciding with the Pope's call for a truce over the public holiday, promised to be a fair augury. In the event, the whole calendar for 1968 was to be marked by a series of peace feelers, proposals, conferences, declarations, and disappointments. To see its efforts in perspective, it is necessary to touch on the initial and largely clandestine attempts at mediation made in the last months of 1967.

Leaving aside the failure of the O.A.U. Committee, the positive moves by Zambia[1] and East Africa,[2] and the frequent spelling-out of terms for a negotiated settlement by General Gowon and Colonel Ojukwu respectively (all of which have been referred to earlier), there remains the role of the Commonwealth Secretariat whose presence was to reappear so prominently in 1968. This skeleton body, representing the vehicle for what formal organization there was within the Commonwealth, was alerted to the sense of shame attaching to another intra-Commonwealth full-scale war like that of 1965 and of potential risibility stimulated by yet another breakdown of stable government in one of its African member states, apparently so prone to friability. As far back as April, before the fighting had broken out, there had been a reported move for mediation through the offices of Mr. A. L. Adu, its Deputy Secretary-General.[3] In July the Secretary-General himself, Mr. Arnold Smith, had flown to Lagos at Gowon's invitation[4] and thence gone on to Accra to discuss the crisis with General Ankrah, who in 1967 had figured conspicuously in attempts to bring the protagonists together. That nothing came of, or was even said about, these reconciliatory moves by the Secretariat at the time, becomes less surprising when one recalls how they were concerned with what Lagos (and, it was believed, official advisers to the British Government) had confidently and publicly assumed to be a 'surgical police action' of a mere week's duration. In October, and again in November, the Commonwealth Secretariat had, it seems, secretly and discreetly arranged for representatives of the two sides to 'coincide' in London as their roving emissaries pursued their round of the world's capitals; but, according to the Federal Government,[5] their three top-ranking men—colloquially referred to in London as 'the

---

[1] *Financial Times*, 14 June 1967.
[2] *Financial Times*, 15 August 1967.
[3] *Financial Times*, 7 April 1967.
[4] *Financial Times*, 7 July 1967.
[5] *The Only Way Out* (Lagos, 1968), p. 12; Arikpo press conference of 25 April 1968.

three musketeers' (Messrs. Ayida, Ahmed Joda, and Asiodu), whose recognized liberal outlook was enhanced by their easy ethnic fusion—waited in vain for Ojukwu's team of Messrs. Mojekwu and Dike to turn up.[1] At the same time there had been renewed speculation on Dr. Azikiwe's potential for leadership and accommodation.[2]

Now, in the new year, it was the turn of the Pope. His Holiness had sent an appeal for peace to both Gowon and Ojukwu on the eve of the war;[3] and when the text of his Christmas message to General Gowon[4] was subsequently released in Lagos,[5] it revealed something more positive than papal good wishes. The two envoys, Mgrs. Conway and Rochau, carried to Biafra a similar appeal to open negotiations.[6] Had not the Church's substantial spiritual empire in breakaway Biafra put His Holiness in a far more favourable position to urge reason than was possible in other Vatican appeals for peace such as those to the non-Catholic Middle East or to Vietnam? Gowon responded to this diplomatic approach by announcing in a brief but highly important statement to the press at Dodan Barracks that there was a group of Ibo leaders 'who I know to be reasonable and who believe in Nigeria':

...We have repeatedly stressed the willingness of the Federal Military Government to work with all Ibo leaders ready to work for reconciliation, unity, and national development. I seize this opportunity to emphasize our earnestness. Ibo leaders such as Dr. Nnamdi Azikiwe, Professor Eni Njoku, Professor Kenneth Dike, Dr. A. N. Ogbonna, Chief Z. C. Obi, Chief A. N. Abengowe, Mrs. Nzimiro, Mr. C. O. Chiedozie, Mr M. C. K. Ajuluchukwu, Sir Louis Mbanefo, Chief Osita Agwuna, Dr. B. U. Nzeribe, Justice A. N. Aniagolu, Dr. J. C. Mbanugo, Archbishop Arinze, Bishop Uzodike, Dr. Ukegbu, Dr. Pius Okigbo, Chief C. A. Abangwu and several Ibo Military Officers, who I know to be reasonable and who believe in one Nigeria, as well as other well-meaning Ibo leaders not mentioned. They are all acceptable to the Federal Military Government to discuss and negotiate how to restore peace and heal the Nation's wounds. We believe that together with such men who would discuss in good faith and keep agreements, effective arrangements could be negotiated to ensure that the territorial integrity of Nigeria is preserved while the safety and livelihood of all its citizens are guaranteed.

For understandable reasons we have pursued the military operations against the rebels with great caution. . . . The operations will be stepped up, but they will be halted as soon as there is a positive response to our appeal from leading personalities and the people in the East-Central State or from the rebels themselves. . . .[7]

---

[1] Dr. Arikpo's statement reported over Lagos Radio, 18 April 1968.

[2] e.g., *Sunday Times* (Lagos), 5 May 1968; *The Times*, 8 November 1967.

[3] *L'Osservatore Romano*, July 1967.   [4] *Le Monde*, 30 December 1967.

[5] *Morning Post*, 6 January 1968; B.B.C. ME/2660 and 2665.

[6] The story is best followed in the Dublin press of the time. See also *West Africa* (1968), p. 205.

[7] Press conference held in Lagos, 5 January 1968. It may be noted that Asika also 'named names', calling on his fellow-Ibos 'to speak up now and save our people from further pain'—broadcast of 28 November 1967.

This hope of splitting the Biafran leadership had been a principal tactic in Lagosian strategy ever since the emergence of a 'Quisling' (in the Biafran view) officer group in the aftermath of the Benin coup.[1] It had been implicit in the careful selection and off-the-record talks in Great Britain and the United States by the Federation's three roving envoys,[2] and had been confirmed in remarks made by Gowon to a U.N. representative at the end of November.[3] To the several general appeals to Ibos to shake off Ojukwu's leadership Gowon had now named those whom the Federal Government would accept as negotiators on the Biafran side. But Ojukwu was still specifically excluded, by name, under Gowon's three earlier conditions.[4] At the same time General Gowon again hinted that 31 March was the date by which, 'with the will to win, the backbone of Ojukwu's rebellion' might and must be broken:

... It is also essential that each of the twelve states should be performing all its functions by the first of April this year. These tasks cannot be accomplished until the rebellion in the Eastern States is finally crushed. The utmost priority will therefore be given to concluding the current operations. We intend to quicken the pace because further delay will be much more destructive of lives and property.[5]

As it happened, this was to be but the first of a number of over-optimistic and unrealized prophecies of a named date in 1968 and on into 1969 for the ending of the war.

Meanwhile, a telling blow was struck at the Biafran economy by the Federal Government cancelling all Nigerian currency notes and issuing differently coloured ones.[6] Within the month Ojukwu had irrepressibly introduced Biafra's own postage stamps and currency,[7] but Nigeria's move had nevertheless shrewdly negatived much of the prize of the two million pounds in old Nigerian notes seized in August 1967 from the Federal Treasury in Benin.[8] Biafra's ever-bubbling emotions were brought to boiling-point by the rumour that a thousand British soldiers destined for Nigeria had embarked on a troopship at Liverpool,[9] and in protest British business offices were burnt and looted in Port Harcourt, at an estimated cost of one million pounds.[10] Molehill that this mountain

---

[1] See pp. 11-12.

[2] e.g., answers to questions put to A. A. Ayida at Oxford in October 1967.

[3] *The Times*, 1 December 1967; *One Nigeria*, vol. iv, p. 50.

[4] See p. 12.   [5] Lagos press conference, 5 January 1968.

[6] *West Africa* (1968), pp. 25, 53, 81; B.B.C. ME/2562 and 2568.

[7] *The Times*, 30 January 1968, with photograph; *West Africa* (1968), p. 141; B.B.C. ME/2683, 2685, 2688. Towards the end of 1969 the Biafran public relations agency in Geneva sought to replenish its funds by offering sets of these currency notes and coins to collectors. Their eventual redemption after January 1970 proved a major economic headache for the Federal Central Bank and at the time of writing [March 1970] the Biafran notes are to all intents and purposes so much worthless paper.

[8] See *The Times*, 25 October 1967, and a useful account in *West Africa* (1968), p. 25.

[9] *Daily Telegraph*, 19 January; *The Times*, 30 January; *West Africa* (1968), p. 113; Radio Biafra, 16 January; B.B.C. ME/2673 and 2674. The report was dismissed by the British Commonwealth Office as 'a complete fabrication'.   [10] B.B.C. ME/2678.

was to be, a neurotic Biafra even submitted a formal protest through its Commissioner for Foreign Affairs to the United Nations:

Your Excellency, information has reached me that the British Government has despatched by sea, at the request of the Nigerian Military junta in Lagos, one thousand British troops to aid the Lagos clique in their invasion of Port Harcourt. These troops are reported to have left Liverpool on the 6th January, 1968, travelled via Cameroons so as to avoid publicity. . . . It is clear from the foregoing that the British Government, by participating directly with the Nigerian military clique in their genocidal war against Biafra has abandoned all pretence of neutrality and is guilty not only of interference in the conflict between Nigeria and Biafra, but of supporting genocide which is an offence under international law. Having encouraged and armed Nigerians in their mad war against Biafra and yet unable to crush Biafran will and resistance, the British are now engaged in a last desperate gamble to maintain and continue their economic exploitation of parts of Biafra by participating directly and actively in the war.

Your Excellency, the action of the British Government is not only an insult to the progressive and independent African peoples, but an outrage to the world conscience, which has already been shocked by the combined military and civilian massacres perpetrated against Biafrans by the Nigerian-British agents. I request Your Excellency to apprise your member-states of the grave situation which has now arisen in the Nigeria/Biafra war by this direct British intervention which is a threat to world peace. . . .[1]

These were, in fact, nothing more lethal than a party of schoolchildren departing on an educational cruise of the West African coast; but the damage was done, in more senses than one, and the incident underlined several points about the Biafran public relations media to those who wanted to note them and recall them in the months of wild allegations ahead.[2] That mercenaries, or at least foreign nationals, were being employed on a minor scale by both sides was substantiated from many sources: a dispatch by *Le Figaro* correspondent,[3] a press briefing in Lagos,[4] statements by and about notorious Congo mercenaries like Mike Hoare and Robert Denard,[5] and disclosures in questions raised in relevant House of Commons debates in January and February.[6]

Press conferences to publicize the claimed progress of the war on either side were held in London by Okigbo and Dike for Biafra,[7] by Tarka as Federal spokesman,[8] and in Washington by the three Federal Permanent Secretaries—the last-named coining a new term for the conflict, 'a modified civil war.'[9] The month ended with a mammoth

---

[1] Biafran Press Release, New York, No. 1/1968.

[2] In May 1968, the Hibernian football team visiting Nigeria were identified by the Voice of Biafra as a unit of paratroopers (B.B.C. ME/2778).

[3] Also quoted in *Daily Graphic*, 12 January 1968.

[4] *West Africa* (1968), p. 173.   [5] *The Times*, 1 December 1967.

[6] Hansard, 30 January 1968, cols. 1062–3, in which reference was made to a Major Wicks and Colonel Peters; *The Times*, editorial, 31 January 1968.

[7] *West Africa* (1968), p. 81.   [8] *West Africa* (1968), p. 113.

[9] Quoted in *West Africa* (1968), p. 116.

address on 27 January by Ojukwu to a joint session of the Eastern House of Chiefs and Consultative Assembly, this time meeting at Umuahia [DOC 142]. Much of it was devoted to attacks on the North's role in Gowon's allegedly exterminist policy, summarized in the assertion that 'They mean to keep Nigeria one in the service of Northern Nigeria.' Considerable publicity was arranged by Biafra, including the chartering of an aircraft by a Los Angeles firm acting for Biafra to carry newsmen and television teams to Ojukwu's elaborately staged press conference.[1] It drew scorn from the Federal Government, still firm in its refusal to treat with Ojukwu as a negotiator, as 'rebel lipservice to peace'.[2] At about the same time, a scurrilous Biafran charge sheet incorporating thirty-nine vicious and malicious accusations against the Federal Government was given circulation abroad [DOC 143].

February was to ring the bells of potential peace louder than ever before. First, Pope Paul sent a new message to General Gowon, by the hand of J. S. Tarka, who had had an audience of His Holiness.[3] Then the two Papal envoys, who had been active in Lagos in December, returned to Nigeria and proceeded to Biafra where, after delivering their message from the Pope, they toured widely.[4] Finally, there was the visit of Mr. Arnold Smith to Lagos twice during the month which, though officially in connection with the Commonwealth Education Conference due to open there on 26 February, gave rise to intensive speculation[5] about his role as potential mediator. Whether, as some saw it, the Commonwealth Secretary-General's visit of 12 February represented the culmination of his discreet efforts since the autumn, but was now sprung too early in the U.K. press, thereby embarrassing the Federal Government, or whether, as Mr. Smith assured journalists in Lagos, his visit was no more than it seemed, Nigeria's information media came out strongly against any Commonwealth peace keeping force patrolling the battle zone:[6]

What are the chances of Arnold Smith's success? The Commonwealth Secretary-General must have been firmly committed to a 'one-Nigeria' solution before the Federal Military Government allowed him to come to Lagos at all. If he puts forward a solution based on the creation of twelve States within the Nigerian Federation, the pirate radio will soon start abusing him just as it did in the case of the O.A.U. Heads of State. This is the dilemma that Arnold Smith faces—either to help the rebels to break up Nigeria, contrary to international opinion and the wishes of Commonwealth countries, or to accept a 'one Nigeria' solution and suffer a rebuff at the hands

[1] The questions and answers at the ensuing press conference were published in Biafra. They are revealing of the Biafran line.
[2] B.B.C. ME/2689.
[3] *West Africa* (1968), p. 173.
[4] B.B.C. ME/2692–8 and 2706.
[5] e.g., in the British press 10–13 February 1968.
[6] *New Nigerian*, 12 February 1968.

of the arrogant secessionist leader. . . . If Arnold Smith realizes that Ojukwu
will not give up unless he knows that he has been beaten hands down, only
then can the Commonwealth Secretary-General hope to succeed.

Another question is the idea of a Commonwealth Military force in the
context of 'one Nigeria'. The whole world accepts Nigeria as one country.
The whole world accepts the Federal Government as the only recognized
government in Nigeria. The Nigerian armed forces are therefore the only
legitimate military force in the country. It follows that a Commonwealth
military force cannot come to Nigeria to separate the combatants, that is the
legitimate Federal armed forces and the rebel forces. This is not a war between the countries, but a war to crush an ill-fated rebellion. The position is
crystal clear in international law: no foreign force can come to Nigeria
except at the invitation of the Federal Military Government.[1]

If negotiations did exist they were now so compromised as to be useless.
Lagos decided to issue a firm denial of any involvement with the
Secretary-General's plans and declared the advance to have been purely
at his own initiative.[2] Striking while the iron was hot, Ojukwu expressed a public welcome to any peace move that would lead to an
honourable settlement:

This war has many angles. In addition to the battlefront, it is also being
fought on the diplomatic front and on several other fronts. Those fighting on
these other fronts have done no less well than those on the battlefront. I
seize this opportunity to thank our representatives abroad who are so ably
presenting our case to the outside world. My sincere appreciation goes to a
number of international organizations, particularly the Vatican, the World
Council of Churches, and the world press, whose representatives have found
time to visit Biafra to see things for themselves and hear our own side of this
tragic story. Biafrans are a peace-loving people. The world is now beginning
to understand that all of us in Biafra have always believed that the only way
of resolving the Nigeria-Biafra conflict is by negotiation. Since this war began
I have always made it clear that we in Biafra are prepared to any time to
accept a ceasefire and negotiate an honourable peace. We did not start this
war. Ours is purely a fight in self-defence.

You will all have heard in the past few days of a number of moves reported
as being made by various international bodies to bring peace to this part of
the world. In accordance with our well-known stand on this crisis, we welcome
any peace initiative that will lead to an honourable settlement. Before this
war our people were slaughtered and driven away from other parts of what
was then the Federation of Nigeria. The 14,000,000 people of Biafra saw in
the establishment of this young republic the only reliable guarantee of
security both inside and outside Biafra. Any formula for an honourable
settlement of the present conflict must therefore take into account this basic
need of all Biafrans. References to constitutional guarantees of internal
security miss this point entirely, because they failed in the past. Any peace

---

[1] Talk over Lagos Radio (B.B.C. ME/2696/B9). See also D O C 145.

[2] *The Times, Guardian, New Nigerian*, 13 February 1968. See also letter from the
Nigerian Deputy High Commissioner in London to *The Times*, 19 February 1968.

plan which does not guarantee to Biafrans security inside and outside our borders will clearly be unacceptable to Biafrans. The challenge to those working on a peace plan is to find a formula which will enable Biafra to live peacefully, not in Nigeria, but with Nigeria.[1]

But Arnold Smith's cool rejection by Lagos was sufficient to prick the ballooning bubble of peace hopes for the time being. Deflation and dismay followed.[2]

In the meantime Biafra had been gathering more and more support among certain classes of Britons and Americans. They were influenced by a number of factors. These included letters in the press from prominent churchmen, reports of the bombing of the Mary Slessor hospital, apparently substantiated accounts of the wanton killing of civilians, but above all the signal superiority of Biafra's public relations agencies in Europe and the U.S.A. In England, this support now crystallized in the formation of a Britain-Biafra Association.[3] This organization was soon to play a markedly activist role by such snow-balling of nuisance tactics as publications, demonstrations, rallies,[4] a Save Biafra sleep-in, lobbying, and a mammoth teach-in.[5] Subsequent bipartisan organizations like the United Nigeria Group and Lord Brockway's Committee for Peace in Nigeria were to be a very different phenomenon; sadly they were far less effective in capturing the public imagination and convincing it of the Federal case.

On the home front, Dr. Asika moved his office to Enugu and broadcast another appeal to his fellow Ibos, calling on them to end this 'useless war'. He praised their spirit ('there is no shame in being beaten after a good fight—the shame lies in not recognizing defeat') and then warned them to lay down their arms before they reached the stage where 'the rule may well be "to the victor the spoils"':

At this stage very little need be said about the question of secession. Your leaders have been asked repeatedly to give up the idea, I have spoken often about the dangers involved, for all of us, if we do not give up the idea. Time is now running out. If your leaders keep up their present childishness of playing with words—one day it is 'Biafran sovereignty is not negotiable;' another day it is 'autonomy' they are talking about; yet another it is 'Aburi Agreements'; then it is 'confederation'; soon it will be something else—if they do not stop this foolishness it will soon be too late. At the rate things are going now if this childish debate continues you will have no secession to give up. You would have been compelled by military victory. Your leaders forget,

---

[1] Broadcast over Biafran Radio, 15 February 1968 (B.B.C. ME/2699/B3).
[2] *Financial Times*, 15 February 1968.
[3] *Africa Weekly Review*, 14 March 1968; *West Africa* (1968), p. 663. The *Sunday Telegraph* of 26 October 1969 tried to analyse the differences in the principal British pro-Biafran groups.
[4] See *Sunday Telegraph*, 4 July 1968; *The Times* and the *Guardian*, 30 September 1968.
[5] *West Africa* (1968), p. 831.

but you must remind them that in the conflict of ideas it is people who die. Does anyone still require to be told that the dead are already too many? Does any one still require to be told that the sacrifice is now enough? Secession was never possible, it has not been possible—in spite of the gallant bravery of thousands of young men dead, it is now hopelessly impossible. Your leaders knew, of course, from the beginning that secession was not actually possible. They believed in secession not as an end in itself but rather as a means towards the seizure of power—by frontal assault—over the rest of the country. To this end, the seizure of power in Nigeria, they planned and gambled on a grand scale. They failed. Not because they did not try. They actually tried very hard—it may be they were even unlucky in places. But there is no doubt as to their failure. Once they were driven out of Benin and the Mid-West the game was up and then was the time to give up. The only other alternative was to convert the means—secession—into the end and to seek to defend it. But they knew already however brave the defence, however clever the strategy, it was inevitable that they would have to keep retreating until there is no place to run. It is so, even now.

There is no Biafra, yet each day hundreds of men go to their deaths because of Biafra. No one has recognized Biafra because it does not exist.... Yet your Biafra, with more than 14 million people as they claim, has not been recognized by one single solitary state, even if only on a temporary basis. It is rather odd is it not? The answer is quite simply that there is no Biafra. A state has to exist before it can be recognized and Biafra does not exist. Now the rebellion is in rout—it has been beaten if yet unbowed. In war as in wrestling there are stages of defeat. A wrestler may be badly beaten and thrown down several times but he may ultimately deny defeat if his back does not touch the sand. No one in the Federal Military Government wants to force our backs to the sand—unless we keep up the fight, then it will and must happen. If we insist on this end, it may be too late to negotiate....[1]

Dr. Azikiwe emerged from three months' silence in a rousing speech to the men of the Biafran Tenth Battalion, quoting as a do-or-die peroration Claude McKay's celebrated call to sacrifice: 'If we must die let it not be like hogs,'[2] and prudently acknowledged Ojukwu's example of resistance: 'May I say that this is the main reason why our young Head of State undertook the mantle of leadership: we, the people of Biafra, gave him the mandate to lead us into victory.'

In the Mid-West, one of the areas most ravaged by the physical impact of the fighting and heir to its own problem of Ibo reintegration, the Governor found it necessary to address the reinstated civil servants on the need for living together, even while the Omo-Eboh Commission continued to receive evidence of guilty collaboration during the August occupation by the Biafran army. Lt.-Col. Ogbemudia spoke sternly:

... Not long ago, the Head of the Federal Military Government and Commander-in-Chief of the Armed Forces observed at the last convocation

---

[1] Federal Ministry of Information Press Release No. 669/68.
[2] Broadcast over Biafra Radio, 26 February 1968 (B.B.C. ME/2707/B7).

of the University of Ibadan that the troubles in the country have been fomented, nurtured, and encouraged by intellectuals in our universities. So too in our own community, civil servants can be an influence for good or evil. Unfortunately a number of civil servants have played an ignoble role and have by their disloyalty and treachery contributed to the creation of the present crisis of confidence in our State. This is a tragedy because civil servants, like the intellectuals, are in a position to exert a healthy influence. Instead of living and working for this ideal many of you have allowed yourselves to be led to treachery by your selfish attitude and stand in the Nigerian crisis. . . .[1]

Nor was there any falling away in the momentum of the peace offensive, only momentarily checked by the Lagos denial of Arnold Smith's assumed moves in February. A major break-through was achieved by the admission of Nigeria's Permanent Secretary for External Affairs to a press conference in London that the Federal Government was after all prepared to drop the third of its original conditions: it would no longer refuse to negotiate with Ojukwu as Biafra's spokesman.[2] The planned peace mission led by Dr. Martin Luther King, which had been welcomed by Biafra at the end of 1967,[3] was dissolved by his assassination.[4] Next, the World Council of Churches and the Roman Catholic Church, having sent separate missions to Nigeria and Ojukwu because of the fear that a single mission might be tainted in the eyes of one government if it had already visited the other (an appreciation that was to prove justified), disregarded abrasive warnings from Lagos and Kaduna radio stations[5] and issued an unprecedentedly joint, uncompromising call for a cessation of hostilities [DOC 144].

With General Gowon's cease-fire target of 31 March only a matter of days away, Federal spokesmen were at pains to hedge its apparent 'deadline' element with qualifications.[6] Happily for them, the fall of Onitsha on 22 March after six months of some of the hardest fighting of the war, resulting in perhaps 10,000 casualties,[7] provided a timely

---

[1] Address to the reinstated civil servants of Ika and Asaba Divisions delivered at Benin, 7 March 1968.

[2] Quoted in *West Africa* (1968), p. 298.

[3] B.B.C. ME/2627 and 2655.

[4] *The Times*, 12 March 1968; B.B.C. ME/2742. Radio Lagos carried a message of sympathy from General Gowon on 6 April and Radio Biafra one from Colonel Ojukwu on the following day; only the latter included a reference to his civil war peace mission.

[5] Titles of the radio talks on this episode included 'Christian Peacemakers' from Lagos (19 March), in which the observation was made that no church delegation had gone to argue with 'Ian Smith, the Rhodesian Outlaw'; and 'British Missionaries and Rebels' from Kaduna (21 March), in which it was asked 'What have these foreign speculators of doom done to stop the rebels from killing Christians in the Rivers and South-Eastern states?' See also *New Nigerian*, 22 March 1968, accusing the two church organizations of 'trying to drive a wedge between [Muslim and Christian] Nigerians.'

[6] e.g., Nigerian High Commission letter to *The Times*, 20 February 1968; Brigadier Hassan Katsina's remarks quoted by Radio Kaduna (B.B.C. ME/2699). The *Financial Times* carried a headline on 29 March: 'General Gowon Misses his Biafra Deadline.' Gowon himself referred to the way it had been 'misinterpreted' (see DOC 145).

[7] B.B.C. ME/2733.

boost to morale[1] and enabled at least one Nigerian diplomat publicly to equate this victory with the fulfilment of Gowon's prognostication:

Major-General Gowon, the Head of the Federal Military Government, in a message to the State Governors in January expressed the hope that by March 31 the Nigerian crisis would be coming to its end. *This wish has been realized.* I can disclose to you that the war in Nigeria has now receded enough to allow the setting up of Administrative machineries in all the twelve states.... Having just returned from Nigeria, I can tell you that the backbone of the rebellion is already broken. The only town of significance still held by the rebels is Port Harcourt. The town of course can fall any time. What remains then is hardly more than mopping up operations. . . .[2]

When the D-Day of 31 March came, invested with the same air of speculative excitement as its 1967 predecessor, both leaders made broadcasts to their people. Gowon spoke moderately of the dawn of a lasting peace and emphasized the birth of the new states [DOC 145]. Biafra's reaction to the ides of 31 March, drowning the would-be prophecy in utterances of sound and fury, was predictably scornful—and abusive.[3] Like Gowon, Ojukwu reviewed the progress of the war in a broadcast, much of it going over old ground. He concluded that:

It is now abundantly clear that Gowon will not willingly agree to the cessation of hostilities and the negotiation of a peaceful settlement. It is clear that he feels no concern for the misery and destruction which the continuation of the war is causing. It is also clear that Gowon will now want to buy more time, fit a new deadline and again step up the scale of his atrocities and achieve practically nothing at the end of it.[4]

Abroad, Biafran satirists, adding to their cruelly satirical 'Biafra-toons',[5] lampooned Gowon in a blasphemous version of the Beatitudes [DOC 146] which enjoyed circulation in some of those western circles where Biafra had made itself 'in' and Nigeria had regrettably chosen to leave itself 'out' through its lower-keyed propaganda campaign.

In Nigeria attention was easily diverted to an event which observers had already noticed[6] as threatening to siphon away some of the country's personal interest, even on occasion at the expense of energies more properly channelled into pursuing the war. This was the implementation of Decree 8 of 1967, for the physical setting up of the new States organization provided problems and opportunities in the redistribution of senior positions. Besides General Gowon's references in his speech of 31 March to the inauguration of his multi-state structure, which was destined to rank as an event as profound in Nigeria's administrative and

---

[1] Cf. editorial in the *New Nigerian*, 22 March 1968.

[2] Statement issued in London by the Nigerian High Commissioner, 29 March 1968 (italics added). See also DOC 145.

[3] B.B.C. ME/2733.

[4] Broadcast of 31 March 1968. The full text is in *Biafra Newsletter*, 12 April 1968, pp. 6–8.

[5] These were principally carried in *Biafra Newsletter*.

[6] *West Africa* (1968), pp. 361ff. Gowon called it 'national complacency' (DOC 175).

constitutional history as 1900, 1914, or 1954 had been, several of the new State Governors made inaugural policy speeches.[1] Lagos Radio carried an important talk on the political landmark, emphasizing the genuineness and likely panacea of the States system:

When on 27 May 1967, Maj-Gen. Yakubu Gowon declared that the Federation of Nigeria had been reorganized into twelve States, most Nigerians admittted that this was a courageous act of statesmanship which must rank with many of the great decisions in history. The alternative courses which were open to the C.-in-C. at that time were few and equally fraught with danger. A federation of four Regions, such as existed before 17 January 1966, was ruled out for two very important reasons. There was the problem of uneven distribution of political power resulting from a lop-sided structure of the Federation. As the Federation then stood, one Region or a combination of the old Northern Region with another Region, could rule the country as long as it wished, however unpolitical the policies they pursued. In the Northern and Eastern Regions, there were substantial minorities who, particularly in the East, were subjected to the political, educational, and economic tyranny of the dominant tribal group. If several million Ibos of the Central-Eastern State do not wish to be dominated or governed by others, it is difficult to see by what process of reasoning they should suppose that the 5,000,000 people of the South-Eastern and Rivers States should not opt for self-determination. . . .

Some cynics have asked whether new States could properly be created without a plebiscite. The history of Nigeria and that of many other countries provide the answer. The old Regions were established without a plebiscite. In particular, the former Eastern Nigeria was created without a plebiscite. The Mid-West, the youngest and the only one left just as it was, was created but confirmed by a plebiscite some months afterwards. Regarding the creation of the new States, it has been stated over and over that where communities, towns, or groups of villages are wrongly grouped, their claims will be examined by an independent state boundary commission, and where justified, there would be marginal boundary adjustment. The war to crush the rebellion in the three Eastern States has made it as yet impossible for the State Delimitation Commission to function. There is no gainsaying that there are a lot of benefits which the establishment of the new States will bring to Nigeria. The old question of imbalance in the political structure of the country has been resolved with the establishment of the twelve States.[2]

Significantly, in view of Biafra's suspicion of the whole operation as a bluff to mask the realities of 'the North's' alleged wish to subjugate 'the South' in perpetuity, the Northern students in the United Kingdom held a party to celebrate the birth of their six new States.[3]

In his speech of 31 March General Gowon had announced that his Government's 'next phase is to usher in lasting peace'.[4] April brought a flurry of renewed activity dedicated to negotiating a cease-fire.

[1] e.g., that by Kano, *Jawabin Kan Manufar Gwamnatin Jihar Kano*, 1 April 1968.
[2] Talk over Lagos Radio, 'The Establishment of the Twelve States', 1 April 1968.
[3] Notice in *West Africa* and author's personal invitation to propose the toast.
[4] See DOC 145.

Biafra's peace feelers were out in a number of capitals, notably those visited by Dr. Azikiwe in an African tour that took in Tanzania, Uganda, Zambia, Senegal, and Ivory Coast.[1] His mission was reasonably queried by Radio Lagos[2] but Nigeria's High Commissioner to Kenya and Uganda attacked his role as 'Ojukwu's messenger', regretting that the erstwhile advocate of Nigerian unity should now 'succumb to the whims of the young ambitious Ojukwu to dismember Nigeria'.[3] Although the E.N.B.S. had rejected Gowon's terms set forth in his speech of 31 March as offering a pistol-to-the-head choice of either talking peace or 'military suppression', Dr. Azikiwe told a press conference in Paris that Biafra was ready to negotiate with the Federal Government without conditions: if Lagos took the same view, 'It could lead to an end of hostilities' [DOC 147]. This was followed by a hint from Mr. Mbu who was reported as saying that Biafra would agree to a plebiscite provided it was conducted by an impartial observer.[4]

Such persistent lobbying both by Biafra's high-powered roving envoys and by her tireless man in Dar es Salaam[5] (who, like his Paris counterpart,[6] had defected from the Nigerian Foreign Service and converted into a most successful spokesman for the Biafran cause), met with a handsome pay-off when, on 13 April, Tanzania became the first country to grant official recognition to Biafra [DOC 148]. Because of the apparent haste[7] of the announcement read out at State House by Mr. Mgonja, Minister for Foreign Affairs, and because of the epoch-making nature of this decision—feared by many to be the opening of Africa's Pandora's Box[8]—it is imperative to note its essentially humanitarian rationale as subsequently expounded by Dr. Nyerere himself [DOC 149].

Amid a hail of press and radio abuse on the 'perfidy' of President Nyerere,[9] whose very skin, Nigerians were reminded,[10] had been saved by the dispatch of Nigerian troops in Tanzania's 'hour of need' after the mutiny of his own forces in 1964, Lagos issued a statement express-

---

[1] Biafra Radio reported that 'In a statement issued at the conclusion of his visit to five African Heads of State at the head of a diplomatic mission from Biafra, Dr. Azikiwe said the mission appealed to the Heads of State to use their good offices to urge upon Nigeria to stop its war against Biafra and accept Colonel Odumegwu Ojukwu's offer of a cease-fire and immediate resort to the conference table for peace talks without pre-conditions on either side. Dr. Azikiwe said the mission emphasized to the various African Heads of State that this peace formula is the only realistic way of restoring peace and stability to this part of Africa and speedily bringing to an end the wanton killing of innocent and defenceless civilians'—broadcast, 2 April 1968 (B.B.C. ME/2738/B2).

[2] Talk on 'Dr. Azikiwe and the Nigerian crisis' broadcast from Lagos on 4 April 1968 (B.B.C. ME/2740/B1).

[3] Quoted in *Uganda Argus*, 22 March 1968.   [4] *Financial Times*, 11 April 1968.

[5] Austin Okwu. See *Daily Telegraph*, 24 April 1968.

[6] Ralph Uwechue. He later again changed sides. See his *Reflections on the Nigerian Civil War* (London, 1969).   [7] *West Africa* (1968), p. 473.

[8] The metaphor was used by *Christian Science Monitor*, 16 April 1968.

[9] *West Africa* (1968), p. 482.

[10] *Daily Sketch*, 20 March; *Daily Times*, 14 April 1968.

I MIND MY OWN BUSINESS, BWANA.

Reproduced by kind permission of the *New Nigerian*

ing regret rather than surprise at this 'hostile act' and recalled her mission in Dar es Salaam.[1] Nigeria's mass-media came out in virulent condemnation of Nyerere, the Lagos radio including a savage talk in which responsibility for much blood was laid at Nyerere's door.[2] So excessive was the style of abuse, that those endowed with the longer look began to wonder how soon such personal wounds could be healed in any post-war return to the spirit of pan-African solidarity.[3]

In Biafra the break-through at the diplomatic level was received with understandable jubilation, even if it was tempered with regret that she had received butter instead of guns. Banner headlines in the *Daily Flash*—now, like most of Biafra's newspapers, grimly printed on cardboard paper or school exercise books[4]—hailed Nyerere as a 'sincere man of honour';[5] Dr. Azikiwe sent him a congratulatory message;[6] and radio programmes were interrupted to carry the special announcement from State House, Aba, where Major-General Effiong was officiating in Ojukwu's absence on what was described as 'a week's Lenten retreat'. The new national anthem, 'composed' by Dr. Azikiwe and set to the stirring music of *Finlandia*, was now heard on the radio for the first time.[7]

[1] Statement issued in Lagos on 13 April 1968.

[2] Lagos Radio, 14 April 1968 (B.B.C. ME/2746/B1).

[3] For a significant beginning of the post-war *détente*, see the conciliatory rationalization of their pro-Biafran stands by the Tanzanian and Zambian governments quoted in *West Africa* (1970), p. 246. An O.A.U.-induced accord of 'Let bygones be bygones' rather than any public recantation seems the likely outcome.

[4] See the description in *The Times*, 8 May 1968, and samples in author's possession.

[5] Quoted in the *Nationalist*, 16 April 1968.

[6] Broadcast by Radio Biafra, 16 April. See *Biafra Sun*, 16 and 17 April 1968.

[7] Subsequently, Dr. Azikiwe was to explain that 'my ode to Onitsha *Ado N'Idu*, "Land of the Rising Sun", was plagiarized and adapted to suit the purpose of the secessionists, who had not the decency to make adequate acknowledgement'—unpublished memorandum on the origins of the Nigerian civil war, December 1969.

A week later Ojukwu, who had returned from his vacation (rumour had also placed him in Tanzania[1]) and naturally looked on this recognition as but one of many more encouragements to come, gave an exclusive interview on 18 April to the three delegates, led by Mr. Geoffrey Birch, from the activist Britain-Biafra Association [DOC 150]. He also held another extravagantly staged press conference at Aba on 22 April,[2] at which he added to his routine allegations of Britain's intervention in the Nigerian war five terms that he would consider for peace:

1. That talks commence without further ado within forty-eight hours;
2. That talks should be either at ministerial or official level;
3. That talks should be at a venue mutually agreed in Africa;
4. That the talks should have joint chairmanship with each of the opposing camps nominating and seeking the good offices of one of the respected Heads of African States;
5. That the first item on the agenda of such a meeting should be an immediate cease-fire.

Ojukwu also claimed that it was only due to the U.K. High Commissioner prevailing on Gowon that caused the latter to amend the text of his speech of 1 August 1966[3] and excise the passage announcing the North's secession:

We in Biafra are convinced that the present crisis would have been resolved by the erstwhile Nigeria but for the intervention of the British Government. It was the British Government's intervention which prevented Northern Nigerians from seceding as they had planned after the 29th July coup. It was Sir Francis Cumming-Bruce, the former British High Commissioner in Nigeria, who prevailed upon Gowon to amend his already-recorded speech of secession. Nevertheless, when Gowon eventually made his first statement on 12th August he categorically—in deference to Northern opinion—stated that the basis of Nigerian unity did not exist. . . . It was the British Government that prevailed on Gowon not to implement the real wishes of the people, as this could complicate the British imperialist and economic interests and policies in this area. This was what happened after the meeting of the representatives of the military leaders on 9th August 1966 when it was agreed that military personnel should be separated to their regions of origin. This was what caused the Northern Nigerian delegation to the ad hoc constitutional conference of September 1966 to abandon its demand for a confederal arrangement, an arrangement which met with the general consensus of the delegation. This was what led to the dictatorial dismissal by Gowon in November 1966 of the ad hoc constitutional con-

---

[1] *The Times*, 19 April 1968.

[2] Biafra Radio, 24–5 April 1968 (B.B.C. ME/2753 and 2755).

[3] See Vol. I, p. 54. The charge, since repeated by different persons, has yet to be proved one way or the other. If true, it would seem to have undertones of wisdom, not treachery.

ference itself. This was what caused the abrogation by Gowon of the agreement reached among Nigerian military leaders at Aburi, Ghana, in January 1967.

This accusation of British involvement was followed up by a radio talk challengingly entitled 'The war is now with BRITAIN'.[1] The Aba press conference was the highlight of another imaginatively organized tour of Biafra at war for foreign correspondents, aware of overseas readers' insatiable appetite for the exploits of any apparent under-dog. Their reports and photographs subsequently filled the columns of the press.[2] They successfully raised Biafra's image in the minds of those who knew or wanted to know little beyond what they hurriedly read at the breakfast table or half-watched at supper time. Exceptionally, Lagos singled out *The Times* correspondent for special praise[3] but once again it failed to seek out the influential world press as an ally in promoting the legality of its own cause.

In the second half of April diplomatic events achieved that publicity so far singularly lacking on the military front. The Federal Government had astutely pre-empted the move for peace talks by a Biafra clearly encouraged through confident expectation of further international recognition; this, in less friendly eyes, was precisely the reason that Lagos suddenly seemed so anxious to take the initiative in peace talks.[4] Hard on the heels of the Tanzanian shock affair, and ahead of Ojukwu's five conditions of 22 April, Dr. Arikpo repeated at a press conference held in Lagos on 18 April that his Government was, 'despite the favourable military situation', nevertheless prepared to hold peace talks 'at any time and at any venue acceptable to both sides'.[5]

Dr. Arikpo now flew to London (generating cynical abuse from Biafra[6]) to meet Government and Commonwealth Secretariat officials on 25 April, three days after Biafra had announced its five-point basis for a peace settlement. Dr. Arikpo, after a personal call at 10 Downing Street, issued a statement declaring that there would be no pre-conditions [DOC 151]. On the day following, the Federal Government published in Lagos its proposed agenda for peace talks, comprising seven points [DOC 152]. Arikpo, still in London, added a supplementary statement at an informal press gathering at which he sought to 'clarify the Federal Government's position'. As a South-Eastern State man himself, he also spoke about the minority areas in Biafra: 'The reaction of the people in all the non-Ibo areas liberated by the Federal troops is clear and unmistakable: they do not want to form part of an Ibo

---

[1] Biafra Radio, 30 April 1968.
[2] e.g., the three special articles contributed to the *Scotsman* by one of the visiting journalists.   [3] B.B.C. ME/2759.
[4] *New York Times*, 10 April; *Observer*, 5 May 1968.
[5] Lagos Radio, 18 April 1968 (B.B.C. ME/2749/B1).
[6] 'They meet to promote genocide.' Text of talk over Biafra Radio, 26 April 1968 (B.B.C. ME/2756/B2).

D

empire.'[1] Then, flying back to Lagos, he made yet another statement on the unsettled venue of the peace talks to heads of diplomatic missions there, explaining why London had been preferred over an African capital [DOC 153].

Although Ojukwu insisted that a cease-fire must be the first item on any peace agenda,[2] he announced the formation of a top-level delegation ready to leave for Dakar at forty-eight hours' notice, and declared that he stood by his reply to the Commonwealth Secretary-General's letter of 24 April stating that he accepted peace talks without any pre-conditions.[3] Gowon now spelt out the Federal stand in a statement in Lagos:

... To the surprise of both the Commonwealth Secretariat and my Government, the rebels have suddenly and unilaterally dislocated all preliminary arrangements that have been made for peace talks. Their radio is now demanding that the peace talks must not be held in London to which they had agreed but in Africa and that they be allowed to nominate an African Head of State to be co-chairman at the talks. ... It is my belief that the rebels are not genuinely interested in peace talks but they merely say so for propaganda purposes.[4]

Relieved that his patient persistence had at last ensured the holding of talks about talks, the Commonwealth Secretary-General now concerned himself with bringing the two delegations together in London so that they might at least agree on the venue and agenda for the proposed peace conference.

The assumption of public disquiet in Britain and the need for the urgent start of negotiations to which Mr. Wilson was presumed to have drawn the attention of the Federal Government in a personal letter to General Gowon,[5] now received substantiation when, during a long debate on Nigeria in the upper House, Lord Brockway urged the Nigerian Government to accept the proposal reportedly made by Presidents Senghor and Nyerere[6] for an immediate cease-fire and a referendum in the non-Ibo areas of Biafra,[7] and again in the debate in the lower House on Britain's arms supplies.[8] A subsequent statement from Biafra listed a long schedule of sophisticated arms said to have been supplied to Nigeria by Britain, a claim that elicited the significant reply from Britain's Commonwealth Office that it was supplying only 'traditional armaments—the sort of items they were receiving before the Biafran secession'.[9] In Lagos, General Gowon—who had just

[1] 'The Nigerian Situation', address by Dr. Okoi Arikpo, London, 26 April 1968.
[2] See editorial, *New Nigerian*, 26 April 1968.   [3] Biafra Radio, 27 April 1968.
[4] Statement issued in Lagos on 2 May 1968 (B.B.C. ME/2761/B1).
[5] Cf. *Listener*, 2 May 1968.   [6] *West Africa* (1968), p. 529.
[7] *Debates*, House of Lords, 29 April 1968, cols. 948ff.
[8] See press round-up in *African Research Bulletin*, p. 1072.
[9] Quoted in the *Nationalist*, 10 May 1968. In January 1970, Walter Schwarz was to challenge this statement in a survey article on arms supplies in the *Guardian*, 29 January 1970.

approved the Federation's Budget for 1968–69[1]—sent a message to heads of African and Commonwealth countries informing them of his efforts to end the war.[2]

The groping progress towards the much discussed peace talks in London received a nasty jolt when the Biafran Commissioner for Information, Dr. Eke, suddenly made a public statement which roundly pre-judged the choice of venue. Rejecting London and Addis Ababa, he proposed Dakar or an East African site:

Since the O.A.U. is not acceptable, other reputable African international organizations like the O.C.A.M. and the East African Common Services Organization, for example, would be quite acceptable to Biafra. If Nigeria prefers O.C.A.M. then the talks should be held in Dakar, the headquarters of that organization. If on the other hand Nigeria wants the talks to be held under the auspices of the East African Common Services Organization, Arusha would be suitable for such peace talks.[3]

But London was on—just. Although the talks started there as scheduled on 6 May, it took two days for the Commonwealth Secretary to advance them from unilateral meetings at his private residence and the submission of proposals for him alone, to an across-the-table confrontation of both delegations.[4] These were led respectively by Nigeria's Commissioner for Information, Chief Anthony Enahoro, who had replaced the Commissioner for External Affairs, Dr. Arikpo, and by Sir Louis Mbanefo, Chief Justice of Biafra. Like the concurrent exploration of peace talks for Vietnam, the search for a mutually acceptable venue jumped giddily round world capitals before finally settling on Kampala. This in itself was seen as a minor triumph for Nigeria, since it effectively 'froze', to quote the Ugandan Minister of Foreign Affairs, President Obote's perceptible leaning towards recognizing Biafra.[5] Although Kampala was mutually agreed upon by 8 May, it took another week before the delegations were able to agree on both the agenda and the date. These were announced by the Commonwealth Secretariat on 15 May [DOC 154]. Yet even this, at the end of an eleven day meeting, failed to show accord over the question of chairmanship that had bedevilled the talks about talks.

[1] *Four Steps to National Stability* (Lagos, 1968) reproduces the full text of the budget speech delivered on 28 April 1968. Its rationale was fourfold: 'First, the civil war, imposed upon this country by a misguided and over ambitious clique of Nigerians supported by foreign adventurers, will be carried to its just and inevitable conclusion. Secondly, funds required for crushing the rebellion must be raised through a combination of fiscal and monetary policies which will leave the economy strong enough at the end of the war for the all important task of reconstruction and development. Thirdly, Nigeria's declining balance of payments position must be protected until new reserves can be built up again. Fourthly, the nation's new found and hitherto unsuspected reserves of confidence and self-reliance must be fully exploited and extended to all facets of the development of the nation's economy.'

[2] Lagos Radio, 2 May 1968.

[3] Biafra Radio, 6 May 1968.

[4] *West Africa* (1968), pp. 535ff.

[5] *Uganda Argus*, 21 May 1968.

Indeed, the Kampala meeting threatened to be killed before it was born, with Nigeria broadcasting uncompromising views to emphasize President Obote's ineligibility for the task of chairmanship because the war was an internal affair,[1] and somewhat provocatively congratulating herself for 'having displayed a rare kind of magnanimity' in taking part in the preliminary talks at all.[2] The Biafrans showed an equal lack of diplomatic sense or sophistication by obstinately reiterating their stand on procedural matters.[3] All the signs were clear that the road to peace would be very hard going; exactly how hard would only be fully revealed over the next twenty months.

Before the peace talks opened in Kampala on 23 May, several events took place on the home front. They followed a ding-dong pattern. Biafra threatened to close down all British firms that did not declare their intentions before 12 May regarding their assets in Biafra:[4]

. . . By the beginning of August, the withdrawal of the expatriate staff of these companies was virtually complete. Most of them made no arrangements for the continuance of their businesses or for the continued employment and payment of their Biafra staff. In most cases bank accounts of the companies used in running the businesses were frozen and the Biafran managers who undertook to look after the businesses are unable to operate them. The result is that in some cases the Biafran staff of the companies have had to be laid off. Some of the companies have not even bothered to correspond with their Biafran managers looking after their businesses or to find out the state of their assets. The action of most of these companies amounts to nothing less than abandonment of their businesses and assets. . . . The Government cannot continue indefinitely to protect these assets when the owners have for nearly one year shown no inclination to maintain and operate them. Accordingly, the Government has decided to give the following notice to all companies operating in Biafra.

Any company that has businesses and assets in Biafra for example, industries, workshops, batteries, buildings, machinery and so forth, should within 30 days from the date of this notice notify the Permanent Secretary of the Biafra Ministry of Commerce and Industry whether or not they still intend to maintain such assets or operate their businesses how they hope to do so and what arrangements they have made for the future operation of the businesses and for the payment of their staff. Failing that, the Government will, after the expiration of the 30 days, assume that the businesses and the assets have been abandoned and will assume responsibility to deal with the property in whatever manner it deems best in the national interest. . . .[5]

This threat was countered by a reassurance from the Federal Government, but both statements of intent prompted a number of anxious questions in the House of Commons throughout the May debates.

---

[1] Spokesmen in Lagos quoted by Kaduna Radio, 13 May 1968.
[2] Talk on Lagos Radio, 15 May 1968.
[3] Comment in *Uganda Argus*, 22 May 1968.
[4] *The Times*, 12 May 1968.
[5] Biafran Government statement issued on 13 April 1968.

Although Ojukwu's deadline passed without incident, he issued a decree on 31 May enabling his Government to take over businesses and assets of all foreign companies that had suspended their active interest in Biafra.[1] While the indisputable military setback to Biafra in the capture of Port Harcourt on 18–19 May by Colonel Adekunle's Third Marine Commando Division, following the fall of Abakaliki and Afikpo in April, made a forceful strengthening of her hand as Nigeria went to Kampala, the blow was immediately discounted in Biafran eyes by the uplifting announcement within less than twenty-four hours of Zambia's diplomatic recognition [DOC 155]. Recognition by Gabon came on 8 May:

. . . Federal groupings inherited from colonisation, or imposed by force, have not been shown from experience to be viable. . . . In the case of Nigeria, the Council of Ministers thinks that the military junta which overthrew the civilian Federal regime has imposed by force an unitary structure in total disregard of well-known rights of the federated states as recognised by the Constitution. . . .

Faced with this situation, the Government of Lagos reacted in the manner every one knows by perpetrating a real genocide with the aim of wiping out the State of Biafra and the Ibo people. Taking into account the atrocities committed with equipment and men supplied by foreign powers, the Government of Gabon considers that the Biafran drama has ceased to be an internal Nigerian problem and should force all African countries to take a stand without equivocation.

The Republic of Gabon could therefore not maintain a guilty indifference in the face of the pogrom organised against fourteen million Africans. . . . When one thinks that in an absolutely unequal fight, hundreds of thousands of innocent civilians, women, old men and children, are condemned to buy, with their lives, the right to existence to which all men are entitled, the Government and the people of Gabon could not without hypocrisy take refuge behind the principle of the so-called non-interference in the internal affairs of another country. . . .

The Government of Gabon deplores the human tragedy that has befallen the Ibo people and denounces the bloody and fratricidal war which is ravaging a portion of the African land. . . . The Government of Gabon expresses its very deep sympathy to the people of Biafra and decided as a result to recognise Biafra as an independent state that must enjoy its international sovereignty.[2]

This was followed a week later by the long expected Ivory Coast decision,[3] only a matter of time after President Houphouet-Boigny's press statements of 25 April and 9 May,[4] with their conclusion that 'as long as Biafra is fighting for its independence there can be no lasting

[1] *West Africa* (1968), p. 677.
[2] Markpress Overseas Division Press Release, 10 May 1968, quoting statements issued in Libreville on 8 May.
[3] Statement issued in Abidjan and broadcast over the radio on 15 May 1968.
[4] *West Africa* (1968), pp. 473 and 482; *Fraternité* (Abidjan), 26 April 1968.

peace in Nigeria.'[1] Here was the third African country to join Tanzania within a month. Furthermore, had not Senegal,[2] Tunisia,[3] and Uganda[4] shown disquieting signs of following suit by continued use of the 'right' vocabulary, and were not the Scandinavian countries known increasingly to incline towards Biafra?[5] The reception of this news by Lagos and Biafra's new headquarters of Aba was expectedly different.[6]

Yet militarily Ojukwu could not shrug off the severance, through Port Harcourt's loss, of this last physical communications link with the outside world. In the final analysis, this deprivation was to be a turning point in the rebels' resistance. Broadcasting on 19 May, Ojukwu declared that the conflict 'cannot be settled by victories won in the battlefield—the breach occurred in the hearts and minds of men', and he went on, in a passage elaborating his belief that 'the second phase of our struggle is about to begin', to promise sustained guerrilla warfare.[7] He then, as usual, summoned the Joint Consultative Committee to hear a similar report and a statement of the line to be taken at Kampala:

... Our stand and approach will be governed by the whole circumstances of our fate and position today. We were driven out of Nigeria after being slaughtered there. We are being slaughtered even in our homes in a most savage and genocidal war. We are fighting for our very survival and security, we want the right of peace and security within and outside Biafra.[8]

The Committee's resolution reaffirmed its faith in Ojukwu's leadership and specifically thanked the four African countries that had now recognized them.[9] It also endorsed Ojukwu's attitude towards the forthcoming peace talks, a point taken up by Radio Nigeria as 'very disheartening and discouraging'.[10]

On the very eve of the Kampala peace talks the foreign press were invited by a Nigeria now waking up to the deep influence of the fourth estate abroad, where danger of further diplomatic recognition appeared alarmingly real, to visit the areas of former Biafra now coming under the administration of Asika. He spoke to the journalists of his aspirations.[11] At the same time General Gowon, speaking in the wake of a

---

[1] There are two texts of this speech, delivered at the Ivory Coast Embassy in Paris on 9 May. The official translation is that given in *Réalités Ivoiriennes*, for a copy of which I acknowledge the help of the Ivory Coast Embassy. The Biafran office in London issued its own translation as a press release on 14 May.

[2] *West Africa* (1968), p. 341.

[3] *L'Action*, quoted in *African Research Bulletin*, p. 1073.

[4] See above, p. 39.

[5] *West Africa* (1968), p. 822.

[6] B.B.C. ME/2768/B2–B3 and *Africa Research Bulletin*, pp. 1073–4.

[7] Broadcast of 19 May 1968 (B.B.C. ME/2775/B2).

[8] Speech of 20 May 1968 (B.B.C. ME/2775/B3).

[9] Biafra Radio, 22 May 1968.

[10] Comment on Lagos and Kaduna Radio, 22 May 1968.

[11] A corrected version of the original hand-out of 21 May is given in *No Victors, No Vanquished* (Lagos, 1968).

signal campaign of military triumph, told a press conference in Lagos that the peace talks in Kampala would in no way halt the military operations.[1]

To the surprise of many the peace talks did manage to open in Kampala on 23 May; the date was almost exactly one year after Biafra's secession.[2] Both sides arrived with a mass of documentation for private distribution in the corridors and at the frequent press meetings. The Lagos literature was focused on—to select actual titles—'The Collapse of Ojukwu's Rebellion' and 'Prospects for Lasting Peace in Nigeria' while the Biafran line was that of 'Biafra Deserves Open World Support' and the 'inherent logic' of its secession; or again, Nigeria's case study of 'A Record of a Rebel' was balanced by Biafra's indictment of 'Nigerian Leadership: a Disgrace to Africa'. The war of words had begun to shift from radio virulence to printed vituperation.

In his opening address President Obote spoke of Nigeria's tragedy demanding the highest priority: 'Whether the war is just or unjust is no longer the question—the principal and over-riding demand is to bring it to an end.'[3] He was followed by the leaders of the two delegations, Chief Enahoro [DOC 156] and Sir Louis Mbanefo [DOC 157], both of whom, as might be expected at this first opportunity to debate *coram populo*, gave extended versions of the history of the crisis as well as outlining their respective opinions on the purpose of the peace talks. As such the speeches rank as important comparative expositions of the case.

Such mutual recrimination immediately engendered gloomy press comments of an inauspicious start, of an opening in anger.[4] Surely enough, the smooth passage of the first two items on the agenda agreed in London was followed by stormy weather caused through the disappearance of a confidential stenographer of the Federal delegation.[5] His decomposed body was discovered three weeks later and murder was established. There was also a Biafran demand for a Nigerian reply to their specific cease-fire proposals. Reputedly,[6] only Mr. Arnold Smith's skilled piloting as a go-between saved the day. Accusing Nigeria of 'delaying tactics' Sir Louis Mbanefo announced his decision to return home.[7] After separate press conferences and a further mediatory meeting with an anxious President Obote, the conference managed to resume. Enahoro now made a two hour statement on proposals for a cease-fire

[1] 21 May 1968 (B.B.C. ME/2777/B3).

[2] The ebb and flow of expectation at Kampala is best followed in *West Africa* for this period.

[3] See the Uganda press, 24 May 1968; B.B.C. ME/2780/B1, quoting Kampala Radio; and Markpress Biafran Overseas Division Press Release No. Gen. 134 for excerpts.

[4] *The Times*, 24 May 1968.

[5] Federal Ministry of Information Press Release No. 1002/1968. See also the Ugandan press of the period.

[6] *Sunday Times*, 26 May 1968.

[7] *Guardian*, 28 May 1968.

and put forward a Federal twelve-point programme [DOC 158].[1]
Mbanefo's comment (unlike Enahoro he gave no press briefing on 28
May[2]) was that this indicated no serious approach to a cease-fire but
rather a naked demand for surrender: Biafra was not prepared to
negotiate 'with a bayonet in our backs'.[3] Nigeria made good use of a
speech by the non-Ibo minority leader, Dr. Ikpeme from Calabar,
assailing the secessionist régime for its ill-treatment of the minorities
in the East who, he maintained, were loth to consider themselves as
part of Biafra.[4]

Despite corridor speculation of another deadlock, the delegates re-
assembled next day. They decided, however, to form a core group, consisting of only the delegation leaders and two advisers each, along with
Mr. Smith and Mr. Odaka, the Ugandan Foreign Minister nominated as
President Obote's non-participating observer.[5] A moratorium on press
statements meant that there was no news about these private meetings;[6]
indeed, for the next two days the delegates did not meet face to face,
even in private, so whatever the proposals gradually gelled with the
intermediary aid of Messrs. Smith and Odaka they never saw the light
of day.

At midday on 30 May Sir Louis called for an immediate plenary
meeting of the conference. It was held next morning, a day that broke
symbolically grey and gloomy. In what was described as a 'hard line,
apparently prepared'[7] speech, Sir Louis emphasized a point that he
made later to pressmen: his delegation saw no useful purpose in remaining in Kampala while more lives were daily lost in this gruesome
war and they would therefore be quitting the talks.[8] In his own press
conference Enahoro was reported to have made an unusually conciliatory reply off-the-cuff[9] but Mbanefo declined the opening door and
announced the withdrawal of the Biafran delegation:

. . . The Biafran delegation believe that there must be an immediate stop to
the mass destruction of life and property and the miseries of war. The
Biafran delegation are convinced that once peace is re-established between
Nigeria and Biafra, it would be possible, in an atmosphere of reduced
bitterness, to explore areas of co-operation with Nigeria. The Nigerian
delegation, despite protestations of their concern for peace and of their
sincerity, have generally treated the conference with levity, employing
tactics of delay to avoid a discussion on the important Biafran proposals for
the immediate cessation of hostilities. When finally the Nigerians produced
their cease-fire proposals, they turned out to be a programme of insulting
arrangements for a Biafran surrender. . . .

[1] No communiqué was issued but see the Lagos summary quoted in B.B.C. ME/2783/
B3, and *Uganda Argus*, 29 May 1968.
[2] *West Africa* (1968), p. 655.   [3] Quoted in *The Times*, 1 June 1968.
[4] *The Secessionist Regime and the non-Ibo Minorities in the East of Nigeria* (Lagos,
1968). For Enahoro's subsequent summary of Kampala, see DOC 171.
[5] *West Africa* (1968), p. 623.   [6] *West Africa* (1968), p. 655.
[7] ibid.   [8] *Africa Research Bulletin*, p. 1070.   [9] B.B.C. ME/2786.

It has become clear that the Nigerians do not want to talk peace. In these circumstances, the Biafran delegation do not see that any useful purpose can be served by their continued stay in Kampala while more lives are daily lost in this gruesome war, and we are, therefore, returning to Biafra.[1]

Enahoro blamed the breakdown on Biafra's tenacious stand on recognition as an independent country and above all on their 'fresh instructions from home' which had put the talks back to square one. In this assumption he was likely right, for Ojukwu's defiant 'State of the Nation' address on the eve of the first anniversary of Biafra's independence, broadcast on 30 May, was scarcely compatible with continued talks of peace [DOC 159]. Its emphasis on the sovereign state of Biafra, deriving strength from the hopes of further international recognition and moral support, left Sir Louis Mbanefo no room for manoeuvring. Ojukwu's grandiose peroration was an unmistakable call to fight on:

. . . Fellow countrymen and women, this Republic was born from tragic and unhappy circumstances. But it was born in faith and great expectations. For the past 12 months it has been put to the most severe and painful test. It has stood that test with increasing and unabashed faith. We have struggled together with unparalleled and indestructive resolve. We have been suffering and dying so that the young Republic may survive and play an honourable role in the comity of nations. May the blood of our youth, the tears of the bereaved, and the sweat of the suffering together water and foster for ever the luxuriant growth of all the principles, ideals and aspirations for which this Republic stands. With our faith fastened on God we shall not fail. Hail the Republic of Biafra!

No less unyielding, in a minor key, were the full-page black-bordered 'In Memoriam' notices published on 29 May in certain Ghana newspapers[2] mourning the 'thirty thousand civilians who were murdered during the pogrom of 1966 in Northern Nigeria'. In contrast, Gowon's own anniversary broadcast, to mark the creation of the twelve States on 27 May 1967,[3] included in its condemnation of 'Ojukwu and his clique' and of their 'so-called diplomatic recognition by dubious characters'—these had also come under fire as 'the tools of neo-colonialists and the instruments of disintegration' in his address on African Liberation Day[4]—a heartfelt appeal for a change of mind by the Ibo people: 'I honestly believe it is in the true interests of the Ibos to return to the fatherland.' Yet neither recrimination nor appeals could disguise the brutal fact that the Kampala peace talks had collapsed: the 'historic reconciliation Conference'[5] was not to be. The cause of any hawkish faction in the Lagos Cabinet had received the necessary justification.

---

[1] Markpress Release No. Gen. 155.

[2] e.g., *Ghanaian Times*, 29 May 1968, p. 5.

[3] Text issued in Lagos, 26 May 1968.

[4] Federal Ministry of Information Press Release No. 1000/1968.

[5] Enahoro's description (DOC 156). Gowon was later to describe 1967-70 as the 'war of reconciliation'.

It was about this time that the International Red Cross Committee had the first of its brushes with the Federal Government—clashes that were to increase in scale and tempo and spill over to all the humanitarian agencies, as they willy-nilly found themselves becoming so involved in the politics of starvation over the ensuing months, that by late 1969 there developed from the protracted procedural wranglings a sub-war in its own right.[1] The official reply by Lagos to the appeal by George Hoffmann of the I.C.R.C. to have the blockade lifted so as to allow the dispatch of two hundred tons of foodstuffs a day to Biafra referred to the acute sense of regret that the organization had compromised its integrity[2]—a charge exploited by Radio Nigeria in its interpretation of 'the new role of the International Red Cross in the Nigerian crisis'.[3]

This phase of intervention by international humanitarian agencies cannot be divorced from Biafra's much publicized accusations that General Gowon, incited by 'Hausa/Fulani monsters', was hell-bent on a policy of genocide for the allegedly hated Ibo race. Indeed, on 28 May the Federal Government rejected an I.C.R.C. protest on this very issue as related to the alleged bombing of civilian targets.[4] Into this argument now stepped the Catholic Church, whose Archbishop in London, Cardinal Heenan, asked in his Whit Sunday sermon at the ecumenical service held in Westminster Abbey, 'How many marchers and demonstrations have there been against the massacre in Biafra?' and went on to cite President Houphouet-Boigny's estimate that 'more people have been killed in the last ten months of the Biafran war than in three years in Vietnam. It is we British who have supplied many of the instruments of death.'[5] In a subsequent B.B.C. interview Cardinal Heenan disclosed that he had already exchanged letters with the Prime Minister on the Biafran war.[6]

Enahoro and his Radio Nigeria at once challenged the Cardinal's figure and started the long-running hare that the Vatican was supporting the rebel cause:

Nigerian Christians of all schools of thought are becoming sick and tired of ill-informed Christians and the partisan intervention of foreign church dignitaries in the Nigerian conflict. The most shocking of these performances was the recent pronouncement of Cardinal Heenan in his sermon at Westminster Abbey. This Cardinal is reported to have said, among other things, that the military operation to crush the rebellion in the East-Central state is a war of unbelievers against Christians. . . .

---

[1] The net result from the Federal viewpoint was, as we shall see, the post-war order to 'pack your bags and depart'.

[2] Lagos Radio report, 28 May 1968 (B.B.C. ME/2783/B4).

[3] Talk on Lagos Radio, 30 May 1968.

[4] Federal Ministry of Information Press Release No. 1011/1968.

[5] Text of sermon by courtesy of Cardinal Heenan's secretary. See also *Daily Telegraph*, 10 May 1968.

[6] Transcript by courtesy of the B.B.C., London.

Is the Cardinal motivated by the love of cheap publicity, a fighter of lost causes? The Cardinal spoke of genocidal war against the Ibos. Surely, the Irish priests who left Calabar, Uyo, Abak, Ikot Ekpene and Ogoja must have told him of the terrorism and atrocities committed by the Ibos against Nigerians in those areas for no reason other than that they desire autonomy for themselves within the Federation of Nigeria and oppose the secessionist attempt of the Ibo leaders. Yet, so far, neither the Cardinal nor his priests in these areas have raised a single voice in condemnation of these acts of brutality and inhumanity. . . . This callous indifference can be traced to the fact that the financial support of the church in the former Eastern Region of Nigeria, had its main source in the large contributions of Ibo political leaders, most of which came from large-scale misappropriation of public funds. . . .

Nigerian Christians, be they Protestants or Roman Catholics, must think deeply about the true meaning of the actions of foreign church dignitaries in the Nigerian conflict. Westminster Abbey, where Cardinal Heenan preached his sermon, is still a relic of communal conflict and the world wars waged by Britain and supported by the Church. The Pope blessed the hordes of Mussolini before they launched their brutal atack on the defenceless Abyssinians in 1935. The late Cardinal Spellman of New York was a notorious supporter of the Vietnam war. Therefore, whatever may be said to the contrary, neither the Church of England nor the Roman Catholic Church is a pacifist organization. Their opposition to the war in Nigeria can only derive from their support for the break-up of this country. . . .[1]

Yet nobody seemed to have noticed that it was neither President Houphouet-Boigny in May nor Cardinal Heenan in June who originated the casualty figures, but a member of the House of Lords who, in March, had quoted 60,000 dead in the first eight months of the war, 'twice as much as the three year figure in Vietnam'.[2] His lordship's source was an article in *The Times*, where the figure was, however, qualified by 'the number of dead is anyone's guess.'[3]

The term 'genocide' had been bandied about for some time by Biafran supporters and propagandists: in articles in the overseas *Biafran*

[1] Talk on 'Foreign Churches and the Nigerian conflicts', broadcast from Lagos on 12 and 13 June 1968 (B.B.C. ME/2795/B2). See also *Sunday Telegraph*, 9 and 16 June 1968.

[2] Quoted in *West Africa* (1968), p. 374.

[3] In an interview on B.B.C. television, 24 August 1968, the figure of 150,000 was attributed to Dr. Azikiwe. The total absence of casualty figures from either side throughout the war has only lent confusion to an issue already clouded by uncertainty over which figures to accept for the May, July, and September massacres of 1966. Visiting Nigeria again in the 'home-coming' months of January/February 1970, I was struck by how many ex-Biafrans of the officer class had happily survived. Hence the sour cocktail-party joke by Nigerians greeting their former brothers-in-arms: 'But was nobody killed in the war?' A large number of their former Nigerian colleagues and class-mates found it hard to list even two or three names of officers on either side who they *knew* for certain had been killed in the war. From this generalization, I except the acknowledged roll of regular officers murdered in January and July 1966 and those killed during the war but not in action, such as Joseph Akahan, Louis Chude-Sokei, Shittu Alao, D. Okafor, Nzeogwu, and Ifeajuna. To the extent that the real casualties, running into their hundreds of thousands, were among the other ranks, the civilians, and above all the Biafran children, it was, in social terms, very much a people's war.

BIAFRATOON

Newsletter,[1] the formation of BIAGEN (Biafran Committee for the Prevention of Genocide) in the United States, a petition by Mr. Mbu to the United Nations,[2] references by the papal envoy[3] and by President Senghor,[4] and of course in speeches by Ojukwu.[5] The charge had been as consistently denied by the Federal Government which, as far back as January 1967, had itself mentioned the concept in its condemnation of the false interpretation of the 'unfortunate pattern' of murder along tribal lines in the two 1966 coups as 'a kind of genocidal warfare'.[6] But it was from May 1968 onwards that the cry of genocide was noisily taken up outside Africa. Nor was its echo even partially stilled until a team of

---

[1] e.g., the issues of December 1967, and February 1968.

[2] *Focus on Biafra*, 18 December 1967, referring to the text of the appeal dated 13 December. This was followed up by a telegram from Mbu to U Thant on 24 February and another multi-page submission on alleged genocide, *Memorandum by the Government of the Republic of Biafra on the Deliberate and Continuous Contravention by Nigeria of the United Nations Charter Provisions on Human Rights and her Practice of Genocide*, submitted, complete with nine documented appendices, through the New York office of the Special Representative of Biafra in February 1968.

[3] B.B.C. ME/2748.   [4] *West Africa* (1968), p. 341.

[5] Notably that of 27 January 1968. See also D O C 63 (*Life* magazine).

[6] *Nigeria 1966*, p. 5.

international military observers, sent at the Federal Government's unique and exemplary invitation in October 1968, concluded that there was 'no evidence of any intent by the Federal troops to destroy the Ibo people or their property'.[1] Even then, as we shall see,[2] the genocide horse had not been flogged to death; though whether the Biafrans or outside do-gooders were the greater wielder of this particular whip remains a matter of opinion. Alarmed by the related mischievous references to the war having religious undertones of a Moslem jihad, the Christian Churches in Nigeria decided to take immediate action by sending a delegation to tour Europe and America[3] and explain the utter falsity of such a charge.[4] Regrettably for most, if anticipatedly by some, a little of this 'genocidal' bird-lime was enough to last for months and entrap not a few of the gullible in the snare.

After the Kampala collapse, expectedly interpreted at variance in Nigeria,[5] Biafra,[6] and East Africa,[7] the scene shifted to London, to where the leaders of both delegations now made their way. Chief Enahoro arrived from Lagos on 6 June to urge a growingly concerned Britain not to stop supplying arms, as the Netherlands and France had.[8] This plea he followed up in a personal letter [DOC 160] sent to all British M.P.s on the eve of their major debate on this issue,[9] ironically the first on a Nigerian subject since the debate on Enahoro's own *cause célèbre* five years before.[10]

In summary, despite the concerted counsel of editorials[11] urging an embargo on British arms as 'the best catalyst for African political rethinking', and the mounting public and parliamentary pressure to change British policy on the Nigerian civil war, the Government stood

[1] Press conference in Lagos, 3 October 1968, to mark the publication of the observer team's first report.

[2] e.g., article in *Spectator*, 24 December 1968.

[3] Statement issued in Lagos on 30 May 1968 and attached in full to Federal Ministry of Information Press Release No. 1020/1968.

[4] The delegation issued another, more important, statement in London in which it reviewed the historical roots of the conflict and discussed the efforts of the *ad hoc* Consultation of Christian Laity set up in Nigeria on 13 August 1966.

[5] The major Nigerian documentation includes the reviewing statement issued by the Federal Government in Lagos on 31 May; General Gowon's personal statement when he welcomed the Federal delegation back to Nigeria on 3 June; the talk over Lagos Radio on the breakdown in Kampala, delivered on 3 June (B.B.C. ME/2787/B2); and the Military Government's post-Kampala pamphlet, *Nigeria: Prospects for Lasting Peace* (Lagos, 1968).

[6] e.g., the talk over Biafran Radio on 3 June 1968 (B.B.C. ME/2787/B4), which makes an important comparative text with that given by Lagos on the same day (see above).

[7] See especially the Ugandan and Tanzanian press between 28 May and 3 June 1968.

[8] See *Africa Research Bulletin*, p. 1099.

[9] The Britain-Biafra Association also heavily lobbied M.P.s in memoranda dated 26 May, 30 June, and 15–16 July. Many, too, received a letter in support of the Federal cause from Sir Rex Niven, formerly Speaker of the Northern House of Assembly.

[10] Comment in *West Africa* (1968), p. 713. Cf. Enahoro's own reference to 'having myself a few years ago been a beneficiary of this [parliamentary] interest and concern'. (letter of 12 June 1968).

[11] e.g., *Guardian*, 12 June, and *The Times*, 13 June 1968.

firm in its belief that it could best retain some influence over Lagos through keeping in with rather than breaking with the Federal Government.[1] The volume of ensuing correspondence in the U.K. press and the number of columns in Hansard occupied by this debate afford some measure of its importance as an index of British public opinion, however well- or ill-informed on the crisis at this time. Both Hansard and the press were to provide a continuing source for the vast and emotional range of British attitudes on the war. These were to be laid bare in all their manifestations over the next eighteen months and, as it turned out, were by no means to cease with the immediate termination of hostilities. The traditional if irrational British conscience was stirred throughout June and July to an unusual pitch by appeals to one of its most sensitive areas: the suffering of children.[2]

Just before the parliamentary debate, Sir Louis Mbanefo was invited to meet Lord Shepherd, Minister of State at the Commonwealth Office. This was the first official contact with Biafra[3] and was enough for the *Spectator*, now to dedicate itself more and more deeply to the cause of what it saw as the Government's betrayal and 'Britain's shame',[4] to implore the British Government to recognize Ojukwu's régime. After the House of Commons debate, Sir Louis Mbanefo gave his critical view on its worth before returning to Biafra:

I should like to say that I was very impressed by the emergency debate which took place last Wednesday in the House of Commons. It was conducted in the true spirit of British justice, at least my memory of it prior to the insane war which has had the support of the British Government. The attitude of nearly all the members engaged in the debate could do a great deal towards repairing Britain's badly tarnished image in Biafra. Admittedly the debate did not result in an immediate decision to cease arming the Nigerians in their ruthless genocidal war against my country. However, there was certainly an improvement in the government's attitude, for as you know, talks are presently going on between myself and Lord Shepherd which is the first time that a member of the British Government has been delegated to do this. I came to London over a year ago, and even though various members of parliament did their very best to persuade the government to talk to me, the government declined to receive me, even unofficially. I do not wish at this stage to make a detailed analysis of the debate, which on the whole was favourable in the sense that [?had] the British government allowed it to come to a vote at that session there is absolutely no doubt that the decision would have been an immediate embargo on further arms shipments to Nigeria.

[1] Speech by the Foreign Secretary in the House of Commons, 12 June 1968.

[2] The documentation over this period is extensive. For an indication of its tone and volume, see the issues of *The Times*, 2, 9, and 12 July; the *Scotsman*, 8 July; the *Daily Telegraph*, 5 July; and *Life*, 12 July 1968.

[3] *The Times*, 11 June 1968.

[4] This was to be the sub-title of the book subsequently co-written with Suzanne Cronjé by Mr. Auberon Waugh, political correspondent of the *Spectator*.

There were certain statements made, however, which did not reflect the true position, and I feel it is advisable to refute them at this time, to keep the records straight. There have been too many misconceptions in the past, which perhaps explains why this unnecessary war has taken place, and certainly its continuation is the result of the lack of accurate information having been given to the public by the British Government. . . .[1]

Then on 20 June Mr. Wilson, seen by some as injecting a note of 'deliberate drama'[2] into the situation, sent Lord Shepherd post-haste to Lagos with a personal message to General Gowon, presumably in answer to one delivered by Chief Enahoro the previous week when the Prime Minister had taken the opportunity to warn him of Britain's anxiety over developments in Nigeria,[3] about to be so forcefully expressed in the House of Commons debate. Lord Shepherd's visit was warmly welcomed by Nigeria (and coldly by Biafra, which spoke of Britain's hypocrisy[4]) and the joint communiqué issued on his departure a few days later[5] elicited mixed comment from both radio systems.[6] This weak, official communiqué[7] was elaborated by a still ebullient Lord Shepherd in a more helpful speech to the House of Lords on his return:[8]

My Lords, with the permission of the House I should like to make a Statement on my recent visit to Nigeria. During my visit to Lagos I had three lengthy meetings with General Gowon and other members of the Federal Government. I was also able to pay visits to Calabar and Enugu to see for myself some of the problems of relief and rehabilitation, and to speak to civilians and prisoners of war in those areas. Unfortunately, because of weather conditions I was prevented from carrying out my plans to pay a similar visit to Port Harcourt, where we have substantial British interests.

In addition to delivering a letter to General Gowon from my right honourable friend the Prime Minister, I had four main aims in going to Lagos. First, I wished to follow up the contacts which I had already made separately with representatives of the two sides in London, with a view to securing a resumption of talks between them after the breakdown of the peace talks at Kampala. I had already been promised by the Biafran representative, Sir Louis Mbanefo,[9] that he would be prepared to assume direct informal talks in London provided that I was able to satisfy myself that the Federal Government were prepared for meaningful negotiations. In Lagos, General Gowon assured me that the Federal Government were ready to start direct talks on an informal

---

[1] Markpress Release No. Gen. 192.   [2] *Guardian*, 20 June 1968.

[3] See *The Times*, 12 June; the *Guardian*, 13 June; the *Financial Times*, 29 June 1968.

[4] Biafran spokesman quoted in Markpress Release No. Gen. 211.

[5] The communiqué was issued in Lagos on 24 June 1968.

[6] Lagos Radio talks on 26 June and 5 July (the latter described the visit, in retrospect, as 'a two-faced affair'); Kaduna Radio talk on 25 June, where Lord Shepherd was referred to as 'playing the mediator'; the press round-up of Nigerian newspapers carried by Lagos Radio on 26 June; and the Biafran Radio report of the visit given on 26 June 1968.

[7] Its contents were couched in the vaguest of non-committal terms.

[8] Hansard, House of Lords, 26 June 1968, cols. 1409–11.

[9] Hansard has 'Mbanafo'.

basis as soon as possible, and to send a representative to London for this purpose with a view to re-convening the Kampala Conference. As a result of my discussions I am satisfied that meaningful talks are possible, and Her Majesty's Government hope that Sir Louis Mbanefo will shortly return to London to take up this offer. I shall be seeing Mr. Arnold Smith to-morrow morning about the practicable arrangements for the resumption of talks.

Secondly, in response to my inquiry General Gowon expressed the readiness of his Government to see, as part of a satisfactory cease-fire arrangement, the introduction of an External Observer Force. He emphasised that the purpose of such a Force would be to give a sense of security to the Ibo people.

Thirdly, I was able in Lagos to emphasise the concern which is felt in this country about the need to avoid unnecessary casualties. I stressed the urgent necessity of achieving a negotiated end to hostilities before the conflict reached a scale likely to cause greater suffering and loss of life to the civilian population. I was given earnest assurance by the Federal Government of their wish to co-operate to this end and to keep casualties to a minimum. General Gowon said that it was not his intention to order further bombing attacks except against important military targets such as airfields being used for arm supplies. General Gowon underlines the responsibility he, personally, felt for the safety and wellbeing of all Nigerians.

Fourthly, I also urged upon General Gowon the need for relief to the civilian population. General Gowon promised his Government's full and ready co-operation in allowing relief supplies to be taken through an agreed corridor in the fighting lines under the control of the International Red Cross, and was ready to put at the disposal of the Red Cross and other organisations whatever airports or sea ports were considered most practicable. Her Majesty's Government are urgently considering what more we can do to relieve the plight of refugees in war-stricken areas. It is the intention of Her Majesty's Government to increase significantly their financial contribution to the relief of distress and they will make a further statement in this respect shortly.

During the Secretary of State's similar explanation to the Commons, a large procession of Biafran supporters marched on Downing Street to protest. Also in London, a high-powered and non-partisan Committee for Peace in Nigeria had been formed by leading public figures[1] and was soon to set out its plan for a peace settlement in a letter to the Prime Minister:

We are deeply concerned, as we know you will be, by the conflict between Nigeria and Biafra and its terrible consequences. We realise that the necessary condition to relieve the hunger is a ceasefire. We feel sure that the British Government will exert its influence towards this end. We believe that two contributions could assist in bringing the hostilities to an end.

The first would be willingness to press upon appropriate governments the provision of an international peace-keeping force. Canada, India and Ethiopia

---

[1] *The Times*, 2 July 1968. See also Lord Brockway's letter to the *Guardian* dated 31 July 1968, in which he set out his Committee's ten-point programme for action demanded from all governments.

have been suggested as acceptable countries for this purpose, and we hope you will encourage this.

The second desirability is a cessation of all arms supplies to both sides. We would like to see the British Government approach the Governments from which supplies are reaching Nigeria and Biafra, and urging that these should be stopped at the points of embarkation. As you will be aware, there is now a very wide feeling in this country that Britain should stop its supply of arms, and we strongly urge this upon the Government. It would be a lead which would influence others.

We recognise that a political settlement cannot easily be realised, but we believe—if there is international pressure to end the war—that an agreement might be reached on the basis of continued association between Biafra and Nigeria, with many common services and a plebiscite in the disputed areas. . . .[1]

At the end of June, press conferences given in London by Dr. Asika and Sir Louis Mbanefo, and a review of the current situation presented by Dr. Ibiam to the World Council of Churches meeting in Uppsala attracted less attention than they deserved, probably because staggering stories of the suffering in Biafra had swept them off the front pages of the world press. The politics of propaganda and the sensationalism of starvation were already well under way.

The war zone had now become the arena for international relief agencies.[2] Motivated by mercy, they operated with characteristic fearlessness and too frequent treading on national toes. Early in June, both Ojukwu[3] and Gowon had held press conferences to air their first reaction to the Kampala breakdown, the latter additionally promising that 'there would be no attempt by the Federal troops to drive into the heart of the East-Central State' and no pursuit of the Biafrans into their homeland except as a last resort after all appeals to Biafra had failed.[4] This remark seems to have been overlooked by *The Times* in its editorial of mid-June, when it took Nigeria to task for displaying 'a desire for revenge and punishment' now that it had militarily secured the upper hand.[5] At the end of the month Ojukwu recalled his joint Consultative Committee to reiterate his opinion that the Kampala talks could not be reopened [DOC 161]. Once more they renewed his mandate:

We, the chiefs, elders and representatives of the 20 provinces of the Republic of Biafra, assembled at this joint meeting of the Advisory Committee of Chiefs and Elders and the Consultative Assembly at Owerri on this 30th day of June 1968, do hereby:

[1] Letter addressed to the Prime Minister on behalf of the Committee for Peace in Nigeria on 30 August 1968 and signed by Lord Brockway and Rt. Hon. James Griffiths, M.P.

[2] Food and medical supplies had been flown into Biafra as far back as November 1967, but it was not till the summer of 1968 when food became really short that such operations began to assume a clamant status.

[3] Press conference of 5 June (B.B.C. ME/2794/B4).

[4] Kaduna Radio, 6 June; *Financial Times*, 6 June 1968.

[5] *The Times*, 13 June 1968.

E

(1) Express our deep thanks to H.E. the Head of State and C.-in-C. of the Armed Forces of the Republic of Biafra for his address, and hereby assure him of the continued loyalty to, and confidence of the people of Biafra in him and his Government;

(2) express our thanks to our delegation to the peace talks with Nigeria at Kampala, and affirm our support for their stand at the talks;

(3) express our satisfaction with the able manner in which the leader of our delegation handled the peace talks at Kampala and the informal talks in London;

(4) deprecate the fact that while we went to Kampala to talk peace, Nigeria went to dictate surrender terms, as evidenced by its 12-point proposal which we categorically reject;

(5) reaffirm our belief in the principle of self-determination and the facts that the issues involved in the present conflict can only be resolved by peaceful negotiations;

(6) reiterate our stand that only a cease-fire can create the necessary atmosphere and confidence for negotiations leading to a lasting settlement of the conflict;

(7) mandate His Excellency, on being satisfied that Nigeria is genuinely interested in a cease-fire without preconditions, to authorise our delegation to participate in talks leading to a cease-fire and thereafter in negotiations for a permanent settlement of the conflict;

(8) reaffirm our determination to continue our struggle for survival and the defence of our fatherland should Nigeria continue its intransigence;

(9) express our deep appreciation to those governments and organisations who have sent aid for our refugees direct to Biafra and advise that only aid sent direct to Biafra is acceptable.[1]

An informal interview with a British journalist granted in Umuahia about this time gave every indication that Ojukwu expected a fight to the finish.[2] Gowon confined his public remarks to a message to his troops commemorating one year of war[3] and to the sanctioning of £1,000,000 to the nine-man Rehabilitation Committee set up in the Cabinet office under Mr. Omo-Bare in March.[4] Its first undertaking was, ironically enough, to advise the over-zealous do-gooders on how to do much better.[5]

One lesson learned by the Federal Government at Kampala had been the sorry quality and ineffectiveness of its publicity[6] in comparison with the Biafran success story.[7] Nigerians themselves had become

---

[1] Resolution passed at Owerri, 3 July 1968.

[2] *Guardian*, 5 July 1968.   [3] *West Africa* (1968), p. 850.

[4] *Morning Post*, 11 July 1968; *West Africa* (1968), pp. 850, 881, and 1170.

[5] Cf. *Foreign Meddlers in the Nigerian War* (1968), p. 7; B.B.C. ME/2821–22.

[6] Cf. *The Economist*, 14 September 1968; letter to *Sunday Telegraph*, 11 August 1968, 'Public relations fog over the Nigerian War'. And note the contemporaneous Federal Government statement: 'When the war went against them [Biafra] they disseminated lies about genocide, religious warfare, etc. They are now beaten. But it is important that the world should know the truth'—*The Collapse of Ojukwu's Rebellion* (Lagos, May 1968), p. 1. See also the remarks of Mr. Nigel Fisher in the House of Commons *Debates*, 27 August 1968, Col. 1461.

[7] Despite occasional articles in the British press and references in the parliamentary

alerted to this failure. Now it was to be rectified, according to a promise made by General Gowon while on tour in Sokoto.[1] It was, as Nigerians urged in their dissatisfaction,[2] obviously no longer enough for Nigeria to depend on the legal cogency of her cause. That this truism was at last appreciated by Lagos was shown in the £5,000 full-page advertised presentation of its case and its efforts placed in *The Times* and *New York Times* early in July. Yet it had taken the Federal Government twelve costly months to appreciate how foreign sentiments could be encouraged to bloom under the hot-house glass of skilled public relations gardeners, their growth forced by the judicious application of the fertilizers of the press and television. Now things were to be changed. In the international escalation of the war an ultimate victory in the field could too easily, as Lagos was learning, be negatived by having lost the battle for men's minds. Ministry rationalization under a first-class Nigerian administrator was progressively carried out over the next few months, coincident with the overdue appointment of a public relations agency in London[3] and of a proven journalist as public relations officer in Lagos. The outspoken arrival of Oxfam and the International Red Cross on the Nigerian scene, stimulated by a well-publicized and sustained radio appeal from Biafra for massive food supplies for its refugees who were now said to be facing 'the highest deathrate in the world'[4] (Lagos took a very different view of this statistic[5]), provided the new public relations men with their first challenge.

---

debates, the full story of H. W. Bernhardt's handling of the Biafran public relations contract from his highly effective office in Geneva has still to be told. The publicity was no less effective in the United States than in Europe, though one Los Angeles public relations firm decided to sever its connection with Biafra, amid considerable comment and speculation in the American press. See *New Nigerian*, 20 August 1968.

[1] B.B.C. ME/2793; *West Africa* (1968), p. 733.

[2] B.B.C. ME/2835; and letters in the Nigerian newspapers.

[3] Messrs. Galitzine Chant Russell. See *Financial Times*, 17 June 1968. One of the first results was the admission by the *Biafra Weekly* that the advent of the new *United Nigeria* had compelled it to close down.

[4] B.B.C. ME/2799.

[5] In a talk over Lagos Radio, 18 June 1968, the speaker declared: 'The rest of the world has known for a long time that Ojukwu's mad political ambition has brought untold sufferings upon the people of Nigeria, especially those who live in the three Eastern States. But curiously enough the rebel leader and his foreign collaborators chose to ignore this fact. Any sacrifice, they said, must be made in order to achieve Ojukwu's ambition. But in recent days the rebel leaders have started singing a different tune. They have finally admitted that the war is pinching their people and have started crying for help. In the past few days they have issued several appeals, begging for badly needed foods, clothing, medicine, and other essential goods to be sent to them. They paint a lurid picture of 4,000,000 refugees dying of starvation and lack of medical attention, and they are now calling on the rest of the world to come to their aid. While nobody denies that the war provoked by Ojukwu's secession is causing a lot of suffering, the two important questions which one must consider are: first, who and what are responsible for all this suffering? Second, what must be done to bring a quick end to it? There is no doubt that the suffering of the people of the Eastern States is the direct consequence of the war Ojukwu has thrust upon the people of Nigeria. . . .'

For suddenly the world remembered the 'forgotten war'. 'The agony of Biafra', it was abrasively reminded, 'is an affront to the conscience of the civilised world.'[1] Divided over Rhodesia, disgusted at the by-now-proverbial savagery of the earlier Congo,[2] dazed by the succession of military coups in Africa, and no more interested in a mini-quarrel 'between the blacks'[3] than it had ever been in the continent even at the apogee of empire, the British public was at last presented with an issue of the Biafran struggle in a vocabulary that it could grasp and react to in a familiar way: the horrors of starvation—and of children at that. In England, Oxfam mounted a heavily advertised appeal for £200,000; Caritas, a Catholic organization that was eventually to assume a hostile political presence in Federal eyes, arranged to fly relief supplies into land-locked Biafra from São Tomé; and the I.C.R.C. prepared an airlift that promised to be on a scale second only to that which saved Berlin in 1948. There was, however, no agreement over the exact route for such relief supplies. A neutral land corridor through the Port Harcourt region was turned down by the Federal Government in favour of road transportation through the Federal lines.[4] Such a cease-fire corridor was not acceptable to Biafra, who went so far as to claim that the Federal insistence on inspecting supplies would allow their agents to poison the food:

The British government has made capital of Biafra's inability to allow relief supplies through enemy territory by means of the so-called sea and land corridors. That the British government should insist on this despite the practical difficulties betrays their real intention of helping Nigeria to achieve its military and political objective. The British government knows that bridges in the areas occupied or menaced by the enemy have been broken in order to impede enemy advance, just as the channels have been blocked for the same reason. To facilitate relief supplies by land or sea corridors would entail restoring the bridges and clearing the channels. In other words, all obstacles to a rapid enemy advance would be removed. . . . All these considerations apart, Nigerians have been known to poison food coming into Biafra.[5]

As the situation deteriorated towards famine level in the coming months, this standing on sovereign sensitivity while thousands died of starvation was to expose Ojukwu to the charge of playing politics with hunger and 'using the misery of his own people to extract diplomatic and other advantages to counterbalance defeats in battles'.[6]

[1] *Sunday Telegraph*, 7 July 1968.

[2] This was a standard of depravity accepted in parts in Nigeria, too. In arguments, warnings about *kada ka yi mini Kongo*, 'don't you dare to bully me', were commonly heard in the early 1960s.

[3] This was the thesis of an article in *Jet* (Chicago, 27 July 1967).

[4] B.B.C. ME/2818; *West Africa* (1968), p. 733.

[5] Biafran Radio, 9 July 1968.

[6] *The Times*, 26 June 1968.

The British Government granted £250,000 for civilian relief in Nigeria and on 5 July Prime Minister Wilson sent Lord Hunt, the conqueror of Everest, to make a fortnight's assessment of how best to deploy the fund. He reported that £1 million would not be 'an unrealistically high figure' for those 'in dire distress' and that the death rate in the South-Eastern state was already 200–300 a day.[1] Ojukwu refused any part of this help. He saw it as nothing more than a plan by Britain to fatten those it then intended to slaughter.[2] The Biafran Ministry of Information, enumerating nine separate instances of how General Gowon allegedly had broken his promises, also asked how, faced by this catalogue of bad faith, Biafra could ever accept any Federal assurance or guarantee even on relief supplies.[3]

If the problem of relief supplies and the ardent pace of Western fund-raising increased throughout July, so did the temper of protestation at the way politics was bedevilling the situation; yet the fears on both sides that such relief operations could, in one way or another, affect the course of the war were real enough.[4] In such a situation, fraught with suspicion and sensitivity, it was not hard for some of the less experienced of the relief personnel to prejudice their position by mishandled protocol, an inadequate grasp of logistics, and sheer over-enthusiastic under-organization.

In Britain, press, radio, and television heightened the sensation as the mass-media suddenly 'discovered' the Nigerian crisis and emphasized their own country's apparently 'criminal' contributions.[5] 'Milk—not murder', shouted a *Daily Sketch* banner headline.[6] 'How can we sit and wait for a million innocent people to die?' asked a skeletal Biafran child from an Oxfam advertisement. 'Biafra: starving children don't care which General wins' proclaimed another poster. Confronted with reports of a weekly death rate in the thousands, British public opinion now suffered the prickings of its uncomfortable humanitarian conscience, suitably stirred by the vigorous application of the swizzle-sticks of mass-media. The British Government's questionable agreement to use R.A.F. planes for flying in relief supplies[7] was not un-expectedly brought to naught by the Federal Government's repeated warning that it would shoot down all unauthorized aircraft violating its air space: 'The Nigerian Air Force has been ordered to shoot and

[1] His report was published as a White Paper, Cmnd. 3727 of 1968. See also debate in Parliament, 22 July 1968.

[2] See also the interview in the *Guardian* 5 July 1968.

[3] Statement issued by the Biafran Ministry of Information, 28 June 1968. Cf. DOC 143.

[4] So, too, I would suggest, was the Federal Government's genuine fear of chaos if it had listened to the pleas of the humanitarian agencies in mid-January 1970 and allowed them to clog up Uli airstrip and its service roads into the Ibo conclave with a massive and uncoordinated airlift.

[5] *Daily Telegraph*, 15 July; *West Africa* (1968), p. 827.

[6] *Daily Sketch*, 22 June 1968.

[7] *The Times*, 9 July 1968.

destroy foreign aircraft, not cleared by the Federal Government, over-flying Nigeria under the guise of dropping relief material to victims of the civil war.'[1]

It was evident by now that the Federal Government had taken just about all it could endure from some of the more 'where-angels-fear-to-tread' humanitarianists.[2] Radio talks, especially against Oxfam, and newspaper articles questioning their impartiality[3] were followed by an acid reference from Chief Enahoro to the campaign as 'overflogged and overplayed'.[4] Finally, after several official 'warnings',[5] their senior representatives were summoned on 19 July by General Gowon, who sternly cautioned two of them, Oxfam and Caritas, against their deepening political involvement.[6] At the same time the Nigerian Government publicized a summary of the protracted efforts it had made to co-operate with the I.C.R.C. in ensuring the receipt of relief supplies by non-combatant sufferers,[7] and reiterated its willingness to re-open a mercy corridor by land through Enugu:

... The method of getting relief quickly and effectively to the secessionist area has been engaging active attention and I can tell you that a road corridor will be opened from Awgu to an agreed point on the Okigwi road where the rebels can take over. Supplies can be airlifted to Enugu and there is a good road to Awgu from there. With a convoy moving these supplies by road to south of Awgu the secessionist area will be quite well served.

Furthermore, it should be possible, at a later stage, and with the release for the exclusive use of the International Committee for Red Cross (I.C.R.C.) by the rebels of some of the Nigerian railways' rolling stock confiscated by Ojukwu, for supplies to be sent by rail from Enugu to supplement or replace the road corridor. The railway line will first have to be inspected and repaired where necessary, and this will probably be a long process especially if the secessionists refuse, as usual, to co-operate.[8]

Certain of Nigeria's missions abroad put out a statement on relief, supplementary to the official one in the press. In Washington, for in-

---

[1] Radio comment on the Government statement issued in Lagos, 5 July. See also the talk broadcast over Lagos Radio on 9 July 1968 (B.B.C. ME/2818/B1) which concluded with the argument: '. . . The proposal to send the British Royal Air Force fighters over Nigerian skies in the name of humanitarianism is vexatious and strange. Even if people believed that the R.A.F. transport would only drop food and medicine, what prevents the Portuguese and South African Air Forces and other adventurers from dropping guns, ammunition and other war supplies following closely in the path cleared by the R.A.F.? The Federal Military Government is alive to its responsibilities.'

[2] Cf. 'Politics and Humanitarianism', *Nigerian Opinion*, June 1968, pp. 302–3, and the lead article 'The Foreign Coalition against Nigeria', ibid., July 1968, pp. 337–40.

[3] *Morning Post*, 19 July 1968; B.B.C. ME/2813, 2817, and 2831.

[4] *Daily Telegraph*, 9 July 1968.

[5] B.B.C. ME/2818.

[6] *Morning Post*, 20 July 1968. The suspicion that the relief air routes could also be used for arms supplies was well-founded.

[7] Recapitulated in *The Way Out of the Civil War in Nigeria* (London, 1968), pp. 14–15, and published at the time in the world press, e.g. *New York Times*, 8 July 1968.

[8] Dr. Arikpo at a press conference in Lagos, 12 July 1968.

stance, the ambassador tellingly developed the American Civil War parallel that had so often suggested itself during the months of crisis and conflict:

. . . The Nigerian ordeal is not without ample and somber precedents. Just over a hundred years ago, there ended in the United States a civil war in which the issue at stake had also been the maintenance of constitutional unity or the acceptance of an act of secession. As in Nigeria, the aching sacrifices of that war were endured not on the battlefield alone.

In these past few days, one has found himself wondering how the people of this country would have reacted, and what impact would have been on later American history, if Lee had met Grant at Appomattox not to end the resistance by his army, but to offer to negotiate an end to the fighting on terms which included (if I may borrow some of the proposals made recently by Mr. Ojukwu's representatives at the Peace Talks in Kampala) recognition of the sovereignty of the rebel coalition, withdrawal of Union troops behind pre-war boundaries, the holding of plebiscites to decide the future of border states loyal to the Union, and the unimpeded and unsupervised admission of massive foreign aid to relieve suffering in the South. This, of course, is fantasy. Lee, unlike the rebel leaders in the east-central state of Nigeria, had the courage to recognize the hopeless plight of the gallant soldiers he commanded. But I believe it is probable that, as he handed his sword to Grant in that simple and famous ceremony, he was also recalling, and relying on, Lincoln's promise to bind up the nation's wounds. And perhaps, also, he looked forward with a sad but firm confidence to the time when the South would once again play an effective and prominent role in a Federal Congress, as all agree it does today, in a truly United States of America. . . .[1]

Yet in Lagos the noisy attitudes of the international relief agencies, for all their honourable intentions, had much of the makings of provoking a conflict in their own right. In January 1970 their curious capacity for giving offence was not to be forgiven by a justly rebukeful General Gowon.

An important diversion was now in sight. Sensitive to the forthcoming O.A.U.'s Consultative Committee on Nigeria meeting, the Biafran Commissioner for Information, Dr. Eke, produced a six-point peace plan at a press conference held in Aba on 11 July:

(1) Britain and Nigeria should renounce the use of force as a means of settling the conflict.
(2) Nigeria should respect world opinion and accept an immediate cease-fire.
(3) Britain should stop supplying arms to Nigeria.
(4) After a cease-fire has come into effect, Nigeria should agree with Britain on arrangements for the conduct of a free plebiscite in the disputed areas of Nigeria and Biafra.
(5) At an agreed time a free and fair plebiscite should be conducted in the

[1] Statement issued by the Nigerian Embassy, Washington D.C., on 12 July 1968.

disputed areas of Nigeria and Biafra to determine whether the people concerned want to be Biafrans or Nigerians.

(6) After the wishes of the people have been so ascertained, true representatives of Biafra and of Nigeria will meet to negotiate a final settlement.[1]

On 15 July the O.A.U. Consultative Committee on Nigeria met in
Niamey. Before leaving to attend the conference (postponed from 5 July)
as head of the Nigerian delegation, Chief Awolowo ruled out the suggested plebiscite.[2] Next General Gowon himself suddenly flew to
Niamey. He made what was described as a frank and convincing address
to the Committee, now in closed session, in which he accepted the idea
of an observer force to give a sense of security to the Ibos [DOC 162].[3]
The Committee was reportedly deeply impressed by his sincerity and by
the delicate balance of his own leadership. After listening to him, the
Committee decided to invite Colonel Ojukwu to meet it in Niamey
'with a view to making a joint and urgent effort to find a satisfactory
African solution to the grave Nigerian crisis'.[4]

Gowon's return to Nigeria before Ojukwu's arrival studiously avoided
the possibility of the two leaders meeting each other for the first time
since Aburi; or, as it turned out, ever again before the war ended.
Ojukwu duly arrived in Niamey on 19 July, flying in President
Houphouet-Boigny's personal aircraft and accompanied by an impressive party of aides. Prior to leaving Biafra, he had held a press
conference in Aba at which he restated, at length, his views on how to
secure peace and the obstacles that he saw thereto [DOC 163].[5] In
Niamey he was courteously but coolly received. After Ojukwu had
delivered a ninety-minute statement to the O.A.U. Committee in
private, it issued a short communiqué on 19 July announcing that both
sides had agreed to an immediate holding of preliminary talks in
Niamey and the resumption of peace negotiations as soon as possible.
These were to be held in Addis Ababa, this time under O.A.U. auspices.[6]
This was followed by an O.A.U. resolution [DOC 164], asserted in some
quarters to have been 'considerably weakened' by the exclusion of a
truce and an internationally policed air corridor after a long session
with General Gowon.[7]

Representatives from Nigeria (five) and Biafra (nine) led by Mr. A. A.
Ayida and Professor Eni Njoku respectively, started talks in Niamey

---

[1] Broadcast by Biafra Radio, 11 July 1968 (B.B.C. ME/2820/B1).

[2] Lagos Radio, 17 July 1968. The daily record of the conference is best followed in
West Africa (1968), pp. 854–909.

[3] Despite rigorous Nigerian protests: see *Sunday Post*, 14 July 1968.

[4] Quoted in *Africa Research Bulletin*, p. 1122. The communiqué announced in English
by Niamey radio has a slightly different wording (B.B.C. ME/2824/B3).

[5] The full text is also available, with the occasional hiatus of 'words indistinct', in
B.B.C. ME/2826/B5–B6 and ME/2827/B1–B5. A useful summary is given in *Africa
Research Bulletin*, p. 1123.

[6] Broadcast from Niamey (B.B.C. ME/2827/ii).

[7] *Ethiopian Herald*, 21 July 1968, quoted in *Africa Research Bulletin*, p. 1124.

under the chairmanship of President Haman Diori on 20 July, and by 24 July had reached some measure of agreement on the proposal, reportedly first put forward by Ghana on 17 July,[1] for a 3–5 mile wide demilitarized corridor along the ninety miles of road from Enugu to Ogoja. However, disagreement on the identity of the six nations to provide the observers for such a corridor and on Biafra's proposed demilitarization of Enugu airfield to allow a direct airlift from Abidjan or Libreville prevented any real advance being made,[2] so that the communiqué issued at the sudden ending of talks on 26 July was again one born from only limited success [DOC 165]. This was not entirely unexpected, given the O.A.U.'s dilemma-bred inability to find a solution to independent Africa's greatest embarrassment. But at least the O.A.U. had managed to get the two sides talking round a table again, a creditable achievement in its own right; furthermore it had always scrupulously held its role to be that of conciliation, never one of mediation. Its continued endorsement of the Nigerian case was to be a welcome source of moral encouragement to Lagos throughout the conflict.

Echoing its censure on Ojukwu for having broken up the Kampala talks by his jingoistic 30 May broadcast,[3] Lagos was quick to blame him[4] for having this time sabotaged the talks by the cocky tone of his Owerri news conference given on his return from Niamey on 21 July.[5] Enahoro, too, quickly slapped down the widely circulating suggestion that Gowon and Ojukwu would personally lead their delegations to the Addis Ababa peace talks due to be held in Ethiopia on or before 5 August.[6] There was concern in some quarters whether Gowon's decision not to meet Ojukwu might not result in a majority of Heads of State on the O.A.U. Consultative Committee themselves boycotting the Addis Ababa talks,[7] especially when Ojukwu pressed home the advantage by announcing that he would not hesitate to lead his delegation in person:

In response to the invitation of His Imperial Majesty Haile Selassie of Ethiopia, who is Chairman of the O.A.U. Consultative Committee of the Nigeria/Biafra conflict, I am leading the Biafran delegation to Addis Ababa in quest of peace. . . . We go to Addis Ababa to seek peace with honour. For fourteen gruesome months the people of Biafra have stood up against a vicious and callous enemy backed by two world powers. We have withstood all forms of atrocities, barbarism and suffering in the knowledge that to do otherwise would mean death and total extermination for our people. The

---

[1] *West Africa* (1968), p. 855.

[2] *West Africa* (1968), p. 882; *Africa Research Bulletin*, p. 1124.

[3] DOC 159.

[4] Lagos Radio, 29 July 1968.

[5] Summary in B.B.C. ME/2829/B1 and excerpts in B.B.C. ME/2832/B2–B6.

[6] Lagos Radio, 30 July 1968. See also Kaduna Radio, 6 August 1968.

[7] *Agence France Presse*, quoted in *Africa Research Bulletin*, p. 1125. See also *The Times*, 22 July 1968 and the remarks of Mr. James Griffiths in the House of Commons. For Gowon's own comment, see *West Africa*, p. 855.

Biafran delegation go to Addis Ababa with sincerity and determination to achieve an honourable and just settlement of the current conflict. We go with a full mandate and shall abide by that mandate.

As an earnest of our sincerity for peace, I have ordered our troops to remain in their positions and to make no attack on the enemy, except in self-defence. In other words, I have unilaterally ordered a temporary truce for the duration of the talks. Our delegation to Niamey had suggested to the Nigerian delegation that a truce be declared by mutual agreement. Well-meaning world opinion has also proposed this. But Nigeria, whose military aims are well known, has not shown any interest in a truce. . . .[1]

Somewhat over-sanguinely, Gowon had allowed himself to be quoted as saying at a diplomatic reception held in Lagos that 'as far as we are concerned the war is virtually over;'[2] his information media, too, were urging Ojukwu that enough was enough.[3]

Meanwhile, Dr. Eke lost no time in rejecting Biafra's responsibility for the Niamey failure and putting the blame on what he called Nigeria's 'conqueror complex'. He listed a number of reasons to explain the breakdown:

(1) Members of the Nigerian delegation openly declared at the conference that starvation was a legitimate tool of war. They said the war with Biafra was 'total' and gave the example of the 2nd World War when Germany was starved by the Allied Powers. Thus they claimed moral and political justification for their action.

(2) The Nigerian delegation insisted on a political settlement first before allowing relief to war victims. They claimed that Biafra's presence at Niamey was dictated by the starvation at present causing untold suffering in Biafra, and insisted on Biafra's renunciation of her sovereignty.

(3) The Nigerian delegation did not understand the seriousness of the refugee problem in Biafra. They likened it to the situation in Nigeria and kept saying that there was sufficient food to feed the refugees.

(4) There was evidence on the Nigerian side of the same conqueror complex exhibited at Kampala, expecting Biafra to beg.

(5) The Nigerians rejected proposals for air-lifting of supplies 'for military reasons', as opposed to the Biafran delegation's proposal for a general agreement on air, land and sea routes, pending further agreement which was to be given priority.

(6) The Nigerian delegation refused to apply principles, governing the setting up of any route, which had been previously agreed upon by both delegations. Such principles include the de-militarisation of a distance of three to five miles on either side of the corridor, the placing of international observers along the corridor to ensure that the supplies were not tampered with, and the de-militarisation of the entire length of the corridor. The Nigerian delegation would only agree to the de-militarisation of the collecting points on Biafran territory. This disagreement on principles led to the fact that there was no agreement reached on any corridor.

[1] Statement of 3 August 1968.
[2] B.B.C. ME/2830.   [3] B.B.C. ME/2828.

Nigeria's new coat of arms?

Reproduced by kind permission of the *Observer*

(7) The determined attempt of the three props of Nigeria—Britain, Russia and the United States—to render the O.A.U. impotent as a mediator. This was well disclosed by Britain's announcement during the preliminary talks, of their determination to continue arms supplies to Nigeria.[1]

A similar explanation was put forward by one of the Biafran delegates at Niamey, who noted how 'we talked of relief but they made relief hinge on a political settlement, so at Addis we will begin with the political relationship of Nigeria and Biafra. If we succeed there we will succeed with a cease-fire and with food.'[2] The Voice of Biafra preferred to blame the British Government for 'wrecking' the Niamey talks, alleging Mr. Wilson's pique at now losing the initiative earlier won by the 'British controlled' Commonwealth Secretariat to the African-run O.A.U.

[1] Statement issued at Aba, 3 August 1968 (Markpress Release No. Gen. 251).
[2] Quoted in *West Africa* (1968), p. 909.

Not unexpectedly, Nigeria's hawks saw the Niamey histrionics as simply another device by Ojukwu to secure a much needed breathing-space for military recoupment. That the army was beginning to show impatience at the Supreme Commander's humanistic tolerance was not hard to identify. In private, field commanders complained that his studious avoidance of the word 'enemy' cut right across a fundamental military precept. In public, press briefings given in July by a senior staff officer, Colonel Danjuma at Enugu, were symptomatic when he acknowledged that 'we will have to go in [to the Ibo heartland] eventually'.[1] Further evidence of military impatience was found in the chafing comments made by two other senior field commanders. Colonel Adekunle's 'as far as I am concerned the war is over—I'm just waiting for the order and in two weeks I'll have captured the "O.A.U." [Owerri —Aba—Umuahia]' was matched by the even more succinct comment of Colonel Utuk: 'I'm only waiting for the order to pitch in—in fifteen days time there will be no more Biafra.'[2] The *Daily Times*, too, came out with an editorial urging 'Let us fight to a finish.'

One more event was to queer the pitch for the heralded Addis Ababa talks; and, in the event, to have such a far-reaching effect that it may in the final analysis be seen to have played a major part, complemented by the relief operations, in greatly extending the length of the war. This was the statement made by the French Cabinet on 31 July calling for a resolution to the Nigerian conflict on—to use the once-sweet, now-bitter hallowed words of so many African leaders in their own struggle of the 1950s against European imperialism—'the basis of the right of peoples to self-determination' [DOC 166]. Indignation in Lagos at this 'deplorable intrusion into the country's internal affairs',[3] especially in this momentous pre-Addis week, was matched by jubilation in Biafra.[4] '*La France, c'est notre seul espoir maintenant,*' Dr. Azikiwe was, incredibly, quoted as saying in Paris.[5] The Lagos and Kaduna radio stations wielded the big stick on 'France and the rebels'.[6] In London, the Nigerian High Commissioner issued a statement accusing France of having supported secession 'from its inception' [DOC 167]. He also claimed to have in his possession 'irrefutable documentary evidence' that Biafra had given away all its mineral resources concession rights. Part of the supporting documentation was later released.[7]

---

[1] *Daily Times*, 8 August; *West Africa* (1968), pp. 850 and 881.

[2] Both cited in *Africa Research Bulletin*, p. 1126.

[3] Statement issued in Lagos, 2 August 1968.

[4] B.B.C. ME/2839.

[5] F. Debré, *Biafra an II* (Paris, 1968), pp. 217–18.

[6] Two strongly phrased indictments of General de Gaulle were carried in talks on 12 August 1968 (B.B.C. ME/2847/B1–B4).

[7] Photostat copies of the agreement were distributed at a press briefing held in Lagos on 8 August 1968. See also *United Nigeria*, no. 2, 1968. It was denied by the Biafran Ministry of Foreign Affairs the next day as 'a piece of intentional blackmail', and they noted that the document carried neither date nor signature. (B.B.C. ME/2540/B6).

The physical implications of France's declaration of moral support were to remain muted for another two months but its timing, falling only nominally short of diplomatic recognition, could not have been more unfortunate. It was enough to encourage an immediate and probably prejudiced hardening of the pre-Addis Ababa attitudes now adopted by the two protagonists in public statements. At a press meeting held in London Mr. Mojekwu, Commissioner for Home Affairs, outlined the three proposals that Biafra intended to put before the peace conference:

(1) Immediate cessation of fighting on land, sea and air. We are prepared to discuss with Nigeria the terms rather than the conditions for a cease-fire.

(2) Immediate removal of the economic blockade mounted by Nigeria against Biafra.

(3) The withdrawal of troops behind the pre-war boundaries to enable refugees to return to their homes.

With regard to (1), cessation of fighting, Biafra will agree to:

(a) the policing of the cease-fire line by an international force the composition of which must be agreed to by both sides:

(b) a supervisory body, the composition and power of which are to be agreed and which will be stationed in the areas from which troops are withdrawn to ensure that the local population are not in any way victimised.

With regard to (2), the removal of the blockade, we shall be ready, if it is agreed, to accept supervision at points of entry into Nigeria and Biafra to ensure that there is no arms build-up by either while talks on arrangements for a permanent settlement continue. The aim should be to restore civilian life and administration back to normal in the war-ravaged areas as soon as possible.

Biafra is still willing to discuss:

(a) Maximum economic co-operation and common services with Nigeria.

(b) Problems relating to the sharing of assets and liabilities (including the external public debt) of the former Federation of Nigeria.

(c) Problems relating to the payment of compensation for the life and property of Biafrans which were lost during the Pogrom and as a result of the war.

(d) The holding of a plebiscite in the disputed areas inside and outside Biafra to determine the true wishes of the people.[1]

These showed little change from Ojukwu's position before the Niamey accord on the Addis Ababa talks.[2] Simultaneously, Chief Enahoro explained his government's position at a gathering in London, warning that too much hope should not be pinned to Addis and reiterating that there was 'no question of General Gowon meeting Colonel Ojukwu in Addis Ababa.'[3]

[1] Markpress Release No. Gen 245.
[2] DOC 161.
[3] Quoted in *West Africa* (1968), p. 910. No text was issued. Commentators noted the reversion to 'Colonel' after the deliberate down-grading to 'Mister Ojukwu' at Kampala.

Thus the 'last chance' peace talks began in Addis Ababa with severely limited prospects of success.[1] In his opening address on 5 August, the presiding Emperor of Ethiopia appealed to both sides for the discussions to be conducted in a spirit of brotherhood and understanding: 'You cannot afford to fail.' At this stage Chief Enahoro limited himself to the formality of a courtesy reply, emphasizing the O.A.U.'s endorsement of the aim of these talks as being 'to preserve Nigeria's territorial integrity and to guarantee the security of all its inhabitants', and noting that this could well be the final opportunity to settle the conflict by negotiations:

... The Federal delegation has come to Addis Ababa determined to make every effort to dispose peacefully of the major issue which divides the two sides to our conflict. Put very simply, the central issue is whether or not the parts of the East Central State of Nigeria still under the control of the other side, can be re-integrated into Nigeria through these talks.

... I assure Your Imperial Majesty that the Federal Government delegation will do all within its power to facilitate the work of this meeting and ensure the success of the O.A.U. Consultative Committee on Nigeria in its search for an African solution to our crisis. We believe, as the Committee does, that such a solution is feasible and ought indeed to be promoted. Given good-will and the courage to face the realities of the situation in our country, the civil war in Nigeria can be brought to a speedy end through the Addis Ababa talks. I feel confident that with the spirit of Niamey behind us, and given an atmosphere of realism in Addis Ababa, we can succeed. Our people and Africa generally expect us to do better here than we did in Kampala where our efforts, assisted by others, to reconcile the differing views of the two delegations, were so abruptly terminated. We are determined to succeed this time because the omens are propitious and this may well be our last chance to resolve our conflict through a negotiated settlement. . . .[2]

Then came a dazzling display of stagecraft.[3] With that heightened sense of *wayo*, 'intelligent craftiness', that he had shown at Aburi, Colonel Ojukwu prefaced his marathon $2\frac{1}{2}$ hour speech [DOC 168] with a telling verbatim passage from the Emperor's own plea of 'defending the cause of all small people who are threatened by aggression' made by Haile Selassie before the League of Nations in that grave June of 1936. Nor did he lose any trick in again going over much of the old ground on the causes of the conflict. Such was the tone of Ojukwu's speech, with its calumny of Gowon as 'the Hitler of Africa,[4] coming on top of the brazen

---

[1] Once again, the best blow-by-blow account is that in the pages of *West Africa* throughout August.

[2] Opening statement by the Nigerian delegation, 5 August 1968.

[3] Lagos Radio was to select the same metaphor when it described the performance as being characterized by 'his usual theatricality' (B.B.C. ME/2843).

[4] In its indignation against this slander, the Nigerian public overlooked the fact that the Government-sponsored *Morning Post* had carried a poem in September 1967 applying the Hitlerian comparison to Ojukwu, and the same analogy was heard among a number of Hausa veterans of the 1939–45 war now re-enlisted in the Nigerian army. The term was also used for Ojukwu by Lagos Radio a year before Ojukwu used it at

insult to Nigeria by the inclusion of Gabonese officials in the Biafra delegation,[1] that Enahoro felt compelled to issue a press statement condemning 'the tirade by Mr. Ojukwu as a gross violation of protocol':[2]

. . . As far as the Federal Government delegation is concerned, we have not come to Addis Ababa for propaganda and in spite of the extreme provocation from Mr. Ojukwu yesterday, I have decided not to descend to his level of polemics and downright lies. . . . As far as I am concerned, the whole affair was really in very bad taste. I am glad that Mr. Ojukwu's performance on this occasion will further help to unmask this man.

We are therefore treating the unfortunate incident of yesterday with the contempt it deserves. In my statement to the next session, when it is convened, I will be concentrating on the Federal Government's proposals for a permanent settlement. I may, however, take that opportunity to correct some of the more serious distortions in Mr. Ojukwu's presentation. For example, it is simply not true to suggest that the Ibos were driven out of the Federation. It would indeed be strange for us to drive them out and at the same time fight to keep them in the Federation. It was Mr. Ojukwu himself who forced Ibos to return to their region of origin and expelled non-Easterners from the East, as part of his secession plan.

Yesterday, representatives of certain countries, notably Gabon, attended the opening session as part of the rebel delegation. This was part of Ojukwu's plan to internationalise our crisis. We did not raise the matter then because we wished to avoid embarrassing the Emperor, but I have taken up the matter with the Ethiopian authorities. I have met the Foreign Minister and I am seeing His Majesty the Emperor later today to inform them that the Federal Delegation will not go back to the conference room until we have received assurances that only Nigerians will attend future meetings as delegates and advisers on both sides. I hope that this matter can be cleared up quickly so that our discussions can be resumed.[3]

It was, indeed, at one time in doubt whether the Nigerians would request a second open session at all.[4] However, the Conference, rocked though it was, had not yet foundered.

In presenting the Nigerian case when talks were resumed on 7 August, Chief Enahoro put forward nine[5] detailed proposals for discussion, similar to those made at Kampala but modified by small concessions and an imaginative face-saving formula of a joint declaration, classified under the three heads of arrangements for a permanent settlement,

---

Addis Ababa (*One Nigeria*, iv, p. 69). Dr. Arikpo was to repay the personal calumny when he addressed the United Nations in October 1968 (D O C 185).

[1] B.B.C. ME/2842.

[2] Cf. the description of 'contrary to all ethics'—*Federal Peace Efforts* (Lagos, 1968), p. 6.

[3] Nigeria House Press Release, 7 August 1968.

[4] *West Africa* (1968), p. 937.

[5] *Africa Research Bulletin*, p. 1151, enumerates ten, but the official listing was nine heads of agreement.

cessation of hostilities, and relief operations [DOC 169]. These may be summarized[1] as:

1. Renunciation of secession.
2. Disarmament of rebel forces.
3. Meeting of Nigerian and rebel military leaders.
4. Rebel area to be policed by mainly Ibo forces.
5. Pledge not to flood rebel area with Federal troops.
6. Armed forces to be used only if there is breakdown of law and order.
7. If policing by external force as suggested by rebels is agreed, Nigeria propose mixed force from Ethiopia, India, and Canada.
8. Military Government to be set up in East Central State and an Executive Council of Ibo civilians.
9. The terms of amnesty to be negotiated. Reinstatement of displaced Federal Government and Statutory Corporations employees included.

After a day's recess to allow consideration of the Nigerian terms, Dr. Eni Njoku, who had introduced himself to the press as the new leader of the revised Biafra delegation on Colonel Ojukwu's departure accompanied by Dr. Azikiwe on 6 August,[2] presented to the conference his seven counter-proposals. These included control of the cease-fire agreement by an international police force drawn from nine African countries and a promise that Biafra would accept a plebiscite in the 'contested regions' of both Biafra and Nigeria [DOC 170]. In a mammoth reply (not delivered until 12 August[3]) which also went over much old history,[4] Chief Enahoro emphasized that the basic principle of secession, which lay at the root of the quarrel, was not negotiable and he rejected the argument that the safety of the Ibo people could be guaranteed only in an autonomous entity outside the nation of Nigeria [DOC 171]. At the end of a week of heavy speechifying the two delegations had broken so little new ground and still clung so tenaciously to their long-prepared positions that the Emperor decided the only way to encourage some break in ideological attitudes was to invite both sides to declare their 'minimum demands'.[5]

On 15 August Dr. Njoku replied to what he called Chief Enahoro's 'long diatribe', by introducing four more papers designed 'to correct the fanciful history', allegedly put forward by the Nigerian delegation. To each of them were attached voluminous appendices, totalling over

[1] From the press briefing issued by Nigeria House, London, on 9 August. A more elaborate summary is to be found in *United Nigeria*, 2, 1968.

[2] For his statement to the press in Paris rejecting Nigeria's call for Biafra to renounce secession, see *Africa Research Bulletin*, p. 1151.

[3] Dr. Njoku charged this delay in replying to Ojukwu's opening address as 'having been merely a ruse to enable him [Enahoro] to take a whole week in preparing a long diatribe'—statement made on 15 August in introducing Biafran Papers Nos. 3–6.

[4] The press release issued by Nigeria House on 15 August is incomplete, comprising only half of Enahoro's speech.

[5] B.B.C. ME/2846; *Africa Research Bulletin*, p. 1152.

200,000 words.[1] His concluding section he significantly entitled 'Nigeria is not penitent':

... Having listened to the reply made by the Nigerian delegation to our proposals, I find that what strikes me most is the continued absence of any sign of penitence by Nigeria for the inhuman treatment which Nigerians have meted out to Biafrans. We are all but human beings and we do make mistakes, grievous ones. But we can repent; we can show penitence. We can even go further and offer atonement and make it up to those whom we have wronged. These are human traits which have so far been utterly lacking on the part of Nigeria. Instead of showing penitence, Nigeria goes out of her way to abuse anybody who shows sympathy for us whom Nigeria has wronged, and turns a deaf ear to all who plead with her to leave Biafra alone. Nigeria has ignored and rewarded by abuse the pleadings of the Vatican and the World Council of Churches. Nigeria has cursed and maligned African States which have shown revulsion at the calculated destruction of African life and property perpetrated by her. The four African countries—Tanzania, Gabon, Ivory Coast and Zambia—which have appreciated the human aspects of our situation and have recognised Biafra as a sovereign and independent nation, have been the subject of particular abuse by Nigeria, and we have seen other African countries being systematically blackmailed by veiled threats to the unity of their countries. When, recently, a European country, France, saw the humanitarian issues involved, and showed the general horror felt by the civilized world because of the inhuman atrocities perpetrated against Biafrans by Nigerians and expressed the view that the Nigeria/Biafra conflict must be solved on the basis of the rights of the people of Biafra to self-determination, Nigeria again took to abuse and even went as far as to allege motives which are more appropriate for explaining the reasons for the arms support they get from the British Government. This is truly a case of their own heart-dealings teaching them to suspect the thoughts of others.

As I have said earlier, all these show lack of penitence and no atonement on the part of Nigeria. But these—penitence and atonement—are the necessary preludes to any reconciliation. When Nigerians say they want Biafra back in Nigeria, it is clear that this is not in a spirit of reconciliation; otherwise, they would first have shown penitence and atonement. Why do they want us back then—to continue their wrongs against us? To make up their bondsmen and slaves? These things cannot be. Biafrans do not want to be slaves and will not be slaves. Nigeria can keep, for the meantime, the slaves they have captured already—the Asikas and others in open or closed prisons. The millions of people in Biafra have tasted freedom and will not give it up. Biafra must be recognised as a free, sovereign and independent nation.[2]

Dr. Njoku now listed five means to guarantee the safety of Biafrans:

1. Internally, maintenance of order and respect of law must be the responsibility of the Biafran government. Biafra rejects any proposal giving the

---

[1] None of these Conference papers 3–6 is included here. Biafran Paper No. 1 was Ojukwu's opening address (DOC 168), and No. 2, Dr. Njoku's peace proposals (DOC 170).

[2] Concluding statement, 15 August 1968.

F

Nigerian government responsibility for creating and maintaining an Ibo police, because the question is seen as a Biafran problem and not an Ibo one.
2. To defend the country against any attack the Biafran army must swear allegiance to the Biafran government.
3. Internationally, Biafra must be a member of international organisations in order to be able to defend at all times its international personality.
4. Economically, Biafra must be able to conclude international agreements. Its economic development must depend only on Biafra. The country must be able to control its immigration services and its industry.
5. Biafra must be able to control its money, economic resources and the rate of its economic development.[1]

This pie-in-the-sky ploy persuaded Chief Enahoro, despite the earlier announcement to explain General Gowon's absence that its delegation enjoyed a full mandate to sign any agreement,[2] to fly back to Lagos for consultations, and the conference was temporarily adjourned. Enahoro's remarks in Lagos indicated little likelihood of, or even advantage in, his returning to Addis Ababa.[3]

Nor had there been any hint of compromise in the interview given in Paris by Dr. Azikiwe in which General Gowon again came under attack for not attending the talks in person.[4] Enahoro had been quick to rebut this:

I have received reports of public statements in Paris, London and Tunis made on our peace proposals by Dr. Azikiwe and Dr. Okigbo. The statements lay down the line for the rebel delegation here in Addis Ababa. We had expected to hear the rebel reaction to our proposals from Dr. Eni Njoku directly here in Addis Ababa and not from rebel leaders who are not here and who obviously had not studied the text of my speech two days ago. This is a repetition of the rebel tactics at the Kampala talks. On that occasion, just when we appeared to be making some progress, Mr. Ojukwu broadcast a hard line which compelled Sir Louis Mbanefo and his delegation to walk out of the talks. . . .

It seems to me grossly unfair to Dr. Njoku to manipulate him like a puppet from so far away. If the rebel leadership cannot trust Dr. Njoku and their delegation to make decisions in negotiations here in Addis, then whoever has the authority to make decisions for their side should come to Addis Ababa. I must say that I sympathise with Dr. Njoku. What can he do now but dress up his conformity with the hard line of publicity laid down for him in his own clothing?[5]

Azikiwe's apparent fence-sitting was also lambasted by the publicity media operating under Enahoro's portfolio.[6] Meanwhile the Federal

---

[1] Quoted in *Africa Research Bulletin*, p. 1152.
[2] Lagos and Kaduna Radio, 6 August, quoted in *Africa Research Bulletin*, p. 1151.
[3] *West Africa* (1968), p. 944.
[4] *The Times*, 9 August; B.B.C. ME/2844 and ME/2847; *West Africa* (1968), p. 944.
[5] Press Release issued by Nigeria House, 9 August 1968.
[6] Talk over Lagos Radio, 'Dr. Azikiwe's role', 12 August 1968, in which some harsh language was directed against the ex-President (B.B.C. ME/2847/B4).

Government lobbied the press in Addis and concentrated on proving the significant rejection of Biafra by the non-Ibo minorities in the East, effectively exploiting their windfall of an uncompromising denunciation of Biafra from no less a person than Ojukwu's former Attorney-General, Dr. Nabo Graham-Douglas.[1]

On 24 August it was announced that both sides had agreed 'in principle' to a compromise plan put forward by the Emperor for land and air 'mercy corridors' to take in relief supplies for civilians suffering from the war.[2] By the end of August, however, the talks showed the two sides to be as far apart as ever, and only the Emperor's indefatigable private contacts and his decision to preside over a session held in his palace instead of in Africa Hall, along with a last minute appeal to the 'rebel [*sic*] leaders to show a spirit of compromise and some flexibility in their approach', saved their complete collapse.[3]

Determined to scotch the accusations of genocide once and for all, Lagos made an almost unprecedented wartime gesture by inviting a team of foreign observers to visit the battle zone for eight weeks and scrutinize the conduct of the Federal troops.[4] This was in the face of earlier demonstrations in Nigeria against this very proposal.[5] At the same time the Federal Government offered to allow direct relief flights to the neutralized Uli-Ihiala airstrip for one week,[6] this again despite the mounting feeling in Lagos and Kaduna against what was seen as meddling in the crisis by foreign wolves wearing humanitarian sheep's clothing.[7] The Federal Government had issued a firm statement on relief supplies [DOC 172] in mid-August and, because of the disquiet voiced abroad, its embassies amplified this with their own publicity, notably in the U.S.A.[8] where the sustained Biafra support was a matter of concern. Finally, Lagos was obliged to give yet another grave official warning to the International Red Cross in reply to the 'peremptory message' it had issued in connection with its flights into Biafra [DOC 173]. The Federal Government also published its own estimate, prepared by nutritional experts at the University of Ibadan and from UNICEF, of the volume of relief (27,750 tons a week over three months to give a daily intake of 1,200–2,800 calories) that would be required by Biafra 'after a final military offensive'.[9]

This 'final push' was dramatically announced at a press conference

---

[1] *Ojukwu's Rebellion and World Opinion.* See also Dr. Graham-Douglas's press conference in London on 22 August 1968.

[2] Ethiopian Radio quoted in *Africa Research Bulletin*, p. 1152.

[3] Lagos Radio, 20 August 1968, quoted in *Africa Research Bulletin*, p. 1153.

[4] Lagos Radio, 30 August; statement issued by Nigeria House, London.

[5] e.g., *Daily Times*, 14 July 1968.

[6] Statement issued in Lagos on 2 September 1968.

[7] e.g., 'One loaf . . . 10,000 bullets: those relief givers ENEMIES ALL'—radio talk by Osimua Ifidon reproduced in *Morning Post*, 6 August 1968.

[8] *Relief Problems in Nigeria*, issued by the Embassy of Nigeria, Washington, D.C.

[9] Quoted in *Africa Research Bulletin*, p. 1153.

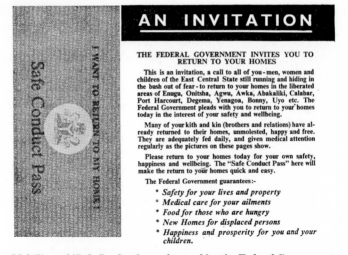

AN INVITATION

THE FEDERAL GOVERNMENT INVITES YOU TO RETURN TO YOUR HOMES

This is an invitation, a call to all of you - men, women and children of the East Central State still running and hiding in the bush out of fear - to return to your homes in the liberated areas of Enugu, Onitsha, Agwu, Awka, Abakaliki, Calabar, Port Harcourt, Degema, Yenagoa, Bonny, Uyo etc. The Federal Government pleads with you to return to your homes today in the interest of your safety and wellbeing.

Many of your kith and kin (brothers and relations) have already returned to their homes, unmolested, happy and free. They are adequately fed daily, and given medical attention regularly as the pictures on these pages show.

Please return to your homes today for your own safety, happiness and wellbeing. The "Safe Conduct Pass" here will make the return to your homes quick and easy.

The Federal Government guarantees:-

* *Safety for your lives and property*
* *Medical care for your ailments*
* *Food for those who are hungry*
* *New Homes for displaced persons*
* *Happiness and prosperity for you and your children.*

Multilingual 'Safe Conduct' pass dropped by the Federal Government over rebel-held areas as part of the 'final push' of August 1968

by General Gowon on 24 August after a meeting of the Army field commanders and Service chiefs at Dodan Barracks,[1] and confirmed in a television interview with the B.B.C. [DOC 174].[2] Then, in an important broadcast to the nation on 31 August, Gowon informed Nigerians that the war was now on the last lap and the Supreme Military Council had decided 'to end the rebellion with the least delay' [DOC 175]. Despite the millions of multilingual safe-conduct passes dropped by the Federal aircraft over both sides of the fighting line, the now declared decision to 'defeat the rebels militarily' and without further ado, could hardly be reconciled with continued discussions on negotiations. With the downgrading[3] of the Nigerian delegation, now left in charge of a junior Commissioner, the Addis Ababa peace talks were ready to justify the gloom of their original Jeremiahs. Opinion in Lagos had hardened: there was now no alternative to a conclusive military solution. Was this final offensive against Biafra's assumed last stand,[4] world opinion could now ask itself in apparent confidence, the beginning of the end of the year-long war?[5] Was the day of reckoning at last just round the corner? Was this, at last, the quick kill,[6] long preferred by the hawks over the nugatory round of peace talks? The war seemed set for its final act.

[1] *West Africa* (1968), pp. 965 and 1029.

[2] See also Gowon's exclusive interview with A.F.P., reported by Kaduna Radio on 27 August, in which he explained, 'I gave the order [on 24th] and left it to the field commanders, on the basis of their state of readiness, to make the necessary move' (B.B.C. ME/2860/B3).

[3] *West Africa* (1968), p. 944.

[4] *Daily Telegraph*, 15 September; *The Times*, 17 September 1968.

[5] *Scotsman*, 22 October; *The Economist*, 26 October, 1968; *West Africa* (1968), p. 1003.

[6] There is, perhaps, an analogy in the quick-kill dilemma in the decision faced by those who had to give the eventual orders to drop the atom bomb on Hiroshima.

In the dying days of August and Addis both Houses of Parliament in London spread themselves in another milestone debate on the Nigerian war. The weight of the members' remarks inclined to the Federal side, in contrast to the pro-Biafran sentiments enjoying concurrent attention in the *Spectator*,[1] *Time*,[2] and the colour supplement of the *Daily Telegraph*,[3] forcing home the message in earlier horror issues of *Life*[4] and the *Sunday Times* supplement.[5] The whole of Hansard for this debate repays examination.[6] Gowon, who was doubtless as aware of the futility of continuing the Addis talks given the present Biafran frame of mind as he was sensitive to the impatient demands of his commanders for a final offensive, could do little but accept their official adjournment on 9 September[7]—this despite the efforts of the tireless Emperor, who had received the delegations separately on no less than thirty-five occasions.[8] Gowon's final determination, after over a year of war and three months of public peace talks in addition to other mediatory moves behind the scenes, to have recourse to a military solution elicited anticipatedly snide sneers from the Voice of Biafra.[9] In London, Dr. Azikiwe defined Biafra's minimum peace terms as absolute control of her security forces, after which she 'might co-operate on social and economic lines with Nigeria,' and reaffirmed her determination to fight to the end against the forces allegedly dedicated to her extermination.[10] Expressing regret at the Addis impasse 'in spite of the Government's major shift in policy and substantial concessions made to bring about a compromise',[11] Nigeria nevertheless went ahead with the publication of its highly important seven-point programme for the reintegration of the Ibos which had been privately discussed at Addis Ababa [DOC 176]. Later it was to add five more promises in its rehabilitation programme:

(i) caring with the utmost compassion for the surviving victims of past disturbances and of present military operations;
(ii) all soldiers, no matter on which side they fought in the civil war, will be rehabilitated and gainfully employed at the end of the military operations;

[1] Summer 1968, *passim*.   [2] 23 August 1968.
[3] 22 August 1968.   [4] 12 July 1968.
[5] 9 June 1968.

[6] It spread over 27 and 28 August: House of Commons, *Parliamentary Debates*, vol. 769, no. 166 and 167, and the parallel session in the House of Lords. Markpress (Geneva) produced an interesting version which contained 'Biafran' comments in the margin.

[7] *Morning Post*, 11 September 1968. The Addis Ababa peace talks were not only the longest of the three public confrontations of official delegations from both sides during the thirty months of civil war; they were also the most complicated and the most heavily documented at the private level. A useful summary of the Addis negotiations is the résumé given by the Nigerian delegation at the end of the talks and reproduced in *Federal Peace Efforts* (Lagos, 1968), pp. 7–11.

[8] Ethiopian radio, quoted in *Africa Research Bulletin*, p. 1185.

[9] Radio talk, 4 September 1968 (B.B.C. ME/2866/B4).

[10] *West Africa* (1968), pp. 1029 and 1044. See also B.B.C. television interview with Dr. Azikiwe on 'Twenty-Four Hours', 26 August 1968.

[11] Comments by the Nigerian delegation on its return to Lagos, quoted from Lagos Radio in *Africa Research Bulletin*, p. 1185.

(iii) those whose properties have been destroyed or damaged, as a result of civil disturbances are to be reasonably compensated;

(iv) all those who fled from their normal places of residence or business will be resettled and assisted to make a fresh start;

(v) all roads, bridges and public buildings which have been destroyed or damaged will be rebuilt.[1]

Furthermore, ignoring another appeal by the World Council of Churches for priority to relief supplies,[2] the Federal Government announced its intention to implement unilaterally the Emperor's personal compromise proposals for sending such supplies to Biafra [DOC 177]. Both plans were, of course, rejected by the Biafran Government.[3]

The Federal Government scored a much-needed propaganda success in bringing about the courageous 'conversion'[4] of one of Biafra's most tireless and hitherto (to Lagos) tiresome friends abroad, Dame Margery Perham, a sympathizer with rather than an uncritical advocate of the Biafran cause. Having studied the situation on the spot in Nigeria, she of her own accord broadcast from Lagos a message to the Ibo people [DOC 178] urging them to cut their losses and surrender now that, as she later told the people of Britain, they no longer had a chance: 'Is it not better for the Biafrans to live not to fight but to work and flourish another day?'[5] This was at a high personal cost, for the published scorn of her disenchanted Biafran friends was but the tip of the abusive iceberg to which this authority on Nigerian affairs was privately exposed for having declared the courage of her convictions.[6] The same counsel to surrender was soon being put out by Radio Enugu, now under Federal control:

This is a public service announcement to the Biafran soldiers. Don't be dead when peace returns. . . . It will be too late if you are dead. . . . Don't retreat from the advancing Federal troops. Just show them you are no longer fighting. Show your hands; you may even hand over your weapons to them. You will be quite safe. You may not be released as yet, being a captured person, but you are not really a prisoner of war. You will get three meals a day. You will see a doctor any time you need one. You will rest and sleep soundly at night. You will gradually be more comfortable. Anyhow, you are better alive than dead. . . .[7]

---

[1] *Ibos in a United Nigeria* (Lagos, 1968), p. 4.　　　　　　[2] B.B.C. ME/2849

[3] Biafra Radio, 16 September 1968 (B.B.C. ME/2877).

[4] *The Times*, 9 September 1968.

[5] Article 'Why Biafran Leaders should surrender', *The Times*, 15 September 1968. For further articles and letters, see M. Perham, *Colonial Sequence, 1949–69* (London, 1970).

[6] Typical of the published rebuffs was: 'If Dame Margery Perham is pro-Biafra, an anti-Biafran defies imagination. But with a friend like Dame Margery, who needs enemies?'—letter in the *Spectator*, 20 September 1968. Private reproof was, I understand, of an even more painful nature. Dame Margery was later to admit in private that she would have been wiser to have used the term 'negotiate' rather than 'surrender' in her broadcast.

[7] Appeal broadcast on 18 September (B.B.C. ME/2878).

In London a letter from Ben Enwonwu[1] in answer to one from Chinua Achebe[2] indicated the deep and distressing dilemma of the Ibo intellectuals over the war.[3]

As if to consolidate this overdue reversal in public opinion, which had shown signs of hardening against a Nigeria too confident in the legality of her cause to bother to argue the moral grounds, the O.A.U. summit meeting held in Algiers in mid-September came out strongly in support of the Federal Government. Encouragingly, Biafra's friends even failed to secure the civil war among the agenda for the Ministerial Council meeting, who at their final session on 12 September rejected the Tunisian call for a resolution on the Biafran situation. In sharp contrast to her behaviour at the Kinshasa O.A.U. summit a year earlier, Nigeria was now no longer reluctant nor afraid to have the question of Biafra's secession discussed by the Heads of State. It could indeed afford to do so on all grounds; and its impressive military occupation of the greater part of Biafra recalled to some Africanist observers the advantages of the 1885 lesson of coming to an international conference armed with evidence of 'effective occupation'. After a diplomatic contretemps over President Kaunda's injured refusal of the vice-presidency of the meeting and after listening to an address by U Thant on the importance of African solutions to Africa's problems [DOC 179], an important resolution based on a report from the O.A.U. Consultative Committee on Nigeria was issued calling on 'the secessionist leaders to co-operate with the Federal authorities' [DOC 180]. At the time there appeared to be some discrepancy between Chief Awolowo's and the official Lagos understanding of the extent of the general amnesty called for by the O.A.U.—'I do not think Ojukwu would be excluded'[4]—but all in all Nigeria this time had every reason to be satisfied with her diplomatic triumph at the O.A.U. summit. The Biafran delegation waiting in the wings never even received permission to enter Algeria.[5]

Any comfort that the Federal Government derived from this diplomatic success, coming encouragingly hard-on-the-heels of its important capture of Aba on 4 September, was sadly limited. On 9 September General de Gaulle included a dramatic reference to Biafran aid at one of his rare press conferences, and intimated that France would support Biafra [DOC 181]. In Biafra, her leaders of thought responded to de Gaulle's uplifting promise by calling for a break with the British

[1] *The Times*, 4 October 1968.

[2] *The Times*, 19 September 1968. See also Dame Margery Perham's reply in *The Times*, 21 September.

[3] Cf. the Asika/Achebe dialogue in *Transition*, 36, 1968; Asika's views 'On being an Ibo' in his collected speeches (Lagos, 1968), pp. 73–9; and Dr. Azikiwe's ambivalence.

[4] *Financial Times*, 17 and 20 September; *West Africa*, pp. 1135 and 1154, quoted in *Africa Research Bulletin*; p. 1174, and Lagos Radio, 19 September 1968.

[5] The Algiers O.A.U. summit meeting is best followed in *Africa Research Bulletin*, pp. 1171–5.

Commonwealth and joining the *Francophonie* community.[1] General
Gowon called an immediate press briefing to reject 'over my dead body'
any meddling suggestions about a confederation for Nigeria,[2] and rude
demonstrations against France gave vent to the nation's indignation
at this encouragement of Ojukwu.[3] Yet it was just possible that with
the fall of Owerri on 16 September and 'the token Republic of Biafra'[4]
reduced to a rectangle a mere 60 × 30 miles wide (a little larger than the
county of Kent or half the state of Indiana) containing but one town,
Umuahia, and two impovised airstrips, the question of this French
quasi-recognition might seem ironically late or laughably academic . . .
unless, of course, moral support was to extend to practical matters like
arms and ammunition. In the event it did—tragically so.

Thus the Nigerian war, which by September 1968 seemed at last to have
a classical military ending in sight, and had been confidently predicted
by General Gowon himself on 24 August as being over 'within the next
four weeks',[5] was suddenly threatened by an internationalizing escalation. With that came the threat, dreadfully fulfilled in the event, of
prolongation. The fighting now became transformed, for the first time
in its course, into a military stalemate through near equality of fire
power. Injured to the quick, Chief Enahoro revealed that Nigeria had
at least learned three lessons from this deliberate protraction of its crisis:

> . . . The first is this . . . never again must we have to rely on external sources
> for the supply of our internal requirements. The second is this: never again
> must any State government be permitted to control its own separate army
> and armed police. And the third is this: by reason of Nigeria's position, we
> are obliged to conduct our public affairs in the full glare of world publicity.
> The situation has its demands. We must meet them.[6]

If September was meant to bring her death-throes, Biafra was an
unconscionably long time a-dying. Yet was the crisis for survival not
over and her capacity for resistance exhausted? Was it not too late for
this French support materially to alter the rebels' desperate military
plight? Could Ojukwu, for all his charismatic leadership, not serve his
people better by quitting and thus allowing negotiations at this eleventh
hour?[7] Reports discreetly circulating in September began to suggest
there was now just a ghost of a chance of his listening to his envoys.
Suddenly recalled to Umuahia, they could not fail to acquaint him with
the altered feeling of many governments towards a Biafra now publicly
disowned in the unequivocal condemnation by African Heads of State

---

[1] Lagos Radio, 10 September 1968; *West Africa*, p. 1123.
[2] Lagos Radio, 14 September; *New Nigerian*, 16 September 1968.
[3] Biafra Radio, 9 September 1968 (B.B.C. ME/2870/B2).
[4] Coined by Lagos Radio (B.B.C. ME/2881).
[5] Biafra Radio enjoyed another laugh at Lagos in its talk 'The latest deadline',
broadcast on 9 September 1968 (B.B.C. ME/2870/B2).
[6] Press conference held in Benin on 23 September (*New Nigerian*, 24 September 1968).
[7] Cf. 'Ojukwu must go', editorial in *Sunday Times*, 6 October 1968.

meeting in Algiers only ten days earlier. Whispers of a cease-fire and negotiation were once more gathering strength.

At any rate, here was enough of a straw in the wind for Britain to send Lord Shepherd—seen by a sullen Biafra as 'that personification of the inhuman callousness and moral bankruptcy of the British Government'[1]—to Lagos on 25 September with another personal message from Mr. Wilson. Within seventy-two hours he was back in London, bearing a chastened tale of 'bitter disappointment'.[2] Lord Shepherd was later to admit[3] that he went to Nigeria after an approach by a group of politicians in Colonel Ojukwu's inner Cabinet who hoped to promote a negotiated settlement with General Gowon and wanted Britain to guarantee the safety of the Ibo people. But the Federal Government had made it clear to him, in no uncertain terms and ones that were to be repeated again and again, that it would consider no peace talks outside the umbrella of the O.A.U.[4]

But it seemed that the long-cherished hope and now faintly audible possibility of a split in the Biafran leadership was not destined to materialize for, despite the unmistakable cooing in the Ibo dovecot on 25 September, Colonel Ojukwu decided that he would fight on. Decrying as 'fantastic', stories of his skulking in a concrete bunker,[5] or his planning a government-in-exile in Gabon[6] or in self-offered Zambia,[7] he told his Consultative Assembly that he refused to surrender. He went on to urge his people, already more tightly knit than ever by frightening propaganda emphasizing how Gowon was intent on killing every man woman and child, 'either with bombs and bullets or by starvation',[8] to counter seductive Nigerian calls for straight-thinking Ibo intellectuals to see the light of day.[9] He called on his people to rededicate themselves to the struggle and foresaw a successful guerrilla movement. Ojukwu no longer aspired to military victory, rather to holding on and so 'delay the

---

[1] Biafra Radio quoted in B.B.C. ME/2890.

[2] See *The Times*, 26 September and 1 October; the *Observer*, 29 September 1968.

[3] *Scotsman*, 8 October 1968.

[4] Statement issued in Lagos, 1 October 1968. A.F.P. reported that Lord Shepherd had indeed brought a message from the British Government urging Lagos to follow up moves with a caucus of Biafran doves who had recently met somewhere in Europe and come out in favour of negotiating an early end to a struggle that now seemed to be futile. Though this is a likelihood believed by many of those on the fringe of such international moves, it has yet to be officially corroborated or described in detail. See p. 78 and DOC 183.

[5] *New Nigerian*, 16 September 1968. The charge was repeated by Dr. Arikpo at the United Nations (see DOC 185).

[6] *Sunday Telegraph*, 15 September; Markpress release dated 27 September 1968.

[7] *Zambia Mail*, 27 September 1968. It is interesting to compare this offer of asylum with the Zambian reaction when in January 1970 Ojukwu fled from Biafra for an undetermined destination.

[8] Biafra Radio talk, 'The Relief of the Assassin', broadcast 17 September 1968 (B.B.C. ME/2877/B1).

[9] Lagos Radio talk of 16 September 1968, 'Let Commonsense Prevail,' quoting extracts from an earlier speech by Asika (B.B.C. ME/2876/B4).

enemy until the world's conscience can be effectively roused', thereby hopefully pressurizing Nigeria into recognition of Biafra's case. 'We are stronger today than we were two weeks ago,' he said, in an allusion to (French) arms supplies, 'and indications are that we shall continue to grow from strength to strength.' He also appealed to the friendly governments and relief organizations to:

re-examine the whole basis of this relief operation in light of the Nigerian determination to frustrate their efforts and to press on to a military solution. It is clear that no relief will be effective without a cessation of hostilities and Nigeria has refused to heed any appeal to this end.[1]

Ojukwu may perhaps have recalled the defiant voice of his new principal prop, General de Gaulle, and echoed the President's broadcast to the French nation at its own moment of supreme crisis four months earlier: 'I will not retire. I have a mandate from the people and that I shall fulfil.' Once more the Consultative Assembly gave Colonel Ojukwu the mandate he wanted to continue the resistance [DOC 182].

Of the disillusioned civilian doves some, like Dr. Azikiwe, returned to Europe; others stayed on and were reportedly kept quiet one way or another.[2] The Biafra propaganda bureau issued a statement[3] claiming that Dr. Azikiwe had pledged his full support to Ojukwu in a letter sent from Paris in refutation of reports in *The Economist*,[4] *The Times*,[5] and the *Sunday Times*[6] that moderate Ibo politicians who favoured a negotiated settlement and a conditional surrender by the Biafran armed forces enjoyed the ex-President's support. However, private papers kindly shown to me by Dr. Azikiwe indicate a very different stand from the interpretation put on his letters by the Biafran propaganda bureau. Indeed, the telex message from Dr. Azikiwe to Ojukwu sent from Paris on 25 September represents a clear attempt to persuade Ojukwu to negotiate [DOC 183]. It also substantiates the reports that prompted Mr. Wilson to send Lord Shepherd as personal envoy to General Gowon at this time.[7] It was this crisis in the Biafran leadership that caused a change of mind in Biafra's successful Paris spokesman, Raph Uwechue.[8]

[1] Exceptionally, the Biafran publicity machinery did not make widely available the full text of Ojukwu's address to the Consultative Assembly and Council of Chiefs at Umuahia on 25 September. An indirect speech account was broadcast by the Biafran Radio on 26 September and Markpress issued selected excerpts on the following day. A fuller version has since become available in *Biafra: Selected Speeches* (1969), pp. 345–57, entitled 'The Failure of Addis Ababa Talks'.

[2] Talk on the reported fate of Sir Louis Mbanefo given by Kaduna Radio on 5 November 1968 (B.B.C. ME/2920/B2).

[3] Biafra Radio, 4 October 1968 (B.B.C. ME/2892/B4).

[4] 21 September 1968.

[5] 24 September 1968.

[6] 29 September 1968.

[7] See p. 77, especially fn. 4.

[8] See his *Reflections on the Nigerian Civil War* (1969). His arrest was reported in B.B.C. ME/2921.

The gravity of this reconsideration of how genuinely tenable and viable Ojukwu's hard-line stand was has still to be fully explored. Meanwhile, there was no doubt on the present outcome: the hawks in Umuahia had won the day.

Ojukwu's unyielding determination was reinforced in a ninety-minute TV interview shown in Paris in which he spoke of Biafra's choice between a slow death and a chance, however minimal, to live;[1] and again in an interview granted to journalists in Umuahia.[2] Clearly he was encouraged in this resolve by the coincidence of the accelerated flow of arms from French sources,[3] often via Lisbon, and by the startling performance of a group of white mercenaries, led by Rolf Steiner.[4] This *chef des affreux* now predicted that the guerrilla fighting would last up to seven years. In the event, he and his aides were soon to be dismissed by an Ojukwu angered at their 'acts of brigandage, acts of indiscipline, and the waylaying of relief supplies'.[5] Lagos was scornful of the mercenary threats, though her continued use of Egyptian pilots restrained her from too strident an attack on the morality of men hired to kill.

In the face of Ojukwu's dogged inflexibility, General Gowon could find little of cheer to include in his message to the nation broadcast[6] on the somewhat empty-sounding Independence Day, now shorn of its customary celebrations, beyond holding on to his repeated belief that the 'end of the war is in sight'. Radio Nigeria was prompted by the Umuahia decision to condemn the Biafrans' apparent suicide psychology:

The decision of the rebel leaders to continue their suicidal resistance to the Federal Military Government reveals the absence of the right kind of reasoning that should reflect the true wishes of the people. The senseless and arrogant rantings of Ojukwu and a few of the rebel top men is a far cry from the desire of ordinary Nigerians still in rebel-held areas. These ordinary men have no illusions about the continued suffering, the deprivation, and the unnecessary deaths that a failure to renounce secession at this stage will mean. They are the men who have borne the brunt of Ojukwu's tragic adventure. It was they who fell victims of Ojukwu's propaganda of hate and needlessly left the other parts of the country where they were living in comfort and security. . . . What is the position today? These men, whose sons and relatives are being sent to their deaths are completely ignored. Ojukwu recalls his henchmen, who have been gallivanting from one European capital to the

[1] *West Africa* (1968), p. 1118.   [2] *Sunday Times*, 6 October 1968.
[3] *Daily Telegraph*, 19 October 1968.
[4] Press release issued by Nigeria House, 25 October; *Africa Research Bulletin*, p. 1189; *The Times*, 16 and 18 November; Lagos Radio talk on 22 October (B.B.C. ME/2906/B7); and Colonel Steiner's interview with A.F.P. (see *Africa Research Bulletin*, p. 1185).
[5] Quoted in *Africa Research Bulletin*, p. 1240. For a report on the presence of Bob Denard, see *United Nigeria*, 5, 1968.
[6] He described the war as having been 'a drama of national discovery'—message to the nation, 1 October 1968.

other since the fighting broke out, and calls on them to come and impose a decision on those who have been daily witnesses of the ravages of war. So no one is really surprised that Ojukwu's globe-trotting henchmen, who have never been exposed to the turbulent dangers of the civil war, should come and make an inhuman decision to fight to a bitter end.

It is all very well for these unrepentant and unfeeling nation wreckers to be smuggled into Umuahia, attend a secretly convened meeting and hop out again. But what about the men who have nowhere to run to? What will be the fate of the men, women and children who have been running for the past 14 months and who have nowhere else to go? Would the women whom Ojukwu has widowed in the prime of life want to carry on the war that is already lost? Would children whom Ojukwu has orphaned in his bid for political eminence ever consent to fight to a finish? Of course not. The rebel leaders can afford to be unreasonable because they have not much to lose. . . . But how many of the common people can afford to live abroad in exile?[1]

In the absence of any acceptable *sors tertia* to the alternatives of peace or war, both sides seemed finally resigned to choosing war.

Despite the absence of hard news from the fighting front in the doldrum months of October and November, there was no lack of informed speculation about the build-up of Biafra's war supplies. These were reliably estimated to be reaching up to one hundred tons a night through a daring airlift to the code-name 'Annabelle' strip.[2] Such reports were matched by others focusing on the unhappy state of the Nigerian Third Division beset by problems of raw soldiery and over-stretched lines of communication. Yet, action or not, it was in the battle zone that the interest was concentrated. First there was the dynamic personality of Colonel Adekunle, the 'Black Scorpion',[3] unable to keep out of the public eye, what with his TV interviews[4] and his noisy expulsions of those simply regarded as nuisances;[5] his publicized execution of a Nigerian officer for the wanton shooting of an unnamed Biafran civilian;[6] his exchange of words with Dame Margery Perham;[7]

[1] Lagos Radio talk, 1 October 1968 (B.B.C. ME/2888/B1).

[2] Kaduna Radio, 24 October 1968.

[3] Cf. Lord Hunt's remarks in the House of Lords debate on 27 August 1968. For one interpretative analysis of Adekunle, see Kenneth Lindsay's paper presented to the symposium on the Nigeria-Biafra Crisis held by the African Studies Association of the West Indies in April 1969.

[4] *West Africa* (1968), pp. 937 and 1029.

[5] B.B.C. ME/2926; *West Africa* (1968), p. 1393.

[6] The controversy over this incident, especially the reported shout of 'hold it' by a TV camera man whose lens was not in focus at the moment the firing squad had come up to the present, was extensive in the British press. See, for example, *The Times*, 3–6 September; *West Africa* (1968), p. 1035; B.B.C. ME/2864; and the pictures in *Morning Post*, 5 September and *Daily Telegraph*, 11 September 1968. A French TV company filmed the murder of the Biafran civilian. The incident of the officer's execution compares with that of the Nigerian officers sentenced and shot in Benin for a similar offence. See *Daily Telegraph*, 27 June, 1968; B.B.C. ME/2807 and 2815; photographs of the gruesome execution in *Jeune Afrique*, July/August 1968; and J. P. Clark's 'Benin Sacrifice'.

[7] *The Times*, 7 September 1968; *West Africa* (1968), p. 1073. Oxford lore relishes the story of how Dame Margery riposted Colonel Adekunle's rudeness with the quip—'Just wait till I have you in my seminar!'

his uncompromising threats to Major-General Raab, to other military observers[1] (which produced an acid skit in the *Spectator*[2]), and to the International Red Cross;[3] and, above all, his alleged Ibophobia derived from his declared intention of 'shooting anything that moves'.[4]

Of far greater importance though less catching to the eye, was the first judgement of categorical rejection of any genocidal plan in the Federal troops' behaviour, pronounced by the team of international observers from Canada, Sweden, and Great Britain[5] [DOC 184]. This they were to follow up by reports submitted later in the month on the other two divisions of the Nigerian army, each unit bearing noticeably different characteristics. Their useful documentation was complemented by a number of subsequent reports from the O.A.U. observers and from the personal representative of the U.N. Secretary-General, as well as by a general report from the international observer teams after their appointment had been extended beyond December 1968. In the same context, attention should be paid to the public statements, frank and reassuring, by the British military observer team's leader General Alexander, with his vital reminder that, 'This is a sovereign country no longer under colonial rule, and whether we like the policies or otherwise of the Federal Government they have a perfect right to run the country as they think fit,'[6] and, more vulnerable perhaps on grounds of historical accuracy, by his successor Brigadier Fergusson.[7] Neither of them was likely to have allowed any wool to be pulled over his no-nonsense soldier's eyes.

Lastly there was the cold blooded shooting, 'unprovoked and inexcusable',[8] by a drunken soldier of four expatriate relief workers at Okigwi. After an 'evasive'[9] press interview by a senior Nigerian Ministry of Defence spokesman, a separate investigation by the observer team was ordered by General Gowon, but its findings[10] failed to elicit either the identification of the officer known to be responsible or the prompt court martial justice that had so impressively characterized two earlier wanton killings.[11] The observers did not accept Colonel Ojukwu's invitation[12] to work on the Biafran side of the firing line but undertook further investigations into the alleged massacre of civilians at Urua

[1] *The Times*, 1 November 1968; *West Africa* (1968), p. 1334. The incident was gladly exploited by the Biafran Radio (B.B.C. ME/2914).

[2] The *Spectator*, 8 November 1968.

[3] *Daily Telegraph*, 24 September 1968.

[4] B.B.C. ME/2878; *Daily Telegraph* 30 and 31 October, and 1 November 1968.

[5] See the *Observer*, 24 November 1968.

[6] Major-General H. F. Alexander, 'The War in Nigeria', Supplement to *United Nigeria* (London), 9 December 1968.

[7] Article in *The Times*, 12 December 1968.

[8] *The Times*, 7 October 1968.

[9] *Sunday Telegraph*, 6 October 1968.

[10] Issued by Nigeria House, 8 October 1968.

[11] *The Times*, 29 October 1968. Cf. the Benin execution (p. 80, fn. 6).

[12] Text broadcast over Biafra Radio, 4 October 1968 (B.B.C. ME/2892/B3).

Inyang by the Federal forces (not proven),[1] and into the conditions of prisoners of war held at Kirikiri and Ikoyi.[2]

In November, too, there was further controversy over the Red Cross intention to continue flying in supplies to the stricken areas, a decision which prompted the Federal Government to ventilate the nation's resentful mind on what was looked on as the unwholesomely partisan role of the I.C.R.C.:

The crisis has gone a long way to reveal the mischief and double-facedness of many international organisations which pretend to work solely for humanitarian reasons. . . .

For some time now the International Committee of the Red Cross has proved beyond doubt that it is in Nigeria for reasons other than humanitarian. The organisation has so sided with the rebels that it has now assumed the role of an agent of the secessionists. . . . The fact is that the rebels and these mischief-making organisations are nothing but partners in crime. The role of the International Red Cross in the Nigerian crisis has clearly demonstrated that it is doing nothing other than aiding the secessionists to sustain their rebellion. . . . Without the co-operation of the Red Cross in solving their foreign exchange and other financial problems the rebels would not have remained so stubborn and unrepentant. . . .

It is definitely true that the International Committee of the Red Cross is not rendering any useful service in Nigeria as far as humanitarian activities are concerned. Quite recently, Col. Adekunle revealed that this organisation was doing nothing in the liberated areas to help the people. He pointed out that the Federal troops were even doing a better job than the Red Cross in helping refugees and displaced persons with food and medical care. And not long ago the Federal Commissioner for Communications, Alhaji Aminu Kano suggested that the Red Cross should be ordered to pack and go, and many Nigerians endorse this view.[3]

Concerned at the mounting tonnage of munitions also being flown privately into Biafra,[4] the Federal Government again warned that it would fire on 'all unauthorised and illegal flights to the rebel-held area',[5] and its air force, hitherto singularly ineffective in the hands of predominantly Egyptian pilots, scored its first night-time success by shooting down two relief aircraft.[6] Advance Christmas card advertisements by UNICEF[7] reminding readers that 'not less than 200,000 children have starved to death in Nigeria' and Oxfam's black-bordered notice in the week-end press[8] of 'Sunday: just another day—and six thousand

---

[1] Report published in Lagos, 2 November 1968.

[2] Report published in Lagos, 3 November 1968.

[3] Lagos Radio talk, significantly entitled 'Partners in Crime' (B.B.C. ME/2885/B2).

[4] The *Scotsman*, 1 November 1968.

[5] Statement issued in Lagos and broadcast over Lagos Radio, 3 September 1968 (B.B.C. ME/2885/B2).

[6] *The Times*, 8 November 1968; *West Africa* (1968), p. 1338.

[7] *The Times*, 13 November 1968.

[8] Leading newspapers, 14–17 November 1968.

will die from hunger in Nigeria/Biafra,' made it clear to all that the humanitarian agencies still had faith in the rightness of their actions.

In the Western State there were rumblings (not for the last time) of subversive separatism aimed at the creation of an independent Yoruba Central State, to comprise the Oyo and Ibadan provinces. This demand had been dormant in Nigeria since the 'Sacred Cow and his Chorus Boys' *affaire* of the previous January[1] for which the Government's own newspaper subsequently had had to print an apology to Chief Awolowo and the Military Governor of the West.[2] This time the incipient discontent was suppressed by Brigadier Adebayo's warnings[3] and stern measures of arrest and newspaper banning, but the Western Region situation remained warningly indicative of the intricacies in re-drawing State boundaries which the Federal Government would have to face on the home front, quite apart from the assumptive ex-Biafran area, once the war was over.

There was a momentary shift of attention to New York in mid-October. This was not so much because of Ojukwu's message to the U.N., in which he implored the President of the General Assembly to invoke Article 8 of the genocide convention,[4] nor because of Dr. Arikpo's confident speech to the General Assembly. In this he compared Ojukwu to Tshombe and Biafra to another 'lamentable tragedy of Katanga in Africa' [DOC 185]. The simile, drawn by Enahoro at Addis in August, had been challenged by other observers. Nor was it because of France's rationalization by M. Debré of her 'significant supplies and valuable medical assistance [to Biafra] in face of acts of unparalleled brutality and a kind of genocide',[5] with its sneer at Gowon's 'phantom states' and its grave undertones of a final French recognition of Biafra. It was rather because the highlight of the 23rd Session of the United Nations was the revealing attitudes of the African states towards Nigeria in their various speeches,[6] along with Canada's overt wish to raise the Biafran issue[7] because of her Parliament's disquiet at the

[1] Article by Dan Zaki in *Morning Post*, 11 January 1968, in which he attacked certain thinly veiled public figures for running the Western State 'as the special patrimony of the sinister Sacred Cow and his chorus boys'.   [2] *Morning Post*, 21 February 1968.

[3] Press conference at Ibadan, 10 September; broadcast over Ibadan Radio, 26 November 1968 (B.B.C. ME/2937/B4).

[4] Text of message in Markpress Release No. Gen. 333.

[5] Quoted in *Africa Research Bulletin*, p. 1212. See also Enahoro's remarks on French arms supplies made in Paris and quoted by Kaduna Radio on 3 October 1968 (B.B.C. ME/2891/B5).

[6] A useful analysis is to be found in Kaye Whiteman, 'The O.A.U. and the Nigerian Issue', *World Today*, November 1968, pp. 449–53.

[7] *The Times*, 9 October 1968; Markpress Release No. Gen. 323. This move had been mooted in mid-September: see Montreal Radio report and the Lagos retort quoted in *Africa Research Bulletin*, p. 1189. The Canadian Secretary of State for External Affairs made a statement before Canada's Standing Committee on External Affairs on 10 October 1968. The Canadian Prime Minister made a clear declaration of his country's support of Nigeria in his speech to Parliament at Ottawa on 27 November 1968 (quoted in *Africa Research Bulletin*, p. 1242).

observers' verdict of 'no genocide', in contrast to the inflamed accounts brought back by two of their M.P.s[1] backed by the tireless lobbying of the Secretary for Overseas Missions of the Canadian Presbyterian Church.[2] In the event this intention—seen by Lagos as flogging yet another dead horse[3]—was dropped, but demands by both Senators Kennedy[4] and Nixon, now President-elect, to 'call an end to this slaughter of innocents', gave further grounds for anxiety [DOC 186].

Add this to the growing Swiss[5] and Scandinavian hostility to Britain on account of her Federal support[6] and it demonstrated to the Nigerian Government that she still had not won over the Western world to her cause—least of all Europe, where a Gallup poll claimed that 42% felt most strongly about Biafra against 17% about Vietnam.[7] Nor, it seemed, had she won all of Africa, as President Obote's hint of taking Uganda into the 'humanist approach to politics' group of those states that had already recognized Biafra,[8] and the reiteration by President Kaunda (presumed by Lagos to have been piqued by his performance at Algiers) of Biafra's own theme that her people had been 'rejected by their fellow Nigerians before secession',[9] made forcefully plain, much to Nigeria's chagrin. Lagos replied with the bitter abuse of disenchantment:

... [Kaunda's] disgraceful show of bad temper ... declined to be one of the eight vice-chairmen of the conference ... alleged that African leaders who spoke before him prejudged the issue of the Nigerian civil war, and lumped him together with the imperialists ... therefore decided to withdraw from the summit.

... In any case, who is Kaunda to talk of the rights of anyone to self-determination in Nigeria? ... Kaunda further confirmed that he is not prepared to repent when he announced that he was considering taking the Nigerian issue to the United Nations. This is a threat which does not move anyone, but one would like to know why Kaunda is considering taking action which runs counter to the O.A.U. resolution calling on all member-states of the O.A.U.

[1] Elaborated on, with clippings from the Canadian press, in Markpress Release No. Gen. 382. See also Releases No. 364 and 366.

[2] *West Africa* (1968), p. 1242.

[3] B.B.C. ME/2880.

[4] *The Times*, 18 November 1968.

[5] The British exhibition in Basle was cancelled for this reason.

[6] For Nigerian reaction to Swedish and Israeli pro-Biafran sympathies see B.B.C. ME/2818 and ME/2814 respectively. See also Markpress Release No. Gen. 325 for Biafran jubilation.

[7] The *Observer*, 17 November 1968. See also *The Times*, 9 September, and Markpress Release No. Gen. 351.

[8] He was quoted as describing the civil war as 'a shame on Africa',*Uganda Argus*, 9 October 1968. See also *West Africa*, pp. 1089 and 1334. Radio reports quoted in *Africa Research Bulletin*, p. 1214, talked of 'possible recognition' by Uganda, which brought a sharp rebuke from Kaduna Radio on 9 October. An indication of the strength of President Obote's genuine pro-Biafran sentiment is to be found in *The People* (Kampala), 26 October 1968.

[9] *The Times*, 5 November; *West Africa* (1968), p. 1334.

and the United Nations to refrain from doing anything which would prolong the Nigerian crisis. Kaunda's motive is, of course, quite apparent. . . .[1]

Nor was there support in the East, either, for the Chinese People's Republic was now speaking out on Biafra's part:

U.S. and British imperialism and the Soviet revisionist ruling clique have committed towering crimes in the past year or more in supporting the military government of the Nigerian Federation in its massacre of Biafran people who have declared their separation from the Nigerian Federation. . . . The Biafran people have been massacred in large numbers, but far from being subjugated, they have been fighting staunchly. . . .[2]

As the French experience continued to prove so alarmingly, this might be a prelude to supplying munitions as well as moral encouragement. Such an injection could, as Nigeria was now learning to her cost, at once change the whole face of the fighting overnight. Much of the Federal Government's frustration at what it felt to be gratuitous intervention by outsiders into a situation that it considered its own sovereign concern is revealed in a publication put out at this difficult time, pointedly captioned *Foreign Meddlers in the Nigerian Crisis*.[3]

It was this fear of a giddy spiralling that prompted the Conservative Party in Great Britain to table a motion deploring the threat posed by France's 'capricious action',[4] which in turn brought about yet another Parliamentary debate on arms supplies from the U.K. Chief Enahoro's prompt arrival in London from Nigeria gave rise to contradictory views on what the British Government may have told him about future supplies.[5] Even the news of a break between the Biafran Government and the American organizer of its Lisbon airlift, Captain Horton,[6] could not bring much comfort to Lagos in its rising fears of a Biafran army, re-armed and possibly resurgent, breaking back to the sea. Such growing belief in further recognition and physical aid, confirmed in the radical shift in the balance of military strength since September,[7] doubtless lay behind the attitude of confidence displayed first by Mr.

---

[1] Talk over Lagos Radio, 21 September 1968 (B.B.C. ME/2882/B1). See also the sharp criticism in the talk carried over Kaduna Radio on 'President Obote's Misfires' on 9 October 1968 (B.B.C. ME/2897/B4). Cf. similar abuse of Nyerere (see pp. 34–5).

[2] Dispatch date-lined Peking, 22 September 1968, given in B.B.C. Monitoring Service Far East/2881/A5/1. See also *Sunday Telegraph*, 10 November 1968.

[3] Published in Lagos, September 1968.

[4] *The Times*, 24 October 1968.

[5] *The Times*, 8 and 9 November; *Financial Times*, 9 November 1968; *West Africa* (1968), p. 1393.

[6] *West Africa* (1968), p. 1301.

[7] The effects were analysed in an A.F.P. report dated 26 October 1968, quoted in *Africa Research Bulletin*, p. 1212. France's motives have been subject to several interpretations, including (oil considerations apart) that of not wishing to see the emergence of a strong anglophone leadership in West Africa. See also editorial in *New Nigerian*, 16 September 1968.

G

Mojekwu in a statement made on arrival in London from Biafra [DOC 187] and then by Colonel Ojukwu at an exclusive press interview granted to a small group of continental newsmen in Umuahia on 27 October.[1] In this, he laughed off as wishful thinking a report that an attempt had been made on his life,[2] attributed to Colonel Adekunle's intelligence, (the same story, *mutatis mutandis*, had been circulated about Adekunle eleven months earlier[3] and about Hassan in the year before). Ojukwu spoke again, in public, on the eve of his thirty-fifth birthday, arguing that with his 50,000 well-armed troops he could not see the war ending for another twelve months, by which time he expected world opinion to have crystallized in favour of recognizing Biafra's struggle for self-determination.[4]

Despite the expressions of support gained from Niger and the Sudan after General Gowon's surprise visit to Maradi on 3 November, in the Lagos view it was still Ojukwu who was the stumbling block. This was reaffirmed by General Gowon in an interview granted to a British M.P. and former leading counsel for the African Continental Bank at the Foster Sutton Tribunal, Mr. W. L. Mallalieu, at which he quoted from a letter attributed to Dr. Azikiwe which implicated Ojukwu in a plot to carry out a military take-over during the constitutional crisis of December 1964.[5] Mr. Mallalieu, endorsing Dame Margery Perham's example, also broadcast from Lagos an appeal to the Ibos to renounce and exile Ojukwu and so resolve the war by finding a new leader.[6] Towards the end of November the I.C.R.C. announced[7] that it needed further funds to extend its relief programme beyond December. Since July, it claimed, the I.C.R.C. had brought in nearly 5,000 tons of supplies and had a further 4,000 stockpiled on Fernando Poo. This appeal followed an alarming Scandinavian Nord Church Aid report to U Thant[8] that without a cease-fire one million Biafrans would die of starvation before the end of the year. Meanwhile, relations worsened between Nigeria and Gabon, which expelled all Nigerian nationals,[9] and the Ivory Coast Foreign Minister gave a press conference in London (where he had talks with the Foreign Secretary and Lord Shepherd) to explain his country's policy of *'le dialogue honnête'* for bringing the Nigerian civil war to an end.[10] In such a tense atmosphere, the reported

[1] Markpress Release No. Gen. 386. A verbatim transcript of a second meeting with selected newsmen was released in No. Gen. 395.

[2] *Observer* and *Sunday Telegraph*, 27 October; *Gaskiya ta fi Kwabo*, 28 October; *West Africa* (1968), p. 1301.

[3] *Focus on Biafra*, 26 December 1967.

[4] Markpress Release No. Gen. 398.

[5] Press release issued by Nigeria House, 21 November 1967. The letter, 'exposing the inordinate political ambition' of Ojukwu, was published in Lagos on 1 June 1968.

[6] Lagos Radio, 17 November 1968 (B.B.C. ME/2929/B1).

[7] *The Times*, 26 November 1968.

[8] *The Times*, 19 October and 22 November 1968; *West Africa* (1968), p. 1273.

[9] *The Times*, 11 November 1968.

[10] *West Africa* (1968), p. 1392.

remark of Chief Enahoro that Federal peace terms might be modified seemed to many a sick joke or no more than a canard.[1] Indeed, the national reaction to this misinterpretation disclosed to the insensitive how sensitive Nigeria was to the matter of a settlement.[2]

Regretfully, observers close to the Nigerian scene began to wonder whether there could be something 'rotten in the state' of Nigeria, especially in the West and at certain levels of military command. That the recrudescent Yoruba riots of these weeks and Brigadier Adebayo's subsequent strong warning to his people[3] confirmed their worry only made matters worse in Nigerian eyes. It was, of course, the very arrogance of this inside semi-informed and outside less informed public opinion that had by now penetrated deep under the legitimately wearing-thin Nigerian skin. Three months after the much heralded 'final offensive' was mounted against Biafra's presumed last-ditch stand in the confident expectation of cutting it in half and seizing Umuahia, the war seemed as far from a solution as it ever had been. The Nigerians found themselves checked on the military plane[4] and rapidly losing the battle for other men's minds at the same time as they were being assailed on the international level. Biafra's would-be last days were proving her longest, too.

The last weeks of 1968 brought an ardent renewal of public interest in Britain, unknown during her period of parliamentary responsibility for the colonies and ironically not voiced till a decade after Nigerian independence, demanding that 'something be done' by the authorities, first to alleviate the apparently monstrous threat of mass starvation in the Ibo heartland (comparisons were sought in Britain's indifference to the Irish famine of the 1840s) where carbohydrate food supplies would, it was reported, as well as proteins, soon be exhausted; and secondly, to bring their governmental influence into play, as promised by the Prime Minister as a collateral for arms supplies, and so effect a cease-fire. A 'Biafran baby' appeal, launched by a Miss Susan Garth with a full page gimmicky advertisement in *The Times*,[5] brought a smart rebuke from the Biafran Government[6] angered at the demoralizing suggestions that could be read into a mass evacuation of children

[1] In the *Financial Times*, 13 November 1968, condemned by Enahoro as 'too scandalous to be excusable'. See also B.B.C. ME/2934, quoting Enahoro's reproof to the *Daily Sketch* (Ibadan), and B.B.C. ME/2936, quoting a talk from Kaduna; *West Africa* (1968), p. 1425.

[2] See the article by Peter Enahoro in the *Spectator*, 24 December 1968.

[3] Broadcast of 26 November 1968.

[4] 'Grave logistical difficulties' was the reason given by the Nigerian Army Chief of Staff in an interview on 4 November 1969, quoted in *Africa Research Bulletin*, p. 1239. Battle reports from the Biafran command on 27 and 28 November spoke of an offensive by the Biafran troops and claims of recapturing a number of villages from Federal hands (Biafra Radio, 28 November 1969).

[5] *The Times*, 12 December, following a report in *The Times*, 5 December 1968.

[6] The *Guardian*, 13 December 1968. An earlier scheme for child evacuation was attacked by Kaduna Radio on 21 October 1968 (B.B.C. ME/2906/B6).

so that the soul of Biafra might presumably live. Oxfam issued further impassioned calls for an immediate end to the fighting, blazoning banners such as 'Do Not Read This If Your Stomach Isn't Strong.'[1] They were irascibly condemned by the Federal Government with the warning that 'Nigerians have had enough of the blackmail approach of the humanitarian organisations:'

... The Federal Government, however, doubts the sincerity and motivation of those behind the latest appeal. ... As a matter of fact, the humanitarian organisations aided and abetted the secessionist leaders in their futile attempt to sustain their armed rebellion. ... It is revealing that Oxfam and Caritas and similar organisations have now come out into the open to take sides in the political questions associated with ceasefire after a long period of clandestine support for the rebel cause of breaking up Nigeria. They behave as if they are concerned with two sovereign nations at war.[2]

The Roman Catholic Church endured equal opprobrium, at the no-holds-barred hands of Lagos Radio, for its 'most despicable role calculated to help Ojukwu break up this country', along with Caritas, accused of 'stepping up its support to help Ojukwu and his rebel gang in the war against their fatherland'.[3] Some Nigerians abroad realized, however, that the puny ineffectiveness of their own publicity had a share in the blame attaching to Nigeria's undeserved unpopularity in certain quarters:

... Outrageously lopsided editorials comments and adverse comment by misguided members of parliament are not countered in anyway either by Nigerian embassy officials or Nigerian public relations agents if such exist anywhere. ... This is a situation that causes absolute agony to those of us who happen to be abroad at this crucial moment of the nation's life.

The claims that Nigerian publicity abroad is succeeding must be exposed for what it is. Nigerian publicity abroad does not exist. Its success is, therefore, imaginary—a fact anybody abroad can substantiate. ...[4]

It was little wonder that General Gowon, weary of outside concern (welcoming only the U.S.S.R. Economic Mission at the end of November) and needfully aware of his own image as the indispensably strong leader, again seized an academic occasion—as he had done at Ibadan the previous year—to deliver a major political speech, this time in Zaria. In round terms he blamed the unexpected protraction of the fighting on certain foreign governments, missionary zealots, and 'misguided humanitarian organizations'. He outlined a programme for

[1] The *Observer*, 1 December; *The Times*, 14 and 19 December 1968.

[2] Statement issued in Lagos, 2 December 1968 (*Daily Times*, 3 December).

[3] Talks on Lagos Radio, 27 November (B.B.C. ME/2937/B5) and 29 November 1968 (B.B.C. ME/2940/B4).

[4] The letters from Mr. C. Abashiya and from M. Kyari Tijani (*New Nigerian*, 27 December 1968) represented an opinion held by many Nigerian students in the U.K. and U.S.A., resentful of the way the Biafran propaganda consistently 'got away with it' with monotonous impunity. Other Nigerian sympathizers were made painfully aware of this.

national reconciliation and promised to announce a new date for a
return to civilian rule as soon as the war was ended [DOC 188].[1] But
Britain's public conscience unfortunately would not let Nigeria alone,
as General Gowon implored the outside world to do. In December,
against a background of renewed pressure at Westminster, mercy
flights were discussed in the House of Commons.[2] Then over 130 M.P.s,
from all parties, signed a motion on 4 December urging the Government
to press both sides to agree to an immediate cease-fire:

> That this House, appalled by the mounting starvation and killing in
> Biafra, urges Her Majesty's Government to press both sides for an immediate
> cease-fire; to seek agreement with the three other Governments still promot-
> ing the supply of arms to the combatants for a joint ban; as proof of its readi-
> ness to do this the British Government should stop the supply of British arms
> forthwith; and should help organize a massive international operation to
> provide food and medical supplies.

Other public figures called on the electorate to lobby their M.P.s for an
emergency debate[3] and call off the quick-kill strategy,[4] while the
Archbishop of Canterbury signed a letter from a group of eminent
humanists calling on the British Government to use 'all the influence
at its disposal for a total international embargo on arms supplies to both
sides'.[5] The foreign affairs debate in the House of Commons in mid-
December inevitably included discussions of the seemingly worsening
Nigerian war. As the Government spokesman put it:

> . . . Our priorities must clearly be relief and a cease-fire. It will probably be
> very difficult to do what the world needs to do concerning relief without
> getting a cease-fire first. Equally, it is extremely difficult to see how we could
> get an arms embargo by all countries and private agencies supplying arms
> without first getting a cease-fire. It would be very difficult, because each side
> would need to be assured that the other was not getting illicit supplies. It
> would be a practical condition in getting that embargo to get, first, a cease-
> fire or a truce. That is why we are concentrating our attention on these two
> points. I accept that the view is sincerely held that if we made a unilateral
> decision to end arms supplies, this would contribute to the two objectives of
> relief and a cease-fire. We need to put the matter in perspective. The supplies
> from this country, which are strictly controlled, are less than 15 per cent in
> value of the arms supplies going to the Federal Government and rather less
> than 50 per cent of the weapons and ammunition going for the ground
> forces. . . .

It is clear that a unilateral decision would not bring about a cease-fire and
would not help relief at this time. Therefore, the Government continue to

---

[1] Also see Epilogue, p. 473.

[2] Debate of 3 December 1968.

[3] Letter in the *Daily Telegraph*, 12 December 1968, from Professor A. J. Ayer and
others.

[4] Letter in *The Times*, 4 December 1968.

[5] Letters in *The Times*, and editorial, 11 December 1968.

supply arms on the same basis as previously. We will, however, use every possible endeavour, because we know that this is the wish of all right hon. and hon. Members, to try to achieve effective ways of getting relief. It is not sufficient, as my right hon. Friend said, to make a donation to the Red Cross. It is essential to do all that we can to see that that is translated into food and supplies where they are needed. . . .[1]

Just as predictably, it concluded with nothing of good cheer, even from the irrepressible Prime Minister himself[2] and, despite a further £700,000 for relief, twenty-two M.P.s abstained in protest against the Government's Nigerian policy.[3] The Labour Party's approach to the crisis was illustrated in its official bulletin published at this time.[4]

As an earnest of how seriously the British Government was viewing the situation of stalemate or worse, Lord Shepherd made his third precipitate visit to Lagos with yet another personal message from Mr. Wilson to General Gowon. But neither Lagos, where Chief Enahoro had bluntly stated he saw 'no hope of reopening peace talks with the rebels',[5] nor Biafra, whose Commissioner for Information had reiterated at a press conference Biafra's refusal to be drawn into 'abortive' peace conferences and had declared that it was a matter of 'give us Biafra or nothing',[6] afforded Lord Shepherd much encouragement in the British Government's anxious efforts at getting peace talks started again. His talks with the Federal Government concluded in a thin joint communiqué which endorsed the O.A.U.'s key potential, regretted Colonel Ojukwu's reluctance to accept a land route for moving in supplies for civilians, and reaffirmed the Lagos intention to 'continue with all necessary measures' the aim of ending secession in the East Central State.[7] He had met with a cool reception in Nigeria,[8] for the Federal Government stood by its conviction that talks could only be held within the formula of the O.A.U. resolution and the issue settled as 'an African problem . . . in an African way'.[9] It went on to deliver a stinging rebuke deploring Britain's endless Parliamentary debates on the civil war as a matter beyond the House's legal competence.[10] At the same time, it

[1] F. Mulley, House of Commons debate, 12 December 1968 (Hansard, cols. 708 and 712).

[2] *Debates*, House of Commons, 17 December 1968, cols. 1162–3.

[3] See commentaries on the debate in *The Times* and the *Guardian*, 13 December 1968.

[4] *Talking Points*, no. 22, December 1968. A number of historical inaccuracies can be identified in its synopsis of events.

[5] *The Times*, 12 December 1968. See also Lagos Radio report, 10 December (B.B.C. ME/2949/B2).

[6] Biafra Radio, 12 December, quoted at length in *Africa Research Bulletin*, pp. 1268–9; *The Times*, 13 December 1968.

[7] Statement issued in Lagos, 16 December 1968. See also Lagos Radio report, 17 December (B.B.C. ME/2954).

[8] e.g., Adamu Ciroma, 'Lord Shepherd, The Communiqué and The Truth', *New Nigerian*, 18 December 1968.

[9] *The Times*, 11 December; *Evening Standard*, 18 December 1968.

[10] *Daily Telegraph* and *Daily Express*, 11 December 1968. Talk on Lagos Radio, 'The Meddlesome British M.P.s', 12 December. See also pp. 106 and 464.

THE CARPET-BAGGERS

Your Excellency, our qualifications for the relief of suffering are impeccable — we did so much to bring it about.

Reproduced by kind permission of the *New Statesman*

stimulated further outbursts in the Nigerian press against 'inhuman humanitarians'[1] and 'missionary zealots'.[2] The stalemate was as unresolved as it had been before the British Government's latest attempt to break it in the face of what the Prime Minister himself roundly condemned as 'the intransigence of those on the spot'.[3]

In a war of this nature an international appeal might not always or readily be distinguished from outside interference, and few regretted the decision of the British Prime Minister, revealed in Whitehall, to abandon his surprising—and possibly disturbing—plan to fly out to Lagos in the role of super-mediator.[4] Instead, the U.K. Government now dispatched a senior envoy (Maurice Foley) to Ethiopia to sound out the Emperor on bringing the two protagonists together for yet one more round of peace talks, this time under the unambiguous auspices of the O.A.U.[5] At Westminster, the Foreign Secretary felt able to say that a Christmas truce would be one way to initiate a cease-fire.[6]

Despite Lagos's resentment at even the whisper of mediation, the drip-drip tears of the world's worry could not fail to have some effect on Nigeria's policy if not perhaps on its clean conscience. Thus, amid all this international brouhaha, further peace offers were made to Biafra in early December.[7] Again, on 11 December, Lagos Radio announced

[1] Letter from 'Insaniyat' in *New Nigerian*, 28 December 1968.
[2] Article by Dan Agbese, *New Nigerian*, 28 December 1968.
[3] Quoted in *West Africa* (1968), p. 1457.
[4] *The Times* and *Daily Telegraph*, 21 December 1968.
[5] *The Times*, 11 December; *Daily Telegraph*, 13 December 1968.
[6] Quoted in *The Times*, 17 December 1968.
[7] Lagos Radio, 3 December 1968 (B.B.C. ME/2942/B1).

that 'It is understood that the Federal Military Government has re-affirmed [to Lord Shepherd] its readiness to accept the invitation to another round of peace talks based on the Algiers [O.A.U.] resolution.'[1] When Ojukwu turned both these overtures down on 12 December, the olive branch was replaced by more character assassination from Radio Kaduna.[2] In the same stigmatizing vein, few seemed to have noticed Nigeria's pot-calling-the-kettle-black lapse in her own regrettably Nkru-mah-like intervention into the domestic affairs of a sister-state when she took the opportunity of Zambia's general election to urge the Zambian electorate to reject President Kaunda, 'the man who has brought nothing but shame to their country.'[3] Meanwhile, realistic editorials in *The Times*,[4] the *Guardian*,[5] and the *Scotsman*[6] not only gave proof of the serious and widespread attention currently shown to a Nigerian problem so prematurely written off as a forgotten war, but also presented succinct and perceptive summaries of the apparently intractable stands of the various parties involved as they appeared to the outside world in the December of 1968.

Then, like an unexpected rainstorm in the dry season of Hausaland, a sudden gust of renewed hope blew through these apparent dogdays, exciting expectations of a real cease-fire at least over Christmas. Follow-ing Dr. Dunwoody as the first British M.P. to have entered the rebel territory since the war started, the octogenarian Lord Brockway[7] and the younger (78) Mr. James Griffiths, one-time Colonial Secretary, undertook a bold visit to Biafra where they had an interview with Colonel Ojukwu [DOC 189]. Then they flew on to Nigeria. They gave their conclusions to a press conference in London[8] in which they dis-cussed their part in encouraging General Gowon's decision to go it alone and call a truce on the two days marking the religious festivals of Id and Christmas.[9] This was in preference to an appeal by the Emperor of Ethiopia for a truce lasting seven days[10] and to a suggestion from Lord Shepherd for one of fourteen days.[11] Colonel Ojukwu countered this by announcing on 23 December that he had issued an order to the Biafran

---

[1] B.B.C. ME/2949/B2.

[2] Talk, 'The Insanity of a Rebel', Kaduna Radio, 13 December 1968 (B.B.C. ME/2952/B8).

[3] Talk on Lagos Radio, 17 December 1968.

[4] *The Times*, 11 December 1968.

[5] The *Guardian*, 18 December 1968.

[6] The *Scotsman*, 6 December 1968.

[7] He described this visit in *New Statesman*, 3 January 1969. The *Morning Post* found the visit a 'great disappointment' and the *Nigerian Tribune* saw no reason why these two visitors should 'poke their noses in our crisis under the guise of a peace mission' (17 December 1968).

[8] Held in the Waldorf Hotel, London, 23 December 1968.

[9] Statement issued in Lagos, 20 December: *The Times*, 21 December 1968.

[10] *Sunday Telegraph*, 22 December; Lagos Radio, 24 December 1968, quoting a Government statement (B.B.C. ME/2960/B5).

[11] *West Africa* (1968), p. 1525.

armed forces to observe an eight-day truce lasting to midnight on 1 January,[1] but neither the undertones of his broadcast nor those of General Gowon's no-illusions letter to the Emperor of Ethiopia about the prior need for a change of attitude by Ojukwu[2] suggested much likelihood of honesty here. Inevitably there ensued mutual accusations of violating the truce.[3]

The year went out like the proverbial equinoctial lion. There was Colonel Adekunle, who again angrily accused a rather dazed International Red Cross Committee of deliberately leaking military intelligence to the enemy[4] (their mercy flights from Fernando Poo had experienced a two-day ban, due to alleged confusion over the Christmas truce).[5] Serious riots again shook the Western State, ostensibly over tax but inseparable from the mounting agitation by Yorubas abroad as well as those in Nigeria for a second State for a people ever more volatile and divisive than they appeared to the unpractised eye.[6] There was a sternly worded complaint from Lagos to the American ambassador over his country's offer of extra transport planes to step up relief operations in Biafra,[7] reinforced by several radio talks on the theme of 'Let the Americans be warned that they will be making a grave mistake by getting actively involved in the Nigerian civil war—they got only their fingers burned in Vietnam, they might get their arms burnt in Nigeria;'[8] an accusing letter from a group of Nigerian professors asserting that the U.S.A. was engaged in 'secret aggression' against their country;[9] and an inspired Government leak that Nigeria would walk out of the forthcoming Commonwealth Prime Ministers' Conference should any member dare to raise her crisis for discussion.[10] Christmas and end-of-the-year messages were broadcast by General Gowon, who called for the nation's rededication of itself in the 'fight for peace' and again promised a 'quick end' to the war, although he warned that this might entail a general mobilization and more sacrifices;[11] and by Colonel Ojukwu, who condemned Nigeria's breaking of the Christmas truce.[12] A week later, however, Ojukwu went on in a longer speech to include two modifica-

[1] B.B.C. ME/2959.

[2] Quoted by Lagos Radio, 24 December 1969 (B.B.C. ME/2960/B5).

[3] Compare Lagos Radio emissions of 24 December with those from Biafra on 27 December 1968.

[4] *Scotsman*, 25 December; *The Times*, 28 December 1968.

[5] B.B.C. ME/2960.

[6] *Daily Times*, 17 December 1968; various reports quoted in *Africa Research Bulletin*, p. 1271. See the reference in General Gowon's New Year message to 'causes extending beyond dissatisfaction with the level of taxation'. The literature in circulation, openly in Great Britain and America but more clandestine in Lagos and the Western State, accumulated to a sizable volume.

[7] Lagos Radio, 30 December; *The Times*, 31 December 1968.

[8] B.B.C. ME/2963.

[9] *Sunday Times*, 29 December 1968.

[10] ibid. See also talk broadcast over Lagos Radio (B.B.C. ME/2951/B7).

[11] *Sacrifice for Unity* (Lagos, 1969).

[12] Broadcast of 22 December 1968 (Markpress Release No. Gen. 459).

tions of Biafra's previous stand, those of negotiated economic links and of a truce for 'a limited and specific period' for relief purposes instead of a general cease-fire.[1]

As the world press and radio surveyed 1968, few failed to draw attention to the tragedy of Nigeria and the worsening conditions in Biafra. The end-of-the-year editorial in the *Nigerian Observer*, published in Benin, claimed that one million Nigerians had already lost their lives through the war and its associated evils. Dazed by such figures and sickened by the stalemate, the world's mind began to boggle at what astronomical total might be reached in another twelve months of attrition and at last began to realize how small Vietnam might be by comparison. *The Times* coined the term 'geno-slaughter' for what it felt was murder that lacked the planning and official hallmark of genocide,[2] and the rabidly pro-Biafran *Spectator* published a special 5,000 word examination of the arguments about when deliberate starvation is not genocide and the extent of Britain's responsibility for what it calculated as the toll of 15,000 deaths a day swelling to an envisaged 5,000,000 dead by early 1969.[3] Aware that its relief stand could less and less escape the charge of not being completely devoid of political motives, the Biafran Government prepared at the very end of the year a special brief on the thorny issue of mercy flights and land corridors [DOC 190]. The target of the Commonwealth Prime Ministers' Conference, due to open a week hence, was implicit in its timing. Whether the ploy was to succeed or not would soon be seen.

[1] Markpress Release No. Gen. 472.
[2] *The Times*, 31 December 1968.
[3] The *Spectator*, 27 December 1968.

LIKE its two predecessors, the year 1969 opened with excited speculation about the chances of a settlement inherent in a round of immediately forthcoming talks. Like 1967 and 1968, too, the hopes of a negotiated peace, or even a cease-fire, were swiftly dispelled, and by mid-January the civil war had in the minds of many reverted to its most unyielding and despairing level.

On his arrival in London for the Commonwealth Prime Ministers' Conference (the successor to the one held in Lagos during that fateful week of murder and mutiny three long years earlier), Chief Awolowo confirmed the agitated sentiments already expressed at home that under no circumstances would the Nigerian delegation brook any discussion of its civil war, held to be essentially and exclusively an internal affair,[1] at the conference table. Dr. Eke's prior appeal to the Conference to press for a cease-fire[2] was already in obvious jeopardy. Leaders of the two Commonwealth countries that had recognized Biafra, Tanzania and Zambia (against whom, together with France and Portugal, the Nigerian radio had maintained a year's vituperative disparagement[3]), retorted that they had every intention of bringing the issue up when it seemed appropriate, and the T.A.N.U. party newspaper the *Nationalist* had warned of Anglo-Nigerian tactics to keep the war out of the Conference hall.[4] In the event, the two Presidents met privately with the Nigerian delegation but without any positive result.[5] Rumours about a planned Commonwealth Peace mission[6] seemed to most observers, given Nigeria's repeated rejection of any body other than the O.A.U. as even a potential mediator, to be mere castles in the air, though more importance could perhaps be attached to a possible discussion of some sort of a Commonwealth peacekeeping force. Biafran envoys who 'happened', as they explained,[7] to be in London at the time delegates were arriving, made ample use of opportunities for lobbying. Their student organizations arranged a protest torchlight parade[8] and then noisily came face to face with a no less voluble show of strength organ-

[1] Lagos Radio, 13 December (B.B.C. ME/2951/B7); *Sunday Times* (Lagos) 29 December; *Financial Times*, 30 December 1968; *Guardian*, 7 January 1969.

[2] Biafra Radio, 4 January 1969 (B.B.C. ME/2968/B2).

[3] In addition to the radio attacks quoted against 1968, two more highly defamatory assaults on Kaunda and Nyerere, questioning their integrity and casting aspersions on their leadership, were now broadcast from Lagos (B.B.C. ME/2897/B2–B5).

[4] *West Africa* (1968), p. 1530. [5] *Observer*, 12 January 1969.

[6] *Sunday Telegraph*, 29 December 1968.

[7] *The Times* and the *Guardian*, 7 January 1969. See also Biafran news conference quoted in *West Africa* (1969), p. 31.

[8] *Daily Telegraph*, 7 January 1969; photograph in *The Times*.

ized by their Nigerian counterparts on the day the Prime Ministers' Conference opened. In quieter, and more telling, terms ethno-areal groups such as the Rivers State Students' Union of Great Britain and Ireland presented protestant memoranda to the Nigerian delegation.

As it turned out, the only reference during the proceedings of the Conference, predominantly perturbed by Rhodesia and the NIBMAR issue, to the rebellion on Nigeria's hands came in a non-committal chronological review by Mr. Wilson, who simply alluded to the 'present time when the hearts of all of us are torn by the tragedy of the fighting in Nigeria',[1] and in the unemotionally factual report by Mr. Arnold Smith of the persistent efforts by his Secretariat to bring the two sides together round a table throughout 1968.[2] But outside the conference chamber there was, in accordance with the protocol of diplomatic strategy, much discussion. Chief Awolowo let it be known that, while he would not go out of his way to get in touch with the Biafran representatives then in London, he would not block any approach from them for private discussion.[3] Later, with his apparent capacity for being misunderstood, he denied that there had been even informal contacts between former friends and colleagues, doubting the calibre of such roving ambassadors as Dike and Nwokedi and inferring that talks with Mojekwu or Azikiwe alone could be profitable;[4] but as he himself was reportedly a last minute substitute for General Gowon, who had originally announced his intention of attending the Commonwealth Conference in person but at the final moment decided against leaving Lagos,[5] the situation threatened to assume the meaningless façade of Hamlet deprived of both Prince and Polonius. The British Prime Minister followed up the studiously balanced week-end house-parties at Chequers with what was officially called a 'discussion over gin and tonic' immediately after the Conference had adjourned, at which Awolowo was reported to have 'shown his willingness' to meet Biafra's representatives 'without pre-conditions'.[6] But nothing came of it, and the reports and denials of who actually did or did not try to get in touch with whom during these ten days (including the muddled messages to newsmen[7]) hinted at a smoke-screen manufactured from elements of, to cite one description, 'suppliant positions' and over-proud sensitivities.[8] As a tail-piece General Gowon felt able to welcome Chief Awolowo on his return to Lagos with the opinion that the Conference had been 'yet another forum for a vote of confidence for Nigeria in her fight against rebellion . . . a victory for sanity and for maturity'.[9] Six weeks later, too, the

---

[1] Quoted in *West Africa* (1969), p. 29.
[2] *Second Report of the Commonwealth Secretary-General* (London, 1969), pp. 22–6.
[3] *West Africa* (1969), p. 31. See also *Africa Research Bulletin*, p. 1290.
[4] Press commentary, 17 January 1969.
[5] *Sunday Telegraph*, 29 December 1968.
[6] *The Times*, 16 January; *West Africa* (1969), p. 81.   [7] *West Africa* (1969), p. 109.
[8] *West Africa* (1969), p. 81.   [9] B.B.C. ME/2979.

Under-Secretary for Foreign and Commonwealth Affairs was to tell the House of Commons that it was the Biafrans who had let slip the opportunity provided by the Commonwealth Prime Ministers' Conference for new peace talks.[1]

The Nigerian delegates were rightly huffed by what they saw as a rudely pro-Biafran handling of television time by the B.B.C.[2] After Awolowo had declined to take part or be represented in a well-advertised panel on 'Panorama',[3] almost a whole hour was allocated on the following evening to the screening of a sensational film on Biafra in 'Twenty-four Hours', followed by a short interview the next evening with Chief Enahoro and—although his chief gave him little opportunity to show his paces—Dr. Asika.[4] The quality of this televised discussion was felt to have done more harm than good to the Nigerian cause, in unfortunate contrast to the stirring timbre of the pro-Biafran film which inspired even a group of tough British dockers to refuse to handle a cargo of arms for Nigeria in protest against Britain's support of the Federal Government.[5] Enahoro's curt rejection of a cease-fire as 'plain stupid' now that 'we have got them on the run'[6] was a chilly curtain-raiser to Mr. Wilson's report to Parliament at the end of the Conference. This was as pessimistic and near despair as it had ever been, matching the mood created by both sides' seemingly wretched failure, in the face of measurable international dismay and souring disgust, to make the most of yet another opportunity, however slender, to avert the tragic suffering inseparable from the slow death of an aborted quick kill.

Support was lent to the odds on this death-by-degrees deduction when reports came in of delays of up to twelve days in unloading relief supplies in Lagos harbour[7] and by obstacles again placed in the way of the International Red Cross operating from an agreed air base in Equatorial Guinea. Here the newly independent Government, who had interrupted relief flights in December, now suddenly served on the I.C.R.C. notice to quit. The mischievous inference that diplomatic pressure had been applied to bring about this ban[8] prompted a denial from Lagos:

The Nigerian Federal Government wishes to state categorically that it brought no pressure to bear upon the Government of Equatorial Guinea in the

---

[1] *West Africa* (1969), p. 257.

[2] Nigeria was to suspend certain facilities granted to the B.B.C. See *Sunday Times*, 12 January, and *Sunday Telegraph*, 26 January 1969.

[3] *The Times*, 9 January 1969.

[4] See comments by Lagos Radio (B.B.C. ME/2970/ii and ME/2977/B3), and the radio talk on 'The Mischievous B.B.C.' on 13 January. Enahoro's reaction is to be found in *Sunday Times*, 12 January 1969. The Nigerian Government's *United Nigeria* described the 'B.B.C. boob' as being worthy of Dr. Goebbels—No. 8, 1969.

[5] *The Times*, 11 January 1969.

[6] Quoted in *Daily Telegraph*, 14 January, and *West Africa* (1969), p. 81.

[7] *The Times*, 16 January 1969.

[8] The *Guardian*, 9 January 1969.

expulsion of International Red Cross personnel from the island of Fernando Po. Recent incorrect and malicious reports have implied that the Equatorial Guinea decision was influenced by representations from the Nigerian Federal Government. It is understood, however, that this decision was the direct result of actions inimical to the national interests of Equatorial Guinea by International Red Cross officials based on Fernando Po.[1]

In the event, it was suspicion and hostility between the Ibo labour force, comprising some 40% of the island's population, and the new President Macias that gave rise to such a penal measure.[2] The Red Cross was now obliged to switch its air-base to Dahomey, twice as far from the key target of Uli. In giving its permission, Cotonou was careful to refer to relief supplies destined for 'the victims of the fratricidal conflict between our Nigerian neighbours',[3] but this did not save the Dahomean Government from reproof by Kaduna Radio for its handling of 'the dirty work' of the Red Cross and from rebukes by other Nigerian organs.[4] The luckless I.C.R.C., long the target of attack by the Federal Government, now felt the lashing tongue of Biafra's spokesmen too,[5] and found itself condemned by both sides as a political organization.

The actual fighting had now entered its fifth month of impasse since the declared 'final push' had been so publicly launched. In Biafra, whose broadcasting station had switched to virulent attacks which made Mr. Wilson[6] (now lampooned as Mr. 'Harold Weasel-ling') and General Alexander[7] rather than General Gowon 'the real enemy of the defenceless Biafran people', and had resurrected doubts about the constitutional legitimacy of Gowon's headship of state[8] ('There exists no basis for his claim or his recognition'), Ojukwu was reported as asserting that 'the next thirty days will be merry hell, but after that I think we can start to win back.'[9] Some of his faith was clearly pinned on Nigeria's vulnerability to ethnic irredentism, currently highlighted by considerable Yoruba violence (and exaggeratedly exploited by the Biafran propaganda machinery[10]), as much as on his hopes that 'another spate of recognition particularly from European countries will force Nigeria to the conference table',[11] and on the near adequacy of

[1] Nigeria House press release, 13 January 1969.

[2] See reports in *The Economist*, 4 January; *The Times*, 27 January; *West Africa* (1969), p. 91; and B.B.C. ME/2988.

[3] Cotonou Radio quoted in B.B.C. ME/2987.

[4] Quoted, along with Enahoro's press briefing, in *West Africa* (1969), p. 165.

[5] Statement by Dr. Eke issued on 16 January 1969 (B.B.C. ME/2978/B8).

[6] e.g., radio talk 'The Bloodbath is Harold Wilson's Responsibility' (B.B.C. ME/2964/B2). See also the analysis 'Wilson and the Commonwealth' issued in Umuahia on 7 January (Markpress Release No. Gen. 479).

[7] Biafra Radio, 11 January 1969 (B.B.C. ME/2974/B4).

[8] Five-page statement issued by Biafra Ministry of Information, January 1969. See summary in Markpress Release No. Gen. 487.

[9] Quoted in *The Economist*, 11 January 1969.

[10] See the alarmist radio report quoted in B.B.C. ME/2957/ii.

[11] Press conference at Umuahia, 25 January 1969.

arms that had since September allowed Ojukwu, in Lord Shepherd's earlier assessment, to reject overtures for a negotiated end to the war.[1] Hence Ojukwu's headlined 'call for peace'[2] made to a small group of journalists visiting him in Umuahia at the end of January,[3] was in reality little more than a further appeal for the internationalization of the moves for a cease-fire and not a change of heart or voice from Biafra. In America, under a new President, the Administration was now beginning to give indications that the House of Representatives would no longer allow itself to remain passive before the country's mounting agitation for a more positive role in the move for peace.[4] January ended with Nigeria's gain of a see-for-yourself tour by four French Deputies[5] offset by the call for France's full recognition of Biafra by two other Deputies just back from there;[6] with an open letter from Dame Margery Perham to General Gowon, suggesting for Biafra 'some interim status as a temporary measure';[7] and with the speculative announcement, issued well after the Afro-Malagasy Common Organization had risen, that it intended to sponsor separate private peace missions to Nigeria and Biafra led by Presidents Diori of Niger and Mobutu of Congo.[8]

Although the existence of any such missions seemed to be in doubt, February brought no slackening in the pace of mediatory moves. Rear-Admiral Wey of the Federal Executive Council was reported to have visited Ghana assumed in order to set fresh moves in train,[9] and there were urgent visits to both sides by United States Congressmen, duly reported and interpreted along drawn lines even when the same Senator was being quoted.[10] Once more addressing the Consultative Assembly at Umuahia in another marathon speech, delivered on 10 February, Ojukwu rejected as firmly as Nigeria had done since Kampala any 'British-sponsored offensive' and warned what would befall Britain's interests in Biafra if she were to assume a leading role in promoting peace.[11] Like Gowon, Ojukwu too assured his people that

[1] Quoted in *Daily Telegraph*, 8 October 1968.
[2] *The Times*, 27 January 1969.
[3] See Markpress Release. No. Gen. 487.
[4] *West Africa* (1969), p. 104; Markpress Release No. Gen. 529.
[5] Nigeria House press release, 29 January 1969.
[6] *The Times*, 3 February 1969; Markpress Release No. Gen. 489.
[7] The *Spectator*, 31 January 1969.
[8] *The Times*, 31 January; *Sunday Telegraph*, 2 February; *West Africa* (1969), pp. 165 and 197; *Africa Confidential*, February 1969.
[9] *Daily Telegraph*, 14 February 1969.
[10] Coverage of remarks by Senator Charles E. Goodell of New York: Nigeria House press releases dated 7 and 12 February 1969; Markpress Release No. Gen. 502 and 515. Compare also Enahoro's address to visiting Congressmen in Lagos (Nigeria House press release dated 14 February 1969) with the unequivocal call on the U.S. Government to 'immediately utilize all of its diplomatic and economic resources for the purpose of bringing about a cease-fire' made by Ohio Representative Donald M. Lukens and newsman Fulton Lewis III at a press conference held in Washington on their return from Nigeria and Biafra (Markpress Release No. Gen. 494).
[11] *The Times*, 12 February 1969; Markpress Release No. Gen. 500 and 501.

'the end is near, the goal is in sight'. As a noisy reaction to Mr. Wilson's visit to Bonn showed,[1] his country was cordially disliked by Biafrans abroad; and at the meeting of the Western European Union the slanging match was reportedly no less vigorous or vituperative between Lord Chalfont and M. Jean de Lipkowski of France than it was between Lagos and Biafran radio stations.[2] The French representative was in some ways simply developing the current anti-British outbursts promoted by a Gaullist Deputy's public accusation of Britain as having 'inspired the 1966 coup' and of having been 'deeply implicated in the assassination of General Ironsi'.[3] Ojukwu's reference in his address before the Consultative Assembly[4] to 'the path of genocide' being pursued by 'Harold Wilson and his clique' was opportunely countered in an editorial in *West Africa* headed 'The World and the War'.[5]

Then, in the middle of February at a private meeting in Oxford, ex-President Azikiwe broke his ten months' silence and put forward a fourteen-point programme for resolving the conflict, which included a plebiscite and direct intervention by a military force raised by the United Nations along the lines of the previous U.N. presence in Cyprus and the Congo [DOC 191]. The 'astonishing haste'[6] and scant courtesy with which Lagos and Kaduna rejected the plan as 'absolute nonsense' and 'another pathetic attempt'[7] within twenty-four hours and assumedly without having more than a news agency report on which to base its decision, was known to have disturbed some ardent Nigerians who had heard the full speech. Perusal of Dr. Azikiwe's private correspondence on this speech reveals that the Biafran Government was no less 'seriously concerned' by it and suggested that it should be called off—a proposal that Dr. Azikiwe castigated as having 'shocked my conscience as being an outrageous invasion of my basic human rights.'[8] Yet in perspective, the Federal Government may not have been so wrong, for all its haste, in writing off the Azikiwe proposals as:

Basically the same as those put forward by the secessionist leaders at the Addis Ababa and earlier peace talks. . . . [They contain] several unacceptable features such as the contemptuous rejection of the O.A.U. efforts and the attempt to involve the U.N. and the U.S.A. in the Nigerian crisis which is

---

[1] *The Times*, 13 February 1969.

[2] *The Times*, 8 February; *Sunday Telegraph*, 9 February 1969. The proceedings of the W.E.U. are not made public.

[3] *Le Monde*, 7 February; *Sunday Telegraph*, 9 February 1969. See also F. Debré's anti-British article published in *Le Monde*, 5 December, and the reply by Dame Margery Perham, 9 December 1968.

[4] Summarized in Markpress Release No. Gen. 501.

[5] *West Africa* (1969), p. 169.

[6] The *Guardian*, 18 February 1969. See also letter in *West Africa* (1969), p. 275.

[7] Kaduna Radio, 14 February; Lagos Radio, 20 February; *The Times*, 18 February; *West Africa* (1969), p. 225.

[8] Correspondence between Dr. Azikiwe (still addressed as 'Your Excellency') and the Office of the Special Representative of the Government of Biafra in London, 16 and 17 February 1969. (By Courtesy of Dr. Azikiwe.)

strictly the internal affair of Lagos. . . . The Government deplores any moves which in effect encourage the rebel leaders to continue to fight for their illusory empire.[1]

Nigerians in the U.S.A., on the other hand, sent a letter to Gowon calling for the quick-kill solution before emotion swept through the United States and brought its military strength in on the side of the secessionists.[2] Senator Kennedy's call for a cease-fire was similarly rebuffed by Radio Kaduna's acid accusation of betrayal: 'the last of the Kennedys has let us down.'[3] Hopes, if any were left, were now to be exclusively pinned to the much-mentioned but seldom-seen 'African solution' through the O.A.U., whose Consultative Committee on Nigeria President Tubman sought to re-activate in mid-February.

Meanwhile Brigadier Hassan's conference of the three 'warlords' (Divisional commanders), followed by General Gowon's remarkably delayed first official tour of the war fronts during the twenty months of fighting,[4] emphasized a no less overdue improvement in the strategical lines of co-ordination hitherto singularly lacking in wielding the Nigerian army into one effective field command. This dramatic and drastic regrouping gave strength to the belief that the Federal forces were about to launch their 'final final push'.[5] To offset this flexing of the High Command muscles, cumulative allegations of 'atrocity bombing' of the civilian population by trigger-happy Egyptian pilots who allegedly regarded Biafra as a 'free bomb zone'[6] were publicized in the Western press.[7] Opinion hardened in Great Britain. It was argued that, at its most generous interpretation, such air raids indicated the extent to which Gowon, despite his repeated and strict instructions against such strafing,[8] was apparently unable to exercise operational control. In the face of reiterated Nigerian denials that any such raids had taken place, a number of British M.P.s felt impelled to raise the matter in the House of Commons. Federal Nigeria's supporters found it progressively harder to deny the force of hostile claims that such civilian-aimed terrorism made a mockery of the Federal proclamation of a forty-eight hour truce to mark the Id festival or to reject the growing thesis that 'if they have any military effect, they must increase the fears of the Ibo people that a Federal victory would be followed by

[1] Statement on the Azikiwe proposals issued in Lagos, 17 February 1969.

[2] Quoted in *West Africa* (1969), p. 166.

[3] Quoted in *West Africa* (1969), p. 197.

[4] Nigeria House press release, 24 February 1969.

[5] *West Africa* (1969), p. 137. See also Hassan Katsina's broadcast cited in *West Africa* (1969), p. 313. Within weeks, however, correspondents found themselves compelled to admit that 'Nobody, not even the most ebullient Federal spokesman, could any longer refer to any Federal attack as "the last push" '—*West Africa* (1969), p. 425.

[6] *The Times*, 26 February, 1969.

[7] *The Times* and *New York Times* led this campaign of 'evidence adduced' in the latter half of February and early March.

[8] *The Times*, 22 February 1969.

H

mass slaughter'[1] or the persuasive argument of critics that 'nothing could be more calculated to stiffen the resistance of this people or to make the achievement of one Nigeria an impossibility.'[2] If they were true, such air raids might well achieve little beyond welding the Biafrans closer than ever in their determined resistance.

In the absence of international observers behind the Biafran lines, these reports from established journalists began to raise unpleasant thoughts that, for all the sincerity of those observers on the total absence of any genocidal plan among the military units, the Nigerian Air Force might be playing a part, however unwittingly, in eroding this truth through their wanton bombing of civilian targets. Certainly there was no doubt that orders had been given to intensify air attacks;[3] the question at issue was what operational control there was over the chosen targets. Coming at this charged period, General Gowon's Id message to the nation and forty-eight-hour truce, his promise to order a cease-fire just as soon as Ojukwu renounced secession,[4] and the offer— interpreted as a move to forestall the alarming plan by Canadian voluntary organizations to raise funds and build an airstrip within Biafra[5]—of free access to a Federal-held airstrip on the fringe of Biafra for use by world relief organizations,[6] all echoed in unreceptive ears more hollowly than they deserved.

Ojukwu chose this moment again to appeal for a peace initiative from the three countries that he saw as having real influence among the combatants, this time emphasizing that it was America that was critical:

I would like to see the new American Administration make a move towards a peace initiative. I think the American people are beginning to realise what this war is about and are beginning to know of our suffering. . . . I think the British people abhor this war and many Members of the Government do too, But it does not seem to make any impression on Mr. Harold Wilson. Frankly. I think that Britain continues this war merely because of vested interests.[7]

His reported new recognition of the Emperor of Ethiopia as the best person to bring about an end to the war[8] seemed to carry him one more important step nearer the Federal Government's continuing faith in the efficacy of the O.A.U. and an exclusively African ambiance. At this very moment, indeed, the O.A.U. Council of Ministers was assembling for its scheduled meeting in Addis Ababa. As it turned out, the O.A.U. was again to achieve nothing more tangible than appeals. While Dr.

[1] *The Times*, 28 February 1969.
[2] *The Times*, 26 February 1969
[3] Lagos Radio report, 10 February 1969, quoted in *Africa Research Bulletin*, p. 1327.
[4] Lagos Radio, 12 February; *West Africa* (1969), p. 225.
[5] Nigeria House press release, 5 March 1969.
[6] *The Times*, 22 February 1969.
[7] Markpress Release No. Gen. 522.
[8] *West Africa* (1969), p. 226.

Arikpo once more ruled out intervention by the United Nations, he did concede that General Gowon would be willing to appear before the O.A.U. Consultative Committee again.[1] In France an 'Action Committee for Biafra' was established and a National Biafra Day nominated amid vast press reportage.[2]

Meanwhile, Chief Enahoro was dispatched on an urgently balancing lecture tour to the U.S.A. where pro-Biafran sentiment, detectable in a perusal of the *Congressional Record* as well as amply expressed by voluntary organizations and in the mass-media, continued to disturb Nigeria. His speech to the World Affairs Council at Boston [DOC 192] was rated by the Nigerian Embassy staff as 'the most important of his whole tour',[3] though many American scholars were more impressed by his performance at Northwestern University, Illinois.[4] Chief Enahoro's timely visit may claim to have had an influence in generating some of the welcomely less narrow views expressed at the seminar on the conflict organized in May by the Center for Strategic and International Studies at Georgetown University in Washington, D.C.[5]

In Britain, a series of stirring and *engagé* articles in the 'I was there' vein from Winston Churchill in *The Times*[6] so underlined the magnitude of the suffering inflicted by the reportedly indiscriminate strafing of Biafran civilians that the Government was forced to seek an explanation of this apparent denial or defiance of General Gowon's orders to his Air Force. In Parliament, Mr. Foley spoke of air raids on civilian targets as 'cruel and militarily useless', and Mr. Wilson went so far as to place on record his determination that 'if we thought we could help to end this war or shorten it by one day, by changing our arms policy, we would not hesitate to consider that'.[7] *The Times*' conversion to the Biafran cause undoubtedly had an effect on public opinion in Britain.[8]

[1] Ethiopian Radio quoted in *West Africa* (1969), p. 257.

[2] G. Varley, 'The French and Biafra', *West Africa* (1969), p. 266; and ibid., p. 258.

[3] Personal letter from the Press Attaché.

[4] Private communication.

[5] *The Nigeria-Biafra Conflict* (Washington, 1969). See also the report in *West Africa* (1969), p. 609.

[6] The advertisement in the *Sunday Times* of the forthcoming series of sensational articles under the heading 'Who [*sic*] Do You Believe?' was made up of photographs of the three personalities involved, respectively captioned:

(i) 'Our pilots have been given the strictest instructions to attack only military targets, and these orders have been repeated'—General Gowon, Head of the Federal Military Government of Nigeria, as reported in *The Times*, 21 February 1969.

(ii) 'None of these places bombed had military targets anywhere near. It is clear that the Egyptian pilots hired by Nigeria regard Biafra as a free bomb zone'—Winston S. Churchill, reporting from Biafra in *The Times*, 26 February 1969.

(iii) 'Killing our people is nothing to him [Gowon]. His attitude is to get Biafra at all costs'—Colonel Ojukwu, Biafran leader, as reported in *The Times*, 27 February 1969. The articles appeared in *The Times*, 3–6 March 1969.

[7] Both remarks made in the debate on Nigeria in the House of Commons, 11 March 1969. Mr. Wilson also referred to the Winston Churchill articles as needing to be taken 'very seriously'.

[8] After the war, serious charges of partisanship were levelled in Parliament against

In the event, when such allegedly bomb-shattered towns as Owerri later fell, there should have been many red faces to answer the pertinent question 'Where DID all those bombs fall?'[1] Nigerians in diplomatic circles were heard to repeat Humbert Wolfe's ditty so popular in Switzerland in the 1938–9 days of European crisis:

> You cannot hope to bribe or twist
> The honest British journalist;
> But seeing what the chap will do
> Unbribed, there's no occasion to.

Winston Churchill became the target for attack by Nigeria's press and radio.[2] But for the present neither Enahoro's denial that civilian targets were being bombed[3] nor a meeting between the international war observers' team and the 'evasive'[4] Head of the Nigerian Air Force nor the Nigerian High Commissioner's public explanation in the press[5] —for all its assurance that any amnesty would now, after all, include Ojukwu too—could stem the mounting discontent in Britain with the country's role in the war. Despite Lord Shepherd's earlier plea that Britain's standing and negotiating strength in Lagos had been gravely undermined by this persistent pro-Biafran lobby,[6] the British Government was now pressurized by a strong but restrained all-party back-bench motion into allowing another emergency debate on the Nigerian situation. The motion, signed by over 150 M.P.s, read:

That this House, deeply concerned about the continued fighting in the Nigerian civil war, calls upon Her Majesty's Government to make a fresh approach to other countries sending military equipment to the combatants, with a view to securing through international action a complete embargo on the supply of arms to both sides:

To use its good offices to try to bring about a meeting between General Gowon and Colonel Ojukwu to discuss an immediate ceasefire; substantially to increase the flow of food and other forms of economic aid to alleviate the suffering caused by the war in both Nigeria and Biafra.

As the March day allocated to this debate approached, so did an air of a Biafran renaissance grow more noticeable. First, there was the

---

the establishment of *The Times* and the B.B.C.—e.g., the remarks made by Mr. Woodrow Wyatt in the House of Commons on 26 January 1970. For a summary press line-up see *West Africa* (1969), p. 302. The writer is but one of several who found it consistently impossible to have letters arguing a pro-Federal viewpoint or correcting a Biafran exaggeration accepted by a number of British newspapers.

[1] *Daily Express*, 8 May 1969 (see pp. 112–113).

[2] *Sunday Post* and *Sunday Sketch*, 2 March 1969. See also the attack by the Nigerian High Commissioner in London: 'If one thing was crystal clear in Lagos, it was that Mr. Churchill had arrived from Europe with a mind fully impregnated there by extensive rebel briefings' (statement of 8 March 1969).

[3] Statement issued on 1 March (*The Times*, 3 March 1969).

[4] *The Times*, 6 March 1969.

[5] Letter to *The Times*, 5 March 1969.

[6] Speech in the House of Lords, 20 February 1969.

Federal admission of the Biafran claim that its troops had been dramatically cut off in Owerri;[1] then came relief organizations like Oxfam and, to a lesser extent, the Save the Children Fund, ready to exploit the current resurgence of pro-Biafran sentiment among the more vocal sections of the British public;[2] and there were even suggestions that Lagos itself no longer believed in its own denials that anything was amiss in the tactical role of its mercenary-manned MIG aircraft.[3] The final prelude to the imminent House of Commons debate was the fillip to the peace lobby afforded by an official protest note from the Americans—reeling from their own Winston Churchill-style assault on their humanitarian emotions[4]—to the Federal Government, expressing its 'deep concern' over the reported bombing of civilians.[5] In Britain, resentment was caused to her somewhat masochistic conscience-keepers at this time by an official statement from the Nigerian High Commissioner, immediately following his talks with the British Foreign Secretary, that air raids would now actually be stepped up.[6] A rather less chauvinistic line was taken by General Gowon himself, who in an interview with a British journalist reassured the world that he would not 'bulldoze' his way into Biafran territory.[7] A few days later, in writing off as 'ridiculous' Colonel Ojukwu's claim that neither side could now win the war, Gowon elaborated this in another exclusive interview with the explanation that 'we are going to win this conflict, we have the will . . . [but] we have been going slowly because we don't want to kill the Ibos . . . we will win in our own time'.[8] Not to be outdone by the newsworthiness of personal interviews, Colonel Ojukwu conceded one to an American magazine in which he ranged over a number of war topics.[9]

Forty-eight hours before the Parliamentary debate was due, the British Government took the unprecedented step of sending its new Head of the Diplomatic Service post-haste to Lagos for consultations with the U.K. High Commissioner and with the Federal leaders.[10] But there was more drama to come in this crowded week before the curtain went up on the House of Commons debate. The international observers published another report, reserving judgement on allegations of indiscriminate bombing of civilians in Biafra since 'it was impossible to receive proof that such allegations are false.'[11] The Federal Government

[1] *The Times*, 5 March 1969.

[2] See advertisements in *The Times*, 6 and 4 March 1969 respectively.

[3] *The Times*, 8 March 1969.

[4] David Reed, 'Must Biafra Die?' *Reader's Digest*, March 1969, pp. 75–80 (English edition: April 1969, pp. 157–62), and the dispatches of Lloyd Garrison in the *New York Times*.   [5] *The Times*, 8 March 1969; *West Africa* (1969), p. 313.

[6] Statement issued in London on the instructions of the Federal Government on 8 March—see *Sunday Telegraph*, 9 March, and *The Times*, 10 March 1969.

[7] *Daily Telegraph*, 12 March; *West Africa* (1969), p. 313.

[8] *Daily Express*, 17 March, quoted in *West Africa* (1969), p. 342.

[9] *Newsweek*, 14 March, quoted in *West Africa* (1969), p. 341.

[10] *The Times*, 11 March 1969.

[11] Quoted in *The Times*, 11 March 1969.

released news of a £1,356 million National Reconstruction Plan for the 'critical years' of 1969–73,[1] which it followed with an international conference at Ibadan[2] where Asika's account of the problem of re-habilitation in the recovered East Central State was among the most interesting papers [DOC 193]. This announcement was quickly coun-tered by Colonel Ojukwu's inauguration of the Biafran Planning Economic Commission.[3] There were also current reports of Russian demands to open consulates in all the states of Nigeria and rumours of a tough Soviet line on a monopoly for supplying arms in quantities that would ensure a quicker-than-quick kill;[4] there were indications that Canada and the U.S.S.R. were both formulating proposed solutions to the conflict;[5] and, schemingly on the very eve of the debate in London, Biafra proposed in a message to the Foreign Ministers of the Common Market countries a one month's truce—unhesitatingly rejected by Lagos[6]—as a prelude to a cease-fire and unconditional talks by both sides.[7]

With its mind buzzing over a question raised by the mass-media, whether in fact there was not after all 'a quarrel to be settled, not a war to be won', or even a war that neither party could win and both sides had already lost,[8] the British Parliament devoted the whole of 13 March to its fifth critical debate of the nation's role in the Nigerian affair—what the Lagos press stigmatized as 'the antics of a vocal section of the British parliament, press and people'.[9] On the previous day, a pro-Nigerian group of M.P.s sent a letter to Brigadier Ogundipe in which they assured him of their support for the Federal Government but asked for an end to indiscriminate bombing [DOC 194]. The debate produced several speeches of a considerable degree of importance to an under-standing of how the Mother of Parliaments viewed, so variously, Nigeria's war [DOC 195]. Those in the pro-Ojukwu lobby included speeches by a former Colonial Secretary and by Mr. Frank Allaun, back from Biafra only a few hours earlier. Often speeches cut clean across party lines. A speech with an added piquancy was that of Mr. A. Lyon, who had accompanied Mr. Barnes to Biafra but returned with a very different assessment of the situation. Any jubilation at the seemingly unexpected result of the forced division of the House, giving the Govern-ment a reassuring majority of 170 out of 294 votes cast, was tempered

[1] Statement issued in Lagos, 6 March. See *The Times*, 7 March; editorial, 'Winning Nigeria's Peace', *West Africa* (1969), pp. 321–2.

[2] *West Africa* (1969), pp. 267 and 347.

[3] Markpress Release No. Gen. 538.

[4] *Sunday Telegraph*, 16 March 1969.

[5] *West Africa* (1969), p. 341, quoting the *Financial Times* report on the U.S.S.R. move.

[6] Lagos Radio report, 14 March; *Daily Telegraph*, 14 March 1969.

[7] Biafra Radio, 13 March; *The Times*, 15 March; 'Gowon Disposes', *The Economist*, 15 March 1969.

[8] *The Times*, 13 March 1969.

[9] *Morning Post*, 14 March 1969.

by the sobering realization of the national meaning of the large number of abstentions: less than half the House voted and over a quarter of the Labour Party failed to support the Government's policy.[1] Some saw in this a telling parallel with the conflict that was being debated: here was another issue that neither side could at that moment convincingly claim to be seen to be winning.

In the event, the British Government were saved from a larger protest vote on 'the burning issue which probably animated many learned members in asking for this debate',[2] by the announcement towards its close that the Prime Minister would himself shortly be flying to Lagos 'to explore the possibilities of an international embargo on arms supplies in the Nigerian civil war, a peace settlement, and the opening of relief corridors to Biafra'.[3] This news prompted the Opposition to warn the Prime Minister that his role must not be that of a 'supercharged dove . . . [all] set to work a miracle'.[4] The argued decision to send H.M.S. *Fearless* into Lagos harbour (apart from its counterbalance to the display of Soviet naval strength then in Lagos roads) was made more understandable[5] when Wilson accepted an invitation to route himself home through Addis Ababa and so talk with the Emperor, as Africa's most influential mediator. Expectedly, both the debate and Mr. Wilson's visit were denounced in advance by Biafra, as respectively 'a characteristically diplomatic gimmick'[6] and 'a step towards an escalation of the war rather than an attempt to make peace'.[7]

No less predictably, the Federal Government decided not to extend an invitation to the Pope to include Nigeria in his forthcoming African tour, for the Vatican's role in flying civil aid to Biafra was sensitively suspect in Federal eyes. To a Zambian goodwill mission Ojukwu declared that his fight was one aimed at breaking 'the colonialist myth of perpetual enslavement of the African race'.[8] It was on this same occasion that Ojukwu revealed Biafra's recognition by Haiti, announced in Port-au-Prince on 24 March. President Duvalier explained

[1] *Daily Telegraph*, 14 March 1969. Copious commentary on the debate can be found in all British dailies and weeklies of the period.

[2] Mr. Maurice Foley, opening the debate on 13 March 1969.

[3] Statement by Mr. Stewart, Secretary of State, in the House of Commons, 13 March 1969. It was anticipated by a report in the *Financial Times* of that morning.

[4] Quoted in *The Times*, 14 March 1969. See also *Daily Telegraph*, 19 and 28 March. The actual date chosen for this visit, 26 March, turned out to have been pre-empted by the Federal Government for a Cabinet Meeting. Those hostile to Sir David Hunt's committed role as our man in Lagos latched on to this as a further proof of how hopelessly out of touch the U.K. High Commission in Lagos was, for Wednesday had long been a regular Cabinet day. See the deserved defence of Sir David in *West Africa* (1969), p. 325.

[5] See *West Africa* (1969), p. 514, referring to the Prime Minister's explanation that the ship's value would have lain in its ability to provide 'an area in which he felt secure and away from Federal control', had talks with Ojukwu—'which looked likely at one moment' —materialized.

[6] Biafra Radio, 13 March 1969.

[7] Statement issued by Dr. Eke in Umuahia, 17 March 1969.

[8] Markpress Release No. Gen. 545.

his Government's recognition of Biafra as a free and sovereign state because of its exponent of the Haitian Government policy of:

Participating in the defence of states and of oppressed countries. Over and above the humanitarian aspects, it aims at a return to a just and lasting peace between Nigeria and Biafra. . . . I must express my fervent wishes that this act of the first free and independent Negro republic in the world serve as a symbol and example, a source of inspiration for the governments and countries of Africa. It constitutes a contribution based on our unique experiences as a Negro nation and aims at the resumption of a formal dialogue between Nigerian and Biafra.[1]

Such an off-beat non-event could bring but cold comfort to Ojukwu; and Haiti turned out to be the last country so to commit itself.

Mr. Wilson flew to Lagos on 26 March, amid some reservations by the press over the value of his visit beyond that of its being another exponent of the modern style of personal diplomacy and of its astute political timing in the U.K. context.[2] The Nigerian press's initial anxiety was quieted by Mr. Wilson's announcement at Ikeja airport that he had come not to mediate but to learn for himself.[3] This followed on an interview given in London in which, in an interesting encapsulation of Britain's position on the civil war, the Prime Minister publicly discounted any expectation of 'spectacular results' [DOC 196]. General Gowon firmly underlined this limited role by including in his speech of welcome the remark that 'the purpose of your present visit is very clear. . . . I expect no dramatic peace initiative on your part' [DOC 197].[4] As promised by the Nigerian Chief of Staff, Brigadier Hassan Katsina, a few days earlier, the Prime Minister's arrival coincided with a 'dramatic new development' in the shape of yet one more major assault by the Federal troops against the Biafrans.[5] Indeed, Ojukwu's temporary capital of Umuahia now came under Federal artillery fire, and reports that the Nigerian Air Force had put a halt to the night airlifts in Biafra and could justifiably claim 'absolute control' of air space over Biafra[6] suggested that Colonel Adekunle was at last about to achieve his triple-top ambition of personally capturing the three 'O.A.U.'[7] towns of Iboland.

[1] Quoted in *Africa Research Bulletin*, p. 1357 and *West Africa* (1969), p. 369.

[2] The Nigerian press of 14 and 15 March had welcomed the original announcement—see the press round-up in *Africa Research Bulletin*, pp. 1355–6. For subsequent British press response, see *The Times*, 24, 27, and 28 March; the *Scotsman*, 25 March; *Daily Telegraph*, 27 March; and the *Guardian*, 3 April 1969.

[3] For an argument of the semantics of this declaration, see *Daily Telegraph*, 31 March and the *Guardian*, 2 April 1969.

[4] See also Gowon's interview with *Financial Times*, 26 March 1969, in which he expressed the hope that the Prime Minister was not 'coming here for any mediation—we know Ojukwu; outsiders do not.'

[5] *Observer*, 30 March; *Daily Telegraph*, 31 March; *West Africa* (1969), p. 313.

[6] *Sunday Telegraph*, 23 March; *Daily Telegraph*, 24 March; *Sunday Times*, 30 March 1969. [7] Owerri, Aba, and Umuahia.

After two non-stop days of discussions and visits to the recaptured areas of the former Eastern Region, the Prime Minister put an end to speculations on whether he intended to visit Biafra[1] by making on 30 March an official offer to meet Colonel Ojukwu 'somewhere in Africa'. The invitation was sent with the knowledge of the Federal Government and was cautiously hedged—bearing in mind the lamented Rhodesian instance—with a proviso that such a meeting in no way implied recognition of a rebel leader [DOC 198]. Twenty-four excited hours later, Radio Biafra (not Colonel Ojukwu himself) turned down the invitation as 'impossible under present circumstances', despite its apparent previously agreed acceptability. Among the reasons put forward was the quite unrealistic insistence on any such meeting being held within Biafra. The statement added that should Mr. Wilson fail to 'honour' his alleged promise of coming to Biafra, 'he will be lending credence to information available to the Biafran government that he had gone to Nigeria to plan with the Nigerian leaders the current military offensive.'[2] Thwarted of further dove-like diplomacy, the British Prime Minister gave another press conference and then left Nigeria in an aura of goodwill.[3] He flew on to Ethiopia to confer with the Emperor in his role as chairman of the O.A.U.'s last-hope Conciliation Committee on Nigeria. Besides reaffirming his belief that 'the task of mediation in the conflict was one for the O.A.U.,'[4] the Prime Minister issued a statement in which he expressed regret at Biafra's rejection of his proposal for a meeting, now confirmed by a message from Ojukwu himself, but stated that he was quite ready to return to London via West Africa if the Biafran leader would meet him at any one of a number of venues outside rebel territory.[5] But nothing came of his final gesture.

Immediately on his return to Britain on 2 April, the Prime Minister reported to the House of Commons [DOC 199] on the generally favourable results of what was still held by some political commentators to have been a puzzlingly inspired decision[6] to undertake personally a week's fact-finding mission to Nigeria without any intention of mediating. Fortunately, the trail of glory he left behind was sufficient to draw a veil over the potential embarrassment[7] sensed by some in the public

[1] *Daily Telegraph*, 25 March 1969.

[2] Quoted in *The Times*, 1 April; the *Financial Times* and the *Scotsman*, 2 April. *West Africa* (1969), p. 397, and *Africa Research Bulletin*, p. 1359 also carry useful summaries of the time-table of this move.

[3] *The Times*, 1 April; Nigeria House press release, 2 April 1969.

[4] Communiqué issued in Addis Ababa on 1 April. It was phrased in cautious generalities.

[5] Report from Addis Ababa (C.O.I. text). See also *The Times* and the *Guardian*, 2 April 1969.

[6] The *Observer* and *Sunday Times*, 30 March; the *Guardian*, 1 and 2 April; and *The Times*, 2 April 1969.

[7] Two months later, Awolowo's dogged defence of a plan for a multiplicity of states based on linguistic grounds resulted in his presence in the Federal Government being attacked in Kaduna as 'greatly embarrassing' (*New Nigerian*, 14 June 1969). Cf. p. 472, fn. 1.

comment by Chief Awolowo, Vice-Chairman of the Federal Executive Council, that he stood by his May 1967 credo that for him acceptance of Biafran secession 'by any case of commission or omission' would be tantamount to the go-ahead for the Western and Lagos States' withdrawal from the Federation even though now at war [DOC 200].

The Federal assault on Biafra's shrinking defences, this time announced with less panache than in heralding previous *soi-disant* 'final pushes' and judiciously left unreported till military gains had already been made, had in the meanwhile been meeting with substantial success as all three of its heavily-armed divisions tightened their pincer-grip on Umuahia. By 12 April there were rumours of the town's partial evacuation. Once again the Federal Government could come to the meeting of the O.A.U. Consultative Committee, scheduled for Monrovia in mid-April, with an impressive military accomplishment compellingly read into its case. In the event, the O.A.U. meeting on 17–20 April was even wishy-washier than its predecessors, and the reports (the sessions were held *in camera*) of the negative statements from the Nigerian[1] and Biafran delegations[2]—the latter had brought Sir Louis Mbanefo back to prominence after six months of silence—were matched only by the practical emptiness of the O.A.U. final communiqué [DOC 201]. The call to renounce secession, in accord with the warmly pro-Nigerian sentiments of the Organization, found no favour in the eyes of the Biafran delegation, whose leader accused the O.A.U. of having neither:

... the ability nor a genuine desire to bring the war to an end. They have not advanced beyond their original stand taken at Kinshasa in September 1967, before we were even heard. Some members, reinforced by the O.A.U. Secretariat, believe that we Biafrans are condemned to die and that we can only get our reprieve by surrender. They are more concerned with maintaining the legitimacy of Gowon's regime than stopping the war. It is now for others interested to take the initiative to bring about peace.[3]

The Biafran delegation was later reported to have said that had the communiqué written in the words 'a solution' instead of 'a united Nigeria' they would have been prepared to accept the Consultative Committee's declaration in principle.[4]

Nigeria, on the other hand, was encouraged by the O.A.U.'s unambiguous endorsement of its fight against secession, viewed by the member states with horror whatever their record of accommodating views on the overthrow of legitimate governments by military coups. The O.A.U. Secretary-General, M. Diallo Telli, attributed the failure of the Monrovia talks to Biafra: 'For the first time we made it a point

---

[1] Lagos Radio, 19 April 1969.

[2] Markpress Release No. Gen. 575.

[3] Statement by Sir Louis Mbanefo, 20 April 1969 (Markpress Release No. Gen. 576, mistakenly numbered 276).

[4] See the account of the Monrovia meeting in *West Africa* (1969), p. 485.

to put responsibilities where they lay.'[1] With any hopes of a non-military settlement once again in smithereens, it was from the war front that late April brought its major announcement: the fall of Umuahia, the third of Biafra's temporary headquarters, to a massive and superbly organized assault by Colonel Mohammed Shuwa's First Division on 23 April.[2] The Nigerian Chief of Staff had fulfilled his earlier promise of 'big news',[3] in time for the Supreme Commander's spectacular wedding in Lagos on 19 April, if late for the Prime Minister's visit. General Gowon could have wished for only one better wedding present: peace itself.

For a moment this seemed just a shade nearer—or at least the end of the fighting did—when President de Gaulle resigned at the end of April.[4] His *sub rosa* personal Biafran support in the shape of directing a steady supply of arms and munitions towards Ojukwu through certain francophone African states had incontrovertibly halted the Federal armies when they were on the threshold of military victory in the previous September. In the first ministerial contact between the two Governments for ten months, Dr. Arikpo was promptly flown to Paris for talks with the Quai d'Orsay.[5] Overduly, too, a pro-Nigerian pressure *groupuscule* got under way in Biafra-conscious France.

But within twenty-four hours of jubilantly announcing the important seizure of Umuahia, the Federal Government had grievously and grudgingly to concede, concealed in an obscure news item and masked as a move 'for tactical purposes',[6] the week-old Biafran claim (earlier dismissed by the Federal Chief of Staff as 'absolutely false'[7]) to have recaptured the strategic town of Owerri.[8] True, this was only the Federal army's second military reverse during the twenty-two months of fighting (their first was the protracted setback opposite Onitsha), a record of which they had cause to be proud given the gravely under-officered and inexperienced state of their troops when war broke out; yet its timing could not help but ironically erode the kudos of one of their most telling military triumphs and give the sorry lie to Lagos's premature description of Umuahia's fall as 'a final mortal blow'.[9] But

[1] Quoted in *Africa Research Bulletin*, p. 1383. The only account so far of this unsuccessful meeting is that given in the chapter 'An African Affair' in Auberon Waugh and Suzanne Cronjé, *Biafra: Britain's Shame* (London, 1969), where Mrs. Cronjé describes the role of M. Diallo Telli and charges him with being personally responsible for 'paralysing' a possible basis for negotiation.

[2] Gowon made the formal announcement to the emirs and chiefs (Kaduna Radio, 23 April). See *Sunday Telegraph*, 20 and 27 April 1969.

[3] *Daily Telegraph*, 31 March 1969.

[4] Cf. Kaduna Radio talk, 'The Mighty Fallen—Good Riddance', 20 April 1969.

[5] *Observer*, 3 May; *Guardian*, 7 May. For subsequent assessments of Pompidou and the Nigerian war, see *West Africa* (1969), pp. 541, 761, and 1359.

[6] Lagos Radio, 28 April; *The Times*, 29 April; *Daily Times*, 1 May 1969.

[7] Quoted in *Sunday Telegraph*, 22 April 1969.

[8] Markpress Release No. Gen. 581; *The Times*, 28 April 1969.

[9] *Morning Post*, 26 April 1969.

it is an ill wind that cannot be put to some use. Perhaps this shock was just what was needed to jolt certain parts and people of the country out of their disturbing war malaise.[1] The *Nigerian Observer* voiced what many Nigerians, at home and abroad, seemed to be thinking about the generally unsuccessful military leadership of the war when it warned that 'what has happened to Owerri can happen to Onitsha, Enugu, Aba, or any of the liberated towns. . . . We think that it is imperative to establish a co-ordinating High Command for the three Divisions close to the war zone.'[2]

It was now a race against time, with the odds on the rains bogging down the slow-moving Federal troops already hampered by their perilously stretched lines of communications.[3] While the Nigerians set their sights on seizing the vital airstrip at Uli, the Biafrans—their high command withdrawing westwards to Orlu, the new capital of the few hundred square miles that now comprised the erstwhile Republic[4]— were ambitiously turning their eyes towards repeating this feat of arms and recapturing Umuahia. If, as all the signs indicated, here was a war that was being fought to a finish, it was hard to find that finish in immediate sight; rather, as one political commentator saw it,[5] it was a case of the quick kill in slow motion.

The month of May, destined to be Biafra's second anniversary and grandiosely interpreted as a 'preliminary to the real war of survival',[6] opened with Colonel (now to be promoted General of the People's Army of Biafra[7]) Ojukwu addressing a meeting—the first for ten months—of the Consultative Assembly, summoned in Owerri to celebrate the town's recapture and elicit a further mandate from them to continue the war until Nigeria was prepared to negotiate for peace.[8] Lagos displayed no official reaction to his call for an international guarantee of any cease-fire settlement.[9] Instead, publicity was given to General Gowon's upbraiding of the Caritas representative and the recurrence of the Federation's suspicions of the 'sinister motives' of charitable airlifts that could likely be ferrying in guns as well as butter.[10] Meanwhile, eye-witness reports of Owerri's desolation and destruction were matched by those describing Umuahia as a ghost town that had lost its reason for existence;[11] but correspondents entering undevastated Umuahia recalled the

---

[1] Cf. the *Scotsman*, 19 February 1969.

[2] *Nigerian Observer*, 28 April. Cf. pp. 101 and 114.

[3] See a realistic appreciation of the military difficulties of the campaign in *The Times*, 2 April 1969.

[4] See the map in *Africa Research Bulletin*, p. 1382.

[5] *Spectator*, 4 April 1969.   [6] Markpress Release No. Gen. 619.

[7] Markpress Release No. Gen. 597 quoted the form 'General of the Biafran Army' but in his published speeches Ojukwu restyled this to 'General of the People's Army'.

[8] Summaries and excerpts in Markpress Release Nos. Gen. 588 and 591, and *Africa Research Bulletin*, pp. 1410–11.

[9] *The Times*, 5 May 1969.

[10] *The Times* and *Daily Telegraph*, 6 May; Nigeria House press release, 8 May 1969.

[11] *The Times* and *Daily Telegraph*, 8 May 1969; Markpress Release No. Gen. 592.

OJUKWU'S RELIEF CORRIDOR!

Reproduced by kind permission of the *Daily Times*

Winston Churchill articles and rightly asked 'Where DID all those bombs go?'[1] Once again the Federal authorities seemed to miss the public relations boat—their well-wishers did not find it hard to imagine how adroitly the lies about razing Umuahia and its Queen Elizabeth Hospital would have been exploited by Biafra's ruthless propaganda machine—and their low-key puff to the testimony of a refugee Ibo chief calling on his countrymen to surrender because 'there is nothing like Biafra left now'[2] made unconvincing showing in comparison with what capital might have been built up from the vindication that was Umuahia.

It was President Senghor of Senegal, currently joint author with Dr. Azikiwe of an appealing foreword to a book on Biafra by one of her former spokesmen,[3] who now came up with the next peace plan; but his proposed balancing of Biafra's renunciation of secession against Nigeria's rescinding of its twelve-state constitution and his endorsement of negotiations to preserve 'the integrity rather than the unity of Nigeria' seemed likely, as he himself said, to lead to his being taken to task by both sides—'but less, I think, by General Gowon and Colonel Ojukwu than by their hawks.'[4] His prophecy was fulfilled and his proposal of the unacceptable was never accepted. The government of the South-Eastern State, secure in its newfound autonomy, resented and now in a new resolution rejected any talk of a plebiscite to sound out the feelings of its non-Ibo peoples towards association with a putative Biafra, for they had everything to gain from the alternative of a multistate structure and nothing to lose in release from alleged Ibo hegemony:

[1] *Daily Express*, 8 May 1969.   [2] Letter in *The Times*, 19 April 1969.
[3] R. Uwechue, *Reflections on the Nigerian Civil War*.
[4] Quoted in *The Times*, 6 May 1969.

As far as our people are concerned, the creation of a South Eastern State which comprises the Ibibios, Efiks, Orons, Annangs and Ekois, all non-Ibo ethnic groups, . . . is the greatest achievement of the Federal Military Government. . . . Our demand for self-determination and a separate, autonomous state was motivated by the discriminatory and selfish methods adopted by the Ibos in and outside the Government against us and the other non-Ibo people of the former Eastern Region. . . . It does not lie in the mouth of any Ibo man to demand a plebiscite or referendum in the South Eastern State on whether the non-Ibo people want to be dominated or governed by Ibos; such a demand is not only unwarranted but provocative. . . .[1]

In the British press, often giving the impression of being more passionately involved in the conduct of and arguments on the war than its Nigerian counterpart, Dr. Conor Cruise O'Brien, back from Biafra, spoke of the Republic's indigenous expression of nationalism and saw Biafra's survival as 'a victory for African courage, endurance and skill, and an opportunity for the further and significant flowering of African talent'.[2] He had been accompanied by Professor Stanley Diamond and Mr. Paul Connet, who in a press conference at Umuahia described Biafra as 'beautiful'.[3] More down to earth than this negritudinal or Black Power idiom was a concurrent analysis by General Alexander of the shortcomings of the Nigerian military field command from staff down to platoon level.[4] This coincided with a dramatic reshuffling of all three of the Federation's Divisional Commanders and the posting back to base of the dynamic 'Black Scorpion'.[5] Adekunle's strategical ambition of capturing Umuahia had over-reached itself, for in achieving this Owerri had cheekily been retaken behind his back. At the civilian level the aftermath of Owerri also had its effect, for an alert Ministry of Information in Lagos did not delay over issuing a correction to a widely publicized shock report that Chief Enahoro had shut the door on any further peace talks.[6] About this time, too, the I.C.R.C. released details of its contribution in feeding over two million people in Nigeria, following up an earlier analysis of the huge sums collected for relief from outside.[7]

[1] Quoted in *The Times*, 2 May, 1969. In the immediate aftermath of peace, the process of Ibo reintegration was to be at its slowest and stickiest in the city of Port Harcourt.

[2] *Observer*, 11 May; *New York Review of Books*, 22 May 1969.

[3] Markpress Release No. Gen. 570.

[4] Major-General H. T. Alexander, 'Why the Civil War in Biafra Drags On', *Sunday Telegraph*, 11 May 1969. Cf. the military evaluation by Michael Wolfers in *The Times*, 2 April 1969.

[5] Full details of the seven top-level postings were given in *Morning Post*, 13 May. See also the Chief of Staff's rationalization of the transfers quoted in *New Nigeria*, 19 May; *West Africa* (1969), p. 569. In the event, Colonel Mohammed Shuwa was not reassigned and he remained as commander of the successful, disciplined, and most 'regular' First Division.

[6] *The Times*, 26 May; *West Africa* (1969), p. 570. Nevertheless, the State Commissioner of Information continued to express a very general dissatisfaction with the inadequacy of Nigeria's efforts to combat the massive Biafran propaganda and described it in terms of 'great disquiet and dismay'—quoted in *West Africa* (1969), p. 822.

[7] The reports are to be found in *Topical Red Cross News*, Information Notes, No. 8 of 31 March, No. 9 of 16 April, and No. 1176 of 30 May 1969.

As an apparent prelude to the approaching second anniversary of Biafra's independence, the seizure of a large group of Italian oilmen at Kwale, an area on the west bank of the Niger which was generally assumed to be safely in Federal hands, and the unexpected air-strikes by a resurrected Biafran Air Force against Benin and Port Harcourt added another dimension to the conflict. Though daring sorties in 'Operation Biafra's Baby' were made by Swedish and Biafran pilots flying single-seater mini-aircraft, led by the controversial Count Carl Gustav von Rosen,[1] their nuisance impact was likely to be more influential on morale than on the actual progress of the fighting—not only in lowering that of the Nigerians but also in raising the Biafrans'. The Government-owned *Morning Post*'s claim that 'the rebel plane was boldly marked in the red and white colours of the International Red Cross' was laughed off in some quarters as another naïveté emphasizing the urgency of improved public relations techniques,[2] and its reference to 'mercenaries' was interpreted by many to accord ill with the 'unaccountable Nigerian denials'[3] of their own undisguised dependence on foreign pilots. The von Rosen gesture was partly aimed at defying Federal efforts to put out of action the crucial airstrip at Uli, perforce by bombing, in the curious absence of Nigeria's ability to launch an Israeli-type commando raid against it which would have measurably shortened the end.[4]

In part, too, Biafra seemed to have declared war against the oil companies.[5] There was, indeed, a hint of this switch in tactics in General Ojukwu's major policy speech delivered on 'Thanksgiving Day', 1 June, at Ahiara to mark his nation's third anniversary, in which he alluded to 'the dramatic re-entry into the war [and] a brilliant series of raids' by the Biafran air force which had set the oil refinery at Port Harcourt ablaze. Indeed this 'Ahiara Declaration', with its emphasis on the revised long-term social objectives of 'the Biafran revolution' and a new commitment to a ten year war, took on the character of a philosophical charter for what Ojukwu envisaged as a renascent and finally triumphant Biafra [DOC 202].[6] Yet for all this hum of renewed activity in the air and cloud-cuckooland speculation of Biafra's chances, the deeper-thinking and realistic editorials of *West Africa* continued to provide

---

[1] *Daily Telegraph*, 26 and 28 May; *The Times*, 27 and 28 May 1969; reports in *West Africa* (1969), p. 628 and *Africa Research Bulletin*, p. 1412. For later revelations, see the article by Suzanne Cronjé in *The Times*, 27 February 1970, and von Rosens's memoirs, *Biafra: Som Jaq Ser Der* (Stockholm, 1969).

[2] Quoted in *Daily Telegraph*, 26 May 1969.

[3] *The Times*, 26 May 1969.

[4] Cf. *West Africa* (1969), p. 1202. In an editorial the *Nigerian Observer* spelled out the belief that 'once the Uli strip is put out of use, the war is over'—16 April 1969.

[5] *West Africa* (1969), p. 671; *The Times*, 7 August; Markpress Release Nos. Gen. 637 and 654. See also *Africa Research Bulletin*, p. 1413.

[6] Cf. *West Africa* (1969), p. 758, quoting from E. Gatacre's report in the *Guardian* that Ojukwu was devoting much of his time to post-war planning and that the atmosphere in Biafra was more civilian than military.

the sanest, best informed, and most balanced assessment [DOC 203].[1]

The Federal Government seemed to offer another Biafra-anniversary hostage to fortune when a senior airport official at Lagos summarily arrested Dr. Lindt, the International Red Cross co-ordinator, on a charge of an unauthorized flight into Nigeria,[2] thereby jeopardizing its image before a world opinion ever susceptible to affront through violation of the internationally accepted code of behaviour towards the Red Cross. Ten days later, the Nigerian air force was featured in the headlines for its 'unexpected and inexplicable' shooting down near Calabar on 5 June of a Swedish Red Cross plane on a relief mission.[3] Lagos issued its own hard-line explanation of the incident, asserting that:

This disaster has long been prophesied by the Federal Military Government to the I.C.R.C., which has repeatedly been approached to discontinue night mercy flights in favour of daylight flights so that their identity could at no time be mistaken for Ojukwu's arms planes, many of which are of the same type.[4]

Hits were also reported on several aircraft belonging to Joint Church Aid.[5] In the face of renewed attacks in the Nigerian press, the I.C.R.C. issued a series of statements denying charges of spying and sustaining Biafra's rebellion and turned to the attack in setting forth its position in the conflict [DOC 204].[6]

Nigeria could offset some of the alarm generated among international opinion through her prima facie arrogant arrest of the I.C.R.C. co-ordinator against the shock spread in Italy through the wanton murder of a few European oil workers by Biafran guerrillas.[7] In subsequently explaining the Kwale incident Ojukwu gave credit to the Pope[8] and to the Presidents of the Ivory Coast and Gabon[9] for their personal intervention to save the lives of the remainder after sentence of death had been passed [DOC 205], but despite rumours of Biafra collecting a useful ransom in a European currency[10] it is doubtful whether in this affair of the oilmen Ojukwu played the important joker card of international goodwill with his customary skill, especially *vis-à-vis* the Vatican.[11] For

---

[1] Cf. 'Two Years of War', *West Africa* (1969), pp. 793–4. See also Michael Wolfers' birthday article in *The Times*, 7 July 1969, and that by Richard Kershaw, 'Nigeria Faces Year Three', *New Statesman*, 6 July 1969.

[2] *The Times*, 29 May 1969.

[3] Statement issued by the I.C.R.C. in Geneva, 7 June 1969. See also the historical review in I.C.R.C. Information Notes, No. 119b, 4 July 1969.

[4] Statement issued in Lagos, 5 June 1969.   [5] *The Times*, 7 June 1969.

[6] The *Scotsman*, 12 June; *The Times*, 21 June and 2 July 1969.

[7] Summarized in *Africa Research Bulletin*, p. 1414, from current press reports.

[8] *L'Osservatore Romano*, quoted in *The Times*, 9 June and *West Africa* (1969), p. 693.

[9] *The Times*, 9 June 1969; Markpress Release Nos. Gen. 642 and 647.

[10] *Financial Times*, 25 June 1969. See also Markpress Release No. Gen. 670.

[11] *The Times* and *Daily Telegraph*, 3 June; *West Africa* (1969), p. 661, quoting the Italian reaction of 'a domestic furore'. Cf. Lagos Radio talk by Uduak Okon, 'Double Standards', on 5 June 1969, in which there was some measure of accord with Ojukwu's implication of double-talk in the West over murder in Africa.

all the not-caring-a-fig attitude towards international opinion, neither the Federal nor the Biafran Government had any illusions about its ultimate importance, for better or for worse, on diplomatic relations and hence internal affairs. Whether one liked it or not, neither Government could survive without some measure of support from abroad; and at no time in the whole course of the war had this credibility gap seemed to widen so unhappily.

For, in this proverbial silly season of mid-summer, neither General gave the impression of displaying his usual polish in diplomatic affairs. If the world—and even, it was hinted, Biafran advisers too[1]—was shocked by Ojukwu's willingness to treat the lives of the non-combatant oilmen as puisne pawns in the game of international blackmail and ransom, it was equally stunned by the disregard of Red Cross immunity revealed in the summary dismissal of Dr. Lindt and his declaration by Gowon as a *persona non grata*.[2] Dr. Arikpo's statement explaining that his Government had taken such unprecedented action because of Dr. Lindt's deepening involvement in Nigeria's politics and of a pro-Ibo statement attributed to him in a Brussels press conference held in April,[3] was rejected by I.C.R.C. headquarters, where *l'affaire Lindt* was taken very gravely.[4] This was followed by a restrained statement by Dr. Lindt himself [DOC 206], who included a request to be relieved of his post as I.C.R.C. Commissioner General for West Africa.[5] Yet this was the climax rather than the cause of months of mounting irritation by the Nigerians at the undeniable relationship (if not a causal link) between relief supplies and the undreamed of protraction of the Biafran defence.

Impatience with Western European susceptibilities was exacerbated by the connection in the Nigerian minds between Count von Rosen's threatening revival of a Biafran mini-air force and intolerable interference by humanitarianists in general. The understandable resentment of Nigerian opinion now found expression in further lambasting of these relief organizations by the Nigerian press, especially the I.C.R.C., as being run 'by thoroughly discredited European humanitarians' and 'hirelings of imperialism', and in the angry demands by student and trade union movements for the Government to remove its kid gloves and end the war forthwith.[6] Dr. Lindt's subsequent condemnation of the rashness of the von Rosen exploits[7] came too late to save the I.C.R.C. relief co-ordinator or indeed the I.C.R.C. itself: it never re-

[1] *Sunday Telegraph*, 22 June 1969.

[2] *Observer*, 15 June 1969.

[3] Lagos Radio report quoted in *Africa Research Bulletin*, pp. 1442–30.

[4] *The Times*, 21 June 1969.

[5] The President's reply to Dr. Lindt is given in I.C.R.C. Press Release No. 989b of 1969.

[6] *West Africa* (1969), p. 661; *The Times*, 26 June. For Nigerian approval of the move, see the Nigerian press excerpts in *West Africa* (1969), p. 725, and Lagos and Kaduna Radio bulletins and talks of the period.

[7] Lagos Radio report, 14 June 1969.

I

gained its position in Nigeria. In retrospect, the event of 5 June was to mark the real beginning of the end of the war.

Such an awareness of the need for a *mouton forfaitaire* was reinforced by reports of growing discontent within Nigeria at the alleged arrogance and corruptibility of the new army class,[1] already brought into the open by Gowon's own severe denunciation of the 'disgraceful acts' of certain 'evil-doers' and their lowered ethics,[2] and of increasing evidence of the 'incompetent pursuit' of the war at all levels.[3] Nor was this malaise peculiar to the Federation. On the Biafran side, the same style of war-weariness and search for sacrificial victims was discernible. There, however, it was qualified by reports of genuine speculation over what value should really be attached to the belaboured Ojukwu thesis—long an article of faith among soldiers and civilians alike—that genocide was in fact the only available alternative to cession of autonomy.

June became a month of sullenness and suspicion. Ojukwu's sudden willingness to agree to a 'surface route' food corridor,[4] long since proposed by the Nigerian authorities, was difficult to accept at its face value—rightly so, as the immediate rider explaining how it had been 'misunderstood' showed.[5] The suggestion that Lagos, angered by Count von Rosen's air attacks, had had recourse to East German mercenaries to man its air force,[6] the aggravated plight of civilians in the rebel areas now that their last food lifeline had been cut by the cessation of relief supplies after the shooting down of an I.C.R.C. plane on 5 June, and the ugly attacks on the Church in West Africa because its Archbishop had, at a meeting in Ghana, signed a declaration urging an end to the fighting[7] were all disturbing, There was too, the expulsion from Lagos of the B.B.C. correspondent for Nigeria, followed by a restrictive ban on reporting[8] and Awolowo's uncompromising yet defensible comment on relief supplies to the rebels—rightly characterized by the British Foreign Secretary as having 'no historical parallel' by any government engaged in total war—that 'all is fair in war and starvation is one of the weapons of war.'[9] These events, attitudes, and undercurrents combined

---

[1] *The Times*, 20 June 1969. Cf. letter from a Nigerian in *West Africa* (1969), p. 643: 'Have we not all seen now that the army have assumed the attitudes which we decried in the old civilian government?' Some of the severest condemnation was carried in the pages of the *Nigerian Tribune*, which declared that those responsible for directing the war 'do not at all appreciate that we are fighting a war' and called on the Government to 'call off relief talks and concentrate on the business of winning the war.' (Quoted in *West Africa* (1969), pp. 849 and 878.)

[2] Nigeria House press release dated 9 January 1969.

[3] *The Times*, 21 June 1969.

[4] Statement issued in Owerri, 18 June 1969 (Markpress Release No. Gen. 664). Cf. *West Africa* (1969), pp. 647 and 725.

[5] Government spokesman in Owerri, 20 June 1969 (Markpress Release No. Gen. 669).

[6] *Sunday Telegraph*, 22 June 1969.

[7] *West Africa* (1969), p. 736.

[8] *The Times*, 25 June. The *Daily Telegraph*, 25 June 1969, carried excerpts from the *New Nigerian* and the *Nigerian Observer* applauding the Federal Government's action as 'long overdue'.   [9] Quoted by Lagos Radio, 25 June 1969.

to exaggerate the air of doubt and despondent disenchantment that settled, harmattan-like, over Lagos and Owerri and spread sinisterly to Western capitals during the sultry month of June.

In the face of this spectacular month of newsworthiness in relief supplies suspended because of the Nigerians' shooting down of a Red Cross aircraft and Italian oilmen shot or ransomed by the Biafrans, little attention was paid either to a report from Geneva of 'direct and secret' talks between the two parties in Europe[1] or to that by the Zambian Foreign Minister that his country was arranging talks to end the conflict;[2] indeed, as these latter were apparently to be outside the O.A.U. and the U.N., it is scarcely likely that Lagos would have paid much attention to them in any case. Nor did the reference by the O.A.U. Assistant Secretary-General, in a throw-away line at Lagos Airport, to fresh peace talks evoke any enthusiasm from either side.[3] Meanwhile, committed involvement with the Biafra cause continued to arouse foreign sentiments. There was the ghastly news of a self-immolation outside the U.N. in protest that 'You must stop genocide—save nine million Biafrans—peace is a state in which fear does not exist;[4]' a coast-to-coast 'Operation Outrage' fund-raising walk in the U.S.A.;[5] a medical aid exhibition in London sponsored by the doggedly pro-Biafran *Spectator*;[6] and there had been the cold-douche warning from Senator Eugene McCarthy to the U.S. Senate which sent a shiver down the Federal spine, 'It is time to examine our policy of "one Nigeria" which has resulted in our accepting the deaths of a million people as the price for preserving a nation that never existed'[7] [DOC 207]. In England, too, reason seemed to be on holiday when the leader of the British Liberal Party proposed that Royal Air Force planes should be sent to fly supplies into Biafra and damn the consequences.[8] The war was in the doldrums; hopes of peace lay becalmed. The wind of a storm was needed to bring life to the torpid scene.

These storm clouds broke on the eve of the war entering its third year. The Federal Government, preceding its move with well-timed reports of another military offensive under way against the remnant Biafran heartland,[9] on 30 June summoned all the humanitarian organizations and, after Enahoro had addressed them on the background to the decision now taken [DOC 208] revealed its new tough line policy on relief operations. The joint communiqué issued on 1 July after the two-day meeting of no less than sixteen relief organizations and the Federal Government showed that Lagos was at last serious in its intention of

---

[1] The *Guardian*, 20 June 1969. [2] *West Africa* (1969), p. 732.
[3] ibid. [4] *West Africa* (1969), p. 637.
[5] Markpress Release No. Gen. 668. [6] *Spectator*, 7 June and 5 July 1969.
[7] See also Markpress Release Nos. 605 and 650; *West Africa* (1969), pp. 678–9.
[8] Quoted in *The Times*, 1 July 1969.
[9] *Sunday Telegraph*, 29 June; *The Times*, 30 June 1969. The fullest account of Enahoro's announcement on the new Federal offensive is that in *Morning Post*, 30 June 1969.

Remnant of the 'Biafran Republic', early 1969.
(Reproduced by kind permission of Galitzine Chant Russell)

stopping any potential plug hole in the Biafran airlift.[1] With relief responsibility now pointedly taken out of the I.C.R.C. hands, except under conditions of surveillance unlikely to be accepted by Ojukwu in his present mood, and handed over to the Federation's National Re-habilitation Committee [DOC 209], the days of Biafran resistance once again seemed certain to be numbered. Scant attention was paid in Lagos to the I.C.R.C. President's piqued summary of the move as 'a conscious affront to all the principles of humanity'.[2] In a rare, full-page leader captioned 'A Policy of Famine', *The Times* of London[3] had taken up the remarks of Nigerian leaders—and few would claim they were the first to argue the legitimacy of famine as a weapon of war—quoting Awolowo's views that in war all is fair, as well as Hassan Katsina's opinion that 'personally I wouldn't support feeding anybody we are fighting'.[4] Gowon, who in a personal interview had said that in view of his objective of 'a happy country in the end' he could not afford to be callous in the way he prosecuted the campaign,[5] felt the need to modify

[1] Text in Nigeria House press release dated 2 July. See also Lagos Radio report, 1 July 1969. The I.C.R.C. representative, however, gave notice that he was 'not in a position to subscribe to this communiqué'. For a Biafran attempt to demolish Enahoro's statement [DOC 84] point by point, see Markpress Release No. Gen. 680 with marginal emendations.

[2] Quoted in *The Times*, 2 July 1969.

[3] *The Times*, 28 June 1969.

[4] Both quoted in *West Africa* (1969), p. 790. See also *Daily Times*, 26 June 1969.

[5] *Time*, 4 July 1969.

the directness of their attitude and to deny that starvation was among his Government's arsenal.[1]

Yet, for all the humanitarian arguments that could be arrayed in support of the nobly conceived I.C.R.C. operation,[2] few would wish seriously to challenge the premiss that through restraint in permitting supplies to be airlifted into enemy territory to a degree unparalleled in the history of warfare the Nigerian Government had positively helped Biafra to prolong its resistance. Whether relief was mixed with arms supplies mattered less than that the Nigerians believed this to be the case. The hawks were not alone in thinking that the time had now come to give some meaning to Gowon's two-year old promise of declaring 'total war' against the rebels.

July thus opened with a week-end of desperate diplomatic flurry to salvage the threatened prestige of the I.C.R.C. and the reputation of Nigeria after the Enahoro bombshell—seen by some as a brutal gaucherie, by others as an inexcusably overdue measure. The British minister responsible for Nigerian relations was sent flying to Geneva 'to mend the Lagos split with the Red Cross';[3] Dr. Arikpo declined the Pope's offer to dispatch Caritas flights direct from Rome; and the U.S. Secretary of State promised that his country would do all it could to avert the 'abhorrent' likelihood of mass starvation in Biafra. In Britain the press[4] (threatened with a 'dressing down' by Enahoro[5]) and M.P.s stepped up the pressure on the Government after the Foreign Secretary's statement to Parliament, in which he argued that if the U.K. continued supplies it would be assumed it supported the Nigerian Government, while to cut off supplies would inevitably be interpreted as support for the view that the rebellion was justified. He finally appealed to Ojukwu to allow daylight flights of relief supplies.[6] In the wake of a premature report that the Federal Government and I.C.R.C. had come to terms in London,[7] the Red Cross in Geneva issued a statement on the inaccuracies of the press coverage on its President's talks with Dr. Arikpo and Mr. Foley in London [DOC 210] and its President flew out to Lagos to negotiate an agreement. The joint communiqué of 13 July stipulated that:

The two parties will co-operate for the transfer to the National Rehabilitation Commission of relief action co-ordination in Federal territory, so far entrusted to the ICRC by the Federal Military Government;

---

[1] Nigeria House press release, 22 July 1969; TV interview in Lagos quoted in *West Africa* (1969), p. 877.

[2] Cf. Enahoro's description of the objective of reliefs (DOC 208).

[3] *The Times*, 3 July 1969.

[4] *Sunday Telegraph*, 6 July 1969. See also *The Times*'s comment on the concurrent Trafalgar Square Medical Aid Exhibition as 'a real subject for protest—the entire nation should demonstrate to save millions of Biafrans'—8 July 1969.

[5] Quoted in *The Times*, 8 July 1969.

[6] Debate in House of Commons, 30 June 1969.

[7] *The Times*, 7 July 1969.

The ICRC may continue its traditional activities in co-operation with the Nigerian Red Cross;

The date of the transfer will not be known before completion of discussions between ICRC experts, the Rehabilitation Commission, and the Nigerian Red Cross;

The ICRC is prepared to consider Federal Nigerian Government proposals for the forwarding of relief to secessionist province; it undertakes not to fly over Federal territory without government authorisation;

The Nigerian Government undertakes to guarantee the safety of the personnel in Federal territory and of aircraft on humanitarian missions flying in the air-corridors assigned for that purpose;

At the request of the ICRC President, the Federal Nigerian Government authorises one liaison flight to the secessionist area to take medical supplies and relieve personnel whose contracts have expired.[1]

In the meantime, on 7 July one more full-scale debate on the Nigerian war took place in the House of Commons. For his part, Gowon marked the second anniversary of the war by a message to the armed forces in which he drew attention to 'the shrinking size of the dream empire of the rebels'.[2]

For the next six weeks, despite patent proof of Biafra's deliberate switching of physical attacks to the oil companies in Mojekwu's public question of 'How many gallons of petrol pay for a Biafran death?'[3] accounts of gun-running from South Africa,[4] and the alarming reports that first the Israeli Foreign Minister had spoken in parliament of his government's 'duty' to send maximum humanitarian aid to Biafra[5] and then the Sierra Leone parliament had passed a resolution calling on its government to use its good offices to secure an immediate cease-fire,[6] it was the I.C.R.C. *cause célèbre* that held the stage. Indignation, discussions, and plans, punctuated by pilots' offers to run the gauntlet[7] and alerts to stand by for immediate resumption of the airlift which were rapidly followed by the cancellation of such instructions,[8] marked the painful and protracted course of negotiations between the I.C.R.C. and the Federal authorities aimed at reconciling what the former saw as 'the legitimate sovereignty of Nigeria and the mandatory neutrality of the I.C.R.C.'[9] Even the United Nations—to whose Secretary-General

[1] From the version released by I.C.R.C.

[2] Lagos Radio, 7 July 1969.

[3] Statement issued in Lisbon, 15 August 1969 (Markpress Release No. Gen. 702, corrected version).

[4] *Sunday Telegraph*, 10 and 17 August; *The Times*, 15 August 1969. The South African Minister of Defence wrote this off as a 'fantasy', but it was accepted as true in Nigeria (Lagos Radio, 13 August).

[5] For this report and a survey of Nigerian press and radio response, see *Africa Research Bulletin*, p. 1470.

[6] *Africa Research Bulletin*, p. 1500.

[7] *The Times*, 17 July 1969.

[8] e.g., *The Times*, 16 and 30 July 1969; *West Africa* (1969), p. 909.

[9] I.C.R.C. spokesman quoted in *The Times*, 22 August 1969.

the British Liberal Party leader had sent a curious cable urging 'personal intervention to arrange and guarantee arrival of relief supplies by air for Biafra'[1]—made an appeal, in vain, to both sides to resume emergency daylight relief flights and to consider opening land and river corridors.[2]

In summary, the problem centred round the need to replace the abruptly halted airlift of relief supplies, after the shooting down of an I.C.R.C. aeroplane on 5 June, by opening up a land and/or river corridor, possibly under international supervision, and to work out some solution on the actual venue of the international supervision of the contents loaded on to the daylight flights.[3] If Lagos rejected Cotonou for the latter lest arms should be mixed in with relief supplies, Ojukwu rejected Lagos lest it closed his sole route for his jet-set emissaries to communicate with the outside world. Despite M. Naville's personal flight to Lagos to speed negotiations, the various concessions over the presence of a neutral team joining in relief aircraft inspection at Lagos, the possibility of flights being supervised from outside Lagos, and Gowon's humane inclination to allow just one more mercy flight and to hell with the hawks,[4] the Federal Government ultimately rejected the I.C.R.C.'s proposed alterations to the flight arrangements agreed earlier in July.[5] These would have made three new conditions:

(i) That an air corridor reserved for the I.C.R.C. mercy flights would be opened across Nigerian air space into the rebel enclave.
(ii) That the safeguard and protection afforded by the distinctive emblem of the Red Cross would be recognised and formally confirmed by the parties to the conflict.
(iii) That the parties to the conflict would pledge themselves to facilitate the mercy flights and to refrain from any intervention either in the air or on the ground, within the limits of the air corridor, during the time reserved for the I.C.R.C. airlift.

En revanche, Biafra turned down relief flights originating from Lagos as 'tantamount to signing our own death warrant'.[6] Thus, with yet another laudatory observers' team report behind them,[7] the Federal Government could allow its military men to have their say in face of the damning evidence of a Biafra revived: the advance into rebel territory was on.

Meanwhile, with no airlift since 5 June, the food and medical situation in Biafra was rapidly deteriorating. The Biafrans' views on the impasse

---

[1] *The Times*, 30 June; *Guardian*, 1 July 1969.

[2] *The Times*, 30 July 1969; *Africa Research Bulletin*, p. 1471.

[3] See also 'Biafran War causes a Red Cross Crisis', *Daily Telegraph*, 19 August 1969.

[4] *The Times*, 14 July 1969; *Africa Research Bulletin*, p. 1469.

[5] Nigeria House press release, 7 August. See *Daily Times*, 8 August 1969.

[6] *Guardian*, 12 July 1969.

[7] For the period 1 May to 27 June 1969. Also issued as a supplement to *United Nigeria*, No. 11, 1969.

were mordantly plain in the statement issued in Owerri on 9 July,[1] even though they glossed over their own attitude to resolving it. It contrasts revealingly with Gowon's reading of the situation[2] and his repetition of the Federal Government's peace terms [DOC 211]. By the middle of August Lagos was still adamant that no checking of loading relief supplies could be allowed on neutral ground, such as Ojukwu was demanding of the I.C.R.C., and that all relief flights into rebel territory must first land in Lagos for a brief daylight checking.[3]

The all too familiar situation of stalemate had once again developed: this time it was in the relief arena as well as on the battlefield. Hard news of the real war remained minimal, and little was heard of the big Federal offensive indicated in Enahoro's press conference of 28 June.[4] Claims and counterclaims of minor military advances aside, three staggering statistical announcements commanded attention. These were Asika's estimate of N£400,000,000 for the rehabilitation of the war affected areas;[5] the Nigerians' revelation that the war was costing the Federation £5,000,000 a month (Gowon)[6] or £340,000 a day (Awolowo);[7] and Dr. Dike's claim in Paris that there would be three million dead if the fighting lasted to the end of the year.[8] (Joint Church Aid had given the remarkable proportion of 1,500,000 civilian deaths to 500,000 soldiers,[9] confirming the 2,000,000 estimated by the newly established Lagos Committee of Intellectuals.[10]) Paris, indeed, in early July became a centre for the Biafran viewpoint, for in addition to Dike's emotive news conference on 'Biafranism',[11] Christopher Mojekwu delivered a series of scathing attacks against the Federal leadership.[12] Nor did a further outbreak of violence in the Western State, which included the murder of the Chief of Ogbomosho, and the consequent criticism of the Governor do much to strengthen belief in the total efficacy of Nigeria's leadership: 'Lagos is now faced with a political

---

[1] Markpress Release No. Gen. 683.

[2] Message in *United Nigeria*, supplement to No. 11, 1969.

[3] Nigeria House press release, 12 August 1969.

[4] See one analysis of the military situation at the end of July, as given by Agence France Presse in *Africa Research Bulletin*, p. 1471. The same source reprints an A.F.P. report on 'Life in Biafra' in August 1969 (pp. 1499–1500). *West Africa* (1969), p. 891, carried a useful comparative note on the attitudes of the French press at this time.

[5] *Financial Times*, 4 August 1969.

[6] *Sunday Independent* (Dublin), 10 August. See also 'Atta Counts the Cost', *West Africa* (1969), pp. 1265–6.

[7] *West Africa* (1969), p. 1038. In March 1970, Awolowo presented his final estimate of the war having cost Nigeria over £300,000,000 (*West Africa* (1970), p. 218).

[8] *Le Monde*, 7 August 1969. See also *West Africa* (1969), p. 1038.

[9] Joint Church Aid press release No. 92.

[10] *Financial Times*, 27 August 1969.

[11] *West Africa* (1969), pp. 831 and 910, and correspondence in *Le Monde*. The thesis that Biafra was a philosophy was repeated by Ojukwu on 26 July when Messrs. Arthur Nwankwo and Samuel Ifejika presented him with a copy of their book *The Making of a Nation: Biafra* (Biafra Radio, 26 July, quoted in *Africa Research Bulletin*, p. 1470 with serious distortion of the names of both authors).

[12] Markpress Releases No. Gen. 676 and 677.

problem and should apply a political solution,' warned the *New Nigerian*. 'It may be necessary to change certain personnel. If the Federal Government again turns a blind eye to events in the West, it does so at its peril.'[1]

A momentary return of hope attached to the Pope's historic visit to Uganda on 1 August when, with the moral support of Presidents Obote and Nyerere, he endorsed Ojukwu's call for a truce[2] and sought personally to bring together the delegations—once more led, in the absence of the invited Gowon and Ojukwu, by Messrs. Enahoro and Njoku— from the two warring sides. On the eve of his departure from the Vatican, His Holiness sanguinely undertook to work out a compromise that would neither diminish the *amour-propre* nor damage the interests of each party yet would be 'in accord with their respective legitimate and essential claims' [DOC 212]. But the very word 'compromise' had assumed in the vocabulary of either side the status of a synonym of betrayal, and the anodyne communiqué issued as His Holiness returned to Rome pre-empted further public statements[3] and barely concealed the message of failure:[4] Europe, represented in the Pope, had had no more success in mediation than had Africa symbolized in the O.A.U.

Far more promising was the reputedly unpremeditated meeting of General Gowon (after flying visits to Accra and Cotonou) and Dr. Azikiwe for private talks with President Tubman in Monrovia on 19 August. En route, Dr. Azikiwe had made a 'surprise' visit to Lagos on 16 August, where he was duly fêted;[5] but the communiqué issued after the Monrovia talks did little more than note that President Tubman and General Gowon had 'renewed their determination to work for the restoration of peace and unity in Nigeria.'[6] Dr. Azikiwe's reference to Gowon's flexibility and spirit of compromise[7] followed up by his public declaration for the Federal cause [DOC 213] was a major feather in the Lagos cap and the most important event in the long cold summer of newsless inactivity on the fighting front.[8] Expectedly,

---

[1] *New Nigerian*, 15 July 1969. For an account of the disturbances and for the challenge in the press on Brigadier Adebayo's statement of 6 July, 'The Truth About Tax Riots', in which he referred to 'the evil machinations of a few individuals', see *Daily Times*, 7 and 8 July 1969. See also *West Africa* (1969), pp. 822 and 830 for a description, quoting the *Nigerian Tribune*, *Nigerian Observer*, and *Sunday Sketch*, of the riots and the murder of the Shoun of Ogbomosho.

[2] *The Times*, 29 and 31 July 1969; Markpress Release No. Gen. 695; *West Africa* (1969), p. 909. [3] *West Africa* (1969), p. 941.

[4] I recall the strong and justifiable feeling found in Uganda immediately after the Pope's visit, that the world press had been unfair in giving so much prominence to His Holiness's inability to mediate in the war and were wrong to suggest that it was Nigeria rather than Uganda that had been the whole purpose of this unique papal visit.

[5] *West Africa* (1969), pp. 985 and 1009; Lagos Radio, 20 August 1969.

[6] *Daily Telegraph*, 20 August 1969.

[7] *Daily Telegraph*, 23 August 1969.

[8] Related documents are his statement made to a press conference held in London on 28 August and his detailed report on his subsequent fact-finding mission to Nigeria, released on 8 October 1969. This latter statement included a list of alleged collaborators.

Azikiwe's 'new posture', as the Federal Government described it,[1] was disowned by Biafra, which issued a long statement on the defection of the erstwhile successful envoy and abrasively condemned what it now wrote off as 'the tragedy of Nnamdi Azikiwe.'[2]

Added to the reasoned rallying call of a group of Ibo intelligentsia in Lagos,[3] Dr. Azikiwe's reappearance on the scene brought nearer hopes of a possible emotional and psychological breakthrough by the Ibo exiles and intellectuals. Such hopes were only partially muffled by the disturbing contemporaneous publication of two articles in influential press circles suggesting impatience and disillusion in Nigeria with its military leadership[4] and by the editorial *volte-face* in a third important weekly journal,[5] along with Dr. Busia's enigmatic promise on his election as Prime Minister that Ghana would 'reconsider' her stand on the Nigerian-Biafran conflict, in the belief that it was 'imperative to do everything to bring about an effective cease-fire'.[6]

September opened with a roll of propaganda drums beaten by the Biafrans to signal the alleged duplicity of Dr. Azikiwe, whose 'treachery' was dubbed 'back to the gilded cage' in a cleverly republicized version of one of his most tellingly chauvinistic Biafran speeches.[7] Yet the considerable attention given to his new support for Nigeria suggested that it hurt Biafra more than they cared to admit.[8] Nor could its meaning for the pro-Biafran sympathizers of Tanzania and Zambia be overlooked.[9] Its significance was echoed in other, less dramatic *volte-faces* such as

[1] Statement issued in Lagos, 30 August 1969.

[2] Statement issued in Owerri, 29 August 1969 (Markpress Release No. Gen. 709) and broadcast over Biafra Radio. Cf. the condemnation by the Britain-Biafra Association in *The Times*, 29 August 1969. See also the letter in *West Africa* (1969), p. 1375.

[3] 'Ojukwu's "Self-Determination"', memorandum from the Committee of Ibo Intellectuals, Lagos, 1969.

[4] A. Hart, 'Nigerian dissatisfaction with Gowon's war policy', *The Times*, 29 August, and Peter Enahoro, 'General Gowon smells trouble', *Spectator*, 30 August 1969.

[5] 'Ojukwu has made his point', *The Economist*, 30 August 1969.

[6] *Guardian*, 1 September 1969. See also the interview with an Ivory Coast journalist in *Fraternité-Matin*, quoted in *West Africa* (1969), pp. 1133 and 1177.

[7] Markpress Release No. Gen. 710. For Dr. Azikiwe's denial of his attributed status as 'special adviser' to Ojukwu, see his letter in *The Times*, 4 September 1969. From private correspondence that Dr. Azikiwe has generously made available to the writer, it is evident that Biafra was intent on making as much capital as it could out of the ex-President's presence and, equally, that he was by no means simply Ojukwu's 'yes-man'. Dr. Azikiwe's forthcoming account of the Nigerian civil war should help to clarify the difficulties of his position.

[8] Cf. the report 'Biafrans' protest turns to "joy"', *The Times*, 2 September, and Mr. Ignatius Kogbara's comment that 'Biafra is a purer and better place without him', quoted in *West Africa* (1969), p. 1069.

[9] 'The significance of Dr. Azikiwe's move lies in its probable effect on President Kaunda, of Zambia, and President Nyerere, of Tanzania. Both leaders were originally persuaded by Dr. Azikiwe—at the time himself a believer in the genocide theory—to recognise Biafra as a new sovereign entity. The fact that the former Nigerian President, who still carries great weight as an African leader, now says he was wrong and that there is no reason for going on with the war is thought likely to make a considerable impact on both Presidents'—Nicholas Carroll, *Sunday Times*, 31 August 1969.

the defection of a former diplomat who had spearheaded the Biafran cause in Paris and of the one-time editor of *Drum* who now switched from the Biafran Directorate of Propaganda to a post in the Federal Ministry of Information.[1] Like the collection of emotional speeches that greeted Zik on his 'I'm home' Nigerian tour,[2] his interview with a Lagos journalist during a nationwide tour of Nigeria in September [DOC 214], and his report on his 'fact-finding mission' [DOC 215], in which he included his own naming of the Biafran hawks, remain important documents for a study of a much longer period than that of 1967–9 alone. In the meantime, an extensive diplomatic offensive was being carried out by Nigeria for the presentation of the Federal case at the O.A.U. Summit meeting scheduled for Addis Ababa in the first week of September. In contrast to Nigeria's low-key handling of the Biafran issue at the Kinshasa Summit of 1967, this time she was expected to give prominence to the civil war.

This sixth Conference of Heads of State of the O.A.U. met in Ethiopia from 6 to 10 September.[3] For the first time, General Gowon was present in person and he addressed the Assembly [DOC 217]. Ojukwu did not attend. Biafra decided to play up the denial of its request for a truce which alone, it asserted, would have allowed General Ojukwu to travel, and took a gloomy view of the usefulness of the meeting even before it was held.[4] Intense diplomatic excitement was caused by President Nyerere's private circulation of his country's radical understanding of the Biafran case [DOC 218]. He asked people to imagine the scale of the African outcry 'if 30,000 Ibos had been massacred by whites in Rhodesia or South Africa,' and went on to warn that unless Africans soon learned to criticize intolerance within their own continent, fascism by African governments against their own people would not only continue but even become acceptable. After a vigorous Nigerian protest by Enahoro [DOC 219] and an 'eyeball to eyeball'[5] meeting between Gowon and Nyerere, the Tanzanian memorandum was officially withdrawn.[6] Further excitement was caused by Gowon's reported breakthrough remark on his return to Lagos that he was ready for unconditional talks—'Let them get there and put all their cards on the table'[7]—but this was quickly denied by Dr. Arikpo as one more instance of misinterpretation to which Nigerian leaders seemed so prone.[8] A further gloss was given by Chief Enahoro, who dismissed the Biafran request for a 'third party guarantee' on relief arrangements as a propaganda

[1] 'Seeing the Light', *United Nigeria*, No. 12, 1969, and *West Africa* (1969), p. 1070.

[2] *Nigeria Welcomes Zik* (Lagos, 1969).

[3] See *Africa Research Bulletin*, pp. 1515–18; *West Africa* (1969), pp. 1075–6.

[4] Statement issued in Owerri, 5 September 1969 (Markpress Release No. Gen. 714).

[5] *West Africa* (1969), p. 1075.

[6] It was subsequently reissued and officially distributed in Dar es Salaam. See also Nyerere's remarks on Biafra quoted in *East African Standard*, 10 September 1969.

[7] *East African Standard*, 12 September 1969.

[8] Quoted in *West Africa* (1969), p. 1133.

stunt. He also revealed that if Ojukwu wrote to the chairman of the O.A.U. Consultative Committee on Nigeria signifying his willingness to negotiate, the Federal Government would do likewise always provided that the Emperor of Ethiopia was convinced of the likelihood of genuinely 'meaningful discussions' emerging from such a Biafran letter.[1]

In the event, the Summit meeting passed a significantly-worded resolution on the Nigerian civil war appealing to both parties to 'accept immediately a suspension of hostilities and the opening of negotiations intended to preserve the unity of Nigeria' [DOC 220]. The voting was thirty-six in favour and five abstentions, the four 'recognizer' countries and Sierra Leone. Indeed, the pressurizing behaviour of Mr. Siaka Stevens, who accused General Gowon of having personalized the discussion,[2] coming on top of the recent motion in Freetown's Parliament calling on the Government to use its good offices and maybe recognize Biafra[3] (Uganda's Parliament had earlier rejected a similar motion),[4] were clearly a matter of fresh concern for Lagos, for all the O.A.U.'s support.

The new relief operations agreement signed on 13 September between the Nigerian Government and the International Red Cross allowed daylight flights from Dahomey under certain compromise conditions for inspection:

(i) All relief flights shall take place in daylight hours;
(ii) A Federal Government inspector shall join two inspectors appointed respectively by the Government of Dahomey and the ICRC to inspect relief consignments at Cotonou;
(iii) The Federal Government inspector has the right, acting alone, to exclude from any flights any cargo or passengers who do not form part of genuine relief action;
(iv) The Federal Government shall call down for inspection in Lagos any aircraft it wishes whether or not the aircraft has been inspected at Cotonou;
(v) Relief material shall be as agreed by the National Commission for Rehabilitation; and,
(vi) Only agreed relief personnel shall be entitled to board aircraft.[5]

The proposals were, however, rejected out of hand by Biafra as being far removed from those she had accepted on 1 August, and she smartingly accused the I.C.R.C. of failing 'to take a firm stand on any issue adversely affecting the public image of the Lagos régime'.[6] In the face of unrelenting propaganda against the humanitarian organizations, one of them was stung into issuing a phrenetic counterblast [DOC 216]. In

---

[1] Enahoro, quoted in *United Nigeria*, No. 12, 1969.
[2] *West Africa* (1969), p. 1075; see also (1970), p. 54.
[3] *Africa Research Bulletin*, p. 1500; *West Africa* (1969), p. 945.
[4] *West Africa* (1969), p. 910.
[5] Quoted from news agency reports in *Africa Research Bulletin*, p. 1530.
[6] Markpress Release No. Gen. 717; *West Africa* (1969), p. 1133. See also 'Dahomey and the Red Cross', ibid., p. 1271.

Lagos, the Chief Justice announced that the Nigerian Red Cross would now take over from the I.C.R.C. as the co-ordinating authority for relief operations.[1] The latter in turn announced its intention of sending a mission to Biafra in an attempt to gain her agreement to the 13 September relief proposals now accepted by the Federal Government. Waning interest in the protracted and frustrating I.C.R.C. negotiations was suddenly swept off the front page news by yet one more 'rebellion' —the dramatic term was that used by Brigadier Adebayo himself—in the unhappy Western State, where the Yoruba propensity for operating on a fine political margin and what the Government called 'sectional combat' came to another climax in the forcing of Ibadan jail and in armed ambushes of the police.[2]

Back in Lagos, General Gowon returned in his Independence Day speech to the theme of an amnesty. This was now to be granted to 'thousands' of Biafran sympathizers detained in Nigeria.[3] He called for rededication after nine years of independence and blamed the humanitarian cause for the painful slowness of the military campaign. In view of the inflamed situation in the West, he also included a reference to his promise of an eventual post-war review of the present twelve-state structure, but asked why the Yoruba should 'give the impression that they relish the taunts of those who disparagingly call the State "The Wild West" ' [DOC 221]. At the October meeting of the United Nations Nigeria's path turned out to be less easy than it had been at the O.A.U. Summit at Addis Ababa. Gabon ignored Dr. Arikpo's warning that any attempt to raise the question would be resisted, declaring it to be 'inconceivable' that Biafra should accept terms tantamount to unconditional surrender; the Zambian, Ugandan, and Ivory Coast delegates all introduced the civil war into their speeches; and thorn-in-the-Federal-flesh Tanzania called on the Assembly to forget its 'legalistic

[1] *The Times*, 3 October 1969.

[2] *Morning Post*, 24 and 26 September; *Daily Times*, 27 September; editorial, 'What's Wrong in Ibadan?' *West Africa* (1969), pp. 1036–7, 1065, 1197, and 1230; and the statement on the disorders issued by the Federal Government in Lagos on 25 September 1969. See also the important report of the Ayoola Committee published in April 1969. For Biafran exploitation of the ugly disturbances, see Markpress Release No. Gen. 721: 'How many dead Yoruba will have to join the Biafran dead before they realise the truth?' For Awolowo's personal meeting with Tafa Adeoye ('Field Marshal'), leader of the cocoa farmers' banned Agbekoya society which had promoted much of the unrest, see *West Africa* (1969), p. 1289.

[3] *Morning Post*, 2 October 1969. *The Times*, 20 October, spoke of 'thousands'. Lagos Radio, 9 October, announced the release of 151 persons in the first week, among whom was Wole Soyinka detained since August 1967 in Kaduna gaol. There had been several calls for his release, from inside and outside Nigeria, but in August Admiral Wey had answered the *Daily Times* appeal by saying the Biafran secession would have to be ended first (*West Africa* (1969), p. 978). Rex Collings' article on Wole Soyinka in the *New Statesman*, 20 December 1968, commemorated Soyinka's award of the Jock Campbell New Statesman prize; it is also one of several appeals by Collings on Soyinka's detention. Soyinka later gave an interview to the *Daily Times* and an important television interview on Ibadan TV—see *West Africa* (1969), pp. 1261 and 1489.

inhibitions' and compel Nigeria to allow immediate relief operations into Biafra.[1]

In Britain, the Labour Party's annual Congress repeated its thwarted 1968 resolution calling on the British Government to stop arms shipments to Lagos. Once again it was pointedly ignored by the Labour Government.[2] The strong Biafran lobby of former expatriate administrators and churchmen from the Eastern Region, now regrouped with a number of eminent 'Nigerians' under the less partisan label of the Co-ordinating Committee for Action on Nigeria/Biafra, presented their closely argued case to the Prime Minister. Mr. Wilson replied disarmingly.[3] Three weeks later, in the traditional survey of Britain's year in retrospect made at the Lord Mayor's dinner at Guildhall, he included an appeal to Ojukwu to allow daylight relief flights:

Lord Hunt went as my personal representative in Nigeria 18 months ago to work out the means of conveying to the hungry the food which was there packed and ready for transportation for those who stood in urgent need of it. In Nigeria last March we worked out in Lagos, in Enugu, in Calabar and Port Harcourt, the means of ferrying that food to where it was needed. It is there today prepacked and waiting. The International Red Cross, with our full backing, have made their proposals. And so far they have been rejected. If Colonel Ojukwu tonight would agree to daylight flights the worst of the starvation, the hunger, could be ended within a week.

If, having refused the still simpler solution of allowing the food under proper safeguards along the road corridors, he continues to reject these daylight flights there will be those who will conclude, as many of us are reluctantly being compelled to conclude, that food supplies are being sacrificed to arms running, that a starving people, and above all starving children, were being used as pawns in the political and military struggle.[4]

A press interview disclosure by his Foreign and Commonwealth Office Under-Secretary that increased arms supplies were being sent to Nigeria[5] involved the Foreign Secretary in a heated exchange in Parliament on 17 November, though he pointed out that the British contribution still remained at 15% of the arms Nigeria received from abroad.[6]

There were also a number of minor outbursts of vacillating interest. These included a report from the Nigerian Red Cross that it was experiencing difficulties in carrying out the relief responsibilities that it had taken on in October from the I.C.R.C.[7] This organization was now

[1] *West Africa* (1969), p. 1197.

[2] Two important debates on Nigeria were held in the Dail Eireann at this period. See the Dail official reports, vol. 241, no. 11, cols. 1881–94 and vol. 242, no. 9. cols. 1488–91.

[3] Private communication.

[4] Quoted in *The Times*, 11 November 1969.

[5] *The Times*, 17 November 1969. An extensive transcript of the press briefing has kindly been supplied by the C.O.I.

[6] See also the editorial, 'Arms for the Slow Kill', *The Times*, 18 November 1969.

[7] *Sunday Telegraph*, 26 October 1969. For a summary of what this entailed, see *Morning Post*, 11 October. See also *West Africa* (1969), pp. 1295 and 1331.

YORUBA CENTRAL STATE MOVEMENT

You may have seen some Yorubas demonstrating last week with placards and banners condemning "One Nigeria" and calling for an 'independent Oduduwaland' (*see West Africa, 11th January, 1969, page 34*) i.e. that Nigeria should be divided into three separate countries —one to retain the name Nigeria, another to be "biafra" and the third "Oduduwaland".

The Yoruba Central State Movement:-

★   dissociates itself from this diabolical move

★   says that the people of Oyo and Ibadan Provinces will NOT be in the dreamland of the Republic of Oduduwaland

★   condemns it as a move to harm the successful execution of the current civil war and cause further chaos in the country

★   says it is designed to give comfort and succour to the rebels in the East Central State

★   says this is treason against Nigeria and that it should be investigated and those responsible dealt with and quickly too

★   says to avert chaos in the West, create the

YORUBA CENTRAL STATE
now inside one Nigeria

Long live ONE NIGERIA; long live the
YORUBA CENTRAL STATE

Typical handsheet issued by one of the 'separate State' organizations.

in its sixth month of inactivity and had been obliged to sell off some of its relief aircraft[1] after the eventual failure of its five-man mission to persuade Biafra to accept the agreement it had negotiated with the Nigerian Government in mid-September—'the very existence of a generation is indeed in peril.'[2] There was too a somewhat damp squib 'Biafra week' in Britain[3] with its anti-oil combine slogans of: 'Boycott Murder, Boycott Shell-BP', and 'Put a Dead Biafran in your Tank'; an unsavoury clash in public between two top Lagos civil servants over alleged big-time corruption and contractor profiteering in the armed forces;[4] another personal political polemic from Chief Awolowo in the Lagos press, denying reports that he was planning to overthrow the Gowon régime;[5] and compulsory registration of all Biafrans overseas.[6] But such trivia apart, there was virtually no hard information from the stalemate, reluctant, 'inching' war.[7] Was this really, in the persuasive phrase of *The Times* leader-writer, no more than 'A Dialogue of the Deaf?'[8]

Then suddenly, in the pattern of hopes' deflation-inflation-puncture to which observers had now become accustomed, another surge of optimism among non-Nigerians swept into front-page prominence. Peace talks, or at least talks about talks, were once again to the fore. First there were reports, however confused, of Gabonese mediation, supposedly at the request of Ojukwu who had apparently agreed to participate personally in peace talks on the sole pre-condition that a truce be observed for the duration of the negotiations.[9] Then there followed a message, including the phrase 'without pre-conditions', sent by Ojukwu through Haile Selassie to Lagos by the hand of the Ethiopian

[1] *The Times*, 8 November 1969.

[2] Quoted in *West Africa* (1969), p. 1353. See statements issued byDr. Sylvanus Cookey, Co-ordinator of Biafran Relief, in Owerri on 14 September (Markpress Release No. Gen. 717) and on 21 October (Biafran Radio report quoted in full in *Africa Research Bulletin*, p. 1560); *The Times*, 23 October. For a useful résumé of the prolonged I.C.R.C. negotiations of mid-1969, see the *Sunday Times*, 26 October 1969.

[3] *Sunday Telegraph*, 26 October; *West Africa* (1969), p. 1290; Markpress Release No. Gen. 731 and 732.

[4] *Daily Telegraph*, 22 October 1969. Statement and counter-statement by the two Permanent Secretaries were released to the Nigerian press, but were hurriedly withdrawn —see *West Africa* (1969), pp. 1321 and 1390. See also Brian Silk, 'Nigeria's Double-talk War', *Daily Telegraph*, 4 November 1969, and the Nigerian press, *passim*.

[5] *Sunday Times* (Lagos), 12 October 1969; *West Africa* (1969), p. 1261.

[6] The notice in the British press ran:
'The Government of Biafra requires all Biafrans resident overseas to be registered with the office of the Special Representative of the Republic of Biafra in their areas. In the United Kingdom, registrations will commence on 1st November, 1969, and end 30th November 1969, after which the register will be forwarded to Biafra. For details of procedure of registration, contact the office of the Special Representative, The Biafra Union and Branches, Divisional Assembly and Divisional Unions.' It was signed by Mr. I. S. Kogbara.

[7] The epithet had been used by the *Sunday Telegraph*, 13 April 1969.

[8] *The Times*, 10 November 1969.

[9] *The Times*, 17 October; *Financial Times*, 18 October 1969. For Nigeria's rejection of Gabonese mediation, see the talk on Lagos Radio, 20 October.

Foreign Minister.[1] There were, too, references to an appeal by Ojukwu urging the United Nations to call for a truce[2] and unsubstantiated reports of secret meetings between French and British diplomats to promote a cease-fire.[3] Then, at Ojukwu's address to his Consultative Assembly in Owerri on 1 November, came the first hard news. Despite his sharp attack on the 'impotent and sheepish' O.A.U. and the alleged duplicity of its Secretary-General, he did express Biafra's readiness to meet Nigeria anywhere and at any time, qualifying this undertaking only by insisting that for any really meaningful talks a concurrent cease-fire was a *sine qua non*.[4] Of far greater significance was the simultaneous report from the Biafra public relations agency in Geneva that a Government spokesman (unidentified) in Owerri had stated that Biafra was willing to compromise on the issue of her sovereignty provided that her safety was assured:

Biafra's only interest in wanting sovereignty is that it provides security for its 14 million people. . . . However, since our attachment to sovereignty is functional and not sentimental, Biafra will be prepared to accept, at the suggestion of no matter who, any alternative arrangement that can guarantee a non-recurrence of the massacres of the past 25 years.[5]

Depending on the value attached to its genuineness, it was not impossible to read a real shift of Biafra's position into this statement. But before its authenticity could be established, once-bitten-twice-shy Lagos had decided to have no truck with yet another likely Ojukwu ploy, and refused to take seriously the offer to give up secession.[6] Their reaction drew apparent justification from the immediate denial by Mr. H. Wm. Bernhardt, head of Biafra's publicity agency in Geneva, that Ojukwu was willing to renounce secession under any terms, and from the growing speculation that Markpress may well have misinterpreted the information received from Biafra.[7] If, as some believed, this was a Biafran kite, Lagos had made it plain that it was useless to fly it again.

Launching his own book on the conflict[8] at a press conference in Owerri (the fact that it was the tenth 'Biafran' book to appear within the year against Nigeria's 'nil return' implied an imbalance in the public record which threatened to be as dangerously lopsided as the consti-

---

[1] *The Times*, 30 October; *West Africa* (1969), p. 1289; *Africa Research Bulletin*, p. 1561, quoting an A.F.P. interview and Biafra Radio reports of 30 October.

[2] Biafra Radio, 25 October 1969.

[3] The *Scotsman*, 4 November 1969.

[4] Biafra Radio, 1 November 1969, quoted in *Africa Research Bulletin*, p. 1586. The Markpress Release No. Gen. 735, quoting from Ojukwu's address to the Consultative Assembly, omitted all references to the readiness for talks and consisted entirely of rebarbative abuse generously extended to all.

[5] *The Times*, 4 November 1969, quoting from a report issued by Markpress in Geneva; *West Africa* (1969), p. 1353; Biafra Radio talk, 3 November (B.B.C. ME/3321/B9).

[6] *The Times*, 5 November 1969. See also the editorial in *West Africa* (1969), p. 1325.

[7] The *Scotsman*, 5 November 1969; *West Africa* (1969), p. 1353.

[8] *Biafra* (New York, 1969), 2 volumes.

K

tutional imbalance had been to the First Republic[1]), Ojukwu admitted that he now saw little prospect of peace negotiations and that the war might after all have to find its solution on the battlefield. If Biafra continued to hold out, he could not see the Nigerians lasting another six months.[2] Yet after six months of suspended relief flights by the I.C.R.C. and with Joint Church Aid alone flying in supplies, the pace was clearly beginning to tell in beleaguered Biafra. 'So the Biafrans suffer on' was the apt title to a contemporary first-hand account,[3] with an estimated 3,000 deaths per day from starvation.[4] Even Biafra's apparent new friend[5] of *The Economist*, misled into viewing the Geneva report as 'the best deal yet available to get talks started', could pose the *num* question of 'Is Biafra ready for peace?'[6]

But in Nigeria the mood was very different: where was any incontrovertible evidence of a change of heart by Ojukwu? Few Nigerians had any doubts about the answer. Availing himself for the third time of the opportunity presented by a university convocation to make a speech of national significance,[7] General Gowon reaffirmed in an address at Ibadan University that the end of the war was in sight. Once again he blamed its excessive prolongation on foreign meddlers who 'place every possible obstacle in the way of peace and support rebel propaganda and intransigence'.[8] But rumours of peace could not be scotched: with Biafra feeling the pinch and Nigeria nervous of the possibility of ugly political reaction to a seemingly endless stalemate on the battlefield, talk about talks was bound to be in the air and seized on in a strawlike fashion. Following reports of a secret peace move by Dr. Busia of Ghana,[9] another momentary spurt of optimism over peace talks sprang up when in late November Switzerland confirmed that a few weeks previously Biafra had indeed asked her to mediate.[10] This chance was buried as soon as it was born, supposedly because of the 'regrettable indiscretion' of a premature leak from a radio and TV interview,[11] but perhaps more realistically because of Nigeria's constant and consistent rejection to treat through any intermediary other than the O.A.U. The Geneva flutter turned out to be yet one more non-starter. But this was not the end of the affair. The order had gone out from the Nigerian Chief of Staff, Brigadier Hassan Katsina, for the army to 'liberate' the remnant rebel area.[12] The offensive was on:

[1] Cf. 'Biafra in Print', *African Affairs*, vol. 69, no. 275, pp. 180–3.
[2] *The Times*, 6 November 1969.
[3] Norman Kirkham in the *Daily Telegraph*, 22 November 1969.
[4] *Daily Telegraph*, 9 November 1969.
[5] This was the interpretation placed by some Nigerians on the meaning of its article published on 30 August 1969. See p. 126, fn. 5.
[6] *The Economist*, 9 November 1969.   [7] See pp. 18 and 88.
[8] *The Times* and *Daily Telegraph*, 18 November; Lagos Radio, 17 November 1969.
[9] *The Times*, 29 November 1969.
[10] *Africa Research Bulletin*, p. 1588, quoting Swiss and Nigerian radio reports.
[11] *The Times*, 27 November; *Sunday Telegraph*, 30 November 1969.
[12] *Nigerian Observer*, 17 November 1969.

whether this was to be the final one or just another semi-final remained to be seen.

It was in early December that that persistent conscience of the war, the House of Commons—some Nigerians were known to comment that the legislature in London gave the impression of taking the war far more seriously than did the Cabinet in Lagos;[1] nor need the stricture be limited to parliamentarians, as Kaye Whiteman's apt phrase of 'the passionate whites'[2] for the busybody polemicists neatly showed—once more began to nag. First came the decision by the Conservative Party to send 'their man in Smith Square' to both Nigeria and Biafra. Whether this was influenced by a letter from the National Young Conservatives to Mr. Heath advocating a complete change of the party's policy on the supply of arms, now hostilely condemned as having produced not a quick kill but only a mass kill,[3] or by the expertise offered from the party's select West African Committee which had urged the early dispatch of a Tory frontbencher to Lagos to express unequivocal support for the Federal Government,[4] is not easy to determine. At any rate, Lord Carrington's clearance by both sides constituted an unusual event among visitors charged with 'finding out the facts for themselves'. His reports on his return to London, though not publicly released, were recognized by those who heard them to be as thin in optimism as his remarks to the press at the airport and to private meetings of senior party members had clearly been.[5] Next came the signing of a motion by over one hundred M.P.s from all parties (though observers noted among the leading signatories those names prominent for the past two years as sympathizing with the Biafran cause), calling for a change of policy by Britain to press, through the U.N. Security Council, for a total embargo on the supply of arms to both sides and setting a time limit for forcing a division on the Government's policy towards Nigeria. Within twenty-four hours a Minister of State in the Foreign and Commonwealth office, the peripatetic Mr. Maurice Foley, was once more on his way to confer with General Gowon in Lagos.

Meanwhile in Geneva on 8 December the World Council of Churches sent a shiver of surprise down the back of the relief agencies and a tremor of pleasure up the spine of Nigerians when it announced its highly significant conclusion that it was 'deeply distressed by the ambiguous position' in which the 'tremendous effort' at relief[6] had placed the Christian people, churches, and organizations. The Council

[1] It is possible to read, as I found some Nigerians did, the same conclusion into the proposal under discussion at the time of writing, that a special thanksgiving service should be held in St. Paul's Cathedral, *London*, to mark the end of the *Nigerian* civil war.

[2] From his article in *Venture*, July 1969, pp. 37–9.

[3] *The Times*, 25 November; *Sunday Telegraph*, 7 December 1969.

[4] Private communication.

[5] *Sunday Times*, 21 December 1969.

[6] See the extensive record of achievement presented in the W.C.C. report on Nigeria/Biafra relief operations issued in Joint Church Aid Press Release No. 113.

went on to ask whether it was justifiable 'to prolong the massive airlift in its present form' [DOC 222]. Many saw this soul-searching as a welcome injection of realism into what had become in danger of being an operation based on misdirected sentimentality.[1] Paradoxically, to provide relief could too easily be to prolong suffering.

In the event, the threatened British backbench revolt fizzled out[2] and a comfortable Labour majority, swollen by solid Conservative support, upheld the Government policy on Nigeria. The debate was full of meat from both sides, with the Prime Minister as well as the Foreign Secretary defending the Government stand with sense and sincerity. There was however a perceptible if unemphasized shift in Britain's rationalization of her presence in Lagos. Instead of the insistence that by supplying arms her High Commissioner in Lagos was in a position to influence an assumedly misbehaving Nigerian Government, the Prime Minister now pointed out that even if this country were to withdraw all arms support immediately not one single Nigerian life would be saved. The debate of 8–9 December also included a proposal from Sir Alec Douglas-Home that the Royal Navy should mount an airlift by helicopters. The idea was quickly written off both by General Gowon, who in a speech at Kano simply rejected it as 'impracticable', and a month later by the Foreign Secretary on the same if more researched grounds.[3]

The Federal Government was understandably tiring of more and more outside suggestions for resolving—or, as they usually saw it, interfering in if not materially prolonging—the conflict. Surely, Lagos felt, the 'best' approach on all counts was quickly to break the gravely weakened Biafran resistance. The same attitude of embittered resentment against intervention, however hedged as humanitarian aid, was felt towards the massive demonstrations staged at Christmas when such gimmicks as a 'Save Biafra Campaign' fast in Piccadilly Circus and Rochester Cathedral and a 'For Whom the Bell Tolls' (they literally did, at the eleventh hour, starting in Canterbury Cathedral) fund stunt[4] which raised £150,000 for victims of the war. Who, Lagos once more began to wonder, were their friends. Did not their latest assurances

[1] In the event, this rethinking was not accepted and the Joint Church Aid Division resolved that 'to stop the airlift now would not only have political consequences but also result in the death of millions of innocent civilians.' It therefore agreed that it had 'no alternative but to continue the relief work for as long as it is an effective means of alleviating the present suffering'—Joint Church Aid Press Release No. 120.

[2] *Guardian*, 10 December 1969. The Government had a majority of 170, with 86 voting against it, although over 150 M.P.s had signed the original all-party motion. The steadfast support of Lagos by the British Government, despite much public disquiet and some dismay in the ranks of the Labour Party, is a notable feature of the war. As with the O.A.U., how touch-and-go endorsement of the Nigerian stand was at times remains for historians to assess once the records are open.

[3] *The Times*, 7 January 1970.

[4] *The Times*, 27 December, 1969; *West Africa* (1969), p. 1594. Advertisement by the United Action for Nigeria/Biafra movement, e.g., *Spectator* (1969), p. 888.

on daylight flights spell out that 'it is not the Government's intention that the Nigerian Air Force should attack Uli when I.C.R.C. aircraft are there during the hours of daylight covered by the agreement; nor is it their intention that Nigerian aircraft should escort or follow the I.C.R.C. flights engaged in relief operations?' 'There is nothing', the statement roundly ended, 'in the agreement [concluded with I.C.R.C. on 30 September 1969] intended to secure any military advantage from the Federal Government from the relief operation.'[1]

Those who resolutely saw little likelihood of the Foley envoy, dispatched to Lagos and beyond in early December, carrying in his briefcase any new tactic acceptable to Lagos,[2] preferred to pin their dwindling hopes on the person of the Emperor of Ethiopia. They had this faith validated when, after forty-eight hours of rumours along the corridors of power, Addis Ababa announced that the Emperor was ready to bring both sides together yet once more and now offered his capital as the venue.[3] Lagos's worried call for 'clarification' on the issue[4] (already clouded by Ojukwu's mischievous broadcast welcoming the Emperor's 'personal initiative'[5]) of whether the Emperor was acting under agreed O.A.U. auspices or in a private mediatory capacity,[6] was exactly the opportunity Biafra sought to enhance her would-be dove-like reputation. With due publicity, a small delegation headed by Dr. Pius Okigbo flew to Addis Ababa; with even greater publicity Ojukwu recalled them three days later, exploiting the Nigerian non-presence as 'conclusive evidence' of an unrelenting policy of nothing less than a military solution to the conflict.[7] But Nigeria remained satisfied that the 'proposed peace talks on the Nigerian crisis' had been called by the Emperor acting within the context of the O.A.U. resolution on Nigeria, and accused Biafra of demeaning the Emperor's status by this fraudulent exploitation.[8] Once again the outcome was an impasse: 'The Emperor's well intentioned attempt . . . has ended in fiasco.'[9] Yet General Gowon

---

[1] This statement, issued in Lagos on 9 December, was dramatically read out in the House of Commons by Mr. George Thomson during the tense debate on the Nigerian war.

[2] *Morning Post*, 9 December 1969.

[3] Announcement by Addis Ababa Radio, 8 December 1969.

[4] *The Times*, 17 December 1969. See Lagos Radio, 16 and 17 December.

[5] Broadcast of 16 December (Markpress Release No. Gen. 766).

[6] Cf. *Daily Telegraph*, 9 December 1969.

[7] Statement issued by Biafran Ministry of Information, 20 December 1969. See *Africa Research Bulletin*, p. 1615, for the comments by Mr. Austin Okwu, Biafran representative in East and Central Africa.

[8] Statements issued in Lagos on 17 and 21 December, quoted by Lagos Radio. For Sierra Leone's major involvement in this abortive attempt at bringing the two sides together, see *Africa Research Bulletin*, p. 1615. This diplomatic failure should be read in conjunction with the earlier remark of her Foreign Minister that Sierra Leone might recognize Biafra if peace negotiations were not in train before the end of the year (quoted in *West Africa* (1969), p. 1353). See also the Lagos Radio attack on Dr. Siaka Stevens' 'gaucherie', 7 January 1970 (B.B.C. ME/3275/B1).

[9] Editorial, *Daily Telegraph*, 19 December 1969.

had never been in two minds where the blame lay. By now he was determined not to have the wool pulled over his eyes any more. 'Let any further peace talk be meaningful,' he had told reporters at Lagos Airport a few weeks earlier. 'Let it be the one that would produce results with which everybody would be satisfied. . . . Ojukwu is the stumbling block.'[1]

It was on this note of smouldering impatience with the effrontery of outside interference that 1969 closed, and with the quiet realization that the possibility of a demoralized Biafra, weakened by six months of drastically reduced airlift, could, if the fates were kind and the rains late, become the probability of a defeated Biafra. In the event, the as yet unannounced incidents of those dying days of the old year were already conspiring to make this probability a certainty; a certainty to be marked by a dizzy succession of happenings on, as it turned out after all, the battlefield and not round the well-worn conference table.

[1] Nigeria House press release, 3 November 1969.

1970

THE New Year opened quietly enough, but to those who had followed the war closely there seemed to be certain straws in the December harmattan that might well augur more than at first sight appeared likely—even to observers by now somewhat cynically inured to the chasmic credibility gap between announcement and actuality or rumour and reality.

A Biafran communiqué boisterously date-lined 'Republic of Benin' and reporting Colonel Okonkwo's tour of inspection in his self-styled role as the Republic's Military Administrator[1] faded into its proper perspective when, at the end of the dying year, Ojukwu admitted at the public opening of the National Orientation College in Owerri that Biafra was currently grappling with one of the toughest military situations in the past thirty months.[2] With the Federal Divisions estimated to number 110,000 men in the field[3] and their morale boosted by the heavy Soviet 122 mm. guns, described by an observer as being 'capable of hurling a shell thirteen miles with pin-point accuracy',[4] now trained on Owerri and awaiting the artillerymen's itching test of their performance in action, it did not seem premature to reconsider the cautious definition of the Federal attack mounted as far back as mid-November as a 'semi-final assault'.[5] With such a shift to the war front, little attention was paid to a rumour from Geneva on 5 January that fresh peace talks were yet again in train[6] and scant heed was given to the report that Dutch legislators and academics were intent on pressurizing Britain into imposing an embargo on arms deliveries.[7] Rather now was the moment to recall General Gowon's quiet statement, confidently made at an exclusive interview in Lagos a few weeks earlier and pushed aside in the European press by its apparent preference for 'good' news from Biafra:

Militarily, politically and economically the balance is very much in our favour ... The end is now very near and just like the Germans today don't like being called Nazis that's how it's going to be here soon—nobody is going to like being called a Biafran.[8]

[1] Markpress Release No. Gen. 761.

[2] *Scotsman*, 25 December 1969. For his Christmas broadcast, see *West Africa* (1970), p. 25.

[3] In the immediate post-war period this figure was raised by one correspondent to 200,000 under arms.

[4] *Daily Express*, 22 December 1969. Cf. *West Africa* (1969), p. 1389.

[5] For its quiet but effective execution, see *The Economist*, 13 December; *Sunday Telegraph*, 21 December; and *The Times*, 31 December 1969.

[6] *Sunday Telegraph*, 4 January; *Guardian*, 6 January 1970.

[7] *West Africa* (1970), p. 25.   [8] Quoted in *West Africa* (1969), p. 1425.

In the event, how near the end already was came as a surprise to all.

Speculation, calculation, and belief in the final cracking of the Biafran edifice received confirmation as hard news at last began to filter through from the battlefront after weeks of empty communiqués or simply no communiqués at all.[1] Reports that the three Federal Divisions were effectively poised to prise remnant Biafra apart were matched by a realization that such a thrust had not only long been strategically imperative but was at last tactically practicable. With Biafra split in two, Owerri threatened, and Uli finally in danger—along with the Lisbon telex, Biafra's sole and vital link with the outside world, and still operating despite the severe reduction of aid flights since June —the Federal Army would be able confidently to expect a military victory before that critical onset of the fourth rainy season of the war. Indeed, were it to be that the course of the inching war would not be decisively altered by the end of the present dry season, the chances of Ojukwu's desperate hope of salvaging the rump of Biafra could be measurably improved, either through a deterioration of the Federal spirit to win the war brought about by Nigeria's vexatious potential for internal disquiet or else through an internationalizing pressure for external intervention compelling the two sides to attend a peace conference. To many, such a non-solution, at least in expectation of any long-term stability for the concept of Nigeria and hence potentially that of Black Africa, seemed to be the worst of compromises and little short of a mere delaying of further disaster.

Speaking to the nation on New Year's eve, from a position of increasingly obvious commanding strength in both the military field and the civilian arena (his Government had just placed an uncompromising and bold ban on all strikes and lockouts[2]), General Gowon reaffirmed his preference for peace talks over a military victory. While he declared that 'we still feel it is better to seek an opportunity for a negotiated settlement', the army had been ordered to press on towards achieving its own conclusion to the conflict and if need be impose by force of arms 'the unalterable objective' of an undivided and indivisible Nigeria.[3] His Chief of Staff took a more exclusively military line. 'It is better to keep quiet and fight,' he was quoted as saying, 'than talk, talk, talk, and depend on the peace talks which bear no fruit.'[4] Clearly Brigadier Hassan Katsina had not forgotten the Hausa proverb that categorizes the warrior as silent and the chatterboxes as gutless bombasts. A new spirit of determination seemed to be abroad. Yet, how imminent the conclusion was, neither the best informed commentators nor the closest

---

[1] The Federal communiqué issued on 10 January was the first war one put out by Lagos for over two months.

[2] Nigeria House press release, 18 December; *West Africa* (1969), p. 1541.

[3] Nigeria House press release, 6 January 1970.

[4] Quoted in *West Africa* (1970), p. 57.

diplomatic sources nor, as it turned out, the Lagos Supreme command itself was really aware.[1]

Suddenly, the news poured in with the bewildering rush of an African tornado. Early in January the Federal Army, in its first properly co-ordinated campaign of the whole war,[2] cut off 500 square miles of the secessionists' territory by means of a strategic link up of the 1st and 3rd Divisions on the Umuahia-Ikot Ekpene road. What was more, this remnant quarter of Biafra was the land that contained the principal food-producing areas. Prisoners told the Federal troops that at the front they had not eaten on an average more than twice a week. Within the first week in January over 150,000 civilian refugees had poured out of the bush in the wake of what could be nothing less than a major Federal offensive. There were delayed reports, too, of the 2nd Division having finally cleared the Onitsha-Enugu road. The way to Uli, at once a symbol and symptom of Biafra's dogged resistance, was now open. Whether it would be truce, negotiation, or armistice that lay ahead, one thing was already clear by the first week in January. The phoney war of the previous months of stalemate and silence was over. The decisive march to Owerri and beyond was on.

Suddenly, too, it was all over. All over bar the starvation, warned *The Economist*;[3] all over bar the reconciliation, the reintegration, and the reconstruction, cautioned others; all over and so back to square one, murmured the comminatory few.[4] But the war itself was over. That not even the most pessimistic of Jeremiahs could deny. This was the indispensable pre-condition to recreating the image and the reality of 'One Nigeria'.

The great news broke on 10 January. It was the 3rd Marine Commando Division, advancing from the south, that found itself confronted by so little resistance that its probing strike developed into an unhalted sweep. Biafran forces had been redeployed to stiffen the defence of Uli, the target of the 1st and 2nd Divisions' pincer assault.[5] Whether, as reported along with the publication of the twenty-six page secret assessment of the war situation (it included full details of the exact operational tasks allotted to each Division in the current 'big push') that had leaked

[1] 'The Government is still recovering from the sudden end of the war'—Chief Ena-horo, quoted in the *Observer*, 18 January 1970. *The Economist* was still doubtful of any military conclusion (13 December 1969) and in December its Lagos correspondent was reporting the Biafran repulse of 'all-out attacks' by the Federal troops (*West Africa* (1969), p. 1565). The last issue of the Biafran newspaper *Jet*, dated 10 January 1970 and printed on exercise-book paper, as had been the practice for some eighteen months, carried the headline 'Nigeria Just Can't Win', culled from a report by Frederick Forsyth in the *Observer*, 7 December 1969.

[2] *Scotsman*, 3 January; *Observer*, 11 January 1970. See the map in *Africa* 1969–70 (London, 1970), p. B545.

[3] *The Economist*, 16 January 1970.

[4] Cf. the remark attributed to President Senghor, that the military collapse of Biafra did not 'alter the fundamental elements of the problem' (quoted in *West Africa* (1970), p. 122).   [5] Often referred to as 'Biafra's umbilical cord'.

from the British High Commission in Lagos,[1] a copy of the Federal order of battle was already in Ojukwu's hands, the disposition of his troops was such that for one reason or another the Biafran High Command found itself caught completely off balance by the simultaneous four-pronged assault. Physically weakened by severe hunger and morally undermined by limited supplies of arms and ammunition, Ojukwu's troops knew as accurately as Lagos did that a crack in her defences could widen into an unpluggable hole as dramatically as with a bursting dam. And so it proved. Within forty-eight hours Biafra was no more.

On 10 January General Ojukwu, after three days of 'long, sad' Cabinet meetings,[2] delivered a dramatic message ostensibly from the Uli runway before fleeing Biafra, announcing that he was 'travelling out of Biafra, to explore with our friends' a negotiated peace rather than to set up a government in exile [DOC 223]. He added that he expected his absence to be but a short one. For those attracted by the neatness of historical symmetry and parallels, there may be grounds for seeing that Cabinet meeting of 9 January as the last in the series of coups that comprise the confines of this book, with Sir Louis Mbanefo reportedly gathering a group of top-ranking officers determined that Ojukwu must go.[3] For the next ten days rumours of the fugitive Ojukwu's arrival came from half a dozen countries in Africa and Europe before it was finally established that he had been granted asylum in the Ivory Coast. Meanwhile, elated by the news of Ojukwu's flight, Gowon called on the Biafran army to surrender and report to Federal field commanders.[4] Late in the afternoon of 12 January Lt.-Col. Effiong, in his colonial-styled capacity as 'Officer Administering the Government', instructed his men to lay down their arms [DOC 224]. Determined that 'the suffering of our people must be brought to an immediate end' he ordered an 'orderly disengagement of troops'. At the same time as he offered un-

---

[1] This is a long story and one which, as this is being written, is not finished since summonses have been served on a number of persons involved charging them with offences under the Official Secrets Act (see *Daily Telegraph*, 18 and 20 March and letter to *The Times* 19 March 1970). The report, 'An Appreciation of the Nigerian Conflict' appeared with very extensive excerpts in the *Sunday Telegraph*, 11 January 1970, along with an account of its authenticity as a secret assessment prepared by the Military attaché to the British High Commission in Lagos (whence he was expelled by the Nigerian Government twenty-four hours later). In view of the delicacy of the case now [March 1970] *sub judice*, no attempt has been made to reproduce the report here as a Document. In the event, the *Sunday Telegraph*'s remarkable scoop turned out to be a damp squib, for on the day of its publication the rest of the world was far more interested in reports of Ojukwu's flight and Biafra's imminent collapse, which overtook the excitement that would otherwise have attached to a report implying that the Federal armies would be hard put to secure victory in 1970. Nigerian press reaction to this gross disclosure revealed the country's horror and the potential British embarrassment of such a breach of confidential material.

[2] See the reports, especially from Boniface Offokaja of A.F.P., in *The Times*, 12 and 14 January; *Daily Telegraph*, 23–8 January; *Sunday Times*, 25 January; *Observer*, 1 February; and *West Africa* (1970), pp. 89 and 101.

[3] *West Africa* (1970), p. 121.

[4] Lagos Radio, 11 January 1970, quoted in *Africa Research Bulletin*, p. 1643.

conditional surrender, he appealed to General Gowon to call a halt to the Federal advance 'in the name of humanity'[1] and announced the dispatch of a civilian mission to Lagos to complete the armistice formalities. In a midnight broadcast on 12 January, General Gowon accepted Biafra's surrender and declared that 'we have arrived at one of the greatest moments of the history in our nation' [DOC 225]. He also declared, in an interview at Dodan Barracks the next day, that there was no question of treating the Ibo as second-class citizens.[2] The rebellion was over. Symbolic, as some saw it, of the real *finis* was the picture[3] of jubilant Federal troops careering down that hateful token of Biafran resistance, the runway at Uli, after its capture on 12 January.

In the meantime, streams of starving refugees, responding to the air-dropped safe-conduct passes, blocked the roads as they dazedly trekked 'beyond' in search of food or in induced fear of the unknown factor of a military occupation; others, too exhausted or too confused to make for relief centres, lay low in the dense bush and wonderingly awaited the penetration of the hidden Ibo heartland by the victorious Federal units. There were, of course, scenes of popular jubilation in Lagos, but General Gowon sensitively ordered a day of national prayer instead of an elaborate victory parade. Later he was to give the important assurance to heads of foreign missions in Lagos that 'there will certainly be nothing like Nuremberg trials here' and to repeat his promise of 'a general amnesty for all those misled'.[4] The British Prime Minister's subsequent tribute to Gowon's 'magnanimity in victory'[5] was to win immediate and warm endorsement over most of the world. In such an atmosphere of genuine relief and reconciliation, Ojukwu's message of defiance from exile [DOC 226] commanded no more support or even attention than another banished African leader had when, in February 1966, he too had vainly promised a triumphant return to where he was already half-forgotten and no longer welcome.

The formal reconciliation ceremony took place at Dodan Barracks, Lagos, on 15 January. An emotion-filled Gowon welcomed his five former brother officers[6] (as it turned out, the civilian delegation from Biafra was not admitted) by their Christian names. Later he embraced the armistice delegates[7] outside on the lawn and congratulated them on

---

[1] The advance was called off on 14 January.

[2] Nigeria House press release, 14 January 1970.

[3] *Daily Telegraph*, 16 January; *West Africa* (1970), p. 128.

[4] Speech made on 12 January 1970 (DOC 225).

[5] House of Commons, 19 January 1970.

[6] Effiong, Amadi, Ogunewe, and Awunah from the army, and Okeke from the police. They announced themselves by their ranks in the rebel forces. On the Nigerian side were Wey, Kem Salem, Hassan Katsina, and Ikwue; the Governors of the South-East, North-Central, and Lagos States; Asika, Elias, Ayida, Joda, and Asiodu (Nigeria House press release, 19 January, and *West Africa* (1970), p. 121).

[7] Mbanefo, Chike Obi, and Emembolu. These civilians were not the same as those first named by Lt.-Col. Effiong (DOC 224).

their 'return to the fold'. 'Biafra now ceases to exist,' declared Effiong. 'We have been reunited with our brothers,' replied General Gowon in a champagne toast,[1] confirming the idiom he had purposely adopted throughout the war in his refusal to refer to the Biafrans as 'enemies'— with all that this unbellicose attitude implied for his sometimes chafing field commanders— but as fellow countrymen who had been led astray by an evil clique. 'But for Ojukwu's madness,' he added, 'such a thing would not have happened to this country.'

On that 15 January 1970, only the morbidly myopic or retrospectively unforgiving few would have endorsed Colonel Ojukwu's defiant call from exile[2] and echoed *Vive le Biafra* to Colonel Effiong's sober surrender of *Biafra est mort*: 'We are loyal Nigerian citizens and accept the authority of the Federal Military Government of Nigeria.' Most, preferring the likelihood of hope to the certainty of despair, shared the optimism of General Gowon as, in a broadcast to the nation, he looked forward to the era of national reconstruction [DOC 227].

The significance of the date of 15 January in its bearing on the terminal speeches in our documentary chronology as well as in its potential Ides-like quality in any future calendar of Nigeria's history, was largely lost in the excitement of the moment. General Gowon aptly drew attention to its talismanic property. For, as the deeply emotional reconciliation took place at Dodan Barracks, it was exactly four years to the day since Lagos had been the stage of an equally dramatic scene, the brutally executed *coup d'état* of Exercise Damisa. If the shots that rang out that night were not the first volley in Nigeria's civil war, they nevertheless brought the final fusillades incontestably nearer. The traumatic events of the ensuing months, culminating in the War of a Thousand Days, have been the focus of this record of Nigeria's crisis and conflict. That war was now over. Rebellion had been crushed; the task had been done, Nigeria had been made one. The world now waited to see how best she could, and should, be kept one.

[1] *Daily Telegraph*, 16 January 1970.
[2] DOC 226.

DOCUMENTS
JULY 1967—JANUARY 1970

120.
Enahoro's Press Conference in London[1]

Before dealing with the subject of our meeting, I would like to take this opportunity to thank the British Press and, through you, the British people for the support which they generously gave me four years ago in my extradition case. I am emboldened to meet you today by the memory of that support and by the knowledge it gave me that once the British Press and people are given the facts, there can be no doubt as to where their sympathies would lie in the Nigerian crisis.

Britain and Nigeria are fellow members of the Commonwealth, with all that this implies in friendly interchange in various fields and at many levels. The British created Nigeria and together we have built it. Britain has substantial commercial and industrial interests in Nigeria; the annual turnover of British trade with Nigeria, for example, is of the order of $510 million a year. Some 20,000 United Kingdom subjects live and work in Nigeria. Nigeria supplies 10% of Britain's oil requirements. For these and other reasons, the Nigerian crisis must be of some concern to people in Britain.

Clearly, from what I have said, there is much else besides oil between our two countries, although oil has come very much to the fore lately because of events in the Middle-East.

Let me say at once that Britain's interest in Nigerian oil is the same as ours—to keep it flowing. I do not doubt that as soon as circumstances permit, the flow will be resumed and will grow.

It is now being suggested in some quarters that the rebel administration in Enugu has de facto control of the area in which most of the oil installations occur and that the Oil Companies might therefore make their payments to Enugu treasury. I need hardly say that such payment would be contrary to the Agreement and would be totally unacceptable to the Federal Government.

As is well known, a Government which has no control of territorial waters and external trade can hardly claim sovereignity over its territory. The effective blockade by the Nigerian Navy has shown that the Enugu Regime does not have control of territorial waters or external trade. Therefore, though Ojukwu may be able to take some action which may temporarily affect oil production, only the Federal Government of Nigeria is in a position to take the more significant action of preventing the off-take and marketing of oil. . . .

What now, about the future?

Let me first correct some misconceptions which I have discovered here. It is said that the so-called Biafra is a gallant little nation fighting for self-determination, threatening nobody, wishing to live its own life, led by a young Rockefeller. Why then not let them go?

This is not the case. Biafra is not and never was a nation and there hasn't been much gallantry in our recent past. We have no Rockefellers, let alone a young one. The act of union which created Nigeria also created Eastern Nigeria and there was Nigeria long before there was an entity known as Eastern Nigeria.

If the union of Nigeria is dissolved, there are no legal bonds to tie together the Ibos and the coastal kingdoms and other tribes of Eastern Nigeria, who would be as fully entitled to self-determination as the Ibos are. What is more, they have shown that they would fight for it.

If Secession by Ojukwu and his group is accomplished, Nigeria will most probably disintegrate. Once fractionalization starts, it certainly will result in the further disintegration of the former Eastern Region of Nigeria. Neighbouring states with ethnic and other problems similar to ours will in due course also disintegrate, and a chain reaction will be set up all over Africa. Africa would end up in petty little principalities. Each successor 'mini-state' would be sovereign enough to acquire foreign protectors and purchase arms. Such a situation, with its inevitable dislocations and frictions over boundaries, trade and division of assets, would produce wars. Foreign countries would intervene on behalf of their 'protectorates' and the conflagration would become bloodier and more permanently damaging to the interests of Nigeria, of Africa, and of foreign countries with stakes in the area.

It is said that Biafra would be self-sufficient economically. There would, of course be no Biafra for any length of time. Only some 5 per cent of Nigeria's oil is produced in the Ibo areas. 60% is mined in the Rivers area and all the pipelines at present run through the Rivers area and 35% is produced in Mid-West State. Of the total value of agricultural exports from the former Eastern Nigeria, the 7,000,000 Ibos produce $25 million and the 5,000,000 non-Ibo peoples produce $48 million. Further, the only 'new lands' left in Eastern Nigeria for settlement is in the non-Ibo Ogoja and Calabar areas. Wiser heads in the Central East (i.e. Ibo) who are at present shut out of public affairs by Ojukwu appreciate therefore that the interests of the Ibos can be best secured in a Nigerian Federation where the industry of their people and the resources of others can be harnessed for the common good.

It is said that the present struggle is one between the largely Moslem North and the largely Christian East. This is an outdated conception of the crisis. The creation of States completely alters the picture. There is now no Northern entity and no Eastern Nigeria identity. Were this not the case, if States had not been created, and if this were a North versus East match, I, for my part, would have found it difficult to accept office at this time. Nigeria is very much a secular state and religion does not play any significant part in Nigerian politics. There is a large number of Moslems in Western Nigeria and Lagos. General Gowon is a Christian. So am I. What is now going on is a struggle for the very survival of our nation. . . .

[1] *Held in the Connaught Rooms, Kingsway, 17 July 1967.*

121.
Ojukwu Exhorts His People[1]

Brave and proud Biafrans, fellow countrymen, in all humility, pride and gratitude I salute you. Two weeks ago at five o'clock in the early hours of Thursday 6th July, Gowon and his Nigerian junta started the long-promised and awaited invasion of Biafra, thrusting almost simultaneously at four different points, three in the Ogoja sector and one, the most crucial and fateful in this struggle, in the Nsukka sector. They brought into the conflict all the might and fury of desperation which they could muster. After 14 grim and long days of successive disaster and bitter disappointment, the Nigerian invading force has found things not as easy as they expected. Within two days of battle, our army wiped out in one sector a whole battalion and one company of the enemy forces. . . .

Since the start of the war, we have as a matter of deliberate policy, refrained from blowing trumpets. Our short, daily releases are always designed to give credit even to the enemy. We are interested in deeds and results, not in words, boasts and false claims. Our aim is to win the war, crush the enemy and exterminate whatever remains of the discredited Nigerian Army.

Now to the heroic armed forces of Biafra. They have excelled in the determination and courage with which they have prosecuted the war. Biafrans at home are proud of their performance to date and assure them of their undying gratitude. My respect and gratitude also go to the militia and the civilians in every walk of life who are playing remarkable roles in this struggle. The dedication of the civil service, the police, doctors and nurses, members of the Red Cross, our scientists and engineers, and hosts of others cannot be overpraised. It is a source of unlimited pride that in this struggle all sections of this young republic are facing the enemy as a united people. The manner in which our people in Ogoja and Nsukka have fought side by side with our regular forces against the enemy is highly praiseworthy. In under six hours after the claim by the enemy that Nsukka had been captured, 61,000 volunteers from all sections of Biafra converged at Enugu, ready to march on Nsukka. It was a touching reaction of a people determined to pay the highest sacrifice in order to maintain and preserve their sovereignty. It is one of the most encouraging aspects of our struggle and something which must give the enemy ill comfort as well as cold discomfiture amongst his ranks. It is a heroic evidence of our nationhood.

Fellow countrymen, all of us know what Biafra means to us. It means the rejection of all that was bad, obnoxious and repugnant in the old Federation of Nigeria. Our young nation stands for the restoration and preservation of the dignity of the individual, for the protection of personal liberty, life and property, and for the guarantee of social equality and justice—particularly, equality of opportunity. Brave and valiant Biafrans, we are fighting for our survival as a nation, and for the preservation of these fundamental values.

Nigeria knows that unless it breaks or takes Biafra it is finished as an entity both politically and economically. Their sense of survival is based on a mission of plunder, loot and the seizure of what does not belong to them. The latest manifestation of Nigeria's greed was shown lately by Gowon, who, immediately after his premature claim that Nsukka had fallen, called in the oil companies and demanded payment of oil royalties already conceded to us by the companies concerned. In the border villages and towns where Gowon's troops have set foot, the story has been one of reckless plunder, loot and rape. These atrocities must sharpen, rather than daunt, our determination to crush and exterminate the plunderers. The task ahead is such as no full-blooded Biafran can afford not to play an active part in it. We require no less than 100,000 volunteers to aid our regular forces. The pride and glory of victory and its rewards await everyone. Those not involved will not have the privilege of sharing in the proud heritage which we must hand down to our children and children's children, indeed, generations upon generations unborn.

L

We must teach Nigeria that they cannot hurt us with impunity. Our victory must be complete and it must be a victory won on the enemy's own land. As commander-in-chief of the Armed Forces, my orders are that our blessed territory be immediately rid of the vermin in Nigerian Army uniforms, and that, once this is done, the enemy must be engaged, attacked and harassed everywhere his presence is known, even in his own land. . . .

It has also been reported that battalions from Lagos and Western Nigeria have been raised to make up Gowon's scratch reserve brigade. It is further reported that that brigade has now been committed in the Nsukka front. There have been speculations about the nationalities of the members of that scratch brigade. But I am convinced that the peaceful Yorubas will not lend themselves to this type of futile, suicidal business, and that the troops concerned are only drawn from Gowon's army of occupation. Now must be the much-needed opportunity for the Yoruba freedom fighters to free themselves from the shackles of Hausa-Fulani domination and oppression.

I am aware of the activities of a few hirelings amongst us who are trying in vain to undermine the oneness of our young republic. Those few black sheep within the fold have been identified and will be dealt with appropriately. Some Biafrans unwittingly advanced the course of the enemy by trying to cause panic, fear and embarrassment through peddling unfounded rumours that innocent, hardworking and loyal Biafrans would be prosecuted for the treasonable acts of a few saboteurs. I am satisfied that all sections and communities in this republic have been working and will continue to work together in mutual confidence and respect.

I am obliged to warn that any Biafran who, by his misguided conduct or attitude, one toward the other, does anything likely to cause suspicion, disaffection and fear among any group, or behaves in any way to cause embarrassment and division among our people, will be regarded as much a saboteur and an enemy of our cause as Gowon and his hirelings. Such people will be dealt with in the severest possible way. In this regard, I must warn against over-enthusiasm on the part of the civil defence organisations. They must bear in mind that theirs is to guard, not to molest, the citizens.

Brave and proud Biafrans, our commitment to this war is total and irrevocable. The general response has been most overwhelming and made a mockery of Gowon's boast to overrun Biafra in 48 hours. It must be clear by now to him that the war has only just started and that he has taken up a little more than he can chew. Fellow citizens, I am proud of you and I have confidence in your ability to carry this war through to victory. Our cause is just and God is on our side. We shall vanquish.

[1] *Broadcast from Enugu, 20 July 1967 (B.B.C. ME/2522/B1).*

122.
Statement on British Arms Supplies from Biafran Students in U.K.[1]

Over six weeks ago Nigeria launched a massive attack against Biafra. Earlier, in 1966, 30,000 Biafrans had been massacred in cold-blood during the pogroms carried out in the Northern and other parts of Nigeria. Two million Biafrans were also driven home as destitute refugees as a result of these massacres. The history of that whole crisis showed that no Federal Government existed in Nigeria which was able to protect the lives and liberty of Biafrans. The current war is a war of survival for Biafrans. The Biafran Army made up mainly of civilian volunteers rose to defend the integrity of their country against the well-armed might of the Nigerian Federal Government.

Just before they launched their invasion, Lt.-Col. Hassan, Military Head of Northern Nigeria, announced that Nigeria would crush Biafra within 48 hours; Gowon himself had declared that it would be a matter of days at the most. The war is now in its seventh week. . . .

With the Nigerian Government's hope for victory now fast disappearing, Britain has embarked on giving massive military aid to Lagos. During the last three weeks, arms and men have continued to be shipped and flown from Britain to Lagos in large numbers. For example, the British Government have given export licences to the Nigerian Government for several B26 bombers, some of which left Britain for Lagos on Friday, 4th August, 1967, ferried across by British pilots and accompanied by loads of heavy armament, rockets and munition. In addition a ship-load of Bailey bridges and other military equipment left Britain for Lagos by sea last weekend in order to assist the war effort of Gowon. Again on Friday, August 4, 1967, with financial credit from the British Government, the Nigerian Government made in Britain a down payment of £280,000 for 60 T-6 fighter planes and also acquired twenty-one T-28 fighter planes. The whole deal was negotiated in London the same afternoon at a cost of several million dollars. There is also a continuing large airlift of military supplies from Britain through Malta.

The British Government have themselves last week confirmed that they supply arms to Lagos. Thus, contrary to their earlier declared policy of 'rigorous neutrality,' the British Government have now openly admitted their active assistance to the Lagos regime.

A few days ago Lagos announced that it would begin a massive air attack on Biafra. Since it is well-known that Nigeria has no trained military pilots and navigators (Biafrans had largely filled these posts in the former Nigerian Airforce), we cannot but conclude that Lagos, which is reported to have been recruiting mercenary pilots from London and elsewhere, has now recruited enough to want to operate an active airforce.

In the last two weeks a number of prominent British newspapers have been suggesting both in feature and in editorial articles that the British Government should demonstrate even more massively and overtly their support for Gowon's government.

We wish through the medium of this advertisement to draw the attention of the British public to these facts. We want the British people to realise the gravity of any direct or indirect assistance given to Nigeria in its unjust and genocidal war to 'crush' the Biafrans in their own home.

The civilised world is watching.

[1] *Issued by the Central Executive Committee of the Biafra Union of Great Britain and Ireland, August 1967.*

123.
Statement on Arms Supplies by the Church of England[1]

1. It is a matter of deep concern to the Churches and Societies we represent both in Nigeria and Britain, that the conflict in Nigeria has reached the point of civil war.

2. We recognise that the Federal Government is the only legal Government in Nigeria. But we are aware that the Eastern Region which is in a state of disagreement with the Federal Government contains more than 7,000,000 people, and consequently the proportions of the dispute surpass the limits of local pacification by the Federal Government.

3. We are aware from Nigerian information that fighting can be of such a widespread character as to lead to an embittered war of sporadic conflict. This can extend to a very long duration with permanent results in estrangement and bitterness between the Regions.

4. We therefore urge H.M. Government not to permit arms to be sent to the Federal Government as the sending of arms cannot but prolong the fighting and increase the bitterness now felt in the Eastern Region. We believe that the paucity of arms on both sides of the conflict is a vital factor which may shorten the period before negotiations bring a solution to the problem now confronting the Federation.

5. Our intimate knowledge of the peoples of the Eastern Region leads us to the conviction that no scale of escalation in the hands of the Federal Government will suffice to subjugate that Region. We are therefore anxious that H.M. Government should not share in a course of action which can only lead to protracted suffering which a cessation of armed conflict and a return to negotiation could prevent.

[1] *Issued on 18 August 1967 on behalf of the Conference of British Missionary Societies, Church Missionary Society, Church of Scotland Foreign Mission Committee, and the Methodist Missionary Society.*

124.
Nigerian High Commissioner States his Government's Case on Arms Supplies[1]

Sir,

It is interesting to read in your paper the statement[2] by some 'inspired' missionaries calling on the British Government not to supply arms to the Nigerian Federal Government. This statement, as prejudiced and onesided as it is, would have made some sense eight months ago.

Right from the beginning of the crisis, General Gowon had made it clear that he was opposed to the use of force. He bent over backwards to amend the Nigerian Constitution to give rebel Ojukwu greater authority. But, determined to secede, Ojukwu would not relent. Like Oliver Twist, he always asked for more until General Gowon was being derided (even by Ojukwu and his rebel collaborators) for his 'excessive piety and indecision'.

Since the war it is only the rebel forces who have bombed innocent civilians in market places and in their homes. Ojukwu wants to make sure that his declaration of total war on Nigeria does not stop with words. Unlike the system of what may be called the democratic militarism carried out by General Gowon before Ojukwu escalated his rebellion, Ojukwu had all along established an uncompromising military rule in the Eastern States, making the minority tribes live in a kind of George Orwell's 1984. It is significant that the missionaries omitted any mention of the five million minorities in the Eastern States when they referred to the seven million Ibos.

All this time our friends the missionaries did not see the need to warn Ojukwu against the murder of innocent civilians. Suddenly their conscience has been aroused because 'no scale of escalation will suffice to subjugate' the rebels. Could the escalation by the rebels have subjugated the Federal Government? If not, why did the missionaries not protest?

Obviously this new move by our missionary friends is based on the out-dated assumption that the present struggle is one between the largely Muslim North and the largely Christian East. But there is now no Northern entity and no Eastern Nigeria identity. Nigeria is very much a secular state and religion plays no important role in the country's politics. General Gowon is a Christian, so are many people from the old Northern Region. What is now going on is a struggle for the very survival of Nigeria as a nation. It is not, as some people would have us believe, any religious warfare.

Yours faithfully,
B. Ogundipe

[1] *Letter to* The Times, *23 August 1967. Text by courtesy of the Nigerian High Commissioner.*
[2] *See* DOC *123.*

125.
Ojukwu Broadcasts on his Seizure of Benin[1]

Brave and courageous Biafrans, on 6th July, just over five weeks ago, Nigeria launched its military aggression on our young republic of Biafra. It was the fulfilment of the long-standing ambition, aggression and threat by Northern Nigeria to attack and subjugate what was then Southern Nigeria. In that aggression, Nigeria brought to bear in full force all the armaments and the resources which the Nigeria Army had accumulated right from its inception. Gowon spent all he could lay hands upon from the suffering Nigerian exchequer to hire mercenaries to lead his rabble army, relying on the superior armaments and numbers available to it and on the expertise and ruthlessness of mercenaries. Nigeria planned to crush this republic within a matter of 48 hours.

My purpose tonight is to take a look at those grim and historic weeks of our war of resistance and survival against a monstrous enemy. The sole purpose of the enemy was to destroy our identity and existence as a people, plunder our wealth, eliminate our menfolk, desecrate our sacred and holy places, defile and befoul our women, and put our children and generations unborn in perpetual serfdom to the Hausa-Fulani hegemony. I also want to take this opportunity to tell the world once more why we are fighting and to restate our aims and philosophy as a responsible member of the world community of nations. . . .

Our general strategy has been to lure the enemy to our territory. When they have been fully committed and trapped for destruction, we then strike. We are now in a position to launch a decisive offensive against the enemy to bring the war to an end. That strategy has already started to bear fruit. The spectacular and lightning liberation yesterday of the entire Mid-West from the clutches of Hausa-Fulani imperialism is the first stroke of our strategy. That operation was carried out with a military precision and minimum loss of lives which have impressed the world and bewildered the enemy.

All through the crisis of last year which led to the birth of our Republic until the present war, the peaceful people of the Mid-West have publicly and consistently declared their determination to keep their soil clear of battle conflicts. This determination was repeatedly made clear in all official utterances and resolutions of representatives of the people. We, on our part, were determined to respect the feelings of those peaceful people. Unfortunately, the Hausa-Fulani imperialists would not allow this. In recent weeks, hostile Northern troops entered that territory in preparation for an attack against us from that sector. We could not tolerate such a situation and therefore decided to move in and liberate the people of the Mid-West. The general welcome and jubilation which greeted our liberating troops everywhere are matters of real satisfaction to me and my people. We went to the Mid-West to liberate and protect the people against aggression from Northern Nigeria. Having done this, the people are free to lead and live their own life in peace and security. Meanwhile, an interim government will be set up until the time when permanent arrangements can be made for the area. Henceforth there will be free movement of people and trade on both sides of the Niger. . . .

We are fighting this war relying on our own resources financially, materially and militarily. Our young scientists have now developed and perfected Biafran bombs, mines, rifles, guns and armoured vehicles. Very soon, our rockets will be in operation. The war has proved an incentive to the resourceful minds of Biafra and the application of acquired knowledge. . . .

If it is possible that the world should be ignorant of our position and why we are fighting, let me take this opportunity to tell them why the people of Biafra are fighting against Nigeria. First, we fight in order to repel naked aggression aimed at complete extermination of our people. Secondly, we fight to secure freedom and dignity for our people. The pogrom of 1966, and all acts of bad faith and recalcitrance shown by Nigeria in all attempts to solve our problems with them, finally made the people of Biafra realise clearly and unmistakably that the road to their progress and survival lay in a separate existence from what was once the Nigerian Federation. Thirdly, having declared our sovereignty and separate identity, it is our duty to defend and preserve the integrity of the new republic. Nigeria is fighting to destroy our integrity and our existence. We are resisting that attempt with resolute determination. Under no circumstances will this republic of Biafra surrender or negotiate its sovereignty. . . .

The war will stop the day Nigeria ceases its aggression against this republic, recognises our right to a separate existence or finds itself militarily defeated. As I have said earlier, the aim of the Hausa-Fulani oligarchy is to subjugate and enslave what was Southern Nigeria. Apart from fighting to maintain our sovereignty, we are prepared to help liberate any part of Nigeria from the domination of the North. Any Yoruba officers or men who are still in the Nigerian Army and who wish to join in this crusade of liberation should report to any Biafran army unit in Biafra or the Mid-West where they are guaranteed full protection. We have established a truly nation state in Africa in contrast to the artificial conglomerations of which the defunct federation of Nigeria was a classical example created by imperialists. . . .

We believe that the UN and its agencies constitute man's best hope for peace and progress. We shall uphold the principles embodied in the Charter of that world body. We hope to continue our association with the British Commonwealth of Nations. With regard to the OAU, we recognise that this is an essential instrument toward the achievement of our idea of meaningful African unity. Unlike the defunct Nigerian Federation, the Republic of Biafra must work more positively for the realisation of the objectives of the Organisation which has thus far eluded that body. We believe that true unity will eventually emerge from the association if each African state, while maintaining its peculiar character and institutions, enters into free association with others to serve their common economic interests. In due course this form of association will help to build up an African political union. . . .

Let us, from now on, think of the things that bind and unite us as a people. We have suffered together, we are fighting the enemy together, and we shall defeat the enemy together. Henceforth, all Biafrans must recognise that they are brothers and sisters with a common destiny. . . .

[1] *Broadcast from Enugu, 10 August 1967 (B.B.C. ME/2541/B1).*

126.
Brigadier Banjo's Broadcast to Mid-West[1]

Fellow Nigerians and Biafrans, I am sure I do not need to introduce myself either to you nor perhaps to many people outside our country. You have already had ample opportunity to hear of my name in January 1966 when this political crisis started in our country. Unfortunately at that time I also only heard about the circumstances under which my name was being publicised at a time when I was in no position to do anything about it. I was then accused of having attempted the life of the late Supreme Commander, Maj-Gen. J. T. U. Aguiyi-Ironsi, and that for the attempt I have been arrested and detained.

Fellow Nigerians, nothing could be further from the truth. The Army mutiny which started the revolution in January 1966 was as such of a surprise to myself as it was to some of my colleagues. I spent all of my time [words indistinct] of the events in ascertaining the true state of affairs in the country. My colleague, then Lt-Col. Yakubu Gowon, was the first officer who gave me precise information about the state of affairs. It then appeared to me that sufficient had taken place to ensure the removal of several Governments of the Federation and that the sum total of the trend of events could be regarded as the beginning of a national revolution. I then considered it my duty to ensure that no further military action took place which might have the effect of totally destroying the stability of the nation.

I felt that the young officers who had started the action were only anxious to destroy what had become a most corrupt and discredited Government. As such, I spent a considerable time in an effort to urge the late Major-General to assume responsibility for the State with the support of the Army to ensure that the Nigerian nation remained together and was protected from national collapse. It was then my view that any attempt to use the Nigerian Army for any military action within Nigeria would only have the effect of breaking the Army into its tribal components of which the Northern component would represent the lion's share. This Northern component, effectively under the control of the Northern feudalists, would then inevitably be employed to impose on the rest of Nigeria the most repressive feudal domination.

I was one of the senior officers of the Nigerian Army who took the decision to accept responsibility for Nigeria. In fact, on that occasion I was the chief spokesman for that decision. I therefore considered it my duty to remain with the General as closely as possible, rather than accept the office of the Military Governor of the West which he then proposed to me and which I declined in favour of the late Lt-Col. Adekunle Fajuyi.

On the day after the General had assumed full responsibility for the State, I was arrested by a few of my colleagues while waiting to see the General. I was never given a reason for my arrest, nor given an opportunity to defend myself against any charges that could be raised. I went to prison for 14 months under a false accusation, the details of which I only found out from the press and radio after I got to prison. I have since had the opportunity of speaking to the so-called actors in that drama of my arrest, and I now appreciate that the action was an act of hatred motivated primarily by fear and suspicion.

I spent a considerable part of my time in prison sending warnings to the late Major-General and my colleagues about the policies that would appear to represent a continuation of the policies of the Balewa Government, which could have the effect of encouraging counter-attempts, which might not only destroy the Nigerian Army but would also, by the extent of the bloodshed and the tribal selectiveness of the [word indistinct], destroy the Nigerian nation as well. The inevitable has now happened, which would seem to confirm that my fears were well founded. There is now an army at the disposal of the feudal North, an army that has lost all the traditions, discipline and standards of a responsible army. There is now a Government of the Federation that is sustained by violence and is therefore tied to the ambitions of the Northern feudalists. There has been a considerable amount of bloodshed, chaos and tribal bitterness among such people. Such tribal rivalry, as used to be exploited by our previous political parties for the harnessing of the opinion of the North and its people, is now translating itself into a most extreme form of brutality and of despicable savagery.

Finally, the dismemberment of our nation has commenced in the breaka-way of Biafra. In August 1966, I wrote to my colleagues from prison to inform them that I did not consider that we, military leaders of this country, had the right to carry out such action as the proclamation of the dismemberment of or presiding over the dismemberment of Nigeria. I still do not think that we have the right to destroy a nation that was handed over to us to save at a moment of crisis. The 29th July 1966 Federal Military Government came into being as a result of a mutiny in which the primary action was directed at the elimination of a particular ethnic group and the supremacy of another ethnic group in Nigeria. This has had the effect of destroying the basic mutual trust and confidence among the people of Nigeria and has created the decen-tralisation of the Nigerian people into tribal groups. This action, more than any other event that has occurred throughout the history of Nigeria, has had the greatest effect on the dismemberment of Nigeria.

The Federal Military Government cannot claim to represent the Govern-ment of the people of Nigeria and to fight for the unity of Nigeria while constantly rejecting fundamental human rights for all people forming parts of Nigeria. The Federal Military Government cannot claim to be seeking a peaceful solution to the problems for achieving Nigerian unity, while at the same time contemptuously ignoring the wishes of the people of the Mid-West and the West in their previous demands for the removal of the unruly troops of the North from their territories in order to allow the unfettered discussion of the present political crisis. The Federal Military Government cannot claim to be genuinely interested in the progress and welfare of the Nigerian people while at the same time inflicting the most bloody warfare on the people of Nigeria and employing unscrupulous foreign mercenaires in a total war that really destroys hundreds of our people and the economy of our nation.

The people of Biafra have a right to fight a Government that has constantly treated its people to the most savage forms of brutality and persists in denying these people its fundamental human rights while claiming to represent other interests. It is my view that the people of Biafra were prepared to remain part of the nation into which they have for so many years invested their resources of manpower and material and with which they had the closest social ties. Provided the people of Biafra could live within such a nation under a Govern-ment that truly represents all sections of its people and truly tries to pursue such measures as are designed to promote the welfare of all Nigerians irres-pective of tribe or religion [sentence as broadcast].

It is the remnants of the old Nigerian Army that broke away in July that now threatens the Nigerian nation. This Northern army is now under the power and control of a group of Northern feudalists who have as their aim the total conquest of Nigeria. The Federal Military Government, having been brought to power and control by that army, is playing to that end. Hence policies are inevitably directed towards achieving the objectives of the Northern feudalists who control that army. . . . It is my idea that the peace-ful settlement of the Nigerian problem will be readily achieved when that fragment of the Nigerian Army now at the disposal of the Northern feudalists has been completely disarmed. Towards this end, the Liberation Army is irrevocably committed.

It is not at all an invasion, and it is not intended to promote the domination of any group of the Nigerian people by any other group through the presence of the Liberation Army. I wish to stress once again what I said during the press conference and previously on the radio that the movement of this Army into the Mid-West is not a conquest. It is also not an invasion. It is to enable the people of the Mid-West to see the Nigerian problem in its proper perspective.

I firmly believe that the people of the Mid-West would prefer to be able to declare their stand in the conflict that has arisen in Nigeria free from any [pressure] either from the North or from anywhere. I believe that the people of the Mid-West would like to be given an opportunity to state their case, free from the coercive influences due to the presence of Northern troops.

It is my view that the political future of Nigeria rests with all the people of Nigeria. It has become a matter of great concern to me, however, to be informed that certain ethnic groups are jubilating as a result of the presence of the Liberation Army in this Region. As a consequence, I also understand that certain other ethnic groups are feeling depressed and frustrated. I wish to assure all ethnic groups in the Mid-West that the achievement of the Liberation Army does not give any ethnic group an advantage over any other. I wish also to appeal to all ethnic groups to exercise restraint and humility and not to indulge in acts which may result in confusion, bringing distress to a large number of our people. Any misbehaviour on the part of any group of persons will give rise to a chain of unpleasant reactions. . . .

I am informed that since the Liberation Army came into the Mid-West a number of civil servants have become so frightened that they have either refused to come to their places of work or reported only for a few hours and then left before the closing time. I wish to take this opportunity to appeal to all civil servants to return to work not later than 15th August 1967, and to assure them of their safety. Those, however, who fail to report on this day will be in danger of permanently losing their jobs. . . .

While on the question of co-operation among the various ethnic groups in the Mid-West, I would like to stress that all tribal meetings should stop, as such meetings are not conducive to peace and mutual understanding. In order to foster co-operation among the people of the Mid-West, I propose within the next few days to invite a cross-section of the people of the Mid-West to a meeting to explain to them the present situation and objectives of the Liberation Army, and I believe this will go a long way to giving them the true picture of the situation and instil confidence in the future of the Mid-West.

I understand that anxiety is being expressed in some quarters about the safety of the Military Governor of the Mid-West, Brig. David Ejoor. I wish to inform you that I have personally held discussions with Brig. Ejoor and to assure you that he is in good health and is not under detention. . . .

I have, therefore, today promulgated a decree setting up an interim administration in the Mid-Western Nigeria. This decree has suspended the operation in Mid-Western Nigeria of the Constitution of the Federation of Nigeria, the Constitution of Mid-Western Nigeria, and other constitutional provisions applicable in Mid-Western Nigeria, except those constitutional provisions absolutely necessary for the efficient functioning of the machinery of State. All legislative and executive powers have been vested in me during the period of interim administration. In order to assist me in the task of administering Mid-Western Nigeria during the interim period I propose to appoint a military administrator and an administrative council. I have also established a Mid-Western Nigerian Army and a Mid-Western Nigerian Police Force, which will for the moment remain independent of the Nigerian Army, the Nigerian Police Force, the Biafran Army or the Biafran Police Force. The Mid-Western Nigerian Army shall, however, during this interim period be part of the Liberation Army. All courts in Mid-Western Nigeria shall continue to function as usual and it may be necessary to establish a court of appeal until it becomes possible to resume [words indistinct] the Supreme Court of Nigeria.

As soon as it is practicable I propose to hand over the administration of Mid-Western Nigeria in order to proceed to the war front and to complete the liberation of Nigeria.

[1] *Broadcast from Benin, 14 August 1967 (B.B.C. ME/2544/B3).*

127.
Major Okonkwo's Address to Mid-West[1]

My dear fellow Mid-Westerners, only yesterday I, Maj. Albert O. Okonkwo, was appointed Administrator of Mid-Western Nigeria. Some of you know me better as Dr. Okonkwo. Indeed, in normal circumstances, I would prefer to continue to be known as Dr. Okonkwo, but, as fate would have it, my duty to this nation surpasses all other things, and I expect that I can confidently count on the support of every one of you in the Mid-West in the performance of the responsibilities which have been thrust upon me. . . .

For several months now we in the Mid-West had hoped and prayed. We thought that our position should be that of a mediator and that we should take the middle course. This was the unanimous will of our people. But what did we find in the last few months? Instead of keeping their heads, those who held the reins of government in the Mid-West succumbed to the fear of the force of arms of the Northern soldiers and gradually dragged the Mid-West into war. It was inevitable, therefore, that the people of Biafra should come to our rescue. . . . Today, we the people of the Mid-West, now have to form a government of our own, independent of the Federal Government and of the Government of Biafra. The new government shall be a government of the people of the Mid-West and for the people of the Mid-West.

There are several reasons why this move has become inevitable. First, we the people of the Mid-West refuse to allow our territory to be used as a theatre of war. We intend to maintain this pledge, and it is undoubtedly true that all our people will support this stand.

Secondly, the previous government has failed us in this respect. Contrary to the wishes and pronouncements of our Obas, Obis, elders, and the representative assembly of the majority of the people of Mid-Western Nigeria, the former government allowed the situation whereby part of our territory was being used by Lagos for the movement of Northern troops and for acts of war.

Thirdly, Mid-Western soldiers were sent to Lagos and deployed for war against Biafra, thereby exposing us and our territory to unknown and unwarranted dangers of war, death and destruction. We of the Mid-West refuse to allow such a course. We refuse to be used by anybody or any government. We do not believe that the best interests of the Mid-West will be served by dragging ourselves into war. . . . If we search our hearts aright, we know that the Lagos Government does not represent the true aspirations of the people of this region. We also know that the Lagos Government does not represent the aspirations of the majority of the people of Nigeria in general. It is to this end that I have been called upon to assume control of the government of the Mid-West. . . . Any miscalculation by the Lagos Government will only lead to unpleasantness to people outside this territory.

It has come to my notice that the Lagos Government is now forcing Mid-Westerners to enlist in an army to fight the people of the Mid-West. I consider this act of the Lagos Government highly criminal in nature. All Mid-Westerners should rise with one voice to protest against this act intended to lead to the destruction of our sons. I am aware that all Mid-Westerners will support our task to keep the war away from the borders of this region. I also note that the Lagos Government has done everything possible to prevent those Mid-Westerners of Lagos and Western Nigeria who wish to return home from doing so. I implore you, all of you, to take heart, and I assure you that this government will take all necessary steps to ensure the safety of the Mid-Westerners resident in Lagos and Western Nigeria.

In carrying out my duties, the government will consist of myself and the administrative council. After consultation with various sections of the community, I have decided on the persons who shall be members of the administrative council and their names will be announced within the next few days. . . .

No price will be too much for us to pay if we, all of us Mid-Westerners, are to survive.

We must be prepared to defend ourselves from aggression from the North and Lagos.

[1] *Broadcast from Benin Radio on 18 August 1967 (B.B.C. ME/2548/B3).*

128.
Major Okonkwo Announces Establishment of the Republic of Benin[1]

My dear fellow Mid-Westerners, on 9th August 1967 we were born anew. On 18th August I spoke to you in my maiden broadcast outlining what this Government stood for, what the problems were, and what we intended to do about them.[2] On 9th September I recounted a few of our achievements and our hopes. Since then your Government has taken further steps, despite the activities of the godless enemy, to ensure the safety of every citizen of this territory while bitter and hard fighting against the enemy by your soldiers continues. During the past few weeks I have been holding a series of discussions with prominent leaders of the Mid-West, including Obas, Obis and chiefs, about our future.

Pressures have been mounting from organisations and youths, mandating me to lead them to the promised land. Only a few days ago I had discussions with His Highness, the Oba of Benin, about these matters and he gave me his unequivocal support. Now I must not hold out any longer. You have expressed your implicit confidence in and support for the policies which this Government stands for. More than that, you are a great people and capable of being even greater. You had a great history in this territory ranging from the Niger river to our boundary with Western Nigeria and from our Northern border to the Bight of Benin. But what happened to that greatness? What happened to that fighting spirit? The Northern vandals, consisting of Gowon's clique of Hausa-Fulani oligarchy, have been allowed to slowly, greedily, viciously and brutally leech on our very existence, sapping us of that vital element of life and of greatness. We will not tolerate any of that, even while the war goes on. We must tell them—and tell them in plain, simple language—of our will to survive and our absolute belief in self determination.

Whereas the people of the Mid-West have exhausted all reasonable proposals in the past for the preservation of Nigeria as one political entity; whereas the representative Assembly of the people of the Mid-West have voted for a loose type of association for the various former Regions of Nigeria; whereas over 10,000 Mid-Westerners were slaughtered or maimed or made orphans by the people of Northern Nigeria; whereas no apology or compensation were forthcoming from the perpetrators of this heinous misdeed; whereas the accords reached at Aburi in Ghana by the then leaders were not honoured by the Lagos and Northern Nigerian Governments; whereas the Lagos and Northern Nigerian Governments forcibly tried to impose an unacceptable type of government on our people; whereas these same Governments then declared war on the Republic of Biafra and the people of the Mid-West; whereas it is common knowledge that weapons of war and destruction have been unleashed on our innocent citizens:

I, Maj. Albert Nwazu Okonkwo, Military Administrator of the territory known as Mid-Western Nigeria including the air space, territorial waters and continental shelf, mindful of the powers vested in me under Decree No. 2/1967 of Mid-Western Nigeria and other subsequent decrees, do hereby declare the said territory of Mid-Western Nigeria as the Republic of Benin, autonomous and completely sovereign.

The Republic of Benin will perform all functions of a sovereign state, make any laws, enter into any treaty with any other sovereign state, prosecute war against the enemy, make peace and agree to enter into association for common services with any Region of the former Federation of Nigeria.

The Republic of Benin shall collaborate with the Republic of Biafra in all military matters. We shall honour all international treaties and obligations, support the OAU, and as soon as possible apply for membership of the UN. We would like to retain our association with the British Commonwealth of Nations and support any other organisations dedicated to peace, the concept of self-determination, freedom of the press, speech, movement and worship. God bless you and long live the Republic of Benin.

[1] *Broadcast made from Benin, 20 September 1967 (B.B.C. ME/2574/B1).*
[2] *See* DOC *127.*

129.
Lt.-Col. Murtala Mohammed Addresses Mid-West on Recapture of Benin[1]

My dear brothers and sisters of the Mid-Western State of Nigeria:

On behalf of Major-General Yakubu Gowon, Head of the Federal Military Government and Commander-in-Chief of the Armed Forces, I, Lt.-Col. M. R. Mohammed, do hereby officially confirm the complete liberation of the Mid-Western State of Nigeria except Agbor and Asaba from rebel soldiers.

The inhuman atrocities suffered by all true Mid-Westerners through the so-called Biafran soldiers, though short-lived, have shocked all Nigerians wherever they may be.

The molestation of innocent civilians and the looting of their property and the indiscriminate killing of men, women and children recently undertaken by the rebel troops has ended.

All Mid-Westerners in the areas where the rebel troops have been crushed are free to move about as they please. No innocent citizen living in any of the mentioned areas will ever be molested again.

The federal troops have been warmly received by the Mid-Westerners everywhere they have gone. We appreciate the friendship of the people and I sincerely hope that this friendship will continue for ever.

I would like to assure the people that my soldiers will do everything in their power to maintain this friendship.

With regard to Emeka Ojukwu and his rebel soldiers, I, Lt.-Col. M. R. Mohammed, do hereby assure the people of Nigeria and the people of the Mid-West in particular, that by the grace of God, we will, in a very short time, crush the rebels in the Central-Eastern State.

To this end, I would like to advise all innocent citizens of the Central-Eastern State to keep out of the way of the federal troops.

The march to Enugu continues, and anybody that stands in the way of the federal troops will be regarded and treated as a rebel.

I have already despatched my forces to deal with the rebels around Agboh and Asaba. I would like to appeal to all my brothers and sisters in the Mid-Western State of Nigeria to assist the federal troops in locating, and in the eventual destruction of the rebels that may be hiding around the Mid-West.

It is necessary to advise the people in Benin City to remain indoors from nine o'clock tonight until six o'clock tomorrow morning as mopping-up operations will continue.

The Administration has suffered quite a lot due to the mischief brought about by the rebel troops.

On behalf of the Head of the Federal Military Government and Commander-in-Chief of the Armed Forces, I appoint Lt.-Col. Samuel Ogbemudia as the temporary administrator of the Mid-Western State of Nigeria.

All officers and men of the Nigerian Army based in the Mid-Western State of Nigeria should report for duty immediately at the Military head-quarters in Benin City.

Brothers and sisters of the Mid-Western State of Nigeria: May God bless you all and good luck.

[1] *Broadcast from Benin, 21 September 1967.* Text by courtesy of a Nigerian soldier.

130.
Biafran Memorandum on Proposed Future Association[1]

TERMS OF REFERENCE

To define possible areas of future association between Biafra and the rest of the former Federation of Nigeria.

POLITICAL ASSUMPTION

In this exercise, an over-all view of the rest of Nigeria breaking up into independent and sovereign units has been taken. It is appreciated that in the scheme of things the nature of the association between Biafra and the States will vary according to the political relationship. It is expected therefore that the recommendations elaborated below might have to be modified accordingly. They, however, could form the basis of discussion at the Conference table.

Too often it has been assumed in certain quarters that the detachment of Biafra from the Federation of Nigeria might lead to balkanization and therefore instability in this part of Africa. This assumption is not borne out by any objective reasoning. Nor does the break-up of the Mali, Central Africa, Malaysian or West Indian Federations, to take a few examples, justify this. Paradoxically, the political structure of the Nigerian Federation was such that it was a source of instability. The painful experience of the past years has shown that only by political disengagement and the promotion of ties that are purely economic, social and cultural can a healthy and fruitful relationship be developed between its various component parts.

PREAMBLE

In the proclamation of May 30th, 1967, which formally established the independent and sovereign Republic of Biafra, His Excellency, Lt.-Col. Odumegwu Ojukwu, Commander-in-Chief of the Armed Forces and Head of State declared, *inter alia*, that this young Republic 'shall keep the door open for association with, and would welcome any sovereign unit(s) in the former Federation of Nigeria . . . desirous of association with us for the purpose of running a common services organization and for the establishment of common ties'.

In spite of the intensified bitterness generated by the outbreak of the present war, the Republic of Biafra still believes that a lasting and mutually beneficial relationship can be established with the rest of the Nigerian Federation or with whatever sovereign state or group of sovereign states that would emerge at the end of the war.

The common experience of over fifty years of political, economic, social and cultural ties between Biafra and these (prospective) states provides a sound and realistic basis for a fruitful relationship. The terms governing such special relationship must be worked out in such a manner that they do not compromise or detract from the sovereign rights of the states concerned.

AREAS OF CO-OPERATION

Given these factors, the Republic of Biafra is prepared to consider and negotiate the establishment of a Joint Services Authority in the following areas; all without prejudice to the right of each state to its own services:

A. ECONOMIC

1. *Railways and Harbours*

These services which already exist can be reopened to serve the mutual interests of member states, particularly those states that might find themselves landlocked as a result of the war, and would require access to the sea for movement of goods.

2. *Inter-Territorial Roads*

An efficient road network linking the states is already in existence, and it would be desirable that this be kept open for freer movement of goods and services.

3. *Merchant Shipping, including Inland Waterways*

All states can participate in the running of a Shipping Line. In this regard the former Nigerian National Shipping Line and Inland Waterways Department provide a nucleus for further expansion.

4. *Airways and Civil Aviation*

Because the running and maintenance of international Air Services by individual states in developing countries is an expensive and often unprofitable venture, it will be in the mutual interest of member states to pool resources together in this respect.

5. *Inter-Territorial Posts and Telecommunication Services*

Existing links and facilities in this respect have reached a reasonable level of development. It would be unwise to sever these links. This arrangement will be without prejudice to the right of each state to develop its overseas services.

6. *Meteorology*

The existence of Joint Air Services makes it desirable for co-operation between member states in matters relating to meteorological services. In this regard, advantage could be taken of existing facilities.

7. *Customs*

In this field the negotiations anticipated could lead to the operation of joint customs services between member states, and special agreements on movement of goods and services. It might be possible to reach an understanding which would eventually lead to a Customs Union.

8. *Currency Matters*

The member states will enter into a Currency arrangement in order to facilitate inter-state trade and commerce. Such an arrangement should not be prejudicial to the right of each state to maintain an independent currency and monetary policy.

B. CULTURAL RELATIONS

1. *Higher Education*

Because institutions of higher learning and educational policies in the former Federation of Nigeria were developed on more or less equivalent bases and standards, it will be mutually beneficial to member states to strengthen cultural and educational links through, e.g. exchanges of students and teachers.

2. *Co-operation in Scientific, Technical and Research Matters*

The former Federation of Nigeria had developed some expertise and institutions in these areas. It would be in the common interest of member states to continue to avail themselves of this knowledge and these facilities rather than stand alone in what is necessarily an expensive undertaking.

3. *Cultural Exchanges*

The member states are already used to common endeavours in the fields of sports, dances, arts, etc. It is therefore expected that exchanges in these fields would foster greater understanding and friendliness amongst the peoples of the different states.

C. DIPLOMATIC AND CONSULAR RELATIONS

1. Subject to agreement, Biafra is prepared to establish Diplomatic or Consular relations at any level to reflect the nature of her relationship with the various states.

2. Agreement could also be reached with any state or group of states to have a joint, Diplomatic and Consular representation in various countries abroad. These agreements will be without prejudice to the separate and individual identity of each state.

D. CITIZENSHIP ARRANGEMENTS

Biafra would be prepared to enter into citizenship arrangements with the various states on the free movement of persons between the states.

INSTITUTIONS

For the effective and smooth running of these joint services the following institutions are envisaged as an example of what could be negotiated:

1. *An Authority*

An Authority composed of the Heads of Government of the Member States is envisaged. It may be vested with legislative functions and the authority to determine policy, subject to individual state ratification.

2. There may be an Executive Board composed of two or more Representatives from each member state. Each member of the Board, in rotation, may be charged with responsibility for one or a group of related services. The Executive Board shall be responsible to the Authority for the efficient performance of their duties. The Executive Board, acting collectively, shall be responsible for the recruitment of staff for the running of the various services.

ASSETS AND LIABILITIES OF THE FORMER FEDERATION

With the break-up of the former federation of Nigeria, the question of the determination of its assets and liabilities will arise, and it will be necessary to discuss this matter.

Matters relating to the pensions, gratuities and National Provident Fund, would also have to be considered.

> [1] *White Paper released in Enugu on 29 August 1967.*

M

131.
Gowon's Address to the Nation on Progress of the War[1]

Fellow countrymen and women,

For eight weeks now, troops of the Federal Military Government have been fighting rebels led by Ojukwu. The fight has raged on several fronts in the three Eastern States and recently in the Midwestern State. The forces of the Federal Government have achieved signal victories. They have captured rebel strongholds like Obudu, Ogoja, Obolo-Eke, Nsukka, Eha-Amufu near the rebels capital, Enugu. They have also captured Bonny and its surrounding islands in the Rivers State.

Recently, there was the disgraceful betrayal of trust by certain Ibo officers in the Mid-West. The military coup they organised enabled rebel infiltrators to occupy the state. The rebels have also in a desperate effort tried to penetrate into the Western State. This has failed. I consider it important to restate at this juncture the objectives of the Federal Government and to explain once again the reasons for the fighting.

You all know that I made every effort, and many Nigerians exerted themselves true to our traditions of timely compromise, to achieve a peaceful settlement. All the concessions I made were rejected by Ojukwu who was bent on secession. We decentralised the Government. We agreed to autonomy for the regions to a greater extent than allowed in our independence constitution. We even agreed that each Regional Governor could exercise a right of veto on decisions of the Central Government. We agreed to look into the question of revenue allocation so as to remove any grievance on the part of any state which felt that it was subsidising any other state. All these efforts which would have prevented the tragedy through which the country is now passing were brought to nothing by the ambition and greed for personal power of Ojukwu and his collaborators.

Whenever reviewing the background to the Nigerian crisis, Ojukwu and his clique conveniently forget the killing in January, 1966 of innocent military officers and of civilian leaders other than members of their own ethnic group. Instead, they widely circulated distorted versions of the unfortunate events in this country in January, May, July and October last year in which many lives were lost in different parts of the country. I condemned these unfortunate incidents. I proceeded to seek a political solution which shall ensure that no one tribe is allowed to become a threat to others. Everybody knows that even now thousands of Ibos are still living in Lagos and other parts of Nigeria.

The rebels have tried to convince the world that they are fighting for what they called self-determination for the Ibos. This is only false propaganda. The Federal Military Government cannot accept that Ojukwu and his clique should force five million Ekois, Efiks, Ibibios and Ijaws into bondage. They cannot drag them along in their so-called secession. These so-called minorities are entitled to equal dignity and equal protection as the Ibos under the laws of Nigeria. What is the explanation which the rebels can offer for the coup in the Mid-West? The Edos, the Urhobos, the Itsekiris, the Ijaws and even the majority of the so-called Midwestern Ibos do not desire to be dominated by Ojukwu agents from the East Central State. The lands and farms of these people in the Midwest have been plundered. Their shops have been looted. All this, and their abortive push towards the West, does not support the false claim of the rebels to be fighting for Ibo self-determination.

It is clear that Ojukwu and his collaborators want naked power for themselves over the rest of Nigeria. This is not acceptable to the rest of Nigeria. Only the new structure of the Federation with twelve states can save this country from continuous unrest and civil war. No proposal based on the former four regions in the country can provide a lasting solution to the Nigerian crisis. All honest Nigerians know this truth.

As far as the world is concerned, the African states have shown a deep appreciation of the problems involved in the Nigerian crisis. The Federal Military Government appreciates the decision of all the leaders of Africa not to recognise the so-called secession of Ojukwu. All friendly countries must appreciate the true facts of the Nigerian situation. There is no alternative to a Federal Union of Nigeria. The only possible alternative is the emergence of several armed camps in this country and continuous fighting for many years to come. There will then be the chaos of an arms race and the tyranny and the petty dictatorship of war lords already exhibited by Ojukwu and his clique. In such a chaos Nigeria will be converted into a theatre for cold war and other disastrous adventures.

Fellow countrymen, we are therefore fighting to ensure that long after the present ugly events shall have passed into history, there shall remain one strong forward-looking and prosperous Nigeria. A Nigeria in which no state and no tribe will be able to try to dominate the others. A Nigeria in which there will be communal harmony. A Nigeria which will then be assured of the stability necessary for economic development to uplift the dignity of man in this part of the world. This is the Nigeria which will be best able to assure peace in this part of the world to the benefit of everybody—Africans and others as well.

Happily, the forces available to the Federal Military Government are adequate to deal with the situation. What Nigeria requires of all of us now are sacrifice and rededication to the cause of the Fatherland. My call is not to the fighting troops alone. All Nigerians are justly proud of their magnificent efforts. My call is to every member of the public as well. We have a unique opportunity in history to create and maintain a large heritage of which future Nigerians, all Africa, and black people everywhere can be proud.

Some people abroad have repeatedly urged that the Nigerian crisis should be ended through peaceful negotiations. The Federal Military Government has always kept the door open for peaceful negotiations and reconciliation. As far as the Federal Military Government is concerned, the military operations can cease immediately if Ojukwu and his collaborators agree:

   (a) to remain part of Nigeria and give up secession
   (b) accept the new structure of the Federation based on the twelve states, including the South Eastern and Rivers States.

I like to emphasise that the Federal Military Government will not negotiate with Ojukwu as the rebel leader. It will be up to the East Central State to produce a new leadership for peace talks aimed at preserving Nigeria as one country.

I have preferred not to talk about the obstacles which have been placed in our way in trying to procure the arms needed to defeat the rebels. The Federal Military Government has never sought military aid from any source. We have purchased all our arms from abroad strictly on commercial terms. Nigeria seeks to maintain her traditional friendships and will continue to pursue with increased vigour its policy of non-alignment.

I must express my deep appreciation and thanks to all friendly countries, especially our brothers in Africa who have shown understanding of the need for the continued existence of Nigeria as one country. I take this opportunity to thank the fighting troops and other members of the armed forces for risking their lives to preserve the integrity of their country. I wish to thank also the general public for their loyalty to Nigeria and support for the Federal cause.

Fellow countrymen, as I have already stated, our forces are equal to the task. We are now mounting decisive operations to crush the rebels everywhere. Victory shall be ours. Victory shall be for one Nigeria. So help us God to preserve our nation united and prosperous.

[1] *Broadcast from Lagos on 2 September 1967 (press release from Nigeria House, London).*

132.
Biafran Memorandum Circulated to Heads of States at O.A.U. Meeting, Kinshasa, September 1967[1]

It is now a fact of history that the Federation of Nigeria which acceded to independence of the 1st October 1960, died a natural death on the 30th May 1967. Over its ruins now stands the young Republic of Biafra and what remains of Nigeria.

Clearly, the peoples of the defunct Federation never really showed a will to live together in one nation. For several years the Government of Northern Nigeria pursued a deliberate policy of replacing fellow Nigerians from the South serving in the North with Northern Nigerians of inferior ability.

Where such Northerners were not available, foreign nationals were preferred. It is a truism that discrimination as a policy never fosters comradeship: and where such practice combines in the same group with recurring hostility against a particular group as occurred in the old Nigeria, there is an inevitable falling apart.

In this connection, the remorseless slaughter by Northerners of several thousand unarmed Eastern Nigerians in May, July and September, 1966, was merely the worst round of a continuing genocide unleashed in Jos in 1945 and followed up in Kano in 1953 against persons of Eastern Nigeria origin.

Understandably, it was also the last straw that decided Eastern Nigerians all over the country that justice, life and property for them could only be guaranteed in the area of their origin and by a Government of their own kindred. In answer to this instinct of self-preservation, some two million refugees fled back to Eastern Nigeria, now Biafra, never again to leave.

Living together with Northerners had been intolerable from the beginning: by the end of 1966 it had become impossible. Mutual confidence had been so shattered that Lt. Col. Gowon in his maiden speech in August, 1966 admitted that the basis for unity no longer existed.[2]

It is thus a matter of reality that, in any consideration of the relationship that can exist between the peoples of the former Federation of Nigeria, the complete absence now of any measure of confidence between them must overshadow all other elements.

However, in spite of the bitter experience of the immediate past, the Government and people of Eastern Nigeria hoped and tried even in the middle of the pogrom of 1966 to salvage whatever common bonds still remained in the Federation.

The first requirement was to re-organise the Armed Forces. Divided by two mutinies, the second of which was directed against troops of Eastern Nigeria origin, it had become evident that officers and men of Eastern Nigeria could no longer, as far as any one could see, safely share the same barracks with Northern soldiers.

Accordingly, the Military Governor of the then Eastern Nigeria proposed that to lessen tension and restore some measure of confidence troops should forthwith be posted back to their regions of origin.

On the 9th August, representatives of the Governors met in Lagos and agreed to this proposal. In view of the heightened distrust that ensued, it is sad to note that this urgent re-organisation unanimously approved by all the Governments of the Federation[3] was subsequently ignored by the Lagos authorities as far as Northern troops occupying Western Nigeria were concerned.

The crisis of 1966 also posed another and more fundamental question: that of discovering a new basis, if possible, for the future association of the different peoples of Nigeria.

Again, it was the Government of Eastern Nigeria which proposed an early meeting to find an answer. When the meeting came to sit in Lagos in September 1966, delegates were asked by Lt. Col. Gowon to endorse one of four patterns of association; a confederation, a federation with a strong centre, a federation with a weak centre, or some novel form of association.[4]

In spite of the difficulties involved, the conference appeared to be making substantial progress towards a confederal set-up when its work was abruptly halted by a new pogrom unleashed by Northern Nigerians against Easterners, some waiting to board planes at airports, others in market-places, and yet some others in places of worship.

One month later, the constitutional conference was formally sacked by Lt. Col. Gowon.

Once more, that is to say, the prospects for peace and reconciliation slid back several jumps. Once more, however, the Government of Eastern Nigeria made fresh proposals for a settlement. The difficulty was that after the third pogrom of September, and given the continued occupation of Western Nigeria by Northern troops, no mutually acceptable venue for a meeting could be found in Nigeria.

So, Governor Odumegwu Ojukwu's new proposal was for a meeting of the Supreme Military Council outside Nigeria. At first the Northern group rejected the idea but after much waste of time, they reluctantly accepted a meeting in Ghana.

And so it was that at Aburi on the 4th and 5th January 1967 Nigeria's highest authority, the Supreme Military Council decided on several issues including the renunciation of force for solving the crisis and the right of consent by the Regional Governors over Supreme Military Council decisions.

The 9th August decision to post troops back to their regions of origin was again restated.

In the matter of rehabilitating refugees, most of whom were in Eastern Nigeria, it was agreed that the Federal Government was to pay the salaries of their fleeing officers until the 31st March 1967.

History must regret that such realistic decisions universally hailed both at home and abroad were never implemented by the Federal Government because a few civil servants in Lagos subsequently advised against them.

If Governments exist to protect rather than persecute their citizens, such a catalogue of faithlessness and indifference on the part of the Federal Government clearly rendered them forfeit of the allegiance of Easterners.

This state of affairs directly led to the Revenue Allocation Edict of the 1st April in which the Government of Eastern Nigeria sought to conserve revenue deriving from the region in lieu of part of its statutory share of Federal Funds long since stopped by the Lagos Authorities.

The whole world now knows that this justified measure of self-preservation subsequently became the excuse for the Northern-controlled Federal Government to impose wholesale economic sanctions against Eastern Nigeria.

By the end of April 1967, therefore, it had become evident beyond doubt that the long suffering people of Eastern Nigeria were no longer wanted in the Federation. But it was not until another month that the Chiefs' Advisory Council and the Consultative Assembly, fully representing all the Provinces and sitting in a joint session, mandated the Military Government at a convenient time to proclaim Eastern Nigeria a separate sovereign state under the name and title of 'Biafra'.[5]

Lt. Col. Gowon's reaction to the inevitable result of his indifference to injustice was a radio division of Nigeria into twelve states.[6] The so-called creation of states is of course a red herring, in no way relevant to the solution of the problems caused by the crisis of 1966. . . .

Lt. Col. Gowon claims that, by splitting his country into several small units, domination of one group by another has thereby been removed. But domination of one, two or three states by any combination of the rest remains still real.

Indeed, Lt. Col. Gowon appears to ensure this by constituting the six Northern states into one administrative unit which he calls the Council of Northern States. Under the constitution which was suspended in January, 1966 but which Gowon nevertheless likes to cite, the creation of any new state requires, among other things, the consent of the peoples concerned as well as the approval of the region from which it is proposed to carve out such state. On the contrary, the so-called creation of states was the act of one single man, Lt. Col. Gowon.

Too often Lt. Col. Gowon announces himself as the legal Government of Nigeria and refers to the fourteen million freedom-loving and industrious people of Biafra as rebels. The truth, however, is that born of an army mutiny and sustained by brute force, Gowon's administration lacks any legal base

It does not and never did control the territory now known as Biafra. In accordance with international practice, a regime established by a coup d'état acquires legal sanction only with either the consent or the acquiescence of the citizens. As far as Gowon's mutiny of the 29th July is concerned, that acceptance never existed in Eastern Nigeria.

On the contrary, a state of hostility persisted between the mutineers and Eastern Nigeria from that date. It is indeed an absurdity to allege that Biafra is rebelling against Lt. Col. Gowon's regime, which is itself a regime of rebellion. Any attempt therefore to argue legitimacy into Lt. Col. Gowon's partial coup of the 29th July, 1966 and to confer on Gowon by legalistic sophistry, an authority over Biafra which he has never established in fact, must end in futility. . . .

Yet Biafra realizes that neither side can achieve complete military victory in a war of this nature, hence she has always stood for a negotiated settlement. . . .

From the foregoing, it is quite clear, first that the people of Biafra had never been welcome in large areas of the Nigerian Federation and secondly that Biafra has successfully defended her right to a separate existence and will successfully defend it in the future against all aggressors.

The third argument that Biafra's example could encourage secession elsewhere in Africa gives to precedent a force that it does not possess. Every Federation that has broken up in history has broken up because of some identifiable local cause and not in consequence of an external factor. . . .

Within the Commonwealth, the Indian Union split at independence into India and Pakistan while Malaysia and the West Indian Federation have more recently disintegrated without anybody suggesting any causal links between them.

There is, besides, no parallel in any other African country with the mass slaughter of several thousand ordinary men, women and children of Eastern Nigeria origin, which forced the rest of their kinsmen to seek refuge in a state of their own.

Nor has there been any other African country so plagued with the series of serious crises as the Nigerian Federation suffered in its six years of independent existence.

Biafra's case is indeed unique. Fourteen million people have been persecuted and hunted from pillar to post, their undeserved sufferings glossed over as regrettable but not serious. For Biafrans, however, there can be no question now of re-entering the Nigerian Federation whatever the terms. No safeguards can work; none ever did. The old Nigerian Federation simply is dead, stone dead. And Biafra is born to stay.

[1] *By courtesy of a Biafran official.*   [2] *See* DOC *37.*
[3] *See* DOC *45.*   [4] *See* DOC *51.*
[5] *See* DOC *112.*   [6] *See* DOC *111.*

133.
Biafra Sees itself as David[1]

History has never repeated itself more clearly as it is now doing in the

Nigeria-Biafra war. When Hitler pounced on the Jews during the last war and sent six million of them to the gas chamber, the world reacted with the usual lukewarm attitude and said, 'It was their domestic affair.' Pregnant women were murdered, children and elderly people were killed. Their only sin was that they were Jews. It took the world more than twenty years after the war to realise that it was, after all, not Hitler's internal affair. But then it was too late to cry when the head was off.

As compensation for this crime against nature, the Jews were later re-settled in what is today known as Israel. Even in their little place which they call 'The Promised Land' they were constantly molested by their compara-tively larger and happier neighbours—the Arabs—who maintain that the Israelis have no right to exist and have not in fact existed. At home the Israelis are two and a half million in population. The Arab neighbours number more than a hundred millions. The Arabs had tried three times to wipe out Israel from the earth, but their efforts were on each occasion abortive.

Today, a similar situation is taking place in the West Coast of Africa. More than 30,000 inhabitants of what used to be Eastern Nigeria were murdered in cold blood. Pregnant women, children, unarmed Christian wor-shippers, were among the victims of the pogrom in Northern Nigeria last year. In Lagos and Western Nigeria, the Biafrans were made to suffer the greatest humiliation in the hands of the Northerners before facing their slow painful death. They were finally driven way with ignominy.

Once again, the world repeated its history and brushed aside this unpro-voked crime of murder in Nigeria and said, 'It is Nigeria's internal and domestic affair.' The champion of the Organisation of African Unity (OAU) in the person of their secretary Mr. Dialo Telli, went to Lagos to see Gowon, and after their dinner-talks, Telli waved his flag of undisputed supremacy over Nigeria, gave a green light for further killing with the assurance that the world would not intervene as it is your own 'internal and domestic affair'.

The Nigerians then started their cold-blooded massacre of the former Eastern Nigerians living among them. The Easterners had no alternative but to rush home to their promised land of 'Biafra'. Even there in Biafra, the Nigerians are still pursuing them. One of their leaders said, 'We will fight and die in our fatherland.' But the almighty God is fighting with the innocent Biafrans.

[1] African Monthly Review, *September 1967, p. 16.*

134.
O.A.U. Resolution on Nigeria, September 1967[1]

(i) The assembly of heads of state and government meeting at its first ordinary session in Kinshasa from 11th to 14th September, 1967;

(ii) Solemnly reaffirming their adherence to the principle of respect for the sovereignty and territorial integrity of member states;

(iii) Reiterating their condemnation of secession in any member state;

(*iv*) Concerned at the tragic and serious situation in Nigeria;

(*v*) Recognizing the situation as an internal affair, the solution of which is primarily the responsibility of Nigerians themselves;

(*vi*) Reposing their trust and confidence in the Federal Government of Nigeria;

(*vii*) Desirous of exploring the possibilities of placing the services of the assembly at the disposal of the Federal Government of Nigeria;

(*viii*) Resolves to send a consultative mission of six heads of state to the head of the Federal Government of Nigeria to assure him of the assembly's desire for the territorial integrity, unity and peace of Nigeria.

[1] *O A.U. communiqué issued at Kinshasa, 14 September 1967.*

135.
Communiqué Issued at end of O.A.U. Consultative Mission Visit[1]

The O.A.U. Consultative Mission under the chairmanship of His Imperial Majesty Haile Selassie I, the Emperor of Ethiopia, and comprising H.E. the President of the Federal Republic of Cameroun, El Haj Ahmadu Ahidjo, H.E. the President of the Republic of Niger, Monsieur Hamani Diori and H.E. Lt.-General Ankrah, the Chairman of the National Liberation Council of Ghana held consultations with H.E. Major-General Yakubu Gowon, Head of the Federal Military Government of Nigeria, today, pursuant to the resolution on the Nigerian situation adopted at the Fourth Session of the O.A.U. Summit Conference in Kinshasa on the 14th September, 1967.[2]

The Mission reaffirmed the decision of the O.A.U. Summit embodied in its resolution condemning all secessionist attempts in Africa. The Mission also reaffirmed that any solution of the Nigerian crisis must be in the context of preserving the unity and territorial integrity of Nigeria.

The Mission considered the terms of the Federal Military Government for the cessation of military operations.

The O.A.U. Consultative Mission agreed that as a basis for return to peace and normal conditions in Nigeria the secessionists should renounce secession and accept the present administrative structure of the Federation of Nigeria, as laid down by the Federal Military Government of Nigeria in Decree No. 14 of 1967.

H.E. Lt.-General Ankrah was mandated by the Mission to convey the text of the O.A.U. Kinshasa summit resolution as well as discussions and conclusions of the first meeting of the Mission in Lagos to the secessionists and report back to the Mission urgently the reaction of the secessionists. The Mission will decide on the next course of action on the receipt of His Excellency Lt.-General Ankrah's report.

It was also agreed that the O.A.U. Consultative Mission will remain in constant touch with the Federal Military Government.

The Federal Military Government was in complete agreement with the conclusions reached at the meeting and the action to be taken to ensure the unity, territorial integrity of, and peace in Nigeria.

[1] *Issued in Lagos, 23 November 1967.*
[2] *See* DOC *135.*

136.
Ojukwu Rules out Surrender[1]

Fellow countrymen, brave and proud Biafrans, today is 29th September, a day to be long remembered, not only in the history of Biafra, but also in that of our heartless association with the defunct Nigerian Federation. It was on this date a year ago that the pogrom started by the Hausa-Fulani vandals in May assumed the proportions which has made it the most hideous in the annals of human cruelty and depravity.

To all Biafrans, then, this date marks two things. It marks our grief for all our losses both in men and materials as a result of the atrocities perpetrated against our people. It also marks the beginning of our realisation that we could not exist as a people within the Federation of Nigeria. Following this realisation, our people found themselves compelled to flee other parts of Nigeria to their own homes. Over 2,000,000 of them returned to us in the process. They found not only welcome but safety, for there is after all no place like home. From then on, we did everything in our power to see that a realistic solution was found to the problems which have beset Nigeria, of which we were then still a part. We did everything to preserve the political and economic identity of that country, provided that the association of its different components was based on a realistic basis. But what did we get for our efforts? Gowon, the mendacious symbol of Hausa-Fulani imperialism, exhibited nothing but recurrent acts of bad faith and hypocrisy. Nothing which could not ensure the perpetual domination of all parts of Nigeria by the North would satisfy him. . . .

One regrettable fact about this present struggle is that some expatriate diplomatic missions have allowed themselves to be used by Gowon as tools. It is unfortunate that they have so easily succumbed to his blackmail. Without the support of some foreign missions for Gowon and the notorious indifference of others, this war would by now have ended. Indeed, as far as the war is concerned, Gowon and his Nigerian clique were defeated over four weeks ago. It was in acknowledgement of this defeat that he frantically sought and received foreign assistance in men and materials to prosecute the war. I do not need to mention the scores of mercenaries leading his Army and operating his Air Force to the utter disgust of Africa. He has been able to obtain the foreign assistance by promising those concerned the wealth of our oil and threatening others with the loss of investments in Nigeria.

Despite all these, however, victory is still illusion. The world still understands our case. Our sister African countries know as well. That was why, despite the efforts of Gowon and his aides, to exclude the discussions or even the mention of our war with Nigeria during the last meeting of the OAU, members of that organisation felt obliged to discuss the matter and appoint a committee to look into it. Awolowo's 'Kinshasa special' was designed to frustrate the efforts of the OAU. . . .

Gowon and his collaborators must realise that, by declaring total war, they have brought misery upon themselves and their people. Gowon's collaborators, particularly the Yorubas who have made themselves tools for the caprices of a mentally sick Gowon suffering from delusions of grandeur and scurrilous allegation, must realise soon that they are doing no more than preparing themselves and their people for perpetual servitude. For our part, we know that victory for Gowon would mean continued genocide for our people, bestiality, disease, and anarchy, ignorance, poverty and desecration of our religion. Those not of the Northern Hausa-Fulani oligarchy and who now choose to collaborate with Gowon must realise that they, too, will not escape this deprivation at the hand of these Northerners. We, the people of Biafra, are fighting to preserve and protect our lives and property, our institutions, our religions and talents, and our progress. We fight to establish our right to live. God knows that we did not start or want this war; but it is our duty, having been forced into it, to pursue this to a successful end. . . .

Faced with the determination of our people to ensure a just and realistic solution to the problems, and embarrassed by the world sympathy for our cause, Gowon resorted to all forms of blackmail as well as distortion and falsification of facts and records. Need we be reminded of the perfidy of the North during the September 1966 ad hoc constitutional conference? Can anyone forget Gowon's dishonesty, duplicity and high-handedness over the famous Aburi agreement? All these failed to achieve Gowon's objective of placing our people and those of other parts of the then Southern Nigeria in perpetual subjugation to the Hausa-Fulani oligarchy. He then resorted to coercive measures, using the central machinery established for the whole Federation of Nigeria to enforce this. That was not all. He tried to subvert our government by sowing seeds of discord and dissension and making unfulfillable promises. All these failed him too. Meanwhile, a stalemate was reached. Our people continued to be insulted and provoked. They were losing in trade and business as a result of the economic blockade, the effectiveness of which was underlined by the attitude of foreign shipping interests.

We reached a stage at which we had no other alternative than to declare our sovereignty. . . . On 30th May this year, we took that irrevocable step. But even in our declaration of sovereignty, we kept the door open for some forms of association of mutual advantage, particularly in the economic fields within Nigeria.

Gowon and his clique would have none of these. Nothing short of complete domination by the North would satisfy Gowon. On 6th July, Gowon unleashed his long-prepared and promised aggression against our young republic. . . . Gowon expected to overrun us within a matter of two short days. In his calculations, he had woefully failed to take into account the historical fact that no people fighting for survival have ever failed. Arms and armies cannot defeat the will of the people to survive. Ours is a war of a people determined to survive.

The people of Biafra, be they in the fighting forces or the public, are all determined to defend their capital city at all costs. The enemy's determination to enter this city is bound to fail. There is no question of our abandoning this capital city.[2] It is therefore the duty of all, when the time comes, to remain in Enugu and help in the war effort while continuing their normal duties as far as possible. Children and women caring for them may leave Enugu. But women engaged in essential services connected with the war as well as those connected with voluntary organisations should remain. In the case of those directly engaged in fighting this war, this Government accepts responsibility for compensation to their families and dependants in the event of death or injury. . . .

God has all along shown his mercies on us. Let us supplement those mercies with our efforts and sacrifices. . . . All Biafrans must now come forward to supplement the efforts of our gallant troops. Biafra relies on all and expects everyone to rally to the call. To fail would mean the certain end of us as a people. Holy Archangel Michael, defend us in battle. Brave Biafrans, proud Biafrans, we shall vanquish.

[1] *Broadcast from Enugu, 29 September 1967.*
[2] It fell within the week.

137.
Gowon's Independence Day Message, 1967[1]

Fellow Nigerians; I wish to call upon you all on this seventh anniversary of our independent existence as a nation to rededicate yourselves to the task of building a strong, united and prosperous Nigeria, a Nigeria in which every citizen regardless of his or her religious belief or ethnic origin will have equal opportunity with his fellow Nigerians.

As you all know, this seventh anniversary is not an occasion for festive celebration. The armed forces of our country have been waging a disciplined but hard campaign to put down a rebellion in the East-Central State of Nigeria—a rebellion conceived, nurtured and executed by Emeka Ojukwu and his collaborators after the failure of their mad bid to subjugate and dominate all Nigeria in the exclusive interest of their ethnic group. Neither the Federal Military Government nor the people of Nigeria wanted this war. Every avenue of peace was fully explored, beginning with the ad hoc constitutional conference of August 1966 and culminating with the last-minute peace move by a number of eminent and representative Nigerians who, in their patriotic desire to find a peaceful solution to the crisis, sent a peace mission to Ojukwu in Enugu. You all will recall how Ojukwu sought the failure of the ad hoc conference on the constitution, first by using his agents to terrorise the delegates by bomb explosions, and then by boycotting the conference totally. From then on the rebels in Enugu were determined to turn their back upon the country and to escalate the crisis by every means at their disposal to a level which would rule out a peaceful settlement.

The government-sponsored radio in Enugu and all the newspapers in the East were organised to whip up the emotion of the people. Rumours were spread of impending attacks on Lagos and on some important installations elsewhere in the Federation. These rumours were subsequently confirmed by the bomb explosions which destroyed Ore bridge, a wing of the Federal Palace hotel and Government residential quarters in Ikoyi. The effect of this campaign of hate and terror was to build up tension, not only in the eastern states, but in many other parts of the country. It was in this charged atmosphere that the story was released about the massacre of a large number of men, women and children of Northern origin resident in the East. This touched off violent actions in the North in September and early October 1966 such as Nigeria had never witnessed before. I strongly condemned this incident, and all right-thinking Nigerians deplored it. Then as now the Government was willing to explore ways in which the survivors of this episode could be cared for and rehabilitated, but Ojukwu and his clique were determined to make that incident the occasion for putting into effect their premeditated plan for the complete breakup of Nigeria after their failure to dominate the country.

Even so, the Federal Military Government did not give up its peace effort, as well as its determination to conciliate the Ibos. It was as a result of this search for a peaceful settlement that the Aburi meeting was held. It is now a matter of history that the Federal Military Government conceded to Ojukwu everything he asked for at Aburi—except one thing, and that was to agree to a breakup of the Federation. This I could not and would never agree to. I am happy that my standpoint on this fundamental question has now been vindicated by the enthusiasm with which Nigerians everywhere have committed themselves to the continued existence of Nigeria as one country. The whole of Africa at the recent OAU conference has also vindicated our stand in its clear commitment to the territorial integrity and unity of Nigeria and in its condemnation of secession. If Ojukwu had sincerely wanted a peaceful settlement of this crisis, he might have used the Aburi decision as a way out of the deadlock. Instead, he proceeded to seize Federal establishments in the former Eastern Region and by an edict of 15th April 1967 he took over all Federal statutory bodies and assets located in the Eastern states. Ibo employees in the Western State and in Lagos were persuaded into returning home while Ojukwu intensified his illegal purchase of arms.

When the clouds of war were gathering fast, a number of eminent Nigerians decided to form a National Reconciliation Committee. The Committee met me in Lagos and also visited Enugu from where they brought back certain conditions which, if fulfilled by both sides, could have arrested the drift to an armed conflict. The main element of their proposed settlement was that the Federal Government should lift the economic sanctions imposed on the East and that the East in turn should end its flagrant defiance of Federal Government authority. It is on record that the Federal Military Government immediately accepted this proposal and implemented it, but it is also well-known that the Post Office vans and postal orders which were sent to the East by the Federal Government in implementation of the Committee's recommendations were seized in Enugu in further defiance of the Federal Government. Ojukwu made no attempt whatsoever to reciprocate. Instead, not only were military provocations stepped up on the border villages of the Benue-Plateau State which had been constantly terrorised by Ojukwu's rebel forces, but Ojukwu went as far as declaring total war on the rest of Nigeria and immediately pursued it with the bombing of defenceless civilians in various parts of the country. In the circumstances, I had no choice but to order police action to arrest the situation and to preserve the territorial integrity of Nigeria as well as prevent Ojukwu from subjugating and destroying the 5,000,000 non-Ibos in the former Eastern Region of Nigeria, who had all along made clear their desire to remain Nigerians.

Fellow countrymen and women, you all know what a marvellous job the Federal forces have been doing. In the military campaign so far we have not lost a single battle. Federal forces now control the whole of Ogoja Province in the South-Eastern State and have also established effective and firm control over most of the Mid-West State. Enugu is at present under siege and is expected to fall any time from now.

It is well known, however, that Ojukwu has been putting out false propaganda about military victories which the rebel forces have never won. Unfortunately Ojukwu's propaganda is being re-echoed in the foreign press and radio with tragic consequences for his rebel soldiers and innocent civilians, who are constantly being pushed by this deceit to certain death at the hands of the superior Federal forces. Only a few days ago he announced that Opi and Nsukka had been recaptured at a time when Federal forces were not only in control of these areas but were, in fact, converging on Enugu. These are certainly not the actions of a man who has the best interest of his people at heart. It is, therefore, foolhardy for the ordinary Ibos to continue this hopeless and suicidal struggle. Now is the time for all those people whom Ojukwu has misled to abandon him and his collaborators, as it is utterly senseless to prolong the fighting and unnecessary suffering of innocent people. In the interest of the younger generation of the East-Central State, I hope that my appeal will soon be heeded. If it is not, the military campaign will continue until the East-Central State is fully integrated with the rest of the Federation.

The Government does not underrate the task before it, and I hope that I can continue to count on your wholehearted support in this fight for the survival of our fatherland and in the work of national reconstruction and reconciliation which lies ahead. The Ibos, when they are returned to the fold, must be given their rightful place and, as a people who have been misguided and misled by their leaders, the rest of us have a duty to bind their wounds and give them our right hand of fellowship. . . .

[1] *Broadcast from Lagos, 1 October 1967 (B.B.C. ME/2582/B2).*

138.
Awolowo's Blueprint for Post-War Reconstruction (1967)[1]

The crisis which hit this country some five years ago has, since it took a dramatic turn in 1965, inflicted enormous damage on our national life. The period of twelve months, beginning with October 1965, had witnessed the exhibition of large-scale violent disturbances in different parts of the country. The calm, which followed this twelve-month period, has now proved, in retrospect, to be our worst national illusion. It is now known that in spite of Aburi; in spite of the constructive efforts of the National Conciliation Committee; and in spite of the Commander-in-Chief's conciliatory gestures and overtures in accepting and implementing, with speed and without reservation, the recommendations of the National Conciliation Committee which were wholly based on the terms dictated by Ojukwu himself,[2] Ojukwu had spent this period of earnest and conscientious search for peace on the part of his fellow-countrymen in making elaborate preparations for war designed not only to take the former Eastern Region out of the Federation of Nigeria, but also, if possible, to subjugate the other parts of the country.

After several violent border provocations at Igumale and Idah, Ojukwu finally launched unprovoked military attack on the rest of Nigeria. In the face of this rebellion, there was only one of two choices open to the Federal Military Government. Either to succumb to Ojukwu's armed rebellion and allow him to take the then Eastern Region out of Nigeria and thereby bring about the total disintegration of the entire Federation, or to put down his rebellion, with all the forces at its disposal, in order to preserve the integrity and oneness of Nigeria. The Federal Military Government chose the latter course. Hence the Police action which, in consequence of Ojukwu's aggravating conduct of his rebellious activities, was later escalated to military operations. . . .

There is nothing we can do about the dead. But there is much—very much —that we can do for the living: for the orphans, the widows, the maimed and the wounded, and for the rest of our people who have loyally and uncomplainingly borne the inconveniences and privations which the crisis and the present military operations have imposed upon them, and who have made contributions in cash and kind for the comfort and relief of the federal troops.

Accordingly the Federal Military Government is committed to the following courses of action:

(*i*) The surviving victims of past disturbances and of the present military operations shall be cared for with the utmost compassion.

(*ii*) The surviving federal troops shall be amply rewarded for their gallant and devoted services to the nation.

(*iii*) All soldiers, no matter on which side they had fought, shall be rehabilitated and gainfully employed at the end of the military operations.

It must be noted in this connection that one of the good things about the present emergency is that it has helped to reduce unemployment throughout the country; it would be a mistaken policy of the worst kind, to allow the federal troops and the rebel soldiers to go back on the scrap heap of the country's unemployment market. It is for these reasons that the Federal Military Government is resolved to keep, and, considerably, improve upon the blessings of the prevailing high level of employment.

(*iv*) Those whose properties have been destroyed or damaged, as a result of civil disturbances, shall be reasonably compensated.

(*v*) All those who had fled from their normal places of residence or business shall be resettled; and, if possible, helped to make a new start.

(*vi*) All the roads, bridges and public buildings, which have been destroyed or damaged, shall be reconstructed with the greatest possible dispatch.

(*vii*) With immediate effect, a special fund into which an amount of £1 million will be contributed annually, beginning with the present fiscal year, has been created for the purpose of:

(*a*) stepping up the training of highlevel manpower in the Nigerian Universities, at the under-graduate and post-graduate levels;

(*b*) raising the secondary school and trained-teacher population in the States which are lagging behind in these respects, and preventing wastes at the secondary school level in the more advanced States, as part of the reconstruction effort; and

(*c*) providing free primary education for the children of all members of the Armed Forces.

In this connection, it is essential to bear three important considerations in mind.

ONE: it is strongly believed by the Federal Military Government that a united Nigeria has all the natural resources and manpower which any people could wish nature to bestow on them. But at present, we are extremely deficient in highlevel manpower. This deficiency can and must be corrected by accelerating, intensifying, and reorientating the university education of Nigerian citizens, so that when the dynamic forces of our total manpower are brought to bear on our latent natural resources, the latter will be compelled to yield their full increase for the benefit of Nigerians. If this desirable end is to be achieved, with the minimum possible delay, many of our youths who have the innate talents, but are unable to obtain secondary as well as university education simply because their parents are too poor to find the money, should be given the fullest possible financial assistance by the Government. This is precisely what the Federal Military Government is determined to do: to give free financial assistance, *not* loans, to all secondary-school pupils and university students who, for good reasons certified by the Authorities concerned to the satisfaction of the Federal Government, are unable to pay their fees. This free financial assistance will be in addition to the usual scholarship awards to deserving pupils and students.

TWO: It may not be generally known that, in the current year, there are only approximately 18,000 pupils in secondary grammar schools in the six Northern States, as against 170,000 in the six Southern States, and roughly 12,000 teachers in training in the Northern States, as against about 24,000 teachers in training in the Southern States. If we are to keep Nigeria one— and harmoniously so, and if all sections of the national groups in Nigeria are to have equal opportunity for contributing to our highlevel manpower needs, this yawning gulf must be closed without further delay. It is for this reason that the Federal Military Government has decided to stimulate, vigorously, the rapid expansion of secondary education and teacher training in the Northern States, by the award of scholarships in large numbers, and the grant of free financial assistance—*not* loans—to qualified pupils in the Northern States.

THREE: It is well known that soldiers, by the peculiar nature of their calling, have to be moved from time to time to different parts of the Federation. Such movements do often entail their being deprived of certain basic amenities which they enjoy in some parts of the Federation, but which are totally absent in other parts. It is in order to minimize this obvious disparity which inevitably arises, as a result of the movement of the members of our Armed Forces to different parts of the Federation, that the Federal Military Government has decided to afford free primary education to the children of the members of the Armed Forces, wherever they may be in the Federation. Children of the members of the Armed Forces and the Nigeria Police Force who lost their lives during the present military operations will also enjoy this benefit.

It will be seen, that the Federal Military Government is resolved not only to win these military operations, but also—and this is by far more important —to secure the peace, which will follow, by guaranteeing political equality and social justice to all Nigerian citizens, irrespective of their State of origin, ethnic affiliation, religion, social status, or the side on which they had fought during the rebellion. It is above all resolved to lay a sound foundation for a prosperous future for our country and our people.

All these things, that is the present military operations and the pro-grammes of reconstruction as well as of development, which I have outlined, do cost money. Already, the military operations have cost the Federal Govern-ment well over £50 million. The cost of general reconstruction, of re-building and, in some cases, widening damaged bridges and roads, has not yet been calculated. But it is assumed that this will run into several million pounds. The same thing will go for the cost of rehabilitation and resettlement. . . .

The problems which confront us, therefore, may be summarised as follows:

(*i*) Whatever the cost, we must finance the military operations until they are successfully concluded or until Ojukwu accepts the peace terms declared by the Federal Military Government. In this regard, it must be borne in mind that our hands are already so long and so justifiably laid on the plough, that it is too late in the day and dangerous for us to look back.

(*ii*) We must find all the money that is required for reconstruction, so as to bring the country speedily back to where it was, before the dogs and the horrors of war were let loose on the country by Ojukwu.

(*iii*) Since we cannot afford to stand still, and since indeed we must, in our own interest, make a big leap forward economically and socially, it is im-perative that we must raise enough money to finance new development pro-grammes.

At the moment, however, our financial situation is far from being a happy one. The gap between expenditure and revenue widens with each day that passes: the one increasing by leaps and bounds, whilst the other steadily falls short of estimates. In the result, the Federal Military Government has had to have recourse to inflationary financing. There is, however, a limit beyond which this method of financing must not be allowed to go, if we are to avoid complete economic disaster.

Furthermore, our foreign exchange position shows a more or less similar trend. Payments for military equipment make an ever-rising demand on our foreign exchange reserve, whilst because of delay in the shipment of our agricultural export products, and of the temporary cessation in the exporta-tion of petroleum products, our foreign exchange earnings are also falling short of estimates.

It is clear, from all that I have said, therefore, that, as a matter of great urgency, the Federal Military Government must do something about our finances. In this connection, it has adopted two lines of approach: to econo-mize our financial resources and to raise additional revenue.

With regard to the first line of approach, it will interest you to know that,

N

ever since the launching of the military operations, the Federal Military Government has embarked on strict austerity measures, some of which are meant only for the interim period, whilst others are intended to remain as a permanent feature of our public life. I will briefly enumerate some of these measures.

(*i*) Every Ministry, other than the Ministries of Defence and Internal Affairs, is enjoined to make 1 per cent savings in its approved estimates of expenditure. But from the next financial year, even stricter economy will be enjoined on all Ministries and extra-Ministerial departments.

(*ii*) The Federal Executive Council has set up a Committee to examine the structure of Government-sponsored Corporations and Companies in the light of the reports and recommendations of the Tribunals set up to enquire into the affairs of some of them. This is done with a view to putting these Corporations and Companies, properly and viably, on their feet. At the moment, most of them are ailing and sick; and the Federal Military Government is determined, not only to cure them, but to prevent a future relapse of their ailments, so that they may be self-sufficient and profitable, and hence cease to constitute an incessant drain on the finances of the Federal Government.

(*iii*) Capital projects in respect of which the Federal Military Government has not irrevocably committed itself are postponed for the time being.

(*iv*) All Federal Commissioners have agreed to observe a stringent Code of Conduct which precludes them from enjoying any benefit, and receiving any allowance, other than their salaries.

(*v*) A Committee has been set up to consider the advisability of reducing the number of our Foreign Missions. These Missions cost us a fortune in foreign exchange, and there is no doubt that some of them are maintained for prestige purposes only.

(*vi*) Steps are being actively taken to recover arrears of income tax and duties. Arrears of income tax amount to well over £4 million, and those of excise duties to over £5 million.

(*vii*) Pending the setting up, at an early date, of a Tribunal of Inquiry for the purpose of recovering ill-gotten gains made by some public officers and their self-employed collaborators, the Inland Revenue has already assessed to tax the amounts of money which some of the persons, who gave evidence before the Tribunals which inquired into certain Corporations, had admitted as having been legitimately made by them as incomes, but which they had not in the past declared as such to the Inland Revenue. As a result of investigation made up to the end of September, a total assessment of about £2 million has been made. Much more than double this amount is expected when the investigation is completed. I would like to say in passing that the taxes collected from these assessments will be offset against the total amount of any individual confiscation.

(*viii*) A much tighter control than ever before is now being exercised in the use of our foreign exchange reserve, care being taken, at the same time, to ensure that our foreign trade is in no way hindered. . . .

It should be clear from all that I have said that in the midst of the present strife which has been forced upon it, the Federal Military Government looks firmly and confidently into a glorious future. A future in which all the national units in Nigeria will live in harmony and unity with one another; a future in which political equality and social justice will be guaranteed to all. These being the declared and ultimate objectives of the Federal Military Government, the present military operations must be consistently regarded and supported for what they truly are. They have been designed, not for the gratification of hatred for any group of Nigerians; not for the extermination of the Ibos, as has been wickedly suggested in some malevolent quarters; indeed, they have been launched for noble and imperishable ends, namely: the federal unity of Nigeria, and the happiness and prosperity of its people.

It follows, therefore, that those who support the Federal Military Government in all its endeavours, including its current search for additional revenue, do the manifest will of God. For, God is the God of unity and progress, not of division and stagnation.

¹ *Broadcast from Lagos, 19 October 1967 (B.B.C. ME/2602/B2). Slightly revised text taken from* Blueprint for Post-War Reconstruction (*Lagos, 1967*).
² *See* doc *106.*

139.
Ojukwu's Address to Consultative Assembly after Fall of Enugu: 'Treachery Within'¹

Respected Chiefs and Leaders of Thought, Learned and Experienced Gentlemen and Ladies, Proud and Brave Biafrans, Fellow Countrymen and Women,

It is impossible for me to find adequate or suitable words with which to thank your Chairman for convening this meeting and you for attending at so short a notice. Our very existence is being threatened both by external and internal foes. Of the two, the latter is the more dangerous because they are within and around us.

At your last meeting held on the 26th and 27th of May, I gave you an up-to-date account of our struggle with Nigeria.² After two days of deliberations, during which you considered all the facts before you, together with the implications and consequences of different alternatives open to us, you passed a number of Resolutions and gave me a mandate.³ . . . The resolutions and mandate, clear and unequivocal, were arrived at without a dissentient voice. The mandate was a clear one by the people to guide me in my dealings, on behalf of our people, with the rest of Nigeria of which we were then a part. In my position as your servant and leader I intended to use your resolutions and the mandate as a basis for bargaining with our opponents. I still believed, even at that time, that there was room for negotiations which could lead to a peaceful and amicable settlement of the problems then besetting Nigeria. I held that belief, in spite of that iniquitous telegram of threat and blackmail which came through from Lagos while I was still addressing you at that meeting of the 26th of May. The text of that telegram was read to you in full.

A number of you will recall my discussions with you and my intention to make further efforts towards a settlement by negotiation, But alas, while these consultations were still going on, and before I had actually received and studied your resolutions and mandate, Gowon promulgated his arbitrary, dictatorial and tendentious Decree on the creation of states, dismissed the Supreme Military Council, declared a state of emergency all over the country and made himself the Fuehrer of Nigeria. The declaration of the state of emergency had two aims, namely, to give Gowon cover to attack us by force and, secondly, to stifle the aspirations of other parts of Southern Nigeria who were fast coming to our position and point of view.

It became clear that Gowon's unflinching aim was to push us out of the then Nigerian Federation. The arbitrary creation of states had been the last trump card towards this end, and was a direct infringement of even his much vaunted Decree No. 8 which purported to guarantee the territorial integrity of the then existing Regions of the Nigerian Federation. . . .

In our declaration of sovereignty, we made it quite clear that we wished to remain friends with what remained of Nigeria. We kept the door open for mutual co-operation and even went further to guarantee whatever might be our own share of debts incurred by Nigeria while we were still a part of it. What more could we have done to show our good faith and continued affection for our former partners of the defunct Nigerian Federation? Gowon and his Northern clique would not leave us to manage our own affairs in an atmosphere of peace, freedom and equality. Nothing short of our complete subjugation to the North, or extermination by it, would satisfy Gowon, who openly vowed to use the military might of Nigeria, a might built over many years with our common resources, to destroy us. To buttress his iniquitous intentions, he set up a puppet Government of ex-politicians, well known for their antagonism against us. Included in his puppet Government were a number of renegades from amongst us. The members of that puppet Government not only endorsed Gowon's evil plans against us but also gave him open support. All of them severally travelled overseas to purchase arms and hire mercenaries for the sole purpose of destroying us. We for our part left no one in any doubt of our intention to fight and die, if necessary, for our freedom and fatherland rather than allow ourselves to be enslaved or made second class citizens by the Hausa/Fulani hegemony.

Meanwhile, our people still resident in Lagos were subjected to increasing and humiliating molestations. They were asked to register as aliens and to go about with passes like slaves. Here, we see another form of Gowon's tact. He singled out the Ibos of Biafra for these treatments not because he liked other citizens of Biafra, but as a subtle means of furthering his determined plan to cause dissension amongst our people by pretending that there were people in this Republic who could be treated differently. In this, Gowon typically underrated the intelligence of our people who could not so soon forget that the Northerners never differentiated between members of ethnic groups in this Republic in their pogrom of 1966.

On the 6th of July, Gowon's hordes invaded the Republic of Biafra at three different points—two in the Ogoja front and one in the Nsukka sector. Because of the long and careful preparation by Lagos, and bearing in mind the superiority of the enemy in arms and numbers, Gowon and his clique planned to overrun this Republic within 48 hours. He called his aggression a 'Police Action' in order that the world might regard it as an internal affair of Nigeria and so fail to recognise and condemn the aggression. Our troops, ill-prepared, inadequate and ill-equipped as they were, displayed such outstanding heroism that within the first two days of Nigerian aggression, they not only withstood the aggression but actually drove the enemy into his own territory. Weeks passed and Gowon could not penetrate beyond the border areas. Contrary to all expectations, Gowon was defeated in his plan to overrun this Republic. The whole world wondered at and admired our heroism. Everywhere, Gowon's troops were humiliated, disgraced and frustrated. The invasion of Bonny after nearly six weeks of war was made possible through the antics and collusion of certain foreign interests. I do not need to go into details of this event because they are well known.

Considering the initial achievements of our troops, their subsequent experience and the supply in sufficient quantities of weapons which our troops initially lacked, we had expected to finish the war in the defeat of the aggressors by the end of August—this in spite of the massive support of Nigeria by Britain and Russia. This expectation was properly founded by our successful liberation of the Mid-West and advance into Western Nigeria.

But hardly could we know that a number of the officers within our army did not share the aspirations of their people and had allowed themselves to be suborned and perverted by the enemy. Those in position of trust in the Army shamelessly betrayed that trust against their people. Because of their positions, nobody could suspect them while they continued with their subtle and nefarious acts of demoralising our troops and causing the destruction of those who could not succumb to their antics. To the astonishment of all, the enthusiasm that our troops had shown from the start began to wane. Instead of making advances, our troops, for inexplicable reasons, kept on leaving the door open for enemy advance. It was in this way that we lost Nsukka town; it was in this way that we lost parts of Ogoja; it was in this way that the door was let open to the enemy through Opi to the suburbs of Enugu; it was in this way that the Mid-West, which later proclaimed itself the Republic of Benin, was abandoned for the enemy. You need to hear the stories of our soldiers to be able to appreciate the degree of sabotage and treachery which a number of our trusted Army Officers were engineering. These young men [a group present on the platform], anxious to fight for the honour and survival of their country, will tell you how their officers were giving them wrong orders or were ordering them not to fight in the face of the enemy. They will tell you how their colleagues were shot and killed from behind, not by the enemy but by their fellow Biafran soldiers. Not suspecting that this sort of thing could be possible among us, I, as the Commander-in-Chief, never suspected such acts of sabotage and treachery. If anything, I put it all down to incompetence which could be forgiven.

These saboteurs and traitors did not stop at that. They entered into a bargain with Gowon and his clique for the overthrow of this Government by a coup. This coup was to take place between the 18th and the 19th of September after which those concerned would have compromised our position with the enemy. But as Providence would have it, this plot was discovered and foiled in time. It was not until after the discovery of the plot that we began to be circumspective and to discover what was happening within our camps.

I repeat that whatever success has been made by the enemy has been a success not of military valour or gallantry, but of treachery by our own men. For days, our own men, using our own weapons were shelling Enugu to cause panic, and acting in collusion with the enemy; they have done the same thing in Onitsha.

Here, let me record the debt of this Republic to our general public whose vigilance has made it possible to foil many efforts by these saboteurs and traitors. We must intensify the vigilance.

Investigations and the vigilance of the general public have shown that there are people outside the Army who either have encouraged these acts of treachery or at least have condoned them. To such people, I can only say woe betide them that they should sell their fatherland for a pot of pottage. It is for the acts of these people that Gowon and his clique have been so confident of defeating us without merit. They know that they cannot defeat Biafra except through the use and help of Biafrans. Having succeeded in getting such support and help by treachery, they appear confident.

It is for you today to decide whether we are to go on with this fight of survival and ensure for the children and posterity freedom, security, fair-play and justice in their own homes and in their own way, or to capitulate to the enemy and for ever remain a conquered, disgraced and enslaved people. The consequences of the latter are clear. Let the few who, whether for money, spite, unpatriotism or sheer wickedness, have helped the enemy find no comfort. The consequence of our capitulation for them, their children, kith and kin and posterity, are clear. Capitulation or surrender would mean acceptance of defeat and slavery; it would mean the surrender of our sovereignty and survival as a people; it would mean perpetual exploitation and expropriation of our wealth by the conquerors; it would mean our ever remaining second-class citizens paying war reparations to the enemy for as long as they wish; it would mean lack of progress and development; it would mean poverty, disease, indeed everything that will make for anything but happiness and self respect.

We do not need to be told that the North do not want us in any association based on equality and respect. It is true that their concept of unity is unity of slave and master. Let us not forget how Major General Aguiyi-Ironsi, whose grave is next door to this building, died. Let us not forget why our officers and men in the Nigerian Army were killed last year; let us not forget the pogrom which cost us over thirty thousand people last year; let us not forget the millions of pounds of investment which our people have lost in other parts of the former Federation of Nigeria by being forced to return home; let us not forget that there is no place like home and that having been killed in other lands and driven away from those lands, history will for ever condemn us for betraying our soil and heritage to the enemy and allowing ourselves to be slaughtered even in our own homes. Most important of all, let us not forget our repeated view that our sovereignty is not negotiable.

As for me, I see no hope for our people without victory in this war. As I told this Assembly on one occasion, I have no personal ambition and have all along carried out what I consider my duty for the people of this Republic. We have in recent weeks heard Lagos call upon you to choose a new leader,[4] a suggestion which I should have thought every man and woman with soul in this Republic would regard as insulting. But if considering what is happening our enemy is echoing what they know to be the feelings in this Republic about leadership, it is for you to take a decision uninfluenced by any external enemy. God knows that I have done my best and I am prepared to continue to serve. But if in this war I am considered the Jonah in the ship of state, I am prepared to step down for another person who will be able to inspire sufficient confidence for the achievement of victory. As a soldier, I know that no man is indispensable and as a soldier I also know that I owe my first duty to my country and my people. We are fighting a war of survival which we cannot afford to lose. If we have personal grievances, if we have personal animosities, should this be a reason for betraying our fatherland and condemning our children and generations unborn to eternal disgrace and servitude? Our sense of patriotism demands of us to fight and win this war in order to maintain our honour and identity as a people. After we should have done this, we can do whatever we like to settle our grievance or redress wrongs.

Finally, in spite of all that has happened, I feel proud of the people of Biafra as a whole. We have worked together, we have sacrificed together. Our young men are dying for our survival. From the resolutions I have received and other expressions of support and determination, the present crisis has brought our people closer together. The differences which had existed between the different ethnic groups are now a matter of the past. If we decide, as we must, to continue in this struggle the enemy will be vanquished sooner than either we or the enemy expect. I commend your deliberations today to God's guidance and await your further instructions.

[1] *Delivered at Umuahia, 11 October 1967.*   [2] *See* DOC *110.*
[3] *See* DOC *112.*   [4] *See* DOC *131.*

140.
'Enough is Enough'—Asika appeals to Ibos[1]

. . . Let me say a few words to the embattled and embittered people of the Central-Eastern State. . . . Some of you, the Ibo of the Central-Eastern State, suffered either directly or indirectly from the acts of some of your brothers, especially in the former Northern Region. It is true the tragedy was not wholly unprovoked. It is true that the tragedy occurred because of the dissolution of the established patterns of order and authority which occasioned and was furthered by the initial coup d'état. But it is also more true that nothing could excuse or justify the terrible horror of those dark days. Out of this terrible experience you resolved, and rightly, that your other Nigerian brothers and sisters must show that they are aware that you have been hurt. They must appease you and they must make amends. This resolve and this decision you made very clear and you demanded of your leaders that they be tough and unyielding in securing these goals so that you, the Ibo people, could once again resume the normal pattern of your lives in security and with hope.

Your other Nigerian brothers were sorry and are sorry, very sorry. They have demonstrated this sorrow in many ways: in public speeches, and in the public actions they have taken and in those actions they have refused to take.

I know that you, the Ibo people, had not lost hope; and that you would not have appeared to have lost hope if you were not unfortunately saddled with an ambitious and irresponsible leadership. A leadership that saw in your sorrow not the challenge for sacrifice, which you expected, but an opportunity to achieve their personal ambitions. A leadership that saw in your resolve for toughness not the grounds for bargaining but rather the excuse for the pursuit of their own goals. They preached to you a gospel of hate and lies. They sought to induce, in you, unnatural fears and unnatural appetites. They tried, with cleverness but with viciousness, to cut all ties between you and your other Nigerian brothers and sisters so that you too would come to believe that there is no hope but death for you in Nigeria. As long ago as September last year, this leadership set you on a road that could only lead to even greater and even more horrible tragedy, to you and to your interests. The road to 'Biafra.' The road to war.

Mr Chukwuemeka Ojukwu and his collaborators in pursuing their wild and criminal policies claimed, and sought to appear as the defenders of your interests, your lives and your property. Yet as a result of their policies, they have achieved the actual destruction of these very interests. A destruction which even now continues. You, the many many thousands of people who had abandoned your homes from Enugu, Nsukka and other areas of the war know the sufferings, the losses you have undergone. Yet, each day this leadership, from the relative safety of their hide-out persist in telling you lies about the fortunes of the war. They persist in asking you to sacrifice yet more losses, lives and property, in defence of an idea called 'Biafra'. They forget, but we cannot forget, that even in the conflict of ideas it is people who die.

Come forward now and let us stop this war. This wanton destruction of lives and property. Enough is enough. You have seen the contrast between the security and prosperity which Ojukwu promised you, by seeking to cut the cords that tie you with the country, and the destruction, the waste and the insecurity in which you now live. I am speaking to you as a fellow Nigerian, an Iboman, who also has suffered. Even as I speak to you I do not know the extent of the waste, the damage, the destruction that has been done to my home at Onitsha, to my families and my friends and to all those very dear to me. Can you imagine that I do not care?

I wish to convey to you the sincere assurances of the Commander-in-Chief of the Armed Forces; the conviction of the many thousands of Ibo people presently living in other parts of Nigeria, and my own certainty that it is not the wish of anyone to seek your surrender so as to treat you as a conquered people. Nor is it the wish of anyone to take your homeland from you either by force or otherwise. All that is required of you is that you give up the idea of secession and the rebellion; that you accept the present division of the country into twelve States as a viable and hopeful basis for rebuilding our country. The rest of the country is waiting, patiently, for you to rejoin them and then together in freedom and with equality, to discuss and resolve the proper relationships that should exist between individual Nigerians, between the individual and the Governments, between the States and the Central Governments, and between the twelve States in an indissoluble Federation.

To those of you who fled from your homes, in Enugu and the areas of

Nsukka I wish to make a special appeal that you now return. Your protection and security are assured. I appeal to the civil servants to return to their posts and to their duties, willing to give service loyally and in the best traditions of Public Service within the framework of one Nigeria. To the teachers, the traders, the artisans and farmers and to the working people to please return and resume their normal life. Your protection and your security are assured, so long as you remain law-abiding.

You have shown your other Nigerian brothers that you were hurt. You have shown, beyond argument, that you cannot be hurt with impunity. You have shown that you are men. Although now Mr Ojukwu with his radio and his talking-soldiers is threatening to turn your manhood into a joke and into a lie, with his ridiculous lies about Enugu, Nsukka, Calabar, Bonny, etc.

By the time I am established in my office at Enugu, which will be very soon, I will have a sufficient number of Nigeria Policemen who would help to maintain internal law and order. It is my urgent desire, and work has already started on some of these, to resume as quickly as possible all essential services; water supply, telephone communications, postal services, health and welfare and electricity. I also plan as a matter of urgency to reopen schools and colleges, to begin work on the rehabilitation of the University of Nigeria, Nsukka so that our sons and daughters who have suffered so much, who have lost so much in terms of education can begin again to study and work for a greater tomorrow.

In the meantime, I can assure all university students that arrangements will be made for them to continue their interrupted studies, in other Nigerian Universities. Already, I have the personal assurance of the authorities of my own University, the University of Ibadan, that they are anxious to have all their old and new students and other students whose careers have been so sadly interrupted.

I ask you now, I will ask you again and often, when next I speak to you from Enugu, you fathers of our families, mothers of our homes, to call home from the battle-field your sons, our sons and our brothers. Tell those who ask you to send your sons to die that when all the sons are dead the lineages and the families die too. And that the lineages and the families must survive. Now the only security, the only hope lies in the return to Nigeria, in the return to your friends, to your brothers, to your sisters, to other Nigerians who are prepared and willing to welcome you back.

The rebels, in arms, are invited to lay down their arms, or better still turn over the arms to the Nigerian Army. All rebels who do so, will be treated with clemency and understanding. Already the Federal Military Government has stated that all soldiers, no matter on which side they fought, would be fully rehabilitated. Indeed I can assure you that it is the decision of the Federal Military Government, to start as soon as peace returns, a general programme for the rehabilitation of all persons displaced as a result of the crises of the past eighteen months.

I wish to assure all those people who had, during the anxious months in the past year, abandoned their property, their places of work in the North, in Lagos and elsewhere within the Federation that they can plan to return to these places. Those of you who out of panic abandoned your positions in the Federal Public Service, in National Corporations, Institutions and Universities can plan to return. The Chairman of the Federal Public Service Commission and the heads of other institutions have in most cases frozen your posts and await the return of most of you. It would be a lie, however, were I to tell you that all persons, including those who planned and are leading the rebellion can return to their former posts. Nigeria does not owe such people a living. They have themselves to blame. . . .

We have before us a country torn by the distresses and the ruins of a civil war. But we also have before us a country, that has through the very agonies of this war won her right to self-determination. We, all have struggled; we, all have suffered. We, have all, now, earned the right to call ourselves Nigerians. I am convinced that when the ashes of the present must have settled; that when our wounds must have been healed, that, it would be said that all Nigerians fought hard and gallantly to achieve and to sustain their common destiny as one people and one nation. And it would be said that the Ibo people of the Central-Eastern State fought as hard, as bravely as other Nigerians, even though they fought on the wrong side. And it is because they fought so hard, and that other Nigerians had to fight harder, that Nigeria survives. It is on this understanding that all Nigerians, without exception, can move forward in confidence and in equality to resume the work of development.

We have before us the difficult, the agonizing, work of reconstruction, reconciliation and the restoration of confidence. The work is immense and challenging. The road to success is littered with obstacles. There will be mistakes, there will be errors but with courage and determination and honesty, we shall overcome these problems. If we look at the history of other places, in other ages, we find other people whose experiences have been similar to and even worse than our present discontents and who have out of the challenge of such experiences emerged as greater and more civil societies. History is on our side. . . .

[1] *Delivered in Lagos on 10 November 1967.*

141.
Biafran Press Conference in House of Commons[1]

. . . Since arriving in London from Biafra a little over a week ago, I have been disturbed at the inaccurate reporting in some sections of your Press and the B.B.C. concerning events in my country, and I therefore welcome this opportunity of correcting some of these errors and answering any questions you may care to put to clarify the situation for you.

In the first place, I want to make it crystal clear that the declaration of the independent Republic of Biafra was not the arbitrary decision of a Military Governor, but was determined by a constituent assembly, representative of all areas of the country and all ethnic groups.

Secondly, it was not a decision taken hastily, but came after many months of attempted settlement following upon the slaughter of innocent people of Eastern Nigerian origin, resident in other parts of the Federation of Nigeria, and the subsequent problem of re-settling the thousands of refugees returning to the East.

I want to refute the impression that has been created that those in charge of the Federal Government have always been so concerned about 'One Nigeria' but that it is the East who are the destroyers of Nigerian Unity. The facts are that it was General Gowon himself who first spoke of secession— secession of the Northern Region—when after continued massacres of Easterners he considered 'there was no longer any basis for unity' and therefore the North should secede. It was on British advice that this policy was abandoned!

Ever since independence in 1960, the idea of 'One Nigeria' had no greater advocates than the Nigerians living East of the Niger. Under the civilian government, concession after concession was made by Eastern Nigeria in the interests of preserving unity. Under the military regime, it was a son of Eastern Nigeria, General Ironsi, who met his death at the hands of Northern murderers because he proposed greater unification within the Federation. We wanted unity based on equality of citizenship irrespective of one's place of origin—a Nigeria where one's suitability for a job depended on qualifications and not on one's region of origin—a Nigeria where one could live and move in any part of the Federation in freedom and security. But the Moslems have shown us that they want a unit based on domination so that they may realise their age-old ambition to reach the sea and control the whole of Nigeria, if necessary by force. This is not unity but oppression and enslavement, and this our people will resist for as long as we draw breath.

Ladies and Gentlemen, I am from Biafra, but I am not Ibo. I come from what is termed 'a minority area', and so it is, I think, appropriate that I should make clear the attitude of the minority groups in this present situation, for again this is something that has been grossly misrepresented in certain organs of your Press. It is incorrect and mischievous to suggest that the minority groups in Biafra are not fully in support of the actions of their Government. Biafra is not a military dictatorship. Full consultation takes place with the civilian representatives of the various ethnic groups and their advice is sought. We who come from the minority areas, know that the attacks in Northern Nigeria were not only made upon Ibos, but on all Nigerians of Eastern origin, and we, along with all other Biafrans, feel that this present struggle is one for the very survival of our people, and for our right to live as free and equal citizens in our own land. . . .

From your Press and radio it would appear that all is over and Biafra has been conquered. I want to tell you that this is far from the truth. Biafran forces have consolidated their positions and are continuing to fight hard to defend their homeland from the invaders—and remember that the troops are fully supported by a mobilised 'citizens' army' with an indomitable spirit. What a picture it is, Ladies and Gentlemen, virtually a people's army defending itself against the Nigerian Army, which is receiving military aid from both the Soviet Union and Great Britain, as well as the large commercial houses whose equipment has been used to transport Federal soldiers to our soil. But our people are fighting back, and successfully too, so don't write us off so easily. . . .

I feel sure that the questions now coming to mind are—What can be done?

What should be done? Might I suggest that as the O.A.U. has failed, here perhaps is an opportunity and a test for the Commonwealth.

If we are truly a family of nations, then here is an opportunity for practical concern to be shown for one of the members of that family. In the first place, the Commonwealth might send an independent team of investigators to look into the charges of atrocities against civilians—particularly in the Mid-West —and to move into areas in the wake of Federal troops to prevent such outrages taking place. This is the most urgent and immediate move that should be made.

Secondly, the Commonwealth Secretariat might explore ways and means of securing a basis on which both parties in the dispute might be brought together, and a cease fire agreed upon whilst talks proceed. But this attempt must be a sincere attempt. Britain, as the mother country, must be completely neutral: military aid to either side should cease whilst the exploratory talks are in progress. Britain's information media must refrain from one-sided reporting. It is only in this context that we would be able to recognise Britain's sincerity and constructive approach to the settlement of the conflict. . . .

[1] *Delivered by Mr. James Udo-Affia in a committee room of the House of Commons on 7 November 1967, under the auspices of the Movement for Colonial Freedom.*

142.
Ojukwu's Address to Consultative Assembly, January 1968[1]

Respected Chiefs and Elders, eminent Ladies and Gentlemen, proud and brave Biafrans.

It once again gives me great pleasure to welcome you all to this meeting which I have had to call at such short notice. As you know it has been my practice to consult you from time to time and to keep you informed about the latest developments in the conflict between our young Republic and Nigeria.

When I addressed this Assembly in October,[2] we were just recovering from the shock of the attempt by some of our misguided sons and non-Biafrans, to whom we had entrusted the command of our forces, to overthrow the Government of this Republic. The disaster of our withdrawal from the capital city of Enugu was the direct consequence of that subversion organized by Gowon and his collaborators.

Our situation at that time was grave. The enemy were in parts of our capital and we needed to drive them completely out of it; the enemy were pressing on us from Calabar where they had landed during the second week of October. We had to push them back to the beaches. In the Ogoja area, the enemy were seeking means of linking up with the forces in Calabar. . . . I pledged my word before you that, subject only to your assent, the Armed Forces would continue to prosecute the war against our aggressors till victory is won. You in this august assembly, signified your unanimous determination to prosecute the war to the bitterest end. For my part and that of the Armed Forces, we took up the challenge.

Today, three months since that date, we have not only succeeded in avoiding what had loomed as grave disaster, we have also been able to hold the enemy down in most of these sectors. In Bonny, we succeeded in pushing the enemy out of all but the southernmost tip of the island. We repulsed the first enemy attack on Onitsha at a cost of nearly three battalions against the enemy; but we were sure that the enemy would make some further attempt on the town. Altogether then, we had war on our hands in every sector. . . .

In November the enemy made another and more disastrous attempt to invade Onitsha. Five ships were sunk and more than two enemy battalions destroyed in the operations.

In the last several days, the enemy have opened a new front in the Nsukka west sector, with the aim of cutting out lines of communication between Udi and Onitsha, and thereby imperilling our defence of the two positions. I am proud to say that our troops have been equal to the new assault and have dealt a drastic blow on the aggressors in that sector. The operation to liberate Ogoja Province continues, and our troops have already liberated several towns formerly held by the enemy. . . .

You have heard of the alleged plan of the British Government to send 1,000 regular marines to aid the Nigerian offensives on that island. The British Government has denied it; and since that denial was made by British Ministers in and out of Parliament we are prepared to accept it in spite of our previous unhappy experiences with British officials denials. . . .

Gowon has been threatening to capture Port Harcourt in the very near future and has even set himself a date. As a man who cannot learn from bitter experience, he is certain to renew his suicidal offensive in the Port Harcourt-Bonny area. We know the strategic importance of Port Harcourt and shall do everything in our power to defend it. War is determination and victory the triumph of that determination.

In the Calabar sector, our forces have gallantly resisted what was obviously a major thrust by the enemy. As I address you, a grim battle is raging in that sector. For over three months of fighting, the enemy were confined to the immediate vicinity of sub-urban Calabar. Following Gowon's New Year desperate orders to his troops, the enemy made more determined efforts to dislodge our forces from their positions and actually succeeded in doing so in a few cases.

The story of enemy presence in the Calabar areas has been the same as in other areas where they were able to set foot. Mass killings, wanton molestation and harassment, wholesale looting and assault have been the order of the day. Reports keep coming in of barbaric crimes and unspeakable cruelties. The enemy have not hidden the fact that it is their desire in this war to annihilate the people of this Republic and expropriate or destroy all their property.

The last few days have witnessed massive and desperate offensive by the enemy against our troops in all sectors, particularly in the Calabar, Nsukka and Nkalagu sectors. They have been able to do this as a result of continued massive assistance from Britain and Russia. Two days ago the enemy virtually razed the Slessor Memorial Hospital to the ground, killing the doctor and patients. But, in spite of these, our troops have remained undaunted and determined to resist until the enemy is vanquished. It is for you in this

Assembly speaking the voice of the people, to renew your mandate to the Government and the fighting forces.

So far for the war.

In spite of the war, we have been doing other things than fighting Gowon and his men. On December 8, 1967, I inaugurated the Biafra Court of Appeal. Our peace-loving people are deeply committed to the rule of law and the proper administration of justice. It is, therefore, essential and proper that, even at this perilous period of our history, the administration of justice should be upheld in all its independence and impartiality. It was a mark not only of our absolute belief in justice and the rights of the common people, but also of our determination to maintain our sovereignty.

As Nigeria wages her war of genocide against the peaceful people of Biafra, Radio Nigeria continued to make the claim that Gowon and his Nigerian and foreign accomplices and collaborators are engaged in the nonsensical task of 'keeping Nigeria one'. It is revealing, however, that immediately after the enunciation of the slogan the Lagos propaganda medium proceeds to spell out in a war song the meaning of 'keeping Nigeria one', namely, to pillage our property, ravish our womenfolks, murder our menfolk and complete the pogrom of 1966. Significantly, and characteristically of Nigeria, this war song is yelled out in Hausa and is not reproduced in any other language of the country which they are claiming 'to keep one'. Not that this bothers us in Biafra; but its significance should be clear to those non-Hausas still remaining part of ill-fated Nigeria.

What concerns us is that the reaction of the world to the genocidal war being waged by Nigeria against Biafra has, for the most part been one of silence and indifference and occasionally of veiled hostility to Biafra. It is however gratifying that signs of change are becoming evident. Expatriate doctors, clergymen, teachers, technicians, businessmen, who have been in Biafra and seen the truth, have gone home to narrate to their people their personal observation and experiences. A number of independent observers and press correspondents have also come to Biafra to see things for themselves and have consequently been impelled to disturb the studied silence of their fellow countrymen. As a result, the case for Biafra has gradually begun to be heard and understood. Only a short while ago, a foreign political analyst cogently saw our case as a fundamental struggle against the attempt by Nigerians to exterminate us in the name of maintaining the territorial integrity of Nigeria. The analyst, Dr. Conor Cruise O'Brien, was the renowned United Nations Representative who incidentally had helped to bring to an end the foreign-organized secession of Katanga in the early 1960's. Concluding his article, Dr. O'Brien remarked:

'A sovereign legitimism which treats its boundaries as more sacrosanct than the lives of stigmatized or refractory peoples is no more attractive in Africa than it was in Europe, and hardly likely to endure long'.

Here, I must crave your indulgence to deal in some detail, upon the background of what has brought us to our present position. It is not a new story; but it is worth reminding ourselves.

Any fair minded observer who had followed or studied the evolution of Nigeria since its creation by the British would not find it difficult to understand the case and standpoint of Biafra in the present conflict. In all spheres of life in the now defunct Federation of Nigeria—economic, social, cultural, political and constitutional—Biafrans (then Eastern Nigerians) were in the forefront of the struggle for unity and equality, justice and progress.

Economically, from the Amalgamation of 1914 down to the late 1950's, Biafra, as an area, was relegated to the background as a destitute area. National installations, projects and utilities were deliberately sited outside Biafra. The siting of military, police and other security establishments are relevant to the present situation. The National Munitions Factory, the Training Base and Headquarters of the Nigerian Army, and the Training Base and Headquarters of the Nigerian Air Force were all located in Northern Nigeria. The National Naval Base was set up in Apapa. The Northern Police Training College was built at Kaduna (Northern Nigeria) and the Southern Police Training College at Ikeja (Western Nigeria). But Biafrans in their un-flinching belief in Nigerian unity were prepared to entrust their security to people in various parts of Nigeria.

Biafrans lost a tremendous lot economically when they were expelled from Nigeria. To the neglect of our home districts we had invested confidently in the economic development of Nigeria. We unreservedly built houses, hotels, market stalls, etc., in various parts of Nigeria, sometimes on the strength of mere Certificate of Occupancy which could be, and indeed often were, re-voked at will in Northern Nigeria.

We provided high and intermediate level manpower for the economic development of the whole country, only to be later frustrated and expelled from positions we had earned on merit. Biafrans built schools and colleges and supplied teachers and lecturers for general education throughout the country. In every corner of the then Federation of Nigeria, we built hospitals and nursing homes and provided doctors and nurses for healing and tending the sick. Culturally, we strove to identify ourselves with the peoples of any areas in which we settled. We spoke their language; we inter-married with them and on the floor of the Northern House of Assembly (in February-March 1964), Northern Nigerians declared that they had conquered us culturally because we wore their dresses. In spite of all these, we were physically and socially segregated from the indigenous people in Northern Nigeria. As for Western Nigerians, they prided themselves on their 'tradi-tional reluctance' to reside in and contribute to the development of places outside their region.

But it is in the struggle for unity, equality and justice, in the field of political and constitutional development that there was perhaps the most striking contrast between the attitude of Biafrans and Nigerians. Ever since the Amalgamation in 1914 of the two Nigerias—Northern Nigeria and Southern Nigeria, the constitutional merger was always 'far from popular' among Northern Nigerians who consistently and openly denounced it as 'a mistake'.

On six different occasions since 1950 onwards—in January 1950, in May 1953, and in May, June, July and September 1966—Northern Nigerians threatened or demanded virtual or actual secession from the rest of the former Nigeria. And at one time during this period, in 1954, Western Nigeria also threatened secession. . . .

Yet again, in the following month of July 1966, Northern Nigerian Army Officers and men organized and carried out a rebellion which had for its motto 'ARABA', the Hausa term for SECESSION. After the murder of General Ironsi and other Biafran Army Officers and men, so the rebels planned, Gowon was to declare himself the 'Supreme Commander' of the 'Republic of the North' and was to fly the Northern Nigerian flag—a piece of cloth with lateral stripes of red, yellow, black, green and khaki. General Ironsi and a large number of Biafran Army Officers and men were indeed murdered, and Gowon did hoist his secessionist flag in front of the Headquarters of the 2nd Battalion of the Nigerian Army at Ikeja, where it flew from the end of July to end of August 1966.

The rebellious Northern Nigerian Army Officers and men only agreed to a cease-fire on two conditions which granted the secession they were demanding, namely: that the then Federation of Nigeria be split into its component parts; and that all Southern Nigerians resident in Northern Nigeria be repatriated to their homeland, and vice versa. In accordance with this demand, all available aircraft at Ikeja Airport were immediately commandeered and used in repatriating the families and belongings of Northern Nigerian Army Officers and civil servants in the Lagos area. Again, it was at my instance that on August 9, 1966, about a week after these secessionist demands and genocidal activities, representatives of Military leaders met in Lagos to seek what should be done 'to keep Nigeria one.'

Lastly, as late as September 1966, Northern Nigeria returned to its earlier proposal of 1953 for the break-up of Nigeria and the establishment of a 'Common Services Organization'. . . .

This was the considered view of Northern Nigeria following detailed and extensive consultation of all sections of Northern Nigerian opinion. While the Conference was still in progress, the Northern Nigerian delegation changed their stand. They now wanted a strong Federal Government which they hoped to dominate. Unfortunately, this new idea ran counter to the feelings and aspirations of the majority of Northern peoples and the impression was created in the popular mind in the North that the Ad Hoc Constitutional Conference was going to recommend a strong Central Government. Rioting ensued in the North, and the September massacres, the most terrible of the series, were unleashed.

And so, for the third time in the same year (1966), Northern Nigerians murdered and maimed thousands of Biafrans resident in their Region, and looted and destroyed their property. This brought the total number of Biafrans slaughtered in the 1966 pogrom to over 30,000. And over two million survivors of this genocide sought refuge in Biafra.

You hardly need to be reminded that on none of these occasions did Biafrans as citizens of the country obtain from the Central Government protection of life and property or redress for wrongs suffered. You need not be reminded that, on no occasion during these pogroms organized with clock-work regularity, did we seek revenge for the injuries inflicted on us. The perpetrators of genocide and other atrocities in Nigeria relished their wicked deeds with abandon. At that point, however, Biafrans painfully realized that in spite of their efforts over the decades 'to keep Nigeria one', the political disengagement which Northern Nigeria and Western Nigeria had been demanding for the past sixteen years was the only means by which Biafrans could survive and the genocide end . . ..

These underlying causes were to be found in the incompatible nature of social values between Northern and Southern Nigeria, in the religious fanaticism of Northern Nigeria and at the centre. As long as these conditions existed, the struggle of units of the Federation for control of power would persist. Violence would continue to be cyclical, and political instability and personal insecurity would be the consequence. There had to be political disengagement if the blood-bath was not to recur. Each Region had to take its fate into its own hands. In particular Biafrans, in the light of their bitter experience, could only be assured of their safety and survival after they had taken their security into their own hands. . . .

The various steps which I took to secure a peaceful solution to the Nigeria/Biafra crisis before and after the meeting of the Supreme Council at Aburi in Ghana are already well-known to you. . . . You will recall that at Aburi, at my own instance, all the Military Leaders solemnly declared that they renounced the use of force as a means of settling the problems confronting the country, and re-affirmed their faith in discussions and negotiations as the only way of resolving the crisis. We in Biafra have adhered to that declaration ever since and have taken up arms only in self-defence.

Even in late May 1966 when we were almost completely driven out of the Federation of Nigeria, this august Assembly was still hopeful of a peaceful settlement of the crisis. . . . But on July 6, 1967, instead of reciprocating this open door policy, Nigeria started a war of aggression against us. . . .

We have indicated that we are the victims of aggression, and that those who started the war should stop it. If they stop attacking us we will stop fighting in self-defence. The truth of course is that Gowon and his men are simply fighting a war of genocide and plunder. . . .

Although Gowon claims that his war against Biafra is an 'internal' affair, its implications already transcend the boundaries of Biafra and Nigeria. For by the very commission of genocide by the soldiers and civilians whom he organized and led during the pogrom of 1966 and by the army over which he has claimed to be Commander-in-Chief since 1967, Gowon now stands condemned before the world. . . . Yet, Gowon claims to be 'a Christian and the son of a Methodist Minister' a claim calculated to impress foreign churchmen and press correspondents who do not know that he is in reality the leader of a Muslim jihad directed towards the annihilation of Biafrans and the islamization of Biafra.

The involvement of certain foreign powers, notably Britain and Russia, in the present Biafra/Nigeria conflict deserves some mention. It is regrettable that these two powers should have openly identified themselves with the regime of force in Lagos and supplied weapons of destruction to Nigeria for continuing the aggression and genocide. In the case of Britain, she has been supplying Nigeria with military, naval and air equipment and personnel before and since the war began. British naval experts planned and executed the operations against not only Bonny but also Calabar. . . . More recently Britain, in spite of her financial difficulties, has granted a loan of £10 million to Nigeria, as was announced at Kaduna, the real seat of power in Nigeria, by Sir David Hunt, the British High Commissioner.

o

Britain's Elder Dempster Lines, and the West African Conference Lines in which the Elder Dempster Lines is the leading firm, started the economic blockade of Biafra even before the measure was officially announced by Gowon. Shell-BP Petroleum Company, a firm in which the British Government has a preponderant financial interest, collaborated with Nigeria in the attack on Bonny in July 1967. A couple of months ago Shell-BP paid to Nigeria the oil royalties that properly belonged to Biafra. This is nothing but an act of war. . . .

As for Russia, she has not had a long enough acquaintance with Africa to understand its peoples. She has had setbacks in the Congo (Kinshasa), Ghana and Guinea and is naturally anxious to regain a foothold in West Africa, and so to further her political strategy in Africa, north and south of the Sahara. Russia and Czechoslovakia stepped in to sell jets to the Nigerian Air Force after the temporary refusal of Britain to do so. Russia has also delivered to Nigeria a number of coastal craft. She and various other East European countries have offered Nigeria a loan totalling £33 million. Hitherto we have had no quarrel with Russia, and one would have thought she would understand the self-expression of our progressive people and our determination to be free from the fetters of neo-colonialism which have immensely contributed to the present conflict.

With regard to African States and the Organization for African Unity, Nigeria has tried intimidation at one time and blackmail at another. For instance, she attacked two African nations through her radio and the press for raising the Biafra/Nigeria issue in the United Nations. She has threatened to foment communal strife within some African countries if they dared to raise their voice in support of Biafra. . . .

More serious still, Nigeria has blackmailed African States with what is variously referred to as the theory of 'disintegrating dominoes', or 'Balkanization'. This is simply the idea that, if Nigeria's disintegration is accepted, other African countries may also disintegrate. It goes without saying that this is a mere ruse. In the history of nations, no country has ever broken up simply because another did. Each case of dissolution of a political union has always been due to unique local factors. . . . The disintegration of the Federation of Nigeria cannot be properly referred to the dismemberment of the Federation of Rhodesia and Nyasaland.

African leaders have also often been warned by Nigeria of their obligation, under the O.A.U. Charter, to respect the territorial integrity of member states. Our understanding of that part of the Charter is that it can legitimately be invoked if one member state attempts to enlarge its territory at the expense of another member state, but certainly not in respect of the emergence of new states arising from the disintegration of a member state.

Africans throughout the continent should waken to the grim prospect that, if the current Nigerian position—'smite to unite'—is allowed to prevail, it may be goodbye to the promotion of peaceful and conciliatory solutions to any serious problems that may confront differing communities of any African state in future. As a well-informed and independent writer has recently observed: 'African and other opinion may yet come to regard the effort to hold the Federation (of Nigeria) together and the means used for this purpose as far more ominous for Africa than dissolution into the major units could have been'. And, whatever the predictions of the pessimists, we Biafrans are satisfied that Biafra may yet prove to be a beacon for the furtherance of unity in other states of Africa—and of the world, for that matter—rather than a precedent for their disintegration. . . . Never again on this Continent of Africa will one section of a political community seek with impunity the total annihilation of another section—for any reason whatsoever—without contemplating the possible consequences of such an act in the light of the Nigeria/Biafra experience. . . .

Gowon has been bewildered by the unity and solidarity of our people. Lagos has been frustrated by the utter failure of its propaganda media to cause dissension and disaffection among our people. The truth is that by inter-marriage, cultural intercourse and economic interdependence, Biafrans have developed common traditions and identity of outlook over the centuries.

And for three-quarters of a century now Biafra has been ruled as a single political unit; so that the vast majority of the population have grown accustomed to the fact of the uniqueness of the political entity which we now know as Biafra. Not even the divisive forces of the turbulent history of Nigeria has broken the cultural and economic homogeneity which has evolved within Biafran territory. Rather, their bitter experience of recent times has further strengthened the solidarity of all Biafrans. We all suffered together in Nigeria and are determined to survive together in Biafra. All Biafrans are today united by a common experience, a common purpose and a common destiny. . . .

The total commitment of all Biafrans to the current war is no longer in doubt. Gowon and his collaborators have tried desperately to talk the world into thinking that this has been the struggle of what they call 'Ojukwu and his rebel gang'. The world however is beginning to understand that as far as Biafrans are concerned, it is a people's war of survival. The Biafra Govern-ment has no War Budget; rather it depends on voluntary donation of the people. We are fighting the war entirely with an Army, Navy and Air Force of volunteers. There is no conscription into the Biafran Armed Forces, instead we are overwhelmed by the large crowds of ablebodied young men who come forward every day to enlist. . . . The Biafran war of survival is not 'Ojukwu's rebellion'. . . .

After their experience of the last half-century, Biafrans can never again entrust their safety and security to people outside their homeland. . . .

[1] *Delivered at Umuahia, 27 January 1968* (Biafra Newsletter, *I*, 7).
[2] *See* DOC *139.*

143.
Propaganda Unlimited: '39 Accusations against Nigeria'[1]

. . . (22) TURNING MINORITY AREAS INTO BATTLEGROUNDS

The sweet love affair between the Northerners and the unfortunate Biafrans whom they have bamboozled into believing they are 'minorities' warms up when the unruly Hausa troops approach any Biafran 'minority' village and start mortaring and shelling. The indiscriminate shelling (as many as 500 in twelve hours!) finds targets among the women and children whom the emirs profess to love and to protect. Those who are not killed are slaughtered, and for the benefit of the press, a handful are carted back to Lagos and Kaduna, away from the 'liberated' areas to somewhere where their services can be more readily dictated.

(23) FLOUTING GENEVA CONVENTION
Ninety per cent of the Hausas, Tivs and Fulanis who make up the so-called Nigeria army have never been to school, can neither read nor write and are not interested in 'Grammar'.

The Geneva Convention to them is nonsense. They have no regard for it except as a bother.

Consequently, all those fighting for Nigeria adopt the code of vandals in place of the international code. . . .

(24) TURNING THE HANDS OF THE CLOCK BACK
The feudalistic Emirs are assuming in their ignorance that no revolution has in fact taken place in Nigeria; that all that is required is a military conquest of Biafra, and the old dead Federation of Nigeria, complete with its corruption and political gymnastics, will again be resuscitated.

This single conviction is responsible for the arrogance, recrimination, and remorselessness of the Hausa-controlled Lagos Junta. It cannot see that the old Sardauna Nigeria is simply no more.

(25) STRIVING TO PROMOTE BACKWARDNESS
The Hausas and Fulanis believe that once Biafrans are exterminated, everybody will be equal. There will be no educated men, no progressive people with new ideas. Those so-called Nigerians who will be left can then settle down to an easy life of indolence in which population will be the basis of merit. Everything in the 'national cake' will then be shared out to those idiots from the most populous parts of that imagined country.

Also, the one element which inspires progress—namely challenge—will have been eliminated and with it the roots of democracy. In short, the fear of progress will have been removed for ever. . . .

(27) RE-INTRODUCING COLONIALISM INTO AFRICA
The Hausas and Fulanis were the most reluctant to achieve self-government and let the British go. Even after Nigerian Independence, the bogey of 'Northernisation' still carved out a kingdom for British and other non-Nigerian nationals to make careers in Northern Nigeria in preference to Southern Nigerians equally qualified and less expensive to maintain.

Today, a Northerner has usurped power in the Central Government of Nigeria and is hastening to undo the Independence struggle which Biafrans successfully fought against British Colonialism.

To make sure of a greater success in plunging Nigeria into the dark ages, the Northern clique has re-admitted Britain in every field, has signed a military pact with Russia and has ensured the final and perpetual return to a pre-Independence colonial status.

The tragedy of it all is that African Nations watch it happening with absolute unconcern.

(28) WAGING A RELIGIOUS WAR

The killings of Biafran officers in the former Nigerian Army and civilians resident in Northern Nigeria, Lagos and Ibadan, were condoned by the Gowon Regime with the smug satisfaction that 'Allah in his infinite mercy' had made it possible for 'another Northerner' to be at the head of affairs in Nigeria.

This attitude was in keeping with the late Sardauna's boast to continue Dan Fodio's jihad till he dipped the koran in the sea.

'To make war on the heathen, if one has the power is a declared duty', the Sardauna said in his autobiography.

In short, convert the heathen Biafrans to Islam, or exterminate them. . . .

[1] *From* Thirty-Nine Accusations (*Enugu, 1968*).

144.
The Churches' Call for Peace[1]

The Roman Catholic Church and the WCC unite in one voice in a most urgent appeal to both contesting parties for an immediate cessation of armed hostilities in this sad conflict and for the establishment of a lasting peace by honourable negotiations in the highest tradition of Africa. . . .

We further point out that war is an inhuman and futile attempt to settle disputes. In this sad conflict, especially, armed hostilities cannot achieve a settlement of the differences; on the contrary they are liable to bring, on a scale that is frightening to contemplate, only further loss of life, starvation, suffering and devastation. Even if, against all right reason, armed hostilities continue, the parties can never achieve peaceful co-existence without a negotiated settlement. The longer hostilities endure, the more innocent human lives will be sacrificed in violence and bloodshed, the more impoverished and devastated will become this beloved erstwhile land of promise. . . .

We appeal in particular to the African Chiefs of State to offer the contribution of their counsel, their suggestions and, should the case arise, their mediation, with a view to the resolution of this sad conflict. . . .

While it is not our part to declare on the issue of contention, we are bound to call the most immediate attention to the sacred issue of the human right to life itself, which is so seriously threatened on such a vast scale by the horrors and effects of the war. We therefore urge governments and international agencies in a position to act effectively in this matter to secure a denial of external military assistance to both parties, an immediate cessation of hostilities, the necessary assurances of security to both sides on the laying down of arms, and a negotiated peace. . . .

[1] *Issued simultaneously in Geneva on behalf of the World Council of Churches and in Rome on behalf of the Roman Catholic Church, 20 March 1968. Text by courtesy of the British Council of Churches.*

145.
'The Dawn of Lasting Peace'—Gowon[1]

At the beginning of this year, I spoke to you about our hopes for 1968. There have been significant developments on the Nigerian scene since then. I would like to review these briefly with you and to redefine the intentions and policies of the Federal Military Government on the targets laid down for the year 1968.

On the political front, as from tomorrow, the 1st of April, ten of the twelve States will be firmly on their feet. I am glad to inform the nation that the whole of the South-Eastern State has been cleared of rebel forces, and the Military Governor, Col. Esuene, has moved to Calabar, the Headquarters, from where he will henceforth administer the State. There, however, remain some difficulties in fully establishing the Rivers and East-Central States before the rebellion is completely crushed. It will not be long before the Military Governor of the Rivers State, Lt.-Commander Diete-Spiff, goes to the Headquarters of the State. I am gratified by the reports I have received from the Administrator of the East-Central State, Mr Ukpabi Asika, that thousands of civilians are now coming back to the liberated areas to join in the work of reconstruction. I am sure that all the three Eastern States will soon be functioning in a peaceful atmosphere.

The Lagos State Government under Col. Mobolaji Johnson has formally taken over the highly developed social services and other State responsibilities in the former Federal territory of Lagos. Lagos will remain the seat of the Federal Government. A Committee is looking into the special administrative problems arising from the dual status of the City of Lagos. The Lagos State has also assumed full administrative responsibility for the parts of the former Western Region now within the boundary of the new State. I wish to thank the Governments and people of the Western and Lagos States for facilitating the smooth transition.

As for the six States in the former North, these are now fully established and each has its own machinery of government. Brigadier Hassan Usman Katsina, the former Chairman of the Interim Administrative Council, is returning to full time soldiering at the end of an important assignment loyally and dutifully executed. I wish to take this opportunity to express my deep appreciation of Brigadier Hassan's splendid performances in leading the Interim Administrative Council which did a magnificent job in establishing the six new administrations out of the former Regional Government in the North. The smooth transition from one administration to six has been made possible through the full co-operation of all sections of the community; the Emirs and Chiefs, civil servants, some of whose career-prospects were affected by the new arrangements, and N.A. officials and the ordinary man in the street. I am grateful to the Emirs, Chiefs, public officers and people of the six States and particularly to the Interim Administrative Council for their unflinching support of the cause of the Federal Military Government and for the smooth establishment of the States administrations. . . .

I wish to reiterate the necessity for the new structure of the Nigerian Federation with the present minimum of twelve States as the only way of removing the major defect in the political structure of the country. Replacing the former four Regions with the new States is the only means of ensuring political stability and social and economic progress in the country. With the establishment of these States, Nigeria has indeed passed through a historic landmark.

I am conscious of the fact that until the rebellion in the East Central State is completely ended, the Federal Government and the Administrations of the twelve States cannot devote all their energies to constructive activities and the urgent task of nation-building. This is why I have been most anxious to see the end of the rebellion and the dawn of lasting peace.

There are only two ways of ending the rebellion—through peace talks or military suppression.

The Federal Government's position on peace talks is very clear. The rebel leaders must give up secession and accept the twelve States structure.

I have been deliberately silent on the various peace initiatives. I am glad to say that most if not all of these peace initiatives, which the Federal Government appreciates, are based on the preservation of the territorial integrity of Nigeria as one country. The O.A.U. Peace Mission is a case in point. There are two peace initiatives which have been given so much sinister publicity of late that I feel compelled to mention them in passing. I have in mind the peace moves by the Commonwealth Secretariat and by the Vatican and the World Council of Churches.

I wish to state quite firmly that at no time did Mr Arnold Smith discuss with me the possibility of using a Commonwealth Peace Force to separate the so-called combatants. That would be untenable in a situation in which we, as a sovereign country, are committed to putting down an internal rebellion. When the rebels show genuine interest in peace by giving up secession, the O.A.U. Peace Mission and the Commonwealth Secretary-General may have a role to play. It will therefore not be in the public interest for me to say more at this stage.

I must say that I have been rather disturbed by the activities of some Christian bodies which, to me appear to have been misinformed about the Nigerian crisis. The World Council of Churches and the Roman Catholic Church have jointly appealed for ceasefire.[2] I respect this appeal. The Christian love of truth should persuade all church leaders that the only road to lasting peace in Nigeria is for the rebel leaders to give up secession. Bishops and other leading church dignitaries in Nigeria went to Enugu on several occasions to persuade Ojukwu not to try to break up Nigeria. It was all to no avail because Ojukwu was secretly building up the rebel army in preparation for secession. The difficulty in a ceasefire without any agreement by the secessionist leaders to retract and to remain part of Nigeria is that Ojukwu and his foreign backers will certainly use the ceasefire pause to re-arm and prepare for a bloodier conflict in which more innocent lives will be lost. Is that what the Christian world wants for Nigeria?

I must say with all sincerity that some Christians are, through their one-sided activities on the Nigerian crisis, doing incalculable damage. The majority of Christians in Nigeria live outside the rebel-held areas. It appears that the feelings of this majority and the future of Christianity in Nigeria and indeed the real needs of the people in the East Central State are being ignored because of the activities of a few supporters of the secessionist leaders.

As I said earlier, there are two ways of ending the rebellion—peace talks or the sad alternative of total military victory.

Since my New Year message to the Field Commanders to quicken the pace of the military operations, the rate of progress in all the war fronts has been most satisfactory. My message about 31 March was misinterpreted by some information media. As a professional soldier, I know that a war cannot be brought to a complete stop on a predetermined date. A commander knows when a war may start, but cannot tell when it will end. I was conscious of the fact that the rebels would try to continue their defiance beyond that date in the hope of impressing their collaborators at home and abroad without caring about the suffering of the ordinary people.

I am fully satisfied that the backbone of the rebellion has been broken with the recent successes of Federal forces and the overall military position. The task of keeping Nigeria one to safeguard lasting peace will be properly finished no matter the cost and how long it takes. If the Federal Military Government must win a clear-cut military victory we shall. But I wish to repeat my promise to the nation that the military operations will be halted as soon as the rebel leaders forget their dream of an empire, lay down their arms and accept the twelve States structure. It should now be clear to the rebel leaders that secession cannot be sustained by military defiance, false propaganda, futile diplomatic manoeuvres, and irrelevant religious appeals.

I know that there are sceptics who claim that a clear-cut Federal victory will make reconciliation and the reintegration of Ibos impossible. We, who are Nigerians, know that this is not so. We fully appreciate that it will make it difficult, but we have the will to succeed in caring and healing our own wounds. This we shall do, God being our helper. Already there is impressive evidence in the return to normal life in the Ibo-speaking areas, and the gradual reintegration of Ibos with other ethnic groups, in the Mid-Western State. Civilians in the liberated areas of the East Central State are returning in large numbers to the towns and villages previously deserted and are being looked after by Federal troops, and the Administrator of the East Central State and his officials. It is a fact also, that thousands of Ibos are still working and living in Lagos and elsewhere outside the former Eastern Region. These are proof of our ability to solve the problem of reintegration.

It is a fact that due to the vile propaganda of the rebel publicity organs, there are many Ibos in the rebel-held areas who fear for their personal safety. Other Nigerians are ready to welcome back Ibos into their midst and to assure them of their personal security. The Government, for its part, is determined to do all in its power to ensure that no Ibo man is molested or intimidated anywhere in this country. We will direct our attention to the physical safety of every Nigerian no matter his State of origin. . . .

The next phase of the Federal Government's operations is to usher in lasting peace in Nigeria and then embark on a programme of post-war reconstruction and rehabilitation. With the support of the people of Nigeria for the Federal Government, we shall succeed. So help us God.

---

[1] *Broadcast to the nation on 31 March 1968, marking the establishment of the 12 states administration.*

[2] *See* DOC *144.*

146.
'The Beatitudes According to "St. Gowan" [*sic*]'[1]

CHAPTER ONE VERSE 1-17

1. And seizing power in July 1966 . . . and after consulting with the Northern Emirs who had come unto him,
2. He opened his mouth and taught his Northern countrymen saying:
3. Blessed are the children of the North; for unto them has been given yet another rule [? ruler].
4. Blessed are the Yoruba opportunists; for they shall grab the jobs abandoned by the fleeing Easterners; rejoice and be exceedingly glad, for today the Biafrans are being bombed.
5. Blessed are the big foreign businesses; for they shall inherit and settle Nigeria's liabilities. . . .
7. Blessed are the Russian Opportunists; for they shall receive opportunities.
8. Blessed are the Egyptian denigrates; for unto them the Scripture has pronounced woos.
9. Blessed are the conscripted Nigerian Soldiers who have been promised an El Dorado to fight for a cause they do not understand; for unto them Biafra is an elusive mirage. . . .
11. Blessed are the Wole Soyinkas who are persecuted for freedom's sake; for unto them the junta openeth the jail gates of Ibadan, Kaduna and Lagos.
12. Blessed are the David Hunts, the Okoi Arikpos, and the Anthony Enahoros who make all sorts of accusations against the Biafran people— ranging from the country's past political and economic ills to the drying up of water supply and who dish out all manner of lies to foreign Press, for propaganda's sake.
13. Damn the Commonwealth peace initiators and be exceedingly glad; for so great is your favour in Britain; for so bullied ye the O.A.U. mission which came months before them.
14. Ye are the tools of big foreign businesses, but if big foreign businesses hath forsaken their tools, from where shall the super profit come? Ye are thenceforth good for nothing, but to be abandoned to rot in grinding poverty and blazing ignorance.
15. Ye are the dreams of Communist and Imperialist adventurers; the dying 'Giant of Africa' cannot be revived. . . .

[1] *From* Africa Weekly Review, *30 March 1968, p. 10.*

147.
Dr. Azikiwe Holds Press Conference in Paris[1]

We visited five African Heads of State. . . . We appealed to them to use their good offices to urge upon Nigeria to stop its war against Biafra and accept Colonel C. O. Ojukwu's offer of cease fire and immediate resort to the conference table for peace talks without preconditions on either side.

We emphasised to the five African Heads of State that this peace formula was the only realistic way of restoring peace and stability to this part of

Africa and speedily bring to an end the wanton killing of innocent and defenceless civilians.

The five Presidents were reminded that the tragic war had lasted more than nine months and has not solved anything; whilst the ruthless destruction of human lives and property has been intensified. Probably, 100,000 soldiers, on both sides, have died in this war. The number of civilians killed has been tremendous and the property destroyed runs to millions of pounds.

My Mission was satisfied that current world opinion is anxious to see an immediate end to this holocaust and destruction of property. We are justified by the recent statements and appeals made by some African Heads of State, the World Council of Churches, the Vatican, some members of the British House of Lords, some members of the United States Congress, and leading European, British and American newspapers.

It is to these appeals and statements that the people of Biafra have responded, and we hope that Nigeria would reciprocate by stopping this war and go to the conference table without preconditions. If Nigeria has no genocidal aims, as it maintains, now is a great opportunity for it to respect responsible and humanitarian world opinion and agree to the following:

(a) a cease fire on land, air and sea,
(b) the lifting of the economic, military, diplomatic and administrative blockades,

so as to clear the atmosphere for peaceful negotiations without preconditions on either side.

Early this year, Colonel Ojukwu stated categorically that Biafra was ready to agree to an immediate cease fire, to be followed by negotiations for peaceful settlement without preconditions, aimed at lasting peace and harmony with Nigeria. The genuineness of this offer has been doubted in certain circles in Nigeria. My Mission affirmed the genuine nature of this offer and we expect Nigeria to reciprocate.

My Mission also confirmed that throughout this conflict between Biafra and Nigeria, the former has maintained that differences between the two combatants could be settled only on the conference table and not on the battle field. We assured our hosts that Biafra still stood by this policy as the only realistic way to stop the tragic loss of thousands of precious human lives.

Finally, my Mission stressed the genocidal aspect of the war and indicated that it would be to the mutual advantage of both Biafra and Nigeria that the war should be stopped now and peaceful negotiations begin. Otherwise, faced with possible extermination, without the chance of peace negotiations, Biafrans would have no alternative than to continue to fight in self-defence and for self-preservation.

[1] *30 March 1968. (Text by courtesy of Dr. Azikiwe.)*

148.
Tanzania Recognizes Biafra[1]

On behalf of the Government of the United Republic of Tanzania, I have the following statement to make:

The declaration of independence by Biafra on the 30th May, 1967, came after two military coups d'etat—in January and July 1966—and two major pogroms against the Ibo people. These pogroms, which also took place in 1966, resulted in the death of about 30,000 men, women, and children, and made two million people flee from their homes in other parts of Nigeria to the tribal homeland in Eastern Nigeria. These events had been interspersed and followed by official discussions about a new constitution for Nigeria, and also by continued personal attacks on individual Ibos who had remained outside the Eastern Region.

The basic case for Biafra's secession from the Nigerian Federation is that people from the Eastern Region can no longer feel safe in other parts of the Federation. They are not accepted as citizens of Nigeria by the other citizens of Nigeria. Not only is it impossible for Ibos and people of related tribes to live in an assurance of personal safety if they work outside Biafra: it would also be impossible for any representative of these people to move freely and without fear in any other part of the Federation of Nigeria.

These fears are genuine and deep-seated, nor can anyone say they are groundless. The rights and wrongs of the original coup d'etat, the rights and wrongs of the attitudes taken by different groups in the politics of pre- and post-coup Nigeria, are all irrelevant to the fear which Ibo people feel. And the peoples of Eastern Nigeria can point to too many bereaved homes, too many maimed people, for anyone to deny the reasonable grounds for their fears. It is these fears which are the root cause both for the secession, and for the fanaticism with which the people of Eastern Nigeria have defended the country they declared to be independent.

Fears such as now exist among the Ibo peoples do not disappear because someone says they are unjustified, or says that the rest of Nigeria does not want to exterminate the Ibos. Such words have even less effect when the speakers have made no attempt to bring the perpetrators of crimes to justice and when troops under the control of the Federal Nigerian Authorities continue to ill-treat, or allow others to ill-treat, any Ibos who came within their power. The only way to remove the Easterners' fear is for the Nigerian Authorities to accept its existence, to acknowledge the reason for it, and then to talk on terms of equality with those involved about the way forward.

When people have reason to be afraid you cannot reassure them through the barrel of a gun; your only hope is to talk as one man to another, or as one group to another. It is no use the Federal Authorities demanding that the persecuted should come as a supplicant for mercy, by first renouncing their secession from the political unit. For the secession was declared because the Ibo people felt it to be their only defence against extermination. In their minds, therefore, a demand that they should renounce secession before talks are begun, is equivalent to a demand that they should announce their willingness to be exterminated. If they are wrong in this belief they have to be convinced. And they can only be convinced by talks leading to new institutional arrangements which take account of their fears.

The people of Biafra have announced their willingness to talk to the Nigerian Authorities without any conditions. They cannot renounce their secession before talks, but they do not demand that the Nigerians should recognise it; they ask for talks without conditions. But the federal authorities have refused to talk except on the basis of Biafran surrender. And as the Biafrans believe they will be massacred if they surrender, the Federal Authorities are really refusing to talk at all. For human beings do not voluntarily walk towards what they believe to be certain death.

The Federal Government argues that in demanding the renunciation of secession before talks, and indeed in its entire 'Police Action', it is defending the territorial integrity of Nigeria. On this ground it argues also that it has a right to demand support from all other governments, and especially other African governments, for every state, and every state authority, has a duty to defend the sovereignty and integrity of its nation. This is a central part of the function of a national government.

Africa accepts the validity of this point, for African States have more reason than most to fear the effects of disintegration. It is on these grounds that Africa has watched the massacre of tens of thousands of people, has watched the employment of mercenaries of both sides in the current civil war, and has accepted repeated rebuffs of its offers to help by mediation or conciliation.

But for how long should this continue? Africa fought for freedom on the grounds of individual liberty and equality, and on the grounds that every people must have the right to determine for themselves the conditions under which they would be governed. We accepted the boundaries we inherited from colonialism, and within them we each worked out for ourselves the constitutional and other arrangements which felt to be appropriate to the most essential function of a state—that is the safeguarding of life and liberty for its inhabitants.

When the Federation of Nigeria became independent in 1960, the same policy was adopted by all its peoples. They accepted the federal structure which has been established under the colonial system, and declared their intention to work together. Indeed, the Southern States of the Federation—which includes Biafra—delayed their own demands for independence until the North was ready to join them. At the insistence of the North also, the original suggestion of the National Council for Nigeria and the Cameroons (the political party which had its centre in the South) that Nigeria should be broken up into many small states with a strong centre, was abandoned. The South accepted a structure which virtually allowed the more populous North to dominate the rest.

But the constitution of the Federation of Nigeria was broken in January 1966, by the first military coup. All hope of its resuscitation was removed by the second coup, and even more by the pogroms of September and October 1966. These events altered the whole basis of the society: after them it was impossible for political and economic relations between the different parts of the old Federation to be restored. They meant that Nigerian unity could only be salvaged from the wreck of inter-tribal violence and fear by a constitution drawn up in the light of what had happened, and which was generally acceptable to all major elements of the society under the new circumstances. A completely new start had to be made, for the basis of the State had been dissolved in the complete break-down of law and order, and the inter-tribal violence which existed.

The necessity for a new start by agreement was accepted by a conference of military leaders from all parts of the Federation, in Aburi, Ghana, in January, 1967. There is a certain difference of opinion about some of the things which were agreed at that conference. But there is no dispute about the fact that everyone joined in a declaration renouncing the use of force as a means of settling the crisis in Nigeria. Nor does anyone dispute that it was agreed that a new constitution was to be worked out by agreement, and that in the meantime there would be a repeal of all military decrees issued since January, 1966 which reduced the powers of the regions. There was also agreement about rehabilitation payments for those who had been forced to flee their homes, and about members of the armed forces being stationed in their home regions.

The Aburi conference could have provided the new start which necessary if the unity of Nigeria was to be maintained. But before the end of the same month, General Gowon was restating his commitment to the creation of new States, and his determination to oppose any form of confederation. And on the last day of January, the Federal Military Authorities were already giving administrative reasons for delay in the implementation of the agreements reached at Aburi. It was the middle of March before a constitutional decree was issued which was supposed to regularise the position in accordance with the decisions taken there. But unfortunately this decree also included a new clause—which had not been agreed—and which gave the Federal Authorities a reserve power over the Regions, and thus completely nullified the whole operation. Nor had any payment been made by the Federal Government to back up the monetary commitment for rehabilitation which it had accepted in the Ghana meeting.

In short, the necessity for an arrangement which would take account of the fears created during 1966 was accepted at Aburi, and renounced thereafter by the Federal Authorities. Yet they now claim to be defending the integrity of the country in which they failed to guarantee the most elementary safety of the twelve million peoples of Eastern Nigeria. These people had been massacred in other parts of Nigeria without the Federal Authorities apparently having either the will or the power to protect them. When they retreated to their tribal homeland they were expected to accept the domination of the same peoples who instigated, or allowed, their persecution in the country which they are being told is theirs—i.e. Nigeria.

Surely when a whole people is rejected by the majority of the state in which they live, they must have the right to life under a different kind of arrangement which does secure their existence.

States are made to serve people; governments are established to protect the citizens of a state against external enemies and internal wrong-doers. It is on these grounds that people surrender their right and power of self-defence to the government of the state in which they live. But when the machinery of the State, and the powers of the Government, are turned against a whole group of the society on the grounds of racial, tribal, or religious prejudice, then the victims have the right to take back the powers they have surrendered, and to defend themselves.

For while people have a duty to defend the integrity of their state, and even to die in its defence, this duty stems from the fact that it is theirs, and that it is important to their well being and to the future of their children. When the state ceases to stand for the honour, the protection, and the well being of all its citizens, then it is no longer the instrument of those it has rejected. In such a case the people have the right to create another instrument for their protection—in other words, to create another state.

This right cannot be abrogated by constitutions, nor by outsiders. The basis of statehood, and of unity can only be general acceptance by the participants. When more than twelve million people have become convinced that they are rejected, and that there is no longer any basis for unity between them and other groups of people, then unity has already ceased to exist. You cannot kill thousands of people, and keep killing more, in the name of unity. There is no unity between the dead and those who killed them; and there is no unity in slavery or domination.

Africa needs unity. We need unity over the whole continent, and in the meantime we need unity within the existing states of Africa. It is a tragedy when we experience to our goal of unity. But the basis of our need for unity, and the reason for our desire for it, is the greater well being, and the greater security, of the people of Africa. Unity by conquest is impossible. It is not practicable: and even if military might could force the acceptance of a particular authority, the purpose of unity would have been destroyed. For the purpose of unity, its justification, is the service of all the peoples who are united together. The general consent of all the people involved is the only basis on which unity in Africa can be maintained or extended.

The fact that the Federation of Nigeria was created in 1960 with the consent of all people does not alter that fact. That Federation, and that basis of consent, has since been destroyed. Nor is this the first time the world has seen a reduction in political unity. We have seen the creation of the Mali Federation, the creation of a Union between Egypt and Syria, and the establishment of the Federation of Rhodesia and Nyasaland. And we have also seen the dissolution of all these attempts at unity, and the consequent recognition of the separate nations which were once involved. The world has also seen the creation of India and Pakistan out of what was once the India Empire. We have all recognised both these nation states and done our best to help them deal with the millions of people made homeless by the conflict and division. One of these things mean that we have liked these examples of greater disunity. They mean that we recognise that in all these cases the people are unwilling to remain in one political unity.

We recognise Mali, Egypt, Syria, Malawi, Zambia, Pakistan and India. What right have we to refuse, in the name of unity, to recognise the fact of Biafra? For years the people of that State struggled to maintain unity with the other peoples in the Federation of Nigeria; even after the pogroms of 1966 they tried to work out a new form of unity would guarantee their safety; they have demonstrated by ten months of bitter fighting that they have decided upon a new political organisation and are willing to defend it.

The world has taken it upon itself to utter many ill-informed criticisms of the Jews of Europe for going to their deaths without any concerted struggle. But out of sympathy for the sufferings of these people, and in recognition of the world's failure to take action at the appropriate time, the United Nations established the State of Israel in territory which had belonged to the Arabs for thousands of years. It was felt that only by the establishment of a Jewish homeland, and a Jewish national state, could Jews be expected to live in the world under conditions of human security. Tanzania has recognised the State of Israel and will continue to do so because of its belief that every people must have some place in the world where they are not liable to be rejected by their fellow citizens.[2]

But the Biafrans have now suffered the same kind of rejection within their state that the Jews of Germany experienced. Fortunately they already had a homeland. They have retreated to it for their own protection, and for the same reason—after all other efforts had failed—they have declared it to be an independent state.

In the light of these circumstances, Tanzania feels obliged to recognise the setback of African Unity which has occurred.

We therefore recognise the State of Biafra as an independent sovereign entity, and as a member of the community of nations. Only by this act of recognition can we remain true to our conviction that the purpose of society and of all political organization, is the service of man.

[1] *Statement by the Government of Tanzania issued on 13 April 1968. Text by courtesy of the United Republic of Tanzania News Service, United Nations Mission Office.*
[2] *Cf.* DOC *133.*

149.
'Why We Recognized Biafra'—President Nyerere[1]

Leaders of Tanzania have probably talked more about the need for African unity than those of any other country. Giving formal recognition to even greater disunity in Africa was therefore a very difficult decision to make. Our reluctance to do so was compounded by our understanding of the problems of unity—of which we have some experience—and of the problems of Nigeria. For we have had very good relations with the Federation of Nigeria, even to the extent that when we needed help from Africa we asked it of the Federation.

But unity can only be based on the general consent of the people involved. The people must feel that this State, or this Union, is theirs; and they must be willing to have their quarrels in that context. Once a large number of the people of any such political unit stop believing that the State is theirs, and that the Government is their instrument, then the unit is no longer viable. It will not continue to receive the loyalty of its citizens. . . .

In Nigeria this consciousness of a common citizenship was destroyed by the events of 1966, and in particular by the pogroms in which 30,000 Eastern Nigerians were murdered, many more injured and about two million forced to flee from the North of their country. It is these pogroms, and the apparent inability or unwillingness of the authorities to protect the victims, which underlies the Easterners' conviction that they have been rejected by other Nigerians and abandoned by the Federal Government.

Whether the Easterners are correct in their belief that they have been rejected is a matter for argument. But they do have this belief. And if they are wrong they have to be convinced that they are wrong. They will not be convinced by being shot. Nor will their acceptance as part of the Federation be demonstrated by the use of Federal power to bomb schools and hospitals in the areas to which people fled from persecution. . . .

As President of Tanzania it is my duty to safeguard the integrity of the United Republic. But if the mass of the people of Zanzibar should, without external manipulation, and for some reason of their own, decide that the Union was prejudicial to their existence, I could not advocate bombing them into submission. To do so would not be to defend the Union. The Union would have ceased to exist when the consent of its constituent members was withdrawn. I would certainly be one of those working hard to prevent secession, or to reduce its disintegrating effects. But I could not support a war on the people whom I have sworn to serve—especially not if the secession is preceded by a rejection of Zanzibaris by Tanganyikans.

Similarly, if we had succeeded in the 1963 attempt to form an East African Federation, or if we should do so in the future, Tanzania would be overjoyed. But if at some time thereafter the vast majority of the people of any one of the countries should decide—and persist in a decision—to withdraw from the Federation, the other two countries could not wage war against the people who wished to secede. Such a decision would mark a failure by the Federation. That would be tragic; but it would not justify mass killings.

The Biafrans now feel that they cannot live under conditions of personal security in the present Nigerian Federation. As they were unable to achieve an agreement on a new form of association, they have therefore claimed the right to govern themselves. The Biafrans are not claiming the right to govern anyone else. They have not said that they must govern the Federation as the only way of protecting themselves. They have simply withdrawn their consent to the system under which they used to be governed.

Biafra is not now operating under the control of a democratic Government, any more than Nigeria is. But the mass support for the establishment and defence of Biafra is obvious. This is not a case of a few leaders declaring secession for their own private glory. Indeed, by the Aburi Agreement the leaders of Biafra showed a greater reluctance to give up hope of some form of unity with Nigeria than the masses possessed. But the agreement was not implemented. . . .

We in this country believe that unity is vital for the future of Africa. But it must be a unity which serves the people, and which is freely determined upon by the people.

For 10 months we have accepted the Federal Government's legal right to our support in a 'police action to defend the integrity of the State.' On that basis we have watched a civil war result in the death of about 100,000 people, and the employment of mercenaries by both sides. We watched the Federal Government reject the advice of Africa to talk instead of demanding surrender before talks could begin. Everything combined gradually to force us to the conclusion that Nigerian unity did not exist.

Tanzania deeply regrets that the will for unity in Nigeria has been destroyed over the past two years. But we are convinced that Nigerian unity cannot be maintained by force any more than unity in East Africa could be created by one State conquering another.

It seemed to us that by refusing to recognise the existence of Biafra we were tacitly supporting a war against the people of Eastern Nigeria—and a war conducted in the name of unity. We could not continue doing this any longer.

¹ *Article in the* Observer, *28 April 1968, and in* Los Angeles Times, *5 May 1968.*

150.
Ojukwu's Interview with Britain-Biafra Association Delegates¹

. . . Here we have for a long time felt that we are abandoned by those who should be our true friends. We felt that of all countries in the world the one with the greatest likelihood of understanding our case was Britain. But unfortunately Government policy as expounded by the British representative in Nigeria, Sir David Hunt, and indeed by British Government action in supplying arms to Nigeria have left us, to say the least, bewildered.

Nevertheless we have not been, as you have noted, bitter against Britain, as we felt:

(1) that there are a number of people in Britain who understand and sympathise with our cause;

(2) we believe that there is a vast number of British people who, once they know the truth of the case would immediately see the justice of our cause.

We have been brought up under an aegis of British fairness and impartiality, and even the events of the past months have not in any way changed us in our beliefs. So that the formation of this society to us was, as it were, a vindication of our innermost belief. I am particularly proud at this vindication because a large measure of myself, my inner self, is British, having been brought up in Britain, done my university education there, and indeed grown to have friends in Britain, and become at times almost a stranger to my own native land. I believe a lot can be done in Britain. . . .

You may ask your questions.

Question: What do you understand the reason to be for British policy?

Lt.-Col. Ojukwu: British policy? I did say in my opening remarks that we find British policy, to say the least, bewildering. That is one, so that whatever I might say of course would be essentially a guess. I think there is this attachment to a creation of theirs:

(1) Federal Nigeria was created by Britain and I think Government policy as run from Whitehall will feel somewhat responsible for its well being.

(2) I think that there is a possible resentment over the fate of Abubakar Tafawa Balewa who was known to the world as a friend of Britain and this quite unjustified accusation to the people of this area that they have in fact conducted the coup that killed Abubakar.

(3) British policy was misdirected by Sir David Hunt. David Hunt's assessment of the two warring or contesting parties was completely wrong and Britain thought that the answer would be to end this thing as soon as possible and therefore supported what appeared the stronger side.

And finally—and I think that this is the most important one because again

P

it is the nearest, the immediate cause for British Government attitude. When the counter coup of July occurred the aim of that coup was separation of the North from the rest of the then Federation. It was Sir Cumming Bruce who made Gowon halt the secession of the North on advice, very strong advice, and made him change his speech which he announced—the famous speech about there being no basis for unity.[2] Having, as it were, led the North into pursuing a policy they were ill prepared for, there is a feeling particularly in Sir David Hunt, the successor of Sir Cumming Bruce, that Britain must do everything in her power to push through what was, at the best, a mistake. . . .

Q: In the last twelve months we have been rather bewildered as observers at the fact that the Nigerian Federation has held together, and we understand that the Government in Lagos represents a coalition of various groups—the Hausa-Fulani, the Yorubas and the minorities of the North, and we are told that Gowon himself represents the accession of the minorities of the North to power in Lagos. Could you give us your own views on this, what type of coalition this in fact is, and whether in fact the old feudal clique in the North still hold the reins in Lagos?

O: I will start my answer from where you started your question. The only thing holding Nigeria together at the moment is Biafra. This is a common bogey with all of them. To the North, should Biafra establish its sovereignty, then there is no point in being saddled with the rest of the Federation. With the Yorubas, should we establish our sovereignty, they would find themselves alone, combating with the giant North, and they wouldn't want that. With the Tivs, the minority of the North, should Biafra succeed, they can see danger because the North would never let them be given an inch to manoeuvre again. As for the Mid-West, the Republic of Benin, its death is a foregone conclusion. The Government of the Mid-West does recognise the impracticibility of trying to integrate the Ibos with the rest, because of the pogrom that occurred after the arrival of the Federal forces in the Republic. It is for this reason that I say Biafra is the cement that holds the Federation of Nigeria, as it is today, together.

The question of power, power in Lagos. It is very complex. Those in power in Lagos are certainly the minority groups who are able to stay in position as long as this bogey exists. The day Biafra is firmly established then these minorities will have no place in the order of things in Nigeria. If you notice the subtlety with which the states were created in the North, you will understand what I mean. It is true that they have announced glibly to the whole world that they have split into six states, but they have maintained the essential machinery of Government of one North. They have maintained that. And it is significant that they insist on a common services organisation. It is equally significant that the newspapers in the South are now very slowly, quietly, beginning to see the danger. . . .

Well, understanding the psychology of the South, particularly the Yorubas, they are under effective occupation, and this is as much as they can see at this time. But they are certainly apprehensive.

The North is continuing its organisation as a separate entity. It hasn't been changed. They are watching very carefully what is happening over here and of course if it goes against and there is no Biafran riches to share then the North will probably decide to stay on its own. The West will definitely want to stay on its own. So that as long as Biafra lasts the coalition of minorities will continue to exist. . . .

Q: You have stated many times that you are prepared to enter into negotiations without pre-conditions. However, during our stay here we have gathered the impression that Biafran sovereignty is not negotiable. Would this in fact be a condition?

O: I don't think one can call it a condition. As far as I am concerned our case is so clear. When we get round a table and we discuss everything I am absolutely certain that what will come out of it will still remain Biafran sovereignty. . . . Yes, we are resolved not to come back into Nigeria, but I don't think that our resolve should be made a pre-condition to negotiations.

Q: Would you ever be prepared to entertain anything like the Aburi agreement?

O: Not now, not now. There will be aspects of it on the economic side of course, yes, but not on the question of political sovereignty. . . .

Q: If the war were to turn against Biafra, is there any point where the slaughter got so bad that you would feel obliged to give it up?

O: Personally, I already consider the slaughter too bad. I think the magnitude of it is really so much, and this is why I have throughout been calling very fervently for peace. But this war is a war in which all the people of Biafra are involved, no matter the amount of carnage. You will have noted each time, in fact stage by stage, I always go back to the people and seek their mandate. And each time for the past four Consultative Assemblies I have put the same question—whenever you are tired let me know. And our people still remain very solidly behind the continuation.

The dangers of mass destruction are so very real we feel that should even one say stop, even lay down arms, the outcome would be death for all of us. There's been nothing to shake us from that belief. All evidence points to the same fact, and being human beings we prefer to take our chance, right to the last, with our arms in our hands. No, knowing my people, I don't really think we will ever reach that point. . . .

[1] *State House, Umuahia, 18 April 1968. (Text by courtesy of the Britain-Biafra Association.)*

[2] *See* DOC 37.

151.
Statement by Arikpo on Talks about Talks[1]

I arrived in London on the evening of Monday, April 22 for discussions with the British Government and with the Commonwealth Secretariat in our efforts to engage in meaningful peace talks with the Nigerian rebels. The Federal Military Government of Nigeria has always followed up any suggestions about the readiness of the rebels to engage in peace talks, because we are very anxious to achieve an acceptable settlement in the context of *One* united Federal Nigeria.

As early as October, 1967, the Commonwealth Secretary-General Mr.

Arnold Smith informed the Federal Military Government that the rebels appeared willing to start peace talks. The Nigerian Government promptly agreed to send three senior representatives with full powers to London. They were to meet a team of rebel representatives as arranged by Mr. Arnold Smith. The venue agreed beforehand by both sides was London. Our representatives waited in vain for one week in London; the rebels and their supporters changed their minds.

Again, in November 1967 when it was clear that rebel forces had been driven out of Enugu, the Central Eastern State capital, we received word again that they were ready to talk peace. Just as our representatives were about to leave Lagos a fresh message came from the Commonwealth Secretariat indicating that the rebels had again changed their minds.

After the outbreak of hostilities, the Kinshasa Summit of Heads of States and of Governments of the Organization of African Unity discussed the Nigerian situation and set up a Peace Mission of six Heads of State to explore with us the possibility of restoring peace to Nigeria. We could have insisted on the OAU Summit not discussing the Nigerian war at all in accordance with the Charter of the Organization. If there was anything the African Heads of State and Governments could do to help bring peace on acceptable terms, we were prepared to let them try. African Statesmen like His Imperial Majesty Emperor Haile Sellassie of Ethiopia, President Hamani Diori of the Republic of Niger, President Ahmadu Ahidjo of the Cameroun Republic and Lt.-General Ankrah of Ghana came to Lagos on the Consultative Mission and after full deliberations, delegated General Ankrah to pass on their findings to Mr. Ojukwu. The message was clear even from the mandate of the Kinshasa Summit Resolution. Africa condemned the attempted break-up of Nigeria and General Ankrah was to try this time on behalf of the OAU, to persuade Mr. Ojukwu to give up secession and accept the new political structure of the minimum of twelve states.

General Ankrah reported later that Mr. Ojukwu refused to talk to him on a direct radio link which, with the consent of the Head of the Federal Military Government Ojukwu maintains with General Ankrah. General Ankrah and the Nigerian Head of State had thought that by maintaining the radio link Mr. Ojukwu would have at his disposal an easy means of contacting General Ankrah any time he was ready for a peace settlement.

Early this month, the Commonwealth Secretariat once more informed the Federal Military Government that there were clear indications that the rebels at last wanted these talks to commence. (Dr. Azikiwe had also earlier announced in Paris on behalf of the rebels, that they were prepared to talk without pre-conditions[2]). The Commonwealth Secretariat stated that the rebels were prepared to send a team of four to negotiate either on official or ministerial level, subject to reciprocity on *all* aspects of the crisis.

I have, since arriving in London, had further discussions in this connection with the Commonwealth Secretary-General Mr. Arnold Smith. I have confirmed to the Commonwealth Secretary-General that the Federal Military Government are prepared to embark on talks without pre-conditions under the auspices of the Commonwealth Secretary-General as soon as the other side are ready. This should be possible by May 1 at the latest.

We really want to get on with the talks. We want to be able to talk to them, to hear from them along what lines peace can return to our beloved country. We have plans and suggestions of our own and we would like to hear their views so that a mutually agreed programme of reconstruction can be under-taken. We want to reassure them that we do not regard them as enemies. The Ibos have never been our enemies. We have a mutual interest in a return to peace and normality. We realize that in order to rebuild our country their advice would be essential and very welcome. Our goal is one of a lasting peace for our country, and our hope is that they would in a spirit of reconciliation come to the conference table to discuss how this can be achieved. Once the talks start we can agree on an agenda and other related matters. I am sure that the moment talks commence we would soon forget even the most recent past events. . . .

¹ *Issued in London, 25 April 1968.*
² *See* DOC *147.*

152.
Nigeria's Agenda for Peace Talks, April 1968¹

After reviewing the latest developments and the reassuring messages of support from African Heads of State and other world leaders, the Federal Military Government has confirmed its readiness to start talks without pre-conditions as soon as the rebels show that they are sincere about engaging in talks meant to lead to a lasting settlement of the crisis.

The Federal Military Government has reiterated that in order to ensure a lasting settlement the proposed talks must concentrate on concrete issues. In the search for a lasting solution, there is no question whatsoever of dis-cussing the existence of an independent Ibo State or a so-called Biafra. It must be clear to all by now that the existence of the so-called Biafra will lead to:

a. permanent fratricidal war between the so-called Biafra and the rest of Nigeria.
b. the continuation of the massacres and other atrocities being committed by Ojukwu and other rebel leaders, especially against non-Ibos in the areas of the Rivers State remaining under rebel control.
c. the creation of a beach-head in the heart of West Africa for the enemies of Africa who have been assisting the supply of arms etc. to sustain the rebellion of Ojukwu and his clique.
d. disintegration of African States.

For these reasons, the Federal Military Government will insist that the talks should concentrate on more positive and concrete solutions likely to produce a lasting settlement to the Nigerian crisis. Therefore the agenda on the proposed talks must embrace the following:

(1) acceptance by the rebels that Nigeria should remain one sovereign united country.
(2) acceptance by the rebels of the new twelve states administrative structure of the Federation.

(3) arrangements for restoring and maintaining law and order in the East Central State such as would remove any genuine Ibo fears about personal safety.

(4) guarantees of equal economic opportunities for all Nigerian citizens regardless of ethnic origin.

(5) arrangements for rehabilitating persons displaced during the crisis.

(6) arrangements for a constituent assembly of representatives of the Federal Government and of the twelve states to work out a new Federal Constitution.

(7) arrangements for the review of revenue allocation and such matters.

Agreement on the above matters will lead to the cessation of hostilities and lasting settlement.

The Federal Government appeals once again to the rebels and their supporters to understand that this is the only possible path to peace and reconciliation. To talk about recognizing rebels as an equal party to the Federal Government or to pursue peace slogans without discussing the issues at stake is only to manifest total insincerity. While the Federal Government is resolved to continue its efforts, military and political, to bring about lasting solutions to the Nigerian crisis, it hopes that the rebel leaders will consider the sufferings and hardships they are imposing on the citizens of the East Central State and embrace this opportunity for an honourable and lasting settlement.

[1] *Statement issued in Lagos on 26 April 1968. (Text by courtesy of Nigerian High Commission, London.)*

153.
Lagos explains why London was preferred over African venue for Preliminary Peace Talks[1]

Your Excellencies must have heard news reports that Mr. Ojukwu, after we had replied to him that peace talks could start without pre-conditions, has now asked, among other things, for such talks to take place within 48 hours and in an African country. On the other hand, I announced in London that the Federal Military Government was willing to meet Mr. Ojukwu's delegates in London latest by the 1st May. I have been given to understand that some African Ambassadors thought that this was a disrespect to African countries and that the Federal Military Government did not want its representatives to meet in an African country. . . . The reason why we agreed to London is very simple. Since October last year, most of the peace initiatives have always been brought to our notice by Mr. Arnold Smith, the Secretary-General of the Commonwealth Secretariat. . . .

I would like to disclose that when Mr. Arnold Smith telephoned me in London and I went to see him, he informed me that one of Mr. Ojukwu's envoys, Mr. Mojekwu, had gone to Umuahia to urge the secessionists to confirm the venue. . . . I would like to disclose further that I was in his office when Mr. Ojukwu's reply for a meeting in 48 hours in an African country came on the Reuters News Service. I accordingly asked Mr. Smith whether this meant that they were withdrawing their request for peace talks. He replied that as far as he was concerned they did not inform him that they were withdrawing the request that he should arrange a meeting.

If we are to examine critically the point of Ojukwu wanting a meeting within 48 hours, with two African Heads of State acting on behalf of either side, we will find that there is absolutely no substance to it. In the first instance, no African Heads of State had got in touch with the Federal Military Government that Ojukwu had requested him to arrange a meeting. The Federal Military Government is not aware which head of state he has in mind. It will be readily agreed that before the said meeting can take place in an African country, the following minimum conditions must be fulfilled:

(1) The African country has to be decided upon.

(2) The African country in question has to agree to play host, and

(3) The date has to be agreed upon.

These conditions, Your Excellencies will agree, are bound to be time-consuming.

From the foregoing, Your Excellencies will see that Mr. Arnold Smith has been acting all the time as a 'go-between' for the secessionists and the Federal Military Government. According to my information his Secretariat has made necessary arrangement as regards the venue and other facilities.

Above all, Your Excellencies, I would like to inform you that all the friends of the rebels in Britain (and there are quite a few), have been carrying out a campaign on their behalf in the belief that the meeting would be held under the auspices of the Commonwealth Secretariat headed by Mr. Arnold Smith. It is for these reasons that the Federal Military Government accepted London as the venue for the peace talks seeing that it will expedite matters if the rebels are really sincere and genuine in their desire for peace. I would like to state with all emphasis that the Federal Military Government has no objection to peace talks being held in any African country except, of course, the United Republic of Tanzania.

As proof of our sincerity, I would further state that even if the meeting should start in London and it is suggested and agreed that it should move to an African country, the Federal Military Government will not object.

Some of Your Excellencies know that very recently I have visited your Presidents with the understanding that Ojukwu's envoys had visited them and stated that they wanted peace talks. If the Federal Military Government harbours any disregard or disrespect towards any African President, these journeys would not have been undertaken. If you would allow me to be personal, the Ambassador of Senegal will bear me out that I visited his Head of State and he gave me the firm assurance that Dr. Azikiwe and his colleagues were returning to Dakar and that I should be ready to meet them in Dakar, but what happened? Instead of coming to Dakar, Dr. Azikiwe issued his Paris statement of the 3rd April. There are many inferences one can draw from this attitude of the secessionist leaders.[2] It is either that there is a division among the various groups with different ideas or they are not serious about peace talks. If it is the latter, then they are merely carrying out their usual propaganda. . . .

[1] *Statements made to diplomats in Lagos by Dr. Okio Arikpo, 27 April 1968.*

[2] *Cf.* DOC 147.

154.
Agenda for the Kampala Peace Talks[1]

The two sides, represented by Chief Anthony Enahoro and Sir Louis Mbanefo, have held several meetings with the Commonwealth Secretary-General, Mr. Arnold Smith, to discuss arrangements for substantive peace talks. The meetings were concluded last night. Agreement was reached as follows:

1. The peace talks will take place in Kampala.
2. The following agenda will be the framework for the talks:
    (i) The question of chairmanship;
    (ii) The question of observers (foreign);
    (iii) Conditions for ending the hostilities;
    (iv) Arrangements for a permanent settlement.

Either side may, under each item, propose for discussion such subjects as it wishes. Either side may at any stage before the peace talks convene, serve notice, through the Commonwealth Secretariat, of the subjects it proposes for discussion under each item. It is agreed that the Secretary-General will transmit such notice to the other side and that he will not publish it.

3. The peace talks will begin in the morning of Thursday, 23 May.
4. The President of Uganda, His Excellency Dr. A. Milton Obote, will be invited to address the opening session of the peace talks.
5. The Commonwealth Secretariat will be responsible for servicing the peace talks.

[1] *Communique issued by the Commonwealth Secretariat, Marlborough House, London, on 15 May 1968. (By courtesy of the Secretariat.)*

155.
Zambia Recognizes Biafra[1]

The tragedy which has befallen the Federation of Nigeria is a most unwelcome event in the phase of Africa's development. The current war and the atrocious exercises committed in waging the war, the loss of human life and property have shaken this continent and there are no prospects yet that Biafra can yield to what has almost become a war of attrition. The Zambian Government has been concerned about the future of this area of Africa. We have been, and are still, most concerned about peace, stability and unity among the people of that area. We have been even more concerned about the amount of blood which is being shed for what is obviously a futile cause. War, in our opinion, will not induce surrender. It will, as has already been seen, continue to widen the gap between the two combatants and increase fear among those who are the victims of war.

Even before the crisis burst into military hostilities, the Zambian Government did everything in its power to prevent the increasing tension from escalating into a shooting war. Since the outbreak of war, Zambia has employed all available means to avert further loss of life and property. But the indiscriminate massacre of the innocent civilian population has filled us with horror. Whereas it is our ardent desire to foster African Unity, it would be morally wrong to force anybody into Unity founded on blood and bloodshed. For unity to be meaningful and beneficial it must be based on the consent of all parties concerned, offering security and justice to all. This Government is convinced that the heritage of bitterness stemming from this horrifying war will make it impossible to create any basis for political unity of Biafra and Nigeria.

The Zambian Government has therefore decided to recognise the Republic of Biafra as a Sovereign and independent state. We hope that the establishment of this Republic will now allow Nigeria and the people of Biafra to work out a better frame-work for cooperation, in order to ensure a better platform for more realistic unity among themselves, in order to live in peace and to foster African Unity in the spirit of brotherhood and mutual cooperation for the benefit of all the peoples of that region.

[1] *Statement by the Zambian Foreign Minister issued in Lusaka, 20 May 1968 (Zambia House Press Release No. 750/1968).*

156.
Enahoro's Opening Statement at Kampala[1]

. . . The Federal Government therefore welcomes the Kampala Peace Talks. The principal task of the peace talks here is to try to resolve our basic differences and arrive at a peace settlement. From this point of view, the Federal Government attaches the greatest importance to item III of the Agenda, 'Conditions for Ending Hostilities'. We shall be circulating a memorandum on this important subject. We can bring the hostilities to an end if we approach these talks with absolute sincerity and in the spirit of give and take. . . .

It is running away from the problem to suggest that hostilities should be ended before we discuss the conditions for ending hostilities. The Evian Agreement which ended the Algerian War, was negotiated while the fighting was going on. The Vietnam Peace Talks are proceeding without a ceasefire.

Both sides in the Nigerian conflict are convinced that they are fighting over great issues. We cannot stop the war without discussing the great issues we have been fighting for.

The delegation of the Federal Government has come to Kampala determined that these talks must succeed in producing a basis for peace and a lasting settlement in Nigeria. It should be clear to the whole world by now that the Head of the Federal Military Government, Major-General Yakubu Gowon and his colleagues on the Supreme Military Council and the Federal Executive Council did everything within their power to arrive at a peaceful solution of the Nigerian crisis and to avoid war. Regrettably, every concession offered to Ojukwu and his group was rejected. As the secessionists' demands were met, they immediately demanded more. They claimed to be convinced that the people in the part of Nigeria over which they had temporary control could no longer live with the rest of the country of which they had formed an integral part for more than half a century. Thus Nigeria found herself in the present situation where thousands of innocent young men have been goaded into rebellion. The Federal Government is determined that everything must be done to stop this strife without further delay.

This is why throughout the course of the war, the Federal Military Government has devoted a great deal of time and energy to working out plans for reconciliation and reconstruction. We will therefore make concrete and sincere suggestions at this conference for a settlement with honour satisfied on all sides to the current conflicts in Nigeria. They will include arrangements for restoring law and order in the East Central State and for guaranteeing security of life and property for Ibos and all other Nigerians with which they and impartial world observers should be satisfied. We must, on the other hand, insist that those representing the group who are unfortunately in rebellion against the Federal Government should adopt a constructive approach to the discussions upon which we are about to embark.

It is necessary for us on all sides to understand the full and accurate background to our crisis. Regrettably, Ojukwu and his group had the field unchallenged for more than two years, engaging in lying propaganda and slander abroad and incitement of tribal hatred at home. In the propaganda which they put out to mislead world opinion and to sustain rebellion at home, Mr. Ojukwu and his group have never addressed themselves to the basic problems which led to the current crisis in Nigeria. On the other hand, the Federal Government, conscious of its responsibilities for the safety of all the citizens of Nigeria, has refrained from matching the tendentious stories put out by Ojukwu regarding the so-called persecution of the Ibos, so as to prevent the possibility of reprisals against that section of the Nigerian community. But at this conference it is necessary for us to talk frankly amongst ourselves in order to base our settlement on a truthful and realistic appreciation of our problems.

One of the root causes of our present difficulties has been the acute regionalism which developed in Nigerian politics from the late 1940s onwards. During that period, with the introduction of the representative system of government, the British and unfortunately many Nigerians began to emphasise the separateness of the three sections into which they divided Nigeria. At Independence, we inherited a very unstable structure. This consisted of three very large Regions with very extensive powers. One of the Regions, the Northern Region, had three-fourths of the total area of the country and more than half of the population. Each Region had one dominant tribal group and numerous smaller tribes. This situation was inherently unstable because:

(a) Each Region was large enough to attempt to dominate the country or at least to blackmail the others during any dispute.

(b) The minority elements within each Region clamoured incessantly for their own States within the Federation and resented the manoeuvres of the dominant tribes to maintain their hegemony. This in turn led to suspicion and abuse of electoral processes by those eager to keep themselves in office.

(c) More than half of the country was dissatisfied with the constituent units of the Federation since the Hausas, the Ibos and the Yorubas were together less than 50 per cent of the Nigerian population.

The leaders of the three 'majority' ethnic groups pursued an increasingly acrimonious policy of regional confrontation regardless of the true needs of the people of the country as a whole. They carefully avoided the essential reform of the country's political structure. There were a succession of crises. ... The late Prime Minister, Sir Abubakar Tafawa Balewa, struggled with all sincerity to accommodate all interests in the country. . . . From early 1965, Nigeria had a broad-based Government, in a territorial sense, in which all sections of the country were represented. But towards the end of 1965, as the cumulative result of the crises already mentioned, the country was in a ferment. It was in this delicate situation that the coup of 15th January, 1966 was staged. . . . A Military Regime under General Ironsi was installed. In spite of the pattern of these killings (only non-Ibos being killed) there were no immediate hostile reactions in any part of the country and military rule was generally welcomed as people hoped that a just and honest administration would result.

However, suspicions were soon aroused in many parts of the country. The coup was described as a mutiny by General Ironsi but he did nothing to bring the mutineers to trial and re-establish discipline in the Army. Many committees were set up to review and make recommendations on various aspects of the administration of the country. The regime promised to review the Constitution only after extensive consultations with the people. Despite all these promises, matters were soon being rushed to the surprise and irritation of many sections of Nigerian society. . . .

Then suddenly, without any warning, and without allowing the Constitution Review Committee which he had himself set up to complete its work and report, General Ironsi promulgated a decree on 24th May, 1966, abolishing Nigeria's Federal structure and imposing a unitary system on the country. Within a few days, widespread riots erupted in the Northern Region and many people, mostly Ibos, were killed.

On July 29th, 1966, there was another military coup which overthrew General Ironsi's regime. Major-General Gowon then assumed the position of Supreme Commander of the Armed Forces and Head of the Federal Military Government with the agreement of all members of the Supreme Military Council with the sole exception of Ojukwu. General Gowon at once promised to restore Nigeria to its Federal structure and to seek an agreed basis for resolving the country's crisis and return the country to civilian rule at the earliest possible opportunity.

Mr. Ojukwu would not accept this. He preached defiance and vengeance. Over the Eastern Region radio, he continuously threatened revenge. He sabotaged all efforts to reach agreement through the conference table. Only reluctantly did a delegation from the former Eastern Region come to the Ad Hoc Constitutional Conference in Lagos in September 1966 which General Gowon summoned only six weeks after assuming office. At that conference it was soon obvious that agreement could be reached but for the intransigence of the Eastern delegates who did not want any effective Central Government to be preserved. Indeed, just before the conference, terrorist bomb outrages organised by Ojukwu's Government occurred in Lagos and at the Ore Bridge on the main road link between Lagos and the Mid-West and East. Some people under his instructions were caught in parts of the North trying to blow up bridges and public installations.

When the Constitutional Conference in Lagos adjourned for two weeks, the

Eastern delegates refused to return to continue the discussions. Meanwhile, the Eastern radio continued its campaign, inflaming the passions of the citizens of the Eastern Region against the rest of Nigeria. By threats and tricks, Ibos outside the East were inveigled into returning home. All these could not but increase tension. Then some elements in the Eastern Region embarked on widespread, organised killings of the people of Northern origin resident in that region. News of this was first broadcast by foreign radios. In these terrible circumstances, riots erupted in the North in which about 5,000 people lost their lives. A majority of those killed were Ibos, but many others were police personnel and Northerners. These tragic and regrettable killings have since been grossly exploited by Mr Ojukwu to compel the Ibos in the East to rebel and take up arms against their country. But it is important to understand the facts.

In his impromptu address to the Ad Hoc Constitutional Conference on October 3, 1966, General Gowon reacted to the October tragedy in the following words: '. . . certainly there has been a damage. I think that is what we never seem to admit when there is something like that. There is a damage and I am very, very sorry about it. I regret it and I am doing everything I can . . .'[2]

Mr Ojukwu himself at the Aburi Conference in January 1967 put the number of those killed in the Northern riots at 10,000 and insisted then that he had fool-proof evidence to support his claim. When it suited his plans later, he raised the figure to 30,000, accused the Federal Government of organising the killings of Ibos, and distributed many malicious publications on the alleged pogrom. The Federal Government does not seek to justify the killing which occurred in the Northern and Eastern Regions. We have always condemned them and regretted those tragedies. But it is clear nonetheless that the circumstances were most unusual.

It is also clear that:

(*a*) the riots were due to mob reaction in very trying circumstances when the Army and Police were fully stretched;

(*b*) the vast majority of Ibos resident in the North were saved from the mobs by their Northern friends and neighbours who could not have been party to any plan for a 'pogrom'; and

(*c*) country-wide communal riots were prevented.

I have spent so much time to set the record straight on the tragedies of 1966 because false and short-sighted significance has deliberately been given to them by Mr Ojukwu to justify secession. . . .

However, all this is in the past, and while the past is useful in determining the nature of our real problems, I suggest that if this Conference dwells too much on the past, we will be in danger of missing the opportunities of the present. The significance of this occasion for our people is that we are at last at this Peace Conference. We sincerely hope that the necessary lessons have been learnt and that we can now honestly address ourselves to realistic solutions to our crisis.

As regards possible solutions, much has been said by secessionist leaders about the so-called Republic of Biafra. They claimed that the Ibos can no longer live with the other ethnic groups in Nigeria and that only the so-called State of Biafra which is sovereign and with its own Army can protect the

Ibos. At the same time, however, they seek to include the non-Ibos of the former Eastern Region in the so-called Biafra. But our brothers on the other side will agree that this concept of a Biafra is unrealistic and untenable.

To begin with, if the argument is that 7 million Ibos in the eastern part of Nigeria must enjoy the right of self determination, surely this same right must be accorded to the 5 million Efiks, Ibibios, Ekois and Ijaws whom the seccessionist leaders wish to force into the so-called State of Biafra. They cannot deny the long-standing demands of these articulate minorities for their own State. There is overwhelming evidence of mass intimidation and brutality conducted by the Ojukwu regime against these people. Hundreds of them have been killed for asserting their separate identity. The liberation of the entire South-Eastern State was accomplished with the enthusiastic support of the Ibibios and Efiks who inhabit that State. The same enthusiastic support for the continued existence of the Federation of Nigeria has been shown in the areas of the Rivers State liberated from rebel control. People from these parts of the former Eastern Region form the bulk of the Nigerian Navy which has distinguished itself in the operations which liberated Bonny, Calabar and Port Harcourt. We are quite sure too that the majority of the Ibos themselves, when peace is restored, will see that their well-being would be better assured in a State within the Nigerian Federation in which they enjoy equality of consideration with all the other tribes and are able to continue their work and business all over the country.

The secessionist leaders know, however, that they were deceiving the world with their stories about the need for an Ibo State called 'Biafra'. They know that there is no way of wrenching the East peacefully out of Nigeria, thereby destroying the social and economic integration that has gone on for more than 50 years. They know that the railways, the telecommunications network, the numerous other assets cannot be divided amongst successor States if Nigeria were to disintegrate. Captured documents now confirm that the intention of Mr Ojukwu and his supporters was first to conquer the former Mid-Western and Western Regions and then later to subdue the Northern Region and so dominate Nigeria. Indeed, during their six-week control of the Mid-West, their slogan was 'Southern Nigeria Solidarity' not 'Ibo survival'.[3] The so-called State of Biafra will only be a staging post and as soon as the rebel leaders have recovered, they will resume their campaign.

It is instructive that many of the agents of Mr Ojukwu concede in private that an independent Ibo apartheid State will be unviable. This is why they insist on retaining the territories of the South-Eastern State and Rivers State. They sometimes disguise this by talking about the need for an outlet to the sea, ignoring the fact that eight of the twelve States in Nigeria are not on the sea coast.

In order to make the so-called State of Biafra sound plausible, they suggest that a sovereign 'Biafra' can have a Customs Union, Common Currency, Common Services including Railways, Post and Telecommunications, Ports, Dual Citizenship and extensive economic relations with the rest of Nigeria as sovereign equals,[4] but they know that this is a specious suggestion because:

(*a*) Sovereign countries resulting from the disintegration of a larger unit and separating in war cannot negotiate, administer, or sustain a Customs Union.

(*b*) Extensive economic relations involve human contact and unhindered travel throughout the territory of Nigeria and this is precisely what the secessionist leaders say is impossible. More than that, they expelled all non-Easterners from their region in October 1966.

(*c*) Any 'Central Organisation' endowed with adequate powers to legislate over and administer common customs tariffs, currencies, establishment and control of industries, Railways, Air Lines, Ports, Posts and Telecommunications, etc., becomes an effective Central Government. These are the business of a Federal Government and these are precisely what the secessionist leaders have so far said that they do not want.

Previous contacts between Federal Government representatives and rebel agents on these matters have shown them to be thus far insincere in their protestations in this regard.

In military terms, the concept of Biafra is now dead. Enugu, Port Harcourt, Calabar, Onitsha are all under Federal control. The rebel regime is now confined to 2 or 3 towns and their environs in the interior of the so-called Ibo heartland. In these circumstances, the concept of Biafra no longer constitutes a serious military threat. We should therefore address ourselves at this meeting to the need for a political solution.

We have always maintained that three principles are of paramount importance in any genuine attempt to find a lasting solution to the Nigerian crisis. These are:

(*i*) that any solution adopted must be conducive to the maintenance of lasting peace. This demands that the solution must be to preserve one sovereign Nigeria and its territorial integrity. To allow the country to be broken up would be to condemn the successor states to the status of military, political and economic protectorates of different power blocks. Such states would be goaded into internecine wars with the supply of arms, and economic and social progress towards genuine independence would be arrested; the support which the enemies of Africa have given to Ojukwu illustrates this clearly;

(*ii*) that the solution adopted must not allow 'tribal apartheid' through any specious theory of tribal protection but must, rather, guarantee equal economic opportunities as well as the same political and other rights for all Nigerian citizens, regardless of ethnic origin—there are more than 200 ethnic groups in Nigeria!

(*iii*) that Nigeria must be re-structured administratively in order to remove once and for all the root cause of political discontent—the fear of domination (or blackmail) by one large Region or ethnic group over the others. Hence we insist on the present minimum of twelve states.

There can be no doubt now that Nigeria must be preserved as one united country if we are serious about achieving lasting peace in order to allow our part of Africa to resume its orderly process of social and economic development. . . .

It is also important to stress why, having renounced secession, those now in rebellion must also accept the twelve State structure. As I said at the beginning, one of the root causes of the Nigerian problem was the fear of domination by one Region or one ethnic group. There is also the long history of the demand for the creation of States in Nigeria.

It was imperative therefore, that the first step in any honest attempt to solve the Nigerian problem was to remove the genuine fear of Northern domination through size, or of Ibo domination through their tightly-knit organisations and their exploitation of the agricultural and oil wealth of the minorities in the East, or of Yoruba domination through the preponderance of the Western Region were only the North and the East split. Thus the only possible solution was to re-organise Nigeria into a minimum of twelve States as promulgated by the Federal Government at the end of May 1967. These states, except the East-Central, are now fully established and functioning. There are more than 100 tribes in the former Northern Region. The present reorganisation of that Region into six states removed once and for all the bogey of Northern domination. Similarly, stability can only be guaranteed in the East with the consolidation of the present South-Eastern and Rivers States which have satisfied the long standing aspirations of the 5 million non-Ibos in that part of the country. These are the underlying factors in the States programme of the Federal Government.

Our brothers who are in rebellion should consider that, in fact, it is only with the success of this exercise that all tribes in the former Eastern Region can co-exist peacefully, continue and even extend their previous level of integration, because they would now be free from the threat of Ibo domination, real or feared, and the resentment it engenders. To insist on denying 5 million people their right of self-determination is to make the problem of reconciliation more difficult. This important aspect of our work will be dealt with in greater detail when we come to the relevant agenda item. I must stress however that there is provision for a machinery—the State Delimitation Commission—which will work out necessary adjustments of States boundaries in order to enhance inter-state harmony.

Throughout this crisis, the Federal Government has been gratified that many thousands of Ibos have continued to live and work as loyal citizens in Lagos and other parts of the Federation. They still serve in the Police, the Prisons Service and even the Armed forces. I believe we have succeeded in educating all Nigerians, except those in rebellion, on the issues at stake in our current crisis and on the real possibilities for lasting settlement and peace. We are also gratified to note that scores of thousands of Ibos who previously fled their towns and villages during the fighting are returning to their homes in areas of the East Central State under Federal control. They are being cared for by Mr Asika, the Administrator of the State, and his officials.

These positive developments encourage the Federal Government to make its proposals for arrangements which will lead to the end of fighting and guarantee the security of Ibos and all other Nigerians in the East Central State and throughout the Federation. We intend at the appropriate stage to disclose the details of our proposals because despite the military victories of the Federal Government, we recognise that certain basic fears of the Ibos have to be allayed. Already, large numbers of people from the East-Central State have been recruited and are being trained in Lagos for the Police Force whose primary responsibility it will be to perform normal police functions in the East-Central State once the rebel Army has laid down its arms. The reinstatement of Ibo civil servants, corporations and company officials who fled from their posts, the rehabilitation of self-employed citizens from the

Eastern States who have suffered as a result of the crisis of the last two years, the re-integration of these people into the communities from which they fled, the reconstruction of damaged roads, bridges, power houses and the restoration of production in factories closed down as a result of the current operations, are priority items for which the Federal Government has prepared plans. I hope that these plans can be improved by constructive proposals from our brothers on the other side.

We wish to discuss arrangements for summoning a body representative of the twelve states and the Federal Government to prepare a new Constitution. The form of the Constitution, including the degree of state autonomy, will be decided by that body. We intend also to discuss arrangements for setting up a Revenue Allocation Commission to review revenue allocation in the new circumstances. We expect that in future safeguards against electoral irregularities and against abuse of Governmental powers will be more clearly spelled out in the new Constitution.

The crisis which has shaken the country since the beginning of 1966 and the war which we are about to end have been an extraordinary phase in the history of Nigeria. The re-organisation of Nigeria into twelve states has removed one of the root causes of discontent, mutual fear and instability. The equality of the new states is emphasised repeatedly by General Gowon, the Head of the Federal Military Government, and is confirmed in the appointment of civilian members of the Federal Executive Council. The bonds of economic and social integration which bind together all sections of the country; the valuable human bridge represented by the loyal Ibos who have worked and struggled together with the Federal Government and other Nigerians throughout this crisis; the new leadership which is emerging; the fact that in national politics, the issues will no longer be controversies between Hausas, Ibos and Yorubas or between a giant North, a giant East and a giant West—these are the grounds for our hope and confidence that we are now at the point of working out a lasting basis for continued progress and harmony in Nigeria. It is in this spirit therefore that we appeal to our brothers that we should jointly approach this historic Reconciliation Conference. We must all endeavour to overcome, even if we cannot forget, the tragedies of the last two years. . . .

Gentlemen, I would like to put the Nigerian conflict, tragic as it is, in its proper historic perspective. The civil war in Nigeria is not the first tragic conflict in human experience. Many countries have had to fight much bloodier civil wars for causes even less worthy than that of national unity. Many African countries which today, appear to condone or rejoice at the misfortune of Nigerians, may tomorrow find themselves fighting their fellow countrymen and the forces of secession in their midst.

We have to come to the Kampala Peace Talks because we believe Nigeria will be saved. We have come to Kampala to talk peace because we firmly believe that a negotiated settlement will enhance lasting peace.

[1] *23 May 1968. Text from* Framework for Settlement: The Federal Case in Kampala (*Lagos, 1968*).
[2] *See* DOC *61.*
[3] *Cf.* DOCS *125–8.*
[4] *Cf.* DOC *130.*

157.
Mbanefo Presents Biafra's Case at Kampala[1]

... We have come to this conference because we believe, and we have said so from the beginning, that the dispute between Biafra and Nigeria is incapable of a military solution. It is a human problem which must be resolved round a conference table. This is a solemn and serious occasion and those of us charged with the task of finding a solution are very conscious of the problem ahead of us. But we cannot get a solution unless we are prepared to face facts—facts on life and facts on history. . . . By the beginning of 1966, Nigeria hovered on the brink of total disintegration. The Constitution had proved unworkable in the hands of corrupt politicians whose sole ambition was to cling to power irrespective of the wishes of the people, and in complete disregard of the innocent blood which was being shed by their actions. These were the circumstances which led to the military coup of January 15, 1966. There is no doubt, as a glance at the Nigerian press of the time could show, that the coup was acclaimed by all shades of opinion in the country as a necessary action to restore order and political stability.

The history of the former Federation of Nigeria clearly shows the futility of trying to keep Nigeria one. Anyone who has followed closely events within Nigeria since independence will notice that crisis followed crisis. . . . The failure of the federation, or rather the causes of these crises, can directly be attributed to the fact that the dominant group in the country, the Northern Nigerians, never accepted the idea of unity. They have demonstrated this both by words and, more tragically, by action. The pronouncements of their leaders and the views expressed in debates in the Northern House of Assembly clearly show their rejection of the idea of a united Nigeria.

The views expressed by these . . . [Northern] leaders have been canvassed and repeated at different times by other leaders and by all the information media in the North, and still represent their stand today. The record of the debates in the Northern House of Assembly is there for all to see in their Hansard. More recently, on assumption of power in Lagos in August, 1966, Lt.-Col. Yakubu Gowon as he then was, now Head of the Nigerian Federal Military Government, declared that there was no basis for Nigerian unity. . . .

It is difficult for a Biafran to speak without much emotion of the pogrom which followed and in which over 30,000 Biafrans were killed and countless others mutilated, maimed and rendered destitute. But, fortunately, these events were well recorded by independent witnesses, especially by foreign correspondents who narrated the carnage they saw in Northern Nigeria. . . .

It is clear that under these circumstances, unity is impossible. Unity with Biafra has been rejected by Nigeria. Nigeria's war of aggression is, therefore, not a war for unity, slogans notwithstanding. It is a war of conquest, a war to 'continue their interrupted conquest to the sea'. It is a war of extermination, a war of genocide. It is difficult for those who have not seen the victims of the pogrom and genocide to form any true conception of what has taken place. This is the case with most Nigerians, including members of the Nigerian Delegation to these talks. For their benefit, I hand round some photographs which describe the events better than words can do. How can one talk of unity with a people you are determined to destroy?

Q

Some people think that assurances can be given that these things cannot happen again. On the question of assurances, our position is quite clear. The experience of over 50 years, in particular the experience of the present war, has clearly convinced Biafrans that the only condition under which they can survive as a people is that in which the protection of their lives, liberty and property is exclusively in their own hands.

Any lasting peace must vest the control of security of life and property in the people of Biafra themselves, not in any external authority. The Biafran Delegation believes that only a separate political existence for the people of Biafra as a sovereign independent state can guarantee this security. Assurances given in the past have availed nothing in securing these fundamental rights which are essential for survival both as individuals and as a people. . . . Furthermore, during the crisis which resulted in the current conflict, several assurances given by Nigerian authorities of the security of Biafran life and property were honoured in the breach rather than in the observance.

Some of the massacres in the North were perpetrated with the active participation, as we have seen, of the law enforcement agents of the Federal and Northern Nigeria Governments. Manifestly, therefore, within the Nigerian political community, no guarantee given by Nigerians can assure Biafrans of the security of their fundamental human rights.

The situation calls for new institutional arrangements, not guarantees by words or on paper. Up to now all that Nigeria has offered is a return to the former Federation with a variation in the number of states. But it should be perfectly clear that as a result of the pogrom, genocide and war, no Biafran can again live freely or make his home with any assurance of safety in Nigeria, especially in Northern Nigeria. To force Biafrans back into the Federation would be like forcing the Jews who had fled to Israel back to Nazi Germany.

Biafrans are forcibly driven out of the former Federation of Nigeria. Freedom of movement and of residence in any part of the country is an essential element for the continued existence of a federation. With its disappearance, it is difficult to see how one can talk of Biafra being part of a Nigerian political entity. The will to federate was strongest in the former Eastern Nigeria; that will no longer exists in Biafra as a result of the pogrom and the genocide. It cannot be resuscitated by war or imposed by conquest.

No state which fails to guarantee the most elementary safety for a substantial number of its citizens has any right to the allegiance of those whom it has rejected. When, therefore, a whole people, like the fourteen million people of Biafra, have been rejected by the majority of the Federal State in which they were supposed to live, they must have the right to live under a different kind of arrangement which secures them the most elementary safety. It is for these reasons that we re-assumed our inalienable right as a people and declared our Independence on 30th May, 1967. It is for these reasons also that we have fought and are still fighting in defence of our new States in the war of aggression unleashed against us by Nigeria.

Our experience of the past ten months of war have strengthened and confirmed us in the belief that only sovereignty can guarantee to Biafra the minimum security required by her people. We are firm in this conviction. This our position has already been supported by a number of African States which have recognized the sovereignty of Biafra. Nevertheless, the Biafran

Delegation will be prepared to examine any other formula put forward by Nigeria which equally and effectively guarantees to Biafrans, by clear and inviolable institutional arrangements, the control of their own security.

Turning to the question of the cessation of hostilities, we believe that talks and negotiations can lead to a lasting peace. But no such lasting peace can be achieved by continuing a war such as Nigeria has been waging against Biafra. The issues involved cannot be settled by force of arms. It is a tragedy that Nigeria attacked Biafra. The pogrom and genocide which preceded the war had already caused enough hatred and bitterness. Nigeria's aggression against Biafrans in their own home-land has made matters much worse, with all the suffering, massacre and bombing of innocent and defenceless civilians.

It is not, however, too late to give up war and return to negotiation as the only means of solving the problems involved. No amount of force, no amount of military operations, can solve the basic issues. That is why the Nigerian war against Biafra has been described by many independent observers as a senseless war. So long as Nigeria continues her acts as aggression against Biafra, peace talks cannot produce meaningful results. Everyday the war lasts, the more difficult it will be to reach agreement. That is why we have insisted that the cessation of hostilities must be the first substantive item on the agenda. We, therefore, propose that there must be:

(1) immediate cessation of fighting on land, sea and air;
(2) immediate removal of the economic blockade mounted by Nigeria against Biafra; and
(3) the withdrawal of troops to behind the pre-war boundaries.

With regard to (1)—cessation of fighting—we shall be willing to agree to:

(a) the policing of the cease-fire line by an international force, the composition of which must be agreed to by both sides;
(b) a supervisory body, the composition and power of which are to be agreed, which will be stationed in the areas from which troops are withdrawn to ensure that the local population are not in any way victimised.

With regard to (2)—removal of the blockade—we shall be ready, if it is agreed, to accept the supervision at points of entry into Nigeria and Biafra to ensure that there is no arms build-up by either side while talks on item 4 of the agenda—Arrangements for a permanent settlement—continue. The aim should be to restore civilian life and administration back to normal in the war-ravaged areas as soon as possible. We believe that given agreement on these points, peace talks can proceed in an atmosphere conducive to success. Since Nigeria is the aggressor in this war, it is only by agreeing to an immediate cessation of hostilities that she can show that she genuinely desires peace.

Once the cessation of hostilities is achieved, the conference will, with confidence, examine whatever arrangements may be suggested for a permanent settlement. As has already been stated, we believe that sovereignty is the only possible way of ensuring that Biafrans have exclusive control of the protection of their own lives, liberty and property. Granted that, the Biafran Delegation will propose for discussion under item 4 of the agenda the following:

(i) maximum economic co-operation and common services with Nigeria;

(*ii*) problems relating to the sharing of the assets and liabilities (including the external public debt) of the former Federation of Nigeria;

(*iii*) problems relating to the payment of compensation for the life and property of Biafrans which were lost during the pogrom and as a result of the war; and

(*iv*) the holding of a plebiscite in disputed areas in and outside Biafra.

It is our hope that the procedural items on the agenda can be cleared as quickly as possible so that we can discuss the substantive items. There are two of these procedural items. There is the question of chairmanship. Both sides have already shown their confidence in His Excellency Dr Obote by agreeing to hold these talks in Kampala. It would be in line with true African tradition that His Excellency, our host, should preside at these talks. On the second question of the presence of foreign observers, by which we mean observers who are neither Nigerians nor Biafrans, it again seems to us to be in accordance with African traditions of peace-making that well-meaning and friendly people should be present, other than the disputants. These two items are so straightforward that I hope that, now that we are talking in the African atmosphere and fully conscious of the spirit of Africa, we can quickly dispose of them.

[1] *Speech made at the peace talks, 23 May 1968 (Markpress Release No. Gen. 135).*

158.
Nigeria's Twelve-Point Proposal at Kampala[1]

1. A date shall be agreed as cease-fire day.
2. A time on cease-fire day shall be agreed as cease-fire hour.
3. Twelve hours before cease-fire hour,

   a. the rebels will renounce secession, order their troops to lay down their arms as from cease-fire hour, and announce the renunciation and the order publicly and simultaneously;

   b. the Federal Government will order the army, navy, and air force to cease military operations as from cease-fire hour and announce the order publicly;

   c. the Commonwealth Secretariat will make the same announcement as at *a.* and *b.*

4. At cease-fire hour, all troops will be frozen in the positions. An observer force drawn from a source agreed at this meeting shall take position at the cease-fire line.

5. Twenty-four hours after cease-fire hour, a mixed force shall enter rebel-held areas for the purpose of supervising the disarming of rebel forces. The mixed force shall consist of:

   a. elements of the federal army and police;

   b. elements of the observer force and

   c. Ibo policemen from police units established in liberated areas.

   The mixed force shall co-operate with elements of the rebel forces.

6. Not later than seven days after cease-fire day, the administration of rebel-held areas will be handed over to the Federal Government.

7. Pending arrangements to bring the administration of the East Central State into line with the rest of the country, the Federal Government will appoint a commission to administer rebel-held areas. The commission shall consist of a chairman who is Ibo appointed by the Federal Government and a number of other members who are Ibos appointed by the Federal Government, half of whom shall be appointed in consultation with rebel leaders.

8. Law and order in the rebel areas will be the normal responsibility of the police.

9. The Federal Government will recruit persons of Ibo origin and integrate them with the Nigerian army.

10. As soon as possible, a person of East Central State origin will be appointed to the Federal Executive Council.

11. The Federal Government will, in respect of the organizers of the rebellion, grant amnesty in appropriate cases, and will, in respect of other persons connected with the rebellion, grant general amnesty.

12. Prisoners of war held by both sides and hostages taken by the rebels will be released.

[1] In the absence of any official text from the Ministry of Information in Lagos or from Nigeria House, this is taken from a secondary source. It is believed to be accurate.

159.
Ojukwu's Speech on Biafra's First Anniversary[1]

A year is a short period in the history of a nation. For us in Biafra, however, the experience of this first year of sovereignty has been that of a century. In one short year we have had to tackle the very grave questions of life and death, war and peace, survival and extermination. We have been blockaded and isolated, shot and shelled, bombed and strafed. We have been insulted and taunted by our Nigerian enemies and their spokesmen, agents and foreign collaborators. Through this period of great trial we have stood up like men and held our heads high. We have fought back against the Nigerian aggressor, scorning his vainglorious threat, defying his borrowed might. Within the year we have made the world aware of our existence as a nation. We have stirred the countries of the world to a just appreciation of our cause. We have earned the diplomatic recognition of our sovereignty and the right to separate existence as a sure guarantee for survival, security and prosperity.

We have a great deal to celebrate this day, a great deal to be thankful for. But as we are still at war we cannot celebrate this occasion with all the spirit and fanfare it deserves. . . .

Let me on this auspicious morning say how proud I have been of you, the people of this Republic, your faith, your courage, your endurance and your loyalty in the crucial months during which I have had the opportunity to lead this nation. I have drawn my own sustenance and strength from the intrepidity of you all. I feel today like 14,000,000 men because I know there are tough lion-hearts behind me. An anniversary such as this is an appropriate time for reflection and projection by the nation. . . .

On this occasion of our first anniversary let me restate these principles and values. First, Biafra believes in the sanctity of human life and in the sacredness of the human person. In our traditional society the destruction of human lives is not only a crime but a sacrilege. Having ourselves been subjected to humiliation, torture and death in the hands of our enemy, we should now and always uphold and strengthen this traditional faith in the sacredness of human life. It is the duty of all Biafrans now and in the future to ensure that this principle is never assailed in their community. . . .

Secondly, we, as a people, believe in hard work and economic initiative. We believe that the property legitimately acquired by an individual through his exertion should not be taken away from him without just cause. This concern for security of personal property derives part of its logic from the view widespread among Biafrans that a certain degree of wantlessness and the possession of personal property is essential to ensure the dignity and respect of the individual and that, conversely, utter destitution and lack of basic personal property reduce that dignity and respect. . . .

Our society, however, believes that every man belongs to this community. Our people have developed a realistic well being which accepts co-operation as the sanest and most logical answer to the question of man's proper place in society. This wide view also recognises a delicate but workable balance between the claims of the individual and those of society. As a result, our society has developed a realistic and effective reciprocal relationship between man and society. Biafra must fight to preserve this relationship.

Thirdly, the ideal of the rule of law is one of the driving forces behind the founding of the Republic of Biafra. The future Biafra will be guided by this knowledge. The law courts will have a crucial role to play in upholding and fostering this rule of law. In this country the process of law and justice will be speedy, efficient and honest. Justice will be accessible to all, irrespective of their personal leaning, and laws will be devised to protect the citizen from exploitation in his search for justice.

Fourthly, we believe in the right of every citizen to participate in the Government of his country as a means of forestalling misrule and securing his rights and liberties. We believe that society should be organised to ensure social harmony and maximum scope for the individual to realise himself and attain personal happiness.

Biafra believes in the communal democracy, national stability and morality to the politics of our traditional society. We have always held that a sound structure of political power and the right relationship between that power and social responsibility hold the scheme to the well being of society and individual. Communal democracy or government by consensus is our own formula for good democratic government. Under this system, which has been with us for centuries, all political authority is derived from the community and political decisions are based not merely on the view of the majority, as in conventional democracy, but on consensus. The result in our traditional society was that the structure of political power and governmental action was aimed at ensuring the good and well being of all people as well as providing stability, peace and justice within society. . . . Consensus will be the basis of government in Biafra.

Fifthly, our society is a progressive and dynamic one. The people of Biafra have always striven to achieve a workable balance between the claims of tradition and the demands for change and betterment. We are an adaptable people because we are convinced as our people say no condition is really permanent, that human efforts and will are necessary to bring about those changes and improvement in the conditions of the individual and of society which they regard as desirable. Where others would accept an inferior position in life or communal backwardness with apathy or even as the design will of the Almighty, the Biafran would see them as a challenge to his God given talent and initiative. He would thus strive relentlessly to improve his lot and raise the general level of his community. . . .

Finally, our revolution has brought home to us the fundamental need for social justice in our community. Our people have always rejected all forms of social injustices and disability. They have been unrelenting in their desire to overthrow all class and sectional privileges and all vestiges of aggression, abuse and corruption. The Government of Biafra is committed to the achievement of a just society in which every citizen will have the fullest opportunity for self-development and self-fulfilment, where a man can reach his just place in the community unimpeded by social, economic or political inequalities, or by the evil forces of corruption and nepotism. . . .

For these values and principles we are willing to endure our present hardship. Let us individually resolve to shape our own lives to accord with these objectives of our nation. The individual Biafran must today resolve to live as the ideal Biafran: a man who believes in the existence of a Supreme God, head over all men, a man who accepts the obligation to work hard; a man who believes in the dignity of work and is diligent in all his exertions; a man who values thrift and uses the resources of his head and hand to find legitimate economic security for himself and his family; a man who is original in his thinking and always eager to experiment; above all, a man who is responsible, disciplined, efficient but simple. . . .

[1] *Delivered on 30 May 1968. The full text was subsequently issued by the Biafran Ministry of Information and appeared, revised, in Ojukwu's selected speeches, Biafra (1969). It is also available, with gaps, in B.B.C. ME/2785. A précis was issued in Markpress Release No. Gen. 156. Its philosophical basis should be compared with that in the 1969 anniversary speech* [DOC *202*].

160.
Enahoro's Letter on Arms Supplies Addressed to all British M.P.s[1]

Dear Member of Parliament,

Much interest and concern has been shown in Britain lately in the events in Nigeria. As you must be aware, there has been some criticism of this interest and concern. For my part, having myself a few years ago been a beneficiary of this interest and concern, I welcome it. . . . It is, however, of the first importance that your interest and concern in Nigeria should be of an informed nature and that you should have the facts correct. This is my excuse for this personal letter to you.

I understand that today the House of Commons will debate a motion dealing with the sale of British arms to Nigeria. This has arisen from the increasing pressure or demand in various quarters in Britain that the British Government should stop the sale of arms to the Federal Government. If I may say so with great respect to those well-meaning persons who have associated themselves with this pressure, the demand is based on ignorance of (a) the significance of British arms in the war, (b) the vast labyrinths of the international arms traffic, and (c) the probable effects of stoppage. Also, in most cases, there is an unfounded fear regarding the use to which British arms may be put in future operations by the Nigerian Army.

I wish to assure you that, so far, British arms have not played a conclusive role in the conflict. Neither the volume nor the variety of British arms could by itself have turned the scale so decisively against the rebels as we have witnessed in recent months of fighting.

As far as the international arms traffic is concerned, the volume, the variety and the sources of arms are considerable and are open to those willing to pay the price. I am afraid there is no prospect that unilateral stoppage by Britain could end the war, because, as I have indicated above, there are alternative sources open to the Federal Government as indeed to the rebels. It may be recalled that when the British Government refused to sell aircraft to the Nigerian Air Force, the Federal Government had no difficulty in obtaining them from other sources. Furthermore, whatever the British Government may feel obliged to do about the sale of arms to Nigeria, it is quite certain that their own existing sources of supply will remain open to the rebels. This would not end our tragic war.

The indiscriminate and ill-founded use of the highly emotional word 'genocide' recalls to the British mind the fate of the Jews in Germany under Hitler and paints a dreadful picture of the use to which British arms may be put by the Federal Army. The evidence of British subjects living in Nigeria, British press and radio correspondents who have visited liberated areas, and priests on the spot, should satisfy impartial opinion that there is no threat of genocide. I cannot avoid a feeling of insult when it is suggested that I or my colleagues (the majority of us Christians) would be party to a diabolical plan to wipe out a 'race' of 8,000,000 people.

So much for what a stoppage would not achieve. It is even more important to consider what the positive effects of stoppage might be. I can immediately foresee four effects.

The first, as I have indicated, would be to compel the Federal Government to turn to other sources of supply at a cost which could conceivably involve British interests. The second is that the stoppage would confirm in the Nigerian mind allegations that the British Parliament and people do not really care whether or not Nigeria remains a united country. In this regard, you must be aware that it is already being suggested that after the liberation of Port Harcourt—securing thereby the oil installations—the British Parliament and Government are indifferent whether or not Nigeria is completely re-united. Thirdly, the stoppage would encourage further rebel intransigence and thereby prolong the war. This would be disastrous at a time when renewed efforts are being made by the British Government and the Commonwealth Secretariat to reconvene the peace talks. Fourthly, I have no doubt in my mind that the stoppage would alienate the vast majority of Nigerians and thereby jeopardise British interests. . . .

I have referred above to the occasion when I was myself a beneficiary of British interest and concern with humanitarian problems. I recall vividly on that occasion how many Members of Parliament refused to accept my warning regarding the ultimate consequences of what was going on in Nigeria. I regret that recent events have proved how right I was. Now on this occasion, when the British Parliament is once again concerned about Nigeria, I say quite solemnly as a well-known friend of Britain that stoppage of the sale of arms to the Federal Government would be a major error of judgement and a serious miscalculation the probable repercussions of which we cannot fully measure at present. . . .

¹ *Sent from London on 12 June 1968. (Text by courtesy of an M.P.).*

161.
Ojukwu's Address to Joint Consultative Assembly, June 1968¹

. . . In spite of all the bitterness of the past year and the grave sufferings we had undergone at the hands of the Nigerians, our delegation went to Kampala in faith and there made genuine and realistic proposals for the settlement of this conflict. We drew attention to the horrors of the present war, to the futility of military adventurism and proposed the cessation of hostilities as a necessary preliminary to any serious talks of a permanent settlement. We therefore proposed as follows [see DOC 157, pp. 231–2]. . . .

From the personal conduct of Nigeria's delegates as individuals, from their official statements and delaying tactics at Kampala, and from the policy guide lines reportedly set out by Gowon in Lagos, it became clear that Nigeria's course was still that of war, conquest and extermination. It is to this policy that we in Biafra must now seriously address ourselves. It is to the implications of this course, also, that we have been asking the world to address itself.

Nigeria, on the other hand, went to Kampala not to seek a peaceful end to the war, but to achieve an accelerated imposition of its genocidal aims. She went to Kampala as a 'conqueror'. Hence the 12-point proposal which the Nigerian delegation presented at the conference. . . .²

These conditions would have to be accepted by our delegation before a cease-fire could be considered. The conditions were obviously unacceptable, and Nigeria must have anticipated this. But so crazed were they with their military power and the strength of the resources of Britain and other powers which stood behind them that they failed to remember that we are not a conquered nation, that we are a people determined, now as at any other time, to fight to the death in defence of our nation, our survival and that of our prosperity. . . .

Let us emphasise here and now that the Kampala talks have ended. Our chief delegate made the position quite clear that he would return to London only in the event of the prospects for a meaningful discussion emerging from the visit of Lord Shepherd to Lagos. In this we were to be the judge. As far as we can see now, such a situation has not emerged. Many interested governments and organisations have sent observers to Biafra since the present war to acquaint themselves with the actual conditions in our republic. Our door remains open for any interested government or organisation to send a mission to Biafra to meet the people of this republic and obtain a first-hand impression of the nature of the conflict and the feelings of the people. . . .

I think we have made it abundantly clear to the world that the only settlement we can accept is one which satisfies the needs and the wishes of the people for whom we speak and on whose undisputed mandate we act. In the early months of this war, our struggle was maliciously called 'Ojukwu's Rebellion' by our enemies. Later, they began to call it the 'Ibo Resistance'. Sooner or later they are bound to accept realities and admit that this struggle has been nothing short of a struggle for survival and self-determination involving all Biafrans. Happily, the world is now beginning to hear something and acknowledge our people's expressions of their right to self-determination.

The issues involved in this conflict affect the very lives of each and everyone of the 14 million people of Biafra. No settlement is therefore valid which does not take very serious cognisance of this fact. It cannot be an agreement among leaders of the two countries, merely on paper: it cannot be simply a face-saving arrangement intended to soothe the conscience of foreign ministers. It must be a settlement which fully satisfies the deepest urges of our men and women who have taken up arms, against mighty odds, to defend their lives and property and ensure that there is a homeland for the security of those that come after them.

It was from this conviction that we challenged the present leaders of Nigeria to accept a plebiscite in the disputed areas of Nigeria and Biafra to determine the true wishes of the people in those areas. Those who now lead Nigeria know too well the reality of the popular support in all the provinces of this Republic for our stand in this conflict to agree to such a plebiscite. It has become abundantly clear to discerning observers inside and outside Nigeria that the leaders of the regime in Lagos are refusing to accept a cease-fire because only as long as the war continues can they hope to remain in power. Because they now control the military machine which Britain and other countries have lavishly made available, these so-called leaders are adamant in their ambition to impose their will on the Biafran people. . . .

[1] *Delivered at Owerri, 30 June 1968 (Markpress Release No. Gen. 220).*
[2] *See p. 232.*

162.
Gowon Addresses O.A.U. Committee at Niamey[1]

Since your meeting in November, when I had the honour and privilege to welcome you to our country, there have been significant developments in the Nigerian situation. I have taken various steps to keep members of the Consultative Mission as well as the entire membership of the OAU fully informed of these developments. Nevertheless this meeting provides another opportunity for the Federal Government to re-state briefly the more important of these events.

Since the rebels refused bluntly to respond to the peace initiative of the OAU, much of the indirect contact with representatives of the rebel regime has been through the Commonwealth Secretariat. In fact, such contact has not been without considerable frustration caused by the insincerity of the rebels who pretend to want a peaceful solution but are not prepared to take the fundamental step that would lead to peace. Twice in October and November, the Commonwealth Secretary-General approached the Federal Military Government with peace initiatives on assurances by the rebels that they were willing to negotiate. On the two occasions, the Federal Government responded favourably and even sent delegates to London to meet the representatives of the rebels. Unfortunately, on both occasions, the rebels changed their minds and did not go to London as promised.

In April when the Commonwealth Secretary-General again informed the Federal Government that the rebels were prepared to talk the Federal Government immediately re-affirmed its willingness to embark on talks with the rebels without pre-conditions. It was this firm commitment to working for a peaceful solution that made the Federal Government agree to the preliminary talks in London followed by the full-scale talks in Kampala Uganda. Members of the Consultative Mission are no doubt familiar with the proceedings and the eventual collapse of the peace talks. . . .

The Kampala meeting disposed of the question of chairmanship and foreign observers mainly because the Federal Government delegation made a concession by proposing that President Obote and the OAU should each nominate an observer. It is indeed revealing that the rebel representatives rejected the Federal Government proposal that OAU Consultative Mission should nominate an observer.

In presenting the Federal proposals on the substantive question of conditions for ending the hostilities the leader of the Federal delegation, Chief Anthony Enahoro, stressed that the mandate of his delegation gave it discretion to be flexible so long as the territorial integrity of Nigeria was not compromised. During the informal off-the-record discussion that followed it was observed that some progress was being made and that given adequate guarantees for the security of the Ibos the rebel delegation might be able to agree to some satisfactory formula for a settlement. This hope was unfortunately dashed when the rebel leader, Mr. Ojukwu, in a broadcast on May 30, announced that the sovereignty of his so-called republic was not negotiable.[2] This broadcast represented a fresh directive for the rebel delegation and the leader of the delegation immediately hardened his position and made it clear that he could no longer continue with the negotiations. He subsequently walked out of the peace talks.

The Kampala peace talks foundered on the important question of a cease-fire. Our basic aim is to preserve the territorial integrity of Nigeria and to guarantee to the different ethnic groups equal status. This necessarily involves the abandonment of secession by the rebel leaders and the ending of the rebellion. The attempt at secession was not only aimed at breaking up Nigeria but also to subjugate the five million non-Ibos in the former Eastern Region to the perpetual domination of the majority Ibo tribe.

Therefore, to agree to an unconditional cease-fire without the rebel leaders' prior commitment to give up their so-called sovereignty will be totally unacceptable to the Nigerian populace. That would be a ceasefire between two sovereign countries. Besides, such a cease-fire can only provide at best, a temporary respite, for the main issue at stake will remain unresolved. The lasting peace settlement has to be in the context of one, not two countries.

One of the most important developments since your last meeting has been the recognition accorded to the rebels by four members of the OAU. The recognition constituted a gross violation of the Charter of the Organisation, and blatant disrespect for the collective decision taken in Kinshasa to entrust the involvement of the OAU in the Nigeria crisis to a Consultative Committee of six brother Heads of State. The rebel leaders have, by the belated recognition, been encouraged to continue their futile war against their fatherland, thus leading to further bloodshed.

Indeed, it is the belief of the Federal Government that the intransigence of the rebels at the Kampala peace talks, and subsequent discussions was due in no small part to the fact that the rebels over-estimated the significance of the 'recognition' accorded by these four African countries. As a matter of fact, Mr. Ojukwu had been promised by his foreign backers that if the rebel forces held on to Port Harcourt for another fourteen days, twelve countries were lined up to recognise the rebel regime, to be followed by eight others. But Port Harcourt fell to Federal forces on May 17, 1968. It is significant that Zambia was the only one of those twelve countries to announce its recognition of the rebel regime on the agreed date in spite of the fall of Port Harcourt. With the fall of Port Harcourt, the last effective link between the rebels and the outside world was broken. This is really the reason why the rebels are talking so much about human sufferings and starvation today.

The Federal Government believes that it would be helpful to the cause of peace in Nigeria, for the consultative Committee to invite, in the name of African Unity, these four countries which seem to have influence with the rebels, to prevail on the secessionists to return to the conference table and negotiate a peaceful settlement. Since it is now quite clear that the Federal Government has done its best to seek a peaceful settlement, the four countries should prove their good faith by advising the rebels either jointly or individually to give up secession and accept reintegration into Nigeria with adequate arrangements for the security of the life and property of Ibos. The four countries can bring effective and maximum pressure on the rebel leaders by withdrawing the recognition accorded the rebel regime if Mr. Ojukwu continues to treat with contempt the OAU peace initiative which the Federal Government has always welcomed. The withdrawal of such recognition is the greatest service these four countries can render to African unity and thereby end the intransigence of the rebel leaders.

I and my colleagues in the Federal Government have been touched by the suffering of Nigerians on both sides in the current civil war. In this respect, the Federal Government has from the start co-operated fully with the International Red Cross and other voluntary agencies and Governments in providing relief for war victims. Shortly after the outbreak of the war, last year the Federal Government allowed the International Red Cross to fly medical supplies into Port Harcourt which was then under rebel control. When the rebels indicated that they would not accept supplies that passed through Lagos the Federal Government allowed the International Red Cross to fly directly from Santa Isabel to the rebel-held areas after inspection by the Nigerian Consul there.

Following the liberation of Port Harcourt by Federal troops, the rebels no longer had under their control any international airport or sea-port; this was at a time when the International Committee of the Red Cross indicated that relief supplies in enormous quantities were urgently required for the rebel-held areas. The Federal Government immediately guaranteed to the Red Cross its co-operation in conveying supplies to rebel-held areas and has even offered to provide vehicles and escorts. The Federal Government agreed that such supplies could be flown to Lagos or Enugu and be transported overland to rebel-held territory through an agreed temporary mercy corridor free from military activity. Fearing that the free passage of relief supplies would deflate his campaign of calumny against the Federal Government, Mr. Ojukwu has rejected the offer. He has, thereby, put a great obstacle in the way of the International Red Cross in trying to provide relief of the suffering masses upon whom he has imposed untold hardship by his mad ambition.

I wish to take this opportunity to express the gratitude of the people and Government of Nigeria to the people and Government of African countries who through public donations and other means have offered relief for the victims of the Nigerian war. The Federal Government realises that the people of Nigeria have to shoulder the responsibility for the emergency relief supplies of food, drugs and other essentials to their less fortunate brothers in the war-affected areas. The Federal Government has accordingly set up a National Rehabilitation Commission for this purpose with an initial financial outlay of £1 million.

We must however, recognise that the rebel leaders and their foreign backers are playing politics with the whole question of human sufferings in the war zones and trying to exploit the sufferings of our countrymen to their diplomatic and military advantage. Once the rebellion is ended by negotiations or otherwise we will heal our wounds and care for the hungry and needy in the war zones.

If the rebel leaders persist in their contemptuous attitude to the conference table the Federal Government will have no choice but to take over the remaining rebel-held areas in which there are only three important towns: Aba, Owerri and Umuahia as shown in the map. In military terms, the rebellion is virtually suppressed already. There is no doubt about that. What the Federal Government is determined to prevent is any diplomatic manoeuvre or political initiative which will enable the rebel leaders to sustain the rebellion and secession which they have lost in the battlefield.

This brings me to the two vital questions of a foreign Observer Force and unilateral cease-fire on which the Federal Government has definite views.

The rebels demand immediate cease-fire together with the immediate removal of the economic blockade of rebel-held areas and the withdrawal of Federal troops to what they call pre-war boundaries. This means in effect that the Federal Government should not only order a cease-fire but withdraw its troops from the two minority States, Rivers State and South-Eastern, and more than half of the East-Central (Ibo) State which the Federal troops have already taken over. The political condition inherent in the rebel proposal for a cease-fire on these terms, is an implicit acceptance of the so-called republic of Biafra by the Federal Government.

A unilateral ceasefire by the Federal Government without any prior commitment by the rebel leaders will give the rebels the opportunity to re-group and rearm and prepare for a bloodier conflict. It will also give them a diplomatic advantage since such a unilateral cease-fire will guarantee the continued existence of the rebel regime in rebel-held areas. Lastly, such a unilateral cease-fire will not in any way relieve the suffering of the people in the rebel-held areas since the rebels will not allow the refugees to return to their homes and villages in the federally-controlled parts of the former Eastern Region of Nigeria. Thus, a Federal Government decision to order a unilateral ceasefire on humanitarian grounds will not in any way relieve the sufferings of the innocent victims of our tragic civil war.

I am fully conscious of the fact that, after the bitter experience of a civil war, the Ibos in rebel-held areas may fear for their personal safety when the rebellion is over. To accommodate this fear the Federal Government has agreed to have an outside Observer Force to give a sense of security to the Ibos. But this foreign Observer Force can only come to Nigeria on the specific invitation of the Federal Government. The proposed external Observer Force is not a peace-keeping force set up to separate the combatants. We are thinking of an Observer Force drawn from friendly Governments to witness the reassertion of Federal authority in rebel-held areas. Such an Observer Force will bear testimony to the fact that Federal troops will not go into the rebel-held areas to 'massacre' Ibos.

To bring an international peace Force into Nigeria on any other basis will worsen the situation and bring false hope to the rebels that they can sustain their rebellion through international backing. An international peace Force will also provide the opportunity for intrigues and 'Big Power' politics in Nigeria, a situation we are most anxious to avoid, judging from the experience in other parts of the world.

The Federal Government and people of Nigeria are more than convinced that the only way out of the war in Nigeria is a settlement based on one country with full protection and equality of status for all ethnic groups including the seven million Ibos and five million non-Ibos in the former Eastern Region of Nigeria. We welcome any OAU initiative which can bring lasting peace to Nigeria in the context of national unity and the preservartion of our territorial integrity.

[1] *Speech made on 16 July 1968. Text by courtesy of a member of the Nigerian delegatio n It was also published in* New Nigerian *and* Daily Times, *17 July 1968.*
[2] *See* DOC *159.*

163.
Ojukwu's Press Conference before leaving for Niamey[1]

... Nigeria sees the pogrom, the expulsion of Biafrans from Nigeria, the economic blockade, sanctions and other hostile acts against Biafrans as steps in the final military solution of the Ibo problem, that is the extermination of 14,000,000 Biafrans. Thus the obstacles in the way of peace may be summarised as follows:

(1) The British Government's desire to maintain its economic dominance over the single Nigeria it has created and its open support and encouragement of Gowon by: (*a*) continuous supply of arms to Nigeria; (*b*) economic, diplomatic and propaganda offensive on behalf of Nigeria; (*c*) dishonest representations of the facts to the British Parliament and public.

(2) Nigeria's intransigence which has resulted in: (*a*) its refusal to agree to a cease-fire; (*b*) its insistence that Biafra must renounce its sovereignty and accept the 12-States structure created without consultation of the people or their representatives; (*c*) the provocative request in the 12-point proposal at Kampala for virtual surrender; (*d*) its continued rejection of all appeals and blackmailing of reasonable African Heads of State and international organisations.

(3) Russia's ambition to establish a communist sphere of influence in West Africa. Consequently Russia, Britain and the United States, countries with diametrically opposed ideologies, are competing to maintain an influence in Nigeria by supplying arms for the genocide of Biafrans.

(4) The unrealistic attitude of the OAU which has the unique opportunity of proving to the world and to the member states that independent African countries are capable not only of defending themselves but also of solving African problems. The OAU mediation committee failed because of its unrealistic attitude of attempting to solve an African problem in an un-African manner. Until a couple of days ago they had not indicated their willingness to listen to both sides in the dispute.

(5) The UN, which has turned a blind eye to evident genocide. The UN Organisation, whose Charter on human rights empowers it to intercede in cases of genocide, refused to accept Biafra's application for intercession to halt Nigeria's genocidal war against Biafra.

Despite all these obstacles to peace, Biafra has offered peace terms which, if accepted, would achieve a lasting peace in this part of Africa. These proposals are: (1) immediate cessation of fighting on land, sea and air—we are prepared to discuss with Nigeria the terms rather than the conditions for a cease-fire: (2) immediate removal of the economic blockade mounted by Nigeria against Biafra; and (3) the withdrawal of troops behind the prewar boundaries to enable refugees to return to their homes. . . .

Biafra is still willing to discuss:

(*i*) maximum economic co-operation and common services with Nigeria;

(*ii*) problems relating to the sharing of assets and liabilities including the external public debt of the former Federation of Nigeria;

(*iii*) problems relating to the payment of compensation for the lives and property of Biafrans which were lost during the pogrom and as the result of the war; and

(*iv*) the holding of a plebiscite in the disputed areas inside and outside Biafra to determine the true wishes of the people.

The Government and people of Biafra believe that the only suitable form of rule is that deriving from the will of the people. . . .

[1] *Markpress Release No. Gen. 242.*

164.
O.A.U. Resolution at Niamey[1]

The Organization of African Unity Consultative Committee on Nigeria meeting in Niamey last Friday, July 19;

Having reviewed the present developments in the Nigerian civil war;

Deeply concerned about sufferings of civilians on both sides;

Considering the urgent need for supplies of food, medicine and clothing to be sent quickly to the affected areas;

Considering further the efforts made by various governments and institutions to convey into the affected areas badly needed supplies of food, medicine and clothing;

Confident that these governments and international institutions will continue to give assistance to the affected areas;

Mindful of its mandate from the Assembly of Heads of State and Government of the Organization of African Unity held at Kinshasa.

Taking note of the decision by the Nigerian Federal Military Government to establish a corridor in the territory it controls to enable the despatch of food, medical and clothing supplies to the affected regions; as well as of its decision to guarantee the security of members of international relief organizations entrusted with the task of transporting and distributing these supplies.

(1) Requests the Federal Military Government to implement without delay its decision to establish a 'mercy' corridor with appropriate collecting points to facilitate the transportation of essential food and medical supplies to the affected areas; to guarantee the safety and freedom of movement of the agents of international relief organizations within Federal controlled territory so as to ensure the effective distribution of these supplies to the needy civilian population in the affected areas; and also to guarantee the safety and security of observers and representatives of international relief agencies who shall inspect supplies at such collecting points.

(2) Appeals to the secessionists to co-operate by accepting relief supplies of food, medicine and clothing transported through the 'mercy' corridor to the collecting points and to provide facilities to ensure the safety and free movement of the personnel of the international relief agencies and guarantee effective distribution to the needy civilian population in the territory under their control.

(3) Thanks those governments and organizations which have so far given assistance for their sympathy and generosity in relieving the sufferings of the civilian population and appeals to these and other governments and organizations to assure the continuation of this humanitarian support.

(4) Urgently appeals to all member states of the OAU to assist in this massive humanitarian relief effort.

(5) Urgently invites both parties, as a matter of urgency, to resume peace talks as soon as possible in order to achieve a final solution of the crisis prevailing in their country, with the object of preserving Nigeria's territorial integrity and guarantee the security of all its inhabitants.

(6) Decides that the Organization of African Unity Consultative Committee shall remain at the disposal of both parties to help them in this direction. The Consultative Committee will remain in contact with the

Federal Government of Nigeria. Colonel Ojukwu or his accredited representatives may at any time contact any of the member governments of the Organization of African Unity Consultative Committee.

¹ *Issued by the O.A.U. Consultative Committee at Niamey, 22 July 1968. Nigeria House Press release, reproduced in* United Nigeria, *no. 1.*

165.
Final O.A.U. Communiqué from Niamey¹

(1) Preliminary peace talks took place in Niamey from 20th to 26th July 1968 in accordance with the terms of the final communiqué issued on 19th July 1968 by the OAU consultative committee on Nigeria.

(2) During their deliberations the two parties have adopted the following agenda for the Addis Ababa peace negotiations under the auspices of the OAU consultative committee:

(*a*) arrangements for a permanent settlement;

(*b*) terms for the cessation of hostilities;

(*c*) concrete proposals for the transport of relief supplies in food and medicine to the civilian victims of the war.

(3) The two parties have examined in detail arrangements for the sending of relief supplies to the civilian victims of the war. No agreement has been reached on certain points in this connection. The two parties, however, agreed to hold additional consultations aimed at taking immediate action which would lead to agreement in Addis Ababa on practical steps on the humanitarian issue whose importance and seriousness have been acknowledged by everyone.

(4) The two parties have agreed on the detailed procedure to be followed at the Addis Ababa peace negotiations.

(5) It has been unanimously agreed upon that the peace negotiations should begin in Addis Ababa on 5th August 1968 at the latest.

¹ *Niamey broadcast, 26 July 1968 (B.B.C. ME/2833/B1). The version issued by Nigeria House, London, on 29 July could be misleading.*

166.
Pro-Biafran Statement by France's Council of Ministers¹

The human drama which is taking place in Biafra is a cause of preoccupation and concern to the French Government. Apart from its desire to take part, to the best of its ability, in the humanitarian efforts now being made, the Government considers that the bloodshed and suffering endured for over a year by the population of Biafra demonstrate their will to assert themselves as a people.

Faithful to its principles, the French Government therefore considers that the present conflict should be solved on the basis of the right of peoples to

R

self-determination and should include the setting in motion of appropriate international procedures.

[1] *Issued in Paris on 31 July 1968. Text by courtesy of the French Embassy, London.*

167.
Nigerian High Commissioner Accuses France[1]

A new situation has arisen in Africa following the decision of the French Government to support the secessionist movement in Eastern Nigeria. Although France has not officially recognised the so-called state of Biafra, there is reason for one to believe that she will attempt to influence some African states to do so and that we are about to witness a diplomatic offensive intended to legalise the existence of a breakaway state in Eastern Nigeria under the pretext of humanitarian considerations.

Of course, we have always known that French interests, as distinct from the French Government, supported the secession from its inception and made it possible by advancing the rebel leaders substantial sums of money which enabled them to acquire large quantities of arms and ammunition. We also knew that French firms extended the rebel authorities important credit facilities for the purchase of vehicles, telecommunication equipment and other materials needed to support their war effort against Nigeria.

Finally, it was through French dealers that the rebel armed forces obtained military aircraft at the beginning of the rebellion. It is difficult to believe that all these deals could have been negotiated without the acquiescence, or at least the knowledge, of the French Government which had officially placed an embargo on the sale of war materials to Nigeria.

What we did not know for certain at the time, though we strongly suspected it, was that this apparently generous financial and material aid to the rebels was granted in exchange for mineral concession rights which had already been ceded by the only legal Government of Nigeria.

Irrefutable documentary evidence has now come into our hands showing that the so-called Government of Biafra actually ceded full and exclusive concession rights to a French group to exploit all the mineral resources of Eastern Nigeria for a period of 10 years. The concession provides for the extraction and exploitation on specified terms of crude oil, coal, uranium, columbite ore, tin concentrates and gold. . . .

It is highly relevant to note in this connection that one of the three preconditions for a settlement of the civil war, officially stipulated by the rebel leaders, is that Federal troops should withdraw to what are described as the 'pre-war boundaries'. These are the boundaries of the former Eastern region of Nigeria which included the present Rivers state where the oilfields are located and where the local population, consisting of non-Ibo minority tribes, has always been loyal to the Federal Government and has greatly suffered at the hands of the rebels. The unrealistic emphasis which the rebels place on this condition, maintaining their claim to the oil-producing area at a time when their military position has become hopeless, confirms, I think, the extent of their commitment to third parties. . . .

In this connection it is to be regretted that France's latest diplomatic move may have the effect of encouraging the rebel leadership to resist peaceful re-unification with greater obstinacy than hitherto in the hope that its claims to independence will be recognised by other African States. . . .

[1] *Statement issued by Brigadier Ogundipe, Nigerian High Commissioner in London, on 5 August 1968. (Text by courtesy of Nigeria House.)*

168.
Ojukwu's Address to Addis Ababa Peace Talks[1]

Your Imperial Majesty, Your Excellencies.

With all humility and the deepest respect, I salute you. I extend to you all the gratitude of the people of Biafra for your concern about the sufferings of our people, following the calculated and systematic acts of genocide and total extermination being carried out against them. We are extremely grateful that you have made it possible for us to state before you, and the world, our case and position with regard to this unfortunate conflict. Speaking for myself and the entirety of the afflicted people of Biafra, and having regard to our love of peace, progress and justice in Africa, we feel totally ashamed that we should be associated with an unnecessary and futile war which has brought considerable discredit and shame to Africa.

'There is no precedent for a people being victim of such injustice and being at present threatened by abandonment to its aggressor. Also there has never before been an example of any government proceeding to the systematic extermination of a nation by a barbarous means in violation of the most solemn promises made to all the Nations of the Earth.

'It is in order to denounce to the civilized world the tortures inflicted upon my people that I resolved to come to Geneva.

'I was defending the cause of all small people who are threatened by aggression . . . It is us today. It will be you tomorrow.'

'Today' was June 30, 1936, the speaker and circumstances are well known to all who have pride in Africa. The appeal was made to a world which seemed to have misplaced its conscience.

The appeal went unheeded to a world already deafened by the cacophony of clanging armour and rattling sabres of a war which was to bring misery to the world on an unprecedented scale. The League of Nations collapsed.

Today I stand before this august assembly because the lessons of this vivid past have not been learnt. I stand before you because the prophetic tomorrow has all too soon become the lot of my people today.

For more than twelve months, a cruel and bloody war has been waged by Nigeria against the people of Biafra. During this period more lives have been lost and more property destroyed than at any other time in the known history of the African continent. An area of our continent noted for its promise and plenty, a region dedicated to justice, peace and progress, is being brutalized and turned into a spectacle of fear and famine, disease and death.

The people of Biafra have always maintained that war can solve none of the fundamental ills which have plagued our part of the continent for decades. If anything, it can only profit the enemies of Africa who dread the progress of the African and his determination to escape from their tutelage and dependence. That is why these enemies of African peace and progress are actively and shamelessly fanning the embers of a senseless and fratricidal war by supplying all the weapons of destruction to one side and are doing everything to obstruct the way and efforts towards a just and honourable peace.

May I with all humility and respect venture to say that Your Excellencies have a special responsibility to both present and future generations of Africans to ensure that this war is brought to an immediate end.

Africa must demonstrate her capacity to settle her own problems free from dictation by foreign vested interests.

She must cast aside attitudes and prejudices inherited from a colonial past.

She must pledge herself to the preservation of those norms and practices that distinguish her from all other peoples.

The world has rightly focussed her attention on this conference taking place in this great African city.

The world challenges Africa to grapple, with sincerity and justice, the problem which she has set out to resolve.

We cannot, we dare not fail without compromising the self-respect, the maturity and the dignity of the African race.

We, the people of Biafra, have come to this conference determined to ensure success for peace. Right from the beginning of the current conflict, and even before, we have always believed that this is an African problem which can only be solved by Africa. We as a people seek nothing but peace and security —peace to save us from extermination, and security to enable us develop our talents for the upliftment of Africa. We are in no doubt that after hearing our case the problem which hitherto had seemed intractable will be easily amenable to your mediation.

Repeatedly, we had made appeals for the intervention of African States into the dispute. A number of African Heads of States had also offered their good offices in quest for a peaceful solution. It was Gowon who consistently and contemptuously spurned all such proposals on the fatuous pretext that the matter was an internal affair of Nigeria. For example, following the controversy resulting from Nigeria's failure to implement the Aburi Agreements we pressed that we moved out of Nigeria into a neighbouring African State to iron out the differences. Gowon would not countenance such a move. Instead, Gowon arranged a meeting of the Supreme Military Council in Benin and wanted to bring in British troops to ensure the security of those attending. It was with difficulty that Gowon was persuaded to agree to the holding of the last abortive peace-talks in Africa. His choice had been London. For chairmanship of the talks, Nigeria wanted a non-African in the person of Mr. Arnold Smith of Canada. When we insisted on an African Chairman, Nigeria preferred to have no Chairman at all.

At this stage, I would like to recall that previous attempts by the O.A.U. to deal with the Nigeria/Biafra conflict were frustrated by the attitude of

Nigeria which made it impossible for the Biafran case to be heard. Since this matter was first raised at the O.A.U. Kinshasa meeting in September 1967, the facts of the conflict have become clear to the world, and open military collusion with, and support of, Nigeria particularly by Britain and Russia has alarmed African nations, which are now anxious and determined to bring an end to the war. The principle that there are two sides to a dispute and that each side has a right to state its case, has now been fully accepted. It is in this spirit that the O.A.U. invited us to Niamey. The position was aptly summarised by President Hamani Diori in a communiqué issued on behalf of the Committee which stated as follows:

. . . the new task entrusted to me is to bring together the representatives of the two sides, each one elaborating his own case before me and I shall try on behalf of the Committee to reconcile the two viewpoints.

It is in this spirit which induced the Biafran Government to send a delegation to Niamey, and it is the same spirit that we are here in Addis Ababa.

The whole background to this conflict is well known to all of you. Yet this being a historic occasion, I implore you, therefore, to bear with me while I recall in some detail the developments which not only form the background to the current conflict, but will best clarify our position and aspirations.

Although the conglomeration of territories formerly known as Nigeria was now and then held up to the world as 'democracy's best hope in Africa', by those who created it, it was never a democracy. What was more, the former Federation of Nigeria indeed encompassed peoples of such vast political, economic, religious and cultural differences as could hardly ever have co-existed peacefully as one independent political entity.

In what was Eastern Nigeria—now Biafra—we found in Christianity much that corresponded to our own traditional outlook on life. We readily accepted the egalitarian and democratic ideas—and other things in their wake—introduced by Christian Europe and America.

On the other hand, as a result of the separatist attitude of feudal Northern Nigeria, a vast section of the Northern Nigerian public was left out of the main stream of educational, technological and industrial development which has taken place in the rest of Nigeria in the last hundred years. The Government, the missionary houses and the business firms wanted men and women to man their new establishments, and naturally they employed those Nigerians who had the requisite education and training. A considerable number of the employable men came from the then Eastern Nigeria whose people had made progress in learning and adopting the new ideas and skills introduced by Europeans and Americans.

Christian education and Western training stimulated and enriched our native resourcefulness, industry and dynamism and so contributed in no small measure to the leading role we played in the development of Nigeria during the half century before 1966. In all spheres of life in the former Federation of Nigeria—economic, social, cultural, political and constitutional—we were in the forefront of the struggle for unity and equality, justice and progress. [The paragraphs that follow repeat DOC 142, pp. 194–5]. . . .

In the field of political and constitutional development, while we advocated

a strong, united Nigeria and had for our watchword one country, one constitution, one destiny, Northern Nigerians consistently and openly maintained
that the Amalgamation of Northern and Southern Nigeria in 1914 was 'a
mistake'. Not surprisingly, in January 1950, at the General Conference
summoned at Ibadan to discuss proposals for the review of the Nigerian
Constitution, the Northern Nigerian delegates announced that, 'unless the
Northern Region was allowed 50 per cent. of the seats in the Central Legislature it would ask for separation from the rest of Nigeria on the arrangements
existing before 1914'. In other words, Northern Nigeria would secede.
Eventually, to avoid breaking up the country, we conceded this demand.

At the Ibadan Conference of 1950 also, Northern Nigerians insisted that
'only Northern Nigerian male adults of twenty-five years or more, resident
in the Region for three years, should be qualified for election to the Northern
House of Assembly'. In reply, our delegates were obliged to enter a minority
report in which they raised an issue of fundamental principle. They asserted:

It is in our view invidious that any Nigerian could under a Nigerian Constitution be deprived of the right of election to the House of Assembly in any Region
in which he for the time being—or permanently—has his abode, merely by
reason of the accident of birth or ancestry.

Three years later, in May 1953, during one of the recurrent constitutional
crises of those years, Northern Nigerians again agitated for secession. They
published an eight-point proposal for the establishment of a 'Central Agency'
to maintain what was in effect a Common Services Organization. To secure
the implementation of this proposal by force, Northern Nigerian leaders
organized and carried out violent demonstrations during which they slaughtered and wounded hundreds of our people then resident in Kano, Northern
Nigeria—acts of genocide which they had perpetrated at Jos in Northern
Nigeria earlier in 1945. In the end, we had to abandon the idea of a strong
and united country which we had been advocating and, with difficulty,
persuaded Northern Nigerians to accept a stronger federal system of government than that which was envisaged by them.

The following year, as a result of its failure to absorb Lagos, Western
Nigeria also threatened to secede and was only prevented from proceeding
to make good the threat by a stern and timely warning from the British
Secretary of State for the Colonies, Mr. Oliver Lyttleton (afterwards Lord
Chandos).

It was in these precarious circumstances that Nigeria acceded to Independence on October 1, 1960. Not unexpectedly, the five years immediately
after that date were marked by successive crises; notably the Tiv Riots of
1960–66, the Western Nigeria Emergency of 1962, the National Census Controversy of 1962–63, the Federal Election Crisis of 1964–65 and the Western
Election Crisis of 1965–66.

By January 1966 it had become clear that, unless the situation was arrested
the successive crises experienced by the country before and since Independence would certainly lead to unutterable disaster.

The existing Independence Constitution gave Northern Nigeria a built-in
50 per cent representation in the Federal Parliament, an arrangement which
assured the Region a permanent control of the Federal Government. The

New Statesman of London aptly described the Northern Nigerian Head of the Federal Government as 'Prime Minister in apparent perpetuity'.

Each crisis had been impossible of satisfactory resolution partly because of the men who handled it. A great number of the politicians and others in public life were known to be corrupt, ostentatious and selfish. Bribery and nepotism were rife. There was widespread inordinate ambition for power, an evil mirrored in the prevalence of thuggery, hooliganism and lawlessness. To win power or to keep themselves in power, public men had sown unhealthy rivalry, suspicion and mistrust among the various communities of the country. Thus the unabashed rigging of the Western Election of October 1965 came to be the last straw. The widespread violence which it precipitated took thousands of lives. Law and order broke down in the Western Region. Since each of the other Regions had an interest in the election, it was obvious that the country was on the brink of civil war. And yet the Northern Nigeria-controlled Federal Government, the last hope of the people, would not discharge its responsibility. Indeed many an objective observer interpreted its inaction in the face of the impending national collapse as virtual abdication.

These were the circumstances in which some young Army Officers and men decided to act. They originated from all parts of Nigeria—the North, West, Mid-West and East. It was a revolt against injustice and oppression. From available information, their aims were threefold: to put an end to the sufferings of Nigerian citizens in Tiv land and Western Nigeria, to dethrone the corrupt and dishonest politicians, and to restore public faith at home and retrieve Nigeria's reputation abroad. They attempted to overthrow the Federal and Regional Governments. In desperation the Federal Government handed over power to the Armed Forces under the General Officer Commanding the Nigerian Army, Major-General J. T. U. Aguiyi-Ironsi, who happened to originate from the then Eastern Nigeria, and had in no way been connected with the Revolution. The Revolution was spontaneously acclaimed in and outside Nigeria. Nigerians basked in the general relief that a corrupt, unpopular and unstable regime had been deposed.

The Military Administration of General Ironsi made the first real attempt to unite the country and its peoples. The General approached his enormous task with transparent honesty, unflinching confidence and unalloyed patriotism. The main organs of the Central Government which he established—the Supreme Military Council and the Federal Executive Council—were representative of all the Regions of the country. Whether it was the appointment of Tribunals of Inquiry into the political activities, financial deals and personal accounts of suspects, or appointments to top posts in the Federal Public Service and Statutory Corporations, or the disposition of command in the Army, General Ironsi promoted the interest of the country as a whole. (For full details see *January 15 ; Before and After*, Government Printer, Enugu, 1966, *passim*.) He endeavoured to accelerate the economic development of Northern Nigeria in order to bring the Region in line with other parts of the country.

On May 24, 1966, Major-General Aguiyi-Ironsi promulgated Decree No. 34. That decree was the implementation of a decision of the Federal Supreme Military Council in which all the Regional Military Governors were represented. The Decree was intended to establish a National Executive Council for the whole country with the Regional Military Governors as members and to unify the top cadres of the Civil Service to ensure the efficient administration of the country for the duration of the Military Regime.

Ironically enough, it was this Decree (popularly known as the Unification Decree) that sparked off wide-spread rioting and violence directed against the lives and property of Eastern Nigerians in Northern Nigeria. It did not seem to matter to the leaders who planned the riots that Eastern Nigerians were in a terrible minority (3 out of 9 members) in the Supreme Military Council that took the collective decision. The death toll of our people in the massacres of that month stood at 3,000. A high-powered Commission was appointed by the Supreme Military Council to investigate the causes and the conduct of the May riots in Northern Nigeria. An English Judge of the Supreme Court was appointed Chairman. Northern Nigerian leaders never allowed that Commission to meet.

In the meantime firm assurances of personal safety for our people in Northern Nigeria had been given by the Supreme Military Council itself, and by the Sultan of Sokoto and the Emirs of the North. On the strength of these assurances, we appealed to our people who had fled their stations to return to Northern Nigeria. They did.

At this point Major-General Aguiyi-Ironsi undertook an extensive tour of Northern and Mid-Western Nigeria, and arranged to round off his tour at Ibadan in Western Nigeria with a meeting of traditional rulers and chiefs from all over Nigeria to seek their advice on matters affecting the future of the country. The meeting was scheduled for July 29, 1966. But in the morning of that day, a well-organized group of Northern soldiers kidnapped the Supreme Commander and his host, Lieutenant-Colonel Adekunle Fajuyi, the Military Governor of Western Nigeria, and subsequently murdered them in very gruesome circumstances. The cruel massacre of over 200 of Eastern Nigerian Army Officers and men also took place.

The pace of violence seemed at the time to be quickening. Its character seemed also to be worsening. Brigadier Ogundipe, then the most senior officer in the Army, was compelled to abandon his responsibility: he escaped from Nigeria and was later posted to London as Nigeria's High Commissioner to Britain. In the confusion and violence which followed all over Nigeria, we made efforts to get Lieutenant-Colonel Yakubu Gowon, the co-ordinator and spokesman for the Northern Nigerian rebels, to stop the bloodshed. The rebels stipulated two conditions for doing so.

1. That the Republic of Nigeria be split into its component units.
2. That all Southern Nigerians resident in Northern Nigeria be repatriated to the South, and all Northerners resident in the South be repatriated to the North.

In pursuance of these demands all available aircraft at Ikeja Airport had been commandeered and used in repatriating the families and belongings of Northern Nigerian top civil servants and other officials the moment the rebellion of the Northern Nigerian Army Officers and men began in the Lagos area.

We had no alternative in the circumstances but to accept the Northern Nigerian terms for a cease-fire in order at least to bring a halt to the mass killings and the general breakdown of law and order in the country. It would also give the Army itself the opportunity to decide on its leadership, a necessary condition for the restoration of normal conditions in the country.

It was well known before May, 1966 that there were very powerful moves in Northern Nigeria for secession from the Federation. With the support of British Government officials these interests—traditional rulers, politicians, civil servants and intellectuals—were known to have planned and led the riots of May and the rebellion of July. Their July *putsch* was given the code name of ARABA or secession. The purpose of the British Government in supporting the riots was to restore the Northern domination of the country. But Northern Nigerians understood this as support for the secession which they had been demanding over the years. In the event, Lieutenant-Colonel Gowon was persuaded by the British High Commissioner in Nigeria, Sir Francis Cumming-Bruce, from making his scheduled broadcast proclaiming the secession of Northern Nigeria. Nevertheless, in his first broadcast on August 1, 1966, Lieutenant-Colonel Gowon declared: 'Suffice it to say that putting all considerations to test, political, economic as well as social, the base for unity is not there.'

On August 9, representatives of the Military Governors held a meeting with those of Lieutenant-Colonel Gowon to propose some urgent steps to halt the pace of violence and destruction and reduce tension in the country. It was decided that an Ad Hoc Constitutional Conference made up of Regional Delegations be convened to recommend in broad outline the future form of association for the different Regions of Nigeria. It was agreed that immediate steps be taken to return military personnel to barracks within their respective Regions of origin. The maintenance of peace and security in the Lagos area was left to Lieutenant-Colonel Gowon acting in consultation with the Military Governors.

Had these basic decisions been implemented, promptly and completely, much of the history of the next several months might have been different. But Lieutenant-Colonel Gowon did or wanted no such thing. With respect to Western Nigeria, for example, Lieutenant-Colonel Gowon refused to repatriate Northern Nigerian soldiers to their Region of origin in opposition to the demands of the Chiefs, leaders and people of Western Nigeria. We implemented the decision fully. In keeping with an earlier agreement, Northern Nigerian soldiers then in our territory left for their home Region with their arms and some quantity of ammunition for self-defence. On the other hand, our soldiers returning from Northern Nigeria were denied both arms and ammunition. Exposed and defenceless, these soldiers became easy victims of ridicule, molestation and torture by Northern Nigerians.

In Lagos it was completely impossible to guarantee the personal safety of our military personnel. Major Ekanem, the Provost-Marshal of Ikeja Garrison, was shot dead at Carter Bridge in broad daylight; at Ikeja Airport another of our officers, Captain Okoye, was captured and subsequently tortured to death. In Yaba two officers, Lieutenant-Colonel Eze and Captain Ilo, obeyed appeals from Gowon to return to duty. Captain Ilo was shot dead; Colonel Eze managed to escape with injuries.

About the same time, armed Northern Nigerian soldiers drove to the Benin Prisons in Mid-Western Nigeria and abducted Army Officers and men in detention there following the January 15 Revolution. Their fellow Northern

Nigerians among them were set free; the others, mainly our people, were murdered under very brutal circumstances.

Throughout this period our territory remained the only part of the former Federation of Nigeria which could boast of peace and order. Though there was bitterness at the treatment meted out to our people in parts of Nigeria there was no attempt on the part of the people to avenge on Nigerians resident among us. Instead our people remained calm and restrained in the face of overwhelming provocation. They were, of course, fully aware of the pattern of events throughout Lagos, Western Nigeria and Northern Nigeria. They saw evidence of genocide in the killings. Somehow, they hoped that it would be possible to check the drift of events and that Nigeria could still be saved.

It is pertinent here to state categorically that we never recognized Gowon as the Head of the Nigerian Federal Military Government. Gowon is a rebel. I made this point convincingly clear during the Aburi meeting of January 1967, and it was in acceptance of this fact that it was agreed at that meeting, that one of the first things to do on our return from Aburi should be the formal election of a Commander-in-Chief, whose duty would be to preside over the meetings of the Supreme Military Council.

As the days passed by in August, the wave of massacres in Northern Nigeria began to gather momentum. From even the remotest villages of the Region, our people were fleeing for dear life to the bigger towns from where to return home. At Kaduna on August 30, and in the early days of September, our people fleeing Northern Nigeria were again attacked—in the railway stations and motor parks where they had congregated in search of transport. Several hundreds were killed. Those who escaped abandoned all their possessions. In Minna and many other Northern Nigerian towns, the African Continental Bank and other businesses owned by our Government and people were attacked and looted. Their agents and owners fled back to their homeland, determined never to return.

These developments notwithstanding, and even though they were taking very serious personal risks, our delegates attended the Ad Hoc Constitutional Conference which began in Lagos on September 12, 1966. In his opening address to the Conference, Lieutenant-Colonel Gowon suggested the following alternative forms of association for Nigeria:

a. A federal system with a strong central government;
b. a federal system with a weak central government;
c. a confederation; or
d. an entirely new arrangement which may be peculiar to Nigeria.

Faced with the realities of the Nigerian situation the Conference was veering towards recommending a loose form of association. The delegation from Northern Nigeria, in its original Memorandum to the Conference, proposed that the country be broken up into 'a number of autonomous states . . . that is to say, Northern Nigeria, Eastern Nigeria, Western Nigeria, Mid-Western Nigeria, or by whatever name they may choose to be called'. The central Government according to the Northern Nigerian Memorandum was to be a mere 'Central Authority' and its powers were to be 'delegated by the component states except that powers connected with external or foreign affairs (and) immigration can be unilaterally withdrawn by the State Government'. 'Nigerian' citizenship should be abolished and replaced by an 'Associate citizenship'; and in any case,

Any Member State of the Union should reserve the right to secede completely and unilaterally from the Union and to make arrangement for co-operation with the other members of the Union in such a manner as they may severally or individually deem fit.

The Joint Memorandum from Lagos and Western Nigeria proposed a 'Commonwealth of Nigeria', if federalism was unacceptable to other Regions. This Commonwealth would comprise 'the existing Regions and such other Regions as may be subsequently created. The Government of each state within the Commonwealth shall be completely sovereign in all matters excepting those with respect to which responsibility is delegated to the Council of State'.

When the Conference adjourned on October 3 for three weeks, it had made some progress in spite of pressures and intimidations. By September 18, within a week of the opening of the Conference, riots had broken out in Makurdi, Minna, Gboko and Kaduna in Northern Nigeria. Our people—men, women and children—became the targets of well-organized and systematic mass murders. Our property fell to Northern Nigerian looters and plunderers. By the third week of September, the reign of terror had spread to Lagos and Western Nigeria. Distinguished Biafrans in Ibadan and Oshogbo were abducted by Nigerian soldiers and killed. In Lagos, too, kidnapping of defenceless Biafran civilians by armed soldiers became the order of the day. The climax came with the massacres of September 29 and after, when the Ad Hoc Constitutional Conference was still sitting. On October 1, at Kano Airport alone, over 400 Biafrans awaiting airlifts home were surrounded by armed Northern Nigerian soldiers and civilians and massacred.

In the five months of massacres and atrocities, May-October, 1966, over 30,000 of our people were shot, hacked to death, burnt or buried alive; hundreds of women and children were ravished; unborn children were torn out of their mothers' wombs. Two million of our people deprived and dejected were forced to seek refuge in their homeland.

The September massacres marked a decisive turning-point in the history of the crisis. Before that, we had hoped that the Ad Hoc Constitutional Conference would lead to some satisfactory solution. After the September massacres we were convinced beyond doubt that our security was entirely in our own hands as individuals, and that our only hope lay in returning to our homeland, where we could be sure of protection from molestation and murder. Hence the mass return home—a mass movement on a scale for which there is no precedent in modern African history. The London *Observer* (October 16, 1966) described the scene in the Eastern Region within a fortnight of this mass return as 'reminiscent of the ingathering of exiles into Israel after the end of the last war. The parallel is not fanciful'. As Dr. Conor Cruise O'Brien remarked in an article in the *New York Times Review of Books* (December 21, 1967), 'If this movement had taken place across international frontiers, it would have attracted world-wide attention. Because it was within the geographical unit called Nigeria, it drew no public comment and won no world sympathy'. The experiences of those who came back were bitter, their hard-ship heart-breaking. Those at home who received them and cared for them were also shocked and embittered; especially when they saw the courtesy and kindness with which they continued to treat Nigerians among them.

The mass movement of population in October, 1966 complicated the problems of the country. It meant that thousands of our people could no longer participate in the functions of the Federal Government through employment with federal officers, statutory corporation and organizations based elsewhere in the then Nigeria. It also meant that thousands of our people who were self-employed were now to make a livelihood out of the re-sources in our homeland and no more.

In short, then, while the Ad Hoc Conference was seeking a short-term solution to the country's constitutional problems, the organised massacres of September and October precipitated a further problem of mass population movements and all the attendant complications. The massacres meant that even long-term solutions were going to be very difficult to reach.

At no better time than during October could Lieutenant-Colonel Gowon and his junta in Lagos have shown an appreciation of the peculiar hardships of the citizens of the former Eastern Nigeria. No more opportune moment could have been wished for by the junta to begin to rethink about the mad-ness of their activities since the previous May. Sad to say, however, it was precisely at this time that Lieutenant-Colonel Gowon and his advisers decided to deal what they hoped would be a death-blow to our people. On October 19, Lieutenant-Colonel Gowon imposed a food blockade on us by prohibiting any diversion to us of what he called 'food meant for consumption in Lagos'. The Police and the Army were summoned to enforce the blockade at check-points throughout Lagos, Western and Mid-Western Nigeria. Thanks to the deter-mination of our people and their capacity for hard work, we had no food shortage. But our people did not miss the lesson of the blockade.

Meanwhile we had looked forward to the adoption of a new form of associ-ation in Nigeria necessitated by the new situation created by Northern Nigerian brutality. We were willing to accept the loose association which the Northern Nigerians had been persistently demanding over the years.

Then suddenly, the situation changed radically. Lieutenant-Colonel Gowon and his fellow Northern Nigerians had been advised by the British that the association they were seeking would not be in the interest of their Region, that their interest lay in a 'strong federal' Nigeria which the Northern Nigerians were to dominate. On the basis of this advice, the Northern Nigerian delegation withdrew its original Memorandum. Subsequently, on November 30, 1966, Lieutenant-Colonel Gowon, without consultation with the Military Governors, unilaterally dismissed the Ad Hoc Constitutional Conference. In its place he appointed what he called a 'Drafting Committee' to draw up a constitution on lines determined and approved by his British mentors. Thus, on top of the constitutional stalemate, complicated by the social and economic effects of the September massacres, Lieutenant-Colonel Gowon was not going to allow the accredited representatives of the Regions—representatives bearing the mandate of their Regions—to suggest in what form they wanted to be associated. By this dismissal of the Ad Hoc Con-ference, Gowon destroyed the one hope we had of being represented in the determination of our place within the former Nigerian Federation. The dismissal of the Ad Hoc Constitutional Conference created the tragic and uneasy impasse that was not broken till the meeting of the Supreme Military Council at Aburi, Ghana, in January, 1967.

THE ABURI SUMMIT

The Aburi Meeting was held at the instance and on the insistence of our people. We had pleaded with our counterparts in other regions that we should meet outside Nigeria (for obvious security reasons) to review realistically the very urgent problems facing the country—Army, the Central Government, finance, population and rehabilitation.

It should be pointed out here that the Aburi Meeting was held under the worst auguries possible. Firstly, the pattern of bad faith had become all-too-evident to us: our people did not believe that Gowon and his fellow rebels had had the kind of change of heart that could give reasonable hope of success at the conference. Secondly, Gowon had begun to talk of the might of the Federal Military machine suggesting that he would use force to achieve his ends. In spite of these doubts and uncertainties, however, the meeting was duly held, and several important and realistic decisions taken. [Here follows a repetition of DOC 86, p. 355–6]. . . .

Commenting on the Aburi episode, the present British Secretary of State for Commonwealth Affairs, Mr. George Thomson, recently said in the House of Commons: 'It has been one of the tragedies of this story that the undertakings entered into at that meeting were given different interpretations by both sides and did not come into effect.' There was no cause for any confusion or misinterpretation, since the meeting was tape-recorded and held before a third party. The truth of course is that there were no differences of interpretation. It is on record that Gowon's Federal Permanent Secretaries and officials mostly of Northern origin advised him not to implement the decisions largely because they were not in consonance with the avowed Northern Nigerian policy of dominating Nigeria under the supervision of the British Government. Gowon consequently drafted decrees which at best circumvented the Aburi decisions, at worst contradicted them. Most dishonourable of all, Gowon included in one of these decrees a clause, not agreed at Aburi, arrogating to himself the power to declare a state of emergency in any Region—a dictatorial measure which completely nullified the whole Aburi Accord.

At this stage in the crisis, I appealed to some African Heads of State to use their good offices to effect a peaceful settlement of the dispute. But Gowon spurned the well-intentioned offers of mediation from those Heads of State.

Gowon even went further. He took positive measures designed to expel us from Nigeria. In the face of the colossal problem of rehabilitating our refugees, his Lagos Government, which was in possession of the central resources of Nigeria, would render no assistance. Instead the Lagos Government complicated matters for our people by denying us the statutory periodic remittances to which we were entitled. In spite of the agreement at Aburi our people in the employ of the Federal Government and its agencies were denied salaries and wages due to them between July 1966 and March 1967. The Lagos Government also stopped the supply of the necessary equipment, material and spare parts for Federal statutory bodies operating in our territory.

On February 16, 1967, I was constrained to address the following letter to Gowon which was copied to the other Military Governors.[2] . . . It cannot here be too strongly emphasized that if the above letter had been heeded and the Aburia greements fully implemented the present conflict would have been averted. No reply to this letter was received.

In the face of the blatant refusal to implement the Aburi Agreements, and of many acts of atrocities against our people, we were forced to pass the 'Survival Edicts'. One of these, Revenue Collection Edict, was to prevent the Lagos Government from owing us the statutory revenues that legitimately belonged to us. The Lagos Government was then indebted to our Government to the tune of £11.8 million. Another, Statutory Bodies Edict, was to ensure the procurement of funds for the maintenance of essential services. It must be stated that these Edicts did not alter the formula for revenue allocation as provided in the Nigerian Constitution. In the Annual Estimates for 1967–68 the revenues expected from Federal sources were shown strictly in accordance with the existing formula.

Gowon's reaction to these Edicts was to impose further punitive measures on us.

Gowon informed major world and African powers that his actions against us were an internal affair, and that their intervention would be regarded as a hostile act against Nigeria. He sealed off our border with the Republic of Cameroun and closed that Republic's Consulate in Enugu. Gowon cancelled the passports of all our people who transferred from the Federal Public Service to our Public Service.

Gowon imposed a total economic blockade on us; suspended Nigeria Airways flights to our territory; closed all our Airports to traffic; froze all our assets in Nigeria; froze all the assets we jointly owned with Nigerians abroad, and withdrew all foreign exchange facilities from us. Gowon closed all our seaports to shipping, and banned all export of produce other than through the Nigerian Produce Marketing Company in Lagos.

The people who were being so shabbily and so callously ill-treated were the self-same people who had virtually created the prosperity and the dignity which Nigeria boasted of abroad. Our traders, businessmen, technicians, university teachers, civil servants and others—men and women who had laboured honestly and diligently for the development and progress of Nigeria —were now the object of Nigeria's gross violence, abject ridicule and ruthless exploitation.

On May 26, 1967 a Joint Meeting of our Consultative Assembly and Council of Chiefs and Elders was convened to deliberate on these latest developments in the crisis and advise our Governor as to what to do. But on May 27, while the Meeting was still in session, Gowon illegally issued a decree arbitrarily amending the Constitution of Nigeria and unilaterally dividing Nigeria into twelve States, three of these being in our territory. Not only was this decree illegal and unconstitutional, it was a calculated slight on our people; it was an act of extreme provocation.

We were now thoroughly convinced that only our separate political existence could guarantee our basic needs of survival and security of life and property. On May 30, 1967, we proclaimed the sovereign and independent Republic of Biafra.

On July 6, 1967 Nigeria opened armed hostilities against Biafra. They massed 3 Brigades on our Northern frontiers and opened four fronts—Okutu and Obollo Afor in Nsukka, Gakem and Obudu in Ogoja. With massive artillery and infantry support the Nigerians were able to overrun these border towns in the first week of fighting. By the second week the provincial capitals of Nsukka and Ogoja fell. Nigerian atrocities began early enough in these towns. Arson, looting, rape and all kinds of torture became the order of the day. Whole villages were remorselessly burnt to ashes, farms and barns completely looted, churches and shrines outrageously desecrated. Defenceless civilians—men, women and children fleeing their homes—gave accounts of their experiences of horror and anguish. Mothers told of the whole-sale massacre and torture of their sons and of the rape and abduction of their young daughters. Children trekked miles of bush paths in tears, wailing the death at enemy hands of mother and father, sister and brother, aunt and uncle.

Since those terrible days of July 1967, the story has not changed. If anything it has been further strengthened by more violent, more gruesome murders made all the more unhuman because they are organized at the highest level and executed with the minutest deliberation. In Benin and Warri, Agbor and Asaba, in August last year, Nigerian soldiers under clear orders from their superior officers machine-gunned hundreds of Biafrans and Mid-Western Ibos. Foreign reporters spoke of the streets of Warri being strewn with dead bodies blocking the flow of traffic. In Calabar, two months later, several hundred non-combatants, many of them school children, were similarly murdered under direct orders from Nigerian officers. Children have been carried away *en masse* from their homes in Biafra to unknown destinations.

Since January this year, Nigerians have intensified their genocidal war with the indiscriminate bombing of civilians in their hearts and homes, in schools and hospitals, in churches and market-places. In February the International Red Cross was so appalled after the bombing of Awgu and Nomeh markets that their representative, Mr. Jean Pierroz, had to lodge a formal protest with the Nigerian Government. The Red Cross observer in Biafra had earlier reported rocket and cannon onslaught on civilians in Aba, Port Harcourt and other towns. These raids, he said, were 'deliberate attacks on civilian population'. Lagos, as usual, denied these charges, but in the week following the recognition of Biafra by Tanzania, Nigerian war planes killed 657 civilians in Aba, Owerri, Umuahia and Port Harcourt. Reporting the bombing of civilians at Aba in the *Sunday Times* of London of April 28, William Norris declared:

I have seen things in Biafra this week which no man should have to see. Sights to scorch the mind and sicken the conscience. I have seen children roasted alive, young girls torn in two by shrapnel, pregnant women eviscerated, and old men blown to fragments. I have seen these things and I have seen their cause: high-flying Russian Ilyushin jets operated by Federal Nigeria, dropping their bombs on civilian centres throughout Biafra.

All the main towns of Biafra have been raided by Nigerian war planes [names follow] . . . By the end of April, some of the tolls were: Aba (279 killed), Port Harcourt (272), Umuahia (214) and Owerri (146). Over fifty villages have been bombed, the most murderous in one single raid being at Awgu (165 deaths) and Nomeh (105 deaths). Gowon's justification for all this? 'To keep Nigeria one'.

Nigeria's conduct of the war has left no doubt in the minds of our people that destruction and death is the mission of the Nigerian aggressors. In thirteen months of war Nigerians have spared no pains to demonstrate that no life in Biafra will be saved, no valuable asset spared in the process of realizing their vain hope of victory. The university of Biafra, Nsukka, has been almost entirely destroyed. The Onitsha Market was completely burnt down by Nigerian soldiers. The industries at Nkalagu, Calabar, Enugu, Port Harcourt, Aba and other Biafran centres have been systematically demolished.

This has been not only a most brutal and ruinous but a most senseless and fruitless war. In all, some 100,000 Biafran civilians have been estimated killed in the past thirteen months of war. In addition to the original 2,000,000 refugees from Nigeria, the Republic has to cater for another 4,500,000 fleeing the towns and villages invaded by Nigerian soldiers. Of these some have found homes with relations of one kind or the other, while the rest are in refugee centres in the country or hiding in the bush. According to the Biafran Red Cross, about one-third to half of the refugees in camps are children who require special foods and medicines.

It has often been suggested that the Nigerian Crisis of 1966–67 followed by the Nigeria-Biafra war had its origins in the Revolution of January 1966. Nigerians have tried to deceive the world into believing that the inhuman atrocities they have been perpetrating against Biafrans since 1966 were a spontaneous reaction to 'crimes' allegedly committed by Biafrans in January 1966.

Nothing can be farther from the truth. The immediate cause of the Revolution of 1966 was the Western Election Crisis of 1965–66. To many Nigerians it was the final test before despairing of constitutional, political and economic reform. In the event the abuses went far beyond the worst predictions of the pessimists. Law and order completely broke down in Western Nigeria. On January 15, 1966, the very day of the Revolution, the West African Correspondent of *the Economist* of London summarized in these words the state of affairs in Nigeria:

> Three months after the disputed election, Western Nigeria shows no sign of settling down to life under its disputed government, and the situation now seriously threatens the prosperity of the region, the popularity of parliamentary institutions, and even the survival of the federation.

In the Revolution the Prime Minister, the Federal Minister of Finance, the Premiers of Western and Northern Nigeria and eight Army Officers of Northern, Western, Eastern and Mid-Western Nigerian origin—twelve persons in all—were killed.

Was it this Revolution that motivated the inhuman atrocities of May to October 1966 resulting in the death of over 30,000 of our people? Was it this Revolution that motivated the following utterances of hate by representatives of various parts of Northern Nigeria in the Northern House of Assembly as far back as February-March 1964?

Mallam Muhammadu Mustapha Maude Gyari:

On the allocation of plots to Ibos, or allocation of stalls I would like to advise the Minister that these people know how to make money and we do not know the way and manner of getting about this business. . . . We do not want Ibos to be allocated with plots, I do not want them to be given plots . . .

Mallam Basharu Umaru:

I would like (you), as the Minister of Land and Survey, to revoke forthwith all Certificates of Occupancy from the hands of the Ibos resident in the Region (Applause) . . .

Mr. A. A. Abogede (Igala East):

I am very glad that we are in Moslem country, and the Government of Northern Nigeria allowed some few Christians in the Region to enjoy themselves according to the belief of their Religion, but building of hotels should be taken away from the Ibos and even if we find some Christians who are interested in building hotels and have no money to do so, the Government should aid them, instead of allowing Ibos to continue with the hotels.

Dr. Iya Abubakar (Special Member: Lecturer, Ahmadu Bello University, Zaria):

I am one of the strong believers in Nigerian Unity and I have hoped for our having a United Nigeria, but certainly if the present trend of affairs continues, then I hope the Government will investigate first the desirability and secondly the possibility of extending Northernization policy to the petty traders (Applause).

Mallam Mukhtar Bello:

I would like to say something very important that the Minister should take my appeal to the Federal Government about the Ibos in the Post Office. I wish the numbers of these Ibos be reduced. . . . There are too many of them in the North. They were just like sardines and I think they were just too dangerous to the Region.

Mallam Ibrahim Musa (Igala North-West):

Mr Chairman, Sir, well, first and foremost, what I have to say before this hon. House is that we should send a delegate to meet our hon. Premier to move a Motion in this very Budget Session that all the Ibos working in the Civil Service of Northern Nigeria, including the Native Authorities, whether they are contractors, or not, should be repatriated at once . . .

Mallam Basharu Umaru:

. . . there should be no contracts either from the Government, Native Authorities, or private enterprises given to Ibo Contractors. (Government bench: Good talk and shouts of 'fire the Southerners'). Again Mr Chairman, the Foreign Firms too should be given time limit to replace all Ibos in their firms by some other people.

The Premier (Alhaji the Hon. Sir Ahmadu Bello, K.B.E., Sardauna of Sokoto):

It is my most earnest desire that every post in the Region, however small it is, be filled by a Northerner (Applause).

S

Alhaji Usman Liman (Sarkin Musawa):

What brought the Ibos into this Region? They were here since the Colonial Days. Had it not been for the Colonial Rule there would hardly have been any Ibo in this Region. Now that there is no Colonial Rule the Ibos should go back to their Region. There should be no hesitation about this matter. Mr Chairman, North is for Northerners, East for Easterners, West for Westerners and the Federation is for us all (Applause).

The Minister of Land and Survey (Alhaji the Hon. Ibrahim Musa Gashash, O.B.E.)

Mr Chairman, Sir, I do not like to take up much of the time of this House in making explanations, but I would like to assure Members that having heard their demands about Ibos holding land in Northern Nigeria, my Ministry will do all it can to see that the demands of members are met. How to do this, when to do it, all this should not be disclosed. In due course, you will all see what will happen (Applause).

The world has seen what has been happening since 1966.

The world has now come to understand that the present war has been nothing short of a continuation of the genocide of 1966 and earlier years. Thanks to the coverage now being given to the war by the world press in response to several protests from us and from many international organizations, the world has been able to read of the brutal nature of the war Nigeria is waging within our borders. The world has had the opportunity to read eyewitness accounts of the barbarity and savagery of this war and has seen photographic evidence of Nigeria's genocidal intentions.

What is quite appalling, in the context of Africa and Africa's aspirations, is that this palpable genocide is being openly financed and directed by major non-African powers whose interest in the event is the economic and political advantage of their own countries. Russia has involved herself fully in the present war on Nigeria's side in return for assurances of military bases and a political and economic foothold in West Africa. In order to further their economic interests and their political influence in Africa, the British Government, that most callous of imperialistic governments, have proclaimed their determination 'to found a single Federal Nigeria'. To this end, they have equipped the Nigerian Government in every conceivable way to wage the present war on such a brutal scale. Every advance of Nigerian troops into Biafran territory has been made possible by the hundreds of British Saladins and Ferrets. With thousands of British artillery shells and mortar bombs, the Nigerians have destroyed many towns and villages in Biafra and rendered their inhabitants destitute refugees. Africa and the world are now in no doubt that Nigeria's war against us is also Britain's war—a war for empire, natural resources and markets.

Accordingly, the British Government have made it impossible for Africa to take the initiative in settling this uniquely African problem. They have used and still use all their political and diplomatic influence to sabotage every honest effort at genuine negotiations. They have refused to stop arms supplies to Nigeria, but have instead continued their policy of imposing their idea of a solution on Biafra and the rest of Africa. In pursuance of their declared policy of support for Nigeria, the British Government have created obstacles in the way of the international and private agencies willing to bring aid direct to us. Adequate relief has not reached our suffering refugees, thanks to the duplicity of the British Government and their schemes for diverting world opinion into a debate on the question of relief.

This question of relief and the larger one of peace between Nigeria and Biafra belong to Africa and cannot be resolved until Africa accepts it on as her own responsibility. To be able to do this, African states must completely insulate themselves from the very baneful influence of these non-African powers who have, in any case, never wished Africa well.

Like many people of goodwill throughout Africa, Biafrans were disappointed to see the former Federation of Nigeria break up. Over many decades, in every sphere of life, we had struggled to make that Federation work. Our disappointment must be taken together with the circumstances and events which made unity in that country impossible. The world is now fully aware of the basic differences of culture, religion, education and social and political organization within that country. We have already given a brief review of the immediate events which, since independence in 1960 made Nigeria's survival as one nation impossible. In fact only the will to federate which was so strong among us saved Nigeria from disintegrating before and since independence. Year after year, we made concessions and compromises to ward off the secessionist threats of Northern Nigerians and save the unity of the Federation. The pogrom of 1966 ended all that, because it killed the will to maintain this precarious and inhuman association called Nigeria. Disappointment, therefore, at the disintegration of Nigeria is not a virtue in itself. It must be placed in a context. The lesson of today is that the incongruous and murderous association called Nigeria cannot and ought not now be restored in unity by either bombs or pious resolutions.

Unity is a sacred word in Africa, and for good reasons. Yet unity is not a miracle, but the consequence of a specific human condition. As President Houphouet-Boigny of the Ivory Coast declared on May 9, this year. 'Unity is the fruit of the common will to live together, it should not be imposed by force by one group upon another. If we all are in agreement in the O.A.U. in recognizing the imperious necessity of unity, unity as the ideal framework for the full development of the African man, we admit, as for ourselves, that it should not become his grave. We say yes to unity in peace, unity in love and through brotherhood. Unity is for the living and not for the dead'.

Will other African countries which are made up of several ethnic groups also break up simply because Biafra has survived? The answer is clearly no.

Firstly, very few countries in Africa have the history of constitutional conflict and tribal power-play such as Nigeria has had. In fact, many of these countries which are multi-tribal in composition have had a common colonial experience or a workable constitutional structure which now unites them in their pursuit of a common independent future. In any case, they have usually had the leadership to realize the need for the fullest co-operation, respect and goodwill among their peoples, and also to realize that political power was never intended to be used to oppress and even exterminate a section of the community. Finally, these African countries can maintain their unity in a progressive environment because they have not come to think, as the Nigerians now do, that 'national unity' should be based on common hatred of one section of the population by all the others. Contrary to the opinion of Africa's detractors, there are many countries in Africa today where unity can flourish because these ideals have been accepted and applied.

Within the past two decades, a number of African countries carved out by the colonial powers have had to break up or had their patterns of association adjusted without bloodshed. In all these cases, it was generally accepted that all political associations have to be based on the will of the associates. From this point of view, every modern African country (including Biafra) is a new willing association of ethnic nationalities. In such countries, the first safeguard against disintegration is the protection of all communities and all individuals under the law. It would be tragic if Africa should consider the territorial structure of existing countries more sacrosanct than the safeguarding of the lives of persecuted communities in those countries. Fortunately, many African statesmen are beginning to realize this and to see that if the conflict between Biafra and Nigeria is solved by 'the application of firepower,' the result would be quite ominous for all Africa. As the Tanzanian Government declared in their Statement of April 13, 1968:

> While people have a duty to defend the integrity of their State, and even to die in its defence, this duty stems from the fact that it is theirs, and that it is important to their well-being and to the future of their children. When the State ceases to stand for the honour, the protection, and the well-being of all its citizens, then it is no longer the instrument of those it has rejected.

This is the lesson of Biafra's bold stand against tyranny and genocide. The loss of this lesson on Africa could well lead to dire harvest of inter-tribal vengeance within our continent.

There are fourteen million people involved in this Biafran resistance. They include the people of all the major tribal groups of Biafra who suffered from the pogrom of 1966 and whose accredited representatives took part in the consultations that led to the Proclamation of Independence. The Nigerians claim that they are waging a war to 'liberate' the so-called minorities. Hence the arbitrary creation of twelve paper states imposed on the people by Gowon without any form of consultation. The world press has rightly seen this action as 'extremely irresponsible' and a 'disastrous political blunder'. As *Africa and the World* of February, 1968 put it: 'The circumstances which led to the secession were created by Gowon and the secession itself was provoked by his unilateral declaration of twelve states'.

The peoples of Biafra have co-existed harmoniously for thousands of years before the creation of the political unit called Nigeria. The common traditions, outlook and identity of Biafrans resulted from their centuries of intermarriage and their cultural and economic interdependence. The cultural and economic homogeneity which has evolved within the Biafran territory remained unshaken even by the divisive forces of the turbulent politics of Nigeria.

The Ibos are of course the majority tribe in Biafra. It is true, nevertheless, that Biafra is the only part of the former Federation of Nigeria where there is no record of civil strife against minority groups. The Willink Minorities Commission, appointed by the British Government in 1958, examined the place of the minorities in the whole of the former Federation of Nigeria. The Commission concluded that the destiny of the 'minorities' in our territory was traditionally and intimately interwoven with that of the rest. In the Rivers area, for instance, of the population of 747,000 (in 1958), 305,000 were Ibo, 240,000 Ijaw and 156,000 Ogoni. The Commission did not recommend the creation of any states in our territory although it strongly recommended the carving out of the Mid-West from Western Nigeria and Middle Belt State from Northern Nigeria. The Mid-West State was subsequently created (in 1963) following extensive consultations, approval by all the Governments of the Federation and a plebiscite among the people concerned. The Northern Nigeria and the Federal Governments controlled by the Hausa-Fulani oligarchy opposed discussion and a plebiscite in connection with the Middle Belt State. The refusal to create this State led to the Tiv riots which lasted from before Nigeria's Independence in October 1960 to the Military Revolution of January 1966.

Biafra has worked out and introduced a Provincial Administration System to meet the needs of local communities. This system was introduced after full consultations and discussions among the people; it has killed any residual fears. The result is that all Biafrans are co-operating fully and vigorously in the prosecution of the present war. It is worth pointing out that the present Provincial Administration System was closely studied and formulated by a Committee headed by Mr. Okoi Arikpo, a member of the Consultative Assembly of Eastern Nigeria who himself originates from one of the 'minority' tribes in Biafra. Mr. Arikpo was later bought over by Gowon who made him his Commissioner for External Affairs.

The uniqueness of the case for Biafra is that from the start of the struggle with Nigeria, the people of the Republic have completely backed the mandate which they freely and unanimously gave to the Government. One only has to consider the various stages of the war to appreciate the fact that no amount of regimentation could achieve the kind of solidarity in Biafra which is immediately visible to those who have visited our country. Fifteen months ago, Nigeria imposed a total economic blockade on our people and since then our businesses and industries—our means of livelihood were completely cut. Yet, our people have remained unflinching in their loyalty. This is the measure of confidence our Government enjoys. In January this year, the Lagos regime announced a change of currency. Overnight the people of Biafra were dispossessed of all their worldly savings. When the Biafran Government called on the people to surrender all the old Nigerian currency in return for mere official receipts the exercise was completed smoothly and in record time. Again that is clear evidence of the people's confidence in their Government. Today, as I have said earlier, Biafra has a refugee population of $4\frac{1}{2}$ million. Let us take even one million or half that number—500,000. I wonder how many countries in the world would harbour that number of destitutes without any ripples in the quietude of the nation. Yet, as all observers have noted, Biafrans have borne their suffering without demonstrations or any breakdown of law and order. Again that is indicative of the confidence which the Biafra Government enjoys.

Some weeks ago, after the enemy had penetrated into the city of Port Harcourt, I summoned all the chiefs of Yenagoa Province, one of the so-called minority areas, and said to them that as a Christian I deplored the shedding of blood. I told them I was anxious to minimise the suffering of our people. I called them to return home and consult their people again on whether they still wished to remain Biafrans. If they had changed their mind I would readily withdraw Biafran troops from the Province because the presence of those troops would make the Nigerians even more blood-thirsty and more blood would be split. However, if they remained steadfast in their loyalty I made it quite clear that I could not promise them safety but all I could promise was that the Government would try its best. The chiefs and leaders wished to give an immediate reply but I rejected this. I insisted that they must return home and consult their people. Well, they did consult and a decision was taken. They reaffirmed their loyalty and their determination to continue the struggle. This mirrors the feelings among all Biafrans for Biafra irrespective of ethnic origin.

The so-called states created by Gowon in our territory were not designed to serve the genuine interests of the peoples but to spite them, cripple them and eventually exterminate them. Early this year, a Swiss correspondent, Dr. Edmond C. Schwarzenbach secured an interview with a Nigerian Commissioner whom he described as 'one of the most impressive in the present military regime in Lagos.' It was an interview which he said, in the *Swiss Review of Africa* of February, 1968, provided him with a 'significant insight into the political aims of the Federal Government.' Dr. Schwarzenbach continued:

The (Nigeria) war aim and 'solution' . . . of the entire problem was to 'discriminate against the Ibos in the future in their own interest'. Such discrimination would include above all the detachment of those oil-rich territories in the Eastern Region which were not inhabited by them at the beginning of the Colonial period, on the lines of the projected twelve state plan. In addition, the Ibos' movement would be restricted, to prevent their renewed penetration into the other parts of the country. Leaving them any access to the sea, the Commissioner declared was quite out of the question.

At the present moment, the Nigerian Army has occupied some non-Ibo areas of Biafra. But this cannot be regarded as a settlement of the 'minority question'. This is why we have suggested a plebiscite. Under adequate international supervision, the people of these areas should be given a chance to choose whether they want to belong to Nigeria or to Biafra. Plebiscites have been used in the Southern Cameroons, in Togo, in Mid-Western Nigeria (and by the British recently in Gibraltar) to determine what grouping is most acceptable to the people of disputed areas. If Nigeria believes that she is really defending the true wishes of the minorities, she should accept our proposal for a plebiscite in the disputed areas of Nigeria and Biafra.

The comparison which the Nigerians make between the Biafran Revolution and the Katanga crisis is ill-founded. In its history, motivation, leadership and organization, the Katanga crisis has no parallels with our revolution. Moïse Tshombe's Katanga was created to frustrate the national independence of the Congo under Patrice Lumumba and was planned and financed by the huge foreign mining combines in that province.

Katanga itself had a long tradition of separation of which its secession in 1960 was simply the culmination. But in the former Federation of Nigeria, it was the Northern Region that had a history of repeated demands for and threats of secession. On the other hand, we made concessions and sacrifices for the maintenance of Nigerian unity, up till the eve of Biafran Independence. Katanga Province voluntarily seceded from the Congo, whereas the massacres and other events of 1966 and 1967 forced Biafra out of the Nigerian association.

Biafra's revolution is, then, an indigenous expression of African self-determination. Dr. Conor O'Brien who supervised the United Nations Force against Katanga, has spoken out against any comparison of Biafra with Katanga:

> The difference is that the secession of Katanga, unlike that of Biafra, had been carried out at the instigation of Western interests and under the protection of an invading force of the former colonial power . . . the secession was not an indigenous but an international phenomenon.

Because our Independence is an indigenous expression of the people's will, it cannot be 'crushed' as the Katanga rebellion was, through the present military campaign. When Nigeria opened armed hostilities against us in July, 1967, we knew she had all the stores and equipment and the bulk of the infantry men of the former Nigerian Army. She had the Naval base in Lagos and the Air Force and Munitions Factory in Kaduna. On this side, we had practically nothing. Our ports were blockaded; our assets held jointly with Nigeria were frozen and contact with foreign Governments was almost impossible. Hence, where the Nigerians invaded our territory with a battalion and supporting weapons, we opposed them with a company and a few rifles. It was no surprise that Nigeria and her foreign advisers concluded that we would be crushed within a fortnight. That prediction has been proved wrong. The will of the people, not fire-power, is the force behind the Biafran resistance.

We, Biafrans, assumed our political sovereignty because we were convinced that this was our only guarantee of safety and protection for our people in and outside Biafra. That conviction grew out of our experience of Nigeria.

Some well-meaning people anxious to maintain some semblance of a united Nigeria, have suggested the provision of guarantees for the people of Biafra within a Nigerian political framework. They admit that it would be tragic for us to give up our sovereign independence without adequate guarantees for our security of life and property.

Two kinds of guarantees have been mentioned. It has been suggested that the Federal Nigerian Government should give direct definite guarantees that the lives and property of Biafrans will be safe everywhere in Nigeria, as if the present Nigerian Government have the ability, sincerity and good faith to keep their word and that all succeeding Governments in Nigeria will be equally able, sincere and willing to honour their pledge.

In colonial Nigeria, not even the British Government was in a position to guarantee these fundamental rights to us. The British administrator who investigated the 1953 massacre of our people in Kano emphasized that the tragic incidents would be repeated in the future.

Independent Nigeria had guarantees for the rights to life and property and the freedom of movement, religion and belief supposedly entrenched in her

Constitution. Independent Nigeria also subscribed to the United Nations Charter and the United Nations Convention on Genocide. Yet these guarantees were unavailing during the pogrom of 1966.

During the crisis of 1966–1967, the present leaders of Nigeria gave several assurances and guarantees to our people about the safety of their lives and property, and about the restoration of political and personal freedom within the Constitution. None of these assurances was honoured. On the contrary, the Nigerian Government went out of their way to demonstrate their repudiation of those assurances. There is, therefore, no precedent to recall and no reason to hope that a Nigerian Government can give adequate guarantees for the security of Biafrans if they are part of Nigeria.

Direct international guarantees have been suggested. According to one suggestion 'the major world powers and the African States should be willing to add their guarantees to those given by the Nigerian Federal Government to ensure the safety of the Ibo people'. The snag is that it is still the Nigerian Government that would have the sovereign responsibility for providing this security. And, in the long run, an international involvement cannot last for ever.

An international force which is used to keep Nigerians and Biafrans apart does not offer any greater security than could be obtained from a cease-fire which Nigeria honours. Even then, such an international force invited into a 're-united' Nigeria would operate under the sovereign authority of the Nigerian Federal Government which could always ask it out of Nigeria. Moreover, an international force would not only have to keep the two armies apart, it would also have to keep the two peoples apart, since no international force can provide security to Biafrans in the day-to-day process of living under Nigerian authority. An international force cannot prevent discrimination and ultimate extermination through pernicious national policies and impositions.

This is why we Biafrans have insisted that only a protective political sovereignty controlled by our own leaders will guarantee us safety at home and protection abroad. In the absence of that sovereignty, we will continue to be regarded as the internal problem of our enemies and die in our thousands as we have done in past years without help or support from the international community.

Today, Nigerians have us to talk to because we have been able to survive the massacres for which they offered no apologies, the total blockade which they have refused to lift, and the 'total war' which they are fiercely waging on us. But for our confidence in God, our belief in our sole responsibility for our survival, and our understanding of our predicament, we Biafrans would long ago have succumbed to the power of the Nigerian junta and to the extermination of our people.

Today, in response to the disturbed conscience of the world, Nigerians are here to negotiate peace with us of the Republic of Biafra. We join in the negotiations in all sincerity believing, as we always have done, that there can be no other way, anyway, for resolving the conflict between us.

While these peace discussions go on, let us not forget that four leading African countries, Tanzania, Gabon, Ivory Coast and Zambia, have carefully considered the issues involved and have accorded us diplomatic recognition.

These countries have also set out their reasons for considering our case just and our independence deserved. Briefly,

they condemn the massacres and the continuing genocide;

they are convinced that we had sought every conceivable constitutional means to protect our lives and property and to get the leaders of Nigeria to accept and implement decisions intended to save the former Federation of Nigeria from collapse,

they believe that self-determination is sacrosanct, and the willing consent of the people a supreme condition for all government; and

they are convinced that the sovereign independence of Biafra will promote humane and democratic rule throughout Africa.

In the words of Tanzania's Statement of Recognition, 'Africa fought for freedom on the grounds of individual liberty and equality, and on the grounds that every people must have the right to determine for themselves the conditions under which they would be governed.' The Statement concludes that only by recognising Biafra as an independent sovereign entity could Tanzania remain true to her 'conviction that the purpose of society, and of all political organization, is the service of man.'

The failure of the Nigerian experiment in political association is not the first of its kind in history. Among the territories of the former British Empire, for instance, several political unions have broken up. These include the Federation of the West Indies, the Federation of Malaysia and Singapore, the Federation of Rhodesia and Nyasaland and the Federation of South Arabia. But it is highly significant that against the disintegration of none of these political associations was a devastating war, wholly supported by Britain, ever fought, as is now the case with the collapse of the Nigerian Federation.

It was certainly because he had the support of the British Government who believed that war could solve the human problems involved in the present conflict that Lt.-Col. Yakubu Gowon could glibly say on March 31 this year that since his New Year message to his field commanders 'to quicken the pace of the military operations, the rate of progress in all the war fronts has been most satisfactory'; that progress, he concluded, would be continued 'no matter the cost and how long it takes'. That progress has indeed continued and Gowon must now be quite happy with its enormous cost in lives and property.

It is always wise to dissolve an unhappy political union rather than to condemn its unfortunate partners to perpetual suffering and misery accompanied by unrelieved bitterness and rancour. Dissolution becomes imperative when one section of a political community is singled out by others for extermination.

The bitter experience of over fifty years of association between Biafrans and Nigerians—experience which reached its climax in the events of 1966 and 1967—has absolutely convinced Biafans that only their separate political existence can guarantee their basic needs of survival and security of life and property as well as of progress. This conviction has been further strengthened by Nigeria's conduct of her current war of aggression and genocide.

There never was very much of a bond of union between us and Nigerians. According to the late Premier of Northern Nigeria, Sir Ahmadu Bello,

Politicians always delight in talking loosely about the unity of Nigeria. Sixty years ago there was no country called Nigeria. What is now Nigeria consisted of a number of large and small communities all of which were different in their outlooks and beliefs. The advent of the British and of Western education has not materially altered the situation and these many and varied communities have not knit themselves into a complete unit.

In the Memorandum submitted to the Ad Hoc Conference on the Nigerian Constitution in September 1966, the Northern Nigeria Delegation declared:

We have pretended for too long that there are no differences between the peoples of (Nigeria). The hard fact which we must honestly accept as of paramount importance in the Nigerian experiment especially for the future is that we are different peoples brought together by recent accidents of history. To pretend otherwise will be folly.

For a long time, we Biafrans continued to act and live as if these differences were not bitterly felt by our fellow Nigerians. We travelled extensively within that country, settled in large numbers in many parts of it, married from among all its people, set up business, provided educational and health facilities in every corner of it. Our investment in men ran to over 3 million, in buildings and other assets to several million pounds sterling. 'If Great Britain had conjured up the entity designated Nigeria from a network of trading routes,' wrote Professor Stanley Diamond of New York's New School last January, 'it was the Biafrans who had dedicated themselves to the proposition of an internally coherent and unified state.'

The massacres of our people in Jos in 1945 and in Kano in 1953 had indeed warned us of the little faith Northern Nigeria had in the idea of 'Nigerian Unity'. The massacres brought home to many of us the immensity of the gulf of differences between our peoples.

Yet, such was our faith and, in retrospect, our folly, that our people ignored these early warnings and continued to preach and fight for a united Nigeria. In our folly we ignored the fundamental differences in religion, the differences in our social organization, the differences in political outlook. We continued to believe that our gestures of brotherhood and compromise, our efforts at understanding and unity, were serving a useful purpose. We continued to invest in Nigeria, and placed all our security—of life as well as of property—in the hands of the Nigerian Government and the Nigerian Constitution.

In 1966 our folly became real tragedy when massacre followed massacre in May, June, July, August, September and October of that year. We lost over 30,000 of our kith and kin. We had to resettle over 2 million refugees, our people who had fled from all parts of Nigeria.

Throughout that period of crisis in 1966, no other people in Nigeria rose to condemn the genocide being perpetrated against our people; none pleaded for our protection. The Nigerian Federal Government, who were expected to honour the Constitution and defend the people, were themselves privy to the planning and the execution of the atrocities.

We came to our senses. We realized that the differences between us and other Nigerians were not only real: they were the perfect circumstances for genocide. We ruminated and resolved to build a security for ourselves, independent of those other peoples of Nigeria who were, and still are, seeking to exterminate us. We were forced to found the Republic of Biafra.

For more than twelve months Nigeria has sought unsuccessfully to destroy that Republic and its people. She has employed every known means for mass extermination which two world powers—British and Russia—have placed generously at her disposal. Biafrans have been bombed out of their homes, schools, churches and hospitals. Their cities have been shelled, pillaged and devastated. Their borders have been sealed off from the outside to ensure that they are totally starved to death. Food treated with arsenic has been passed from Nigeria to them for consumption. The war has claimed over 100,000 Biafran civilian lives; between 200 and 300 Biafran men, women and children are dying daily from starvation and disease; over 4,500,000 have become refugees in the areas still under our control. Can it be doubted that the war has increased the bitterness between us and Nigeria? Is it possible to imagine that our people would now be ready to accept Nigerian rule? What kind of confidence can Biafrans repose in the present Nigerian leadership after all that has happened?

We accuse Gowon of murder, for plotting the death of his benefactor, Major-General J. T. U. Aguiyi-Ironsi, late Supreme Commander and Head of the Nigerian Military Government.

We accuse Gowon of duplicity and bad faith for consistently failing to honour agreements mutually arrived at.

We accuse Gowon of genocide for seeking to exterminate 14 million Biafrans in a most gruesome manner.

We accuse Gowon of aspiring to be the Hitler of Africa.

This is the case of Biafra. It is the case of 14,000,000 people. We are a people who have suffered more ravage and endured more wrong from our fellow Africans than from our former European colonial oppressors. We seek nothing other than what every people in Africa have struggled to achieve for themselves—peace, self-determination, security and progress. We have come to this ancient African country convinced that the rest of Africa cannot justly deny us what they themselves enjoy. We are confident that if left alone Africa can resolve this problem. Let therefore the people of Africa be the sole judges; let them resist the promptings and dictates of foreign vested interests; let them exercise the impartiality which alone can enhance the moral authority of the O.A.U.

Against all the background of suspicion, hate, conflict and war, our survival cannot be separated from the sovereign independence of our State. No one who has studied the past contribution of our people to the cause of African freedom and unity can doubt our awareness of the need for the whole of Africa to unite. Nevertheless, we have learnt by bitter experience that unity must come in stages through co-operation and mutual understanding. This was the purpose for which the O.A.U. was established. In fulfilment of that purpose we offer to discuss with Nigeria the closest form of association which does not detract from our right to ensure our security at home and abroad.

All along we in Biafra have made several proposals for a peaceful settlement of the crisis even before the start of the shooting war. All those suggestions have been spurned by Gowon. I can see no better opportunity than now to ask Gowon to bring forward his own proposals for peace.

Finally, Your Imperial Majesty, Your Excellencies, as we sit here thousands of God's sacred creation are perishing in Biafra. They are dying not so much from bullets supplied by Britain and Russia, as from starvation imposed upon them by this inhuman war. God and humanity are owed a debt, a duty, an immediate end be put to the suffering. The situation is of immediate urgency. The adversaries of Biafra are doing their best to exploit the sufferings of these helpless people for their political and military ends. I therefore call upon you, in the name of God, of humanity and of Africa to expedite your deliberations and action at this conference.

[1] *Delivered on 5 August 1968. Text from Biafran Ministry of Information. See note to* DOC *171 and cf. the historical review in* DOC *110.*

[2] *See* DOC *89.*

169.
Enahoro Sets out Nigeria's Terms for a Settlement[1]

Two days ago, in my courtesy reply to the address by His Imperial Majesty, I urged that if we are willing to live up to our responsibilities as leaders and representatives of our people we must accept the inescapable fact that the Addis Ababa peace talks represent probably the last opportunity in our long search for a negotiated settlement of the Nigerian crisis.

I am convinced that if we lose this opportunity through miscalculations by either side or for some reason such as reliance on promises of support from neo-colonialist sources and their agents, another round of peace talks can hardly be organised before the Nigerian conflict is resolved by other means available to either side. I would like to assure you that I do not say this as a threat, but in order to emphasise the importance which we must attach to the present talks and the need for us here to work out an agreement on the basic issue which divides us. It is in the hope that this general approach will be accepted by the other side that I will endeavour to set a moderate and conciliatory tone in my statement.

We came here hoping that our discussions would be conducted in the new spirit which was emerging at Niamey. I was, therefore, quite astonished at the printed speech of Mr. Ojukwu,[2] and I have already apologised to his Imperial Majesty for the ordeal to which he was subjected, in violation not only of the undertaking not to engage in polemics, let alone in downright insults but also for our previous practice at these peace talks.

I can only describe the speech as quite an extraordinary performance in the circumstances not only because it was so patently false in parts and needlessly virulent in others but also because it was so destructive, advancing nothing new and offering no proposals whatever for the peaceful settlement of our crisis. Indeed, I cannot imagine what constructive purpose this speech was supposed to serve since it must be obvious now, judging by the world press, that even as a publicity stunt it fell flat. It may be that the speech was calculated to irritate, provoke and annoy, in the hope of again abruptly terminating these discussions. If so, it has failed. I have assured His Majesty and I will not go back on that assurance, that I have no intention of descending to the level of that speech.

We have to bear in mind that this was Mr. Ojukwu's first opportunity outside Nigeria to present a case which he probably thought had not been properly presented by Sir Louis Mbanefo and Dr. Eni Njoku at Kampala, and he must have felt himself under great compulsion to use the opportunity to unburden himself of some propaganda. I doubt very much whether Sir Louis Mbanefo or Dr. Njoku would again have inflicted on us substantially the same speech—down to the same phraseology—as we heard at Kampala, including even the liberal use of such highly emotive words as 'pogrom' and 'genocide' which were hardly calculated to facilitate discussion or negotiation here. I am quite certain that neither of them would have thought they could advance their case or their cause by being abusive.

Mr. Ojukwu seems to have misunderstood the nature of these discussions, in two senses. He seems to have believed that there was to be mediation. Of course His Majesty promptly corrected him on this score. He also seems to have thought that anyone was really interested at this stage of our sad conflict in listening to a partial account, in many respects even a distorted account, of past events which I assure him was presented in a much more civilized manner in Kampala.[3] Again, as His Majesty so appropriately said, if any solution is to emerge from Addis Ababa, we must be prepared to look forward and not backward.

As I have said, there were many inaccuracies and many distortions of fact in Mr. Ojukwu's speech. I have no intention of protracting our discussions here by dealing with them orally but I have a full statement which corrects parts of that speech and it would be quite easy for me to inflict a three-hour speech on you. Indeed, I had thought of calling for an open session for this purpose, but on reflection, I have come round to the view that to do so would be to pursue a course bound to end where Mr. Ojukwu obviously wants these talks to end, namely in failure. I am determined to satisfy the other side that we desire a peaceful settlement. If we are to fail the whole world must see where the blame lies. Therefore I will submit my statement only for the purpose of the record as an answer to Mr. Ojukwu, and proceed to a more constructive theme.

Before doing so however, here are one or two points in Mr. Ojukwu's speech which are relevant to what I will later have to say. First of these are the sad events in our country in the last two years. It is my firm conviction that these events cannot recur. If there is a fear on the other side of a recurrence my answer is that in order to have a recurrence, we would require to experience the same succession of events as we have passed through—namely, a constitution providing for an unbalanced structure, an alliance of tribal political parties, agitation by minorities for self-determination, destruction of opposition forces, rigged elections, the assassination of the Prime Minister and all non-Ibo State Premiers, the liquidation of the non-Ibo Higher Command of the army, the accession to power in the country of an inept ruler who is Ibo after such assassinations, the emergence of another Ojukwu with his wild ambitions, and various other developments. I firmly believe that all these cannot happen conjointly again.

Second, the probable effect on other African states of the disintegration of

Nigeria. Mr. Ojukwu claimed that there was no comparison between the probabilities in other African countries and the events in Nigeria. Quite the contrary. Those who are more familiar with the African scene agree that the repercussions of Nigeria's disintegration on the rest of Africa would be catastrophic. We would in all probability witness the disintegration of African states as we know them today and another scramble for Africa. If Mr. Ojukwu is as concerned about the independence of African states as he pretends and desires a purely African solution to our crisis, why has he made an ally of Portugal, whose hands are stained with the blood of Africans in Angola and Mozambique? Why does he want to make a French puppet out of parts of Nigeria? There is little point in quoting obscure, vicariously subsidised publications . . . as impartial authorities on Africa let alone on Nigeria. If we have the welfare of Africa at heart, we must maintain a united Nigeria.

Third, the desires and aspirations of the minorities in Eastern States. Those who have been in public life for many years in Nigeria know that there is a long-standing demand amongst the non-Ibo peoples of what was Eastern Nigeria for states of their own. I am afraid that if Mr. Ojukwu's authority for diluting this is a handful of captive chiefs, two of whom he has brought to these talks, he really must be very naive regarding the role of chiefs in the politics of Nigeria long before independence, and since then chiefs have been accustomed to supporting the de facto authorities who controlled them, and in every part of Nigeria it has always been possible for the administration of the day to produce chiefs like rabbits out of a hat to support its policies. No, the long history of separate state movements among the Rivers people cannot now be falsified by a couple of lightweight chiefs.

Fourth, the Nigerian crisis has been presented by Mr. Ojukwu as a 'Biafran' problem. He knows as we know that there is no 'Biafran' problem. There is however an Ibo problem. Whether it is other tribes who fear or hate Ibos or Ibos who fear that other tribes hate them, such fear or hate indicates the existence of an Ibo problem. It is not a problem of cultures or traditions but quite simply an economic problem in the sense that Ibo-land by itself cannot sustain the teeming population of Ibos at the level of economic activity to which they have become accustomed in the Nigerian association. Let me hasten to assure you that I am not and never have been anti-Ibo. But we have surely reached a stage in our existence as a nation and in our crisis when this problem must be looked at squarely in the face so that putting our heads together, we can work out solutions. For example, it has never been suggested that non-Ibos of the so-called 'Biafra' experience any difficulties in other parts of Nigeria, nor do they believe that other Nigerians hate them. If we are to be realistic at these talks, we must reduce our crisis to its proper proportions and recognise the problem facing us as an Ibo problem. The quotations by Mr. Ojukwu from debates in the old Northern House of Assembly only serve to emphasise this point.

Fifth, Mr. Ojukwu claims that the Ibos are fighting a war of survival which is precisely what Hitler claimed when his hordes marched into Austria, Czechoslovakia, Poland and France. The rebels' ill-fated incursion into the Mid-West and Western States revealed quite clearly that the Ibos were fighting a colonial war. Never having organised an empire, some of their leaders thought they would now do so with at least all of Southern Nigeria as their vassals, and the oil of the Mid-West and Rivers Areas to sustain the new Herrenvolk machine. It is the collapse of this adventure that we are witnessing today.

Six, Mr. Ojukwu spoke of some still-born Federations. Was it ignorance, I wonder? How can we possibly compare an attempt to federate separate sovereign states with an exercise in the reverse direction? No amount of vituperation can wish the Federation of Nigeria out of existence.

Seven, Mr. Ojukwu has offered a plebiscite in the non-Ibo areas. Why does it not occur to him that Ibo leaders to demand a plebiscite in the territory of other ethnic groups [text as released by Lagos]? The creation of a Rivers State and a South-Eastern State means that those areas now have their own administrators, officially recognised leaders and accredited spokesmen, who are more than competent to speak for their people. The sooner Mr. Ojukwu releases his captive chiefs to make their peace with their people, the better for them.

Lastly, I must refute Mr. Ojukwu's allegation that we on this side were opposed to African assistance in our efforts to find a settlement. I do not know what report he was given by delegates to the London and Kampala talks. But either they deceived him or he is guilty of deliberate falsehood. The records are clear and Mr. Ojukwu ought to read them. We proposed in London that the Commonwealth Secretariat or the OAU Secretariat should service our peace talks. Sir Louis Mbanefo rejected the OAU. We proposed in Kampala a nomination by the Emperor of Ethiopia or by the OAU of an observer. Sir Louis Mbanefo categorically rejected both. We proposed a long list of venues including several African capitals and of course Addis Ababa. From our list the other side accepted Kampala. The Federal Government has also given the OAU Consultative Committee every co-operation. Clearly therefore Mr. Ojukwu's allegation is false.

Having disposed of these eight points let me now turn to the part of my speech which I hope will at least provide a basis for success at these talks. We were invited in the last gasp of Mr. Ojukwu's speech to state our proposals for bringing the civil war to an end. In doing so let me confess at once that I cannot conceive of any mutually acceptable proposal which does not envisage the unity and territorial integrity of Nigeria. Indeed, I find it difficult to foresee an immediate end to our civil war unless we can agree here that we all belong once again to the same country. I further confess therefore that my proposals are based on the ending of secession and the reintegration of rebel controlled areas with Nigeria. If the other side are to renounce secession we must examine at these talks a number of contingent problems. The first of these is the form and manner of renunciation of secession. At the Kampala talks we had reached a stage where we were examining the possibility of a formula which would provide for renunciation of secession without necessarily imposing on the other side an obligation to declare publicly in so many words that they had renounced secession. This was a face-saving device for the other side which we thought might ease their return to one Nigeria. If there is any lingering fear in their minds that they would be required to renounce secession in a grovelling manner let me dispel it. Notwithstanding the undisputed Federal advantage in the field we are prepared to negotiate at these talks a formula, possibly based on a joint declaration which will have the effect of bringing secession and rebellion to an end without necessarily imposing on the other side an obligation to take or make some unilateral grovelling act or pronouncement which they might regard as impossible to accept or undertake.

Accordingly we propose the following joint declaration to which both sides should subscribe: 'Both sides agree to maintain the unity and territorial integrity of the Federal Republic of Nigeria with external boundaries as established at the 1st day of October, 1963 and to ensure for all time the security of the lives and property of all its inhabitants.' We regard this formulation as negotiable. I have no doubt in my mind that such a joint declaration given agreement in other areas could be immediately followed by the cessation of hostilities. For example, it would be necessary to agree not only on the formulation of the declaration but also on the authority and mandate of the signatories and on the date and time for the cessation of hostilities.

Second: The declaration and the cessation of hostilities would have to be followed by the disarming of rebel troops. Clearly if we are to be one united country again it will be generally accepted that there can be no question of any of the constituent units of the country having or maintaining its own separate standing army or armed forces. We propose a meeting of military officers from both sides at a venue to be agreed here to work out the details of disarming of rebel forces.

However, in our present circumstances, especially given the fears regarding their personal and collective security which Ibos entertain, it is obvious that some form of guarantees which are convincing, practicable and effective would have to be offered to the rebels. I shall come to that in a moment.

Third: If rebel forces are disarmed consideration must be given to the policing of rebel held areas in the East Central State. In the atmosphere of general fear which has been promoted among Ibos they may well be extremely reluctant to place themselves at the mercy of Federal troops especially after their own troops have been disarmed. In any case it is not part of the normal functions of the army in Nigeria to undertake police duties. We propose therefore that the normal policing of rebel held areas should be the responsibility solely of the police and that the police units in these areas will consist mostly of persons of Ibo origin. There is no intention on the part of the Federal Government of flooding Ibo areas with police units composed mainly of Nigerians from other ethnic groups. Naturally the police in the areas would be an integral part of the Nigeria Police Force with the same functions as in other states. We are prepared to negotiate as to the mechanism for the police to call for support from the armed forces in the event of a breakdown of law and order.

Fourth: Of particular importance in the consideration of the problem of physical security of Ibos at any rate until mutual confidence is restored is an external force. I was rather taken aback when Mr. Ojukwu declared in his speech that no form of guarantees in this respect would be acceptable to his side. I hope that this was said merely for public effect on the occasion. In the past, representatives of the other side have demanded the presence of an external force as an insurance for their security. We on our side have in previous exchanges proposed such a force. This has been common ground between us for some time and I cannot imagine that the other side would now wish to go back on it. We now again propose an external force and we are prepared to negotiate here the functions of such a force, its composition, numbers, command, financing and the duration of its presence. Such a force would have to be drawn from sources acceptable to both sides. We can think of many such countries. Subject to further negotiation and the consent of the countries concerned we propose that the external force should be drawn from Ethiopia, India and Canada. In addition, we are prepared to examine any other sources which the other side may suggest.

Fifth: As a consequence of the renunciation of secession, or if you like of an end being put to secession, it will be relevant to consider the administration of the East Central State. I hope it will be agreed that if we are one country then that administration must be brought into line with the administration of the other eleven states. It is well known that the entire country including that part of it which is represented by the other delegation is at present under military administration. Therefore a military governor will have to be appointed. He will need to assist him an Executive Council composed mainly of civilians. As an earnest of our assurance that there is no intention of imposing on the Ibo people ruled by another tribe we are prepared to undertake that the military governor and members of his executive council will be Ibos. Furthermore in recognition of the part to be played by the East Central State, we are prepared to agree that the Executive Council should be drawn in part from among persons who have been loyal to the Federation and in part from among persons who have supported the rebel cause in proportions to be agreed by negotiation.

Sixth: The question of amnesty is vital to the decision-making process at these talks. We have already stated at previous talks that we are prepared to grant a general amnesty in most cases and to examine other claims for similar treatment. However, we are to discuss this matter further at these talks and to try to reach agreement on it.

Seventh: In thinking of re-unification, we cannot avoid discussion of the future of Ibos who fled other parts of the Federation either because they were recalled by the rebel command or because they feared for their security. Of these persons, public servants constitute an important group. We are prepared to undertake that such public servants will be re-absorbed into public employment and that the Ibos as a people will be assured of a fair share of employment in the Federal Public Service including Federal Statutory Corporations. In regard to self-employed persons we are prepared to guarantee their freedom of movement but if for any reason this guarantee is not acceptable to the other side then we would like to hear and we are prepared to examine any proposals they may put forward. The rehabilitation and resettlement of such persons and of all displaced persons in Nigeria in areas of their choice will be the responsibility of a rehabilitation commission assisted financially within the means at the disposal of the Federal Government and the States Governments concerned.

Eighth: It may be argued that the foregoing are interim proposals and that there cannot be a permanent settlement until a new constitution is worked out and the degree of association between the various peoples and tribes of Nigeria is agreed. We are prepared to discuss at these talks arrangements for a constitutional conference including the composition of such a conference,

T

selection procedure for delegations and various other matters. The Ibos of the East Central State will have the same right of representation as other ethnic groups and states at such a conference.

Ninth: One of the many subjects for discussion at these talks, is the question of relief operations. I do not myself think it an impossible or insuperable problem, once the major question of secession and re-unification is resolved. If there is no war and we are one country then there is absolutely nothing to stand in the way of relief supplies reaching the innermost recesses of rebel-held areas. If the stories which are current about starvation and suffering are true, then there is a duty on all of us here to expedite our deliberations to agree on the re-unification of Nigeria, and to open up all routes by land, sea and air for relief to be rushed to the needy areas. To summarise then, my proposals mean that we should discuss the following matters at these talks:

1. Under the item 'Arrangement for a permanent settlement.'
   a. Form and manner of renunciation of secession.
   b. Disarming of rebel troops.
   c. Policing of rebel-held areas.
   d. Security of Ibos.
   e. External force.
      (*i*)   Functions.
      (*ii*) Composition.
      (*iii*) Numbers.
      (*iv*) Command.
      (*v*)   Financing.
      (*vi*) Duration of presence.
   f. Administration of East Central State.
   g. Amnesty.
   h. Future of Ibos who fled other parts of Federation.
      (*i*) Public servants.
      (*ii*) Self-employed persons.
   i. Constitutional conference:
      (*i*)   Conference composition.
      (*ii*) Selection procedure.
      (*iii*) Date and venue.
2. Cessation of hostilities: Date, time and mechanics.
3. Relief operations.

I would like to end my speech as I have taken every opportunity to do at our peace talks, with a personal appeal to members of the other delegation. There were on both sides at our opening session here people who have been engaged in the business of building Nigeria for very many years. Much of what has happened in the last two years has been distressing to all of us. Nevertheless, this is the price which we have to pay for our own short-comings. It may be that history will decide that there are no angels on any side in the recent history of Nigeria. We have all made mistakes, grave mistakes. If we cannot overcome them, if we cannot learn from them, then we will be adjudged guilty not only of the failures which have brought us to our present situation but even more of the greater failures of today, namely our unwillingness or inability to come to terms and to begin to undo the evil which our generation has done. For, make no mistake about it, when the history of our times come to be written, it will be the failures of our generation as a whole that will be recorded. You and we will be equally guilty, unless we who are here at these talks can agree to open a new page in the lives of our people. At the opening session, I saw sitting before me persons who have been concerned with public affairs in our country for almost as long as I myself have been, and in at least one case even longer. I still see before me some with whom as friends and associates I shared youthful dreams about our nation. I know that some of them were not directly involved in planning the gamble for secession. I appeal to them in the name of our common heritage and in the name of all that Nigerians have tried to achieve in the past, to take this opportunity to bring the suffering of our people to an end. Let us jointly create a new Nigeria worthy of our people and worthy of the dreams which we have shared.

Sometimes, it takes great courage to fight, sometimes it takes even greater courage to stop. Certainly it takes wisdom to know when to stop. Let us show the greater courage and that wisdom. I assure you that there is no need to continue fighting. There is no cause for continued war. I cannot believe that the people behind rebel lines do not want to see an end to the fratricidal war of the last fourteen months. I am satisfied that on the Federal side, there are enough elements in positions of responsibility, authority and influence who want to work for peace and reconciliation, but there is even more on the other side a crying need for persons of courage and influence who can say to their people: 'Let us stop; let us see whether we cannot put the pieces together again.'

I assure you that if I did not myself believe that we can bring the war to an end, and that living under the same banner we can create a happy future for the next generation, I would not be here. If my word is of any value, please believe me that there is a genuine desire on the part of the Federal Government and on the part of those whom you know either personally or by reputation, to bring this whole sad business to an end, and to start afresh.

I invite you, in the name of all that you hold dear, in the name of that same God whom Mr. Ojukwu invoked two days ago, to save our country and our people from further bloodshed and suffering, and to join the Federal Government in this enterprise.

---

[1] *Speech delivered at Addis Ababa, 7 August 1968. (Text from the Federal Ministry of Information.)*
[2] *See* DOC *168.*
[3] *See* DOC *157.*

170.
Biafra Puts Forward Counter-proposals[1]

1. We have learnt by bitter experience that unity must come in stages, through co-operation and mutual understanding. We therefore propose that the existence of Biafra as a sovereign and independent nation should be accepted. We believe that, as bitterness dies down and mutual understanding grows, a closer association may again be possible.

2. There should be maximum economic co-operation and common services between Nigeria and Biafra. Details of these areas of co-operation should be negotiated at this conference.

3. Other matters consequent on the separation of the two countries, such as the sharing of the assets and liabilities (including the national public debt) of the former Federation, should also be negotiated at this conference; as well as matters relating to the payment of compensation for the lives and property of Biafrans which were lost during the pogrom and as a result of the war.

4. In order to promote a lasting peace and to avoid a further increase of bitterness, we should now agree on:

(*i*) immediate cessation of fighting on land, sea and air;

(*ii*) immediate removal of the economic blockade mounted by Nigeria against Biafra;

(*iii*) the withdrawal of troops behind the pre-war boundaries to enable refugees to return to their homes.

5. Until more permanent arrangements are made, the cessation of fighting on land, sea and air should be policed by an International Force drawn from the following African countries—Ethiopia, Liberia, Ghana, Niger, Cameroun, Congo (Kinshasa), Tanzania, Gabon, Ivory Coast, Zambia. We regard the composition of the International Force as negotiable.

6. We should agree on the holding of a plebiscite in disputed areas inside and outside Biafra to determine the true wishes of the people, i.e., whether they wish to be in Biafra or Nigeria. The details of the arrangements for a plebiscite should be worked out at this meeting.

7. Immediate agreement should be reached on the transportation of relief supplies by air, sea and land to the civilian victims of the war, whether they be in Nigeria or Biafra.

On all these points, we are prepared to submit to the conference memoranda n further elaboration of our proposals.

[1] *Speech by Professor Njoku at Addis Ababa, 9 August 1968. Text by courtesy of a member of the delegations.*

171.
Enahoro Puts Federal Case at Addis Ababa[1]

When I spoke here last Wednesday,[2] I said I did not wish to inflict on this meeting a lengthy opening statement in reply to Mr. Ojukwu's speech, particularly as I had hoped that we could quickly get down to the serious business of negotiation. Since then, the acting leader of the delegation on the other side has repeatedly made references to Mr. Ojukwu's speech, to buttress his argument for a separate sovereign state for the Ibos. As I promised when we last adjourned, I have studied Dr. Njoku's statement carefully, and I propose to show that his suggestions are untenable. However, we have to bear in mind that Dr. Njoku's proposals[3] are predicated upon the case which Mr. Ojukwu tried to make. If that case is right, then the conclusions to be drawn from it are those drawn by Mr. Ojukwu and Dr. Njoku, and both the proposals submitted by Dr. Njoku and his reaction to our proposals flow inescapably from those conclusions.

It is clear therefore that in order to show that Dr. Njoku's proposals cannot be the answer to our problem, I cannot ignore their case as stated by them and the conclusions upon which the proposals are based. If I can show that the true facts are not as stated by Mr. Ojukwu, then from the correct facts, we can draw a different set of conclusions from which a different set of proposals—namely, the Federal peace proposals which I have presented—would emerge. For this reason, I have already informed Your Imperial Majesty that I propose to speak at some length this afternoon, and in the course of my speech, I shall submit substantially the same facts and arguments as would have been contained in the written statement which I promised to make a few days ago. That statement will not now be necessary. Your Imperial Majesty, what is the correct historical background of the Nigerian crisis, and what are the true facts?

Although Nigeria was the creation of European ambitions and rivalries, its peoples had their own ancient history before the arrival of the Colonizers. This newly-created country contained, not just a multiplicity of pagan tribes, but a number of great kingdoms which had evolved complex systems of government, independent of contact with Europe. Within its frontiers were the great kingdom of Bornu, with a known history of more than a thousand years; the Fulani Empire, which had existed for a hundred years before its conquest by Britain; the Benin Empire, stretching at its zenith from east of the Niger and to well beyond Nigeria's western borders; the Yoruba Empire of Oyo, which had once been one of the most powerful of the states of the Guinea Coast; the kingdoms of the Niger Delta and Calabar, the loosely organised Ibo peoples in the hinterland of the former Eastern Region, and the dukedoms and small tribes of the Plateau. Of the three most populous ethnic groups of Nigeria, therefore, (Hausa/Fulanis, Ibos, Yorubas), only the Ibos never had an organised state, an imperial past or a 'golden age.' They had not centralized political administration or loyalties and never had an era of kings, dukes or conquerors. Nor did they have an early start in either Western or Missionary (Islamic or Christian) education. The greater part of the North was Moslem.

The British tried to weld together these kingdoms and territories with such diversity of languages and cultures and at such different stages of civilization as has been described above. On 1st January, 1900, the administration of Nigeria was formally taken over by the British Government. The British ruled the country for almost sixty years. During the colonial period Nigeria went through different stages of administration. The Colony and Protectorate of Lagos first became part of Southern Nigeria. A Protectorate was established over Northern Nigeria. The Protectorates were then merged with Lagos into the Colony and Protectorate of Nigeria. In the forties, a regional pattern of Government was introduced and the Northern, Eastern and Western Regions were established. Constitutional changes which followed in the forties and fifties introduced Regional Legislatures and Regional Governments. Self-government was granted to the Regions in the fifties. The Independence Constitution was introduced in 1960 and the Federation of Nigeria became an independent and sovereign state on 1st October, 1960.

Unfortunately, during the years of British occupation, Nigeria did not produce one nationalist movement in the classic sense, as was the case in India and Ghana, to mention only two former British colonial territories. Instead, Nigeria produced three nationalist movements which, unfortunately, were based on the three major tribal groupings. The major political parties grew out of these movements, and political developments during the struggle for Independence therefore took the shape of compromises between these political parties which were different in their outlook and programmes and which were regionally entrenched. The only common factor among them was the struggle for independence. In their common desire to win independence, many vital problems were left unsolved.

One of these outstanding problems was the creation of more states which would have provided a more lasting foundation for stability of the Federation of Nigeria. The British Government pointed out at the time that if new states were to be created, the new states must be given at least two years to settle down before independence could be granted. On reflection, Nigerian leaders have admitted that the British were right and they were wrong on this vital issue in hurrying to independence without solving the problem of stability of the Federation.

Nigeria's attainment of independence on 1st October, 1960, was greeted with world-wide acclaim in the great expectation that this new nation would eventually emerge as a model of unity and strength in a developing continent. Despite these expectations, Nigeria was plagued with a deep-seated imbalance in its political structure, stemming from the inequality of its component units which placed one of the regions in a dominant position in the Federation. The failure of the Nigerian Constitution at independence in 1960 to recognize the strong desires of minorities and other communities for self-determination affected the balance of power at the centre.

There were other causes which affected the stability of the Nigerian Federation soon after independence.

Among the most important of these were:

i. The existence at the Centre of a very powerful executive which weakened the Central Legislature in its role of safe-guarding the interests of component units of the Federation.

ii. The abolition of the Judicial Service Commissions, the precipitate termination of appeals to the Judicial Committee of the Privy Council in London and the subordination of Public Prosecutions to political control.

iii. The restrictions imposed on the emergence of truly national political parties and the refusal of regional authorities to accept or work with political parties with roots in other regions.

iv. The electoral systems which left the control of elections to machineries dominated by politicians who could and did manipulate elections to the advantage of their supporters.

v. The abuse of power, such as the power to control the Police Forces, and the use of Courts and appointments of Judges for political ends.

vi. The ineffectiveness of the Federal Parliament in the discharge of its function and the misuse of the powers of Parliament.

vii. The avoidance of public accountability and public examination by Ministers.

viii. The division of powers between the Federal and Regional authorities, which in certain cases left vital areas of conflict between them and, in others, failed to allocate to the Federal authority functions which would have promoted national unity.

ix. The absence of codes of conduct for public functionaries and the absence of democratic traditions.

x. The collapse of normal safeguards against misrule, in particular:

    a. the right of public protest;

    b. free Press and Radio;

    c. free public discussion;

    d. the ultimate sanction of an alternative government.

xi. National traits of sycophancy and deference support.

xii. The psychological impact of coups in neighbouring African States.

xiii. Tribalism, tribal discrimination, nepotism and corrupt practices, particularly in appointments to public offices and in the distribution of amenities.

xiv. The desire of ethnic linguistic groups for separate states within the Federation.

xv. The continued economic and ideological interests of, and intrigues by, the old colonial regime and other foreign countries in Nigeria.

xvi. The slow pace of social integration among the various population groups.

xvii. The problem of the Army:

    a. the dichotomy in social origins between the majority of the rank and file and the majority of officers;

    b. political interference with the role of the Army as guardians of legitimacy;

    c. the unanswered question of the peace-time role of young, educated, politically conscious but largely idle officers.

The situation in Nigeria less than three years after the attainment of independence was therefore disturbing. Of the three main political parties, two formed the Government and the leaders of the third were in prison. There was increasing agitation in certain areas for self-determination, leading for example, to the creation of a Mid-West State out of the Western Region in 1963 and the imprisonment of a large number of people agitating for a State of their own in a part of the North. The Government and Parliament of one Region were suspended by Federal action. There were census disputes. Due to population pressure and the shortage of arable land in the central part of the East, many of its Ibo people had moved out and settled in large numbers among other communities, but they did not become integrated with the host communities. Parliament and Regional Legislatures met infrequently, public meetings were banned at random, and the Press was under siege.

In December, 1964 there was a controversial and much disputed Federal Election. Two political alliances had emerged in 1964 on the eve of the Federal Election. The alliance which won claimed to rule legitimately. The alliance which lost claimed that the elections had been rigged. Then followed another hotly-disputed election in the former Western Region. That election resulted in widespread rioting, arson and lawlessness. By the end of 1965, five years after independence, all those factors had combined to produce an explosive situation little short of a breakdown of law and order. It became increasingly clear that sooner or later there would be a fundamental, and probably violent, change. That change came on 15th January, 1966.

Historians will continue to debate whether what happened in Nigeria on 15th January, 1966, was a rebellion, a coup or a mutiny. Whatever it was, there was a change of Government. The civilian administration was removed from office. In the morning of that date, the Prime Minister of the Federation (Sir Abubakar Tafawa Balewa), the Federal Minister of Finance (Chief F. Okotie-Eboh), the Premier of the Northern Region (Sir Ahmadu Bello), the Premier of the Western Region (Chief S. L. Akintola), the second and third ranking officers in the Nigerian Army (Brigadier Maimalari and Brigadier Ademulegun), other senior officers (Colonel Ṣodeinde, Colonel Pam and others) were seized and murdered. All of them had one thing in common—they were not Ibos. The Premier of the Eastern Region (Dr. Michael Okpara), the Premier of the Mid-West Region (Chief Dennis Osadebay), the Head of the Army (Major-General Aguiyi Ironsi), the Federal Minister of Trade (Dr. K. O. Mbadiwe), and others in like position were not killed. They had one thing in common—they were Ibos.

However, in the morning of the fateful date, and for some time afterwards, these facts were not generally known in the country. Major-General Aguiyi-Ironsi established a Federal Military Government after January 15. He promised to restore law and order, to put down what he described as a mutiny, to deal with corruption and to restore civilian rule 'as soon as practicable.' In assessing the motives as well as the consequences of the Military coup of 15th January, 1966, attention should be drawn to the various interpretations and excuses offered. Firstly, some people saw in it an attempt to end Northern domination. Secondly, some regarded it as an attempt to remove corruption in Government. Thirdly, others hoped that it would introduce an honest and just programme of political and administrative reform to correct the structural imbalance in the Federation. No one quarrelled with these aims.

Consequently there was an atmosphere of general relief immediately after the coup of 15th January, until the pattern of killings which emerged, when the dust had cleared, revealed that this was a coup organised by young Ibo officers in the Army. Whatever they may claim was their basic plan, its effect was that civilian leaders and senior military officers from other areas and ethnic groups were killed while those from Ibo areas were spared. All non-Ibo senior military officers above the rank of Major who were accessible were killed in the January 15 coup. There was only one exception to this when a junior Ibo officer, half-awake through his midnight sleep, was killed in Apapa for refusing to hand over the key of the armoury. Therefore, to most Nigerians, the incidents of 15th January were a clumsily camouflaged attempt to secure Ibo domination of the Government of the country. This impression was later reinforced by certain appointments and actions of the new regime under Major-General Ironsi, himself an Ibo.

The opportunities of January 15 were misused in several ways by the Ironsi regime in the months that followed. For a while every Nigerian hoped that the country would go on to achieve greater progress in its development generally. Unfortunately General Ironsi allowed matters to be taken out of his hands by prominent Ibo leaders in the army, in the public service, and in public life. Affairs in the public service and the armed forces appeared to lend colour to the impression that the coup of January 15 was designed to install Ibos in positions of power. Out of twenty-one promotions in the Army in April, 1966, for example, eighteen were Ibo officers. General Ironsi drew his principal advisers from the Ibo ethnic group. Ethnic groups tend to be chauvinistic but the Ibos were the most militantly chauvinistic and this naturally created apprehensions in the minds of the others.

Although public inquiries were instituted into the conduct of certain public officers, some of these men remained in positions of power. The public was disenchanted. In the Army itself there was growing resentment about officers killed in the January 15 coup. Non-Ibo officers and rank and file resented the killing of officers from their ethnic groups while those from the Ibo ethnic group were spared. Major-General Ironsi did little or nothing to answer this resentment which rapidly became widespread in the Army. There were continued reports that January 15, 1966 was inconclusive and that plans were afoot to 'complete the job' by the liquidation of surviving senior non-Ibo Army officers.

The leaders of the Opposition remained in prison, whereas it was freely said that some Yoruba Army officers had participated in the coup expressly for the purpose of securing their release. In the North, after January 15, the people had adopted an attitude of 'wait and see.' In several parts, especially Kano, Katsina and Zaria, some of the former Ministers of the Regional Government had been molested and jeered at on their return to their Provinces. But the situation soon changed because of measures introduced by the Ironsi Government which many Northerners believed were inimical to their interests, and because of the publicly provocative and taunting attitude of Ibo traders and workers living in the North who paraded themselves as the new masters of Nigeria. All advice to the Ironsi Government to rectify the situation was ignored. Major-General Ironsi did nothing to remove the impression that the January 15 coup was part of an Ibo Master Plan to dominate the country.

This was the state of affairs in the country generally, and in the North in particular, when the unification decree was announced by Major-General Ironsi on 24th May, 1966. The decree (Decree No. 34), a major constitutional and political step which contrary to traditional practice, had not been widely discussed, announced a unitary system of government, the dissolution of political and tribal parties and other measures. But the fateful words in the announcement were: 'the Regions are abolished.' Before promulgating this decree, Major-General Ironsi did not even allow the Constitutional Committee, which he had appointed and which had begun to sit in regional centres, to complete its work, despite his public and written undertaking that no constitutional changes would be introduced until after the fullest consultation with the people of the country. All this caused great disquiet in all parts of the country and led to the May 29 disturbances in the North in which a number of Ibos were killed.

There was an uneasy calm after the May disturbances. The Governor of the then Northern Region, in co-operation with the Native Authority administration, did everything possible to put down the disturbances and hostility to both the Ironsi Government and people of Ibo origin resident in the North.

But there was political uncertainty regarding the future of Decree No. 34, and widespread tension and mutual suspicion in the Army. Regular channels of communication were being deliberately by-passed by the Ironsi government in the transmission of instructions. Military officers of the Ibo ethnic group had advance information about vital matters of state while superior officers from other ethnic groups were kept in the dark. Then there was the sudden decision by Major-General Ironsi that he would rotate the Military Governors and appoint Military Prefects, even after this proposal had been rejected by the Supreme Military Council.

Amid all this, the economic situation rapidly deteriorated. The country, which had welcomed the change of January 15 soon realised that the events which followed January 15 had not justified the hopes and aspirations of that change. It became clear after a few months, that the country had no satisfaction from the events of January 15, 1966. Once again, conditions were ripe for a change.

In the last week of July 1966, the change came. During the week, there were widely circulating rumours that the 'unfinished job' of January 15 was to be completed by the elimination of the remaining senior army officers of non-Ibo origin. Although many such officers had been killed in January, a number had escaped being murdered. Some of them were out of Nigeria in January 1966 and had since returned to the country. They were now holding some key positions in the Army and still prevented an all-Ibo command at the top of the Nigerian Military administration. There were also rumours of a countercoup to reverse the effects of the January 15 coup. By 28th July, 1966, there was strong evidence that one group or the other would move. In the country at large, people expected a change because of dissatisfaction with the manner the Ironsi Government had handled national matters since January 16. It was generally agreed that the opportunities of the change of January 16 had been hopelessly misused.

A mutiny started at the Army Barracks in Abeokuta in the former Western Region in the morning of July 29. An officer of Northern origin heard a telephone discussion between two Ibo officers. After the discussion, the Ibo officer at the Abeokuta Barracks ordered all Ibo soldiers at the barracks to take up arms and 'be ready.' This was believed to be the signal for the elimination of the remaining non-Ibo officers in the Army—the 'unfinished job' of January 15. The officer from the North in turn asked all soldiers from other ethnic groups to take up their arms. An argument followed between the officers and their supporters and shooting broke out between the two sides.

These disorders spread to other barracks in the rest of the country and continued all through that week-end. Major-General Aguiyi-Ironsi, who was then visiting Ibadan, and his host, the Military Governor of the West, Lt.-Col. Adekunle Fajuyi, were kidnapped at the Government House in Ibadan. The net result of all this was another coup. Following the coup, Major-General Yakubu Gowon (then Lt.-Col.) succeeded Major-General Aguiyi-Ironsi on 1st August as Head of the Federal Military Government. In a broadcast to the nation that morning he promised to bring the disorders in the Army under control, stop further bloodshed, restore law, order and confidence in all parts of the country with minimum delay, and seek a new basis for unity. Major-General Gowon also analysed the roots of the Nigerian crisis and announced that a unitary form of Government did not provide a basis for Nigerian unity. He promised that with the concurrence of the Military Governors and other members of the Supreme Military and Federal and Executive Councils a decree would soon be issued to lay a sound foundation for Nigerian unity. July 29 was welcomed by the nation, particularly because of the events which followed it.

On his assumption of office, Major-General Gowon set in motion the machinery for finding a lasting solution to Nigeria's problems. He ordered:

a. the release of Chief Obafemi Awolowo who was Leader of the Opposition in the Federal Parliament until his imprisonment in 1963, Chief Anthony Enahoro, and other political prisoners and detainees;

b. an immediate return to the Federal system of government;

c. the summoning on 12th September, 1966, of an Ad Hoc Conference on Constitutional Proposals, comprising representatives of all the Regions of the Federation. This conference was preceded by Consultative Conferences in all areas in the Regions. At these Consultative Conferences, the issue of the creation of more States in the Federation was revived and memoranda were submitted demanding that the basic cause of dissatisfaction—i.e. the imbalance in the Federal structure—should be removed.

Major-General Gowon also announced that the country would return to civilian rule as soon as it could be arranged.

The Constitutional Conference already referred to was preceded by terrorist bomb outrages in Lagos and at the Ore Bridge on the trunk road from Lagos to the East, organised by Ojukwu's administration. Plans for large scale sabotage in several parts of the country were uncovered. Some senior Ibo officials under the direction of Ojukwu's Government were actually arrested in the process of blowing up the Railway and Road bridges in Kaduna, the Kaduna Stadium, Waterworks, Post Offices and power houses. Quantities of explosives were discovered and impounded by police in Kaduna, Kano and Jos. In the midst of all this, Mr. Ojukwu continued recklessly to inflame passions. His radio was preaching hate, defiance and revenge and all Ibos were being publicly called back to the East because, as he alleged, they were not safe elsewhere in the country. A few heeded the official call, but most were pressured by threatening telegrams in the East to return home. Towards the end of September, 1966, Constitutional Conference which Major-General Gowon had set up had made good progress, justifying his hopes for an early return to civilian rule. Unfortunately, the work of the Committee was rudely interrupted by the outbreak of disturbances late in September, 1966.

At this time, Nigerians of Northern origin living in the former Eastern Region were attacked by Ibos. Many of them were killed, others maimed and injured. This was between 20th September and 28th September, 1966. The attacks on the Northerners took place in Port Harcourt, Abakaliki, Oji River and Onitsha. News of these attacks was first broadcast over Radio Cotonou in Dahomey and other foreign stations and subsequently over Radio Kaduna. Northerners in Iboland fled back to the North. Many of those who tried to escape were collected, massacred and dumped into Imo River by Ibo assailants. Then Northerners retaliated by attacking Ibos living in the North.

The riots of 29th September and the resulting death toll might have been avoided if Ojukwu and his group had recognised 29th July, 1966, as the antithesis of 15th January and genuinely sought a basis for saving the country. On the contrary, they were full of threats of revenge, and rumour set several dates for it. A bomb incident in Lagos in mid-September 1966, in which an Ibo official tried to blow up public buildings, designed to prevent the meeting of the Constitutional Conference called by General Gowon, confirmed such fears. Such an explosive atmosphere could only produce further tragedy. It has since become clear that Ojukwu deliberately provoked this tragic chain of events in order to justify his plot to pull the former Eastern Region out of Nigeria.

This description of the sequence of events is not an attempt to excuse the death toll of Ibos in the North or Northerners in Iboland during the tragic riots at the end of September. The Federal Government and the then Northern Region Government publicly condemned the killings and acted decisively to stop them while Ojukwu offered no regrets.

Indeed, in his impromptu address to the Constitutional Conference on 3rd October, 1966,[4] General Gowon said:

Gentlemen, I will tell you this: certainly there has been a damage. I think that is what we never seem to admit when there is something like that. There is a damage and I am very, very sorry about it. I regret it and I am doing everything I can . . . As I said, for God's sake, don't lose hope. If we are alive and if we are determined, we can get this country back to its proper shape. I am determined to do that even if it means my life. I give you my word for it. . . . To our Eastern friends, for God's sake, please don't lose hope. Let us try and see what we can do to mend what has happened. Give me a chance and I am quite convinced I will be able to do something very shortly.

It is regrettable that the rebel regime has viciously exploited this tragedy in their propaganda while conveniently ignoring killings of other Nigerians in Iboland. From the tragic events of 1966, all sections of Nigeria have learned their lessons. There is no reason why the pattern should be repeated, given the will to overcome them. Nigerians must forgive one another, even if all sections of the country which suffered in one way or another from these events, cannot forget.

It is necessary at this stage to recall the long history of efforts at conciliation from October, 1966 to May, 1967. The decision of the Federal Military Government, even when there was no military capacity in the East, to refrain from action against the illegal actions and defiance of Federal Government by Mr. Ojukwu, illustrates clearly the conciliatory approach of the Federal Military Government. In spite of the following outrageous acts directed by Mr. Ojukwu, the Federal Government continued its efforts to persuade the East to see reason and co-operate.

The seizure within the Region of more than one-third of the rolling stock of the Nigerian Railway, including 800 wagons and 115 oil tankers;

The denial of port facilities to exports from the Northern Region;

Persistent obstruction of the movement to the North of oil products from the Refinery (owned by all the Governments in Nigeria, including that of the Northern Region);

The seizure of property belonging to a foreign government—the neighbouring Republic of Chad;

The seizure of barge-borne traffic on the international waterway of the River Niger bound for the friendly Republics of Niger and Cameroun;

The expulsion since October, 1966, of all non-Easterners from the East.

All these outrageous acts were overlooked by the Federal Government in the belief that time was needed for Mr. Ojukwu and his group to come round to discuss how best to restore the country to normal conditions.

Again, after the Aburi Conference held in Ghana in January 1967 a Decree (No. 8) was introduced which completely decentralised the country even beyond the original demands of Mr. Ojukwu and beyond the provisions of the Nigerian Federal Constitution. The Decree was unacceptable to Ojukwu because it contained a clause which provided against secession.

One by one, these efforts were completely frustrated by Mr. Ojukwu and his group who, from the very beginning, had set their minds on secession. More regrettably, the long time spent in genuinely trying to appease them was used by them to engage in a massive arms build-up in preparation for Civil War.

The warlike actions of the rebel leaders before the first shots were fired testify to their responsibility for starting the war, as clearly manifested in the words spoken by Mr. Ojukwu to the National Conciliation Committee Peace Mission which met him at the State House, Enugu on the 6th of May, 1967. Mr. Ojukwu said:

I started off this struggle in July 1966 with 120 rifles to defend the entirety of the East. I took my stand knowing fully well that in doing so, whilst carving my name in history, I was signing also my death warrant. But I took it because I believe that this stand was vital to the survival of the South. I appealed for settlement quietly because I understood that this was a naked struggle for power. Quietly I built. If you do not know it, I am proud, and my officers are proud that here in the East we possess the biggest army in black Africa. I am no longer speaking as an under-dog, I am speaking from a position of power.

In answer to a specific query by Chief Awolowo, the leader of the Peace Mission, regarding the attitude of the Leaders at Enugu to the former Northern Region and secession, Mr. Ojukwu replied: 'On the specific question of whether there is a possibility of contact with the North, the answer is on the battle-field.'

Meanwhile, every conceivable concession was made to Ojukwu who was then the Military Governor of the East. The concessions included the following:

i. The sum of half a million pounds was paid as first instalment to help Ojukwu's Government in the rehabilitation of its refugees. Ojukwu promptly expended the money in buying arms and recruiting mercenaries.

ii. The meetings of the Constitutional Conference were postponed several times in order to persuade Ojukwu to allow the Eastern delegates to continue participating in the meetings. The Heads of all other delegations to the Conference and religious leaders made individual and joint appeals to Ojukwu but he flatly rejected every mediation and ordered the Eastern delegates not to attend further meetings. This brought the Conference to a standstill and imposed a period of tension and anxiety on the whole country.

iii. Efforts were made to persuade Ojukwu to attend meetings of the Supreme Military Council. These failed. Major-General Gowon then agreed to the extraordinary procedure of holding a meeting of the Supreme Military Council outside Nigeria. That meeting was held in Aburi, Ghana on 4th and 5th January, 1967. Ojukwu had hardly left the Conference hall before he began to twist the Aburi Agreements. The agreements reached at Aburi were subsequently embodied in Decree No. 8 promulgated on 17th March, 1967. The decree conferred greater powers on the various Regional Governments in a deliberate effort to restore confidence among the then component units of the Federation. The new decree exceeded in decentralization anything ever before attempted in Nigeria. It was introduced to placate Ojukwu. Yet Ojukwu completely rejected the Decree and instead demanded the right of separate sovereign existence for the former Eastern Region, co-operating only in a few common services with the other Regions as sovereign states.

iv. On 15th April, 1967, a group of eminent Nigerians formed a National Peace Committee and urged Major-General Gowon to continue in his efforts for a peaceful settlement of the crisis in the country. The Committee then visited all the Regional Governors including Ojukwu. Ojukwu promised to attend other meetings called by Major-General Gowon. He never fulfilled this promise.

v. The Federal Public Service Commission rescinded a previous directive in order to enable Ibo officers to continue after 15th October, 1966 to enjoy the rights and benefits of the Federal Civil Service, including their remunerations, while in fact they had deserted the Service to the Eastern Region from other parts of Nigeria. Originally the Commission had ordered that all those who did not return by that date should be dismissed.

vi. A group of six leading Obas (Natural Rulers) from the former Western Region went on a peace mission to all the Regional Governors and the Head of the Federal Military Government. They met Ojukwu in Enugu and urged him to seek a peaceful settlement of the Nigerian crisis by attending the meetings of the Supreme Military Council. Ojukwu rejected their advice after making false promises to the delegation in Enugu.

vii. Another Committee (the National Conciliation Committee) was set up to make yet another effort to bring Ojukwu back to the fold. The Committee included the Chief Justice of the Federation, Sir Adetokunbo Ademola; Chief Obafemi Awolowo and Chief Jereton Mariere, Adviser to the Mid-West Military Governor. A Delegation of the Committee led by Chief Awolowo met both Major-General Gowon in Lagos and Ojukwu in Enugu. After the delegation had conferred with Ojukwu, it recommended that the Federal Military Government should lift its economic sanctions imposed on the former Eastern Region and that Ojukwu in his turn should revoke all measures taken over Federal institutions and departments in the East. The Federal Military Government accepted all the recommendations of the Committee and revoked its economic sanctions against the East. Ojukwu flatly turned down all the recommendations of the Committee. In addition, he seized all the Federal postal vans which carried mails to the East.

While concession after concession was being made to him, what was Ojukwu's attitude towards the Federal Military Government?

i. On 11 September, 1966, an agent of Ojukwu who was an Ibo explosives expert in the employ of the Federal Coal Corporation at Enugu, one Edmund Agu, blew up part of the £1 million Federal Palace Hotel in Lagos and the

Ore Bridge on the Ijebu-Benin road. Edmund Agu, not satisfied with the wreckage he had caused thus far, was assembling other explosives in a house in a residential suburb of Lagos when he blew himself into pieces.

ii. Many Ibos were caught trying to plant explosives at certain public places in the former Northern Region. These places included the bridge linking Kaduna North with Kaduna South, the Hamdala Hotel in Kaduna, the Kaduna Stadium, the main Post Office at Jos and the Waterworks in Kano. Other acts of sabotage were perpetrated by Ibo engineers at the Post Office and the Electricity Corporation of Nigeria in the North.

iii. Consignments of arms and ammunition from the East to Ibos in the North, including some to the Head of the Eastern Students' Union of the Ahmadu Bello University in Zaria, were intercepted.

iv. All mass media under Ojukwu's control in the former Eastern Region mounted a campaign of hate against the rest of Nigeria. They called the Head of the Federal Military Government dirty names, libelled and blackmailed senior Government officials in the Federal Public Service. Ojukwu himself indulged in the crudest abuse of Major-General Gowon and other members of the Supreme Military Council.

v. One of the agents of Ojukwu, yet another Ibo man, was caught dressed like a Northern Chief and hiding explosives in his dress at the entrance of Lugard Hall, Kaduna, during a meeting of Northern Leaders.

vi. Ojukwu expelled all non-Easterners from the former Eastern Region, contrary to the entrenched provisions of the Constitution.

vii. In January, 1967, Ojukwu seized about £206,000 worth of produce belonging to the Northern Nigerian Marketing Board, awaiting shipment overseas at Port Harcourt.

viii. Also in January, 1967, Ojukwu impounded about one-third of the entire rolling-stock of the Nigerian Railways, including 115 oil-tankers, and completely disrupted the services on the Eastern District of the Nigerian Railways.

ix. Ojukwu's Government disrupted the supply of oil products from the refinery near Port Harcourt to the Northern Region, although the refinery is owned jointly by the Federal Government and all the former Regional Governments.

x. Ojukwu's Government also hindered the passage of goods to Nigeria's neighbouring countries and seized goods belonging to these foreign countries, thus flagrantly violating normal international practice and disturbing friendly relations with Nigeria's neighbours.

xi. On 30th March, 1967, Ojukwu published an Edict seizing all revenue payable in the East to the Military Government. In addition he seized all Federal Installations in the Region. These included Harbours, the Federal Broadcasting Corporation, the Central Posts and Telegraphs Department, the Federal Railway Corporation and the Federal Coal Corporation.

xii. On 5th April, 1967, a Nigerian Airways DC3 Aircraft which left Lagos Airport earlier in the day was seized at Port Harcourt on Ojukwu's instruction.

xiii. On 13th April, 1967, a Nigerian Airways F27 Aircraft which took off from Benin, capital of the Mid-West State, and was flying to Lagos with twenty-six passengers was hi-jacked by Ibo gunmen and diverted to Enugu.

The aircraft was seized by Ojukwu in Enugu, and the passengers sent off by road.

xiv. Ojukwu's agents attempted to hi-jack another Nigerian Airways aircraft flying to Lagos from Ghana. Their plans leaked and their attempt was foiled by security men at the Accra Airport.

xv. On 23rd May, 1967, Ojukwu rejected the proposal of the National Conciliation Committee for a negotiated settlement of the Nigerian crisis.

xvi. On 30th May, 1967, Ojukwu declared the illegal secession of the former Eastern Region from the Federation of Nigeria.

Immediately after Ojukwu declared the secession of the former Eastern Region on 30th May, 1967, the Head of the Federal Military Government and Commander-in-Chief of the Armed Forces, Major-General Yakubu Gowon described the secession as an act of rebellion which must be crushed. Major-General Gowon ordered general mobilization of troops. He regretted that some innocent Nigerians in the three Eastern States would suffer considerable hardship and possible loss of life as a result of Ojukwu's rebellion.

Major-General Gowon assured Nigerians from the three Eastern States resident in Lagos and other parts of the Federation of their safety and asked them to feel free to go about their normal business. He warned that anyone molesting them would be dealt with on the spot by the Army and Police. Major-General Gowon emphasized that the three Eastern States remain an integral part of the Federal Republic of Nigeria. He warned all countries and international organisations to respect the territorial integrity of Nigeria and to refrain from giving any support whatsoever to Ojukwu's rebel group. Major-General Gowon reimposed the economic sanctions against the Eastern States which had been lifted in the spirit of conciliation. Other sanctions were also imposed. These included a ban on the importation and exportation of Nigerian currency notes, the tightening of foreign exchange control and the stoppage of bank transfers from the Eastern States payable in other parts of the Republic. Any new currency notes issued in the Eastern States would be illegal tender. The Federal Government pointed out that the measures were not punitive but were aimed at safeguarding the stability of the Nigerian Pound.

On 31st May, 1967, the Federal Government suspended public telecommunications services and postal services with the three Eastern States. The Government, however, allowed existing private teleprinter services and private fixed radio services for which licences had been granted to continue to operate as long as these services were used for the purpose for which the licences were granted. Ojukwu illegally ordered oil revenues and royalties payable to the Federal Government to be paid to his illegal regime in Enugu.

On 3rd June, 1967, the Federal Government replied by instructing all oil-tankers proceeding to the Oil Terminal at Bonny to call first in Lagos for clearance from the Nigerian Navy. Naval Commanders were ordered to intercept any tankers proceeding to the prohibited zone in the three Eastern States without prior clearance at Lagos.

On 10th June, 1967, Ojukwu's agents planted quantities of explosives and accessories at a bulk oil installation in Apapa, Lagos. The explosives included cases of gelignite cortex fuses, battery packs, thirty-six electrical fuses and time-relay packs. The Federal Government further tightened security measures in all public buildings and places in and around Lagos. Movements of vehicles into Lagos between 7 p.m. and 6 a.m. was prohibited.

On 22nd June, 1967, Ojukwu tried his hands at piracy. A vessel, 'Richard Lander,' owned by the British firm of United Africa Company of Nigeria, was seized at Onitsha by Ojukwu's gunmen. The vessel had twenty persons on board and carried two barges of Northern Nigeria Marketing Board groundnuts of about 400 tons. Ojukwu neither returned the vessel nor the groundnuts, despite protest by the United Africa Company to the Federal Military Government.

On 24 June, 1967, several Ibos, agents of Ojukwu, were arrested in a village near the University of Ibadan in the Western State for planting ten packages of explosives near the University.

On Friday, 30th June, 1967, Ojukwu boasted that he would wage total war against the people of Nigeria. He immediately unleashed terrorist activities in Lagos and other parts of Nigeria. Ojukwu's agents blew up the Igumale Bridge in Idoma Division and attacked several villages in the neighbouring Northern States. These villages included Ofante, Akpanya, Obale and Oguru in Igala Division.

Ojukwu also carried out acts of terrorism and intimidation against the innocent minority people of the Rivers State and South-Eastern State for supporting their own States. Ojukwu's rebel army looted their Treasuries and Post Offices and imprisoned their leading civilians. These acts of terrorism also included wholesale murders, pillage, arson and seizure of personal properties of the citizens of the Rivers and South-Eastern States.

On 1st July, 1967, Ojukwu was dismissed from the office of Governor, East-Central State, and from the Nigerian Army with ignominy, by the Federal Government and the Army Council.

On 2nd July, 1967, two Ibo agents of Ojukwu attempted to blow up the Nigeria Police Force Headquarters in Lagos under the pretence that they were senior Police Officers returning to work in the evening. But the explosives they carried in their car blew up, killing three Ibos and destroying a petrol station as well as doing great damage to a nearby hospital. Almost simultaneously, there was another explosion at a petrol station in Yaba on the Lagos mainland. Several people were injured.

Ojukwu's rebel troops opened fire on Nigerian Army positions in the Benue/Plateau State in the East-Central State in the early hours of 6th July, 1967. The Federal troops immediately returned fire. Major-General Gowon then ordered the Nigerian Army to penetrate into the East-Central State and capture Ojukwu and his rebel gang. The Armed Forces and the Federal Police were ordered to take adequate measures to safeguard security of the citizens in the Rivers, South-Eastern and the East-Central States. This was the beginning of a 'police action' against Ojukwu's rebellion.

On 15th July, 1967, Major-General Gowon issued a special appeal to officers and other ranks, the true leaders of the people and the general public in the three Eastern States to disown Ojukwu and his rebel collaborators in order to prevent loss of life of innocent citizens of these States in the Police action against Ojukwu.

He urged civilians, in their own interest, not to fight or provoke Federal troops. He advised them to abandon Ojukwu's conscript army and join

U

forces with all true Nigerians to save the country from further suffering. He reassured Ibos of the East-Central State that, with the new States structure and other reforms under the programme of the Supreme Military Council, they would have full equality of treatment with all other communities anywhere in Nigeria.

On 18th July, 1967, Ojukwu's agents replied to the appeal of Major-General Gowon by causing another explosion in Yaba, Lagos. An oil-tanker owned by an Ibo was left in front of a cinema house by an Ibo driver with explosives inside the tank. The explosion caused great damage to the Inland Revenue buildings, the Cinema House, killed many people and wounded several others.

Ojukwu cut off the electricity supply to the Mid-West Textile Mills at Asaba, and to Asaba town, which normally came from the Afam Power Station in the Eastern States. The Federal Government had to restore electricity supply through other sources on 20th July, 1967.

On 23rd July, 1967, Police discovered another petrol tanker loaded with explosives outside a house in Lagos. The Police established that the tanker belonged to the same company—Morris Chima and Sons of Aba in the East-Central State which owned the tanker which earlier caused the explosion in front of a cinema house at Yaba.

On 9th August, 1967, Ojukwu's rebel planes bombed innocent and defence-less civilian population in Lagos, Kaduna, Kano, Lokoja (raided on a Sunday when people were at Church) and several towns in the Northern States.

Also on 9th August, 1967, Ojukwu's rebel soldiers infiltrated into the Mid-West State and, in collaboration with Ibo Officers of the Army in the State, staged a coup against the legitimate Governor of the Mid-West. This coup enabled rebel infiltrators to occupy the state from 9th August to 20th September, 1967. The rebel soldiers, during their occupation of the Mid-West State looted the treasuries and the Central Bank, despoiled markets and killed many innocent civilians.

On 11th August, 1967, Major-General Gowon had no alternative but to instruct the Nigerian Army, Air Force and Navy to carry out full scale military operations against the rebel forces of Ojukwu wherever they might be. General Gowon recalled that while the friends of Nigeria were urging a cessation of fighting and while the Federal Government tried to keep damage to life and property to the minimum, Ojukwu and his rebel gang boasted of total war. Their bombing raids of defenceless villages and their acts of terrorism in the Mid-West emphasized their determination to involve as many Nigerian people and their properties as possible in total destruction. Major-General Gowon said it was necessary to arrest the destructive madness of the rebels with the minimum delay.

During the operations to crush Ojukwu's rebellion, the forces of the Federal Government have achieved signal victories. They have cleared the Mid-West, South East and Rivers States, and parts of East Central State, of the rebels. They have liberated rebel strongholds like Obudu, Ogoja, Onitsha, Nsukka, Calabar, Port Harcourt and the Bonny Oil Terminal. Rebel aircraft, including their B26 raiders used for bombing defenceless civilians in Lagos and other parts of Nigeria, have been destroyed.

The movement for the creation of many states in Nigeria has a long history.

This was a problem for the British in their very early days of administration in Nigeria. There were open discussions among British officials and Nigerians on the most suitable basis for dividing the country for administrative purposes, so that each ethnic group might retain its identity and develop culture. In 1945, Dr. Nnamdi Azikiwe, himself an Ibo, advocated in his book *The Political Blueprint of Nigeria*, a federal form of government for Nigeria and the division of the Federation into eight States.

By 1947, when the Richards Constitution was being considered in Government circles in Lagos and the Colonial Office in London, ethnic group consciousness had become a fact of life in Nigeria. The first ethnic cultural organisation, the Ibibio Union, was born at this time. Others sprang up but, like the Ibo Union, became more political in character than the pioneer Ibibio Union. Unfortunately, Sir Arthur Richards ignored the diversity of the cultures and peoples of Nigeria, and a federation of three massive regions was imposed on Nigerians on 2nd August, 1946, when the Richards Constitution was promulgated. Agitation for ethnic group self-determination and cultural sovereignty grew in the late 1940s. Events fed the flames of agitation.

In 1945, a prominent Ibo lawyer, Charles Onyeama, a member of the Central Legislative Council, said in a public statement in Lagos that the Ibo domination of Nigeria was only a matter of time. This statement sparked off attacks on Ibos in other parts of Nigeria. This statement intensified the growth of ethnic and cultural unions throughout Nigeria. There sprang up the Edo Union, the Calabar Improvement League, the Egbe Omo Oduduwa, the Ijaw Progressive Union, etc. The fear of domination of the rest of Nigeria by any one ethnic group reinforced the search for a form of government in Nigeria which would prevent it. In 1947, Chief Obafemi Awolowo, a Yoruba, in his book, *Path to Nigerian Freedom*, suggested the division of Nigeria into forty states, with cultural and linguistic affinity as the basis of division.

The National Council of Nigerian Citizens (N.C.N.C.), a political party then known as the National Council of Nigeria and the Cameroons, issued a Freedom Charter in 1948 advocating a federal form of Government with units based on ethnic and linguistic affinity. In the same year, Dr. Azikiwe, who was National President of the N.C.N.C. accepted presidency of the Ibo State Union and declared at the Aba Convention of the Union that the God of Africa had specially created Ibos to lead Africa out of bondage. This statement by Dr. Azikiwe, coupled with the emerging overbearing behaviour of the Ibos, created distrust of Ibo intentions and heightened the clamour by other ethnic groups, especially in the former Eastern Region of Nigeria, for their own states.

Although the creation of more states as a basis for nation unity was again ignored during the review of the Richards Constitution in 1949, the demand for new states was not abandoned. The introduction of the Macpherson Constitution in June, 1951, was followed by much articulated dissatisfaction with the constitution by organisations from minority ethnic groups in the country. The most important of these were the Middle Belt State Movement in the former Northern Region; the Mid-West State Movement in the former Western Region, and the Calabar-Ogoja-Rivers (C.O.R.) State Movement in the former Eastern Region.

The demand for more states was again drowned at the London Constitutional discussions in 1953, but it soon received new impetus. Discrimination against the minority areas by regional governments which were dominated by the three major ethnic groups made it crystal clear that these governments could not be just and fair to minorities. Because of the numerical strength of the larger ethnic groups, it was apparent that they could rule perpetually. This intensified the demand for separate states. In fact, the Ibo-dominated Eastern Nigeria Government had planned in 1960 to discontinue news relays in the Efik language in the Region—a step in the direction of cultural suffocation. The measure was abandoned only because of the united protest from the Efik-speaking people of the former Eastern Region.

Chief Awolowo proposed in 1953 the division into nine states. The Western Region was to be broken into two, the Northern Region into four and the Eastern Region into three. In 1959, the Action Group called for the creation of more states, and in addition to cultural and linguistic affinity, proposed a new criterion of viability as bases for division. During the 1957 election into the Eastern House of Assembly the then Premier of the East, Dr. Nnamdi Azikiwe, restated the right of all minorities to self-determination, and affirmed the right of the minorities of the people of Calabar-Ogoja and Rivers Provinces to self-determination. But after the election and at the N.C.N.C. Convention at Aba in October, 1957, Dr. Azikiwe opposed what he called the 'dismemberment' of the Eastern Region.

At the 1953 Constitutional Conference in London the Camerooneans demanded a separate region in order to escape victimization by the government of the former Eastern Region. The Secretary of State for the Colonies promised Dr. Endeley, the Southern Cameroon leader, a separate region if Dr. Endeley and his supporters won an election on the platform of a separate region. When the election was won on this slogan, Southern Cameroons was separated from the Eastern Region.

The fears of minorities were explained in great detail and set out in the report of Sir Henry Willink's Commission appointed by the British Government in 1958. But the Commission was told not to recommend the creation of more states unless as a very last resort. At the end of the inquiry, known as the Minorities Commission, the British Government said that if they were to create more states in Nigeria the new states must be given time to settle down and Independence for Nigeria would be delayed for about two years. This was rejected by Nigerian leaders.

In the 1959 General Election in Nigeria, the Action Group party which campaigned for the creation of more states won unexpected victories in the minority areas of the North and East. Although no new states were created before Nigeria achieved independence on 1st October, 1960, the agitation for the creation of more states went on after independence. In 1963, as a result of the 1962 crisis in Western Nigeria and the declaration of a State of Emergency in that region, the Mid-West Region was created out of the Western Region. Towards the end of 1965, the grumblings in Kano in the heart of the Hausa North and the demand for the creation of a Kano State became louder.

Following the creation of the Mid-West Region in 1963, minority groups all over Nigeria renewed their demand for their own States. One of the major factors which contributed to the collapse of the Ironsi Government was the fact that this basic issue of the creation of States was ignored by him, on the advice of his Ibo advisers. When Major-General Gowon set in motion the process for the review of the Constitution by the setting up of the Ad Hoc Conference on Constitutional proposals, the demand for the creation of more states was one of the major issues raised everywhere in the country. There were extensive discussions in the Regional Consultative Committees and Leaders-of-Thoughts Conferences all over the country. Resolutions were adopted demanding the creation of states in the North and Lagos. There were petitions from minorities in the East which had been subjected to violent intimidation by the former Eastern Military Government under Ojukwu. The minorities in the Eastern Region who numbered 5.4 million out of a total population of 12.4 million were, because of the refusal of the Ibo majority, denied the States they had been demanding all along. The Northern Region was at that time opposed to the creation of states in its area and therefore supported the Eastern majority. However, the North eventually came round to accept being split into smaller units. The Ibo majority in the East, however, did not move from their determination to 'hold' their minority peoples. When the Constitutional Conference in 1966 considered the issue of new states, the North, West, Mid-West and Lagos delegations supported the creation of more states.

The Eastern Nigeria Consultative Assembly agreed in principle at its meeting in the first week of October 1966 to the simultaneous creation of more states in the country. However, Ojukwu, acting alone, qualified this on the 25th October, 1966, by adding: 'provided the criteria for the creation are mutually agreed by everyone . . . Provided that is agreed, I go with it.' Meanwhile the East Regional delegation refused to attend the resumed Conference in Lagos on 24th October, 1966 and all efforts to persuade Ojukwu to send delegates proved unsuccessful. The memoranda exchanged between delegations at the Conference were significant in that the East Regional Government's memorandum included the following paragraph under the heading 'Units of Association and Power'; 'Constitutional arrangements for Nigeria as a whole should be made on the basis of the existing Regions, namely Northern, Eastern, Western and Mid-Western Nigeria. This must be so having regard to the present situation and the necessity to save the existence of Nigeria as one political entity before it is too late.'

As, in spite of all our difficulties, there had never been any doubt about the continued existence of Nigeria as one entity, this statement by Ojukwu was the first intimation of his intention to break up the country. Furthermore, by insisting that the units should remain as they stood, he gave a clear indication that his own will must prevail over that of the people, including the Eastern Assembly, who wished to split up the country into more states. With this attitude of Ojukwu, backed by his illegal Army, it became more than ever impossible for the five million non-Ibos in the East to achieve their known desire for a state of their own.

It was against this background of the Ibo leaders refusing the right of self-determination to the minority peoples of the East and their refusal to accept the Northern Region's declaration that it was prepared to be split up into smaller units that the Federal Military Government created new states by decree on 27th May, 1967.

This decree was received with acclaim by the vast majority of the fifty-five million Nigerians, with the exception of Ojukwu and his henchmen. The extreme patience of General Gowon and the never-ending hope that Ojukwu would return to the ways of peace was shown when, in appointing Military Governors of the States, General Gowon made Ojukwu Governor of the East-Central State, thus giving him an opportunity to promote the welfare of his own people as an integral part of the Federation. Legally, however, Ojukwu no longer had any authority over the areas which became the Rivers and South-Eastern States.

From the foregoing account, it is clear that the creation of States is not a punitive measure against Ibos. On the contrary, it is a condition of further political progress in Nigeria and a new basis for national reconstruction, as it allows for the development of a stable order based on equality of the States and a common expectation of justice among the tribes. The decision of Major-General Gowon to create twelve States on 27th May, 1967, was a courageous act of statesmanship. The alternative courses which were open to him were few and fraught with danger. A Federation of four Regions such as existed before 17th January, 1966, was ruled out for two very important reasons. Firstly, there was the problem of uneven distribution of political power resulting from the lopsided structure of the Federation. As the Federation then stood, one Region could rule the country as long as it wished, however unpalatable the policies which it pursued.

Secondly, even in each of the old Northern and Eastern Regions there were substantial minorities who, particularly in the East, were subjected to the political and economic domination of the majority tribal groups.

As to the idea of a Conference or loose association, or a 'pulling apart' which Ojukwu's clique suggested, there was no apparent or real reason why Nigeria, if it disintegrated, should have broken into only four parts. The indications were that the four Regions would in turn have broken up into their component ethnic groupings. The issue therefore was how to redraw the political map of Nigeria in such a way as to establish a balanced Federation in which no ethnic group would be dispossessed or dominated. In his decision to create twelve States out of the former four Regions, Major-General Gowon responded to a long-standing and increasing vociferous demand by most Nigerians.

Dr. Eni Njoku has produced some strange claims about the economy of the Eastern States. What are the true facts? In the former Eastern Region of Nigeria, the Ibos numbered about seven million and the Efiks, Ibibios, Ekois and Ijaws about five million. Half of the land area of the Region belonged to these five million so-called minorities. The minority areas produced about £16 million out of £25 million of annual agricultural exports from the East before the outbreak of hostilities. The bulk of crude petrol exported from Nigeria comes from the Rivers State and the Mid-West and not the East-Central (Ibo) State. Moreover, the fact must be stressed that all the pipelines run through the Rivers area, which is unfortunately the most neglected and the most embittered portion of the former Eastern Region. Also, the only 'empty' lands left in the East for settlement are in Ogoja and Calabar minority areas.

It can be seen, therefore, that one of the motives of some Ibo leaders in declaring secession was to ensure that the Ibos appropriated these enormous benefits from the so-called minority areas. This situation could not endure, and any attempt by the Ibo leaders to perpetuate it would have failed, but after much bloodshed. Once group frustrations are removed, there is no reason why the Ibos cannot continue to live in peace in the so-called minority areas and other parts of Nigeria, contributing their quota to the economy of the state of their residence.

With regard to the latest phase of the crisis, the reassurance must be given that the position of the Ibos is best guaranteed on a long-term basis in a Nigeria with twelve equal States. If seven million Ibos are entitled to self-determination, equally so are five million Efiks, Ibibios, Ekois and Ijaws. In the present circumstances, even if the Federal Military Government did nothing, those around Ojukwu could never have enough power to contain the so-called minority of five million perpetually. Instability due to rebellion from the non-Ibo minorities would be inevitable. If the situation is not resolved now, the resulting bloodshed and chaos would be infinitely more disastrous to everyone concerned.

With regard to the consequences which Ibos fear of the economic effect of 'losing' the minority areas, in particular regarding the distribution of industries, stress must be laid on the peculiarities of the next stage of industrial development in Nigeria. The simple import substitution industries have already been established. Next are large basic and intermediate industries like iron and steel, petro-chemicals, fertilizers, large plantation-based industries which require massive inflow of foreign capital. Such capital can only be attracted towards well-conceived viable projects. Therefore, in the next phase of development in Nigeria there should be less room for 'distortions' of location of industries mainly for regional or political reasons.

Moreover, under the auspices of the O.A.U. and the E.C.A., the efforts of all African States are now directed towards integration of sub-regional and regional units to create the basis for effective industrialisation and genuine progress of Africa. A united Nigeria will be in a better position to co-operate with the rest of West Africa to achieve these noble and imperative objectives.

The secessionist leaders claim that they are fighting for 'Ibo survival.' This is simply not true. Before they embarked on armed rebellion, they ought to have realised that there was no peaceful way of wrenching the East out of Nigeria and destroying the substantial economic and social integration that had gone on for more than 50 years. For example, the railways, communication links, and numerous other assets could not be divided amongst successor sovereign states easily. Boundary disputes would be widespread. Most probably, war would result for which Ojukwu had 'confidently' prepared.

Captured documents now confirm that the intention of the former Eastern authorities was to conquer the former Mid-Western and Western Regions and then in a later phase subdue the former Northern Region. This was not surprising. Ibos need to work and trade over the whole of Nigeria which they have always known in this century as their country. The rebels did subvert the Mid-Western State and occupy it for six weeks in August and September 1967. Then their slogan was 'Southern Nigeria Solidarity' not 'Ibo Survival' until the march to the West and Lagos was halted at the decisive battle of Ore in the Western State.

The so-called 'Biafra' of the rebels is not a homogeneous tribal state. As I have said, five out of its twelve million inhabitants are not Ibos. They are Ibibios, Efiks, Ekois and Ijaws. Rebel leaders argue that they all support 'Biafra.' Then why the mass intimidation and brutality conducted by the Ojukwu regime against them, all to no avail?

At the recent Kampala Peace Talks, Dr. B. J. Imkeme from Calabar, a retired Senior Medical Officer in the employment of the former Eastern Nigeria Government, who is well known to the other side, gave a résumé of rebel atrocities in the South-Eastern State in the following words:

It was clear to all right thinking people that these people (the minorities) wanted to remain within the Federation of Nigeria but with States of their own in which they enjoyed the right of self-determination. This did not suit the Ibos of the newly declared 'Republic of Biafra' and so they were determined either to force the 5 million non-Ibos into their Republic or to exterminate them systematically. To this end, Ibo soldiers were quickly sent to all non-Ibo areas with instructions to keep down the people, detain or even kill all who dared raise a voice in protest against the idea of 'Biafra.'

The Provincial Secretary for Calabar, an Ibo man, called a mass meeting in June, 1967 and addressed the Calabar people thus, and I quote: 'You Calabar people say you want a State of your own. Let me tell you that by the time the Federal Troops come here to enforce this mad idea there will be no one left but grass and weeds, for we shall have flattened your land and killed all you Efiks.'

From then on the non-Ibos of the Eastern Region were subjected to torture, detention, all forms of human indignities and even killing.

In Asang, a town in Enion Division where I come from, and which is just a mile from Okpo, my own village, all the inhabitants numbering about 400 were carried away to an unknown destination. Two women, one a relation of mine, who had been bed-ridden for two years were slaughtered in cold blood because the soldiers said it would be a burden to carry them along and they were under instructions not to leave alive any person in the town. On the way out a woman gave birth to a babe, Adee, and was groaning in her travail. The soldiers bundled her out of the canoe which was taking them away, shot both mother and the innocent child only a few minutes old.

In Attan Onoyon, another town in Enoing Division, the whole town was burnt down together with all the people the Ibo soldiers could lay hands on. An uncle of mine was killed together with his wife and four of five children. The only surviving child is a girl of 10 years—her right arm severed—who now lives to tell the tale of how they were all lined up by the river bank and shot. Luckily for her she did not die and is being cared for by me now.

In Ikot Ekpenyong, three miles from my home town, the Ibo soldiers rang the church bell one Sunday afternoon and forced everybody in the village at gun point to assemble in the church building for a special prayer for the survival of so-called 'Biafra.' When all were assembled the Ibo soldiers surrounded the church, set it on fire, burning down the villagers and shooting those who tried to escape. It is estimated that more than 300 men, women and children were massacred, in and around that church that day.

At Ikot Okpot, two wells were filled with the bodies of men, women and children all thrown in there by Ibo soldiers to die.

In Idro—a village four miles from my village—the men folk were forced to dig three large pits each seven feet deep. All the men and women were tied hand and foot and thrown into them. Children were dumped in with their parents. Five men were left to cover each pit with earth. When this task was done, the men were themselves all shot dead and their bodies placed on the mounds. I saw these bodies and the mounds myself when I arrived there three days after the gruesome and inhuman incident.

On the day Federal Troops landed in Calabar (that was 18th October, 1967) there were 169 civilians in detention by so-called 'Biafran' soldiers in the Calabar Army Barracks. They were all lined up and shot dead by Ibo soldiers. Those dead include Mr. Effiong Spatts, ex-Member for Calabar in the Nigerian Parliament and Mr. Ekpenyong, a Senior Lecturer in Nsukka University well known to Professor Njoku.

Even as I speak, these acts of genocide are still being carried on by the Ibos in minority areas still under their occupation. When they were being chased out of Port Harcourt the so-called 'Biafran' soldiers killed off almost all the Rivers people they could lay hand on, in accordance with instruction from their high command. The killings continue now in the Riverine areas not yet under Federal control.

Recently, 200 Ibibio men and women who had been under detention in Umuahia were taken out to face a mob who brutally murdered them in cold blood outside the Progress Hotel. There are many other gruesome incidents of children and pregnant mothers killed in market places by Ibo soldiers. of houses and property of non-Ibos wantonly destroyed.

Similar stories of atrocities in the minority areas have been told by other prominent Nigerians from the South-Eastern and Rivers States including Chief Holmes and Dr. Graham Douglas former Attorney-General of the former Eastern Region Military Government under Governor Ojukwu. Contrary to Dr. Njoku's claims, the minority peoples have always welcomed Federal troops with enthusiasm. The bulk of personnel in the Nigerian Navy including the Commander, Rear-Admiral J. E. A. Wey, come from these minority areas of the former Eastern Region. The Chief of Staff, Supreme Headquarters of the Armed Forces of Nigeria, Brigadier E. Ekpo, is an Efik from the South-Eastern State. Many Federal Troops now fighting in the East are from the former Eastern Region. There are even some Ibo personnel fighting in the Federal Armed Forces and many more are in active service in the Police, Prisons, Service etc. The war to crush the rebellion is not a tribal war against Ibos. Even secessionist leaders concede that the concept of an Ibo 'apartheid' state or 'Ibostan' is untenable. If the Federal Government were to concede an independent state embracing only Ibo land, that state would not be viable and the secessionist leaders would not accept it.

Consequently, they talk of 'Biafra' embracing all of the former Eastern Region because of the agricultural wealth and 'empty' lands of the South-Eastern State and the oil of the Rivers State, and because of access to the sea. It is 'however, to be noted that eight of the twelve states of Nigeria, with 80 per cent of its population, have no seaports. The East-Central State is therefore not unique in having no seaport within its boundaries.

Secessionist leaders also advance the argument that the so-called 'Biafra' can be sovereign but have a customs union, common currency, common services including railways, posts and telecommunications, ports, dual citizenship and extensive economic relations with Nigeria. This is a specious suggestion because:

a. Sovereign countries resulting from the disintegration of a large unit and separating in war have little hope of successfully jointly administering or sustaining a customs union.

b. Extensive economic relations involve human contact and unhindered travel throughout the territory of Nigeria, and this is precisely what the secessionist leaders say is impossible.

c. Any 'Central Organisation' endowed with adequate powers to legislate over and administer common customs tarrifs, currencies, establishment and control of industries, railways, airlines, ports, posts and telecommunications, etc., begins to have the character of an effective Central Government. These are the business of a Federal Government, which the secessionist leaders do not want.

The concept of 'Biafra' as a military proposition is dead. Secession cannot therefore be sustained militarily. After one year of fighting, more than two-thirds of the former Eastern-Region is now under the control of Federal Troops. In Iboland, these areas include the capital of the so-called 'Biafra,' Enugu, the largest Ibo town, Onitsha, Abakaliki, Awka, Nsukka, Nkalagu, Awgu, etc. In the so-called minority areas, the whole of the new South-Eastern State comprising the old Ogoja and Calabar Provinces of the former Eastern Region has been cleared of rebel troops and the Military Governor of the State, Col. Esuene, an indigene of the State, has taken up residence in Calabar, the State Headquarters and set up an administration. In the Rivers State, Port Harcourt, Bonny, Ahoada, Degema, Abonnema, Okrika, etc. have all been liberated. The State administration is settling down in Port Harcourt. However, it was not the purpose of the Federal Government to plan a total military victory or inflict humiliation on the Ibos as a group. Our main purpose is genuine national reconciliation within the context of One Nigeria. This is why the Federal Military Government prefers a negotiated settlement, if it can be obtained within this context.

As an earnest of this desire, the Federal Government has consistently responded to or taken peace initiatives towards a just and lasting solution to the Nigerian conflict. The Government responded fully to the peace moves by the historic Consultative Mission of six Heads of State appointed last year by the Kinshasa Summit meeting. The work of the O.A.U. Mission was neither welcomed nor appreciated by the secessionist leaders. The Commonwealth Secretary-General, Mr. Arnold Smith, began his peace initiative as far as July, 1967 before the outbreak of hostilities. The Federal Government has always responded favourably and co-operated fully with Mr. Arnold Smith in his efforts last October. The Federal Government sent three high ranking representatives to London for preliminary peace talks organised by the Commonwealth Secretary-General, but after waiting in London for a whole week, they had to return to Lagos because representatives of the rebels failed to turn up.

Again, in November, 1967, there was another invitation from the Commonwealth Secretary-General indicating that the rebels were ready for talks. The Federal Government responded promptly by instructing its representatives to get ready to leave for London, But they were informed by Mr. Arnold Smith at the last minute that the representatives of the rebels were no longer available. The Federal Government responded within twenty-four hours to the invitation from the Commonwealth Secretary-General which resulted in the successful preliminary peace talks in London on a venue and agenda leading to the Kampala Peace Talks. The subsequent Peace Talks in Kampala ended abruptly because Ceasefire Proposals submitted by the Federal Government delegation led by Chief Anthony Enahoro and those submitted by the other delegation, led by Sir Louis Mbanefo, conflicted. Sir Louis had proposed immediate ceasefire and the immediate removal of the economic blockade against the rebel regime to be followed by the immediate withdrawal of federal troops behind the pre-war boundary line; in other words, Federal Troops were to withdraw from the minority areas of the South-Eastern State and the Rivers State and nearly half of the East-Central State, currently administered as part of the Nigerian Federation.

These proposals were incompatible with those submitted by Chief Enahoro to the effect that the rebels should abandon secession on ceasefire day and that an international observer force should be stationed along the Ceasefire Lines. A Mixed Force drawn from the international observers and elements of the Federal Army and Police in co-operation with elements of the rebel forces were to move into rebel areas to disarm the rebel forces. The introduction of a foreign military presence by the Federal Government was to allay the fears of the Ibos about their personal security.

The two sides in Kampala then retires to off-the-record private discussions to see how the two proposals could be reconciled. In the estimated view of the Federal Government delegation, some progress was being made, thanks to the good offices of the Commonwealth Secretary-General, Mr. Arnold Smith and the Uganda Foreign Minister, Mr. Sam Odaka acting as foreign observer, when suddenly Sir Louis Mbanefo and his delegations called a plenary session at which he categorically stated that his delegations could not continue with the talks unless the Federal Government accepted his ceasefire proposals and the 'de facto' recognition of the sovereignty of the so-called Republic of 'Biafra.' The leader of the Federal delegation to Kampala pointed out that that was a sudden change of mind by the other side, presumably on the new instructions broadcast the day before to the whole world by Mr. Ojukwu.[5] The fundamental conflict in the Nigerian crisis is whether a settlement and other discussions are to be based on the preservation of Nigeria as one sovereign country or whether such discussions were to be conducted between two sovereign countries, Nigeria and the so-called 'Biafra.'

The choice before Nigeria during the present crisis is one between unity and disintegration. Should the country be allowed to disintegrate into weak, small quarrelsome, sovereign states? Or should there be a new framework to ensure stability and unity? Ojukwu and the clique of Ibo leaders supporting him have preached secession. Major-General Gowon, supported by all the other leaders of the country (including the vast majority of ordinary Ibos who have been silenced by Ojukwu's tyranny), have opted for a united and strong Federation of Nigeria. The issue really has been narrowed down. It is simply: what is the case for the so-called 'Biafra' and of what value is one Nigeria?

The problem of Nigeria since independence has been the problem of some Ibo leaders and how to make them accept a basis of equality for every ethnic group in the Federation. The lie has been sold abroad by the clique of Ibo leaders behind Ojukwu that there is no place for the Ibos in the new set-up and that all other ethnic groups in Nigeria want to exterminate the

Ibos. Ojukwu and these leaders have also spread the lie that they are hated because they are hard-working, Christians and more Westernized than any other ethnic group in Nigeria. It has also been falsely stated by them that nobody has ever expressed regret for the events and disturbances of September, 1966. The fact, of course, is that the Ibos were late starters in some respects. Group action was new to them. At last there was an Ibo consciousness and an Ibo 'nation-hood.' Consequently on the eve of independence, some of their leaders felt that they must act as a group in order to progress. This was to be the 'golden age' which their people had never had.

Apart from what the Ibos did to provoke the killings in September, 1966, there has been no excusing the killings, either in official quarters or among the Nigerian public generally. The Head of the Federal Military Government, Major-General Gowon, the former Military Governor of the Northern Region, Brig. Hassan Usman Katsina, and all the leaders of delegations to the Ad Hoc Constitutional Conference expressed regret at these killings, both publicly and in private. I have already mentioned Major-General Gowon's own impromptu address to the Ad Hoc Constitutional Conference on October 3, 1966. Col. Hassan not only sent troops from Kaduna to Kano to suppress the riots, he went personally and faced a mutiny of a section of his own troops in Kano although he was warned by Ojukwu not to go.

In Nigerian history, riots and killings are not so rare as may have been generally believed abroad. There were the Mid-West riots of 1961. There were the Adelabu riots in Ibadan in Western Nigeria in 1958; the Enugu riots, the Kano riots in the North of 1953, the Ogoloma riots and the perennial Obosi and Okrika riots of the former Eastern Region, the post-election riots in Western Nigeria in 1965 and others. Many Nigerians died in these riots and the Ibos were not the only people who lost lives in the events of 1966. Many Hausas and people of other ethnic groups of the former Northern Region were killed by the Ibos in the East in 1966 and also during the suppression of the September, 1966 riots in the North.

To those outside Nigeria who do not really grasp the facts of the Nigerian crisis, the case for the so-called 'State of Biafra' is simple and is this: the Ibos who inhabit the so-called 'Biafra' are another race of Jews who want to form a state of their own because of oppression by fellow countrymen in Nigeria. This is complete falsification of the real issue involved in the Nigerian crisis.

First, the former Eastern Region of Nigeria is not inhabited by only Ibos. Of a total population of 12.4 million there are 5.5 million people who are not Ibos, and who have always resented the tribalism, nepotism and sheer injustice of Ibo leaders.

Secondly, there are thousands of Ibos outside the former Eastern Region, and many of these are still to be found in other parts of the Federation of Nigeria enjoying the full rights of citizenship.

The Ibos in the main now occupy the present East-Central State of Nigeria. In the past, because of shortage of arable land in their own part of the country, thousands of Ibos migrated to other parts of Nigeria. But this was not peculiar to the Ibos. Other ethnic groups like the Yorubas, the Edos, the Kalabaris and the Hausas have also left their own areas, though in smaller numbers than Ibos, and settled in other parts of the Federation. On the eve of independence some Ibo leaders, as I have said, unable to look back to any 'golden age' or era, looked forward to the 1960s as their own golden era. This was why the principal Ibo leaders in politics, in commerce or trade immediately after independence did everything to monopolize public offices and trade, as against other ethnic groups. This trend continued until the end of 1964.

A new alignment of political forces in 1965 halted the excesses of these Ibo leaders, but soon the military intervention in January, 1966, offered them another opportunity. They used the Ironsi Government to pursue their ambition to dominate other ethnic groups. The removal of the Ironsi Regime in July 1966 upset their plans and since then Ojukwu and his clique of advisers resorted to the destruction of the Federation of Nigeria by every means at their disposal. Now Ojukwu and his clique dream of an Ibo empire in so-called 'Biafra,' depending on the revenues from oil and other minerals and the lands in the minority areas of the former Eastern Region. That is the secret of the ambitions of the Ibo leaders around Ojukwu and that is why they prefer that Nigeria should disintegrate. But there is another school of Ibo leaders, growing up around Mr. Ukpabi Asika, the Administrator of the liberated areas of the East Central State. They share our dream of a modern, united nation-state in Nigeria. They are blessed with a wider mental, emotional and psychological horizon than the narrow tribal outlook of the chauvinists around Ojukwu. They have outgrown the village mentality of the other side. Together, we work for peace and reconciliation, and for something greater than the other side seem capable of appreciating today.

Ethnic strife is not peculiar to Nigeria. Examples abound in history and currently in other parts of the world. The mark of a people's genius and greatness is their ability to overcome divisive influences. As His Imperial Majesty said in his opening address, 'in the life of a family, as in that of a community, there occur conflicts which disturb their harmonious growth.' So it has been in Nigeria. Only a generation of small men with small minds would succumb to such conflicts. Major-General Gowon has given repeated assurances that there is no intention on the part of the rest of Nigeria to wipe out the Ibos. All the actions of his Government have pointed to the fact that no tribal group will be oppressed or dominated under the new dispensation. But at the same time, no ethnic group will be allowed to have a domineering position of privilege and advantage in the new Nigeria. Ibo leaders too must allow the people of the Rivers State and the South-Eastern State to enjoy freedom and equality, unmolested by Ojukwu and his rebels.

Apart from the money which had been given to the former Eastern Region Government under Emeka Ojukwu for the rehabilitation of displaced persons during the 1966 disturbances, the Federal Government continues to protect all Ibos outside the former Eastern Region. These Ibos continue to enjoy every amenity and remain undisturbed and unmolested. The only alternative to disintegration is a Federation of States, united in the cause of one Nigeria and affording equal opportunities to all. This is the desire of all Nigerians. The economic, political and social advantages of this United Nigeria are so overwhelming that they should need no recapitulation.

Nevertheless, recent publications especially in Western Europe and the United States of America have tended to ask: Why One Nigeria and why not

4, 5, or 6 Nigerias? There are many reasons why Nigerians desire one united, great Nigeria. Among them are:

i. There are Nigerians who only know one Nigeria. They have been born into one united country, they have had their education in one united country and they have always pursued their livelihood in one Nigeria. They are united by the bond of common experience. These Nigerians will be found in all walks of life—teachers, doctors, lawyers, academicians, trade unionists, artisans, engineers, farmers and school children. They know no fatherland other than one Nigeria. Many Nigerian heroes have worked and died for one Nigeria. Not to uphold this united country would be a betrayal of their memories.

ii. A strong and united Nigeria will be an invaluable asset to the cause of a united Africa.

iii. If Nigeria breaks up, it will definitely be the beginning of the collapse of many African states. The result would be chaos on the African Continent and a set-back for the Organisation of African Unity.

iv. The main powers have borne and continue to sustain the economies of several countries in Africa and Asia. A united and strong Nigeria with her resources fully developed will help to relieve them of this burden, especially in Africa.

v. The economic advantages of a united Nigeria with its agricultural and mineral wealth and other potentialities speak for themselves. These advantages, if properly exploited, would result in benefits to all the component parts of the Federation and reflect great credit-worthiness overseas.

vi. One Nigeria, a potentially powerful and rich black nation, will raise the dignity of the black man throughout the world and be more able to champion the cause of the black man against oppression and discrimination by countries like Portugal.

vii. A united Nigeria will be better able to develop democratic political institutions and uphold the rule of law.

viii. The stability and political unity of Nigeria will be an eloquent testimony that Africans can govern themselves and maintain their unity and territorial integrity.

ix. A united Federation of Nigeria will be a more effective force in world affairs, to the advantage of Africa and the black man.

x. Balkanization of Nigeria will be a liability to the African race and only give joy to the racists in South Africa and their fellow travellers in Africa and Europe.

xi. A strong and united Nigeria, co-operating with other African States, will constitute a bulwark of defence against re-colonization of African states and the spread of apartheid from the South to the rest of Africa.

xii. A strong and united Nigeria will serve as a much desired umbrella for her various ethnic groups to live together in peace and harmony under democratic institutions, the rule of law and freedom from domination and oppression.

xiii. The tensions in Nigeria which are pleaded in justification of so-called 'Biafra' exist to an even greater degree in Eastern Nigeria and can only be contained and eliminated in a greater Nigerian family.

xiv. A strong and united Federation of Nigeria is the only hope for present and future Nigerians, and such a Nigeria would be better placed to plan for prosperity, full employment and a welfare state for all.

xv. A strong and united Africa needs a united and stable Nigeria. The world would be a poorer place without one strong and united Nigeria.

Your Imperial Majesty, let me now turn to the proposals submitted by Dr. Njoku before our weekend adjournment.[6] I am not sure how seriously Dr. Njoku expected us to take them. As I said last Friday, I prefer to think of the proposals as Dr. Njoku's opening gambit in our negotiations. If they represented the final position of the other side, there would be very little scope for negotiation. Secession is the basic issue which divides the two sides to the Nigerian conflict and Dr. Njoku's position on this basic question is totally unrealistic.

Although there is nothing new or unexpected in the peace proposals, I have nevertheless examined them very carefully, as I undertook to do, especially against the background outlined by Mr. Ojukwu and Dr. Njoku. I find the proposals entirely out of place here. Since the other side agreed in Niamey to talks under the 'auspices of the O.A.U. Consultative Committee on Nigeria' they should treat with less levity the mandate of the Committee which enjoins it to assist in the search for a solution which will preserve the unity and territorial integrity of Nigeria. This mandate precludes the Consultative Committee from condoning secession or what Dr. Njoku referred to as the acceptance of the existence of the so-called 'Biafra' as a sovereign and independent nation. Not only that: the Niamey resolution of the O.A.U. Consultative Committee on Nigeria urged the two parties to the Nigerian conflict to resume peace talks with the objective of preserving Nigeria's territorial integrity and guaranteeing the security of all its inhabitants.

It is perhaps necessary to remind Dr. Njoku of the terms of the Consultative Committee's mandate. At the Kinshasha summit in September 1967, the assembled Heads of State and Government 'reiterated their condemnation of secession in any member state, and resolved to send a consultative mission of six heads of State to the Head of the Federal Government of Nigeria to assure him of the Assembly's desire for the territorial integrity, unity and peace of Nigeria.' At Niamey, the Consultative Committee took and published a resolution which read, in part: 'The Organisation of African Unity Consultative Committee on Nigeria meeting in Niamey on 18th July, 1968, having reviewed the present developments in the Nigerian civil war, mindful of its mandate from the Assembly of Heads of State and Government of the Organisation of African Unity held in Kinshasha, requests both parties, as a matter of urgency, to resume peace talks in order to achieve a final solution of the crisis prevailing in their country, with the objective of preserving Nigeria's territorial integrity and to guarantee the security of all its inhabitants.'

The vital weakness in Dr. Njoku's proposals is that they are in conflict with this mandate and this resolution.

With due respect, the O.A.U. Consultative Committee on Nigeria is therefore not competent to preside over the liquidation of the Nigerian Federation. If, for purposes of argument, the two parties to the Nigerian conflict agreed to discuss the breakup of our country, they could not do so under the auspices of the Consultative Committee operating under its present mandate. Unless Dr. Njoku and his colleagues have come to these talks under false pretences or under an illusion, therefore, they must reconsider their peace proposals which are based on the proposition that the existence of their so-called independent republic has to be accepted. As far as the Federal Government delegation is concerned, we have not come to Addis Ababa to grant independence to the Ibos in the East Central State and to hand over to them as colonial possessions the minority peoples in the South Eastern State and the Rivers State.

It is really expecting too much for Dr. Njoku to seriously propose that the Federal Government should now accept and recognise the sovereign status of the rebel regime at the very moment of its impending collapse. I want to make it abundantly clear that any proposals which do not accept the unity and territorial integrity of Nigeria as the starting point are totally unacceptable to the Federal Government.

The other basic assumption in Dr. Njoku's peace proposal is that the security of Ibos of the East Central State can only be guaranteed in an independent country physically separated from the rest of Nigeria. I find it very difficult to believe that Dr. Njoku is convinced in his mind that the tragic events of 1966 can recur in Nigeria. In a federation of twelve or more states, will young Ibo officers again stage a military coup in which a non-Ibo Prime Minister, all non-Ibo State Premiers are murdered while Ibo State Premiers and other politicians are left alive? Will Ibo officers again liquidate their senior military colleagues from other ethnic groups while sparing their own, in the same manner as they did in January 1966? If they do all this, and the same public behaviour by Ibos in the North as in 1966, and the same killings of Northerners in the East, then I am afraid we must expect retaliations and consequences similar to the occurrences of 1966. For my part, I do not believe that this is the sort of chain Ibo officers will again set in motion after being reintegrated into Nigeria.

If the people of the East Central State fear for the security of their lives and property because of the number of civilians who lost their lives in the tragic events of 1966, we must ask, can these events be repeated? The number of Ibos killed in the mob riots of September, 1966 appears to vary with the propaganda value of the occasion. The official estimates available to the Federal Government puts the total number of persons of all tribes killed at about five thousand. The majority of them were Ibos. In the first official publication from Enugu, the figure was stated as seven thousand. During the Aburi meeting of military leaders, Mr. Ojukwu inflated the number to ten thousand, a figure which was challenged at that meeting as being exaggerated. On the eve of secession, he increased the number to thirty thousand, and we have since been told of other figures rising to one hundred thousand. Let me say that the whole incident is tragic and regrettable, irrespective of the number killed.

Rebel leaders have stated in their official pronouncements that nearly two million refugees were repatriated from the then Northern Region to the East, following the tragic events of September, 1966. Even if we accept that figure, does Dr. Njoku not think the world must ask how two million defenceless civilian Ibos got back to the East alive if the Federal Army and Police and the Northern Region administration organised the killings of Ibos in the North? How can he now speak of the Federal Army as an army bent on genocide if, as he says, they killed thirty thousand people out of over two million Ibos said to be in the Northern Region? If these mob riots are put in their proper perspective, the Federal authorities and the law enforcement agencies deserve some appreciation for the speed with which they contained the violent mob reactions of 1966 arising from very difficult circumstances. It was the Northern Region Government which organised the airlift and transportation of the two million people who got back to the East alive. If the Government and the Army organised those killings, the number of those who lost their lives would have been much higher.

I want to emphasise that the Nigerian civil war is not a war of genocide. If it were a war of genocide against the Ibos as a people, over fifty thousand Ibos would not be living in Lagos today, going about their business as law abiding citizens without molestation. One of the most vicious statements by Dr. Njoku is that the Nigerian Army is an instrument of genocide against the Ibos. The full account of the course of events which I have given shows that it is the secessionist leaders who tried to convert the Nigerian Army into a political instrument for fulfilling their tribal ambition.

The restlessness in the Nigerian Army since January 15, 1966, arose from the attempt to introduce tribal and power politics into the Army. This attempt failed and members of the Nigerian Armed Forces are at present drawn from all the ethnic groups in Nigeria, including Ibos who believe in the Federal cause of keeping Nigeria one. It is a statement of fact that there are Ibos fighting side by side with their counterparts from the rest of Nigeria, to crush the rebellion in the East Central State, just as there are Ibo civilians who believe in the Federal cause and are assisting the Federal Government in its programme of re-unification. Mr. Asika, the Administrator for the liberated parts of the East Central State, is building up an administration manned wholly by Ibos from the area. Both Mr. Asika and the Ibo public officials working with him and thousands of Ibo civilians are being protected by the Federal Army in the parts of the East Central State under Federal control. How can this Army be referred to, as Dr. Njoku repeatedly does, as an instrument of genocide against all Ibos?

Dr. Njoku and other spokesmen of the rebel regime have been proclaiming that Ibos as well as people from minority groups in the former Eastern Region were killed in the tragic events of 1966. Because some Efiks, Ibibios and other minority peoples in the East lost their lives, the secessionist leaders argue they should join the Ibos in the so-called republic of 'Biafra'. But it is on record that some Yorubas and Mid-Westerners also lost their lives in the mob-riot. By Dr. Njoku's logic, all of Yorubaland and the Mid-West should also be in their still-born republic.

As a matter of fact, it is most revealing to recall that when the rebels occupied the Mid-West, the secessionist leaders changed their political objective from that of Ibo survival to that of Southern Nigeria solidarity. They argued in those days that the people of Southern Nigeria should form a new front. In those days, Dr. Njoku and his colleagues made no reference whatever to 'disputed areas' between the secessionist leaders in the East Central State and the rest of Nigeria.

Dr Njoku pretends to think, or at least he urges, that military position today is, as he says, 'irrelevant'. When they acquired a handful of obsolete aircraft and helicopters, and bombed defenceless citizens and areas (including

x

Lokoja on a Sunday, with Christians at worship), they described their B.26 planes as 'masters of the Nigerian skies'. When they sneaked into the Mid-West in the hours of darkness, they spoke of a 'Republic of Benin' and boasted that they had 'the best army in Black Africa'. When they marched to Ore, scenting Lagos in the distance, they spoke of 'Southern Nigeria solidarity'. They intended to impose their solution by force of arms on the rest of Nigeria. We were not told then that their military adventure was irrelevant. Now that superior planning, superior generalship and superior valour have all but vanquished them and liberated the minorities and even half of Iboland, they seek to neutralise by empty words the realities of today.

Much of the difficulty in which the rebels find themselves is due to the fact that they have become victim of their own propaganda, just like the Nazis in the last World War. For example, Dr. Njoku claims that Federal forces have been driven out of Uyo, Annang and Eket. I am reminded of Sir Louis Mbanefo's ludicrous claim at a press conference during the Kampala peace talks when he gleefully announced that the rebels were in control of Port Harcourt, yet they had been driven out of the city several days before. Sometimes I think that even rebel leaders do not grasp the enormity of the predicament into which they have led the Ibos. When will they realise that they are being deceived by their high command?

I hope that we at these talks can at least avoid personal insults to one another. There will doubtless be occasions when we have to speak in the strongest terms, but I hope we can avoid personal insults. In this connection, let me say that I regard the very idea of equation with Mr. Ojukwu as a personal insult. I have far greater regard for Dr. Njoku's attainments and personality than for Mr. Ojukwu's, and I can see absolutely nothing in Mr. Ojukwu to excite admiration. His political leadership of the Ibo people has brought only disaster to them, his generalship, in spite of the five rows of unearned decorations on his tunic, has been non-existent; his personality radiates immodesty, and his appearance and performance here lacked refinement and restraint. I assure you I would rather equate myself with Dr. Njoku than with such a man. As I said at Kampala, however the Nigerian crisis is resolved, the Ibos have a problem on their hands in Ojukwu.

We are definitely faced in Nigeria with another Katanga. Here, it was copper and Belgium. In Nigeria, it is oil and France. The objective is the same—to break up a potentially great African country, mortgage its mineral resources to neo-colonialists and create an appendage to a European power. Tshombe's symbol was the rising sun of Katanga. Ojukwu, lacking originality, adopted the rising sun of so-called 'Biafra'. Tshombe depended on European mercenaries, so has Ojukwu. Tshombe declared secession, so did Ojukwu. There is only one difference between Tshombe and Ojukwu. Tshombe was said to be always loyal to his colleagues. What did Ojukwu do for his colleagues of January 15, 1966? What did he do with Col. Banjo, Col. Ifeajuna, Philip Alale and so forth? They were eliminated on his orders. At Kampala, I said Ojukwu fancied himself as a Hitler. Again lacking originality, Ojukwu now retaliates by describing General Gowon as Hitler.

Dr. Njoku has made much of bombing of rebel areas. He claims his side did not bomb civilian targets. The 'military' targets they bombed included a Lokoja church. Their military objectives included such 'vital targets' as Casino Cinema and the Federal Palace Hotel in Lagos.

Dr. Njoku has referred to my presentation of the Federal case. In doing so, he has misrepresented me again. I have at no time spoken of Sir Louis Mbanefo or Dr. Njoku as moderate. In fact I have tried as much as possible to avoid comments on either of them across the table. All I said (and the text of my speech bears me out) was that Ojukwu's presentation here had been much less civilised than Sir Louis's and Dr. Njoku's at Kampala.

Dr. Njoku speaks of the extermination of Ibos. As I implied earlier, what is Mr. Asika? What about the fifty thousand Ibos in Lagos? What are our Ambassadors in Brussels and New Delhi, and many others who have remained in the service of their country but Ibos? Have they been exterminated? What about some half a million Ibos in the Midwest State, their two State Commissioners living in Benin, and various persons in the Public Service of that State? Have they been exterminated?

At the Kampala talks, I explained the reference in General Gowon's broadcast, on his assumption of office, to the question of unity. I am somewhat surprised that Dr. Njoku has not himself discovered the simple explanation that General Gowon was referring to a unitary system rather than to unity itself when he spoke in August 1966, of a state of affairs for which there was no basis. Clearly General Gowon could not say that there was no basis for unity and in the same breath promise that he would introduce measures designed to lay a sounder foundation for unity. In any case, even if General Gowon had said, on assuming office that he did not believe in unity, and then to the relief of most Nigerians, he became persuaded that unity was possible and desirable, is it not something in his favour?

My reference to captive Chiefs does not seem to have been well understood by Dr. Njoku. I chose my words with great care, and if Dr. Njoku would care to read them again, he will find that I spoke of Chiefs, not chieftaincies. Indeed, the chieftaincies of Bonny and Buguma are ancient institutions. The King of Warri and their Princes had visited Europe in the 15th century, but that is by the way. The point I was making is also unintentionally made by Dr. Njoku. All he has said is in eulogy of the chieftaincies and stools of Bonny and Buguma, not of the present occupants of the stools. And it is with the occupants that we are concerned. The chieftaincies are not captive. The Chiefs are. The thrones are not lightweight. The occupants have been made so. The chieftaincies represent the best in the history, the culture, the traditions and the ambitions of their people. The Chiefs oppose these. What is there to say in their defence? As for me, Dr. Njoku knows very well that I am not a natural ruler and I do not therefore owe my office or my position here to my chieftaincy.

I repeat again that when the secessionist leaders were holding high office in Lagos and sharing power with Northern leaders for some 14 years before they turned round to murder them on January 15, I opposed some of the things the North stood for then. But the old North is dead and in its place we have six states run by young men with ideals and vision of a united Nigeria. They stand for high ideals of a united country and that is why I am here. It may interest Dr. Njoku to know that out of 19 members of the Federal Executive Council today, only four are of Hausa-Fulani extraction and out of the 20 members of the Supreme Military Council, including twelve State Governors, only three are Hausas. One would like to ask Dr. Njoku: would his people have behaved with the same moderation and restraint?

If our discussions here are to be taken a bit more seriously, Dr. Njoku must forget all about the so-called disputed areas between the rest of Nigeria and the secessionist leaders in the East Central State. Dr. Njoku should make up his mind whether the so-called disputed areas are being contested on the principle of ethnic grouping or on some other basis. If he is asking that all the Ibos of Nigeria should form one state, he cannot on that wave-length speak about the fate of five million non-Ibos in the former Eastern Region. If, on the other hand, Dr. Njoku is asking that the former Eastern Region should remain intact under Ibo domination, he should be honest enough to say so.

Before leaving the question of disputed areas, let me refer briefly to Dr. Njoku's call for a plebiscite, and remind him of the history of plebiscites in Nigeria. The former Eastern Region of Nigeria was established in 1954 without a plebiscite. The other Regions were similarly established without plebiscite. As regards the Midwest, the Region was created by law and an interim administration was set up for a period of six months before a confirmatory plebiscite was held. During that interim period, the Midwest administration was run by Midwesterners and the plebiscite was organised by the Federal Government. If Dr. Njoku is calling for a similar plebiscite in the Rivers and South Eastern States, he should say so. If the minority peoples in the former Eastern Region want a confirmatory plebiscite, it is for them to call for such a plebiscite. The Ibo leaders in the East Central State have no moral or political right whatever to demand a plebiscite in the territories of the five million non-Ibos of the former Eastern Region.

It has been argued by the other side that the Federation of Nigeria should be allowed to disintegrate because the Federation of West Indies, the Federation of Malaysia and Singapore, the Federation of Rhodesia and Nyasaland and the Federation of South Arabia, have all broken up. The Nigerian Federatin is different from the examples given. Before the Federal Constitution was introduced in 1954, Nigeria as a colony, was governed from Whitehall in London as a single administrative unit for about fifty years. On the other hand, each of the other Federations listed was made up of separate colonies which were governed as such for many years until the Federation was imposed on them by the metropolitan power for a brief period. For example, Jamaica, Trinidad, Barbados and the other West Indian islands were for centuries administered by Britain as separate colonies until they tried to federate. Nyasaland, Northern and Southern Rhodesia were similarly ruled as separate colonies for about 60 years until Britain imposed the ill-fated Federation on them. In the case of Malaysia and Singapore, both tried to form the Federation of Malaysia after each had attained independence.

It has been suggested by the secessionist leaders that another justification for their rebellion is that at one time or another both the Northern and Western Regions threatened to secede from Nigeria. In the case of the Northern Region, it was over its demand, based on population distribution, for 50 per cent representation in the Central Legislature. Western Nigeria was said to have also threatened to secede 'as a result of its failure to absorb

Lagos' in 1954 but was prevented from doing so because of a 'stern and timely warning from the British Colonial Secretary'. If secession by any section of Nigeria was not permitted fourteen or fifteen years ago, how does that justify secession today?

I will now return to the peace proposals by Dr. Njoku. I have already rejected the corner-stone of these proposals, namely the acceptance of the independence of the so-called 'Biafra' which can meaningfully refer only to part of Ibo areas of the former Eastern Region. Once Dr. Njoku's proposal for the reognition of so-called 'Biafra' is untenable, his other proposals based on this cannot stand. We cannot discuss the sharing of assets and liabilities. We do not accept the premise of two countries. The question of common services between such two countries does not arise.

As for the totally unrealistic proposal for withdrawal of troops to pre-war boundary lines, this cannot stand serious examination except in the context of two countries. How can the Federal Government be expected to hand over five million non-Ibos of the Rivers and South-Eastern States back to the reign of terror which they have just experienced at the hands of the rebel forces?

Dr. Njoku's proposal for an international peace force to separate the armies of two sovereign countries does not arise in the context of one Nigeria. When Dr. Njoku is interested in the security and safety of Ibos within Nigeria, he will see that our proposal for an external observer force to give a sense of security to the Ibos is the only way to meet their genuine fears in our present circumstances.

Dr. Njoku's only proposal deserving of consideration is the appeal for immediate agreement to be reached on the transportation of relief supplies to civilian victims of the war. I suggest that the details of this agreement can be negotiated under Item 3 of our agenda. The Federal delegation is prepared to renew the offers we made at Niamey. As far as we are concerned, the land corridor is already established and is available for transporting food to civilian victims of the war in rebel-held areas as soon as the secessionist leaders allow the International Red Cross to operate through the corridor. The problem of other corridors can be discussed when we come to Item 3 of the agenda.

If I may summarise, I would say that once we do not accept Dr. Njoku's basic proposal for a separate and independent existence for the Ibos, he has to re-submit a new peace plan. Here I would suggest that as soon as Dr. Njoku is prepared to face the problems arising from re-integration of the rebel-held parts of the East Central State into Nigeria, he should have a second look at the peace proposals by the Federal delegation.

If I were in Dr. Njoku's shoes, I would not treat in an off-hand manner the Federal Government's offer of an amnesty. I am sure there are many people on the other side who would welcome our proposal at the appropriate time when we are all ready to discuss the problems in realistic terms. In the same way, there are those in rebel-held areas who will be interested in our offer of employment for displaced public officials and for the rehabilitation of self-employed persons. Dr. Njoku probably does not need a job because of academic connections, but I doubt very much if he was speaking for the majority of the displaced public officials and self-employed persons in rebel-held areas who stand to benefit from our offer of employment opportunities and freedom of movement.

Your Imperial Majesty, we have seen examples in our time of countries which have broken up in circumstances rather like ours. There, hopes of an early rapprochement—like Dr. Njoku's five years—have not been realised. On the contrary bitterness has continued, the successor countries have armed with the assistance of the big powers and the resultant wars have escalated beyond the communal strife which was pleaded in justification of separation. In the long run, more damage has been done than would have been the case if the countries had not broken up. This is not what we want for Nigeria.

It is not what we want for Africa.

Our peace proposals are based on a one-country solution. It accords with the aspirations of our people and with the mandate and the Niamey resolution of the O.A.U. Consultative Committee on Nigeria. As soon as Dr. Njoku is prepared to give up his republic for a 'one Nigeria' solution he will find that the Federal peace plan is the only way to preserve Nigeria's territorial integrity and guarantee the security of all its inhabitants including the Ibos.

I regret that I have had to take up so much of Your Imperial Majesty's time.

[1] *Delivered in Addis Ababa on 12 August 1968. The text here is an amalgam of the various excerpts made available by the Federal Ministry of Information. The first half of Enahoro's statement is now avalaible in* Africa 1968–69, *edited by Colin Legum and John Drysdale, pp. 672–9. This extract does not make it clear that it is only half the speech. In the same way, the verbatim text issued by Nigeria House on 15 August 1968 glosses over the fact that it also is only half the full speech. In view of the fact that the Enahoro statement of 12 August and the Ojukwu speech of 5 August provide the final and most passionately held presentations of the respective Federal and Biafran cases and so constitute comparative documentation fundamental to the whole issue of war and peace, no apology is needed for their inclusion in toto.*

[2] *See* DOC *169.*
[3] *See* DOC *170.*
[4] *See* DOC *61.*
[5] *See* DOC *158.*
[6] *See* DOC *170.*

172.
Lagos Defines its Stand on Relief Supplies[1]

The Federal Military Government categorically rejects the suggestion that any individual or organisation or country can be more concerned about the events in Nigeria and the sufferings of civilians than itself. It has demonstrated its concern by agreeing to the establishment of two temporary road corridors for relief supplies, that is, one, from Enugu southward to Awgu and thence to any agreed point in rebel-held territory, and the other from Onitsha southward to any point in the rebel-held territory.

The International Red Cross and other relief organisations have confirmed that significant quantities can only be conveyed by road. The Federal Military Government has also established the National Rehabilitation Commission with an initial disbursement of £1m. out of a budget of £5m. to enable it carry out relief and rehabilitation in all the war-affected areas. It has further allowed the ICRC to carry out its relief work in all areas under Federal control without placing any restrictions in their way.

Stocks of food and relief materials have been built up in Enugu and a large fleet of lorries has already been assembled there. As soon as the rebel authorities agree large quantities of supplies will begin to flow through Awgu southward to any agreed point in rebel-held areas. People genuinely concerned with the sufferings of civilians in the rebel-held areas should appeal to the rebel leaders themselves to show some humanity by accepting the Federal Government offer.

The rebel insistence on neutralised airstrips and air corridors is, therefore, mainly to relieve military pressure on them and to strengthen their false propaganda. It is clear that in order to support the false propaganda on genocide and their campaign for separate existence they wish to avoid any evidence that the Federal Government is helping to expedite relief supplies to civilians in rebel-held areas.

The Federal Government cannot accept the proposal to fly relief supplies to a so-called neutralised air strip in the rebel-held areas. The suggestion that any portion of Nigeria should be internationalised and handed over to a foreign agency is unacceptable. The Federal Government, as already indicated, will only permit flights of supplies to Enugu from where they will be carried southward by road.

The Federal Military Government again emphasizes that the distribution of relief supplies donated by foreign organisations is carried out by ICRC personnel. Therefore any repetition of the rebel propaganda that the Federal Government will poison such supplies or take military advantage of the land corridors will only serve to demonstrate the rebels' lack of concern for the sufferings of the civilians.

It is hoped therefore that the rebel leadership will stop playing politics with the lives of our people, and accept the mercy corridors offered by the Federal Military Government. It is also hoped that the ICRC will make the full facts known to the world in view of the aid interest which has been aroused in this matter.

[1] *Statement issued in Lagos and London simultaneously on 16 August 1968.*

173.
Federal Government's Warning to the International Red Cross[1]

The Federal Military Government has received a peremptory message from Dr. A. R. Lindt, Chief Co-ordinator of the International Red Cross Committee in West Africa, informing it that he intended to lead personally, five I.C.R.C. planes carrying supplies from Fernando Po to Obilagu airstrip in a rebel-held area with effect from Tuesday, 3rd September, 1968, between 0900 and 1700 hours. Four of the five aircraft were provided by Nordic countries of Denmark, Sweden, Norway and Finland and the fifth by Switzerland.

The Federal Government and the Red Cross themselves have consistently and repeatedly stated that the best way of bringing in massive supplies into the rebel-held area is by a land corridor. However, in view of its concern for the suffering civilians whose fate is being callously exploited by the rebel leaders, and the untiring efforts of the Emperor Haile Selassie at the Addis Ababa peace talks, the Federal Government has agreed to allow the use of the airstrip in the Ihiala-Uli area which is known to be the best airstrip held by the rebels at the moment for direct emergency air-lift of relief supplies for a period of one week. It is in fact, this very airstrip which it is claimed the I.C.R.C. uses by night to fly in supplies from Fernando Po. The Federal Government has repeatedly stated that Obilagu airstrip is not acceptable as it is now in the direct line of immediate advance of Federal troops. Its use for relief operations will be precarious and short-lived. It is therefore difficult to understand the insistence of the I.C.R.C. on Obilagu.

The Federal Military Government had invited Dr. Lindt four days ago to discuss the matter and the invitation is still open in order to find an agreeable solution to the air corridor problem. The Federal Government states categorically that it absolves itself from any responsibility arising out of the consequences of any unauthorised and illegal flights intended to land at Obilagu airstrip. The Federal Government appeals to all countries which have any influence on the I.C.R.C. to urge them not to carry through the action, unprecedented in the history of the Red Cross, of over-flying Nigerian territory and the positions of Federal troops without the agreement of the Government. Such internationally illegal action could lead to grave incidents for which the Nigerian Government cannot be held responsible. The I.C.R.C. can advance the humanitarian ends we all desire by appealing to the rebel leaders to change their present attitude of being more insulting and intransigent while the Federal Government delegation at Addis Ababa make more conciliatory proposals and offer numerous concessions. The Red Cross should urge them to accept the compromise package deal proposed at the Addis Ababa talks.

[1] *Statement issued in Lagos on 2 September 1968.*

174.
Gowon Announces the 'Final Push'[1]

B.B.C.: It's reported that your final military push has already started, is that true?

Gowon: That's correct.

B.B.C.: When did it start?

Gowon: Today [24 August 1968].

B.B.C.: And where's it taking place?

Gowon: All fronts from the north southwards, southwards northward, north western pushing south eastern.

B.B.C.: Can you say how many troops are involved in this push?

Gowon: No, this is a military secret which I would not like to divulge.

B.B.C.: And how long as a soldier, would you expect it to take to take over what's left of the eastern region?

Gowon: Well it's usually very difficult for any soldier to say in this sort of operation, to say how long that it would take before the remaining area is taken. But if one would like to hazard a guess, within the next four weeks.

B.B.C.: What sort of equipment are you using? Helicopters—armoured vehicles?

Gowon: Certainly, but we are just using the minimum conventional in arms and equipment which the Nigerian army is equipped with or has been equipped with since the beginning of the war.

B.B.C: Aren't you being affected though, by these very heavy rains, the heaviest on record I think?

Gowon: Yes, that's correct, pretty heavy rain, rainfall we're having this year. But it doesn't seem to disturb the boys at all they seem to like it very much indeed. It seems as though it cools them off you know, after a hard day's job.

B.B.C.: What's your latest report on the situation?

Gowon: Excellent progress, according to the plan. . . .

[1] *Interview, 24 August 1968, shown in B.B.C. programme 'Twenty-Four Hours', 26 August 1968. Transcript by courtesy of B.B.C. London.*

175.
Gowon Broadcasts to the Nation on 'The Last Lap'[1]

Fellow citizens. The theme of my address to you today is on the ending of the war—the last lap.

The Supreme Military Council held an important meeting last week. Members of the Council reviewed the progress in putting down the rebellion of some of our fellow countrymen and in laying the foundations of a better future for the nation.

The nation was plunged into Civil War by Ojukwu thirteen months ago. This bitter and tragic development followed one year of appeasement. One year in which the Federal Military Government and many national leaders made every effort to conciliate Ojukwu. We offered numerous concessions which tended to destroy the authority and personality of the Federal Government. This was a deliberate policy pursued in the hope of reducing tension, and dissuading Ojukwu from pushing the former eastern region into secession, war and the terrible tragedies which would necessarily follow.

We failed. Ojukwu's ambition for personal power was insatiable. Feeding on that ambition and at the same time encouraging it were the evil influences of foreign meddlers and the conspiracy of certain foreign powers against Nigeria.

We have been fighting for thirteen months. Our troops have won resounding victories: they have completely liberated the South-Eastern State and the Rivers State and the major portion of the area of the East-Central state itself. Today, as is well known, the rebels are confined to less than five thousand square miles, which is a very tiny portion of the territory of Nigeria. But we have conducted this war in a very deliberate fashion, giving adequate opportunity at every juncture for the rebel leaders to stop and reconsider the tragedy to which they have plunged the nation as a whole and, in particular, the Ibos whom they claim to serve. At this time when the supporters of the rebels are busy spreading calumnies abroad about the policies of the Federal Military Government, when the enemies of Nigeria falsely accuse us of wishing to exterminate Ibos and are exploiting the sufferings and starvation of innocent civilians in parts of the Eastern states for vicious propaganda, it is perhaps necessary to recall the great goals for which the Federal Military Government is fighting. We are fighting this war in order to avoid disintegration of the country into several mini-states which will become protectorates of foreign powers. Everyone knows what the consequences of such disintegration will be. The tiny states will all recklessly acquire arms from their protectors. There will be continuous war, insecurity of life and property and much greater sufferings than we have yet experienced. The degradation of Nigerians and Blackmen everywhere would follow.

Then the ignominy of re-colonialisation. Such a backward development would have meant good-bye to economic progress and the hopes of a higher standard of living for all Nigerians. Even if foreigners refuse to understand us, we of this generation have no right to make such a choice for Nigerian posterity. Victory will enable us to consolidate the new twelve-state structure, remove the fear of domination by one tribe or region which destroyed the first republic, and equal status and opportunity for all ethnic groups will be guaranteed thus laying a sounder foundation for political stability and more rapid and even development. I am therefore happy that we have successfully established an effective administrative machinery in each of the twelve states. This achievement is, in fact, the most radical reform in our social and political development over the past 50 years. The Governor of the Rivers State has taken up his duties in Port Harcourt. All the twelve states are now being administered from their respective capitals. As you all know, the Federal Military Government has explored from the beginning every possible avenue for a peaceful settlement of the crisis. This we have done consciously because we must look ahead to the peace which we must win and ensure national reconciliation. It is the policy of the Federal Government that every Nigerian community should participate fully in the Development of the Nation. There will be no second class citizens in this country. This is why I sent fully mandated delegations to London, to Kampala, to Niamey and now to Addis Ababa to seek peace and agree to an arrangement for a permanent settlement. The basic conditions of the Federal Military Government for a peaceful settlement remain unchanged. They are: that the rebels must agree to become reintegrated into one United Nigeria, and that they must accept the twelve-state structure subject, of course, to any agreed marginal adjustments to the boundaries of the states. These two conditions of the Federal Government for a peaceful settlement are essential if we are not to repeat the tragic process towards Civil War.

Boundary rectifications will enable small towns and villages to be regrouped at their request in more appropriate states for the removal of all doubt and mischievous speculation. Let me stress here that Port Harcourt will remain the capital of the Rivers State. Its port facilities as those in Lagos and other ports in the country will, of course, remain the responsibility of the Federal Government and available to all users in one United Nigeria. The issue of so-called land-locked states does not arise. The existing rights of personal and company property in Port Harcourt as in other parts of the country remain inviolate and will be guaranteed by the Federal Government.

Regrettably the rebels have at all stages since found one reason or another for refusing to engage in serious talks that can lead to a peaceful settlement although they claimed that they tried to secede from Nigeria because the security of the Ibos could not be guaranteed.

The rebels have refused to discuss what guarantee they consider necessary for the security of the Ibo; instead they have insisted at peace talks on (1) Immediate cease fire (2) Withdrawal of Federal troops to what they call pre-war boundaries and (3) The recognition of their so-called sovereignty. They claim—against all evidence to the contrary—that Federal troops wish to annihilate all Ibos. They also disseminate lurid accounts of the sufferings and starvation of the Ibo people and so forth.

It is a great disservice that some respectable people in Europe and else-where seem to see wisdom in these obstinate and unrealistic demands and to encourage the rebels. What is the use of a temporary cease fire in the circumstances, of a small section of the country containing one ethnic group of seven million wishing to break away after a bitter war, not even alone, but insisting on dragging with them against their will other tribes numbering five million and at the same time laying claim to more territory in the Mid-west State and elsewhere? Are these not the seeds of future bloody wars if the claims are conceded? One can only conclude that those who support them do not do so for the sake of peace or for the love of the Ibo man.

Most regrettably even on the limited question of relief supplies the rebels have refused to accept the one effective way of taking adequate quantities of food and medicine to the suffering civilians once they accept the 'mercy' land corridor proposed by the Federal Government. The fleet of relief lorries already assembled can carry the essential supplies quickly to the few towns and villages still remaining under rebel control in the East-Central State. To make matters worse they have also rejected the offer of Nigerian foodstuffs to be contributed by the Federal Government to international agencies to distribute in their area.

The sufferings of the innocent civilians in these places are apparently only to be exploited by Ojukwu for propaganda and international manoeuvres for recognition. While recognising the good work done by the Red Cross and some other relief organisations, we must therefore express our disappointment at the political activities of some agents of these foreign relief organisations. They avoid urging the rebels to accept the land corridors which they admit is the best answer to the problem. Instead there is diversionary insistence on air corridors alone and many statements have been issued to embarrass the Federal Government. It must be emphasised again that the food most needed by the suffering civilians are things like yams, *garri*, beans and dried fish: these foodstuffs which they are used to are available locally and must be carried by road: hence we continue to appeal to the rebels to accept land corridors. However, the Federal Government will approve a neutralised air-strip in the Uli/Ihiala area under strict conditions of control which will ensure that it is needed only for handling relief supplies. We reject any other airstrip offered merely as a trick to hamper the advance of Federal troops. We remain confident that good sense will prevail and a way found very soon for taking relief to those who need it most, using every available means of transport. Moreover, the troops in the field are under orders to pay maximum attention to the movement of relief supplies to the areas they liberate. Despite the urgency of the situation and the increasing interference of certain countries the Federal Military Government has been very patient: but the time has now come when in the interest of humanity and in the interest of the Nigerian citizens, suffering under Ojukwu's terror, we can no longer allow Ojukwu to use their fate so callously to achieve a political and diplomatic personality. Much has been said about the question of a military solution. I owe it to the nation to remind the world that in August 1966 I agreed to withdraw Nigerian Army units from Enugu. If I was bent on reducing Ojukwu and the opposition of his clique to Federal authority by military means I could have done it then in a very brief campaign. Again, in February 1967, when it was clear that Ojukwu had abused the purpose and the decisions of the meetings of the Supreme Military Council at Aburi, in Ghana, I could have ordered military operations to bring back Ojukwu under Federal authority. I did not. Again, in April 1967, when Ojukwu outrageously seized all Federal revenues and Federal property in the former Eastern region, I could have ordered military action: I did not. Even when Ojukwu declared secession at the end of May 1967, I did not order military action because I had hoped that sooner or later reason would prevail and Ojukwu would agree to bring back the former Eastern Region into the fold of a United Nigerian Nation. The fact is that it was Ojukwu himself who launched the attack on Federal Government troops in July 1967 and began the war. It was he who declared total war and introduced aerial bombing by attacking Lagos, Idah, Lokoja, Kano and Kaduna with his B.26 bombers. So much is history. It is therefore wrong for anyone to accuse the Federal Government of desiring and planning for a military solution of the Nigerian problem.

It should be clear to the world by now that after the liberation of Nsukka, after the liberation of Enugu, after the liberation of Port Harcourt, enough time was given to the rebel leaders for reflection. The respite was always used by the rebels to acquire more arms and to regroup their troops. Enough opportunity was given at the meetings in London, in Kampala and in Niamey for an honourable settlement of our crisis. Meanwhile, the result of our patience has been further sufferings for thousands of our innocent people and more foreign interference in our domestic affairs threatening to bring even greater catastrophe. Nigeria is now threatened with aerial invasion by transport planes escorted by fighter planes instructed to do battle with the Nigerian Air Force for the so-called humanitarian reason of delivering supplies to the rebels. This is an outrage; of course it will not be the first time in the history of Africa when European nations have violated the rights of African countries with impunity. But Nigeria is ready. We will defend our sovereignty. We will continue to do what is right to restore order to the country and save all Nigerians including Ibos from greater disaster. While we have sought peace at Niamey and Addis Ababa they have acquired more sophisticated arms and increased their activity. Obviously the Federal Government must act in time to prevent a sharp deterioration in the military situation. Together with my colleagues in the Supreme Military Council and the Armed Forces we have therefore resolved that we must now press on with all our might to defeat the rebels militarily and remove all traces of the tyranny and terror of the rebel regime from the face of this country. Because of the position in the field it can be said with confidence that victory is in sight. However, there are still great odds before us which we must not underestimate. One of the obstacles is the consequences of foreign interference. Foreign interference in the Nigeria crisis has taken many forms since 1966 and it poses serious threats. Millions of pounds have been spent by foreign interests in financing the rebellion against us. Enormous quantities of arms have been delivered to the rebels enabling them to sustain their fighting against Federal troops. The flow of arms to them continues while obstacles are placed in the way of the Federal Government. We have always been aware of the manoeuvres of commercial and other interests in France and the apparent indifference or complicity of commercial interests in some other countries. There has also been a conspiracy especially in the countries of Western Europe to misrepresent the policies of the Federal Government on their mass media in order to whip up sympathy for the rebellion. They have suppressed the truth which is favourable to the Federal Government. There have also been diplomatic pressures to turn our friends against us. I must warn all concerned that these activities apart from being hostile and against the aspirations of all Nigerians are short-sighted and not in the interest of those foreign countries themselves. To seek to provoke chaos in Nigeria is to cause further bloodshed among over 50 million Nigerians and a disservice to all humanity. People whose business interests are protected by our laws cannot continue to subvert the Federal Government with impunity. We must deplore the announcement of French Government support for the rebels. We also note with regret that some of our traditional friends failed to declare unequivocal support for the aspirations of all Nigerians earlier in the crisis and remain enigmatic. There are also a few misguided African leaders who claim to support the rebels. I am happy however, that the great majority of the members of the organisation of African unity and all members of the Consultative Committee of the organisation set up at the Kinshasa summit conference last year recognise the primary need to maintain the territorial integrity of Nigeria and the fairness of the settlement which the Federal Military Government offers to the rebels. Mischievous claims of humanitarianism have been used to justify foreign interference, but the result of such interference has been far from humanitarian in encouraging the intransigence of the rebels and wickedly dangling before them a false hope. It has only meant the prolongation of the painful war and more death and misery for innocent Nigerians. Another excuse offered, is the principle of self-determination: but they refuse to recognise that self-determination for all the ethnic groups in Nigeria is the basis of the new twelve-state structure and it will be a travesty of the principles of justice and self-determination to force five million Annangs, Efiks, Ekois, Ibibios, Ijaws and others into the so-called Republic proclaimed by the secessionists and supported by Neo-Colonialists and the racist regimes. I must re-emphasise that all our resources will be devoted to ensuring that we achieve as quickly as possible a complete victory over the rebellion and that the goals of the Federal Government are attained. Our resolution in this respect is unshakable. I therefore appeal to the foreign countries which are trying to interfere in our crisis to desist from doing so in their own interest and in the interest of the humanitarian principles which they claim to espouse.

The second obstacle is the tendency to national complacency. There is too much complacency all over the country. Outside the immediate war zones, it is difficult for a visitor to Lagos and some of our cities to be aware that this is a nation at war. It is sad: we must realise the seriousness of the crisis through which the nation is passing and the sufferings of many Nigerians in the war zones. Although we have won so many important victories the threats against us remain serious and much vigilance and austerity must therefore be the watchword. We must always remember that until the last village is liberated from the rebels or until they agree to a negotiated peaceful settlement there can be no respite. I must, therefore, remind the nation that many more sacrifices may still be required. Sacrifices in men, sacrifices in money. The task of maintaining the dignity of the Nigerian nation and of securing its greatness and unity cannot be accomplished lightly. There may be many more agonising moments in the days and weeks ahead before complete victory against the rebels is achieved.

I have issued instructions that security should be tightened all over the country to ensure that the nation remains vigilant against the evil designs of the enemies of our unity and freedom. You will all continue to co-operate with the security forces as you have done in the past. It is in the interest of your own safety. Moreover, even after the war, there will be the great task of healing the nation's wounds. This will call for more sacrifices, more devotion, more national discipline, more understanding, more patriotism.

A great and noble task of rehabilitation and reconstruction is before us. It is Nigerians who must perform this task.

We cannot rely on foreign assistance. The federal government will therefore soon launch a national relief corps.

When the time comes I expect that thousands of our youth will volunteer. They will receive intensive training for a few weeks and they will march out to the farms and factories, villages and towns damaged by the war and by deeds will spread forth the message of a re-awakened country rebuilding itself and of new brotherliness.

Fellow citizens, I have told you of the decision of the supreme military council to end the rebellion with the least delay. Orders have been given to the armed forces to press on, as vigorously as possible with the military campaign. At the same time, a full mandate has been given to our delegation at the Addis Ababa talks because we would still prefer a negotiated settlement to the harsh alternative of a total military victory.

I will sum up our policy as follows:

i. The goal of national unity remains the same.

ii. The conditions for peace (first, that the rebels must acknowledge that Nigeria remains one united nation and second, that they accept the new structure of twelve equal states in the federation) remain the same. We shall make all necessary arrangements to ensure the security of all Nigerians wherever they choose to reside and take all measures to enhance reconciliation and national unity.

As soon as the war ends we shall pursue the arrangements for a constituent assembly which will produce a new constitution for the country. At the assembly, all the states will be represented adequately and fairly. It is also our intention to review the revenue allocation formula to ensure equity in the distribution of national revenue and to enhance national development. Indeed, the machinery for this review has already been set in motion. Meanwhile, the thousands of Ibos who have remained in our midst outside the East Central State contributing loyally to the progress of the nation, the many more millions of civilians who have returned to their homes in liberated parts of the East Central State and are being resettled and given new hope are eloquent answers to the foreign sceptics who doubt the possibility of the successful reintegration of the Ibos in a reconciled nation. After the war, we are confident we will continue to emphasise by all we do that a generous and warm welcome awaits all Ibos still in rebel-held areas as they return to the fold of the nation.

I repeat here the offer we have made at the Addis Ababa talks. That there will be a general amnesty for all who reaffirm their allegiance to the Federal Government. We shall forgive the errors, we shall forget the divisions of the past.

To achieve our great goals, we are resolved to overcome all obstacles and all enemies. At the end of our present struggle we are confident that we shall have built the foundations for a virile nation, progressive and truly independent, which will be able to co-operate in dignity with all friendly countries. I therefore urge all the citizens of this country to remain vigilant and resolved. God is with us. God will see us through. Long live one Nigeria.

[1] *Broadcast on 31 August 1968. The texts in* United Nigeria, *3, 1968, and* Ending the Fighting (*Lagos, 1968*) *omit the opening sentence (included here) of the original broadcast.*

176.
Federal Proposal for Guarantees and Integration of Ibos in Biafra[1]

How can the people in the areas under the control of the other side be reintegrated into Nigeria? This formulation enables us to concentrate on the essentials and the problem is that of guarantees on the basis of one Nigeria. It is obvious that a different set of solutions will be inevitable if there are two sovereign countries.

GUARANTEES

i. The Federal Government in a reunited Nigeria will not be a foreign government as it appears to the delegation on the other side at present. Ibos from the East-Central State will participate in the Federal Government on the same basis as people from other states in the executive, administrative, military, police, judicial and other aspects of government. The present composition of the civilian members of the Federal Executive Council is one Commissioner from each of the eleven states, for example—Chief Awolowo (West), J. S. Tarka (Benue-Plateau), Aminu Kano (Kano), Chief A. Enahoro (Mid-West). The only state not represented on the Federal Executive Council at present is the East-Central State. A person will be appointed from the State into the Federal Executive Council. Such a person will be appointed Federal Commissioner with a portfolio as soon as possible. As in the other eleven states a Military Governor will, as soon as possible, be appointed to East-Central State. He will be an Ibo and will be a member of the Supreme Military Council on the same basis as the other military governors. Furthermore, consistent with the national aims of the Federal Government and especially with its already made offer to grant general and specific amnesty it is the policy of the Federal Government to seek to reinstate and re-employ former Federal Public Servants, both in the government service and in the corporations who for one reason or other had to leave their posts in the past two years.

ii. A stable means of livelihood for individuals in a society is a precondition for the functioning of a viable social order and any proper system of law and order based on justice. It is for this reason that the Federal Government lays great emphasis on its proposals and policies for the rehabilitation of persons displaced from their stable sources of livelihood as a result of the tragic events of the last two years, up to and including the current civil war. A National Rehabilitation Commission has already been set up which has responsibility, in co-operation with the state governments, to rehabilitate all displaced persons.

iii. The Administration of the East-Central State will be in the hands of the people of that State. The Federal peace plan ensures that some of the State Commissioners will be drawn from people on the other side. In addition, the law enforcement agencies, the judiciary and civilian administrators will be Ibos of East-Central State origin as is the case in other states. It should be stated that already under the Asika Administration in the East-Central State returning public servants of the former Eastern Regional Government are currently being reinstated and re-employed.

iv. The policing of the East-Central State will be provided by the Nigeria Police Force in which the rank and file in each State are normally people drawn from the indigenes of that state. In the case of the East-Central State, it will be guaranteed that all the policemen and officers would be drawn from people of East-Central State origin. These are the people who come into daily contact with the ordinary people as the instrument of law and order. This pattern of policing is already adopted in the Rivers and the South-Eastern States, areas of the former Eastern Region now under Federal control.

v. Possible guarantees regarding the Armed Forces are indeed limited. The Armed Forces must remain one since there cannot be two standing armies under independent and sovereign command in one country. On the other hand, after the bitterness of the civil war and the consequent propaganda from the other side, it is natural for many people on the other side to fear for their lives until mutual confidence is re-established. It is in recognition of this that the Federal peace plan includes the establishment of an External

Observer Force to provide added confidence of security for the people in areas at present under the control of the other side. The details of such a force in the context of one country, its functions, composition, be negotiated during these talks.

vi. As already stated, the Federal Army will not normally perform ordinary policing duties and their presence will only be required where there is a threat to peace or breakdown of law and order. There is therefore no need to station Federal forces in all parts of the East-Central State. The Federal Government delegation are prepared to negotiate the number of strategic places where Federal forces are to be stationed in the East-Central State. The presence of Federal forces will not be felt by the ordinary man under these arrangements until confidence is restored.

vii. As for the disarming of rebel troops it should be explained that the intention of the Federal Government is to reabsorb Ibos on individual basis in the Federal Armed Forces as is the case with the other ethnic groups. The purpose is not to disarm the forces under the control of the other side and debar the Ibos as a people from even participating in the Armed Forces of their country. The Federal offer of amnesty is relevant here. It will facilitate the reabsorption of Ibos into the Federal Armed Forces as confidence is slowly re-established. The role and duration of the External Observer Force are equally relevant considerations here.

The Federal Government delegation was prepared to consider any additional guarantees the other side may propose in context of a 'one country' solution without which there can be no meaningful negotiations on the question of guarantees for the security of people in areas at present under the control of the other side.

There is no problem of guarantee in areas of the East-Central State under Federal control, since Federal forces including policemen and officers of Ibo origin in these areas are protecting the lives of the civilians there even under wartime conditions. In the Abakaliki Province alone there are well over 600,000 Ibos under Federal control. In the villages around Enugu there are over 100,000 civilians. In the Mid-West, there is an Ibo population of about 500,000. In Lagos and Western States, there are over 50,000 Ibos under Federal control. In all, there are at present about 2 million Ibos in all the areas under Federal control but they do not require any special guarantees now and will not require any special arrangements when peace has been restored.

¹ *This undertaking was originally given in closed session at Addis Ababa in August 1968. It was published in Lagos on 11 September. The text here is taken from the* Ibos in a United Nigeria *version (Lagos, 1968).*

177.
Nigeria Accepts Emperor's Proposals for Relief Supplies¹

1. Direct airlift from Fernando Po to Uli-Ihiala airstrip in the rebel-held area of the 3,500 tons of relief materials already accumulated on that island. This

Y

operation is to be undertaken by the International Committee for the Red Cross in conjunction with the Organisation for African Unity Consultative Committee.

2. The immediate handing over to the international team of supervisors of relief depots in Lagos, Warri, Asaba and Enugu for the purpose of accumulating all materials preparatory to the operation of all road, air and sea corridors proposed by His Imperial Majesty and accepted by the Federal Government.

3. Movement of relief supplies by the international team of supervisors along all land and water corridors, namely:

a. the Enugu/Awgu land corridor;

b. the Asaba-Onitsha land corridor;

c. Warri/Sapele, Asaba/Oguta.

4. After the evacuation of the 3,500 tons of supplies on Fernando Po Island, the I.C.R.C. and the international team of supervisors will continue the airlift of relief supplies accumulated at the Lagos depot from Lagos to Uli-Ihiala airstrip for a period of two weeks subject to weekly renewal.

5. All international relief agencies will be formally invited to make their relief supplies available under the auspices of the international team of supervisors. The international team of supervisors will be representatives of the Organisation for African Unity Consultative Committee of Six and representatives of the International Committee for the Red Cross.

[1] *Statement issued in Lagos on 11 September 1968.* (*Press release from Nigeria House, London, dated 12 September.*)

178.
Margery Perham's Broadcast to Ojukwu[1]

This is Margery Perham speaking. I am speaking to you, Emeka Ojukwu, and to the Ibo people with you.

You know—for you have written to me—how many Ibo friends I have and how I have tried to put the Ibo case in Britain for many months. I know that many wrongs have been committed both against your people and by your people since this conflict began. But it is no time to speak of these things now when your Biafra is being surrounded by Federal troops, and it cannot be long before you and your people will have to face defeat.

If you try to fight to the end, many thousands of lives which Nigeria cannot spare will be sacrificed, both on your side and on the Federal side. More than this, if you insist upon holding out to the end, then thousands, perhaps millions, of women and children may die, or be wounded, or have their health fatally destroyed by hunger and hardship. And those people who have come from Britain and elsewhere to help you—doctors, nurses and others—they too might be killed or wounded. It is feeling for your people, and especially the innocent women and children, which has so deeply stirred the sympathy of people in Europe and America who have seen their suffering on television. The world which is watching would condemn you if they now believed that you were using your leadership to prolong a hopeless struggle at their expense: there would be not only sorrow, but indignation against you.

You might say that I have been put up by the Federal Government to make this appeal. It is not so. I think I am too well known in Britain and by many of your own people for it to be thought that I would act or speak in any other way than upon my own judgment and initiative, and as a Christian. I cannot speak for the Federal Government. I can only say that from what I have seen and heard, not only in Lagos but in visits to other parts, the East and the North, I do not believe that your people would be in danger of massacre or revenge. You must know, even if your people do not, that an immense effort is now being made to prepare the way back for your people into life in Nigeria.

I therefore beg you not to take upon yourself the terrible responsibility of refusing to surrender and of fighting to the end.

[1] *Broadcast over Lagos Radio, 7 September 1968. (Text by courtesy of Dame Margery Perham.)*

179.
U Thant's Address to the O.A.U. at Algiers[1]

If I am unable to conceal my concern about developments stemming from the persistence of colonial and racial policies in Africa, even less can I refrain from expressing my distress and dismay at the mounting toll of destruction, starvation and loss of life resulting from the tragic fratricidal strife in Nigeria over the past year. As has been verified from impartial sources, a very large number of people, combatants and non-combatants alike, are either dying or undergoing acute suffering; many, particularly children, are dying from, or are on the verge of, starvation. In the name of humanity, it is essential that everything be done to help relieve the impact of this tragic conflict.

It will be recalled that I had the privilege of attending the fourth session of the Assembly of Heads of State and Government of OAU in Kinshasa last year when this issue was discussed. The Assembly adopted a resolution which recognized the 'sovereign and territorial integrity of Nigeria' and pledged 'faith in the Federal Government'. It further recognized the Nigerian crisis as an internal affair and expressed 'concern at the tragic and serious situation in Nigeria'. This resolution is a basis for my attitude and approach to this problem, and I believe that the OAU should be the most appropriate instrument for the promotion of peace in Nigeria. In order to co-ordinate efforts and thus undertake the most effective action, it has been agreed by a number of organizations, both governmental and private, that all the humanitarian aid to the victims of the Nigerian conflict should be channelled through the International Committee of the Red Cross and this arrangement still stands.

In addition, deeply disturbed by the extent of human suffering involved in the present conflict, and wishing to determine in what way I might contribute towards a solution of the relief problems, I appointed a representative who proceeded to Nigeria over a month ago in order to assist in the relief and humanitarian activities for the civilian victims of the hostilities. Similarly, in co-ordination with the International Committee of the Red Cross, other organs within the United Nations family have been active in sending supplies and in trying to speed up their distribution to the distressed areas. However, it would appear that, apart from the need for larger shipments of relief supplies, there is an urgent need for greater efforts and fuller co-operation on the part of those bearing responsibility in the areas of the conflict as regards facilities for the movement and distribution of supplies.

Even so, it goes without saying that there can be no quick end to the present plight of the people in the areas affected by the conflict unless concrete measures are taken with a view to bringing about the cessation of hostilities and the negotiation of arrangements for a permanent settlement. In this connexion, I wish to pay tribute to the efforts of the O.A.U. and in particular to its six-member Consultative Committee under whose auspices useful preliminary talks recently took place at Niamey and Addis Ababa. It is my earnest hope that, pursuant to the practical steps and procedures thus far agreed upon, fruitful negotiations will take place leading to a just solution which would guarantee the security of all the people of Nigeria.

In expressing this hope I am also taking into account the possibility that situations of this type can be easily—as indeed the present situation has been in some circles—misrepresented or exaggerated to the disadvantage of Africa as a whole. Already the Nigerian conflict has created difficulties in relations between African States, and its continuance is bound to affect badly needed co-operation and unity among African countries. As I have said elsewhere, the many problems that the African peoples are facing are by no means all of their own making. Nevertheless few, if not all of them, can be solved except by the African countries themselves showing the qualities of maturity and restraint which they have often displayed, and using these qualities to engender the greatest spirit of co-operation and willingness to work together which is essential to the fulfilment of Africa's destiny. . . .

[1] *Delivered at Algiers on 13 September 1968. (Text by courtesy of the United Nations Press Services Office, New York.)*

180.
O.A.U. Resolution on Nigeria (Algiers)[1]

The Algiers meeting of the Heads of State in September 1968:
1. Expresses its gratitude to all Heads of State who are members of the Consultative Committee and particularly to His Imperial Majesty Emperor Haile Selassie I, for their invaluable efforts to carry out the mandate entrusted to them by virtue of the Kinshasa resolution.
2. Notes the Consultative Committee's report on Nigeria.
3. Appeals to the secessionist leaders to co-operate with the Federal authorities in order to restore peace and unity in Nigeria.
4. Appeals for cessation of hostilities.
5. Recommends that the above being accomplished the Federal Military Government of Nigeria declare a general amnesty to co-operate with the Organization of African Unity in ensuring the physical security of all people of Nigeria alike until mutual confidence is restored.

6. Appeals further to all concerned to co-operate in the speedy delivery of humanitarian relief supplies to the needy.

7. Calls upon all member states of the United Nations and O.A.U. to refrain from any action detrimental to the peace, unity and territorial integrity of Nigeria.

8. Invites the Consultative Committee, in which it reiterates its confidence, to continue its efforts with a view to putting into effect the Kinshasa and Algiers resolutions.

[1] *Adopted by the Conference on 16 September 1968.*

181.
De Gaulle Announces Support for Biafra[1]

Question: The drama taking place in Biafra seems to grow more tragic every day. You have alluded several times to the Biafran problem. Mr. President, could you give us your point of view on this problem?

De Gaulle: I am not sure that the system of federation, which sometimes, in certain parts and from a certain angle replaces that of colonization, is always a very good and very practical system, particularly in Africa. But not only in Africa, for in fact it consists in arbitrarily joining together peoples who are sometimes very different or even opposed to each other and who, therefore, have no desire whatever to be joined. We see this in Canada, in Rhodesia, in Malaysia, in Cyprus, and we see it in Nigeria. Indeed, why should the Ibos, who are generally Christians, who live in the south in a certain way, who have their own language, why should they depend on another ethnic fraction of the Federation? Since this is what one ends up with once the colonizer has withdrawn his authority. In an artificial federation, one ethnic element imposes its authority on the others.

Even before the present drama in Biafra, one could wonder how Nigeria would be able to live, in view of all the crises the Federation was experiencing. And now that this appalling, enormous drama has occurred, now that Biafra has proclaimed its independence and that, to subdue it, the Federation is resorting to war, blockade, extermination and famine, how can it be imagined that the peoples of the Federation, Ibos included, can resume life together?

France, in this affair, has done what was possible to help Biafra. She has not performed the act which, to her, would be decisive, of recognizing the Biafran Republic, because she regards the gestation of Africa as a matter for the Africans first and foremost. Already, in fact, some States of Eastern and Western Africa have recognized Biafra. Others appear to be moving in that direction. This means that, where France is concerned, the decision which has not been taken is not ruled out for the future. And indeed, one can imagine that the Federation itself, recognizing the impossibility of keeping on its present organization, may turn itself into some kind of union or confederation that would reconcile Biafra's right to self-determination with continuing ties between it and the whole of Nigeria.

[1] *Remarks made at a press conference, Paris, on 9 September 1968. (Text by courtesy of the French Embassy, London.)*

182.
Ojukwu Receives Mandate to Fight on[1]

We, the chiefs, elders and representatives of the 20 Provinces of the Republic of Biafra, assembled at this joint meeting of the Advisory Committee of Chiefs and Elders and the Consultative Assembly at Umuahia on this 26th day of September 1968, do hereby:

1. reaffirm our implicit confidence in and loyalty to our Military Governor, C-in-C of the Armed Forces and Head of the Republic of Biafra, Lt.-Col. Chukwuemeka Odumegwu Ojukwu;

2. express our deep appreciation of the able way in which His Excellency has prosecuted the Nigeria-Biafra war up to date;

3. place on record our deep sense of appreciation for the gallantry and devotion of our armed forces, and offer them our heartiest congratulations;

4. express our thanks to His Excellency and members of the Biafran delegation to the peace talks at Niamey and Addis Ababa, and support their stand;

5. express our disappointment at the outcome of the peace talks, confident that truth and righteousness will vindicate itself in the course of history; and

6. reaffirm our determination to ensure the security of life and property for ourselves and prosperity, and reiterate our original mandate to His Excellency and his Government to continue the struggle until victory is won.

[1] *Resolution passed by the Biafran Consultative Assembly, 27 September 1968 (B.B.C. ME/2887/B4).*

183.
Azikiwe Tries to Persuade Ojukwu to Negotiate[1]

Your Excellency,

With due deference to the considered opinions of your military and political experts, I am constrained to address you, today, from purely patriotic and humanitarian motives. . . .

Therefore, I am obliged to appeal to you and your advisers to analyse critically and reassess the military situation and also reappraise its political implications. The question arises: what are we fighting for, if it is not intended to protect precious human lives and then safeguard an imperishable heritage of respect for individual freedom under the rule of law?

In view of the present military situation, I am asking Your Excellency for definitive guidance as to what specific alternatives, if any, you may have to offer so as to offset the terrible carnage and holocaust that are now in the offing? These should serve as guidelines to me and other envoys abroad to convince the world of our honesty of purpose and our sincere concern for human life.

The world expects us to demonstrate our maturity and statesmanship in preventing our country from becoming transformed into a massive cemetery. Tell me, Colonel Ojukwu, to assure the world that we have a rendezvous with life and not necessarily with death. Let me tell the world that we shall not wantonly sacrifice the lives of our gallant youth, our brave women, our wise elders, and our innocent children, when we can prevent same by being more realistic and by doing the honourable thing, which an alternative solution to the present military encirclement can prevent.

May God guide you to think straight and to be humane in framing your answer to me. . . .

[1] *Unpublished letter from Dr. Azikiwe to Colonel Ojukwu, sent from Paris on 25 September 1968. (By courtesy of Dr. Nnamdi Azikiwe.)*

184.
First Report by International Observer Team[1]

Summary
In the areas of 1st Nigerian Division that the observers visited they found:
a. Genocide:
There is no evidence of any intent by the Federal troops to destroy the Ibo people or their property, and the use of the term genocide is in no way justified;
b. Conduct of Federal troops:
The troops in the area are taking positive action to obtain the confidence of the local population and assist them in re-establishing a normal life;
c. Conduct of civilian inhabitants:
An increasing number of the inhabitants of the villages, almost all of whom are Ibo, are returning to their homes. The people who have returned to the villages display no fear of the Federal troops;
d. Food and medical assistance:
These are being provided by the civilian population through the combined efforts of the army, the Civil Administration and the Red Cross. While the supply of food has been adequate, the supplies of drugs and medical assistance in the area seem to be inadequate because of a shortage of transport, particularly air transport. This situation could become serious if an expected large increase in the number of refugees and people requiring such assistance takes place;
e. Destruction of property:
The observers received no evidence of deliberate and unnecessary destruction of property by Federal troops. There has, however, been considerable destruction as a result of the war, and the work required to repair this situation, which is just beginning, will be very expensive.

[1] *Report dated 2 October 1968, on the First Nigerian Division. (Full report by courtesy of the Foreign and Commonwealth Office.)*

185.
Arikpo's Address to United Nations[1]

It does not require any effort of imagination to recognise the fact that Nigeria is a sovereign entity which attained political independence on October 1, 1960, and was admitted to membership of this Organization as a Member-

State on October 9, 1960, as a corporate and indivisible entity. When therefore a group of its citizens, motivated by narrow selfish interests and supported by foreign economic and neo-colonial interests, resorted to armed rebellion and declared war on their fatherland, it was the duty and responsibility of the Government of Nigeria to quell that rebellion. Similarly, my Government expects that the Government of any Member-State will do the same if any province of such State were to proceed to secede from it in armed rebellion.

Over the last fifteen months my Government has watched with increasing horror and dismay how the facts and events of our national life have been reported and frequently distorted by certain sections of the world press. Many of these reports are based on hear-say and several others on the work of public relations firms who have been hired by the rebels in my country to promote their secessionist cause. Through their skilful and clever propaganda, emotions of otherwise well-meaning friends have been aroused and manipulated at will. The concern and compassion for the human sufferings arising from our internal conflict that have manifested themselves have therefore sprung from reasons of diverse interests and motives of uneven quality— frequently tendentious, subjective, irrational and at times based on reasons of pure financial consideration. The impression is given that the causes of our internal conflict no longer matter and that the survival of a nation no longer counts. The impression is also given that the conflict is merely to inflict death and starvation on innocent women and children. Hiding, therefore, behind the cloak of humanitarianism, a curious combination of neo-colonialist, political, economic, religious and ideological interests is today assailing our national sovereignty, political independence and territorial integrity.

Never before in history has a rebellious faction in a sovereign state been accorded diplomatic recognition for so-called humanitarian reasons. Never before have otherwise reputable relief organisations chosen their fancy to act and speak without regard to accepted norms and their constitutive laws. Never before have honest and reasonable men been so much beguiled by contrived pictures and stories of death and starvation used as blackmail to sustain and support an armed rebellion and war against a fatherland. Our recent experience should serve as an object lesson to all the small and militarily and economically weak countries of the world.

As the rebel leader retires into a concrete bunker, reminiscent of another false hero, it is relieving that the world has begun to realise that the internal conflict in my country concerns the concept and acceptance of the fact of national sovereignty and territorial integrity of all African States. Were we to permit secession and armed insurgence based on tribal states, Africa, so much in need of union and unity, would again be fragmented into thousands of tribal principalities; Africa, again weakened and uncertain of itself, would be recolonised and more intensively exploited by foreign powers. . . .

The task of crushing the rebellion in my country is now almost completed. We have therefore begun to turn our attention to the more important task of rebuilding the human and material bridges that have been broken and to the reconstruction of our national life in fuller dignity and freedom. We are sparing no efforts or resources in doing this. Urgent relief supplies of food, medicine and clothing to those in need is the immediate and overriding preoccupation of my Government. We have prepared plans which are now being implemented and have made substantial budgetary provisions for the relief and rehabilitation work in the war-affected areas. A National Rehabilitation Commission, headed by a Commissioner of Cabinet rank, has been established to supervise and implement the relief and rehabilitation programme for the victims of the conflict. In fact, as of now, and even when the conflict was at its height, the Federal troops carry not only their rations but vital relief supplies for the civilian victims as they fight on against the rebel elements. The International Committee of the Red Cross, UNICEF and a number of other charitable organisations have been rendering a most signal service in this respect. I salute them on behalf of my Government. . . .

Mr. President, . . . my Government has never and will never stand in the way of any humanitarian organisation or men of goodwill who genuinely want to help us in alleviating the sufferings of the civilian victims of our internal conflict. We have never placed any obstacles in their way. Indeed we warmly welcome them. We shall continue to do so and to provide them with every possible facility and assistance. My Government assures them of its continued service and full co-operation. We do insist, however, on full respect for Nigeria's sovereignty and territorial integrity. We also demand strict adherence to the established norms of international law and behaviour in the fields of international co-operation and humanitarian assistance.

Mr. President, my delegation has listened with interest to the distinguished speakers before this august Assembly who have had cause to refer to the situation in my country. Much as we do appreciate that some of them have been prompted by humanitarian considerations, my delegation takes a firm and categorical objection to any incursion into matters which are essentially within the domestic jurisdiction of my country. References such as we have had to the so-called 'tragedy of Biafra', the so-called 'martyrdom of the Ibo people', the so-called 'incontestible personality of that people', and the suggestion founded on a patently erroneous construction of certain provisions of the Charter of this Organisation that a solution must be found to our internal problem so as to give effect to certain imaginary rights, amount to a flagrant violation of the basic principle of non-intervention in the internal affairs of Member States.

Self-determination for a so-called 'people of Biafra' has been canvassed. But what is 'Biafra' other than a manifestation and an ugly repetition of the lamentable tragedy of Katanga in Africa? What is it other than a cancerous symbol of disunity and disintegration—a concept which only exists in the aberrant imagination of those who refuse to accord Africa the dignity and recognition which they reserve for themselves? It is neither a political entity nor even a geographical location.

They talk of the so-called 'Biafra' as the land of the Ibos, deliberately losing sight of the fact that the former Eastern Region of Nigeria which those now in rebellion against their fatherland purported to incorporate into their dream empire consisted not only of the Ibos, but also of other ethnic groups amounting numerically to more than five-and-a-half million people. Indeed their dream empire was to include the Mid-West State and the Western State which they proceeded to invade and occupy in August, 1967, before they were later driven out in October of the same year. . . .

The Ibo-speaking people of the former Eastern Nigeria constitute the third State—the East Central State. Over two-thirds of the area of this State has also been liberated from rebel control and reintegrated into the federal structure. The liberated areas are currently administered by an Ibo admini-strator assisted by other Ibos who, *inter alia*, man all the law enforcement agencies now effectively operating in such areas. Significantly, in all such areas, the civilian Ibo populations, now realising the barrenness of rebel propaganda, are coming out in large numbers to co-operate with the Federal authorities and indicating in very certain terms their willingness to take their rightful places in the Federation of Nigeria. Besides, Ibos participate on equal status as other Nigerians in the national life of the country and hold responsible positions in the Federal services of Nigeria.

There can therefore be no question of denial of human rights to any section of the Nigerian population. The much canvassed right to self-determination of the East Central State is sacred and only relevant in the over-all national context of Nigeria—in just the same way as, for instance, it is in Brittany or Alsace-Lorraine.

It is the view of my delegation that it is mischievous to characterize as martyrs the people of any section of my country in the current national conflict. If one were to look for martyrs in the recent history of colonial Asia and Africa it is to the people of Indo-China and Algeria that one would readily turn. . . .

There has appeared on the African political scene another Moïse Tshombe. Behind this reincarnation are some of the financial circles that inspired and attempted to sustain Katangese separatism. Alike with open expressions of support and sympathy and clandestine financial assistance—in money and in arms and ammunition—and by complicity in foul propaganda, these circles have attempted, and continue to attempt, to sustain the rebellion in my country. By urging the rebels to hold out in spite of the realities of the situation in the hope of gaining ultimate victory through world intervention, they have encouraged them to exploit human suffering for political advan-tage. . . .

As for those of our brothers in Africa and the Caribbean who have thought fit to meddle in our internal affairs, I can only forgive them. I am sure that the cause of world order would be better served, if they paid a little more attention to the solution of their own internal problems. . . .

[1] *Delivered to the 23rd Session of the General Assembly in New York, 11 October 1968.*

186.
Nixon's Call for American Action on Biafra[1]

The terrible tragedy of the people of Biafra has now assumed catastrophic dimensions. Starvation is daily claiming the lives of an estimated 6,000 Ibo tribesmen, most of them children. If adequate food is not delivered to the people in the immediate future hundreds of thousands of human beings will die of hunger. Until now efforts to relieve the Biafran people have been thwarted by the desire of the central government of Nigeria to pursue total and unconditional victory and by the fear of the Ibo people that surrender means wholesale atrocities and genocide.

But genocide is what is taking place right now—and starvation is the grim reaper.

This is not the time to stand on ceremony or to 'go through channels' or to absorb the diplomatic niceties. The destruction of an entire people is an immoral objective, even in the most moral of wars. It can never be justified; it can never be condoned. Voluntary organisations such as the Red Cross, the church world service and Caritas have rushed thousands of tons of protein high rich nourishments and baby foods to the vicinity of the stricken region. Much of the food remains nearby while these children starve to death.

The time has long passed for the wringing of hands about what is going on. While America is not the world's policeman, let us at least act as the world's conscience in this matter of life and death for millions.

The President of the United States is a man charged with responsibilities and concern all over the world, but I urge President Johnson to give to this crisis all the time and attention and imagination and energy he can muster. Every friend of humanity should be asked to step forward to call an end to this slaughter of innocents in West Africa. America is not without enormous material wealth and power and ability. There is no better cause in which we might invest that power than in staying alive the lives of innocent men and women and children who otherwise are doomed.

[1] *Statement as distributed in Markpress Release no. Gen. 300.*

187.
Mojekwu Reports on the State of Biafra[1]

I have just returned from Biafra, and I am very concerned to see the extensive distortions and misconceptions which prevail in some quarters, on the present situation of our fight against the Nigerian invaders. I feel duty bound to try to put the record straight.

I visited all the battlefronts, I spoke to our commanders, I talked with several members of our Consultative Assembly and the Council of Chiefs and Elders, I discussed the situation with our Head of State, Lieut.-Col. Ojukwu and members of the Biafran Cabinet. I spoke to the foreign correspondents, the Canadian Members of Parliament and to other fact-finding visitors, who were in Biafra at that time. I held two meetings with the major foreign relief organizations in Biafra—the Caritas International, ICRC and the WCC, together with representatives of the Biafran Red Cross and our Rehabilitation Commission. I held extensive discussions with Provincial Administrators of the twenty Provinces in Biafra, and received fresh reports on the encouraging activities of our people behind the enemy lines.

One must agree that this is a pretty fair cross-section of reliable opinion and a good up-dating of the situation. So I use it today to shoot down some of the inaccurate statements which have appeared in print, some of them probably emanating from Lagos.

One of the less happy flights-of-fancy lately said that His Excellency Col. Ojukwu and his family were no longer in Biafra, that they had left for Gabon or some other destination. I met His Excellency several times—alone, with his family, with foreign correspondents, and at Cabinet meetings. I would like to repeat His Excellency's assurance that he intends to remain with his people.[2]

Another example of peoples' statements being falsified is the report which appeared in the press that Doctor Nnamdi Azikiwe had become a 'Dove'. Doctor Azikiwe categorically denied this. He added 'I associate myself completely with the support voted in the Resolution of the last meeting of the Consultative Assembly and Council of Elders in Umuahia. No Biafran politician has discussed the question of Dove-like politics and none have my support as some people try to suggest'. I would remind you this resolution that Dr. Azikiwe mentioned favoured fighting on to the bitter end. This should make it clear enough that Dr. Azikiwe was badly mis-represented.

Another story which is circulating claims that 80 tons of arms are supposed to be arriving every night in Biafra from Gabon. Sad to say, this just is not true. I only wish it *were* true. If it were, believe me, every Nigerian soldier would have fled back to Nigeria by now. The reason for these reports is probably that some people are trying to justify the policy of Mr. Wilson's Government, of continuing massive arms supplies to Nigeria, which as you know is against the wishes of the British people themselves, members of both Houses, leaders of the Church, including the Archbishop of Canterbury himself. On the other hand, it is no secret that our Government is able to receive some smaller amounts of arms supplies from various sources, with which to defend ourselves against the very much more heavily-armed enemy.

Another inaccuracy, which seems to be rather in the realm of wishful thinking, is the appearance of maps showing the war situation. I often wonder who draws these maps, but I feel on the whole that it could never be a military strategist who knows something about the conflict.

You see, certain basic principles of African warfare are not understood. People, especially those with memories of European-style warfare, apparently assume that when the Nigerians capture a town, they have taken at the same time not only the surrounding area but possibly the entire Province of that name. The Nigerians have in fact only captured a number of isolated and usually empty towns. A great number of these represent for the Nigerian Commanders positions of weakness rather than of strength. They are linked with each other by tenuous supply lines which are continually being harassed by regular units and guerilla fighters of the Biafran Army. A good example is the fact that the Nigerians are having to send military supplies via a 1,000 mile road detour because they are unable to control a 4-mile section of the Onitsha-Awka Road.

One thing which I think everyone will agree must be classed as a Nigerian 'inaccuracy' is the succession of predictions from General Gowon's side as to the date of their final victory. I think most people must be losing count of the number of these predictions. If I can manage to count them correctly myself, I seem to remember that they started off with a snappy little boast of 'just 48 hours' and then went on with three weeks—three months—six months—a year. March 31st, May 30th, August 31st, October 1st, and now

October 31st, 1968. Didn't Gowon say he would be drinking a cup of afternoon tea in Umuahia about the beginning of this month? But then, I hear
that one of our senior army officers recently told a Canadian correspondent
'There's one thing about Nigerians and dates—they have absolutely no sense
of time'.

We know that Nigeria has recently become very sensitive to world opinion.
They wish to muffle the outcry against their treatment of Biafrans at least
until they achieve a military victory. But their record of genocide is a
historical fact, established during the period when they cared nothing for
world opinion. A leopard does not change its spots. It is really very naïve to
imagine that from now on and especially after the war, the Nigerians will
change their attitude to us: it is too deeply ingrained in them. The heavy
losses they have suffered during the war and the bitterness of the past two
years will, if anything, result in increased repression and slaughter—unless,
after a peace is finally worked out, Biafrans are in a position to defend themselves. No nation should be left at the mercy of a military attack by a neighbour, so Biafra should not be left at the mercy of a military Junta in Lagos.

Lieut.-Col. Ojukwu has repeatedly suggested a referendum under International control which would allow the people of Biafra to vote on the
question of whether they would rather remain Biafran or become Nigerians.
The Nigerians and Mr. Wilson's Government never even deigned to comment
on this. The referendum would give anyone in Biafra, both in occupied and
unoccupied areas and of all ethnic groups, a chance to state their preference.
Surely Lieut.-Col. Ojukwu would not have persisted with this suggestion if
he were a tyrant governing against the wishes of his people. He has repeatedly
asked the Biafran Consultative Assembly to give their vote of confidence and
to express their wishes. Had the Consultative Assembly wanted to accept
Nigeria's terms of unconditional surrender so shamefully stated at Kampala
and repeated thereafter, they are free to have said so. The record shows that
Col. Ojukwu has never acted against their wishes. He stands firmly for
democratic principles.

It is clear the military Junta in Lagos does not concern itself with such
democratic institutions as Consultative Assemblies, or other forms of regular
government. This is still the position today. In fact, it is even more so than
before. It would be revealing if Lagos, who rules ruthlessly by military might
and without civil support of any form, ever did accept a referendum. We
Biafrans see this proposal of a referendum as a solution that world opinion
too would back wholeheartedly. Such procedures are not new to Africa: in
1960, the people of the territory formerly known as Southern Cameroons
voted not to be part of Nigeria but part of the Cameroons, while the territory
known as Northern Cameroons voted to become part of Nigeria. Again, in
1956, the people of the former British mandate of Togoland were allowed to
vote: they decided to become part of Ghana.

The all-important point to bear in mind, when one considers the present
situation in Nigeria and in Biafra, is that here you have two countries where
the people have the right to live. We agree that Biafra is a young nation. A
young nation created because of genocide. A young nation, nevertheless, with
a burning desire to live in peace. Many world leaders, of respected nations
and of important international organisations, have spoken out supporting

the right of Biafrans to live. This has encouraged us enormously, believe me, to know that what we are fighting and dying for is recognised by others also as a just cause. But now is the time to act and to insist on the idea of a referendum under some form of international control, supported militarily, since the Nigerians have so far refused to show good faith in this proposal. . . .

[1] *Statement made on 23 October 1968* (News from Biafra, *1, 2, 1968*).
[2] *Cf.* DOCS *223 and 226.*

188.
Gowon Speaks on Post-War National Reconciliation[1]

The theme of my address to you today is National Reconciliation in post-war Nigeria. The task of nation-building in Nigeria has never been an easy one. It will even become more difficult after the civil war.

One of the crucial tests by which the leadership of this country will be judged after the war, is the extent we can achieve national reconciliation and reintegration of the Ibos as a people. Our friends and foes alike have expressed concern about the prospect of national reconciliation in Nigeria in view of the bitterness of the current conflict. Many people have often asked me whether the Ibos can ever be integrated into Nigerian society again. My personal conviction and that of my colleagues in the Supreme Military Council and the Federal Executive Council is that national reconciliation is possible. As a result of the vile and unscrupulous propaganda of the rebels, it will not be an easy task to demonstrate to the ordinary Iboman that he still has a place in Nigeria. However, I sincerely believe that reconciliation in this country will be achieved in a comparatively short time. What is important for us is how soon can we do it after the war. . . .

We cannot, however, achieve national reconciliation in Nigeria by just quoting the experiences of other peoples. Honestly, I believe it is part of the African character to forgive and try to forget. Unless we try to forget, it will be more difficult to truly forgive. If only the outside world will leave us alone to find an African solution to our problem!

Outside the rebel-held areas of the country, Nigerians have never been as united as they are today. This is the real basis of my hope. Nigerians have demonstrated their identity of interest in the preservation of the unity and territorial integrity of this country.

The experience of Federal troops in the Central Eastern State so far shows that the ordinary Iboman will have no guilty conscience after this war, because he was not responsible in any way for the one-sided coup of January 15 and its tragic aftermath. The ordinary Iboman was not responsible in any way for planning secession and its equally tragic aftermath. Secession and rebellion were planned and executed by the elite comprising some ex-politicians, university intellectuals, senior civil servants and, I regret to say, military officers. Once these people who abused the power which knowledge brought them agree to lead their people to work for national reconciliation, the ordinary Iboman will find a ready place in the heart of other Nigerians in all parts of the Federation.

The Federal Military Government on its part, will play a positive role in leading the nation to carry out a comprehensive programme for national reconciliation. The main planks in our programme of national reconciliation will include the following:

i. While recognising our ethnic differences in the country, the leaders and people of post-war Nigeria should concentrate on actions which will promote national consciousness and the evolution of Nigerian nationhood. I am convinced that Nigeria means more to most of us today than the 'mere geographical expression—created by the British'. We have shed our blood for the nation and we must all now admit that as of today Nigeria is a living reality. Nigeria will certainly become one of the modern states in Africa. Nigerians will not therefore agree to have their country weakened by foreign vested interests in order that the country might remain the 'economic outpost' of any foreign power.

ii. Already, the Federal Government is actively involved in the humanitarian relief measures and rehabilitation effort aimed at providing food, health and shelter to the needy in the war zones. The National Rehabilitation Commission and other Federal agencies and the State Governments concerned are to expand their relief work to cover the resettlement of people on the land, and the provision of job opportunities for the displaced in the war damaged areas. The Nigerian Red Cross is being strengthened to take over the voluntary relief activities of the ICRC and similar bodies which will fade out of field operations with the end of hostilities.

iii. After the war, the Federal Government will embark on a programme of economic and social reconstruction not only in the war damaged areas but in the whole country. It is easier to achieve national reconciliation in prosperity rather than poverty. Fortunately for us we have the potentialities for development in this country once our resources are properly managed. . . .

iv. It is wrong to think of national reconciliation purely in economic terms. Reconciliation will involve a struggle for the minds of people. Wherever we are in the country, whoever we are, we must be prepared to show kindness to our less fortunate brothers who have suffered most in the armed rebellion in the Central Eastern State. In re-educating people, in readjusting their minds to their new environment, the universities have a major role to play. The reintegration of Ibos into the rest of Nigeria will be that much easier if we can get positive leadership from the universities, from the academic community and the intellectuals.

The ordinary man is no problem. I maintain he has never been directly involved in the struggle for power and jobs in the country; although as I used to warn Ojukwu in the days before secession, it is the innocent ordinary man who has suffered most from this conflict.

Students have an important role to play in the process of national reconciliation. . . . They should . . . re-assure Ibo students abroad that there is a future for them in Nigeria. . . .

In looking at the problems of national reconciliation in post-war Nigeria we have to recognise at all times the main political issues which led to the civil war. All Nigerians accept the need for constitutional and political reforms after the war. This will be done on the basis of the present twelve states. The Constitution Assembly to be set up after the war, will have to complete its assignment as quickly as possible to pave the way for civilian rule. The Ibos will, like other groups, have their say in Constituent Assembly. The Supreme Military Council will review its Political and Administrative Programme at the end of the war and set a new target date for the return to civilian rule since the war has upset the former time-table of restoring civilian rule early in 1969.

As a soldier, I still intend to go back to barracks when our mission has been accomplished. In this context I must emphasise that the Nigerian Armed Forces will not hand over power in chaos or to any individual or group of individuals except those who have been duly chosen by the people of this country. The Military are holding power in trust for the entire people of Nigeria and not for any group or sectional interest.

The civil war has lasted much longer than anticipated mainly because of the support which the secessionist leaders have been getting from certain foreign governments, some missionary zealots and misguided humanitarian organisations. In spite of this support Federal Forces are making progress mile by mile and day by day, and we are as determined as ever to crush the rebellion and reunite the country. I want to assure you, there is no so-called stalemate in the war. It is a foreign bogey so that they can have an excuse to intervene. I say to them 'Keep out'.

While the war lasts, however, I must remind all sections of the Nigerian community that the state of emergency remains in force and we should therefore avoid partisan political activities and controversies capable of weakening our military efforts. I would also like to take this opportunity to warn those who are over-anxious for the return of partisan political activities, to wait until the end of the period of emergency. Those who ignore this warning will have themselves to blame for the consequences of their action.

It seems to me that in Nigeria today there are far too many people who have not learnt the right lessons from the present civil war. The less we learn from our past mistakes and current experiences, the more difficult it will be for us to achieve lasting peace and national reconciliation.

It is now up to all Nigerians in privileged positions to do their best to heal the wounds of the Ibos as a people. On the other hand, our Ibo brothers must also learn from their past mistakes and strive to live in harmony with other Nigerians as equal partners for national progress. The rebel leadership has done incalculable damage to the Ibo people.

The time will soon come, with the end of the rebellion, for all of us to repair this damage. Let us start now. . . .

[1] *Convocation address at Ahmadu Bello University, Zaria, 30 November 1968.*

189.
Brockway and Griffiths Visit Ojukwu[1]

Ojukwu: . . . One thing I want to say at this opening is that we have had a long history of association and friendship with the British people. This struggle has not altered our feelings towards the British people. It is the present administration under Mr. Harold Wilson that we find the enemy. Any criticism you hear from us is directly at the Harold Wilson administration which we firmly believe does not reflect the public will of Great Britain. . . .

Brockway: Your Excellency, I wonder whether I might say this, that both Mr. Griffiths and I have been to many African countries. I do not think we have ever loved a country or loved a people more than we have during this last week in Biafra. . . .

I think you know that we came quite independently of our Government. We come from a peace committee which is very broadly representative of British people. When we sent a letter to the Prime Minister, among other things opposing the British Government's policy of sending arms to Nigeria, we had signatures to it of 250 of the leading personalities in Britain. The Archbishop of Canterbury, the Archbishop of York, 20 Bishops, the leaders of the Catholic Church, the leaders of the Free Churches, members of all political parties, scientists and distinguished personalities. Among those 250 figures there were only six who dissented from our call to the Government to stop sending its arms to Nigeria. From the first we opposed this policy. We took the view that the role of the British Government should be that of a mediator in the Commonwealth, that the role of the British was not to send arms but to seek methods for a just mediation and to send the aid that was necessary.

Your Excellency, may I indicate the political position of our Committee [for Peace in Nigeria]. We took the decision that at this moment it was desirable that a deputation should come here and afterwards that this deputation should go to Lagos. Three months ago it was a common belief in Britain that the Nigerian forces would sweep over Biafra within a few weeks. We never took that view. Both Mr. Griffiths in the House of Commons and I in the House of Lords have said that if there is to be a military solution it will be a long and a terrible war. Therefore, we are doing our best to seek a political solution.

Our first proposal is that there should be a cease-fire. We have found during our visit to Biafra that everyone we spoke to would welcome a cease-fire. We are actually going to make a proposal immediately we return to Britain that there should be a truce over Christmas and we already have the support of religious leaders in this country to that proposal. We are confident we can get the support of the Churches and others, not only in Britain but in Europe. I know the doubts which will arise as to whether that cease-fire will be kept, but it would not be to the credit of the side which broke it.

Secondly, we are suggesting that a cease-fire should be followed by an international, impartial peace-keeping force. We have discussed with your Ministers the conditions of such a peace-keeping force and we hope we may have the opportunity of discussing it with you.

Thirdly, we have urged that this must be followed by negotiations and dialogue between Biafra and Nigeria, at which the problems of the nationhood of Biafra and its relationship with Nigeria in the future should be discussed. We appreciate that this may take a long, long time.

Lastly, we want to see massive aid to the hungry, to the starved and the

z

diseased. We are very proud of the work which the Churches have done in this respect—Caritas, the Catholic International, and the World Council of Churches. We are perfectly sure that there will be a response from world opinion even greater and we are discussing with representatives of the relief organisations how this massive aid can be made in time. . . .

Ojukwu: . . . I agree that the most urgent matter is that of a cease-fire, and an immediate cease-fire. I am not quite in agreement with the appeal to religious leaders. It sounds to me once again like the shadow boxing that has bedevilled everything that has happened in this struggle. The opinion of the Church in this struggle is quite clear. They have not had any influence on the other side. An appeal for a cease-fire, if it is going to be effective, must go to Russia and Britain. . . .

[1] *Verbatim report of meeting in Umuahia, 10 December 1968. (Text by courtesy of Lord Brockway.)*

190.
Biafra's Brief on Relief Flights and Mercy Corridors[1]

Nigeria has been actively canvassing daylight flights and land corridors to bring relief into Biafra. In this she has, as usual, received the fullest support of Great Britain, including the entire propaganda machinery of that country which has mischievously sought to misrepresent the Biafran leadership as unreasonably intransigent and cynically indifferent to the sufferings of its own people. Unfortunately, these malicious distortions and misrepresentations appear to be gaining acceptance in certain countries and among individuals some of whom are not necessarily unsympathetic to our cause. It is absolutely necessary that these erroneous impressions should be erased and the Biafran position on relief—both with respect to daylight flights and through the so-called land corridors—carefully stated.

RELIEF

On the question of relief in general, the following points should be emphasised:

a. Nigeria is not genuinely interested in seeing that relief comes into Biafra. This can be proved by the fact that since the beginning of the war, she has placed all conceivable obstacles to obstruct, frustrate or delay the efforts of those international organisations anxious to provide relief. Furthermore, Nigeria's leaders have openly stated that starvation is a legitimate weapon of war. Finally, Nigerian field commanders . . . have openly derided relief operations and expressed their determination to prevent such relief from reaching the people for whom it is intended. Nigeria air force jets have, in accordance with this policy, been used to bomb relief and refugee centres.

b. The Biafran Government is genuinely concerned about the welfare of the people partly because of the religion and traditional custom of the people which place the highest premium on human life and the pride which the government takes in a people noted for their industry and ingenuity. It would be self-defeating and counter-productive for the Biafran leadership and Government to adopt any policy that would undermine the capacity to prosecute the war or facilitate a return to normalcy and reconstruction. The priority which the Government attaches to refugee and relief work, and the way and manner in which the Government has mobilised all its available resources to alleviate the sufferings of the people, should also be emphasised.

c. Concerned as the Biafran Government is over the need to provide relief for those who are suffering, it is also mindful of the fact that the entire people of Biafra are fighting a war of survival, a war in which if Nigeria obtains complete mastery would result in the extermination of the whole Biafran people. Any proposal for relief must, therefore, be examined carefully so as to ensure that it would not give Nigeria considerable military advantage leading to eventual total victory and extermination of the entire people.

d. That relief, no matter how massive, is at best a palliative and that the only way to ensure that relief is brought in on the massive scale required or to minimise or even obviate the need for such relief is to agree on a cease-fire so that millions of displaced Biafrans can return to their homes, where there is food only awaiting harvesting. If conditions are even relatively normal, Biafra is assured of an appreciable degree of self-sufficiency as far as food supply is concerned.

DAYLIGHT RELIEF FLIGHTS

With particular respect to proposals for daylight relief flights, it should be emphasised that the security of the people and the Republic of Biafra would undoubtedly be unduly compromised in the following respects:

a. Nigeria demands before agreeing to any daylight flights that intending international relief organisations should furnish her with the flight plans. Consequently, it would be possible:

i. For enemy aircraft to try and penetrate into our air space by mingling with or following such relief planes in order to promote its war aims, including harassing the civilian population.

ii. For enemy aircraft to attempt to effect a landing on Biafran airport and/or territory under the cover innocuously provided by daylight flights.

iii. For enemy aircraft, bearing illegally markings of the relief planes and utilising code signs obtained from relief organisations, as a price for permitting such relief flights, to penetrate Biafran air space or effect a landing on Biafran territory or airport. Even if flight plans are not communicated to Nigeria directly, experience has shown that Nigeria would, as usual perfiduously exploit the situation in the manner outlined above. In this connection, it pertinent to stress that the enemy has of recent taken advantage of the facilities for night flights in its attempt to destroy Biafran airstrips, etc. The risks would be accentuated were these attempts by the enemy made during the day and not at night.

b. The indiscriminate bombing of civilians and civilian locations have instilled in all Biafrans an alertness for enemy aircraft. The implementation of proposals for daylight flights would confuse the civilians and undermine their vigilance, thereby laying them open to enemy air attack, for there is no doubt, from past experience, that Nigeria would seize such an opportunity to promote her diabolical plan of exterminating the people of Biafra.

c. Biafran anti-aircraft batteries would be immobilised as we would not wish to shoot down aircraft which might turn out to be those of our benefactors. This would make it possible for enemy aircraft to penetrate Biafran airspace with impunity and carry on its self-appointed task of destruction.

d. The facilities at present offered by night flights have not yet been fully utilised. The airstrip and night facilities at present available can cater for any number and tonnage of aircraft which the relief organisations are in a position to provide. Until these facilities prove inadequate or are fully utilised there is really no need to risk the security and lives of the entire Biafran population by permitting daylight flights.

The aforementioned serious objections notwithstanding, the government of the Republic of Biafra is prepared to agree to daylight relief flights in principle. To this end the Government is prepared to make available to any relief organisation, which does not find the existing night facilities adequate, an area in Biafra where they can build an airport for daylight flights. Although, due to the blockade, Biafra has neither sufficient money nor materials to do this on her own, she has enough skilled manpower and expertise— engineers and other technicians—which she is prepared to place at the disposal of any organisation wishing to take up this offer. In addition to this, Biafra shall make available any other facilities within her competence. There is no doubt, as experience has shown, that with money and materials available the construction of the airfield for daylight flights can be completed within a very short time.

LAND CORRIDORS

On the question of land corridors for relief, our objections are based on military, practical and humanitarian considerations. These objections are:

a. That bridges have been destroyed and channels blocked along whereever the so-called land and sea corridors may be established.

b. That none of any such routes within Biafran territory, including those areas where Nigerian troops have established their presence, is under the full control of the Nigerians. Agreement on a land corridor would, therefore, mean yielding to the enemy an unimpeded communications line for their military operations—something they have been striving for without success since their lines became extended and our guerrilla and commando units went into operation. Further, all the Biafran routes in Nigeria-held territory are hotly contested by our forces and this will continue until the enemy pulls out,

c. That the purpose of destroying bridges and blocking channels is to frustrate the progress of Nigerian troops into the Biafran heartland. The establishment of the so-called land and sea corridors would remove obstacles in the way of Nigerian troops and create routes through which the Nigerian war machine can roll easily into the Biafran heartland.

d. That even if the idea of land and sea corridors were acceptable, it would require the hardest industry and considerable length of time to restore normal communications before supplies could get through. By then, more people would have died.

e. That, apart from political and military reasons, there is also the question of the need to safeguard the people of Biafra from mass extermination through the poisoning of food reaching them from occupied by Nigeria. As disinterested observers who have visited the Republic of Biafra have noted, items of food like salt, milk and sugar, which have found their way into Biafra from Nigeria, have been proved to contain arsenic. Under the circumstances, it would be the height of folly for the Government of Biafra to throw its borders open to relief supplies which have passed through Nigerian lands. Biafrans believe that they will be poisoned if such food gets to them through Nigeria and no arrangement for aid can ignore this fact. Instead the people may even become suspicious of all relief food.

In spite of these, the Biafran government has been willing to consider only such corridor which would not give Nigeria serious military advantages or have disastrous military consequences for Biafra. The only possible route which falls within this category is for supplies to be sent through the River Niger up to Oguta where they can be discharged direct into Biafra. Ocean going vessels (as had been shown by the trading practice of the Royal Niger Company for about a century) could carry their cargoes to the estuary of the River Niger from where the cargoes would be transferred into a smaller craft through River Nun and up the Niger to Oguta for distribution within Biafra. This proposal was made by Biafra both at Niamey and Addis Ababa, but Nigeria refused to consider it.

It must be emphasised in particular that relief is at best a palliative, and can only be a temporary solution of the problem, no matter how massive the relief may be. Biafra is rich in food, both protein and carbohydrates, and all that is required is for conditions to become more or less normal for the million of refugees to return to their areas at present disturbed by enemy presence. It is, therefore necessary that there must be a cessation of hostilities so that refugees can return to their homes. Furthermore, a cessation of hostilities would make it possible for relief to be brought in by daylight flights and through land and sea, as the need to ensure that Nigeria does not take military advantages of such facilities would not arise. A cease-fire would also prevent the wanton destruction of lives and property (including civilians)— a pursuit in which the Nigerians are now actively engaged.

Accordingly, Biafra is willing to agree with Nigeria on a cease-fire in principle. She is also willing, after accepting the idea of a cease-fire in principle, that both sides should discuss the details, arrangements and implementations of the cease-fire. To achieve the desired objective, which is to prevent further loss of lives either through starvation or military action, it is imperative that forces of both sides must be withdrawn from each other's territory. Biafrans who believe that Nigerians are bent on exterminating them would be unable to return to their homes until the Nigerian soldiers have been withdrawn. For the purpose of observing and enforcing the cease-fire, Biafra is willing to agree on an international peace-keeping force, the composition and strength of which should be the subject of negotiations and agreement.

With the cessation of hostilities, it would be possible to open negotiations for a permanent settlement of the conflict, in more conducive atmosphere.

[1] *Statement issued at Umuahia, 29 December 1968.*

191.

Azikiwe's 14-Point Peace Proposal[1]

. . . It is my considered opinion that the argument in certain circles that the United Nations and its organs cannot properly interfere in the internal affairs of its member states is illogical. . . . The United Nations should not present a distorted image of helplessness, vacillation and timidity. It is now obvious that the solution to the civil war between Nigeria and Biafra lies in international mediation and not regional conciliation.

As a positive and practical move towards a permanent settlement of the war, I propose that the United States of America, as a confirmed neutral, should take initiative, without further delay, and call attention of the Security Council of the United Nations to the deteriorating situation in the Nigerian crisis, with a view to the Council taking effective measures to bring the armed conflict to a speedy end. This done, the United States should move the Security Council to constitute a Committee of 19 to study and recommend ways and means.

This Committee should comprise three categories: (1) permanent members of the Security Council (China-Taiwan, France, United Kingdom, United States, and the Soviet Union), (2) non-permanent members of the Security Council (Algeria, Colombia, Finland, Hungary, Nepal, Pakistan, Paraguay, Senegal, Spain, and Zambia); (3) particular members of the United Nations (Gabon, Ivory Coast, Portugal, and Tanzania). Four of the continents of the earth are represented on this Committee of 19: Africa 6, America 3, Asia 3, and Europe 7. Of the nineteen countries mentioned, four are committed to Nigeria (United Kingdom, Soviet Union, Algeria and Senegal); five are committed to Biafra (France, Gabon, Ivory Coast, Tanzania, and Zambia); whilst nine are neutral and Portugal is passively neutral.

The terms of reference of the Committee should be framed with due regard to the legitimacy of Nigeria as a member of the United Nations, whose internal affairs are sacrosanct and could not be interfered with, excepting under extremely special circumstances which affect not only the peace and security of the world but also the conscience and morality of mankind. Surely, the fact that 1.7 million human beings, mostly children, had died, after 83 weeks of a brutal civil war, should aid in placating Nigeria and persuading this African giant to be humane and not to exercise its power like a giant in pressing its legitimate claims. As President Emile D. Zinzou of Dahomey remarked . . . he is against secession but he does not support a union of the dead.

It is now necessary for me to make a personal appeal to General Gowon, as one of his predecessors in office. He should consider the social, economic, cultural and political effects of this disastrous civil war. He and his advisers should be pensive and ponder on the grave situation facing Nigeria due to its involvement in this war. General Gowon should not press for his pound of flesh in advancing any claim, no matter how legitimate, to prevent this issue from being handled by the United Nations due to its being an internal matter. . . .

The Committee of 19 should be charged with responsibility: (1) to study and suggest to the Security Council, within seven days, how Nigeria and

Biafra could be persuaded to call a truce immediately so as to lay down their arms and assemble round a conference table to discuss peace terms; and (2) to make recommendations to the Security Council how the following proposals for peace could be implemented with immediate effect:

PROPOSALS FOR PEACE

Definition of terms.

'Biafra' means the territory now under the jurisdiction of Colonel Ojukwu. 'Nigeria' means the territories occupied by Nigeria which were formerly part of Eastern Nigeria, but does not include territories at present within the jurisdiction of Biafra.

Terms of the Armistice.

1. That the Security Council should declare a total arms embargo to prevent Nigeria and Biafra from being further supplied with arms by member states of the United Nations. Since Nigeria has its own ordnance factories for the manufacture of small arms, the Security Council should secure the co-operation of Nigeria and other countries to implement this arms embargo in the greater interest of stability in Africa and peace in the world.

2. That the Security Council should proclaim an armistice embracing a cease-fire on land, sea and air, and also persuade Nigeria, in the overall national interest for which it had languished in a civil war, to revoke the economic and other forms of blockade and sanctions it imposed immediately before the outbreak of hostilities.

3. That the Security Council should establish an international peace force stationed in the war zones: (*a*) to keep the peace; (*b*) to provide adequate security to the persons and property of the inhabitants in the war zones; and (*c*) to maintain law and order.

4. That the Security Council should assume administration of the war zones with the aid of indigenous and expatriate personnel during this period of transition.

5. That the Security Council should demobilise all Nigerian and Biafran troops in the war zones, as soon as the armistice becomes operative.

6. That the Security Council should obtain acceptable official assurance from Biafra of its unqualified acceptance of the principle of the creation of states, provided it accords with the wishes of 60% of the inhabitants of the area or areas concerned, without prejudice to the future modification of the present twelve-state structure, as far as Port Harcourt is concerned.

7. That the Security Council should conduct a plebiscite in the war zones requesting the adult inhabitants therein to answer the following questions:
a. Do you want Nigeria to remain one country which shall include Biafra: yes or no?
b. Do you want Biafra to become a separate country from Nigeria: yes or no?

8. That if the overall majority opinion of the plebiscite is in favour of Nigeria remaining one country, which shall include Biafra, then the Security Council should guarantee the protection of the fundamental freedom and basic human rights of those concerned, by maintaining that their incorporation in Nigeria would crystallize only on two mandatory conditions, that:

a. Nigeria signs, ratifies, and accedes to all the nine international conventions if it had not already done so . . . [not listed here.]

b. Nigeria and Biafra sign a *modus vivendi* accord, to be enforced by the Security Council, creating a political union, based on the Aburi agreements and establishing a joint services authority in certain demarcated areas of government and administration.

9. That if the overall majority opinion of the plebiscite is in favour of Biafra becoming a separate country from Nigeria, then members of the Committee of 19 should support the membership of Biafra into the United Nations, on the mandatory condition, that Biafra signs, ratifies and accedes to all nine international conventions enumerated in paragraph 8 (*a*) above.

10. That the international peace force should supervise the orderly transfer of territories, where necessary.

11. That as soon as the transfer of territories has been completed, all the armed forces in the areas concerned should be demobilised and civilians should resume control of government, under the supervision of the Security Council.

12. That if majority opinion of the plebiscite favours Nigeria remaining intact, then arrangements should be made by the Security Council, with the co-operation of the Federal Military Government:

a. to demobilise the armed forces engaged in the civil war and provide them with compensation, in the form of gratuities, honoraria, pensions, etc, in accordance with the current laws and regulations;

b. to rehabilitate the soldiers who were wounded or incapacitated during the civil war;

c. to rehabilitate the civilians who were physically or mentally handicapped during the various disturbances in the country from January 1966 to the end of the civil war;

d. to arrange for compensation to be paid to the civilians who were dispossessed of their property or whose property was damaged during the disturbances in the country from January 1966 to the end of the civil war;

e. to rehabilitate the children and dependants of civilians who lost their lives or were incapacitated as a direct result of the disturbances referred to above;

f. to undertake an efficient, reliable, scientific and most up to date census of the whole country as a basis for future demographic calculations;

g. to establish a most modern system of births and deaths registration everywhere in the country;

h. to convene a constituent assembly comprising:

  i. Members of the Supreme Military Council,

  ii. Members of the Federal Executive Council,

  iii. Members of the Biafra Executive Council,

  iv. Governors of the twelve states,

  v. Two members representing each of the twelve states, to be nominated by the Supreme Military Council, after consultation with the State Executive Council,

  vi. Members of the erstwhile Regional Executive Councils (North, East, West, and Midwest), now suspended, *vii.* Members of the Federal House of Representatives, now suspended,

viii. Members of the Senate, now suspended,

ix. Governors of the erstwhile regions, now suspended,

x. President of the Federal Republic, now suspended,

to deliberate and decide the form and nature of a new constitution for the country.

13. That the international peace force should remain in the country and supervise the federal and regional elections, in collaboration with the regular Nigerian armed forces and also witness the handing over of the government and administration of the country to the civilians who are to form the new government.

14. That the international peace force should exist for a period of one year, in the first instances, and its maintenance budget should be the responsibility of the United Nations and Nigeria, provided that its tenure may be extended, from time to time, until the new civilian government has re-established control for the maintenance of law, order and good government in the country

These fourteen point proposals are intended to placate the extremities of Nigeria and Biafra which had made a cessation of hostilities virtually impracticable. My aim is to adapt the proposed solutions offered by both sides on to a matrix which should reflect the wishes of both parties but at the same time clear the atmosphere of much bitterness and propaganda. In as much as the questions of territorial integrity, self-determination and security of the person and property loom ominously in the reckoning of the combatants, it would be more democratic to allow the people of the areas concerned to determine their future, by expressing their opinion, apart from the views held at present by the two military regimes. I think that this would be a fair criterion.

The Nigerian argument about the preservation of its territorial boundaries is sound, as long as it is based on the accepted frontiers artificially created after the Berlin Conference 1885. This relates to external boundaries. But it is an undisputed fact that the majority of the people who inhabited what later became known as Nigeria were never consulted when that part of Africa was partitioned by the European powers. This view applies equally to the rest of Africa.

As for the internal boundaries, the majority of the inhabitants were not consulted as to their wishes when constitutional changes, with their territorial demarcations, were made intermittently during the period 1886 to 1960. But there are recent precedents for ascertaining the wishes of the majority inhabitants of a particular area in Nigeria for the purpose of adjusting internal boundaries. I have in mind the referenda in 1960, with reference to Southern and Northern Cameroons, and that of 1962, with reference to the creation of the Midwest region. In each of the above three cases, the ascertained wishes of those concerned were respected both by the United Nations and Nigeria, in respect of their responsibilities. . . .

[1] *From a lecture delivered before the Ralegh Club in Rhodes House, Oxford, on 16 February 1969. (Text by courtesy of the speaker immediately after the meeting.) The lecture was subsequently printed privately.*

192.
Enahoro Presents Federal Case to U.S.A.[1]

I am, as you may know, a Minister in the Federal Government of Nigeria and to that extent those who contest the views which I shall express may contend that I am not an impartial commentator. However, I have played some part in the political and constitutional development of my country for some twenty-five years, and I believe that my duty, on occasions such as this, is to make a presentation which transcends partisanship as far as possible and promotes a deeper understanding of the forces at work in Nigeria and the nature of our problems. The opinions and judgments I shall express are therefore mine and not necessarily those of the Federal Government. . . .

In the case of Nigeria, the circumstances and the course of events do not fit snugly into either category. On the one hand, the army majors who seized power in Nigeria in January 1966 were not, in my opinion, agents of imperialism or of international communism. On the other hand, their *modus operandi* (namely, the assassination of so many civilian and military leaders) and the end result of their actions (namely, that all those assassinated had the singular distinction of not being from the Ibo tribe) could not be described as the popular will of the people of Nigeria. What then is the answer? What was it all about? What led to our present tragedy?

One fatal error into which commentators on the Nigerian crisis fall is oversimplification. They seek a simple, all-embracing answer to what is a complex question. Thus, some of them speak of a religious war, some of a tribal war, and some of an oil war. Unfortunately it isn't as simple as that, and one may, with diligent analysis identify at least six distinct bodies of causes of the Nigerian crisis.

The first is rooted in our very being. Nigeria consists of over two hundred tribes. . . . Each of these tribes has a separate language and a separate group culture. Before the European advent, they were all at different stages of civilization. . . . Of the major tribes, only the Ibos had not as yet evolved organs of centralised administration or the institutions of a higher group existence or a consciousness of group interest. The British brought all these tribes together some seventy years ago and made a country out of them.

From this circumstance has arisen the popular description of Nigeria as 'an accident of history'. . . . The same accident of history produced the United States of America, Canada and states of South America. Other accidents of history (Roman colonisation, Moorish colonisation, dynastic marriages) produced the states of Europe. Therefore, Nigeria is not peculiar as an 'accident of history' or in the history of accidents.

The territorial extent of Nigeria is about 350,000 square miles, and its population about fifty-five million. Even if there were no other consideration, the vastness of territory and the size of population would obviously have dictated some form of decentralization of authority. The British solution, in which we as Nigerians gradually came to acquiesce, was to create three regions—North, East and West and establish three regional administrations subordinate to the Central Authority. Each of the three geographic regions was dominated by one of the three major tribes. Here was the foundation for the sectionalism which later plagued Nigerian politics and which was to

facilitate the rebellion in one part of the country. The British paid no heed
to the desires of the minority tribes within each group. Thus, the 13 million
who were not Hausa-Fulani in the North, the two-and-a-half million non-
Yorubas in the West and the 5 million non-Ibos in the East, came under the
dominance of the three major tribes.

To further complicate matters, sections of the population within each
major tribe resented domination by other sections within the same tribe. . . .
[There was] an element of religious difference between the leading politicians
in the north and those of the south. . . . We shall see later what consequences
this mixed grill had on the development of Nigeria.

The second body of causes may be identified as the economic motivations
for secession. In retrospect, it seems clear that whichever part of Nigeria
appeared for the time being to enjoy a comparative economic advantage
vis-à-vis the rest of the country tended to develop a secessionist tendency.
Thus, before economy of the Northern parts picked up, and when it appeared
that the leaders in Northern Nigeria were slow to identify themselves with
growing nationalism, there were leaders in the South who felt that the
country did not need the north. When the balance of advantage seemed to
shift to the North with groundnuts and tin playing a greater role in our
economy, Northern leaders were inclined to feel that they need not carry the
burden of Nigeria on their back. In the late forties, during the great cocoa
boom in the Western part of the country, some western leaders suggested
that their area should go it alone. Now in later years, with the discovery of
oil in the Eastern part of the country, their leaders too developed secessionist
tendencies. Unfortunately, this occurred contemporaneously with other
influences and events facilitating secession, which we shall shortly examine.
It will be seen, therefore, that oil was an important factor in the present
attempt by a part of the country to secede, because it encouraged the dream
of separate viability.

Another economic factor arose from two population movements in Nigeria.
The eight million Ibos are crowded into a small area of land, resulting in
Iboland having the greatest population density in all tropical Africa. The
effect has been to make the Ibos a hardy, energetic people, and to generate
among them a migratory movement not only to other parts of Nigeria but to
distant parts of West Africa. This was one population movement.

The second population movement came about in this way. As I said earlier,
the northern parts of the country were largely Muslim and insulated from
European influences by the Sahara Desert and also by southern tribes who
acted as a buffer between the Muslim potentates of the North and the advancing tide of the Western and Christian civilization. This was an arrangement
which suited the British administration as well as the traditional authorities
of the North. But the outcome was that European education, a Europeanised
way of life and European-style economic forms were first established in the
South, with the assistance of Negroes from West Indies and Sierra Leone.
They helped to train Southerners as Clerks, Shopkeepers, Accountants,
Interpreters, Locomotive Drivers, to grease the wheels of imperialist rule and
British commercial activity, and as Catechists and lay preachers for the
missionaries. Consequently, when the time came for the British to develop
their interests in the North, they were able to draw upon a reservoir of

Southerners already trained. We see, therefore, the coming together of two movements of a demographic nature. The first was a movement of Ibos caused by the exigencies of life in Iboland, and the second was the movement of trained personnel and their dependents, relatives and hangers-on into administration, commerce, industry and religion in the North.

Unfortunately, these immigrants, instead of settling among the local populace in the native cities, established separate communities of their own on the fringes of the native cities. These settlements were promoted by the British, who did not wish the educated upstarts from the South to corrupt and contaminate the Northerners; by the missionaries, who did not wish to lose their hold on the Southern converts; and by the traditional rulers of the North, who feared that the presence of these enlightened pagans from the South might generate developments threatening the established order. There came a time, however, when these combined forces could no longer resist the desire of the people of the North themselves for enlightenment and progress. Younger men became Emirs, schools were opened, colleges came into being, hospitals and training institutions were started, and the northern areas began to produce their own sons and daughters. In the atmosphere of general under-development, there were no employment opportunities for these people, as most jobs were already taken by Southerners, who were mainly Ibos. Consequently, there was a growing reaction against 'stranger elements' who dominated the economic life of the northern areas. Here was a fertile source of friction.

The third body of causes to which I have already briefly referred, was the lack of social integration among the tribes. In particular, the historically and culturally more advanced tribes tended to look down on the less developed. In practice, this meant that many Hausas, Yorubas, Edos, Efiks and others looked down upon the Ibos as newcomers to the scene of civilization and as people without a corporate history of any value. The Ibos had not, after all, organized empires or kingdoms. But this attitude was counter-productive, because it drove the Ibos to work even harder, to help one another at the expense of others, and to acquire the modern symbols and levers of power. In time, the Ibos became more united than any other tribe, and they too began to despise the other tribes as effete and unprogressive.

The Yorubas are, as we know, well in advance of any other Nigerian tribe in modern development. The majority of doctors, lawyers, bankers and persons qualified in the arts and humanities, are Yorubas. This tended to leave the technical field and the Armed Forces and Police clear to the Ibos. Given their newly acquired sense of common purpose and their psychological need for group achievement to give them a sense of pride and place in Nigeria, the Ibos rapidly improved their position by the singular process of ensuring that where an Ibo person was employed he made sure that all others around him were Ibos. Here was another source of friction.

The fourth body of causes arose from the pattern of political and constitutional development during the years of struggle for Independence. We did not manage to evolve a single or unitary nationalist movement in the classic sense, like the Indian National Congress. We did not even produce a dominant movement like the CPP of Ghana. On the contrary, we produced three major movements revolving round the three largest tribes in the three regions.

Consequently, each national movement increasingly became an expression of tribal will. Thereby, we as a people missed the advantage and the unifying experience of common endeavour. . . .

As the fifth body of causes, I would mention all those effects which together may be attributed to under-development. Poverty, which meant a shortage of employment, which led to bribery, corruption and nepotism. Bad roads, which meant that goods could not be moved quickly and efficiently which slowed down exports. Shortage of indigenous capital, poor education, low wages. The nett effect was to create increasing loss of confidence in the ability of the Government to provide the necessities of life for the people. Meanwhile civil servants, army officers, police officers, business managers, and the political class rode in big cars from the U.S.A. and Europe at a time when the majority of the people were growing poorer. All this produced economic unrest.

Finally, as the sixth body of causes, I would identify the collective failures of Nigerians, irrespective of tribe, in the years 1960–1966. Let me mention a few. There were the political devices, like the rigging of elections which political parties used to maintain themselves in office, whence it rapidly became clear that no party in power could, in the forseeable future, be removed from office by the process of elections. There was the ineffectiveness of Parliament, because ministers refused to summon Parliament for several months and when they did, would not permit sessions to last more than a few days. Parliament became a farce. There was the Army problem. As a result of the departure of the British, very young men in their late twenties and early thirties, had rapidly been promoted to positions of responsibility in the army, police, civil service. In the army, these educated, politically conscious young officers, having no wars to fight turned their minds to public affairs. There was the failure to grant the minority tribes their demands for separate states. Instead many of their people were killed and thousands imprisoned. There was the arbitrary removal from office of the elected constitutional government of one Region by the Federal Government. The courts themselves were brought into disrepute when Parliaments overruled decisions of the courts. Political parties might win elections, but their opponents were declared the winners. Public meetings were banned throughout the Federation for almost two years, the right of public protest was abrogated. There was widespread corruption. Then the psychological impact of coups in neighbouring states produced impatience among our people. Compromise became disreputable. It was now thought that the short cut to a better existence was through a coup.

To summarise, therefore, it will be seen that the causes of Nigeria's misfortunes are for the most part rooted in the very history of Nigeria, in the mistakes which the rulers of Nigeria made in the year 1960–1966, in the desire of some of the leaders of the Ibos to create an Ibo history comparable to the past of the other competing tribes in Nigeria. . . .

Upon the declaration of secession, the Federal Government was confronted with two questions. Should the secessionists be allowed to go? If not, how could secession be effectively brought down as quickly as possible? As to the first question, there were a number of considerations. The Leader of the Yorubas, Chief Awolowo, had declared that if the Ibos were allowed to go, his people too would secede. Within the Eastern Region, the minority tribes, who made up five million as against eight million Ibos in the Region, had no desire to secede. In any case, with the reorganisation of the Eastern Region into three separate states, it was no longer open to the Ojukwu government in Enugu to speak for these five million. Further, among the Ibos, a large number of them had stayed on in other parts of the Federation refusing to associate themselves with secession, many of them remaining in the public service of the Federation. The Federal Government could not betray them. In addition, it was clear that once the right to secede was conceded, not only Nigeria but all the other multi-ethnic states of Africa would disintegrate. For these reasons, the Federal Government had to resist secession. . . .

Mr. Chairman, I began this address by protesting the irrelevance of secession to the solution of our problems. It is clear that whether or not secession succeeds, we will still be confronted, as the rest of Africa is, by the major problem of unifying in a modern state people of different tribes, cultures and languages. We will still have the problem of democratic institutions, a decision to make in regard to Parliamentary forms of Government and the responsiveness of authority to the popular will. We will still have other human problems: for example, what shall we do with our standing armies in Africa, led as they often are by politically minded young men in their twenties and thirties? We will still have the problem of political parties: can we develop a viable multi-party system of government or are we doomed to the single party system? Secession will not answer any of these questions. For no matter into how many parts we break Nigeria, these problems will remain to be solved. . . .

If it was right for Abraham Lincoln to crush secession and to lay the foundations for the United States as it has come to be today, is it so wrong for us in our own time equally to resist secession and to seek to make out of Nigeria something comparable on the African Continent to the life which you provide for your own people and the leadership which your country gives on the American Continent? Many of us in Nigeria were born into an age when Nigeria as a whole has come to represent to us our homeland. We are not petty little tribesmen, hunting with spears, bows and arrows, knowing no higher loyalty than to our immediate tribal surroundings. We have grown up in the new nationhood and we are determined to defend that nationhood with all that we possess.

Pay no heed, I beg of you, to those who argue that so much bitterness has been generated by this civil war that we cannot live together again. I think that the Western mind underestimates the African's capacity to forgive and forget. Within our experience, barely 15 years ago there was a holocaust in Kenya which was attributed to the Mau Mau rebellion. Today the tribes of Kenya are reconciled and even the British are still there as businessmen and farmers. A few years ago, there was an even worse conflict in the Congo, but today among the Congolese it has become a page of history. Or shall we talk of Algeria, where the French killed, by their own estimation, over one million Algerian nationalists in eight years of struggle? Today, Frenchmen are going back to Algeria in increasing number as businessmen and farmers. Already millions of Ibos are back in their homes and in Lagos and other parts of Nigeria, fully welcomed by us all. Our National Athletic Team for the Olympics and our National Football Team again contains Ibos. Ibos have returned to Northern Nigeria and reclaimed their properties valued at over a quarter of a million dollars. These are the grounds for our contention and our faith that we in Nigeria can live together again as brothers, that we can together re-establish Nigeria and that we can together make the greater Nigerian dream a reality. Upon what is based the contrary view that we cannot do it, saving the ill will of those who secretly nourish a yearning for the discomfiture, disunity and subjugation of Africans?

[1] *Excerpts from a speech delivered to the World Affairs Council at Boston, Massachusetts, in March 1969. (Text by courtesy of the Nigerian Embassy, Washington D.C.)*

193.
Asika Looks ahead to Reconstruction in East-Central State[1]

. . . The genesis of our problems for which rehabilitation and resettlement are being offered as solutions is in a series of social upheavals beginning with the social disturbances and communal riots of 1966, unto the present on-going civil war. Social upheavals involving inter-ethnic and inter-communal relationships, and which take the extreme form of a civil war inevitably throw up complex human, sociological and political problems that significantly limit, if they do not wholly determine, the form and the content of post-crisis social policy. It is therefore crucial to our discussion of rehabilitation and re-settlement in the present Nigeria situation that we first explore the social context and background which have given rise to these expressions of public policy.

Before proceeding I should perhaps make some qualifications to the analysis. Firstly, no attempt is being made to provide an exhaustive social history of Nigeria. Secondly, although the problems which may require rehabilitation and resettlement are more general, the present discussion is limited to the area of the former Eastern Nigeria. Thirdly, I have limited my discussion of the political factors to a statement of the effects, without discussing the causes. This limitation should be no great loss since it can be presumed that most people are broadly familiar with the political causes of our crisis—even if there is disagreement on some points.

In the period before the crisis which started in 1966 the population of the area of the former Eastern Nigeria was very unevenly distributed, with the major contrast being between the very heavily populated Ibo-speaking and Anang areas and the rest of the region. On the one hand, while the population density exceeds 1,000 per square mile in Orlu, Okigwi and Anang areas, indeed in some places it approaches 3,000 per square mile. On the other hand, the density of population in Ikom, Obubra and Rivers province was below a hundred per square mile. This uneven distribution is significant in that it corresponds with ethnic cleavages, most significantly in that the areas of high density are also, broadly speaking, the areas of the Ibo-speaking people while the areas of low density are inhabited by the minority ethnic groups. This convergence of ethnic and demographic factors is further complicated by the fact that the areas of high density also correspond with the sand lands which are very poor in quality and which are already heavily exhausted. Thus in gross terms the Ibos are to be found on areas of already exhausted low yield land in dense concentrations while the non-Ibo people occupy areas of great fertility with low population concentrations. It is not quite clear how this unusual and internally unstable pattern of population distribution evolved. It is probable that the dense populations located on poor soils may have been, as it were, stranded in their present locations by the fact of colonial conquest and the institution of *Pax Nigeriana*.

Most of the population of the former Eastern Nigeria lived in 7,500 village communities which formed the traditional or rural economy. . . . The economy of most of these rural villages was stagnant. There was a little or no invest-ment in these villages except in the building of private houses by individuals. On the contrary the last decade before the crisis was a period of intensive urban investment which increased significantly the gap between urban and rural conditions and thus contributed to a retrogression of the rural economy. Furthermore, in the decades before the crisis, especially weaving and pottery, foundry and smithery, had been displaced by the importation of manufactured substitutes. Also in the same period considerable farm land had been given up to urban and industrial development. . . . Where attempts at economic organization and cultivation were practised these were handicapped by a general insecurity of land tenure characterised in some places by year to year leasing and by other complex legal and sociological ambiguities. The sum total of all these factors therefore was a built-in tendency in the rural areas with high population density and low agricultural yield towards out-wards movement and migration.

In the decades before the crisis patterns of migration had developed to foreign countries: Western Cameroons, to Fernando Po, to Ghana; to other areas of Nigeria; to the new towns within Eastern Nigeria itself. Such migration which achieved its highest rate in the immediate post second world war period was usually on a more or less permanent basis, at least for the active life of the migrant, in search of work or employment. Towards the end of the decade political considerations had already started to limit further migration outside the territorial limits of Nigeria with the assertion of autarkic economic policies by these newly sovereign states. It may therefore be assumed that such outward migration is no longer a significant viable option. Migration into other areas of Nigeria especially the Northern region, Western region and Lagos continued although in the years immediately before the crisis the stability of such patterns of migration had already become threa-tened by political factors. In a situation of rather intense inter-ethnic political rivalries, the interculary status position of, especially, the Ibo migrants in the former Northern Nigeria engendered considerable tensions. Increasingly there was a blocking off of opportunities and avenues for employment and income, hitherto available to migrants in these areas. However, in the same period there was an increase in what may be called internal migration from the rural areas of the former Eastern region into the urban areas in the same region. The decade before the crisis was a decade of relatively rapid and expensive economic development in the former Eastern region, a pattern which was accelerated towards the last years by the discovery, exploitation and pro-duction of mineral oil. In this decade the urban centres of Port Harcourt, Aba, Onitsha and Umuahia and Enugu almost all more than doubled in population, and it is perhaps significant that the greatest expansion took place in Port Harcourt.

In addition to these cases of more or less permanent migration into urban centres or to areas outside the region, there was also another pattern of migratory adjustment to the ecological and demographic pressures of the rural economy and one which may be called regional seasonal migration. Each year hundreds and thousands of agricultural workers moved from the areas of high density and low yield to the areas of low density and high yield such as Ogoja and Obubra in the areas of Cross River. There they hire or otherwise acquire land parcels temporarily for the purposes of cultivation and at the end of the farming season they depart with their harvested crops and return to their own areas. . . . Quite apart from factors of political rivalry engendered by the coincidence of ethnic and economic cleavages it would appear that with the increased monetization of the economy, and the increase of social solidarity based on division of labour the various village communities had grown less permeable and more resistant to migrants. The present war, as we shall note has accelerated this process towards closure. . . .

Thus in the period before the crisis private and public efforts had not succeeded in any measure in changing the broad pattern of the economy of Eastern Nigeria as outlined above. That is to say that there was rural stagnation and under-employment, there was a high level of migration out of the rural into the urban areas and there was an even higher level of urban unemployment and underemployment in the region. And this was so in spite of the fact that in contrast to the other areas of the country the East had been enjoying a relative economic boom, largely as a result of oil and superior fiscal policies. The co-existence of conditions of boom and conditions of stagnation and mass underemployment must have induced particularly intense levels of frustrated expectations. It is to this already unstable and explosive Region that large and sudden inputs of repatriated populations were destined as a result of the crises in 1966.

As a result of all the social disturbances of 1966 especially these in the former Northern Region several developments occurred. Firstly, there was repatriated to the Eastern region and in particular to the high density Ibo areas of the Eastern region about 2 million persons in destitute or more or less destitute conditions. Quite apart from the sudden increase in the general population and the pressure on already stretched resources, the return of the migrants cut off a substantial source of transfer income which the migrants used to send back to their village communities and which provided a significant proportion of the gross income of such communities. Thus those who were in a large measure dependent on the more affluent migrants were suddenly obliged to accommodate, feed and maintain the migrants who had returned in poverty or worse. . . . Initially the structure of segmentary lineages and kindred groups proved admirably able to absorb the returnees and to cushion the impact of their presence and thereby prevented immediate breakdown or explosion. However with the increasing complication in the political situation and the apparent closure of outward re-migration as an open choice, the returned population who were in most cases already urbanised, or at least socially mobilised, began to drift into the urban centres of the Eastern Region—very urban centres which as we have noted were

2 A

already congested with the under-employed, unemployed and unemploy-
ables. . . .

The inability and the failure of the Eastern Military Government to absorb
or rehabilitate these displaced persons was highly functional for its policy of
political extremism which eventuated in the declaration of secession. It may
not have been a deliberate Machiavellian policy, but it is nonetheless true
that by successfully absorbing, resettling and rehabilitating the civil servants,
the educated, professional, university types this Government thus succeeded
in disarming the articulate groups, who out of a sense of deprivation might
have been expected to provide an alternative programme and policy to that
of the Government. The masses of the people, displaced, destitute and
thus without alternative leadership formed a combustible and easily manipulated body for the propagation and pursuit of extremist political goals. . . .
For our present purposes it is sufficient to simply identify what appear to
be the major consequences of the war for these three States as these affect
possible programmes of rehabilitation and resettlement.

In a sense it can be said that the war has been a struggle for the control of
the cities and the access routes to the cities. In consequence much of the
actual physical destruction as a result of the war is localised to the cities and
the villages and towns on the routes to the cities. . . . Altogether the pattern
has been very uneven, some cities are barely scratched yet in some cases
the destruction has been of such magnitude that were the population to
return they would be rendered homeless. It is sufficient to note that the pace
of rehabilitation and of return to normalcy will be directly affected by the
pace of restoration of these destroyed and disrupted urban facilities.

We have noted the admirable manner in which at the initial period of
repatriation the structure of kinship groups and segmentary lineages was able
to absorb and cushion the sudden input of millions of displaced persons. But
even before the outbreak of war the strain on the kinship structure had
already become too much and the drift into the urban areas had already started. It is my very strong impression that the cumulative effects
of the earlier pressures and that of wartime displacement and disruptions on
the structure of the family may have proved fatal and excessive. It would
seem that there is a considerable fragmentation and individuation of family
units, a breakdown and an erosion of social norms with regard to family life
and other aspects of communal existence, and that one must expect in the
post-war situation considerable social anomie. The break-up of what is known
as the extended family, together with other factors, will considerably limit
if not wholly negate the contribution and the absorptive capacity of the
family as units of welfare and rehabilitation. . . . In the long run the breakdown of the family may have positive consequences for economic development since it has as its obverse a qualitative leap in the scope of social
mobilization. . . . It may be expected that as a result of this war a significantly
larger proportion of the population in these areas, now fragmented into
nuclear family units, would have been structurally displaced into urban
existence and orientations. In the long run this transformation into what
Daniel Lerner calls a participant society should have positive significance
for the ability and the willingness of the people of these areas to adopt new
techniques, new innovations and to accept the strains of rapid industrialisa-

tion. It should also facilitate the processes of social reintegration since such integration will no longer be mediated either by the corporate lineage groups, or by groups based on the kindred system.

Another important consequence of the war is the elimination of migration, whether seasonal migration or long term migration, as a significant means of adjustment to the ecological and demographic pressures of Iboland. . . . In all the war affected areas, whether in the Mid West State, the Rivers State or the South Eastern or the East Central State the consequence of war has been the exodus of the migrant Ibos from non-Ibo areas and from the new urban centres to return, where they can, to the traditional villages. . . . Until the present wounds in the relationship of Ibos and their closest neighbours in the other two Eastern States have been healed, outward migration into these areas, whether long term or seasonal, may not be significant. It should be stressed that this closure of the option of migration to the Ibos of the East Central State is bound to be temporary. . . . But for so long as it lasts it effectively precludes migratory adjustment to the ecological and demographic pressures of Iboland, which in turn eliminates the use of re-settlement as a strategy of rehabilitation with regard to the Ibos. This factor is probably the single most important consideration that should determine our programmes of rehabilitation. . . .

There are and will be other consequences of the war. All I have sought to do in this section is to highlight these aspects which seem to have major relevance to our problems. My analysis has been rather selective but I hope it has been adequate to its purpose which was to define the form of the problem and the social and political context within which it has to be tackled. . . . The Nigerian Civil War has brought great destruction to life and property and to the texture of social life and has traumatically re-defined the opportunities and circumstances of millions of Nigerians in the war affected areas. From my experience I can state without equivocation that these problems of peace will be much greater and more complex than the problems of the present war. The processes of rehabilitation and resettlement contain a crucial even if less tangible socio-psychological dimension. They involve not merely the restoration of the capacity for economic well-being to persons, the restoration of destroyed or distrupted materials and services, but also in the circumstances of a civil war also include the need to re-assure the people that they do in fact have a future. . . .

[1] *From a paper 'Rehabilitation and Resettlement' presented to the Conference on National Reconstruction and Development in Nigeria held at Ibadan University, March 1969. (Text by courtesy of a delegate.)*

194.
British M.P.s Write to Ogundipe[1]

The debate which will take place in the House of Commons tomorrow is of momentous significance in the history of Anglo-Nigerian relations. The compassion of the British people has been aroused by the heartrending suffering brought to Nigeria by the tragedy of civil war, and in company with the whole civilized world, we are desperately anxious to help end the killing on the battlefield and the agony of innocent deaths.

The M.P.s signing this letter have no doubt that once the joy of peace returns to your country we shall see Nigeria serving as a beacon to independent Africa. We believe that once the paramount danger of tribal secession and national disintegration has been overcome, all the peoples of Nigeria will have the opportunity to work together in peace, freedom and mutual harmony. We do not accept that genocide has ever been the policy or the practice of the Federal Government.

Because we believe that the cause of the Federal Government is just—and is necessary for the sake not only of Nigeria but of Africa as a whole—we are bound to experience grave misgivings over the bombing incidents in recent weeks when civilians, including women and children, have been killed.

We believe that such acts of destruction are wholly at variance with the philosophy of your Government, and we accept that they are the unfortunate accidents of war waged from the air in terrain where military targets are poorly mapped and difficult to identify.

The bombing onslaughts on cities during World War II demonstrated that attacks upon civilians are barbarous. Furthermore, they both fortify the morale and fighting spirit of the enemy, and discredit the perpetrators of such action. We therefore urge your Government to avoid indiscriminate aerial bombardment, which can only do grave harm to the cause of Federal Nigeria.

[1] *Letter sent by a group of pro-Federal M.P.s to the Nigerian High Commissioner in London on 12 March 1969, on the eve of a major House of Commons' debate.*

195.
Britain's Foreign Secretary Winds up Debate[1]

The Secretary of State for Foreign and Commonwealth Affairs (Mr. Michael Stewart): We have had a debate in which right hon. and hon. Members have spoken with great breadth of knowledge and great depth of feeling. There have been some bitter passages in the debates, but I believe that we are now, at the end of it, all in the mood to accept that this is a question on which humane, well-intentioned and well-informed people can form very different conclusions and that we shall get nowhere if we start accusing others with whom we disagree of being callous, hard-hearted, immoral or hypocritical. We must try to do better than that.

This cannot be represented as an argument between the humane and the moral on the one hand and the hard-hearted *realpolitiker* on the other. We are aware of the struggle that is going on within us all; that there are issues of right and wrong actually struggling with each other on this question. This is what indeed makes it a tragedy—this conflict of rights and of feelings of morality.

The situation in the end means that one must make a judgment knowing that when one has made it, although one will stick firmly to it one is bound to do so with some distress and regret. I believe that this is in the minds of us all.

However, it does not remove from us the necessity to make a firm decision, despite the distress and regret that it may cause.

It is in that spirit that I wish, first, to try to state the essentials of the problem and the essentials of Government policy, and, secondly, to take up what I think have been the two main presentations by the House to the Government. They are, first, the question of what steps we can take in the interests of humanity to bring this war nearer to a conclusion, and, secondly, the plain question of what we should do about the supply of arms.

Anticipating the main course of my argument, and in response to a point made by the right hon. Member for Bridlington, I will say a word about initiatives and steps to end the war, though I shall have more to say about this later. I believe that the House will accept that if we are to take such steps we must keep closely in touch with the Nigerian Government; otherwise it will simply be an empty exercise.

It is to be expected, therefore, that at some stage there will be a meeting of my right hon. Friend the Prime Minister with the Prime Minister of Nigeria. [*Interruption.*] It was well known and it was public knowledge at the time of the Commonwealth Prime Ministers' Conference that such a meeting might occur. Indeed, I can tell the House that there is to be such a meeting.

The details of the meeting have not yet been arranged, and I should have been entirely happy, as would my right hon. Friend, to have left any announcement of this until later. However, in view of the questions that have been put by hon. Gentlemen opposite and in view of what has already been made public knowledge, I am now confirming for the House that this is a correct report.

In the course of the debate it has been urged on us that we should take initiatives to end the war. Those who have asked that presumably know that if it is to be done to any purpose there must be consultation between Her Majesty's Government and the Federal Government of Nigeria. It is not reasonable, that request having been made—indeed, it is ungenerous and departs from what I said at the beginning of my speech about the mood of the House—for us to be asked to try to take initiatives to end the war and then for it to be assumed that anything that may be necessary in the course of that is adopted merely for the purpose of influencing the debate. If there are hon. Members who really advance that argument, they are thinking and speaking unworthily and out of tune with the general mood of the House.

While I wish to take up what I said at the outset about dealing with the essentials of the problem, I should, perhaps, first say that the immediate occasion of the debate is the natural concern of the House about the bombing in the rebel-held territory in Nigeria. . . .

The Under-Secretary of State, who opened the debate, on the question of bombing, stated very clearly our refusal to condone and our condemnation of indiscriminate bombing. He further detailed the instructions given by General Gowon to his officers, the determination of the Nigeria Government to proceed most resolutely against any officer guilty of disobedience of these orders. That is one point which has been established. It has also been brought out during the debate—and this is an unhappy fact we must realise—that the bombing of civilians has not in the course of this war been confined to one side.

I say that not because one set of cruelties excuses another, but for the reason that I do not think all hon. Members have fully realised that there are a number of Africans who notice the great concern about the recent bombing of civilians in rebel-held territory and are saying, 'Where were the consciences of these Europeans when the hopsital at Ore was bombarded by the rebels? Where were the consciences of the Europeans when there was bombing on Lagos and repeated incidents of this kind at the beginning of the war?' When we weigh up all this, the conclusion we have to come to, and which was voiced by a number of hon. Members, is that we know very well that if there is war at all there will be cruelties inflicted on innocent people, whether deliberately or through recklessness, or sometimes inevitably in the mere course of warlike operations. This will be true whether the war is waged by land, sea or air.

Our real concern, therefore, if we are concerned—and who is not?—about the suffering caused by the bombing, must be to try to bring the war to an end. . . .

I ask the House now to consider what I call the essentials of the problem. Here it cannot be said too often that this is a problem affecting Nigeria and Africa as a whole. There have been some references to the boundaries or existence of Nigeria. We should remember this. When Nigeria came to dependence she was accepted without cavil by every nation in the Commonwealth as a fit member of the Commonwealth and by every nation in the United Nations as a fit member of the United Nations. She was not regarded as an artificial, ramshackle creation, but as a genuine State. That is a fact that we cannot set aside.

In the light of that, we must all accept how serious a principle is raised if it is suggested that a particular people out of the many peoples of Nigeria should be able to carry out a successful secession. This was a point very strongly and rightly emphasised by the right hon. Member for Kinross and West Perthshire (Sir Alec Douglas-Home). We must remember not only what the effect would be of a successful secession on Nigeria, but also its effect . . . on other African countries. . . . What I am saying now I say out of a deep conviction formed over many years as to what is one of the most important points in world politics today. That important pivotal point is that the peoples of Africa, who have for so many centuries been bullied, enslaved, kicked about by more powerful and sophisticated peoples, should now be able to take their proper place in the world. I do not believe that they will be able to do that unless they have a structure of efficient viable States.

I believe that, if the existence of those States is threatened by tribal secessions, we shall find ourselves living in a world in which Africa is for ever dragging behind other continents. This, I believe, would be profoundly wrong. This surely is one of the essentials of the problem. I know that not all hon. Members accept it, but they must accept that many of us do believe this sincerely and deeply. They must also be prepared to realise that this is very much the African view of the problem.

It is in the light of this that Her Majesty's Government took from the start, and still take, the view that this attempt by the Ibos, whatever their grievances, at rebellion and secession to remedy their grievances, was a tragic and disastrous error and that therefore the Nigerian Government were right to resist it. But with that right there goes a duty—the duty on the Nigerian Government so to frame the structure of their State that there is the fullest possible degree of autonomy and development, not only for the Ibos, but for the many other peoples of whom the Nigerian Federation is made up. . . .

The right hon. Member for Stafford and Stone (Mr. Hugh Fraser) said that one of the objects of British policy has been to maintain a unitary Nigeria. Here, with respect, he really has got it wrong. Nigeria is and always has been a Federal State. It is most important that the Federal character of it should be emphasised so as to provide the Ibos with their proper place in it. This is exactly what the Federal Government are now prepared to do. The reconstruction of the State of Nigeria into 12 States gives the opportunity for the many peoples in it to co-operate in building up what could be one of the most prosperous and fortunate nations in Africa.

We held that view, that the rebellion was tragic and disastrous and that the Nigerian Government, at one and the same time, had the right to resist it but the duty so to construct the State that there was a proper place for the Ibos. This, I think, is what many hon. Members mean when they speak of a political solution, that while the Nigerian Government are in our view right to resist secession, they must seek a political settlement, that is, a federal structure of such a kind that none of the peoples of Nigeria can say that they are unfairly deprived of opportunities for their own development and their own culture or the opportunity to play their proper part in Nigeria as a whole.

Although I realise that what I have said will not command the agreement of all hon. Members, I do not believe that anyone can say that the position which I have advanced is inhumane or unreasonable, and I believe that, even for those who cannot accept it, it must have a great basis in the real facts of the situation.

Granted that, the decision which we had to take about arms supply followed. We could not have said to Nigeria, 'We gave you to understand that you would be able to obtain from firms in this country certain kinds of arms, but now, because you are faced with a rebellion, a rebellion which is in our view and in yours evil for Nigeria and dangerous for Africa, we shall cut them off'. If we had said that, it would have been in Nigerian eyes and in fact tantamount to supporting the rebellion, supporting something which we believed to be wrong. . . .

I wish to make this quite clear because it has always been the Government's position. We have never claimed that we were neutral in the sense of taking no view as to the rights and wrongs of the issue. We believe that the rebellion was wrong and that it was right, therefore, not to take the deliberate act of cutting off arms from a Government faced with a rebellion of so disastrous a character.

Anyone who advocates that we should have taken the other view, that we should have cut off arms, must look at what the results would have been. There would certainly have been a profound estrangement of ourselves from Nigeria and from Africa as a whole. It would have involved a great increase of Russian influence in Nigeria, and it would have involved a great risk to British people and British interests in Nigeria.

The House knows that I have on other occasions taken the view that there are circumstances in which it is entirely right for a country to say, 'We must push our economic interests aside because there are overwhelming moral considerations.' That is the view which the Government took over the sale of

arms to South Africa, the view which I expressed in the House. But in this
case, who can say that it is axiomatic that it is morally right to cut off arms
supplies from a country facing a rebellion of this disastrous character? It is
not axiomatic, and I do not believe it to be true. . . .

It has been suggested that if we had taken a different view about arms we
could have acted as mediators. Let us look at what actually happened. There
are a great many countries which are not supplying arms to either side. There
are a number which are either supplying or allowing arms to be supplied to
Colonel Ojukwu. Have they been able either to mediate or to exercise influence on Colonel Ojukwu? Have they been able to say to him, 'Will you
open your country to mercy corridors for relief?', the main thing required to
prevent starvation in Biafra? If we had refused to supply arms, any chance of
acting as mediator would have gone at once. I say that I have never pretended, the Government were in the position of a mediator. For the very reasons
I have just set out. I understand that that cannot be so. If my hon. Friend
will read what the Government had said he will see that he has not been misled
on this point. . . .

It is not true that the Government's policy amounted only to the decision
on arms. If I have had to spend some time on that it is because of the emphasis many hon. Members have laid on it. But it was furthering our aim, so
far as we could, to seek a peaceful solution, and this had to be done in consultation with the Nigerian Government. Since the suggestion has been made
that we have never had any influence, that we have never worked for peace,
I must remind the House that we brought about the conversations at Aburi.
I must tell the right hon. Member for Stafford and Stone that his allegation
that the British High Commissioner encouraged, persuaded or in any way
influenced the Nigerian Government to go back on that agreement is wholly
without foundation. We further brought about the talks at Kampala, which
could have brought peace if it had not been for encouragement to the
secessionists from people outside.

In 1968 there were the meetings between my noble Friend, Lord Shepherd
and Sir Louis Mbanefo, and the visits of my hon. Friend the Under-Secretary
of State and my noble Friend, Lord Shepherd. More recently, at the Commonwealth Prime Ministers' meeting, it was with our help and encouragement that Chief Awolowo said explicitly that he would meet the representatives of Colonel Ojukwu here without any pre-conditions.

The Leader of the Liberal Party was somewhat scornful on the question of
whether we have had any influence. I would put the matter like this. It is
obviously not possible to say, when one looks at the whole record of the
Nigerian Government's behaviour, how much of it has been due to persuasions of ours and how much of it they might have done anyway. Whilst we
have rightly criticised and condemned them for the recent bombing incidents,
let us look at the whole record of their behaviour, remembering that they are
a Government facing a rebellion and fighting for the whole structure of their
country. Let us notice what they have done. Throughout the whole struggle
they have made it clear that they will talk and compromise about anything
short of the dismemberment of Nigeria. They have admitted—and I think
that this is unprecedented—international observers to go about with their
forces to supervise the behaviour of those forces, and it is those observers who

have torn to pieces the allegations of genocide. They have made it quite clear that they are willing, when a settlement is reached, to give guarantees for the safety of the Ibos, and would even have an observer force or something of that kind to see that those guarantees are kept.

On the question of relief, the Nigerian Government have made the generous offer of Obilago Airport. It is not they who stand in the way of pouring in relief by land. I am bound to say, remembering the strain under which they are placed—and I think we all know the terrible fact that when human beings wage war they are always likely to become more callous in the process— that I do not think one can condemn—far from it—the general record of the Nigerian Government, and I am not prepared to believe that the persuasions of this country, which has been in close touch with them throughout and which has always urged on them counsels of moderation and humanity, have been of no effect at all. . . .

Now there does lie on us the need to try to seek peace and settlement. If we are to do that, can we get an arms embargo? I should be deceiving the House if I pretended that getting an embargo was anything but very difficult. Many of my hon. Friends will remember that the attempts to bring about the policy that was known as non-intervention in the Spanish Civil War in practice worked entirely to the advantage of one side. But we have not been idle about this.

We know the Russian view, which is that they are prepared to go on supplying in all circumstances. The French view is that they are not in fact supplying. We have raised this matter in Western European Union, and it is interesting to note that the recent decision of W.E.U. was that its wisest approach was to handle this in consultation with the O.A.U.

Governments which support the rebel cause hold strongly to their point of view. The Portuguese Government, for example, provide important transit and other facilities and presumably see this policy as part of their long-term defence of Portuguese colonial interests in Africa. Similar considerations arise in the case of other countries.

In this situation—and I hope I carry hon. Members with me here, for I am pointing out, as I must, the difficulties—it would be easy to pretend that we could make a striking initiative for an embargo tomorrow and try to conceal the fact that the chances of success are not very great. [Hon. Members: 'Why?'] If we want success, the embargo has to be supervised inside Nigeria itself. There is no other way of making it effective.

That means, if the supervising job is to be done properly, that the international arms embargo would have to be accompanied by a ceasefire, and the same thing works the other way, because a ceasefire without an arms embargo would so clearly work to the advantage of the rebels that one could not reasonably ask the Nigerian Government to agree to it.

It seems to me, therefore, that the object of any steps must be a combination of the following things: an international arms embargo, a ceasefire, the meeting of the two sides without pre-conditions and, one ought to add to that, the opening of the 'mercy' corridors for relief. I am bound to say that if Colonel Ojukwu maintains his opposition to that it would be difficult to place much reliance in good faith on the other issues.

As to meeting without pre-conditions, I must tell the House that the positions of the two sides on this have changed and it is difficult to be certain at any one moment that one is giving a completely accurate and up-to-date account of what their view would be. I simply remind the House that, at the time of the Commonwealth Prime Minister's Conference, Chief Awolowo of Nigeria was prepared to meet Colonel Ojukwu's representatives on those terms. What we must try to work at is for such a situation to recur and, when it does recur, for there to be this time, as there was not at the Commonwealth Prime Ministers' Conference, a response on Ojukwu's side.

By what mechanism could this be achieved? I must tell the right hon. Member for Kinross and West Perthshire that the problem of trying to do this through the United Nations would be that we would be tackling an international arms embargo, which, for reasons I have already mentioned is unwelcome to a number of countries, through a mechanism which would be extremely unattractive to the participants and to African countries who feel that the proper regional organisation is the Organisation of African Unity. I do not rule out an approach to the United Nations, indeed, I do not think one can give immediately a blueprint as to how we should try to reach the objectives I have mentioned. I do not rule out the United Nations. I have pointed out the difficulties of it.

Above all, we must try and work, as much as we can, through the Organisation of African Unity. As for the part that the Commonwealth, the third agency mentioned by the right hon. Gentleman, could play, it seems that it could play a part in any observer or peacekeeping forces that will be required after a settlement is reached. Our willingness to provide our contingent to such a force has already been announced.

I have tried to describe to the House what is the nature of a possible settlement that might be reached. I have not attempted to disguise the enormous difficulties, because there are here deep and profound differences of principle which divide the Nigerians from Ojukwu and his followers.

What I am suggesting could be attained if there is a real effort in other directions. We shall endeavour to do all we can to produce that result. The House knows that Britain does not hold this issue in the hollow of its hand, but we are more likely to be able to help if we accept the need for Africa, for the unity of her peoples and for the movement away from tribalism towards modern nationhood. That is why I feel obliged—and I do not do this with malice, but one must be plain—to say that I have not found it possible to accept the proposition of an immediate cut-off arms supplies, which would not save a single life, which would make negotiations for an agreed embargo impossible, and which would weaken rather than strengthen our hands in anything we seek to do.

[1] *Speech made to the House of Commons, 13 March 1969 (Hansard, 13 March 1969, cols. 1682–94).*

196.
Prime Minister Summarizes Britain's Stand on Nigeria[1]

Q.: Prime Minister, Why are you going to Nigeria?

P.M.: The Nigerian war is a matter of world concern. It's a matter of deep concern in Britain. We are linked with the Nigerian Government by very long ties going back even to colonial days but very close ties since Nigeria got her independence. But there is concern about the bombing of civilian targets. There's concern about the relief supplies, of getting relief, the relief lines, the relief supplies through to the areas where food is needed because the whole world including Britain have provided food and we would like to see that food go through. There are other anxieties. I'm not going with the idea of mediating. I don't think that the present situation really admits of mediation and indeed if there is a case for mediation it must be African mediation, through the Organisation of African Unity headed by the Emperor of Ethiopia. But I really intend to try and find out for the British people all that's going on and to be able to express some of the anxieties that the British people and the British Parliament are feeling in their hearts.

Q.: So you don't expect spectacular results from this visit?

P.M.: No.

Q.: When you're over there you are going to see General Gowon. Will you also take the opportunity of seeing Colonel Ojukwu if you have that opportunity?

P.M.: I think if General Gowon who is after all the Head of Government of Nigeria felt that this would be helpful, and if Colonel Ojukwu with his colleagues felt it would be helpful of course I would be glad to do any thing I could to arrange it, but I am not going for any spectacular mission of mediation between them as I have said. I think there are important questions that ought to be put on behalf of the British people, on behalf of a much wider world opinion to all concerned in Nigeria because there's nothing so bitter or so malevolent as a civil war and I think the whole world wants to see it moderated and to see a peaceful solution.

Q.: We've been criticised, Britain's been criticised, for not having enough influence on the course of events in Nigeria. What sort of influence can the British Government have, Prime Minister?

P.M.: Well you know this is a Nigerian problem. It's a problem of a great Federation one of the richest countries in Africa one which for many years worked, despite all other internal difficulties, and their tribal problems work very well as an independent Nigeria, and at the end of the day the problems must be solved by Africans.

We have this friendly relationship with Nigeria and our friendship goes out not only to the Federal Government but to the Ibo tribe and we have tried to exercise our influence but not to the point where we could ever consider becoming a colonial power or attempting to put illegitimate pressures upon them. We have represented the views of the British people and I believe a world opinion, for example in saying that when there is a settlement that there must be a settlement one day, there must be no recrimination, there must be no genocide to the Ibo people, who may have made mistakes under the leadership they have, must not be subject to threats, massacre, genocide, to any interference to their life, liberty, pursuit of happiness, and these are the things we have pressed upon them, but we are not in a position to dictate and I don't want to dictate.

Q.: On the eve of your departure for Nigeria could you briefly define again what the British Government's position really is on Nigeria?

P.M.: In a sense I've already done it in answer to the last question. We are friends of Nigeria, we created a unified Federal Nigeria, it is our purpose to help preserve the integrity of Nigeria but within that, with the tribal problems, with proud peoples, and very fine peoples too, we believe they should have the right of self expression within that united Nigeria. It is our policy, we continue to supply on a limited scale arms, not bombs, not aircraft, to the Government of Nigeria because we have always been their suppliers. To have cut it off would have been an un-neutral act, it would have been an anti-Nigerian act, we knew that, but that's not the main part of our policy, our policy is to try with so many others all over the world, particularly in Africa to bring the two sides together; it is our policy to try to moderate the vehemence of this fighting to try and protect civilian targets from attack; it is our policy to above all perhaps, perhaps all we can do, to help to get the vast supplies of relief foods and medical equipment and medical supplies which we and others have joined together in supplying to get it through to the people who need it. These are the things they are going to be talking about. The House of Commons recently debated Nigeria, endorsed this policy, I want to make this policy real in all its aspects.

Q.: It is a unified Nigeria that we want?

P.M.: Yes.

¹ *Interview given in London on his departure for Lagos, 25 March 1969. (Text by courtesy of the London Press Service Verbatim Service.)*

197.
Gowon's Welcoming Address to Wilson¹

It is with great pleasure that I welcome you on your second visit to Nigeria. We recall the equally warm welcome accorded you in January 1966. Today, however, my country is in the throes of an internal rebellion similar in nature to that in Rhodesia which I understand your Government is equally determined to crush.

In spite of the war, you will find here in Lagos and in other parts of the country outside the small area still under rebel control, that my people are engaged in their normal pursuits; they are resolved to bring the war to a speedy end and to concentrate their energies on rehabilitation and reconstruction.

The purpose of your present visit is very clear and I look forward to having fruitful discussions with you in the next few days. I expect no dramatic peace initiative on your part, and I have noted, with great interest and appreciation, your remarks that you were not coming to Nigeria to mediate in the civil war. Nevertheless, I wish to assure you that my Government is as willing as ever to go to the conference table for negotiations at any time provided these would bring about a lasting solution to our present crisis.

As you know, it was never the intention of my Government to seek a military solution to the present crisis knowing fully well that such a solution was hardly necessary in putting down an internal rebellion in this country.

Our doors have remained open for alternative solutions but if there are none, this country will have no choice but to intensify its military operations until the rebellion is completely crushed.

It is to the credit of the British Government that it relinquished its sovereignty over Nigeria as one nation. It was a wise decision, and for the good of all Nigerians and posterity, my Government is irrevocably committed to the preservation of Nigeria's territorial integrity. I know too that this is the wish of the many Ibos at present oppressed by the rebel leadership. It should also be the desire of those who have vast economic interests in the country.

It is my wish and prayer that the sufferings and hardship which the present conflict has brought on all Nigerians both here and behind the rebel lines should not be prolonged one day longer than is absolutely necessary, and you may be assured that the Federal forces will stop further action the moment the secessionists show a genuine willingness to negotiate in the context of one Nigeria. Successful negotiations can only come about if there is mutual agreement on basic issues. It is, indeed, unfortunate that no one has been able to persuade the rebels to engage in meaningful negotiations.

At this point, Mr. Prime Minister, I must say that my Government and the people of this country, consider our relationship with Britain as a special one for obvious reasons. Consequently, we expect the United Kingdom Government and the British people to understand, better than others, the true nature of our crisis and the danger in any arrangements or suggestions which can only lead to the dismemberment of Nigeria in the long-run. We are very grateful for the support which your Government has given to us in the task of protecting Nigeria's sovereignty and territorial integrity. You have personally been most courageous and we commend your efforts in maintaining— in the face of tremendous political odds both at home and abroad—your support for the cause for which we are fighting this tragic civil war in Nigeria.

We are conscious of the genuine humanitarian ideals to which some people in your country subscribe. Contrary to the vile propaganda of the rebels, however, I wish to assure you and the whole world that all true Nigerians rightly regard the entire populace of the secessionist area as fellow citizens and not enemies as Ojukwu calls other Nigerians. We believe, and I have always said, that nobody outside Nigeria can be more concerned about the welfare of our citizens than the Nigerians themselves. My Government has accordingly offered, time and again, all possible facilities for increasing the flow of food and other relief materials to the area still under rebel control.

It is as much to the distress of all Nigerians as to that of genuine humanitarians abroad that Mr. Ojukwu continues to disallow daylight flights and the use of land corridors for the supply of relief materials. These, it is generally agreed, are the most practical and effective means of alleviating distress and privation in the secessionist area. The reason for Mr. Ojukwu's refusal, of course, is not far to seek. He wishes to continue to exploit the misery of the helpless populace in the area under his control to achieve his political ambitions. In this regard, we note with regret that he has been considerably assisted by those in Britain and other countries of the Western world who are either ignorant of the true facts or who conceal their sympathy for his political aims under the cloak of humanitarian concern.

It is now fashionable for the supporters of Mr. Ojukwu's political ambitions abroad to talk and write in terms of a so-called 'Biafra' over which Mr. Ojukwu has been attempting to establish his sovereignty and impose his dictatorship; and in complete ignorance of the realities of the Nigerian situation and the prospects, they also talk about a so-called 'Aburi Agreement' and of 'Confederal Arrangements'. We have no illusions about the objectives of 'humanitarians' of this kind—their purpose is plainly to break up our country, discredit Nigerians and Africans and exploit a divided Nigeria to impose their will. We will not succumb to this blackmail.

You will meet, during your short stay with us, many Ibos who have been living and working happily in Lagos throughout the present crisis. They enjoy the same rights and privileges as other Nigerian citizens. You will also meet in the liberated areas of the former Eastern Region displaced persons who are being resettled and rehabilitated. The liberated areas of the East Central State are already under an Administration composed entirely of Ibos. I hope you will also be able to see something of the work of our National Rehabilitation Commission, the Nigerian Red Cross, and some British medical and relief teams in the field. My Government has repeatedly given assurances that there is an honourable place for all Ibos in a united Nigeria. They will not be treated as a defeated people or as second-class citizens at the end of the war.

You have just met the Governors of most of the new States and members of the Federal Executive Council who are drawn from all the States. The twelve-State structure of the Nigerian Federation is here to stay. It is the surest guarantee for peace, progress, stability and unity in this country. There can be no looking back. . . .

[1] *Delivered in Lagos, 27 March 1969 (Nigeria House press release).*

198.
Wilson's Offer to Meet Ojukwu[1]

I have today sent a message to Colonel Ojukwu expressing my willingness to meet with him while I am here in Africa, for a discussion of any points he wishes to raise with me and a number of questions I should wish to put to him. It would be clear that if I were to meet him this would not of course involve recognition of what is called 'Biafra'.

I think there are those in this room who will recall that I have had meetings in the past—indeed HMS Fearless is not very far away—which did not involve recognition of that regime. There will be no question, therefore, of recognition. There would be no question of mediation or negotiation. I have no cut and dried plan to put forward to anyone in Nigeria. I regard this as a matter for the Nigerians.

I would feel that if mediation is wanted and is asked for it is best supplied through the medium of the OAU: and, of course, I shall be discussing the lessons of my visit with His Majesty the Emperor of Ethiopia in a day or two's time, and I hope also to have the opportunity, while there, of discussing it with the OAU itself.

As to where such a meeting would take place I would not propose to go into the part of Nigeria controlled by Colonel Ojukwu. This has been made quite clear from the outset. But I have indicated to him a very wide variety of areas where I would be prepared to meet him. He has his own problems of transit and communications and security.

It could be that there are one or two areas he would not be keen to go to, and I have indicated a very considerable number of African venues where I would be agreeable to meeting him. Naturally, I have discussed this matter with General Gowon. The Federal Military Government have no objection in principle to such a meeting. They are aware, of course, of the basis on which the meeting would take place which I have just outlined.

¹ *Extract from the Prime Minister's press conference held in Lagos on 30 March 1969. (Text by courtesy of the Central Office of Information Overseas Press Division.)*

199.
Wilson Reports on his Nigerian Visit[1]

Mr. Speaker, with permission I should like to make a statement on my visits to Nigeria and to Addis Ababa.

My main purpose in Nigeria was to see at first hand and to discuss with the Federal Government something of the problems which have aroused anxiety in this House and more widely.

As I had previously made clear to the House, I did not go to mediate between the Federal Government and Colonel Ojukwu. This is a conflict between Nigerians and, if outside help is needed, the Organization of African Unity is the appropriate agency for mediation.

But, on the question of negotiations, I received from General Gowon a clear assurance that his government is prepared, unconditionally, to sit down with Colonel Ojukwu or his representatives, to discuss a settlement. It remains Nigerian Government policy that they would not agree to any settlement which breaches the principle of Nigeria's unity and territorial integrity, but there are no prior conditions for entering into negotiations.

Secondly, I received an equally clear assurance that the Federal Government stands by the guarantees it has given for the safety and security of all Ibos and remains ready to include in any final settlement such further guarantees as are required, in the shape of observers, for example, from the O.A.U. General Gowon stated categorically that, after the fighting had stopped, the Ibos would not be treated as a defeated people but would enjoy the same rights and privileges as any other Nigerian citizens.

Thirdly, I received most specific assurances about Federal willingness to facilitate the flow of relief supplies to the war affected areas. At a joint meeting I held with the international relief agencies and the Federal Government, I was given the evidence I wanted about that Government's readiness to consider any appropriate route, by sea, land and river, or by air, including daylight flights.

Fourthly, on bombing I expressed the deep concern which had been shown by hon. members in the recent debate, and more generally, about the bombing of non-military targets. I have no doubt about the determination of General Gowon and his colleagues, about the strict instructions which have been given, and reaffirmed, that bombing attacks should be restricted to strictly military targets, and about General Gowon's assurances that stringent measures would be taken to deal with anyone found disobeying those instructions. I have more doubt, and I strongly expressed this doubt, about the adequacy of control of air operations and about the quality and efficiency of some of the personnel entrusted with the bombing.

In lengthy discussions on this issue, I stressed the need for still stricter control and felt it right to ask whether such military advantages as the present bombing operations produced were sufficient to compensate for the political damage to the Federal cause resulting from inaccurate bombing which caused the death of innocent civilians. The question of extending the role of observers has been raised in the House. I discussed with General Gowon—as I would have hoped to discuss with Colonel Ojukwu—the possibility of extending to the results of aerial bombing the observer system now operating in Federally controlled areas. There are, however, great difficulties in getting an effective system of observation of bombing operations and when I met the team of international observers they emphasised these difficulties.

I made clear to General Gowon that the bombing issue as a whole might have to be raised again.

For the rest, the observers when I met them stated that they felt their work to be a success and worthwhile. They drew attention to their regular and unanimous reports confirming that they had found no evidence whatsoever to support allegations of genocide, or, after a few early and localised cases of individual indiscipline, of reprisals against the inhabitants of the areas where the federal advance had taken place.

On questions of relief and rehabilitation I had, in addition to my own meetings with members of the various relief agencies, as well as with a fully representative group from the Christian Churches of Nigeria, the advantage of a series of reports from Lord Hunt, who accompanied me on my visit in order to follow up the work he did as a special representative on relief questions last summer. Besides meeting Federal and State Commissioners and officials, he devoted as much time as possible to seeing the work in the field, in the three areas we visited which had been the scene of heavy fighting, and to discussing the work on the spot with international and British relief workers and doctors.

I visited, briefly, three relief and rehabilitation centres—one of them 100 percent Ibo—in three different states and saw the fine work being done, not least the proud achievements of young British volunteer workers, men and women, working in arduous circumstances and in very difficult climatic conditions. There is still a need in these areas for supplementary food rations for displaced persons, but both Nigerian and international agencies are now placing more emphasis on rehabilitation and on the need to get displaced persons and others robbed of their livelihood back to work. This will mean more concentration on the supply of the tools of production—farming, fishing and simple manufacturing—and on the supply of the equipment needed for education and other social services. In the spending of the money allocated by our own Government, the question of changing priorities will be constantly watched.

But in the area at present controlled by Colonel Ojukwu the first emphasis will have to be on food and medical supplies, and a rotating stock is being built up in Federally-held areas, ready for immediate use following a settlement or cease-fire. And, still more urgent is the need to get supplies in now. The alternative routes proposed by the Nigerian Government and international agencies were examined in detail by Lord Hunt, and this is one of the questions I would have wished to discuss as a matter of urgency with Colonel Ojukwu.

Sir, I should inform the House of the attempt to arrange a meeting with him. Before I left London messages had reached me through reliable channels indicating his willingness to meet me. During my discussions with them in Lagos, the Federal Government told me that they had no objection in principle. Accordingly on Sunday afternoon, I sent a message through Colonel Ojukwu's London representative proposing that such a meeting should take place early this week, and indicating no less than ten possible meeting places. This invitation was repeated in further messages on Monday and Tuesday indicating my willingness to fly back from Addis Ababa to West Africa for a meeting today.

I should perhaps make clear again that Colonel Ojukwu's representative had been told before I left London that I would not visit Biafra. Indeed alternative meeting places were being discussed before I left.

I very much regret that Colonel Ojukwu in the event felt unable to accept my invitation. There was much to discuss.

Finally, Mr. Speaker, as the House knows, I went on from Nigeria to Addis Ababa for meetings with His Imperial Majesty the Emperor. My delegation was received by him with the warmth and deep courtesy which marks all his dealings with representatives of this country.

In our discussions I gave him full details of the Lagos talks and of my impressions. He gave me a comprehensive account of all his attempts on behalf of the O.A.U. to mediate between the parties to the fighting, and of his marathon effort to reach agreement on the entry of relief supplies to the affected areas.

We analysed all these problems and I can tell the House that there is a full identity of view between her Majesty's Government and the Emperor on this analysis. The O.A.U. Consultative Committee, at its Monrovia meeting later this month, will be discussing the next steps in the Nigerian situation.

I also had a useful and lengthy talk with the Secretary-General and senior officials of the O.A.U.

Sir, while in Nigeria, I took every opportunity to ensure that the Federal Government and its representatives, as well as others I met, were made fully aware of the deep anxieties which have been expressed in the House. Having now seen something of the Nigerian tragedy at first hand, I am more determined than ever that Her Majesty's Government should make every appropriate effort to help those seeking to bring peace to this war-torn land.

[1] *Statement made in the House of Commons, 2 April 1969.*

200.
Awolowo Repeats his Political Testimony[1]

Since it is the vogue with some Nigerian political analysts and commentators to see my political aspirations at work in practically every public issue, and

2 B

to construe my public conduct and pronouncements on the basis of supposi-
tions and hypotheses which are not at all in accord with such aspirations, I
would like to take this opportunity to disclose some of these aspirations.

First: I am irrevocably committed to federal politics, no matter what the
constitutional structure of the Federation is. On March 15, 1957, I declared my
intention to leave regional politics for good. I stand, as hitherto, inflexibly by
this declaration, today and for the rest of my life.

I want to make it abundantly clear that I nurse no secret ambition to rule
the Western State, as it is at present, or as may be enlarged by future constitutional arrangements.

I am, by nature, too proud to descend from the pedestal of being the first
premier of the Western Region, which embraced practically the whole of the
present Western, Mid-Western and Lagos States, to the lower level of being
the premier or governor of the present Western State, or of an enlarged
Western State which, under my formula, embraces all those, in the present
Western State, Kwara State, and Mid-Western State, who speak Yoruba as
their mother tongue.

I have, since 1959, burnt my boat as an aspiring ruler of any constituent
state in the Federation of Nigeria. I am not looking back; and I have no
cause to regret my action.

Second: Even at the federal level, I have no desire whatsoever, and I
certainly cannot be tempted or induced to develop one, to head, or participate
in, an unelected or even an electoral college—elected civil administration in a
military or any setting.

At the moment, I am participating in the activities of the Federal Military
Government because I have been invited, and I also think it is right. so to do.

I had once declared, and I still stand by the declaration, that, if by any
acts of commission or omission the Eastern Region (now the East Central
State) was 'allowed to secede or opt out of Nigeria, then the Western Region
and Lagos must also stay out of the Federation.'

Furthermore, the Commander-in-Chief and my other colleagues know the
view I hold very strongly that, in any negotiation for peace, no concession
should be given to the Ibos which we are not prepared to extend to each of the
other ethnic groups in the Federation.

I am, therefore, obliged, morally and for the purpose of keeping Nigeria
united, to take part, as fully as I can, in any measure designed, in particular,
to keep the Ibos as a constituent ethnic unit in the Federation of Nigeria,
enjoying equal and identical status and benefits with other ethnic units, and,
in general, to preserve Nigeria as an economic and political entity.

Third: I have no intention whatsoever to participate, as a member, in the
deliberations of the Constituent Assembly, whenever it is set up, unless its
members are duly elected throughout the country, on a franchise based on
universal adult suffrage.

A Constituent Assembly whose members are nominated or appointed by a
government functionary, however well-intentioned and whatever his rank,
would be unrepresentative and its deliberations are more likely than not to
come to grief like those of the Ad Hoc Conference.

Fourth: It is my unshakable and irrevocable resolve [not: *omitted from
original*] to participate in any governmental activities after the return of

civil political life, unless: general elections are held throughout the country on the basis of universal adult suffrage; and the first general elections are organised, conducted, and supervised by an Electoral Commission, which is not only independent, but is seen to be so.

I will certainly not participate in any election in which the basis for franchise differs in one part of the country from the rest, and the conditions for unimpeded campaign and canvassing for votes throughout the country and for free and fair voting, are denied or not sufficiently demonstrated before the commencement of electioneering activities.

Fifth: I am quite satisfied in my own mind that, whether I am in government or not, I now, by the Grace of God, occupy a position whereby my thoughts and ideas are bound to have, now and for a long time to come, profound, pervasive, and persuasive influence, and impact on the affairs of the country. . . .

The only reason why I aspire, and will continue until I am 75, to aspire to participate effectively in government activities, is that, by such participation, it would be possible for me to translate my thoughts and ideas into realities much more quickly than would otherwise be the case.

So, if, on the return of civilian rule, I am in government, well and good. If not, I will mount a most vigorous campaign to the end that those who are in power should give very serious, sincere, and favourable consideration to what I believe should be done to cater to and advance, the welfare and the best interests of the masses of our people.

Fortunately in this connection, the country has reached a stage of enlightenment and articulation under which it is not going to be easy, at all, for any ruler or group of rulers in Nigeria to silence the voice of reason and progress which, under God, many right-thinking people and I claim to typify.

[1] *Letter to* Sunday Times (*Lagos*), *30 March 1969.*

201.
Communiqué from the O.A.U. Consultative Committee on Nigeria[1]

Upon the request of the Consultative Committee of the O.A.U. on Nigeria the two parties to the civil war accept, in the supreme interest of Africa, a united Nigeria which ensures all forms of security and guarantee of equality of rights and privileges to all its citizens.

Within the context of this agreement the two parties accept an immediate cessation of the fighting and the opening without delay of peace negotiations.

The Consultative Committee of the O.A.U. on Nigeria offers its good offices in order to facilitate these negotiations.

The Consultative Committee noted with satisfaction that the Federal Government of Nigeria accepted the proposals. The committee regrets that the representative of Colonel Ojukwu did not accept the proposals.

The Consultative Committee again solemnly appeals to the leaders of the

secession and all their supporters to accept and implement the declaration so
that reconciliation, peace and unity may be restored to Nigeria.

[1] *Issued in Monrovia, 20 April 1969 (Nigeria House press release).*

202.
Ojukwu: the Ahiara Declaration[1]

Today, as I look back over our two years as a sovereign and independent
nation, I am over-whelmed with the feeling of pride and satisfaction in our
performance and achievement as a people. Our indomitable will, our courage,
our endurance of the severest privations, our resourcefulness and inventive-
ness in the face of tremendous odds and dangers, have become proverbial in a
world so bereft of heroism, and have become a source of frustration to Nigeria
and her foreign masters. For this and for the many miracles of our time, let
us give thanks to Almighty God. . . .

Fellow countrymen and women, for nearly two years we have been engaged in a war which threatens our people with total destruction. Our enemy
has been unrelenting in his fury and has fought our defenceless people with a
vast array of military hardware of a sophistication unknown to Africa. For
two years we have withstood his assaults with nothing other than our stout
hearts and bare hands. We have frustrated his diabolical intentions and have
beaten his wicked mentors in their calculations and innovations. Shamelessly,
our enemy has moved from deadline to deadline, seeking excuses justifying
their failures to an ever credulous world. Today, I am happy and proud to
report that, all the odds notwithstanding, the enemy, at great cost in lives
and equipment, is not near to his avowed objective.

Proud Biafrans, I have kept by promise. Diplomatically, our friends have
increased and have remained steadfast to our cause: and, despite the rantings
of our detractors, indications are that their support will continue. . . .
Fellow countrymen and women, the signs are auspicious, the future fills us
with less foreboding. I am confident, with the initiative in war now in our
own hands, that we have turned the last bend in our race to self-realisation
and are now set on the home straight in this our struggle. We must not flag.
The tape is in sight. What we need is a final burst of speed to breast the tape
and secure the victory which will ensure for us for all time, glory and honour,
peace and progesss.

Fellow compatriots, today, being our Thanksgiving Day, it is most appropriate that we pause awhile to take stock, to consider our past, our successes
notwithstanding, to consider our future, our aspirations and our fears. . . .

Fellow Biafrans, I have for a long time thought about this our predicament
—the attitude of the civilized world to this our conflict. The more I think
about it the more I am convinced that our disability is racial. The root cause
of our problem lies in the fact that we are black. If all the things that have
happened to us had happened to another people who are not black, if other
people who are not black had reacted in the way our people have reacted
these two long years, the world's reponse would surely have been different.[2]

In 1966, some 50,000 of us were slaughtered like cattle in Nigeria. In the
course of this war, well over one million of us have been killed: yet the world

is unimpressed and looks on in indifference. Last year, some blood-thirsty Nigerian troops for sport murdered the entire male population of a village. All the world did was to indulge in an academic argument whether the number was in hundreds or in thousands.

Today, because a handful of white men collaborating with the enemy, fighting side by side with the enemy, were caught by our gallant troops, the entire world threatens to stop. For 18 white men Europe is aroused. What have they said about our millions? Eighteen white men assisting the crime of genocide: what does Europe say about our murdered innocents? Have we not died enough?

How many Black dead make a missing white? Mathematicians, please answer me. Is it infinity?

Take another example. For two years we have been subjected to a total blockade. We all know how bitter, bloody and protracted the First and Second World Wars were. At no stage in those wars did the white belligerents carry out a total blockade of their fellow whites. In each case where a blockade was imposed, allowance was made for certain basic necessities of life in the interest of women, children and other non-combatants. Ours is the only example in recent history where a whole people have been so treated.

What is it that makes our case different? Do we not have women, children and other non-combatants? Does the fact that they are black women, black children and black non-combatants make such a world of difference? Nigeria embarked on a crime of genocide against our people by first mounting a total blockade against Biafra.

To cover up their designs and deceive the black world, the white powers supporting Nigeria blame Biafrans for the continuation of the blockade and for the starvation and suffering which that entails. They uphold Nigerian proposals on relief which in any case they helped to formulate, as being 'conciliatory' or 'satisfactory'.

Knowing that these proposals would give Nigeria further military advantage, and compromise the basic cause for which we have struggled for two years, they turn round to condemn us for rejecting them. They accept the total blockade against us as a legitimate weapon of war because it suits them and because we are black. Had we been white the inhuman and cruel blockade would long have been lifted. . . . That Nigeria has received complete support from Britain should surprise no one. For Britain is a country whose history is replete with instances of genocide.

In my address to you on the occasion of the first anniversary of our independence,[3] I touched on a number of issues relevant to our struggle and to our hope for a prosperous, just and happy society. I talked to you of the background to our struggle and on the visions and values which inspired us to found our own state.

On this occasion of our second anniversary, I shall go further in the examination of the meaning and import of our revolution by discussing the wider issues involved and the character and structure of the new society we are determined and committed to build. Our enemies and their foreign sponsors have deliberately sought by false and ill-motivated propaganda to cloud the real issues which caused and still determine the course and character of our struggle.

They have sought in various ways to dismiss our struggle as a tribal conflict. They have attributed it to the mad adventurism of a fictitious power-seeking clique anxious to carve out an empire to rule, dominate and exploit. But they have failed. Our cause is transparently just and no amount of propaganda can detract from it.

Our struggle has far-reaching significance. It is the latest recrudescence in our time of the age-old struggle of the black man for his full stature as man. We are the latest victims of a wicked collusion between the three traditional scourges of the black men—racism, arab-muslim expansionism and white economic imperialism. Playing a subsidiary role is Bolshevik Russia seeking for a place in the African sun. Our struggle is a total and vehement rejection of all those evils which blighted Nigeria, evils which were bound to lead to the disintegration of that ill-fated federation. Our struggle is not mere resistance —that would be purely negative. It is a positive commitment to build a healthy, dynamic and progressive state, such as would be the pride of black men the world over.

For this reason, our struggle is a movement against racial prejudice, in particular against that tendency to regard the black man as culturally, morally, spiritually, intellectually, and physically inferior to the other two major races of the world—the yellow and the white races. This belief in the innate inferiority of the Negro and that his proper place in the world is that of the servant of the other races, has from early days coloured the attitude of the outside world to Negro problems. It still does today. . . .

It is this myth about the Negro that still conditions the thinking and attitude of most white governments on all issues concerning black Africa and the black man: it explains the double standards which they apply to present-day world problems: it explains their stand on the whole question of independence and basic human rights for the black peoples of the world. These myths explain the stand of many of the world governments and organisations on our present struggle.

Our disagreement with the Nigerians arose in part from a conflict between two diametrically opposed conceptions of the end and purpose of the modern African state. It was, and still is, our firm conviction that a modern Negro African government worth the trust placed in it by the people, must build a progressive state that ensures the reign of social and economic justice, and of the rule of law. But the Nigerians, under the leadership of the Hausa-Fulani feudal aristocracy, preferred anarchy and injustice.

Since in the thinking of many white powers a good, progressive and efficient government is good only for whites, our view was considered dangerous and pernicious: a point of view which explains but does not justify the blind support which those powers have given to uphold the Nigerian ideal of a corrupt, decadent and putrefying society. To them genocide is an appropriate answer to any group of black people who have the temerity to attempt to evolve their own social system.

When the Nigerians violated our basic human rights and liberties, we decided reluctantly but bravely to found our own state, to exercise our inalienable right to self-determination as our only remaining hope for survival as a people. Yet because we are black, we are denied by the white powers the exercise of this right which they themselves have proclaimed as inalienable. In our struggle we have learnt that the right of self-determination is inalienable, but only to the white man. . . .

What do we find here in Negro Africa? The Federation of Nigeria is today as corrupt, as unprogressive and as oppressive and irreformable as the Ottoman empire was in eastern Europe over a century ago. And in contrast, the Nigerian Federation in the form it was constituted by the British cannot by any stretch of imagination be considered an African necessity. Yet we are being forced to sacrifice our very existence as a people to the integrity of that ramshackle creation that has no justification either in history or in the freely expressed wishes of the people.

What other reason for this can there be than the fact that we are black? . . . Because the black man is considered inferior and servile to the white, he must accept his political, social and economic system and ideologies ready made from Europe, America or the Soviet Union. Within the confines of his nation he must accept a federation or confederation or unitary government if federation or confederation or unitary government suits the interests of his white masters: he must accept inept and unimaginative leadership because the contrary would hurt the interests of the master race: he must accept economic exploitation by alien commercial firms and companies because the whites benefit from it. Beyond the confines of his state, he must accept regional and continental organisations which provide a front for the manipulation of the imperialist powers: organisations which are therefore unable to respond to African problems in a truly African manner. For Africans to show a true independence is to ask for anathemization and total liquidation.

The Biafran struggle is, on another plane, a resistance to the Arab-Muslim expansionism which has menaced and ravaged the African continent for twelve centuries. . . .

Our Biafran ancestors remained immune from the Islamic contagion. From the middle years of the last century Christianity was established in our land. In this way we came to be a predominantly Christian people. We came to stand out as a non-Muslim island in a raging Islamic sea. Throughout the period of the ill-fated Nigerian experiment, the Muslims hoped to infiltrate Biafra by peaceful means and quiet propaganda, but failed. Then the late Ahmadu Bello, the Sardauna of Sokoto tried, by political and economic blackmail and terrorism, to convert Biafrans settled in Northern Nigeria to Islam. His hope was that these Biafrans of dispersion would then carry Islam to Biafra, and by so doing give the religion political control of the area. The crises which agitated the so-called independent Nigeria from 1962 gave these aggressive proselytisers the chance to try converting us by force.

It is now evident why the fanatic Arab-Muslim states like Algeria, Egypt and the Sudan have come out openly and massively to support and aid Nigeria in her present war of genocide against us. These states see militant Arabism as a powerful instrument for attaining power in the world. Biafra is one of the few African states untainted by Islam. Therefore, to militant Arabism, Biafra is a stumbling block to their plan for controlling the whole continent. This control is fast becoming manifest in the Organisation of African Unity.

On the question of the Middle East, the Sudanese crisis, in the war between Nigeria and Biafra, militant Arabism has succeeded in imposing its point of view through blackmail and bluster. It has threatened African leaders and governments with inciting their Muslim minorities to rebellion if the governments adopted an independent line on these questions. In this way an O.A.U. that has not felt itself able to discuss the genocide in the Sudan and Biafra, an O.A.U. that has again and again advertised its ineptitude as a peace-maker, has rushed into open condemnation of Israel over the Middle East dispute. Indeed, in recent times, by its performance, the O.A.U. might well be an organisation of Arab unity.

Our struggle, in an even more fundamental sense, is the culmination of the confrontation between Negro nationalism and white imperialism. It is a movement designed to ensure the realization of man's full stature in Africa.

Ever since the 15th Century, the European world has treated the African continent as a field for exploitation. Their policies in Africa have for so long been determined to a very great extent by their greed for economic gain. For over three and half centuries, it suited them to transport and transplant millions of the flower of our manhood for the purpose of exploiting the Americas and the West Indies. They did so with no uneasiness of conscience. They justified this trade in men by reference to biblical passages violently torn out of context. . . . This brutal and unprecedented rape of a whole continent was a violent challenge to Negro self-respect. Not surprisingly, within half a century the theory and practice of empire ran into stiff opposition from Negro nationalism. In the face of the movement for Negro freedom the white imperialists changed their tactics. They decided to install puppet African administrations to create the illusion of political independence, while retaining the control of the economy. And this they quickly did between 1957 and 1965. The direct empire was transformed into an indirect empire, that regime of fraud and exploitation which African nationalists aptly describe as neo-colonialism.

Nigeria was a classic example of neo-colonialist state, and what is left of it, still is. The militant nationalism of the late forties and early fifties had caught the British imperialists unawares. They hurried to accommodate it by installing the ignorant, decadent and feudalistic Hausa-Fulani oligarchy in power. For the British, the credentials of the Hausa-Fulani were that not having emerged from the middle ages they knew nothing about the modern state and the powerful forces that now rule men's minds. Owing their position to the British, they were servile and submissive. The result was that while Nigerians lived in the illusion of independence, they were still in fact being ruled from Number 10 Downing Street. The British still enjoyed a stranglehold on their economy.

The crises which rocked Nigeria from the morrow of 'independence' were brought about by the efforts of progressive nationalists to achieve true independence for themselves and for posterity. For their part in this effort, Biafrans were stigmatised and singled out for extermination. In imperialist thinking, only phoney independence is good for blacks. The sponsorship of Nigeria by white imperialism has not been disinterested. They are only concerned with the preservation of that corrupt and rickety structure of a Nigeria in a perpetual state of powerlessness to check foreign exploitation. . . .

Fellow countrymen and women, we have seen in proper perspective the diabolical roles which the British Government and the foreign companies have played and are playing in our war with Nigeria. We now see why in spite of Britain's tottering economy Harold Wilson's Government insists on financing Nigeria's futile war against us. We see why the Shell-BP led the Nigerian hordes into Bonny, pays Biafran oil royalties to Nigeria, and provided the Nigerian army with all the help it needed for its attack on Port Harcourt. We see why the West African Conference readily and meekly co-operated with Gowon in the imposition of a total blockade against us. We see why the oil and trading companies in Nigeria still finance this war and why they risk the life and limb of their staff in the war zones.

And now, Bolshevik Russia. Russia is a late arrival in the race for world empire. Since the end of the second world war she has fought hard to gain a foothold in Africa, recognising, like the other imperialist powers before her, the strategic importance of Africa in the quest for world domination. She first tried to enter into alliance with African nationalism. Later, finding that African nationalism had been thwarted, at least temporarily, by the collusion between imperialism, and the decadent forces in Africa society, Russia quickly changed her strategy and identified herself with those very conservative forces which she had earlier denounced. Here she met with quick success. In North Africa and Egypt, Russian influence has taken firm root and is growing. With her success in Egypt and Algeria, Russia developed an even keener appetite for more territory in Africa, particularly the areas occupied by the Negroes. Her early efforts in the Congo and Ghana proved still-born. The Nigeria-Biafra conflict offered an opportunity for another beach-head in Africa.

It is not Russia's intention to make Nigeria a better place for Nigerians or indeed any other part of Africa a better place for Africans. Her interest is strategic. In her challenge to the United States and the western world, she needs vantage points in Africa. With her entrenched position in Northern Nigeria, the central Sudan of the historians and geographers, Russia is in a position to co-ordinate her strategy for West and North Africa. We are all familiar with the ancient and historic cultural, linguistic and religious links between North Africa and the Central Sudan. We know that the Hausa language is a lingua franca for over two-thirds of this area. We know how far afield a wandering Imam preaching Islam and Bolshevism can go. . . .

Fellow Biafrans, these are the evil and titanic forces with which we are engaged in a life and death struggle. These are the obstacles to the Negro's efforts to realise himself. These are the forces which the Biafran revolution must sweep aside to succeed. . . . We do not claim that the Biafran revolution is the first attempt in history by the Negro to assert his identity, to claim his right and proper place as a human being on a basic of equality with the white and yellow races. We are aware of the Negro's past and present efforts to prove his ability at home and abroad. We are familiar with his achievements in pre-history; we are familiar with his achievements in political organisations; we are familiar with his contributions to the world store of art and culture. The Negro's white oppressors are not unaware of all these. But in spite of their awareness they are not prepared to admit that the Negro is a man and a brother. . . .

In world context, this is Biafra—the plight of the black struggling to be man. From this derives our deep conviction that the Biafran revolution is not just a movement of Ibos, Ibibios, Ijaws, and Ogojas. It is a movement of true and patriotic Africans. It is African nationalism conscious of itself and fully aware of the powers with which it is contending. . . .

We have indeed come a long way. We were once Nigerians, today we are Biafrans. We are Biafrans because on May 30, 1967, we finally said 'no' to the evils and injustices in which Nigeria was steeped. Nigeria was made up of peoples and groups with very little in common. As everyone know, Biafrans were in the fore-front among those who tried to make Nigeria a nation. It is ironic that some ill-informed and mischievous people today will accuse us of breaking up a united African country. Only those who do not know the facts or deliberately ignore them can hold such an opinion. We know the facts because we were there and the things that happened, happened to us.

Nigeria was indeed a very wicked and corrupt country in spite of the glorious image given her in the European press. We know why Nigeria was given that image. It was her reward for serving the economic and political interests of her European masters. Nigeria is a stooge of Europe. Her independence was and is a lie. Even her Prime Minister was a Knight of the British Empire; but worse than her total subservience to foreign political and economic interests, Nigeria committed many crimes against her nationals which in the end made complete nonsense of her claim to unity. Nigeria persecuted and slaughtered her minorities; Nigerian justice was a farce; her elections, her politics—her everything—was corrupt. Qualification, merit and experience were discounted in public service. In one area of Nigeria, for instance, they preferred to turn a nurse who had worked for five years into a doctor rather than employ a qualified doctor from another part of Nigeria. Barely literate clerks were made Permanent Secretaries. A university Vice-Chancellor was sacked because he belonged to the wrong tribe. Bribery, corruption and nepotism were so widespread that people began to wonder openly whether any country in the world could compare with Nigeria in corruption and abuse of power. All the modern institutions—the legislature, the civil service, the army, the police, the judiciary, the universities, the trade unions and the organs of mass information—were devalued and made the tools of corrupt political power. There was complete neglect and impoverishment of the people. Whatever prosperity there was, was deceptive. There was despair in many hearts, and the number of suicides was growing every day. The farmers were very hard-hit. Their standards of living had fallen steeply. The soil was perishing from over-farming and lack of scientific husbandry. The towns, like the soil, were waste-lands into which people put in too much exertion for too little reward. There were crime waves and people lived in fear of their lives. Business speculation, rack-renting, worship of money and sharp practices left a few people extremely rich at the expense of the many, and those few flaunted their wealth before the many and talked about sharing the national cake. Foreign interests did roaring business spreading consumer goods and wares among a people who had not developed a habit of thrift and who fell prey to lying advertisements. Inequality of the sexes was actively promoted in Nigeria. Rather than aspire to equality with men, women were encouraged to accept the status of inferiority and to become the mistresses of successful politicians and business executives, or they were married off at the age of fourteen as the fifteenth wives of the new rich. That was the glorious Nigeria, the mythical Nigeria, celebrated in the European press.

Then worst of all came the genocide in which over 50,000 of our kith and kin were slaughtered in cold blood all over Nigeria and nobody asked questions; nobody showed regret; nobody showed remorse. Thus, Nigeria had become a jungle with no safety, no justice and no hope for our people. We decided then to found a new place, a human habitation away from the Nigerian jungle. That was the origin of our revolution.

From the moment we assumed the illustrious name of the ancient kingdom of Biafra, we were rediscovering the original independence of a great African people. We accepted by this revolutionary act the glory, as well as the sacrifice, of true independence and freedom. We knew that we had challenged the many forces and interests which had conspired to keep Africa and the black race in subjection for ever. We knew they were going to be ruthless and implacable in defence of their age-old imposition on us and exploitation of our people. But we were prepared, and remain prepared, to pay any price for our freedom and dignity. . . .

Our revolution is a historic opportunity given to us to establish a just society; to revive the dignity of our people at home and the dignity of the black man in the world. We realize that in order to achieve those ends we must remove those weaknesses in our institutions and organisations and those disabilities in foreign relations which have tended to degrade this dignity. This means that we must reject Nigerianism in all its guises. . . .

The Biafran revolution is the people's revolution. 'Who are the people?' you ask. The farmer, the trader, the clerk, the businessman, the housewife, the student, the civil servant, the soldier—you and I are the people. Is there anyone here who is not of the people? Is there anyone here afraid of the people—anyone suspicious of the people? Is there anyone despising the people? Such a man has no place in our revolution. If he is a leader, he has no right to leadership, because all power, all sovereignty, belongs to the people. In Biafra the people are supreme; the people are master; the leader is the servant. You see, you make a mistake when you greet me with shouts of 'power, power'. I am not power—you are. My name is Emeka, I am your servant, that is all.

Fellow countrymen, we pride ourselves on our honesty. Let us admit to ourselves that when we left Nigeria, some of us did not shake off every particle of Nigerianism. We say that Nigerians are corrupt and take bribes; but here in our country we have among us some members of the Police and the Judiciary who are corrupt and who 'eat' bribes. We accuse Nigerians of inordinate love of money, ostentatious living and irresponsibility; but here, even while we are engaged in a war of national survival, even while the very life of our nation hangs in the balance, we see some public servants who throw huge parties to entertain their friends; who kill cows to christen their babies. We have members of the armed forces who carry on 'attack' trade instead of fighting the enemy. We have traders who hoard essential goods and inflate prices, thereby increasing the people's hardship. We have 'money-mongers' who aspire to build on hundreds of plots on land as yet unreclaimed from the enemy; who plan to buy scores of lorries and buses and to become agents for those very foreign businessmen who have brought their country to grief.

We have some civil servants who think of themselves as masters rather than servants of the people. We see doctors who stay idle in their villages while their countrymen and women suffer and die.

When we see all these things, they remind us that not every Biafran has yet absorbed the spirit of the revolution. They tell us that we still have among us a number of people whose attitudes and outlooks are Nigerian. It is clear that if our revolution is to succeed, we must reclaim these wayward Biafrans. We must Biafranize them. We must prepare all our people for the glorious roles which await them in the revolution. If, after we shall have tried to re-claim them, and have failed, then they must be swept aside. The people's revolution must stride ahead and, like a battering ram, clear all obstacles in its path. Fortunately, the vast majority of Biafrans are prepared for these roles.

When we think of our revolution, therefore, we think about these things. We think about our ancient heritage; we think about the challenge of today and the promise of the future. We think about the changes which are taking place at this very moment in our personal lives and in our society. We see Biafrans from different parts of the country living together, working together, suffering together and pursuing together a common cause. . . . We see our ordinary men and women—the people—pursuing, in their different but essential ways, the great task of our national survival. We see every sign that this struggle is purifying and elevating the masses of our people. . . . We see many bad social habits and attitudes beginning to change. Above all, we find a universal desire among our people not only to remain free and independent but also to create a new and better order or society for the benefit of all.

In the last five or six months, I have devised one additonal way of learning at first hand how the ordinary men and women of our country see the revolu-tion. I have established a practice of meeting every Wednesday with a different cross-section of our people, to discuss the problems of the revolution. These meetings have brought home to me the great desire for change among the generality of our people. I have heard a number of criticisms and com-plaints by people against certain things. I have also noticed groups forming themselves and trying to put right some of the ills of society. All this indicates both that there is a change in progress, and need for more change. Thus, the Biafran revolution is not dreamt up by an elite. It is the will of the people. The people want it. Their immediate concern is to defeat the Nigerian aggressor and so safeguard the Biafran revolution.

I stand before you tonight not to launch the Biafran revolution, because it is already in existence. It came into being two years ago when we proclaimed to all the world that we had finally extricated ourselves from the sea of mud that was—is—Nigeria. I stand before you to proclaim formally the commit-ment of the Biafran state to the principles of the revolution and to enunciate those principles. Some people are frightened when they hear the word revolution. They say: 'revolution? Heaven help us, it is too dangerous. It means mobs rushing around destroying property, killing people and upsetting everything.' But these people do not understand the real meaning of revolu-tion. For us, a revolution is a change—a quick change—a change for the better. Every society is changing all the time. It is changing for the better or for the worse. It is either moving forward or moving backwards; it cannot stand absolutely still. A revolution is a forward movement. It is a rapid forward movement which improves a people's standard of living and their material circumstance and purifies and raises their moral tone. It transforms for the better those institutions which are still relevant, and discards those which stand in the way of progress.

The Biafran revolution believes in the sanctity of human life and the dignity of the human person. The Biafran sees the wilful and wanton destruction of human life not only as a grave crime but as an abominable sin. In our society every human life is holy, every individual person counts. No Biafran wants to be taken for granted or ignored, neither does he ignore or take others for granted. This explains why such degrading practices as begging for alms were unknown in Biafran society. Therefore, all forms of disabilities and inequalities which reduce the dignity of the individual or destroy his sense of person have no place in the new Biafran social order. The Biafran revolution upholds the dignity of man. The Biafran revolution stands firmly against genocide, against any attempt to destroy a people, its security, its right to life, property and progress. Any attempt to deprive a community of its identity is abhorrent to the Biafran people. Having ourselves suffered genocide, we are all the more determined to take a clear stand now and at all times against this crime.

The new Biafran social order places a high premium on love, patriotism and devotion to the fatherland. Every true Biafran must love Biafra, must have faith in Biafra and its people, and must strive for its greater unity. He must find his salvation here in Biafra. He must be prepared to work for Biafra, to die for Biafra. He must be prepared to defend the sovereignty of Biafra wherever and by whomsoever it is challenged. Biafran patriots do all this already, and Biafra expects all her sons and daughters of today and tomorrow, to emulate their noble example. Diplomats who treat insults to the fatherland and the leadership of our struggle with levity are not patriotic. That young man who sneaks about the village, avoiding service in his country's armed forces is unpatriotic; that young, able-bodied school teacher who prefers to distribute relief when he should be fighting his country's war, is not only unpatriotic but is doing a woman's work. Those who help these loafers to dodge their civic duties should henceforth re-examine themselves.

All Biafrans are brothers and sisters bound together by ties of geography, trade, inter-marriage, and culture and by their common misfortune in Nigeria and their present experience of the armed struggle. Biafrans are even more united by the desire to create a new and better order of society which will satisfy their needs and aspirations. Therefore, there is no justification for anyone to introduce into the Biafran fatherland divisions based on ethnic origin, sex or religion. To do so would be unpatriotic. Every true Biafran must know and demand his civic rights. Furthermore, he must recognize the rights of other Biafrans and be prepared to defend them when necessary. So often people complain that they have been ill-treated by the police or some other public servant. But the truth very often is that we allow ourselves to be bullied because we are not man enough to demand and stand up for our rights, and that fellow citizens around do not assist us when we do demand our rights. In the new Biafran social order sovereignty and power belong to the people. Those who exercise power do so on behalf of the people. Those who govern must not tyrannize the people. They carry a sacred trust of the people and must use their authority strictly in accordance with the will of the people. The true test of success in public life is that the people—who are the real masters—are contented and happy. The rulers must satisfy the people at all times.

But it is no use saying that power belongs to the people unless we are prepared to make it work in practice. Even in the old political days, the oppressors of the people were among those who shouted loudest that power belonged to the people. The Biafran revolution will constantly and honestly seek methods of making this concept a fact rather than a pious hope. Where, therefore, a ministry or department runs inefficiently or improperly, its head must accept personal responsibility for such a situation and, depending on the gravity of the failure, must resign or be removed. And where he is proved to have misused his position of trust to enrich himself, the principle of public accountability requires that he be punished severely and his ill-gotten gains taken from him.

Those who aspire to lead must bear in mind the fact that they are servants and, as such, cannot ever be greater than the people, their masters. Every leader in the Biafran revolution is the embodiment of the ideals of the revolution. Part of his role as leader is to keep the revolutionary spirit alive, to be a friend of the people and protector of their evolution. He should have right judgement both of people and of situations and the ability to attract to himself the right kind of lieutenants who can best further the interests of the people and of the revolution. The leader must not only say but always demonstrate that the power he exercises is derived from the people. Therefore, like every other Biafran public servant, he is accountable to the people for the use he makes of their mandates. He must get out when the people tell him to get out. The more power the leader is given by the people, then less is his personal freedom and the greater his responsibility for the good of the people. He should never allow his high office to separate him from the people. He must be fanatical for their welfare.

A leader in the Biafran revolution must at all times stand for justice in dealing with the people. He should be the symbol of justice, which is the supreme guarantee of good government. He should be ready, if need be, to lay down his life in pursuit of this ideal. He must have physical and moral courage and must be able to inspire the people out of despondency. He should never strive towards the perpetuation of his office or devise means to cling to office beyond the clear mandate of the people. He should resist the temptation to erect memorials to himself in his life-time, to have his head embossed on the coin, name streets and institutions after himself or convert government into a family business. A leader who serves his people well will be enshrined in their hearts and minds. This is all the reward he can expect in his life-time. He will be to the people the symbol of excellence, the quintessence of the revolution. He will be Biafran.

One of the corner-stones of the Biafran revolution is social justice. We believe that there should be equal opportunity for all, that appreciation and just reward should be given for honest work and that society should show concern and special care for the weak and infirm. Our people reject all forms of social inequalities and disabilities and all class and sectional privileges.

Biafrans believe that society should treat all its members with impartiality and fairness. Therefore, the Biafran state must not apportion special privileges or favours to some citizens and deny them to others. For example, how can we talk of social justice in a situation where a highly-paid public servant gets his salt free and poor housewives in the village pay five pounds for a cup? The state should not create a situation favourable to the exploitation of some citizens by others. The State is the father of all, the source of security, the reliable agent which helps all to realize their legitimate hopes and aspirations. Without social justice, harmony and stability within society disappear and antagonisms between various sections of the community take their place. Our revolution will uphold social justice at all times. The Biafran state will be the fountain of justice.

In the new Biafra, all property belongs to the community. Every individual must consider all he has, whether in talent or material wealth, as belonging to the community for which he holds it in trust. This principle does not mean the abolition of personal property but it implies that the state, acting on behalf of the community, can intervene in the disposition of property to the greater advantage of all. Over-acquisitiveness or the inordinate desire to amass wealth is a factor liable to threaten social stability, especially in an under-developed society in which there are not enough material goods to go round. This creates lop-sided development, breeds antagonisms between the 'haves' and the 'have-nots' and undermines the peace and unity of the people.

While the Biafran revolution will foster private economic enterprise and initiative, it should remain constantly alive to the dangers of some citizens accumulating large private fortunes. Property-grabbing, if unchecked by the state, will set the pattern of behaviour for the whole society which begins to attach undue value to money and property. Thus a wealthy man, even if he is known to be a crook, is accorded greater respect than an honest citizen who is not so well off. A society where this happens is doomed to rot and decay. Moreover, the danger is always there of a small group of powerful property-owners using their influence to deflect the state from performing its duties to the citizens as a whole and thereby destroying the democratic basis of society. This happens in many countries and it is one of the duties of our revolution to prevent its occurrence in Biafra.

Finally, the Biafran revolution will create possibilities for citizens with talent in business, administration, management and technology, to fulfil themselves and receive due appreciation and reward in the service of the state, as has indeed happened in our total mobilization to prosecute the present war. The Biafran revolution is committed to creating a society not torn by class consciousness and class antagonisms. Biafran society is traditionally egalitarian. The possibility for social mobility is always presented in our society. The new Biafran social order rejects all rigid classifications of society. Anyone with imagination, anyone with integrity, anyone who works hard, can rise to any height. Thus, the son of a truck pusher can become the Head of State of Biafra. The Biafran revolution will provide opportunities for Biafrans to aspire and to achieve their legitimate desires. Those who find themselves below at any particular moment must have the opportunity to rise to the top.

Our new society is open and progressive. The people of Biafra have always striven to achieve a workable balance between the claims of tradition and the demand for change and betterment. We are adaptable because as a people we are convinced that in the world 'no condition is permanent' and we believe that human effort and will are necessary to bring about changes and improvements in the condition of the individual and of society. The Biafran would, thus, make the effort to improve his lot and the material well-being of his community. He has the will to transform his society into a modern progressive community. In this process of rapid transformation he will retain and cherish the best elements of his culture, drawing sustenance as well as moral and psychological stability from them. But being a Biafran he will never be afraid to adapt what needs to be adapted or change what has to be changed. The Biafran revolution will continue to discover and develop local talent and to use progressive foreign ideas and skills so long as they do not destroy the identity of our culture or detract from the sovereignty of our fatherland. The Biafran revolution will also ensure through education that the positive aspects of Biafran traditional culture, especially those which are likely to be swamped out of existence by introduced foreign influences, are conserved. The undiscriminating absorption of new ideas and attitudes will be discouraged. Biafrans can, in the final analysis, only validly express their nation's personality and enhance their corporate identity through Biafran culture, through Biafran art and literature, music, dancing and drama, and through the peculiar gestures and social habits which distinguish them from all other people.

Those then are the main principles of our revolution. They are not abstract formulations but arise out of the traditional background and the present temper of our people. They grow out of our native soil and are the product of our peculiar climate. They belong to us. If anyone here doubts the validity of these principles let him go out into the streets and into the villages, let him ask the ordinary Biafran. Let him go to the army, ask the rank and file and he will find, as I have found, that they have very clear ideas about the kind of society we should build here. They will not put them in the same words I have used tonight but the meaning will be the same. From today, let no Biafran pretend that he or she does not know the main-spring of our national action, let him or her not plead ignorance when found indulging in un-Biafran activities. The principles of our revolution are hereby clearly set out for everyone to see. They are now the property of every Biafran and the instrument for interpreting our national life. But principles are principles. They can only be transformed into reality through the institutions of society, otherwise they remain inert and useless. It is my firm conviction that in the Biafran revolution principles and practice will go hand in hand. It is my duty and the duty of all of you to bring this about.

Looking at the institutions of our society, the very vehicles for carrying out our revolutionary principles, what do you find? We find old, jaded and rusty machines creaking along most inefficiently and delaying the people's progress and the progress of the revolution. The problem of our institutions is partly that they were designed by other people, in other times and for other purposes. Their most fundamental weakness is that they came into being during the colonial period when the relationship between the colonial administrators and the people was that of master and servant. Our public servants as heirs of the colonial masters are apt to treat the people today with arrogance and condescension. In the new Biafran social order we say that power belongs to the people, but this central principle tends to elude many of the public servants who continue to behave in a manner which shows that they consider themselves master and the people their servants. The message of the revolution has tended to fly over their heads. Let them beware, the revolution gathering momentum like a flood washes clear all impediments on its way. . . .

Our experience during this struggle has brought home to us the need for versatility. Many of our citizens have found themselves having to do emergency duties different from their normal peace-time jobs. In the years after the present armed conflict, we may find that in the defence of the revolution the general state of mobilisation and alertness will remain. One of the ways of preparing ourselves for this emergency will be to ensure that a citizen will be trained in two jobs—his normal peace-time occupation and a different skill which will be called into play during a national emergency. Thus, for example, a clerk may be given training to enable him to operate as an ambulance-driver during the emergency or a university lecturer as a post-master. We realize here that the problem is more than that of providing narrow, technical training. It has to do with re-orientation of attitudes. It has to do with the cultivation of the right kind of civic virtues and loyalty to Biafra. We all stand in need of this.

It is quite clear that to attain the goals of the Biafran revolution we will require extensive political and civic education of our people. To this effect, we will, in the near future, set up a National Orientation College (N.O.C.) which will undertake the needful function of formally inculcating the Biafran ideology and the principles of the revolution. We will also pursue this vital task of education through seminars, mass rallies, formal and informal addresses by the leaders and standard-bearers of the revolution. All Biafrans who are going to play a role in the promotion of the revolution, especially those who are going to operate the institutions of the new society, must first of all expose themselves to the ideology of the revolution.

The full realisation of the Biafran ideology and the promise of the Biafran revolution will have the important effect of drawing the people of Biafra into close unity with the Biafran state. The Biafran state and the Biafran people thus become one. The people jealously defend and protect the integrity of the state. The state guarantees the people certain basic rights and welfare. In this third year of our independence, we restate these basic rights and welfare obligations which the revolutionary state of Biafra guarantees to the people.

In the field of employment and labour, the Biafran revolution guarantees every able Biafran the right to work. All those who are lazy or refuse to work forfeit their right to this guarantee. 'He who does not work should not eat' is an important principle in Biafra.

Our revolution provides equal opportunities for employment and labour for all Biafrans irrespective of sex. For equal output a woman must receive the same remuneration as a man.

Our revolutionary Biafran state will guarantee a rational system of

2 c

remuneration of labour. Merit and output shall be the criteria for reward in labour. 'To each according to his ability, to each ability according to its product' shall be our motto in Biafra.

Our revolution guarantees security for workers who have been incapacitated by physical injury or disease. It will be the duty of the Biafran state to raise the standard of living of the Biafran people, to provide them with improved living conditions and to afford them modern amenities that enhance their human dignity and self-esteem. We recognize at all times the great contributions made by the farmer, the craftsmen and other toilers of the revolution to our national progress. It will be a cardinal point of our economic policy to keep their welfare constantly in view. The Biafran revolution will promulgate a workers' charter which will codify and establish workers' rights.

The maintenance of the health and physical well-being of the Biafran citizen must be the concern and the responsibility of the state. The revolutionary Biafran state will at all times strive to provide medical service for all its citizens in accordance with the resources available to it, it will wage a continuous struggle against epidemic and endemic diseases, and will promote among the people knowledge of hygienic living. It will develop social and preventive medicine, set up sanatoriums for incurable and infectious diseases and mental cases, and a net-work of maternity homes for ante and post-natal care of Biafran mothers. Furthermore, Biafra will set great store by the purity of the air which its people breathe. We have a right to live in a clean, pollution-free atmosphere.

Our revolution recognises the vital importance of the mental and emotional needs of the Biafran people. To this end, the Biafran state will pay great attention to education, culture and the arts. We shall aim at elevating our cultural institutions and promoting educational reforms which will foster a sense of national and racial pride among our people and discourage ideas which inspire a feeling of inferiority and dependence on foreigners. It will be the prime duty of the revolutionary Biafran state to eradicate illiteracy from our society, to guarantee free education to all Biafran children to a stage limited only by existing resources. Our nation will encourage the training of scientists, technicians and skilled workers needed for quick industrialisation and the modernisation of our agriculture. We will ensure the development of higher education and technological training for our people, encourage our intellectuals, writers, artists and scientists to research, create and invent in the service of the state and the people. We must prepare our people to contribute significantly to knowledge and world culture.

Finally, the present armed struggle, in which many of our countrymen and women have distinguished themselves and made numerous sacrifices in defence of the fatherland and the revolution, has imposed on the state of Biafra extra responsibility for the welfare of its people. Biafra will give special care and assistance to soldiers and civilians disabled in the course of the pogrom and the war. It will develop special schemes for resettlement and rehabilitation. The nation will assume responsibility for the dependants of the heroes of the revolution who have lost their lives in defence of the fatherland. . . .

Again and again, in stating the principles of our revolution, we have spoken of the people. We have spoken of the primacy of people, of the belief that power belongs to the people, that the revolution is the servant of the people. We make no apologies for speaking so constantly about the people, because we believe in the people; we have faith in the people. They are the bastion of the nation, the makers of its culture and history. But in talking about the people we must never lose sight of the individuals who make up the people. The single individual is the final, irreducible unit of the people. In Biafra that single individual counts. The Biafran revolution cannot lose sight of this fact. The desirable changes which the revolution aims to bring to the lives of the people will first manifest themselves in the lives of individual Biafrans. The success of the Biafran revolution will depend on the quality of individuals within the state. Therefore, the calibre of the individual is of the utmost importance to the revolution. To build the new society we will require new men who are in tune with the spirit of the new order.

What then should be the qualities of this Biafran of the new order? He is patriotic, loyal to his state, his government and its leadership. He must not do anything which undermines the security of his state or gives advantage to the enemies of his country. He must not indulge in such evil practices as tribalism and nepotism which weaken the loyalty of their victims to the state. He should be prepared if need be to give up his life in defence of the nation. He must be his brother's keeper, he must help all Biafrans in difficulty, whether or not they are related to him by blood. He must avoid, at all costs, doing anything which is capable of bringing distress and hardship to other Biafrans. A man who hoards money or goods is not his brother's keeper because he brings distress and hardship to his fellow citizens. He must be honourable, he must be a person who keeps his promise and the promise of his office, a person who can always be trusted. He must be truthful. He must not cheat his neighbour, his fellow citizens and his country. He must not give or receive bribes or corruptly advance himself or his interests. He must be responsible. He must not push across to others the task which properly belongs to him, or let others receive the blame or punishment for his own failings. A responsible man keeps secrets. A Biafran who is in a position to know what our troops are planning and talks about it is irresponsible. The information he gives out will spread and reach the ear of the enemy. A responsible man minds his own business, he does not show off.

He must be brave and courageous; he must never allow himself to be attacked by other without fighting back to defend himself and his rights. He must be ready to tackle tasks which other people might regard as impossible. He must be law-abiding; he obeys the laws of the land and does nothing to undermine the due processes of law. He must be freedom-loving. He must stand up resolutely against all forms of injustice, oppression and suppression. He must never be afraid to demand his rights. For example, a true Biafran at a post office or bank counter will insist on being served in his turn. He must be progressive; he should not slavishly and blindly adhere to old ways of doing things. He must be prepared to make changes in his way of life in the light of our new revolutionary experience. He is industrious, resourceful and inventive. He must not fold his arms and wait for the government to do everything for him—he must also help himself.

My fellow countrymen and women, proud and courageous Biafrans, two years ago, faced with the threat of total extermination, we met in circumstances not unlike today's at that august gathering. The entire leaders of our people being present, we as a people decided that we had to take our destiny into our own hand, to plan and decide our future and to stand by the decisions, no matter the vicissitudes of this war which by then was already imminent. At that time, our major pre-occupation was how to remain alive, how to restrain an implacable enemy from destroying us in our own homes. In that moment of crisis we decided to resume our sovereignty.

In my statement to the leaders of our community before that decision was made, I spoke about the difficulties. I explained that the road which we were about to tread was to be carved through a jungle of thorns and that our ability to emerge through this jungle was to say the least uncertain. Since that fateful decision, the very worst has happened. Our people have continually been subjected to genocide. The entire conspiracy of neo-colonialism has joined hands to stifle our nascent independence. Yet, undaunted by the odds, proud in the fact of our manhood, encouraged by the companionship of the Almighty, we have fought to this day with honour, with pride and with glory so that today, as I stand before you, I see a proud people acknowledged by the world. I see a heroic people, men with heart-beats as regular and blood as red as the best on earth.

On that fateful day two years ago, you mandated me to do everything within my power to avert the dangers that loomed ahead, the threat of extermination. Little did we, you and I, know how long the battle was to be, how complex its attendant problems. From then on, what has been achieved is there for the entire world to see, and has only been possible because of the solidarity and support of our people. For this I thank you all. I must have made certain mistakes in the course of this journey but, I am sure that whatever mistakes I have made are mistakes of the head and never of the heart. I have tackled the sudden problems as they unfold before my eyes and I have tackled them to the best of my ability with the greater interest of our people in mind.

Today, I am glad that our problems are less than they were a year ago, that arms alone can no longer destroy us, that our victory, the fulfilment of our dreams, is very much in sight. We have forced a stalemate on the enemy and this is likely to continue, with any advances likely to be on our side. If we fail, which God forbid, it can only be because of certain inner weakness in our being. It is in order to avoid these pitfalls that I have today proclaimed before you the principles of the Biafran revolution. We in Biafra are convinced that the black man can never come into his own until he is able to build modern states based on indigenous African ideologies, to enjoy true independence, to be able to make his mark in the arts and sciences and to engage in meaningful dialogue with the white man on a basis of equality. When he achieves this, he will have brought a new dimension into international affairs.

Biafra will not betray the black man. No matter the odds, we will fight with all our might until black men everywhere can point with pride to this republic, standing dignified and defiant, an example of African nationalism triumphant over its many and age-old enemies.

We believe that God, humanity and history are on our side, and that the Biafran revolution is indestructible and eternal.

Oh God, not my will but thine for ever.

[1] *Speech delivered at Ahiara, 1 June 1969. The text in Markpress Release No. Gen. 632 at the time was subsequently reprinted as* The Ahiara Declaration: the Principles of the Biafran Revolution (*Geneva, 1969*). *When originally delivered, the titling was 'Commander in Chief of the Armed Forces of the Republic of Biafra', but when subsequently republished the rank of 'General in the Biafran Army' had given way to 'General of the People's Army'. The frontispiece of Ojukwu in his books suggests a conscious Castro-like image. The philosophy preached in this speech may be compared with that of the first anniversary address* (DOC *159*).

[2] *Cf.* DOC *218, p. 438.*

[3] *See* DOC *159.*

203.
Entering the Third Year: Two External Views[1]

(*i*)

After two years of war the area under Col. Ojukwu's control is not much more than a hundredth part of Nigeria, or a tenth of the area he once controlled. From such a base, totally landlocked and lacking even food for the people, how can he still be a military threat to the Federation? The fortitude of the people, their continued fear of genocide, and the inflexible outlook of the leaders are important factors. So is the leaders' belief that, if they hold out the world will rally to their cause, while the Federation will disintegrate politically (even Col. Ojukwu cannot now believe that the Federation will meet economic disaster, however long the war continues). But the main direct factor supporting organised resistance in Biafra can only be physical assistance from outside—food, drugs, supplies of all kinds, and arms, as well as money.

For the Federal Government, therefore, the nature of this assistance and the methods by which it comes are of the highest military importance. Anybody who ignores that can only be assuming that the Federal Government has no interest in winning the war. And anybody who thinks that the Federal Government should permit Biafra to have unhindered communication with the outside world is assuming that Lagos has already accepted the sovereignty of the area under Col. Ojukwu's control.

In fact, the most vociferous critics of the Federal, and the British, Governments are really claiming just that—claiming that Biafra's sovereignty is established and that the Federal Government no longer has any rights or responsibilities in Col. Ojukwu's territory. The critics are saying, in short, that Col. Ojukwu has won the war and that the Federal Government should recognise this.

Others, however, who have opposed Biafra's secession, and who understand the Federal Government's case, are, after these two tragic years, beginning to ask whether the Federal Government, in its own interest, should not recognise that 'no military solution is possible' and so negotiate some arrangement with Col. Ojukwu which would leave Iboland in a special status. Some Africans who strongly support the Federal Government in its attitude to outside bodies ask this question. Even some Nigerians, anxious to avoid more casualties, on the Federal as well as the Biafran side, ask it. And if such an arrangement were possible, and could be permanent, it should at least be considered.

It is, however, clear that no such arrangement can be made. For the Biafran leaders, as their territory has shrunk, have widened their claims. They would demand to negotiate not only on behalf of the territory they hold and all the rest of Iboland, but on behalf of the whole area of the former Eastern Region, and now, on behalf of the Ibo people of the Mid-West. It would be a considerable concession on the part of the Federal Government to allow them to negotiate for Federally-held Iboland, where millions of Ibos live under an Ibo civilian administration, and where thousands happily 'collaborate' with the Federal Government. It would be impossible for the Federal Government to accept Col. Ojukwu as spokesman for the non-Ibo peoples of the former Eastern Region, whose deep attachment to their new states, and anger at their treatment when they were part of Biafra, is a political factor which can never be ignored. It would be unthinkable for the Federal Government to accept Col. Ojukwu as spokesman for any part of the Mid-West state, whose non-Ibo people are keener than any in Nigeria to see Biafran secession ended.

Even if the Biafran leaders did limit their claims to the new, Ibo, East-Central State, what sort of agreement can be imagined? The Federal Government cannot possibly allow establishment in the centre of Nigeria of a land-locked sovereign enclave, ruled by bitter enemies of Nigeria, ready to inspire and support any separatist group in the Federation. Nor could Federal leaders accept, any arrangement which would allow a sovereign Biafra to arm itself without hindrance, with the assistance, one can be sure, of those who have shown in the present war that they will stop at nothing to destroy independent Africa's most powerful country. For such a Biafra would certainly, as soon as the leaders felt strong enough, attempt to 'rescue' the Ibos of the Mid-West, to reassert Biafran claims over the Rivers and the South-East State, and particularly over Port Harcourt.

The only arrangement, indeed, which the Federal Government could possibly concede is one very like the arrangement now existing between the new states and Lagos, with such modifications in the matter of army and police control as a later constituent assembly might agree. And the Biafran leaders reject this arrangement completely. We hope that the Federal Government will feel able to make inspections of relief supplies outside Federal territory, and that Col. Ojukwu's friends will persuade him to accept daylight flights on that basis. We consider urgent the planning of an international force, which can, when the time comes, be an assurance to the Ibos that there is no danger of genocide. We pray that when victory comes the victors will be magnanimous. But after two years of war we still see no outcome to the conflict except a military one.

(ii)

Next week sees the second anniversary of the Nigerian invasion of Biafra, the event which marked the start of the bloodiest war on the face of the earth. It may also prove to be a week in which more innocent children die than ever before in the history of the world. This is no fanciful exaggeration—would that it were. Last Tuesday the sober, reticent, Swiss President of the International Red Cross, M. Naville, summoned a special press conference in order to warn the world that in his own words, 'hundreds of thousands of children will starve in the next few days alone, unless food supplies to Biafra can be resumed.' And this will occur, he added, because of the policy of the Federal Nigerian government and the 'role of some non-African powers.' The policy to which M. Naville referred is that of the deliberate starvation of the civilian population of Biafra. The role of the non-African powers is that of providing the military means to enable the Nigerian government to implement this murderous policy. And the non-African powers who are the subject of M. Naville's unprecedented public indictment are Russia and Britain.

Less than twenty-four hours earlier the Foreign Secretary had been given the opportunity to present to Parliament the British government's case. Reports of starvation in Biafra are greatly exaggerated, he assured the House of Commons, calling in aid Colonel Ojukwu's statement of 1 June that 'we seem to have overcome the imminent danger of mass starvation and now it appears after this crisis that we can look forward to comparative plenty'. . . . Mr. Stewart has certainly succeeded in proving Colonel Ojukwu a poor prophet, but this hardly justifies a deliberate attempt to mislead the House about the true situation in Biafra.

Perhaps Mr. Stewart, who has no direct evidence of conditions there, considers M. Naville and the representatives of the Churches on the ground (who have) to be liars. If so, it would be interesting to know his reasons. It would also be interesting to know how many child deaths a day through starvation Mr. Stewart considers tolerable. This we have not yet been told. Mr. Stewart did, however, find time to praise the Nigerian government for having been prepared to allow, over the past two years, breaches in its blockade of Biafra. 'I know of no historical parallel,' he enthused to the House 'to a government engaged in war being prepared to do that'. The truth of the matter is that at no time have the Nigerians willingly allowed their attempted total blockade to be breached. . . .

If the Nigerians, once they discovered that a quick military victory was beyond their capabilities (for all their lavish supplies of arms from Britain and Russia), had ever wavered in their policy of starving the Biafrans into submission, however great the cost in human life, why is it that they bombed Obilago airstrip within hours of its being demilitarised by the Biafrans and handed over to the Red Cross exclusively for relief work? Why is it that they have kicked the distinguished Red Cross representative out of Nigeria altogether, and announced that in future all relief supplies must be handled entirely by the Nigerian military government? Why, indeed, is it that both Nigeria's Chief of Staff and the leading civilian in its government have in the past few days openly admitted to a deliberate policy of starvation? . . .

As a result, Britain stands in the dock alongside Russia, indicted before the whole world by the President of the International Red Cross for the most inhuman crime known to man. When government spokesmen discuss the Brooke affair, they claim to be motivated by the fact that we have different values, more humane ethics, attach a greater importance to the sanctity of human life than do the Russians. Hundreds of thousands of starving Biafran women and children must be hard put to tell the difference. Yet why is it that the overwhelming majority of Members of Parliament see no reason to demand that the British government at last gives evidence of its much-vaunted influence with Lagos by insisting that this mass starvation is averted and Red Cross and Joint Church Aid relief flights resumed without further delay? A failure of imagination? This, certainly, is part of the answer.

But there is more to it than that. . . .

Today, we stand, alongside Russia, in the dock of responsible world opinion, branded as a country without a conscience.

[1] *Excerpts from editorials: 'Two Years of War'*, West Africa *(1969), p. 793, and 'A Country Without A Conscience?'* Spectator, *5 July 1969.*

204.
Nigeria/Biafra Relief Action: the I.C.R.C. Standpoint[1]

(*i*)

For over a year, the International Committee of the Red Cross, with the support of National Red Cross and Red Crescent Societies, UNICEF and many voluntary agencies, has been undertaking a large-scale relief action for the victims of the fighting between the Federal Government of Nigeria and those calling for an independent Biafra. For over a year, teams of volunteers from various parts of the world have been working alongside their comrades in Nigeria and Biafra to give food and care to women and children as well as aiding the wounded.

These efforts pursued in most difficult conditions have gradually shown results. Food supplies have arrived as well as medicine and also the necessary funds for the purchase of transport—lorries, boats and aircraft—and for the continuation of a vast relief operation over land and sea. Between teams from wherever they may come, co-operation has been established, the staffs responsible for orders, transport and the distribution of food have acquired experience and set up co-ordinating machinery which functions with the authorization and help of governments directly concerned. The situation of the population has improved and the number of persons assisted on both sides of a fluid front has increased. Two million in all in the first months of 1969, two million and a half in April, not counting those receiving aid direct from the Churches. The fight against epidemics has been engaged and is being pursued, whether it is a question of measles, smallpox or tuberculosis.

However, this operation which after having overcome numerous obstacles is in full development, must face a new and redoubtable danger; the weariness of public opinion.

Already now, when the warehouses are full, money is beginning to lack in order to ensure the distribution of relief and medicine. Financing for the six month plan (1 March–31 August) is not yet assured. Whilst the United States have amply done their part by contributing 52 million Swiss francs out of a total of 84 million and the Swiss Government has, for its part, decided to make a payment of 6 million francs, for the whole of the period, and if other governments have promised useful contributions although still on too low a scale, Europe is still far from having supplied an amount corresponding to the emotion it feels and the sentiments which it expresses.

Now this population, over whose fate opinion has been moved and which we have helped to survive, has still been given respite. Should, however, the airlift slow down and lorries and vessels come to a halt, then famine which always threatens will return. Just because things seem to be going better and other sufferings require attention, will one allow the impetus of the action to be broken and abandon women and children who have again learnt to live?

The action on behalf of the victims of the Nigeria-Biafra conflict must be pursued. No one can ignore the fact that even if the concerted efforts of all the governments concerned in Africa or elsewhere were to lead to a cease-fire, many months will be necessary to help the population re-organize its existence. On the level of the present relief there will succeed another which the ICRC has the duty of preparing, which it is indeed preparing and for which it intends to obtain the support of governments and public opinion. It is a question of knowing now whether the aircraft which we have had to buy, the vessels we have chartered and the pilots we have engaged will be able to continue to bring relief to the population in danger. The ICRC cannot be content with fine words. Also, all surpluses generously offered are of no avail, if funds are lacking to cover transport costs to the place of distribution. The responsibility which it assumes towards the population, the engagements it has had to undertake and which amount to tens of millions of francs oblige it to speak out clearly and to ask governments which have not yet decided to give definite answers. Of the 84 million francs necessary for the financing of the present plan, there are still twelve lacking. It must be known now at this moment, before the European holidays begin, whether we can count on their support in the autumn.

(*ii*)

In the climate of tension and crisis engendered by the sudden intervention against Nigeria of the aircraft under Captain von Rosen's command and following the destruction in the air of an aircraft engaged in the relief action for Biafra, the International Committee of the Red Cross (ICRC) have been the object of unjustifiable and unacceptable attacks.

Engaged in relief actions on behalf of the civilian populations in the war-stricken areas on both sides of the front in Nigeria, the ICRC have consistently taken every precaution, in conformity with the rules of conduct which they have established in the course of over a century's experience in the field, against adopting any position of a political character. The ICRC constantly exercise close control over all their operations and consignments and can give every formal assurance that they have never, under any circumstances whatsoever, transported either arms or munitions or any other equipment which could have—directly or indirectly—been used to further the conduct of military operations. Furthermore, the ICRC have taken precise and careful measures in order to avoid any transmission of information or military intelligence. Hence, they formally deny all and any insinuations whose object it is to pervert the purely humanitarian character of their mission.

Indeed, since the outbreak of this conflict, the ICRC's unique aim has been to operate openly, in agreement with the parties to the conflict, in order to ensure satisfactory conditions for the transportation and the distribution of relief supplies.

That is why the ICRC have never ceased to demand and demand once again the authorization to switch their operations from night flights to day-time flights. If the ICRC have pursued their night flights at their own risk and peril, this was because they felt that they did not have the right to abandon populations, of whom they were the support, to their fate, pending the result of these protracted negotiations.

All that the ICRC wish, now as in the past, is that pending peace, the parties to the conflict accept to make the necessary concessions, in order to allow the ICRC to aid and protect the civilian populations from the effects and consequences of the war. In the final analysis, moreover, it remains with the governments to create the necessary climate and conditions propitious to the development of a humanitarian action.

(iii)

Following the destruction in flight of one of the aircraft operating on the airlift into Biafra and the death of the crew, the International Committee of the Red Cross has been the subject of unjustified press criticism which it flatly refutes.

In the course of the humanitarian mission which it has been carrying out without any distinction of race or opinion since the beginning of the conflict, that is to say for almost two years, the ICRC has always remained faithful to Red Cross principles and the tradition it has maintained for over a century. It has never transported troops, arms and munitions, or supplied military information.

The relief operation which the ICRC is conducting in co-operation with national Red Cross Societies and other organizations, and with the financial backing of several states, has so far saved the lives of more than two and a half million innocent victims of the war. The ICRC expects governments and responsible authorities to enable it to continue doing so until peace is restored.

Distribution of relief supplies, however, is not enough. Non-combatants must be protected against the hardship of war. The ICRC therefore again draws attention to the principles recognized by all nations and embodied in the 1949 Geneva Conventions which today are universal. Those principles require that surrendering combatants shall have their lives spared and shall not be ill-treated, that the wounded shall be cared for, that hospitals and the sign of the Red Cross shall be respected, that civilian populations shall be spared and not attacked. There again, the ICRC expects instructions to be given, or repeated, that these rules shall be strictly applied in all circumstances. It will be possible thereby to save many human lives.

[1] *Composite document from International Red Cross Committee Press Release Nos. 977b of 30 May, 982b of 11 June, and 983b of 13 June 1969. All issued in Geneva. (By courtesy of the I.C.R.C. Press and Information Department, Geneva.)*

205.
Ojukwu Interprets the Kwale Incident[1]

A few weeks ago, during an operation at Kwale across the Niger, gallant Biafran troops captured and brought into Biafra fourteen Italians, three Germans and one Lebanese. From the reports of our field commanders in that sector and from evidence produced during investigations and the subsequent trial of the men concerned, they were captured fighting alongside Nigerians against our troops. In addition, they assisted in constructing roads and other means of communication to aid the enemy in their operations against our republic.

As all of you now know, these men were duly tried for crimes against the Republic of Biafra. A total of eleven charges were preferred against them. Of these, they were acquitted on nine and found guilty on two. The two counts on which they were convicted carried, in accordance with our law, the death penalty. They were accordingly condemned.

In response to the direct appeal by His Holiness the Pope and the intercession of our friends, I, two days ago, on June 4, 1969, exercised my prerogative of mercy and granted the men a reprieve. We meet today, on this happy but solemn occasion, to witness their release. They will be released and handed over to our friends of the Republic of the Ivory Coast and the Republic of Gabon who have kindly agreed and undertaken to take them back to the Republics of Ivory Coast and of Gabon where arrangements will be made to fly them to their respective countries. All of us, in Biafra, are happy and proud that we have been able to perform this Christian and magnanimous act in spite of all provocations and injuries of the greatest and varied magnitudes which we have suffered at the hands of our enemies. Our action has been influenced by humanitarian considerations and respect for the sanctity of human life. In all our actions and conduct right through the whole period of this episode, we have placed three considerations and factors above everything else, namely (*i*) the fact of our sovereignty; (*ii*) the indispensability of our security; (*iii*) the image of our country and that of our friends. The men to be released have been described as 'oil men', that is to say, people working for oil companies in Nigeria and Biafra. This immediately brings to mind the significance of 'oil' in the current Biafra/Nigeria conflict. Oil is the mainstay of the Nigerian economy and it is on oil that they obtain all the credits necessary for the prosecution of this futile war. Anyone, therefore, who does anything to sustain Nigeria in its genocidal war against Biafra, is the enemy of Biafra pure and simple, and will be treated as such when apprehended. . . .

There is a significant side-line to the events connected with the release of these men—a situation from which all Africa should draw a healthy and wise lesson. For the lives of eighteen individuals, the entire white population of the world—from east to west, north to south—have risen in an impressive solidarity. Even those who for these two years of war have actively supported Nigeria in the slaughter of thousands and thousands of black lives in Biafra, have raised passionate voices and made desperate moves. I am not a racist. Far from it. But it is impossible to avoid the need to point to these facts and to make appropriate deductions.

I appeal to Nigeria and all countries of Africa to draw a useful lesson. Those countries who instigate and encourage Africans to destroy fellow African lives, no matter the pretext, are no friends of Africa. In this issue, Africa and the black race should emulate the action of the white world, as clearly brought out over the fate of the eighteen lives now spared, and rise up in concert to end the current bloodshed in Africa. With the incapability of the O.A.U. as an organisation to stop the conflict, and the reprehensible indifference of the Secretary-General of the U.N.O., I hereby take this opportunity to call for a cessation of hostilities and negotiations leading to a permanent solution—the negotiations to be without pre-conditions. If it is impossible for the two sides to do so directly, then I suggest that friends of the warring parties should get together for preliminary discussions which would facilitate a peaceful confrontation of the conflicting view points. We repeat that this war is futile. The war will, and can, never solve anything. The current conflict can only be resolved round a conference table. . . .

¹ *Statement made at Owerri, 6 June 1969 (Markpress Release No. Gen. 653).*

206.
Statement by Dr. Lindt on Tendering his Resignation[1]

From the beginning I was aware of the difficulties to be overcome in order to maintain a relationship of confidence with each of the parties in conflict, exacerbated by the bitterness present in all civil wars. I have always endeavoured to draw public attention—directed too much, in my opinion, towards Biafra—to the suffering among the population on the Nigerian side of the front. It was not assistance to governments which was required, but to victims wherever they were and whatever their ethnic origin.

My determination to remain objective was not always appreciated in this conflict where propaganda and psychological warfare play an important part. Our work was therefore the butt of attack sometimes from one party, sometimes from the other, and even from both simultaneously. Nevertheless, co-operation with the civilian and military authorities was always possible and in spite of the many crises and obstacles, the work was supported by men of good will, whose friendship, although not publicly displayed, I shall treasure.

When Count Von Rosen intervened, his exploits considerably changed the situation. First a campaign was launched against me in the Nigerian press; then an ICRC aircraft was shot down without any notification to anybody by the Nigerian government of a change of policy. These events resulted in the Nigerian Federal Government's decision to declare me persona non grata. I shall not dwell on the Nigerian Federal Government's accusations by which it tries to explain its decision. The work achieved is sufficient in itself to exculpate me.

I would however reply to one reproach. In private as in public I have said that the conflict should be resolved by peaceful means. I cannot consider this as a political attitude; it is merely common sense. I have learned sufficiently to appreciate the negotiating genius of independent Africa to reach the belief that it is able to show the world an example of a pacific and humanitarian settlement of a conflict.

It is not given to me to retreat easily when confronted with obstacles, but the desire I have most at heart is that the relief operations continue. Otherwise, international assistance so far given will only have served to prolong for a few months the lives of hundreds of thousands of children. The cessation of operations would for them mean an inevitable return to famine. As the Nigerian attacks are concentrated on me in person, I consider that I can no longer act as a neutral intermediary in keeping with the ICRC's character, and that were I to remain in office the continuation of operations would be even more difficult. . . .

[1] *Statement issued in Geneva quoting from a letter by Dr. Lindt on 19 June 1969. (By courtesy of the I.C.R.C.)*

207.
Senator McCarthy Urges American Intervention[1]

Mr. President, during the past year, the horrors of the Nigerian-Biafran war have become clearer. Widespread starvation has resulted from the compression of millions of refugees into an area one-quarter of the original homeland, from disrupted planting, and from the cutting off of trade routes by the Nigerian forces. It is reported that over a million Biafran civilians have perished from starvation and a million more deaths may occur within the next few months. Not since World War II has a civilian population been so affected by war.

The American people have responded compassionately by contributing to relief efforts, which operate under the most difficult conditions, to airlift food and medicine to Biafra. The U.S. Government also has donated food and equipment to relief organizations on both sides of the fighting line.

Unfortunately, this relief effort can alleviate only a fraction of the suffering, for as long as the fighting continues only a small part of the desperately needed supplies can be brought in. As long as official U.S. policy awaits a 'military solution,' present relief efforts will remain superficial and inadequate, if not contradictory to official policy.

It is time to re-examine our policy of 'one Nigeria,' which has resulted in our accepting the deaths of a million people as the price for preserving a nation that never existed.

The pattern of American diplomacy in this area is a familiar one, not very different from that in Vietnam. It began with misconception, was followed by self-justification, and is ending in tragedy. Political preconceptions have kept us from realistic examination. They have kept us from recognizing that the boundaries of Nigeria imposed artificially by a colonial power are not so sacred as to justify the deaths of several million people. The price of unity is too high.

When independence was attained in 1960 Nigeria was a colonial amalgamation of several hundred relatively autonomous peoples, who had by no means developed a national consciensness. It was the Easterners who were the best educated and who had left their crowded homeland in large numbers to occupy middle-level skilled jobs throughout the country, who most looked forward to 'one Nigeria.' It was the people of the northern region, where indirect rule had strengthened the conservative and authoritarian structure of the society, who were most regionally oriented and who threatened frequently to secede from the Federation of Nigeria unless they dominated it.

The first 6 years of the Nigerian Republic were characterized by shifting political coalitions, ethnic conflict, regional jealousies, and governmental corruption. . . .

In the fall of 1966, 30,000 Ibos and other easterners residing in the north were killed. The easterners living outside their homeland lost trust in the federal government and 2 million of them returned to the east, suffering loss of jobs and property and in many cases physical injury. They understandably moved away from the commitment to the federal government which had not restored mutual trust among the regions and tribes.

At a conference at Aburi, Ghana, in January, 1967, a confederated union with equality among the regions was agreed upon. However, the Aburi agreement was soon abrogated unilaterally by the government in Lagos with the promulgation, without consultation with the east, of a 12-state system particularly designed to confine the Ibos to a small area and to break their influence. The Easterners felt excluded from the government and seceded in May, 1967, declaring the independent Republic of Biafra. . . .

Secession was followed quickly by war in July 1967. The 'quick, surgical police operation' of ending secession, expected to take several weeks, has been followed by five 'final offensives' and a war which is now almost 2 years old. Armed with British tanks and bullets and with Russian Mig's piloted by Egyptians, the Nigerians have surrounded the Biafrans and cut them off from traditional sources of food and outlets to the sea. A strategy of siege, designed to produce military victory, has produced massive starvation unparalleled in modern warfare. . . .

The Nigerians claimed originally that the Biafran leaders represented a small, elitist clique who acted in their own self-interest without popular support, and this claim was accepted by the British and American Governments. It was thought that the secession would end soon. Now, although their capital has been moved three times, although they are surrounded and completely cut off from normal sources of food and trade, although they are bombed daily by jet fighters, although their young and old have died of starvation, the Biafrans have survived. They make their own oil for transport and their own crude weapons to fight with. They desert their towns to the enemy rather than collaborate. They fight on despite the human misery. This is not an elitist struggle.

From the beginning of the civil war, the British have supported the federal military government of Nigeria, partly for economic reasons and partly because of an emotional or intellectual stake in a unified Nigeria, which is represented as a triumph of the British colonial technique of indirect rule and of the successful transition from colonial rule to independence. The U.S. Assistant Secretary of State for African Affairs, Joseph Palmer, who was our first Ambassador to Nigeria, personally shared this commitment to 'one Nigeria.' He accepted the analogy of the secession of Biafra to the secession of the American Confederacy, entirely overlooking the fact that Nigeria, unlike the United States, was not unified by a common language, culture, and historical tradition, and had no background of stable, capable government.

Furthermore, 30,000 South Carolinians had not been massacred in 1861, and the inhabitants of the Southern States were neither pushed out of the Union nor were they living in fear for their physical security as is the case with the Biafrans in Nigeria. The U.S. State Department accepted a historical analogy without taking into account the complicated background to the secession. By putting its diplomatic and political weight behind the Nigerian position, the United States has committed itself to a purely military solution. . . .

We were and are, in fact, not neutral. The United States has been neutral only in refraining from shipping arms. Whereas Great Britain and the U.S.S.R. continue to send in arms, we have officially accepted the Nigerian explanation of the situation and have used our influence to gain acceptance, for this viewpoint among other African nations.

Any review of past events clearly demonstrates the bankruptcy of American policy of 'one Nigeria—at any cost.' The 'one Nigeria,' which upon the most optimistic projections might survive from the war would have little resemblance to the carefully balanced federation of regions which many people had envisaged as essential to independence. The 'one Nigeria' of the future would have to be postulated upon the inequality of different tribes. The Ibos and other eastern tribes who co-operated in forming Biafra would be stigmatized and penalized in many ways. The Ibos would—according to the new proposed division of the country into states—be confined to a crowded, infertile region smaller than their ancestral homeland, with no access to the sea. They would be deprived of all but token participation in the reconstituted unitary state. At a recent planning conference in Nigeria, it was declared that it will be 25 years before Ibos can be given positions in Nigeria. . . .

The United States should immediately call for an arms embargo. We should actively seek a truce. We should use our good offices to promote negotiations for resolving the differences. We should press for a de-escalation of great power involvement. We should seek to form a multinational effort to provide the logistic support required for an adequate relief effort. We should accept Biafra's right to a separate national existence and look to possible early recognition of Biafra by the United States and other nations.

The reaction to these proposals by those who have shaped American policy in West Africa heretofore can be anticipated.

They will say that Biafran independence will be a first step toward the Balkanization of Africa.

They will say that the Rivers tribes and other minority tribes of the east will suffer if Biafra gains its independence.

They will say that these proposals will undermine the position of our British ally in Africa.

They will claim that U.S. diplomatic recognition of Biafra will constitute intervention into a purely African problem.

Let us look at each of these objections.

The prediction that Biafran independence would lead to the Balkanization of Africa is obviously the discredited domino theory transferred to a new locale. There is no more reason to think that it is correct or that it is an adequate basis for present policy in West Africa any more than it is in Asia. Local grievances, local animosities, and local injustices are more important than outside influences in accounting for revolutionary developments within a country. It is significant that four African countries—Tanzania, Zambia, Ivory Coast, and Gabon—have recognized Biafra. Each of them has large minority groups, but none of them seemed to fear that its recognition of a secessionist regime elsewhere would encourage secession within its own boundaries.

As regards the question of economic stagnation and retrogression, it should be recognized that eliminating the hostility generated by an artificial political union could release energy for economic development. Certainly the technical ingenuity of the Easterners will be stimulated by the independence of Biafra. Furthermore, independence does not preclude economic association. The Biafrans have already indicated their willingness to co-operate with Nigeria on vital problems of transportation and communication, particularly the use of the Niger River. Almost any advantage that can accrue from 'one Nigeria' can also be achieved by regional economic arrangements such as a common market and a regional development board for redistributing revenues. Even without such arrangements it is clear that Nigeria is viable without the eastern region, since it has great resources, including vast amounts of oil in the midwestern region; it has been able to forego the eastern oil revenues for 2 years while fighting a costly war, and it would evidently be in far better economic condition without the expense of the war.

It is hard to credit the claims of the Federal Government of Nigeria that Biafra is governed solely by and for Ibos, who subjugate the minority tribes. In any case, the national preference of the minority tribes is a question which can be settled through plebiscites supervised by the United Nations or the Organization of African Unity. Even without some minority tribes, Biafra would be a populous country by African standards, larger than three-fourths of the African countries. Only 10 of some 40 African countries would be larger.

The argument that American recognition of Biafra would undermine the position of our British ally depends upon two premises, both doubtful. The first is that essential British oil interests would be threatened by Biafran independence. However, as pointed out before, much of the oil is in the Midwest, nor have the Biafrans expressed any intention of expropriating British oil. In any case, this should hardly be a major consideration of American foreign policy in this case.

The second premise is that the British support the Federal Government of Nigeria has diminished Soviet influence upon that government. However, all that can be said with assurance is that the Federal Government of Nigeria has shrewdly played off the Soviet Union against Great Britain in order to receive as many arms as possible from both. Who will come out ahead in this game of influence is uncertain. . . .

To argue that diplomatic recognition of Biafra would constitute intervention into purely African affairs is irrelevant; nonrecognition is also intervention. There are faults of omission as well as of commission. The United States has already intervened repeatedly in the area: first by propping up General Gowon when he assumed power; later by backing him when Nigeria abrogated the Aburi agreements; and also by exerting pressure on a number of African nations not to recognize Biafra.

The steps I propose are diplomatic, not military. Our goal should be the recognition of Biafra which has demonstrated that it represents the interest of its people. We should begin by seeking an arms embargo. Our goal should be a truce with a view to reasonable negotiation. We should seek to de-escalate great power involvement. We should provide massive relief. The alternative—to continue to give passive military support and active diplomatic support in the name of unity—is no longer defensible.

[1] *Speech to Congress, 16 May 1969* (Congressional Record: Proceedings and Debates, *91st Congress, First Session, vol. 115, no. 80*).

208.
Federal Government Briefs Relief Organizations on its New Policy[1]

I welcome you all to this important meeting with the representatives of Voluntary Relief Agencies operating in Nigeria. I hope that, after this meeting, relief operations in all parts of Nigeria will be conducted in a more orderly manner with duly regulated procedures for ensuring that relief activities are removed from the arena of politics, diplomacy and propaganda in the current conflict in Nigeria.

The provision of certain relief supplies for needy innocent persons in a war situation, especially a civil war, may be viewed with sympathy. In any armed conflict, non-combatants displaced from their homes in the fighting zones, helpless refugees and innocent victims of military operations may be cared for by their more fortunate brothers not directly caught up in the disruptions of war. But the Federal Government has noted with regret that there are far too many people, including the secessionist leaders and their foreign supporters, who seek to use the humanitarian cover to sustain the rebellion in parts of the East Central State.

Nigerians as a people have always been proud of the fact that Nigeria feeds itself. Nigeria is determined to continue to feed itself.

The aim of this meeting is to examine ways and means of ensuring that genuine relief supplies and operations are separated, and *seen* to be separated, from those so-called humanitarian activities which strengthen the will of the rebels to fight on and reinforce their means of sustaining their rebellion as well as the illusion of world diplomatic approval and *de facto* recognition.

I have, in the circumstances, been authorised by the Federal Government to announce that the Federal Government and the people of Nigeria will henceforth assume the main responsibility for providing relief to needy persons in the war zones. Because of the current war situation, however, the Federal Government will continue to welcome genuine relief assistance from

2 D

outside the country provided that the donors agree to adequate arrangements for such relief to be channelled exclusively to needy civilians. Such outside relief assistance will henceforth be regarded as supplementary to whatever we ourselves can do for our less fortunate brothers.

In considering the organisation of relief assistance to needy persons in the war affected areas, two distinct sets of problems emerge. Firstly, there are the problems associated with the organisation of relief supplies to displaced persons in areas under lawful authority. Secondly, there are those problems associated with foreign relief operations in the pockets of territory still held by the rebels. The two sets of problems should be considered separately. For those agencies which operate exclusively on the national side, only the first set of problems will be of special interest.

One major need, in organising relief for displaced persons and other needy civilians in the war-affected areas under federal control, is to identify and vitalise the appropriate administrative machinery for the collection and distribution of relief materials. At present, there are far too many agencies operating in this field without effective co-ordination. There are nearly twenty organisations represented at this meeting. Some of you here, in fact, represent several organisations. The Federal Government has, therefore, decided that the National Rehabilitation Commission will henceforth be the co-ordinating authority for all relief operations on the national side of the fighting line.

You may be aware that the International Committee of the Red Cross was, at a certain stage, invited by the Federal Government to co-ordinate foreign relief supplies to civilian victims of the war on both sides. It is true that some of you operated outside the umbrella of the I.C.R.C., but many foreign Governments supported the I.C.R.C. in a massive way because of its status as co-ordinator. The Federal Government has decided that the co-ordinating role of the I.C.R.C. shall cease forthwith. The I.C.R.C. will, therefore, no longer be competent to appeal for any aid from the international community and foreign donor Governments on behalf of the Government and people of Nigeria.

Any foreign government or agency interested in assisting the civilian victims on the national side of the current conflict must henceforth deal with the National Rehabilitation Commission and the appropriate Federal Ministries, not the International Committee of the Red Cross.

The Federal Government has also decided to strengthen and reorganise the National Rehabilitation Commission. Steps are also being taken to strengthen the Nigerian Red Cross which will be expected to play a more effective role under the control and general direction of the revitalised National Rehabilitation Commission. . . .

I wish now to turn to the set of problems posed by efforts to organise relief supplies to rebel-held areas. The Federal Government did not invent economic blockade as an instrument of war. It is as old as the history of war itself. If carried to its logical conclusion, total economic blockade implies an embargo on all supplies which can assist materially the ability of the rebel group to resist federal authority or prefer continued war to capitulation. However, in the peculiar circumstances of our civil war, the Federal Government realises that it is necessary to demonstrate to the Ibo that Federal

Forces are not fighting them as a people. Besides, the Federal Government also believes that it is necessary to demonstrate that after the current war, Nigerians intend to live in peaceful and equal compatriotism with their Ibo brothers still trapped in rebel-held areas. Therefore, if supplies can be properly organised, the Federal Government will continue to allow relief to civilian victims of the civil war in such areas.

Having set out this noble objective, I must add that our experience so far is that the secessionist leaders, in their calculated indifference to the hardships of the people in the areas they control, have turned the aid given to them by humanitarian relief organisations into the means of continuing their rebellion. Thus for example, they procure arms under cover of 'mercy' flights. Some unscrupulous 'mercy' flight operators have publicly admitted that when space is available in their aircraft they are under no moral obligation to vet the type of cargo which the rebels and their friends may wish to transport in their aircraft, even where arms are involved.

Another major advantage of relief supplies and donations to the rebels has been that they and their friends have used this as a veritable source of foreign exchange earnings. It is known that they charge astronomic prices for local services rendered to relief agencies and their personnel. The relief agencies sometimes buy food in rebel areas for distribution to innocent civilians, but such purchases are made in a way which entails the exchange of worthless rebel currency for hard foreign currency which the rebels promptly use for arms purchase and their other foreign exchange expenditure in furtherance of their rebellion. From information available, it is estimated that the direct and indirect foreign exchange earnings which the rebels have derived from the activities of relief agencies so far total more than £50 million. Most of this has been expended on arms and the financing of vicious propaganda and other rebel activities in prosecution of their rebellion.

The present course followed by foreign relief agencies is therefore counter productive. By indirectly prolonging the war, more lives are being lost, thus cancelling out the value of saving some lives through relief operations. On its part, the Federal Government can no longer allow this situation to continue. On your part, notwithstanding your concern at human suffering, I am sure you will wish to prevent your charity from being used in the furtherance of secession.

All relief supplies to the rebel-held areas must therefore be so organised that the rebels cannot abuse it for their arms trafficking and other military purposes or to their political and diplomatic advantage. Henceforth, only authorised relief operators who satisfy the Federal Government on the necessary details will be permitted to take relief supplies to rebel-held territory. It will also be necessary, apart from other details, for such authorised relief agencies to agree with the Federal Government on the permissible relief items which are henceforth to be restricted to certain necessities. All war materials, including such items as fuel and spares for radios, vehicles and aircraft which the rebels can commandeer for military purposes will be excluded. If the rebels can find fuel for their military vehicles, they should be able to meet the essential fuel requirements of the relief agencies.

I should like to add that so-called 'mercy' flights must no longer be used for facilitating communications between the secessionist regime and the outside world. Non-relief personnel will be specifically prohibited from using relief flights. The rebel regime has in the past tried to pretend that it is still functioning as a modern government by using the facilities provided by humanitarian organisations to maintain psychological and other essential links with the outside world. This must be brought to an end.

Many voluntary relief agencies operating in Nigeria have given the impression that their moral and religious obligation is to bring pressure to bear on the Federal Government. In their negotiations to get relief supplies to rebel-held areas, they usually do not bring comparable, or indeed any visible, pressure to bear on the rebel leadership who in the final analysis must bear the heavy responsibility for the hardship in the areas they still terrorise. . . .

Humanitarian organisations and relief agencies must henceforth desist from allowing their employees and agents to be used by the rebels for propaganda and diplomatic manoeuvring. It has been suggested that if the voluntary agencies and church organisations are to succeed in raising funds for their relief operations, their spokesmen are obliged to whip up public emotion in their countries about starvation and disease in the disturbed parts of Nigeria. But there is nothing in true religion which requires such spokesmen to become so emotionally involved as to become rebel sympathisers and the strongest advocates of the secessionists' political cause. Unless relief agencies can control their functionaries who engage in pro-rebel publicity stunts it will be impossible to reorganise relief supplies on a basis satisfactory to the Federal Government.

I hope that we will have a successful meeting.

[1] *Statement issued simultaneously in Lagos by Chief Enahoro and in London by Mr. Allison Ayida on 30 June 1969 (Nigeria House press release).*

209.
Lagos Announces New Policy on Relief Supplies[1]

The Federal Government of Nigeria has reviewed the relief and other activities of voluntary agencies operating in all parts of Nigeria and has decided that these should henceforth be properly supervised, effectively controlled and co-ordinated in the interest of national security and efficient operations, and in order to safeguard the genuine foreign relief agencies and their personnel working on both sides of the fighting lines.

The Federal Government in collaboration with all the States Governments and the entire people of Nigeria will do all in their power to help the displaced persons and other civilian victims of the current conflict in Nigeria. The question of relief supplies is therefore a national problem and a challenge first and foremost, to the Government and people of this country. The services of volunteers from students unions, trade unions, private employers, the public services and corporations will be mobilised.

It is customary in a situation of national disaster and national emergencies or other serious disruption in the normal life of a people as in the war affected parts of the country, for the international community and Governmental and non-governmental organisations to come to the assistance of the innocent victims of such tragic situations. The Federal Government will therefore continue to welcome foreign relief assistance to needy persons in the war affected areas but the Government regards such assistance as supplementary to the effort expected of the Government and people of Nigeria.

It is against this background that the Federal Government has taken the decisions listed below in respect of

i. the organisation and administration of relief supplies to displaced persons and other needy civilians of the war-affected areas under Federal control; and

ii. the authorisation and control of foreign relief operations in the rebel-held areas of Nigeria.

i RELIEF SUPPLIES TO NEEDY PERSONS IN FEDERAL AREAS

a. The National Commission for Rehabilitation shall assume full control over, and co-ordinate, all relief activities in the areas under Federal control. The membership of the reconstituted Commission will be made up of one representative from each of the twelve States, representatives of the Federal Ministries closely associated with the work of the Commission and about six persons drawn from other walks of life. This nation-wide representation on the new Commission will bring home to all sections of the community their involvement and primary responsibility for relief assistance to their less fortunate countrymen particularly the children, the women and the aged. The functions of the Commission are:

i. the supply of food, clothing, drugs and other essentials to needy persons particularly women and children, in areas affected by the war and its aftermath;

ii. the determination of priorities for all emergency relief operations and rehabilitation work in all parts of Nigeria;

iii. the co-ordination of the activities of all voluntary agencies engaged in emergency relief operations and rehabilitation work and facilitating the field operations of such agencies in all parts of Nigeria;

iv. the co-ordination of the administration of properties abandoned by displaced persons in the Federation; and

v. the collection and the distribution of emergency relief supplies of food, drugs and other 'humanitarian' gifts from foreign donor Governments, international and non-governmental agencies, and the receipt of financial and technical aid through the appropriate Federal Ministries.

An appropriate Decree establishing the Commission will be promulgated.

b. In assuming full control and co-ordination over all relief agencies in the country, the National Commission for Rehabilitation will take over immediately from the International Committee of the Red Cross its role as co-ordinator of external relief aid for Nigeria; it will also take over from the I.C.R.C. its relief and related activities in Federally controlled areas in the shortest time possible. No relief agency will henceforth be allowed to contribute to relief operations in Nigeria except with the approval of the Commission on such terms and conditions as the Commission may decide.

c. The Nigerian Red Cross will be strengthened and given the necessary administrative and financial support, but the Nigerian Red Cross Society like other voluntary relief agencies, will operate under the direction and control of the Commission.

d. The Nigerian Red Cross will henceforth collaborate with the World League of Red Cross Societies in Geneva in respect of normal Red Cross activities.

e. All the twelve states, notably the four most affected—East-Central, South-Eastern, Rivers and Mid-West—will in collaboration with the Commission have as their primary task, the rehabilitation of displaced persons and other civilian victims of the crisis in the country.

f. The Federal Government wishes to place on record its appreciation to the I.C.R.C. for its valuable contributions to the relief and rehabilitation of the needy persons in the war zones, notwithstanding the unfortunate activities and involvement of some of its personnel in the Nigerian crisis.

ii. FOREIGN RELIEF OPERATIONS IN REBEL-HELD AREAS

The Federal Government reiterates its position that relief supplies to rebel-held areas whether by air, sea, river and land, must be cleared by the Armed Forces and Police after thorough inspection in Lagos or other approved points in Federal areas. Any agreed route must be such that the rebels cannot abuse it for arms trafficking or other military purposes or for their political, psychological and diplomatic advantage.

The Federal Government is most anxious to remove relief supplies and human sufferings from the arena of political and diplomatic intrigue and propaganda. This is the main consideration of the Federal Government in summoning the meeting with the representatives of all relief agencies operating in Nigeria.

The Federal Government recognises that many innocent Ibo civilians in rebel-held areas are using the opportunities available to them to escape to Federal areas where they are being properly cared for. The Government is aware that the secessionist forces are doing all they can to prevent such civilians who are not politically committed to the rebel cause, from escaping from the hardship in rebel-held areas. As long as this situation exists and in order to demonstrate that Federal Forces are not fighting against the Ibos as a people, the Federal Government is prepared to allow relief supplies under its strict control to rebel-held areas. Adequate arrangements will have to be made to ensure that the permissible relief items are limited to essentials such as food and drugs. The Federal Government must satisfy itself that such relief supplies do not prove a cover for the transportation of arms and other war materials such as spare parts for radio,vehicles, aircraft and fuel for the use of the rebels.

The Federal Government takes this opportunity to remind all loyal Nigerian citizens and the international community that the total economic blockade of the rebel-held areas of the East-Central State of Nigeria remains in force. The Nigerian Army, the Navy, the Air Force and the Police Force are under strict orders to enforce the total embargo on all supplies by air, sea, river and land. The Federal Government will not therefore bear responsibility for any attempt to break the blockade.

[1] *Statement issued in Lagos, 11 July 1969* (United Nigeria, *11, 1969*).

210.
I.C.R.C. Criticizes Reports of its Director's Press Conference[1]

Certain newspapers having inaccurately reported statements made by the President of the International Committee of the Red Cross during his press conference on 1st July, Mr. Marcel A. Naville wishes therefore to make clear the following:

1. The Nigerian Federal Government's right to entrust the co-ordination of relief operations to a National Rehabilitation Commission was never in question. Plans for such a transfer were being worked out.

2. No particular country was mentioned as being responsible for the prolongation of the war. The right of every country to ensure its own defence was never contested. The allusion to armaments manufacturers was intended uniquely to serve as a reminder that even the activities of the ICRC, an important humanitarian organization, cannot morally atone for the suffering engendered by the production of weapons of death.

3. President Naville stated that the ICRC's relationship to donors is that of a trustee assigned to deliver relief in Nigeria and to provide for storage and distribution. This work has, moreover, been carried out in close co-operation with the Nigerian Red Cross. The ICRC has never claimed to have any other mandate.

[1] *Statement issued in Geneva, 5 July 1969.*

211.
Lagos Repeats its Peace Terms[1]

1. PARTICIPATION IN FEDERAL GOVERNMENT
Ibos from the East Central State will participate in the Federal Government on the same basis as people from other states in the executive, administrative, military, police, judicial and other spheres. Each of the states is represented by one civilian Commissioner on the Federal Executive Council, and the twelfth place, now vacant, will be filled by an Ibo from the East Central State.

2. MILITARY GOVERNOR
As in all the other states, a military governor will be appointed in the East Central State. He will be an Ibo and will be a member of the Supreme Military Council with the same status as the other military governors.

3. REINSTATEMENT OF CIVIL SERVANTS
In accordance with its offer of a general and specific amnesty, it will be the policy of the Federal Government to reinstate and re-employ former Federal public servants, both in the government service and in public corporations, who for one reason or another had to leave their posts in the past two years.

4. REHABILITATION OF DISPLACED PERSONS
The Federal Government attaches the greatest importance to its plans for the rehabilitation of persons displaced from their stable sources of livelihood

as a result of the tragic events of the past two years. A National Rehabilitation Commission has already been set up and will co-operate with state governments in carrying out the policy.

5. ADMINISTRATION OF EAST CENTRAL STATE

The military governor will be assisted by a civilian council, drawn from the people of the state. In addition the law enforcement agencies, the judiciary and civilian administrators will be Ibos of East Central State origin.

6. POLICING

Policing of the East Central State will be by the Nigerian police force, whose rank and file are normally recruited locally. In the case of the East Central State it will be guaranteed that both officers and other ranks are drawn from natives of that state.

7. EXTERNAL OBSERVER FORCE

To give additional confidence to the population, an External Observer Force will be stationed in areas at present under rebel control.

8. ARMED FORCES

The Federal Army will not normally perform policing duties and its presence will only be required if there is a threat to peace or breakdown of law and order. It will therefore be stationed only at a number of strategic points in the East Central State and its presence will not be felt by the ordinary person.

9. DISARMING

Since there can be only one army in a united Nigeria, it will be necessary to disband the rebel forces, but the intention of the Federal Government is to reabsorb individual Ibos into the Federal Army, as confidence is re-established, on the same basis as other ethnic groups. The Federal Government has also offered to consider any additional guarantees the other side might propose in the context of a 'one country solution'.

In addition the Federal Government stated again in January that if the rebels laid down their arms then there would be general amnesty for everyone including Mr. Ojukwu. But should they continue fighting to the end, the law would take its course and all the leaders of the rebellion would be tried for treason.

[1] *Confirmed in a statement by General Gowon contained in* United Nigeria, *July 1969.*

212.
The Pope Announces His Aim of a Peace Settlement on his African Tour[1]

A question was put to Us, and it was like a stab in Our heart. We were asked why the Pope does not first of all go to those parts of Africa where there is most suffering, especially to those where a tremendous struggle has been going on for years, followed by the entire world with great trepidation, where whole populations are under the threat of being destroyed by arms and especially by the agony of starvation? Why does not the Pope go and see for himself, with his own eyes, how entire generations, children, babies, women, are being reduced to conditions of unimaginable want because of a terrible lack of food, of elementary health assistance? Why does not the Pope cry out for help and peace? So a Bishop, one of Our many informants, has spoken to Us.

Dearly beloved children, how painful this suggestion has been for Us!

Do you think that We are indifferent to such disasters, and that We prefer to go where everything seems calm and orderly, where We shall be met by joyful and festive people? . . .

Well, We can tell you that when We decided to make this unusual journey, We had in Our heart the hope and indeed the desire to contribute to the settlement of that conflict in some way, and that hope and desire are still in Our heart. At all events, during the painfully thoughtful time of preparation for Our journey, We have increased Our efforts, contacts and initiatives on the practical plane to try to open a way to honourable negotiations.

We would add that there is no political partiality in Our mind in this regard. The relief work begun at Christmas 1967 for the victims of the conflict and the populations which have been thrown into confusion by it, was at once supported by Us and has been carried out with wonderful enterprise and magnificent courage by Our 'Caritas Internationalis', aided by various Catholic charitable organizations from several countries. In this work of giving relief it has been Our intention to offer succour to both one side and the other, without any discrimination—preference being given solely to places where the need was greater, more extensive and more urgent.

This undertaking really has drama and heroism in it. It has perhaps earned Us some unpopularity in Nigeria, which is most dear to Us; perhaps it gave rise to suspicions that the flights arranged by 'Caritas Internationalis' were carrying arms and information. But that is not true. Food, medicine, clothing and comforts, yes, but nothing else. And they had no other purpose than that of saving human lives in the civilian population, the frail and innocent lives of children especially, and to predispose minds, if possible, towards solutions through negotiation, not through shedding of fraternal blood and the sufferings of hunger.

The region which is the theatre of war became isolated by land and sea; it became more and more necessary but also more and more difficult and expensive to send in relief supplies. It was necessary to turn to air transport, to save thousands of people from starving to death. It was then that 'Caritas Internationalis' and other Catholic relief organizations joined up with other relief and confessional organizations to set up an air bridge. This was a very risky and costly undertaking (about three thousand flights have been completed). It has succeeded in saving a great number of poor people who were destined to die of hunger.

In spite of all this, resources are still below the level of the needs, not so much through lack of supplies, which come partly from the United States' generosity, but due to technical obstacles in air transport. It is still hoped that agreements may finally be arrived at for river transport and day flights, with proper control and guarantees of freedom from attack. We Ourself took steps to aid the effort of the Red Cross to provide this service.

But the situation is still tragic. It appears impossible for Us to make a visit to the tormented region, because of logistic difficulties and the political interpretations which would be given to it and which would make the situation even graver, taking away that little hope that Our impartial concern may perhaps still permit.

We have tried another way: an approach to the parties in conflict. We did so not without hope of favourable result, but without assuming the part of a mediator. On the contrary, We called on others, who are in a much better position than We are to act as peacemakers, to mediate. But the opposing positions upon which the conflict is based still seem to be too far distant from each other. We will keep on doing everything possible to persuade the adversaries that it is necessary to make a truce, which can be guaranteed, if necessary, by a neutral African Power; that a 'compromise' honourable for both sides will not harm their prestige, will not hurt their interests, and can be made to accord with their respective legitimate and essential claims. We have repeatedly taken steps in this direction, in many directions; and We will keep on doing so. Even though results may be nil, they will at least go to show Our good will and above all remind Africans and world opinion of the one idea that is worthy of being professed by all: the idea of peace, in justice and fraternity. . . .

This will make clear to you, dearly beloved, that Our journey to Africa, far from being made in forgetfulness of the wound from which Africa is bleeding, fills Our heart with sharp paternal sorrow, tempered only by hopes which are sustained by the common prayers of the good. By your prayers! With Our Apostolic Blessing.

[1] *General audience given by His Holiness in the Vatican, 30 July 1969, on the eve of his departure for Uganda* (L'Osservatore Romano, 7 August 1969).

213.
Azikiwe on Ojukwu's 'April Fool'[1]

I desire to place on permanent record my impressions after six days' visit to West Africa last week. My object in doing so is fourfold . . . and to affirm the safety and security of the Ibo and non-Ibo people who now live in the Federal Territory of Lagos as well as those who reside outside of what is now left of former Eastern Nigeria. It was a thrill to walk once more on the soil of my native land. Only a true patriot can appreciate this feeling.

I was happy to meet General Yakubu Gowon and many friends, who cheered me and made me feel at home. By the grace of God, I will soon return to my country and help to repair the damage done to my people by this illwind which has brought us nothing but disaster. . . .

This visit has enabled me to observe at first hand the complex problems of Nigeria. I must record my appreciation of General Gowon's flexible attitude and his willingness to see the other fellow's point of view without necessarily compromising on fundamental issues. This is a mark of true greatness in a leader and it presages hope for the rebuilding of a united country based on respect for the idiosyncrasies of its components.

I have been strengthened in my faith in 'One Nigeria'—an expression I believe I coined in the halcyon days before the attainment of our independence as a sovereign state. I believed then, as I believe now, in one Nigeria, which is indivisible, indestructible, and perpetual, provided adequate security is ensured to all its citizens and inhabitants in their persons and property.

Naturally, no sane person can support a policy which seeks to exterminate the Ibo or any other linguistic group in Nigeria by means of genocide or otherwise. When our 'Young Turks' reacted the way they did early in 1966, I expressed my deep concern at the use of violence to solve our political problems; but I was misunderstood. It will be remembered that from 1961 to 1965, I sounded warnings of the coming storm; but they were derided, distorted and ignored. Howbeit, I deeply regret all the killings of 1966, from January to October. In spite of any opinion to the contrary, I submit that they constitute an egregious blunder which has defaced our national image. They should never have been committed.

Having said that much, I am bound to confess that I would resist to the limit of my mental and physical abilities any concerted attempt to exterminate any linguistic group, whether Ibo or non-Ibo, for any reason. In the same line of reasoning, I cannot be expected to support any policy which is based on calculated falsehood to deceive the Ibo or the non-Ibo to believe that they are destined to be exterminated, when it is obvious that this is an artful propaganda destined to buttress the questionable claims of those who may wish to foist an unpopular leadership on an improverished, destitute and unarmed people.

Knowing that the accusation of genocide is palpably false, but bearing in mind the widespread killings of 1966, which must always haunt our memories, why should some people continue to fool our people to believe that they are slated for slaughter, when we know that they suffer mental anguish and physical agony as a result of their being homeless and their places of abode having been desolated by war and their lives rendered hapless?

The civil war should be ended as soon as possible, so that all our hands should be on deck to heal the nation's wounds and bind together in one common brotherhood and sisterhood all members of the various linguistic groups of our nation. This appears to me to be the most prudent thing for any leader of consequence to advocate and to work for its attainment. Otherwise, it means that the sufferings of millions and the deaths of thousands are of no intrinsic value, when they conflict with the inordinate ambition of those who would rather fool some of our people some of the time, knowing full well that they cannot fool all the people all the time.

I want all the Ibo people and their non-Ibo brothers and sisters who now live in the various theatres of war in what is now left of former Eastern Nigeria to know that, as far as I have been able to ascertain, there is no concerted plot to exterminate them or any of their leaders. I want them to believe me when I say that the world has taken cognisance of their fortitude in the face of extreme suffering in addition to the valour and gallantry of their soldiers. There can be no doubt that they fought and died in the conscientious belief that they and their people were slated to be exterminated. Blood has flowed freely because of this false propaganda. The killings should stop now, now. Enough is enough.

All evidence made public by experts and lay persons, after extensive investigations, indicate that the claim that certain people are to be exterminated is false and unfounded. These witnesses of truth represent the most unimpeachable international organisations of the world, who have nothing to gain by the shedding of Ibo and non-Ibo blood; and I am not in a position to decipher why they should tell lies to the world, if such a criminal plot has been hatched.

For thirty-five years, I have associated myself with other compatriots in the vanguard of the nationalist struggle for freedom in our country. Thus I have a vested interest in the preservation of the precious lives of our people. I cannot join in destroying our people, and I shall not encourage anybody to continue to deceive my people that there is a concerted plan to destroy them. As far as I know, there is no such plan.

Commonsense indicates that discretion is the better part of valour. Having fought valiantly for one hundred and eleven weeks for our survival, and having sustained heavy losses through the supreme sacrifice paid by thousands of our youth, the glory of any nation, not reckoning the untimely deaths of hundreds of thousands of our innocent children and forebears, the destruction of our homes and the desolation of our shrines, wisdom counsels that all Ibo and non-Ibo who are now adversely affected and are suffering privations of the civil war, should have second thoughts and urge their leaders to go to the conference table and negotiate for a just and honourable peace, which shall give them a respectable place in Nigeria as worthy citizens of one united country.

In the circumstances, I am obliged to testify to all who listen to me and who may have doubts about the personal safety of the Ibo people, as I was obliged to have up to one year ago, that the information is a cock-and-bull fairy tale. They should regard it as pure propaganda, because there is no concerted plan to commit genocide against the Ibo and the non-Ibo who inhabit that part of Nigeria which is at war with the nation. Alas, we have been victims of a hoax—a sort of April fool! . . .

[1] *Text of statement released simultaneously in Lagos and London, 28 August 1969.*

214.
Azikiwe Speaks his Mind on his Role in Biafra and Nigerian Crisis[1]

Question: Sir, I think I ought to lay the proper foundation for the series of questions I like to put to you on the present situation in our country. With due respect sir, I do not regard such foundation as raking up old wounds; rather I see it as essential background to this morning's exercise.

I know that you regarded the immediate causes of the first of the crises in Nigeria as (*a*) the incompetent manner in which our electoral machinery was operated, (*b*) the undemocratic nature of the electioneering campaigns featuring violence and lawlessness and (c) the threat of secession by one of the four regions that made up the Federation.

You also detected a number of remote causes related mainly to the exercise of executive, legislative and judicial powers: the enjoyment of fundamental human rights, the creation of more states and the status of Head of State.

All these, sir, you spotlighted at a time when you were in office as President of the Republic who enjoyed no executive powers. The newspapers have reported you as advocating a strong Federal Government, on your historic come-back to Nigeria. Will you like to expatiate on this, bearing in mind the observations I have just credited to you and the constitutional changes you envisage for the new Nigeria you have vouched to help rebuild.

Azikiwe: For forty years (1914–1954) we experimented on the unitary system of government. From October 1954 to March 1966, we tried a loose federation. From April to June 1966, the unitary system was reintroduced and since July 1966, we have continued with a loose federation.

The civil war was made possible because the federation was too loose and it enabled a component of the federation to levy war against it. A tight federation is the logical alternative.

I suggest that the powers of the Federal Government should be enumerated, whilst the powers of the constituent states should be residual. In addition, the Concurrent List should include the following subjects: administration of justice, Agriculture, Co-operatives, education, electricity, health, housing, information and publicity, labour, police, prisons, social security, transport, and welfare.

In so doing, the Federal Government would be in a position to deploy its greater resources to provide all the population with the necessities and amenities of modern living.

Q: I will be the last person to label our distinguished former head of state as a prophet of doom. But Sir, I recall at least two significant statements you made as head of the Nigerian federation.

The first, you made as Governor-General when you told the Commonwealth Parliamentary Association Conference in Lagos something to the effect that events in the world did not make for confidence due to conflict of interest and subversion against constituted authority.

The second, I think, you made as President of the Republic on the eve of the controversial 1964 elections. You warned that, should the politicians of the time fail to heed the series of warnings you gave about the conduct of the elections, the experience of Congo would be child's play compared with the calamity that would befall the country. How do you relate the present catastrophe with the soothsayer's prediction made by Nigeria's President in 1964?

A: As a political scientist, I meticulously observed the political trends in the country, in the light of historical occurrences elsewhere, and their sequences, I made my deductions and drew inferences accordingly.

Q: I think you did speak of possible break-up of the country on that occasion? This could be interpreted as reference to possibility of secession; but certainly not to the creation of states. Which is which, Sir?

A: I had in mind both. Since the nineteen-fifties there had been demands for either secession or the creation of more states.

Q: How successful would you say you were in projecting the image of

Father of the Nation who was far removed from partisan politics in that turbulent period when things went so bad that the politicians were seen crossing swords with the President?

A: I did not take sides but I reserved to myself the right to enjoy fundamental freedom of expression without fear or favour.

Q: I recall that shortly after the 1964 election, it was reported from the State House that the President was indisposed. Not long after, a statement was issued by the State House physician that His Excellency had fully recovered and was capable of fulfilling all his engagements both inside and outside the State House. . . .

Are you aware, sir, that several meanings were read into this report of indisposition? . . .

A: Frankly, I was seriously indisposed and efforts were made to fly me to the United Kingdom or to the United States. Nevertheless, I was able to perform the routine chores of a constitutional Head of State. Until I had left the country no other person could perform such functions, unless I resigned or was removed. Naturally, the situation led to speculations. . . .

Q: One of the six point formula agreed upon in resolving the crisis was the formation of a broad-based national government. This description of that government was the subject of ridicule in some newspapers. Looking back, sir, any regrets on this, or the fact that you did not resign in the heat of the crisis, or that the constitution made the President so impotent?

A : A broad-based national government could be a government comprising representatives of the major parties or representatives of all political parties. It depends upon the meaning attached by those concerned. The late Prime Minister preferred the former, I preferred the latter. Had I resigned as a result of this, it would have intensified rather than resolved the crisis. And I would be blamed for perpetuating the crisis.

Q: You have spoken about Ojukwu's prompting that you should set up a provisional government after the election fiasco. You knew of course that this was unconstitutional as the President had no such power. But you also said he assured you of Army backing? What was it that worried your mind that you had to turn down this offer?

A : It was both unconstitutional and illegal to subvert the armed forces for such a political end. . . .

Q: Like most Nigerians, you welcomed the military regime of 1966, describing its predecessor as corrupt and nepotic. What were/are your reasons, sir?

A : I welcomed the military regime because it would inject discipline into the body politic. Without discipline, any human organisation would degenerate. Corruption and nepotism are manifestations of political degeneration which a corrective force can cure.

Q: As a follow-up, it has been suggested by some Nigerians that politicians of the First Republic, often described as the 'Old Brigade' should not be allowed to hold public office in future. What is your view, sir?

A : Not all politicians are bad and not all politicians are good. Therefore, some politicians are good. Must the good ones suffer with the bad? Is it fair? I think that some distinction should be drawn between the good and the bad. . . .

Q: But then, suddenly you became closely associated with his rebel regime —or so reports said: how come?

A: I was never closely associated with the Ojukwu regime on my own volition. But living under his jurisdiction I was commandeered to proceed on missions always under surveillance.

Q: For a fairly long time, there was mystery about your where-abouts in the Central Eastern State. There were, naturally, guesses about your movement. Not a word from you, or about your activities. Will you like to comment on this 'silent period?'

A: From February 26, 1966 to July 9, 1967, I lived at Nsukka. From July 9 to October 4, 1967, I lived in Onitsha. From October 4, 1967 to February 21, 1968, I lived in Adazi Nnukwu, when I was officially informed that my safety and security were a responsibility of the state. Thereupon, I was placed under house arrest and was evacuated to Nekede, near Owerri, by two armed escorts. There, I resided closely guarded until August 1968.

Q: I like to link this one with the question you have just answered. I wonder if you recall what, at least to those of us here, appeared to be a mystery letter said to have been written by your good self and published in the London *Times* in reply to William Norris sometime in 1967.[2] . . .

A: An armed escort and a senior police officer handed me a letter at Adazi from Colonel C. O. Ojukwu instructing me to reply to the article published by *The Times*. That was the first time I ever saw this article and it contained quite a number of mis-statements. I replied immediately and the news media disseminated its content.

Q: Will you please describe your life in 'Biafra' with particular reference to your position, your participation in the administrative affairs of the regime, your security etc?

A: I was never a member of the 'Biafra' Executive Council or its Civil service or Statutory bodies or its establishment. I was never consulted before any official policy was formulated or implemented; but occasionally, I was ordered to do certain things: for example, proceed on a mission abroad, join the delegation to Niamey and Addis Ababa.

Of course, I had but Hobson's choice. In some cases, I had to read prepared statements, in others, I was allowed to prepare my own statements. But by and large, I always acted under duress.

Q: You were out on a number of occasions on rebel missions; did you ever return to the rebel territory at any stage and back again on your mission? Or did you take the first opportunity to move out never to return to Nigeria until that fateful Sunday morning.

A: I was out on a prolonged mission twice. This enabled me to have an idea of the mechanics of such missions. On the third occasion, I decided to sever my connection with the rebels and I informed Colonel Ojukwu accordingly. On October 2, 1968, I arrived London a free man. On August 17, 1969, I stepped on the sacred soil of my country.

Q: What form did this message take? It couldn't have been personal, otherwise. . . .

A: I sent him a telex message from Paris making suggestions and advising him that a ruler was remembered best in history, by preserving human lives. The untimely deaths of children, youths, aged men and women did not reflect credit on any government of human beings. I suggested that he negotiate for a just and honourable settlement. He invited me to return to Owerri for consultation. I refused because I realised what it meant. I decided to proceed to London for a medical check up and for an escape to freedom.[3]

Q: I am interested in what I like to call 'A day in Ojukwu's Consultative Assembly'. Will you oblige, please?

A: The Consultative Assembly and the Advisory Council of Chiefs and elders have no locus standi in law. They were not established by any edict or decree. They were the brain-children of Ojukwu. They do not have any set procedure or any standing rules and orders. To my knowledge, verbatim reports of proceedings are not taken or published.

At first, the Consultative Assembly comprised of four members representing each of the 28 administrative divisions. All of them were nominated members appointed by Ojukwu in his absolute discretion. Then the easterners complained that Ojukwu was becoming too dictatorial.

In September 1966, after the Kano disturbances, he agreed that each division should elect six members to serve, but ruled that the hand-picked nominated members must continue their membership.

I was elected to represent Onitsha Urban. I attended the meeting of the Consultative Assembly only once, on October 4–5, 1966. It is on record that five natives of Onitsha who came to report to me at Nsukka that I had been elected to represent Onitsha Urban were subsequently detained by Ojukwu. . . .

Since there is no set procedure, whatever deliberation which takes place is restricted to a 'motion of thanks to His Excellency for His Gracious Speech.' Usually, a resolution is prepared in State House, either by Mr. Onyegbula or Mr. Ugwumba or Mr. C. C. Mojekwu. This is put before the 'house' for 'debate'.

Usually, it is unanimously carried by acclamation. Naturally, no votes are taken as such and almost every meeting of the Consultative Assembly unanimously carries a written vote of implicit confidence in the leadership of Colonel Ojukwu. If anybody dares contradict the contents of such a previously prepared written resolution, he runs the risk of being detained. That was the experience of Mokwugo Okoye at Owerri in June 1968. . . .

Q: And a bit of what you saw of the fighting. Did you really see action and where, sir?

A: No, I was not allowed to see any action. Early in March 1968 or thereabout I was commandeered to read a prepared statement before groups of recruits at two training camps near Agwu.[4]

On each occasion they broke ranks, shouting 'Zeek! Zeek!' I understand Ojukwu thought it more discreet not to send me to such morale boosting missions because he was advised that it made me to appear to be more popular than he.

Q: What is your experience of foreign participation in the war; I mean on the 'Biafran' side?

A: Not much, excepting the mission to some African States and a visit to France, Portugal. The latter claims to assume a neutral position, allowing either side staging facilities. France toes the line of Ivory Coast and Gabon.

Q: If newspaper (foreign and local) accounts were correct, and I have no doubt they were, you passionately argued the case for 'Biafran' sovereignty in world capitals, particularly with your revered contemporaries like President Senghor, and far away from the local Fuehrer's dictatorial eyes; this culminated into recognition of rebellion by a few African countries.

What motivated this? Were you not so clear in your mind then, sir, about the issues involved? . . .

A: Up to April 1968, we were told that the Federal Military Government refused to negotiate with Ojukwu and also refused to negotiate without pre-conditions. This seemed to me then to be a negative approach. Moreover, an 'atrocities tribunal' under the chairmanship of G. C. M. Onyiuke, former Federal Attorney-General published evidence by witnesses that certain leaders of Eastern Nigeria were earmarked to be liquidated. My name was included. Naturally, I became apprehensive of my safety.

However, when the Federal Military Government decided to negotiate without pre-conditions, and International observer teams reported that there was no genocide and there was no intention to liquidate any Ibo leaders, that put a different complexion on the issues.

When now Ojukwu refused to negotiate without pre-conditions and insisted on the sovereignty of 'Biafra' being not negotiable, it made some of us to realise that the war was precipitated not necessarily for the survival of Easterners but for a more sinister purpose. Thus some of us retraced our steps. I felt I had been bamboozled. So did many others. . . .

Q: You were at the first Addis Ababa conference, and on the front row with Ojukwu? I know you will want to offer a brief comment on this.

A : I was ordered to accompany Ojukwu which I did. And I was seated next to him on his instruction. A closer look at the photograph of the occasion should tell a lot.

Q: The secession was hatched at Nsukka, in the university campus. True or false? Who were the main brains behind the rebellion; who were Ojukwu's principal collaborators?

A: It is possible that Nsukka was one of the places the secession was hatched. I do not know. I was completely isolated and my residence was under very close surveillance. Perhaps his principal collaborators might include the present 'hawks'; that is those who would not compromise under any circumstance, like [here follow a dozen names of prominent 'Biafran' personalities, some of whom have been mentioned elsewhere in these volumes in one role or another]. My impression is that the 'hawks' might have a vested interest in the continuation of the civil war, probably because they have a lot to account for at the end of the war.

Q: Listening to the pirate radio one gets the impression of an orderly government of 'Biafra', full of governmental activities, with commissioners making statements and mass rallies taking place. What is the true position?

A : It is all false. There is, of course, a façade of government but it all starts and ends with the person of Ojukwu. . . . But he is based in Lisbon. It is all a ruse intended to deceive the world.

As for the rallies, most of them are stage-managed, whilst some of them are productions of the fertile imagination of Messrs Ojukwu and [. . .]. Naturally, commissioners must make prepared statements, what with Decree No. 5 dangling over their heads like the Sword of Damocles.

2 E

Q : A word about the security around the arch-rebel himself and his bunker or bunkers, sir?

A : He is one of the most guarded tyrants in contemporary world history. At Enugu, he spent a lot of money for his comforts and shelter. At Umuahia, he is said to have spent £15,000 for his modernly-equipped bunker. He is said to have spent £10,000 for his bunker at Owerri. I am assuming that he spent a lot at Orlu or somewhere near there. When you get close to Ojukwu you will realise that in spite of his blusters, he is a confirmed coward. During an air raid, I saw him run into his bunker at Owerri and I complimented him for his speed!

Q : Were you aware of the news of Ojukwu's seven days lenten retreat sometime in April 1968? What was the April fool about?

A : Yes. It was just one of his histrionic displays.

Q : What famous names can you remember as having been murdered or in detention in the rebel held areas today? Recall, sir, your description of Ojukwu's empire as Internment camp, or what Nikita Khruschev would call a vast cemetery?

A : I can make some forty or more names available, including Lt.-Col. H. M. Njoku, . . . Dr. Chike Obi etc. . . .

Q : In the story of your impression of your visit to Nigeria and Liberia, you said: 'The civil war should be ended as soon as possible, so that all our hands should be on deck to heal the nation's wound and bind together in one common brotherhood . . .' This seems to be what everyone of us has been saying for months. What exactly do you prescribe for ending the war quickly?

A : Intensified psychological warfare; intensified publicity at home and abroad; intensified conventional and sophisticated warfare. . . .

Q : You spoke of 'conference table' and negotiation for just and honourable peace, do you really believe this is possible with the consistent uncomprising stance of Ojukwu?

A : Yes in spite of Adolf Hitler, the allies and the German High Command negotiated a peace settlement. After all, until Hitler got out of the way, the impression was that all Germans were behind him. . . .

Q : What will you suggest should be done with Ojukwu if (*a*) he surrenders (*b*) he is captured as a prisoner-of-war?

A : That is the decision to be taken by the Commander-in-Chief, the Supreme Military Council, and the Federal High Command. After all, I am just a humble civilian. . . .

[1] *Exclusive interview*, Sunday Times (*Lagos*), *21 September 1969.*
[2] *See p. 18.*   [3] *See* DOC *183.*   [4] *See p. 30.*

215.
Azikiwe Appeals to his Fellow-Easterners[1]

My considered opinion, after my observations, is that there is a genuine desire, which is widespread throughout Nigeria, for the following changes:

1. *Restoration* of peace in Nigeria, whose territorial integrity shall be preserved intact, provided the rebels retraced their steps and negotiated for a just and honourable settlement, where there will be neither victor nor vanquished.

2. *Reconciliation* of Nigeria with what is left of rebel-held territory on the basis of settlement which will not be featured by social humiliation and will not condone victimisation or vengeance.

3. *Restitution* to all Nigerians, including the rebels, without any distinction or discrimination, of their Fundamental Freedoms and Basic Human Rights, under a Federal Constitution which shall not permit the erosion of such freedoms and rights and shall not abridge same excepting under the due process of law.

4. *Rehabilitation* of all Nigerians, including the rebels, for losses sustained by them either through death or injury or destruction of property during the civil war.

All the Heads of Government and Natural Rulers, together with other distinguished personalities, including those in authority, made it clear to me that they desired the Ibo and non-Ibo displaced persons to return to their places of domicile and resume their normal activities. They gave assurance that they shall be secure in their persons and in their properties. This strengthened my faith in the emergence of a New Nigeria that would be united, indivisible, indestructible and perpetual.

The Federal Public Service Commission assured me most solemnly that all displaced persons who left their employment either in the public service or in the diplomatic service or in the service of statutory bodies, as a result of the civil war, shall be reinstated and their period of absence shall be officially treated as 'leave without pay.' I was assured that the promotion prospects of those concerned will not be adversely affected. They would enjoy the benefits of an innovation now introduced as 'notional promotion.' . . .

I observed also the business-like manner in which the State Governments handled the properties of displaced persons. It was at Benin that this system was first explained to me; but it is widespread in all the States of the Federation, excepting the Rivers State, South Eastern State and East Central State, which are just finding their feet administratively. Comprehensive records were kept, which indicated the name of the owner, valuation, location, address, and rent receivable for each property. Abandoned Properties Committees were established to take custody of these. The damaged ones were repaired and having been made tenant-able, they were rented out and the rents collected were pooled together in a fund administered by the appropriate local authority. After deducting legitimate expenses in respect of repairs and maintenance, including commissions to realtors, the balance was credited to the accounts of the owners to await their return. This means that in certain cases, some of the displaced persons had earned from £100 to £1,500, held in trust for them by the various State Governments. In Kano, for example, £83,000 was collected. In most of the Northern States, over £40,000 was collected. The same holds good for Western State, Mid-Western State and Lagos State.

From the above, I am fair and reasonable in concluding that the intention of the Governments concerned is to give assurance to displaced persons that not only are their persons safe and secure but their properties are also intact with some accumulated earnings in addition. Therefore, it is not far-fetched for me to continue to appeal to the displaced Ibo and non-Ibo people to return to the Federation instead of their wandering in the bush aimlessly like vagabonds, running from place to place without comfortable shelter and sufficient food to eat.

My visit has made it clear to me that all of us have now realised the mistakes we made in the past by fighting one another. There is a general feeling, which is widespread, that all are now determined to turn a new leaf and help repair the damage we have inflicted on ourselves. Not only that, there is now a deep-seated desire to have an effective central government which will hold the Federation intact so that, in the future, no component of it shall be in position to challenge the Fatherland to a mortal combat.

It will gladden the hearts of many to hear that the Federal Public Service Commission has introduced a 'Federal Public Service' where all Nigerians can work without discrimination and they will be eligible to be seconded to the State Governments anywhere in the Federation as federal civil servants without losing their promotion prospects or any of their entrenched privileges. This is a death knell to the regionalisation of the public services of the federation because it enables the States to draw from a common pool to enable them to operate the machinery of government competently and efficiently.

Since I had the courage of my conviction to express my faith in One Nigeria, and to expose the false propaganda employed to bamboozle Eastern Nigerians, I have been called names not only by those who have a vested interest in the continuation of the civil war, but also by people who should know better. As I said on August 28, now that our nation is aflame, I am not in the mood for retaliation. Let my disclosures speak for themselves because abuse is no answer to argumentation. . . .

The world has been shocked that an enterprising people, like the Ibo, have been tongue-tied and emasculated that they have allowed tyrants to blindfold and hoodwink them so that in a war alleged to be fought for their survival, more than 1·5 million of their children had died of starvation and disease. It sickens me to see the advertisement of skeletal Biafran babies on the pages of newspapers and on the TV screens, begging for charity and relief. It hurts my pride as a human being.

There are plausible reasons for this strange behaviour of the Ibo elite. In the first place, the events of 1966 made it possible for them to be convinced that they had been earmarked for physical annihilation and social humiliation. Then they were persuaded to believe that their properties in federal territory have been confiscated; and they were told that they had been dismissed from their jobs in the Federal and Regional Public Services of Nigeria; and they were scared into believing that they would be treated as socially undesirable persons and second class citizens. Thus, the propagandists converted them to have faith that only a sovereign and independent State, like Biafra, can guarantee them security in their persons and property, employment, and in the enjoyment of Fundamental Rights as citizens of a free country. Those who propagated the dismemberment of their country had mixed motives. Some of them had genuine fears for the security of their lives. Some had inordinate ambition to hold public office. Some cultivated an extraordinary desire to be associated with those who exercise power. Some had excessive zeal to display authority. Some had tangible apprehension of punishment arising from the findings and recommendations of public tribunals of inquiry. Some were uncertain about their future prospects of employment and advancement in life. Some were anxious about the preservation of their properties. And some were apprehensive that if they did not support the Ojukwu regime, their families would be victimised, their houses would be demolished, and they and their families would be ostracised for ever. . . .

Surely, if my second son and I are free to move about the regions of Nigeria, without any fear and without any harm being done to our persons, I think that it is sufficient evidence to conclude that all Ibo and non-Ibo displaced persons should leave rebel territory and come out of their hiding places and rejoin their brothers and sisters to rebuild our wounded nation.

Therefore, I advise all the displaced people who used to be classified as 'easterners,' to come at grips with truth and seriously consider the following realities:

1. It has never been the intention of the Federal Military Government to commit genocide against any linguistic group in Nigeria, including the Ibo. When the Ibo killed the non-Ibo and the latter retaliated, the Federal Military Government expressed deep concern and regrets for the tragedy.

2. People with axes to grind have deceived Ibo people to believe that they were to be massacred and their properties were to be confiscated. This has conditioned their minds to be apprehensive of their safety and security.

3. Reputable representatives of the United Nations, the O.A.U., the United Kingdom, Canada, Poland and Sweden, after expert investigations, from September to December 1968, produced unanimous reports, based on their observations on the spot, in the war zones, that the allegations of genocide against the Ibo were baseless and without foundation.

4. After two visits to Nigeria, I can say, without fear of contradiction, that thousands of Ibo-speaking people have returned to their homes in different parts of Nigeria, and they have not been molested by anybody. Instead, the Federal and State Governments have arranged to rehabilitate them.

5. General Gowon, the Military Governors, the Federal and State Commissioners, together with the leading traditional rulers of Nigeria, have assured me of their genuine desire to welcome the Ibo people back into the Nigerian fold as equal citizens of one undivided country; and I have no cogent reason to doubt their integrity.

6. The Federal Public Service Commission have assured me that they would welcome back into the Federal Public Service and the Diplomatic Service all displaced persons who vacated their jobs during the war; and their absence will be treated as 'leave without pay', without prejudice to their promotion prospects.

7. The State Governments have taken custody of the buildings of displaced persons, repaired them, rented them out, and collected rents on their behalf, pending their return to claim their properties.

8. The Federal Military Government has released hundreds of detainees, who are displaced persons, in honour of the third anniversary of the Federal Republic. This was done as an earnest of its willingness to forgive those who

were misguided to take up arms against the Fatherland. If they retraced their steps now, laid down their arms, and returned to the fold of One Nigeria, they will not be humiliated.

I went to Nigeria on a fact-finding mission. The above facts are true and unassailable. They demonstrate the good faith of General Gowon and his colleagues. They vindicate statesmanship of a high calibre. I hope that displaced Ibo leaders, students and people, at home or abroad, will appreciate the generosity and patriotism of the Federal Military Government and reciprocate without further delay.

In conclusion, I believe that the hall-mark of any great leader, at any period of history, is his ability to preserve human life, to guarantee the fundamental freedoms and the basic rights of humanity, to secure the welfare of the under-privileged, and to make life to be a boon and not a bane for the greatest number of human beings. This is the challenge that his people offer to General Ojukwu. I wish he would have second thoughts and inscribe his name in contemporary world history as a brave soldier and beloved leader, instead of disfiguring the pages of Nigerian history as another political impostor and petty tyrant.

[1] *Statement issued in London on 8 October 1969, on his return from his first official visit to wartime Nigeria.*

216.
Joint Church Aid Rejects Anti Humanitarian Agencies Propaganda[1]

Never since the days of Dr. Goebbels has propaganda—in his sense of the word—played such a primordial role in warfare as it is playing on both sides of the Nigeria/Biafra conflict.

To attack humanitarian agencies which have raised hundreds of millions of dollars for the relief of starving refugees on both sides of a conflict presenting neither political nor economic interest to them is both in bad taste and absurd. Because of its very absurdity, this libel is frequently left unanswered. And so it goes on recurring at regular intervals until the most unlikely publications and people are found believing it—or at least passing it on.

In a recent letter published by a leading Canadian newspaper, for example, it was reported that both Church and Red Cross relief to Biafra serves as a screen for collecting military intelligence. Even more incredibly, the writer continues: 'In fact, Caritas admitted openly that they provide space for rebels armaments in their relief planes'.

Caritas General-Secretary Monsignor Carlo Bayer answered this old allegation some time ago. He said: 'The universally recognised function of Caritas is to extend Christian charity to the world, and it would be ridiculous and false to believe that an organisation with purely humanitarian ends would lend itself to arms traffic'.

All funds collected in Europe, United Kingdom, Australia and the Americas by Catholic and Protestant agencies have in fact been spent in buying and transporting food and medicines for war victims. Protestant and Catholic agencies send foods and medicines to Nigeria and to Biafra irrespective of the province of origin or the religious denomination of the refugees. The relief to Biafra is sent by specially chartered planes from the base of Sao Tomé in Portuguese West Africa. JCA has no other bases for planes. Before each flight, all planes are subject to control and inspection to prove that they carry nothing but humanitarian supplies.

No less absurd in the eyes of Church and Red Cross workers who have been in Biafra since the relief operations were organised is the statement that humanitarian supplies end up with Biafran army units. More plausible, perhaps, at first sight, than the arms-running libel, this allegation is also seen on closer scrutiny to imply that church leaders, missionaries and relief workers on the spot are liars. Because, say these people, humanitarian relief is so organised in Biafra that it would be impossible for food to end up anywhere else than in the feeding centers—or for medicines to end up anywhere else than in the hospitals.

Since the International Committee of the Red Cross suspended its flights and the Joint Church Aid airlift was reduced to a minimum, less than one-third of minimum requirements can be sent to Biafra refugees. Most of these supplies are medicines, which are unloaded by Protestant and Catholic personnel at Uli Airstrip and transported under their close supervision—and under escort—to church supply centers and thence on to hospitals and to distribution centers in different parts of the country. These supplies do not leave the hands of the relief workers until they reach the sick and starving civilians who are their ultimate destination.

The only way in which supplies could possibly reach the Nigerian/Biafran Army would be through military hold-ups on the road. Incidents of this kind have been extremely rare—and individual offenders have been punished by the authorities concerned. Were large-scale looting to be allowed by the Nigerian/Biafran authorities, then obviously the humanitarian agencies would be thwarted in their aims and their intervention would stop.

Taking into consideration the fact that, at the last estimate published some weeks ago, Joint Church Aid has sent only $28 millions worth of supplies into Biafra as compared with $60 millions worth of food and medicines channelled by its member agencies into Federal Nigeria, this kind of propaganda is unlikely to influence world opinion. It may thus be considered 'bad public relations'.

[1] *Joint Church Aid Press Release No. 89.*

217.
Gowon Addresses O.A.U. Heads of State[1]

. . . It is a great honour for Nigeria and myself to be given the opportunity to address the opening session of the O.A.U. Assembly of the Heads of State and Government and to respond to the moving opening address of Your Imperial Majesty. I am personally gratified as this is the first time the situation in Nigeria has permitted me to attend the O.A.U. Summit meeting. I have always felt that my first presence at an international gathering outside

Lagos should be under the auspices of the O.A.U. which has played such a laudable and significant role in African affairs. In this regard, permit me, Your Imperial Majesty, to make a few remarks on the Nigerian situation.

The Kinshasa and Algiers resolutions of the O.A.U. have facilitated the efforts of the Federal Government of Nigeria to contain the imperialist plot against the territorial integrity of my country and the undue foreign interference in the Nigerian crisis.

It has been suggested that the O.A.U. Consultative Committee on Nigeria has not succeeded so far in finding a solution to our civil war because of the restrictive nature of the Kinshasa mandate. I do not believe that this is the case. The first question which faces any peace-maker in the Nigerian conflict is to decide whether the civil war in Nigeria is to be settled on the basis of one country or two or more countries.

Any organisation interested in offering its good services must, first of all, adopt an attitude to the vexed question of secession. This is the only question that divides the secessionist leaders from the rest of Nigeria.

There is no doubt that the Ibos as a people, as well as other ethnic groups in Nigeria, are entitled to the security of their persons and property. As of now, there are four to five million Ibo-speaking Nigerians in parts of the East Central State under Federal control, and they are very safe. The security of the Ibos as a people is therefore no longer in dispute.

I have had occasions to declare publicly before that the constitutional settlement which will follow the war is a matter for Nigerian leaders from all parts of the country to decide in a constituent assembly.

We are, therefore, fighting a war, not about constitutional procedures but against armed rebellion and secession. It is thus not possible for us to compromise on the principle of the territorial integrity of Nigeria.

On the progress of the war since the Algiers Summit, Federal forces have recovered much of the remaining area under secessionist control. The secessionist forces are at present confined to an enclave less than one-tenth of the former Eastern Region of Nigeria. Unless the secessionist leadership gives the O.A.U. the opportunity to settle the Nigerian war by peaceful negotiations on the basis of the Kinshasa and Algiers mandate, the Federal Government will have no option but to carry on the military operations to their logical conclusion, no matter how long. I have been asked, now and again, what is holding up the military operations. There have been four major factors responsible for the prolongation of the war. There are many others, of course:

Firstly, there are the well-known international conspiratorial and racialist elements who are committed to the disintegration of Africa, starting with Nigeria, after they had failed in the Congo.

Secondly, the activities of some of the humanitarian organisations and relief agencies have helped to sustain the secessionist regime through moral and material support, including the direct supply of foreign exchange, arms and military equipment. In spite of this, the Federal Government will continue to allow genuine relief supplies to the innocent civilians in the secessionist enclave.

Thirdly, many of those behind secessionist lines have been misled by vicious propaganda and unparalleled falsehood into believing that they are fighting for their own survival. The myth of genocide had been exploded.

Fourthly, the conduct of the war has been guided by our strong desire to quell a rebellion and not to destroy our people. Our action has never been motivated by malice or hatred. We are not fighting a non-discriminatory war or one of total destruction as would have been the case in a total war against an external enemy.

Your Imperial Majesty, I shall be having the opportunity to discuss further the Nigerian situation with you and my other brother Heads of State. . . .

[1] *Speech made to the Sixth Assembly of O.A.U. Heads of State, held in Addis Ababa, on 6 September 1969.*

218.
Tanzania's Memorandum on Biafra's Case[1]

In arguments about the Nigeria/Biafra conflict, there has been a great deal of talk about the principles of national integrity and of self-determination; many analogies have been drawn with other conflicts in the world, and particularly in Africa; and finally, there has been a considerable amount of discussion about the role of the O.A.U. and other international organizations in relation to the present conflict. It is my purpose to discuss some of these problems and to examine the lessons which are, and which I [President Nyerere] believe should be, drawn from the analogies.

Let me look first at the analogies and their relevance to the principles which are under discussion.

The British give three reasons for their opposition to the demand for the incorporation of Gibraltar into the Spanish State. First is the Treaty of Utrecht 1713 (to which the Gibraltarians were not a party); second is the opposition of the Gibraltarians; and third is the dictatorship in Spain. . . .

In the political climate of the modern world, the opposition of the Gibraltarians is the more important matter for winning world support for Britain's case. But the Treaty argument also has an importance.

Look now at the analogy with the Nigeria/Biafra issue. Britain appears to be arguing that she is helping Nigeria to stop the Ibos from unilaterally breaking the 'Treaty' under which all the peoples of Nigeria agreed to accept independence as a single Federation. In this case, in other words, she is leaving out the question of self-determination, although it is the main plank of her argument on the Gibraltar question.

But in the case of Nigeria and Biafra, the issue is not some minor, technical issue about the legalities or morality of a Treaty. It is an issue of life and death, involving a massacre by one party to that Treaty of more people among another party to the Treaty than all the inhabitants of Gibraltar. After the failure of several serious attempts to secure reassurance for the resultant fears, the people who had been the victims decided to break away to form their own State. If the principle of self-determination is relevant in the case of Gibraltar—as it is—then surely it is relevant under these circumstances? But the rest of Nigeria objects, and says: 'These Ibos must remain part of Nigeria'. Surely we should be saying to Nigeria: 'Get their consent'. Instead, what we are saying is: 'Shoot and starve them into submission'.

It may be argued that all those involved in a Treaty should be consulted about any change in it, and that therefore in this case the Nigerians should be consulted as well as the Biafrans. That is not actually my argument, but let us look at it in these two cases. Consult the people of Spain about the incorporation of Gibraltar: I do not know what their verdict would be. Consult the people of Britain: they will vote against Spain—not because of the Treaty of Utrecht but because the Gibraltarians do not want to be part of Spain. They would vote, I hope—indeed I am sure—in support of the self-determination of the people of Gibraltar as it has been so freely expressed, not for Spain's claims. Then ask the Nigerians about the forcible incorporation of the Ibos. At worst their answer would be equivalent to that of the Spanish Government, and of their own Government now: 'Keep them part of Nigeria, even against their will'. Ask the people of Britain about this issue: in this case I am not sure what their verdict might be, in spite of the clear determination of the 8 million Biafrans to be left alone. But neither is Wilson sure, so we shall never know. What we do know is that the 29,000 Gibraltarians have been asked their opinion about the dispute in which they are involved, and they have given their answer. The 8 million Biafrans have not been asked, and will not be asked their opinion on their conflict; but they have given their answer nevertheless—with their blood.

Britain invokes the principle of self-determination in the case of Gibraltar, because it serves her interests to do so. She must justify her stand on some acceptable principle (international law, plus self-determination) because she still wants the Rock. Nevertheless, the principles she advances are valid. I am not going to say that they are not valid because they are advanced by Britain. In the case of Nigeria, Britain invokes a different principle—the principle of territorial integrity—because it suits her own interests to do so. The choice of principle is the result of a decision taken on the basis of British interests, not because one principle is more valid than another. If British interests had been different, we would have self-determination being advanced as a reason for supporting Biafra.

What, then about the analogy which is sometimes drawn to the American Civil War? Like the Nigerian Civil War, it was about secession. Like that in Nigeria it caused very dreadful suffering. But we do justify wars, or condemn them, because of what they are about. And in America, the South was not trying to break away because Southerners had been rejected in the North, and had been massacred in their thousands with the connivance or the assistance of the forces of law and order. The Southern States were not swarming with millions of refugees who had fled from the North leaving their property behind, in order to save their skins. Of course it is true that Lincoln fought to save the Union. But he believed, even before the war, that that Union could not last half free, half slave. He was concerned to make it what it had proclaimed itself to be—a society of free and equal men. Had there been a Lincoln in Nigeria, he would have fought the prejudices which led to that inordinate and almost pathological hatred of the Ibos which made secession inevitable and justifiable.

A politically more serious comparison, however, is made between the secession of Biafra and that of Katanga. Tanzania, in particular, is accused of the most blatant inconsistency because it opposed Katanga and recognizes Biafra. I know that there are similarities between Katanga and Biafra.

But these similarities can be grouped into those which are superficial and irrelevant and those which are real and crucial. An examination of the real and crucial similarities reveals some apparently unnoticed facts.

First, let me acknowledge the similarities which are advanced by the opponents of Biafra, but which I believe to be superficial and irrelevant to the main issue. Katanga was part of a United Congo; Katanga decided to secede; the Centre objected; a war then broke out between secessionist Katanga and the Centre. (Notice that I am not trying to say why Katanga decided to secede; I am merely stating the fact of secession). Similarly, Biafra (or the Eastern Region of Nigeria) was part of a federated Nigeria; Biafra decided to secede; the Centre objected (this is not quite correct, but I must admit a few similarities); a war broke out between secessionist Biafra and the Centre.

Now for a different and more fundamental group of similarities. Katanga had vast copper resources; the former colonial power was very much interested in this vast amount of wealth; her economic interests were threatened by Lumumba at the Centre; when war broke out between Katanga and the Centre, Belgium supported one side in an effort to safeguard her economic interests; she joined the side supported by the copper companies. No need to go further.

Now for the conflict in Nigeria. Biafra had vital oil resources; the former colonial power was vitally interested in this vast amount of oil; her interests were threatened in the conflict (the really vital matter was the threat, not whether the threat came from the Centre or the periphery; this is only important in deciding who is going to be ally and who enemy); but in this case, due to relations between the British and the Ibos, the threat came from the secessionists. When war broke out between Biafra and the Centre, Britain, like Belgium, was on the same side as the Foreign Companies—in this case the Oil Companies.

Let those who love the superficial similarities of secession have the courage and honesty to accept this unpleasant fact also. In Katanga, Belgium and the Copper Companies were on one side; in Nigeria, Britain and the Oil Companies are on one side. This is the one constant and crucial factor in both cases, around which everything else can be variable. In both cases, the former colonial power and the vested economic interests are on one side. Tshombe was a stooge of the Copper Interests. They filled his coffers with their vast financial resources. Ojukwu is not a stooge of these interests; they refuse to pay him a penny from the wealth they derive from Biafra oil. This vital contrast is the corollary to the decision to support the Centre instead of secession. In the one case it was the Centre under Lumumba which was the threat to the economic interest if the Congo remained united; and therefore it was the Centre which had to be starved of Revenue. In the other case it was a separate Ibo state which was the threat, and it was Biafra, therefore, which had to be strangled. Is this really so difficult to see? Only great simplicity—or even extreme naivety—could lead anyone to accept that Britain is defending the unity of Nigeria, or African Unity in general. She is defending her own economic interests. That may be natural and even understandable, but it is as well that it should be understood and not camouflaged by talk of a particular principle.

The Netherlands decision to stop the supply of arms to Nigeria after the capture of Port Harcourt and its oil-rich surrounding areas is a reflection of her assessment that the oil supplies were then assured. But the British wish to be more certain. I am told that Britain expects to get 25 per cent of her oil supply from Nigeria by 1972. With her traditional Middle East suppliers being (in her view) unreliable, this is a very serious matter indeed for industrial Britain.

From Britain's point of view what is vital is her oil interests; as she decides on her own policy, this is what the war is about. The Biafrans are fighting a most unequal war, and if they go on fighting, God alone knows what their end will be. Completely blockaded as they are, Nigeria no longer needs to shoot them into submission. Starvation and disease can fight for Nigeria, and Britain can go on explaining to the world that this is inevitable and justifiable because it is part of warfare. Those who want peace before the Biafrans are wiped out must convince the British of one of two things. They have to be convinced that, in their present helpless position, the Biafrans are no longer a threat to British interests. And truly, the Biafrans know how weak they are; they are less interested in the oil than in their lives. This is the relatively easier thing to try and convince the British. The more difficult one is to try and convince Britain that her oil interests would be safe in an independent Biafra. But how could they know that Russia would not help Federal Nigeria to win total victory against the Biafrans? and if that happened, where would Britain be?

These are the vital issues, and those who are saying that O.A.U. can solve this problem are being fooled, or are conveniently fooling themselves. Britain is the vital force in this conflict; more important even than Federal Nigeria. The Biafrans believe they are fighting for their very survival; they are fighting to live in freedom and security. The Nigerian people are not quite sure what they are fighting for. Some of their leaders hate the Ibos; some may have ambitions of being Lincolns; some may even believe that they can force others into a United Nigeria and still have a meaningful nation. But that is all. Without Britain's military and in particular her diplomatic support, the Nigerians would have no hope of winning against the Biafrans. The Soviet Union would not have been able to help them secure victory. Indeed, without Britain the Soviet Union would have become a huge diplomatic embarrassment to the Nigerians (and Nigeria would have become a wee embarrassment to Russia). For if Russia had supported Lagos and Britain did not most of the Western world would have been anti-Lagos; and since there is so much popular sympathy for Biafra in many Western countries, it is hard to think of a reason which would have prevented Western Governments supporting Biafra. After all, they would be fighting against communism. Under these circumstances it would not have mattered whether African Heads of Government had continued to fear the effect of an example of successful secession; the Western powers, the only ones who have real power in Africa, would be fearing a different example, and one more vital to their own interests.

But if this argument is not convincing, those who believe that there is a direct and valid comparison between Katanga and Biafra must be able to answer some few questions. Which tribe in Katanga is the equivalent of the

Ibos? Azikiwe, an Ibo at the Centre, was trying hard, under very difficult circumstances, to co-operate with the dominant North to build a United Nigeria; who was his equivalent in the Congo? The Ibos, because of their education, industry, enterprise (and consequent arrogance?) were almost universally hated in Nigeria. Who in Katanga represented this educated, industrious, enterprising, arrogant and almost universally hated people? Who in the Congo represented the 30,000 massacred Easterners? Who in Katanga represented the 1.5 or 2 million refugees? What in the Congo represented the National Council for Nigeria and the Cameroons (N.C.N.C.) a party led mainly by Ibos it is true, but one which was nevertheless truly aimed at Nigerian Unity? Who in the Congo was the equivalent of the Sardauna of Sokoto, so powerful that he did not even bother to go to the Centre but governed the Federation through lieutenants while he himself governed the vital North? What in Katanga was the equivalent of the Northern Peoples Congress (N.P.C.)?

Or again, who is Biafra's Tshombe? Who in Biafra represents the Copper Companies? Africa appealed to the United Nations to support Patrice Lumumba; why are we not appealing to the United Nations to support General Gowon who on this analogy would be Nigeria's Lumumba? Perhaps the true answer is that it is not necessary; he already has strong support. But why is it not necessary? Because the Ibos are simply fighting for their own survival and therefore have no strong supporter. That is their strength and weakness; it is the major difference between Katanga and Biafra. In the one case, foreign economic interest was on the side of the secessionists and that made them very strong; in the other case, foreign economic interest is on the side of the Federalists, and makes them too very strong. They can even quote the O.A.U. Charter on non-interference in the internal affairs of a member state. The devil can quote Scripture—when it suits him. In the one case a despicable African stooge allowed himself to be used as a tool of foreign economic interests; in the other case, a brave African people are fighting against immense odds purely and simply for their own survival and their own self-respect and dignity. How does this analogy stand up to examinations?

The break-up of Nigeria is a terrible thing. But it is less terrible than that cruel war. Thousands of people are being shot, bombed, or seeing their homes and livelihood destroyed; millions, including the children of Africa, are starving to death. (It is estimated that possibly more people have died in this war in the last two years than in Vietnam in the last ten years). We are told that nothing can be done about this. It is said that the sufferings of the Biafrans in the war are regrettable, but that starvation is a legitimate war weapon against an enemy. Yet by this statement you have said that these people, the Nigerians and the Biafrans are enemies, just as Britons and Germans in Hitler's war were enemies. If that is the case, is it rational to imagine that, once a Federal victory is obtained, they can immediately be equal members of one society working together without fear? Or is the logic of being enemies not a logic which leads to conquest and domination when one side is victorious?

We are told that Ojukwu should end the terrible sufferings of his people by surrender. We are told that he should reason thus: 'The Nigerians are stronger than we are and they have stronger friends than we could ever hope to get.

If we go on resisting, a combination of bombing, starvation and the inevitable epidemics, would exterminate us'. Perhaps he should add, kindly: 'Even if the Nigerians never intended to exterminate us'. He should then convince the Biafran people about the wisdom of surrendering and then duly send the appropriate notice to the Nigerians. When the Federal Government gets this note, they presumably say: 'At last you have come to your senses. As you rightly say, we never intended to exterminate you: but had you gone on resisting we would have continued the bombing and the blockade and the result would have been exactly the same as if we had intended to exterminate you'. Perhaps they would add, kindly: 'But, of course, the fault would have been yours'. Then the Biafrans surrender and all is well.

Historically and logically, however, surrender on such terms as these—with the alternative being exterminated—is for the purpose of creating empires. Surrender to an implacable enemy on his own terms, with the only condition being that you should not be killed, cannot lead to any kind of friendship, or even toleration. If it is a battalion which surrenders, the soldiers become prisoners-of-war; if it is a people, they become a colony, or an occupied territory, or something like that. Those who surrender cannot become an integral part of the conqueror's territory because they did not do so of their own free will; they did so as the only alternative to death.

The argument is being advanced that if Biafra is allowed to exist, Nigeria cannot exist. Nigerian leaders themselves have advanced this argument. If the Ibos are allowed to go, so the argument runs, Nigeria will break up completely, for the others will also go. To deal with this argument seriously, let us assume the worst; let us assume that, if the Biafrans leave the Federation, all the others will also secede and set themselves up as separate States. What this argument amounts to is that only two things bind the Hausas and the Yorubas (these being the major elements) together. These two facts are, firstly, the recent historical accident that all (plus the Ibos) were conquered by, and then governed by the British; and secondly, the more recent historical fact that, when the Britain left, they left these peoples as one Nation. If these accidents of history were in fact the only reason for Nigeria, and if there is no feeling of mutual benefit arising from the political unity, then the secession of the Biafrans would certainly and inevitably lead to the break-up of the Federation as the Yorubas and the Hausas(?) secede. In using this argument, therefore, we are in effect saying: 'The Yorubas, the Hausas (and the others) cannot remain together without the Ibos; we want the Yorubas and the Hausas to remain together; therefore we must forcibly prevent the Ibos from breaking away—even if this attempt to prevent them, together with their stubborn resistance, may lead to their extermination.'

This is an extremely logical and nice argument. But it must be directed to people other than the Biafrans. They cannot be asked to sacrifice their freedom in order that two peoples, who are not otherwise willing to attempt the building of a nation together, may carry on a precarious united existence. It is bad enough to force the Biafrans to make immense sacrifices for their own freedom; it would be worse than absurd to expect them to surrender the freedom for which they are dying in order to maintain a precarious unity among other peoples—whose own commitment to that unity must be very slight if this argument has any validity at all.

In fact, the argument 'If you allow the Ibo to go, the others will also go', inevitably provokes the question: 'Who are these others, and where will they go?' For properly considered, this argument is an Imperialist argument. I can well imagine Winston Churchill saying: 'If I allow India to go, the others will go, and I was not appointed the King's First Minister in order to preside over the liquidation of the British Empire'. But how can this kind of thing be said of Nigeria—most of all by Nigerians? Who in the Nigerian issue represents Churchill? And who represents the 'Others' who would break away if the Ibos are allowed to go? And who is the imperialist metropolitan power in Nigeria?

Those who advance this argument assume the Hausas to be the Churchill and the 'Others' to be the Yorubas in particular, and also the smaller groups. They assume that the Hausas would like to complete their conquest of the South, which was interrupted by the British, and are saying that the only way the Hausas will be able to continue to dominate the Yorubas and the smaller ethnic groups is if they also succeed in dominating the Ibos.

If this is the basis of the argument, and if it stated the actual position, I would be amazed at Africa's reaction to an African Imperialism abetted and supported by British Imperialism. Indeed, it would be very shameful if Africa, which is still groaning from the yoke of European Imperialism, was to make a cynical distinction between that and an internal African Imperialism. Such an argument must be rejected by the whole of Africa. Not only would it make nonsense of the principles we have been proclaiming; it is also an insult to the people of Nigeria—the Hausas, the Yorubas, and the others.

Let us reject the Internal Domino Theory in relation to the Nigerian question. For it assumes that the people now in the Federation of Nigeria are, and wish to be, imperialists. I cannot believe that. I still believe that they are capable of recognizing the tragedy which has caused one part of the Federation to break away, and of acknowledging that very different tactics are necessary if the old Nigeria is ever to be re-created. For surely they could decide to leave the Biafrans to go their own way and, by the kind of Nigeria which they create, to show the Biafrans what they are losing by remaining separated from their brethren. For if the other peoples of Nigeria decide to work together, they will continue to be a strong and powerful force in Africa; they really have the opportunity to build a good nation of which every Nigeria—indeed every African—can be proud. Then it may be that at some time in the future the Biafrans will wish to rejoin the peoples from whom they now wish to part; if this happens, it will be the accession of a free people to a large and free political unit. For if the secession of Biafra is a setback to African Unity—as of course it is—no one is suggesting that we should consequently stop working for African Unity on the basis of willing commitment. Why then are we suggesting that our Nigerian brethren have a different conception of unity, and that they want a unity of conquest only? I am not making such an argument: I am saying that, although our Nigerian brothers want to maintain one Nigeria, including Biafra, on the basis of equality of citizenship, they are wrong in thinking that this can be done now. I refuse to impute bad motives to General Gowon; I believe he is mistaken in his judgment and that Africa must not make the same mistake.

There is another Domino Theory which relates to the rest of Africa. We are told that, if we allow 'tribalism' to break up Nigeria, no African country would be safe; for every African nation consists of tribes which find themselves in the same country by an accident of history and by the grace of the Imperialists. I fully accept the danger of tribalism in Africa. When we started TANU in 1954, the first of the objectives of our Party was preparation for independence, and the second was 'to fight against tribalism'. We have not completely succeeded in eradicating tribalism from our society; indeed I was recently forced to remind our people of this objective, and to warn them about certain tendencies.

But the dangers of tribalism are so well-known that, although I would never wish to minimize them, I do not think it is now necessary to expound them afresh. There is, however, a different fact which can be equally dangerous. Sometimes, indeed very often, the spectre of tribalism is raised by the enemies of Africa against Africa. It is dangerous for Africa to accept the argument of tribalism without examining its relevance in every given case. Indeed to the extent that we need to learn from Nigeria's 'tribalism', I have a feeling that Africa is being bamboozled or mesmerized into learning the wrong lesson.

But first, what is a tribe? And how comparable is Nigeria's position to that which exists elsewhere in Africa? Are Hausas a tribe? Are the Yorubas a tribe? Are the Ibos a tribe? It may be said that they are not 'nations', but are they tribes? There are Scottish clans, but the Scots are not a tribe simple because of the fact that they are not a nation. The Welsh: are they a tribe? Are the Protestants of Northern Ireland a tribe? The Hausas, the Ibos, and the Yorubas, are not nations in the legal sense; but they are not tribes either. Each one of them is a 'people' which could easily become a very coherent nation. Each one of these 'peoples' of Nigeria has a better chance of forming a really viable and stable bation than many of the legal nations of Africa and other parts of the world.

Indeed, those who glibly compare Nigeria with other African countries show that they did not begin to understand the immense significance for the rest of Africa of the Nigerian experiment. Nigeria was trying (and if they do not allow themselves to be convinced by the internal Nigerian Domino Theory, they may continue trying) to building a Nation which incorporates several peoples who could have become Nations on their own. Had Nigeria succeeded (and Nigeria can still succeed if she rejects the argument of all or none), Africa would have a great example before it. We would be able to say: 'Within Nigeria there are several peoples, each conscious of itself and conscious of its ability to be a nation on its own. If they have nevertheless succeeded in submerging their natural unity into a larger artificial unity, for the greater benefit of them all, then the rest of Africa can submerge its smaller artificial units into that greater artificiality (indeed that more natural unit of all Africa) which holds greater promise for all the peoples of Africa.' In other words any success in Nigeria—even if partial is a demonstration of the practicability of our declared aim of African Unity—even though a Nigerian failure would not make this aim impossible of achievement. This, I repeat, is Nigeria's real significance to Africa.

No other political unit in our continent has the same significance for Africa; not even the Sudan, although the two cases are similar in one respect. Both have a basic problem of 'peoples' in the sense that the North of Sudan is different from the South, racially, religiously, culturally, and socially—although the one 'people' of the South are divided into several different tribes. The Sudan's problem, therefore, is very serious—just as Nigeria's problem is.

But fortunately for the Sudan, and for Africa, Southern Sudan is not blessed (or cursed) with immense mineral wealth. As a result, foreign economic interests are not involved in this conflict. However agonising the problem may be for the authorities in Khartoum—and for the people of the country—the former Colonial Power is most unlikely to pour arms into the Sudan to help maintain Sudanese unity. It is also unlikely to intervene in support of any attempt at secession. This situation will continue irrespective of the ideological leanings of the Government in Khartoum, and irrespective of what Russia does. In this case Sudanese leaders, and African leaders, have a real chance of solving the problem—provided we do not make the same mistake as we made in Nigeria and act as if there is no genuine problem to be solved.

The solution, as the present Government in the Sudan has rightly foreseen, lies in a constitution which recognizes both the unity of the Sudan, and the legitimate interests of the South. This is what Eastern Nigeria was asking for before it seceded, this is what the Aburi Agreement was all about; it was the refusal, by Lagos, to accept this necessity that finally led to secession and the present situation.

The fact is that the peoples of Nigeria have less in common, historically, linguistically, culturally, and as regards religion, than the peoples of Scandinavia. The only thing that the peoples of Nigeria have in common is that they are all Africans and all have been under British rule for a few decades—and Britain governed them virtually separately. It would be infinitely easier for the peoples of Scandinavia to form one nation than for the peoples of Nigeria. Those who do not see this do not understand Nigeria's significance for Africa.

One final point must be made about this tragedy. In spite of attempts on both sides of the quarrel to bring in religion, the conflict between Nigeria and Biafra is not a religious one. Yet if it were, that would be simply an additional complication: it would not justify the war. In fact, however, there are Christians and Muslims on both sides; religion cuts across the divisions between the Peoples.

I said earlier that Africa is learning the wrong lesson from the Nigerian tragedy. We are saying that if Biafra is allowed to secede, every country in Africa is going to have its own Biafra. But what we are doing is looking at results without looking at the cause of those results, and then saying that the same results will happen elsewhere without there having been any causes. That is nonsense. But there is a very serious lesson to be learned from the present tragedy. We should learn that where in any African state there is a dominant group, whether that group is ethnic, religious or otherwise, it must wield its power and influence on behalf of all the elements which go to form that country. In particular, it should be very solicitous of the interests of the minorities, because they are the ones which need the protection of the State. If a dominant group does not act in this protective manner, then civil

2 F

strive and consequent Biafras become inevitable. That is the lesson Africa should learn from the Nigerian tragedy.

We African leaders had a golden opportunity at the O.A.U. Summit Conference in Kinshasa, but we missed it because we were confused by the tribal domino theory. At that time the whole of Africa, including those countries which now recognise Biafra, supported the territorial integrity of Nigeria. Yet I believe that all States had some sympathy for the Easterners, who had already experienced a massacre of some 30,000 of their brethren, and who were trying to absorb nearly 2,000,000 refugees in the Eastern Region. Since we were all supporting Nigeria in its main objective of maintaining national unity, we should have used our moral stength to urge Nigeria to listen to those demands. We should have pointed out that under the circumstances of the two coups and the massacres, what they were asking was not only understandable but was also justifiable. Since we were supporting the Nigerian authorities in their efforts to keep Nigeria one, and since by that very support we were rejecting any claim by the East to secede, we were in a very strong position. We did not have to worry about Domino Theories and the Charter of the O.A.U. But we were so obsessed, bewitched and terrified by the Domino Theory that we did not dare raise a voice for the Ibos even when we all supported the Federal Authority.

That opportunity was lost. But we must not therefore even appear to acquiesce in the present situation of war and suffering. The least we can do is now to ask our brethren in both Nigeria and Biafra to stop fighting and to begin talking about their future relations. It is being said that the situation has changed from what it was two years ago, and that Biafrans need no longer fear for their future. If that is the case, we should ask Nigeria to convince the Biafrans of it at a conference table. You cannot convince people that they are safe while you are shooting and starving them.

The O.A.U. was established by Heads of African States. But it is intended to serve the peoples of Africa. The O.A.U. is not a trade union of African Heads of States. Therefore, if it is to retain the respect and support of the people of Africa, it must be concerned about the lives of the people of Africa. We must not just concern ourselves with our own survival as Heads of State; we must even be more concerned about peace and justice in Africa than we are about the sanctity of the boundaries we inherited. For the importance of these lies in the fact that their acceptance is the basis for peace and justice in our continent, and we all have a responsibility to the whole people of Africa in this regard.

Many African Governments, some of them very good governments, have been overthrown through coups. Some countries have had more than one coup; but none of them has broken up. Only the Nigerian Federation is in danger, and this from the effects of a failure to meet the legitimate interests of the Easterners, not directly because of the coups. And the fall of African Governments, however regrettable, is not the same thing as the disintegration of African countries. We must not be like the French monarch who said 'L'état c'est Moi'—'I am the State.' The O.A.U. must sometimes raise a voice against those regimes in Africa, including independent Africa, who oppress the people of Africa. In some countries in Africa it might be the only voice that can speak on behalf of the people. If we dare not do that, even in private, we shall deserve the scorn of those who accuse us of double standards.

In this connection we could learn a good lesson from our former masters. For European Governments are not often very polite to European regimes which fail to show respect for basic human rights within their own countries. Europeans do care about what happens to Europeans. (Sometimes, as in the case of Stanleyville, we are reminded of that fact rather unpleasantly). I think that is a lesson worth learning.

Thus, for example, European Governments do not invade Greece, for they respect the territorial integrity of fellow European States; but they have not left, and will not leave, the Greek regime in any doubt at all about what they think of it. Yet what have the Greek Colonels done? They have carried out a military coup against a constitutionally established government, and are detaining and persecuting the supporters of the constitution—an occurrence so familiar in young Africa that it is hardly considered wrong any more.

If we do not learn to criticise injustice within our continent, we will soon be tolerating Fascism in Africa, as long as it is practised by African Governments against African peoples. Consider what our reaction would have been if the 30,000 Ibos had been massacred by whites in Rhodesia or South Africa. One can imagine the outcry from Africa. Yet these people are still dead; the colour of those who killed them is irrelevant. We must ask Nigeria to stop more killing now, and to deal with the problem by argument, not death.

Justice is indivisible. Africa, and the O.A.U., must act accordingly.

[1] *Circulated privately to the O.A.U. Summit Meeting held at Addis Ababa, 4 September 1969. It was subsequently published in Dar es Salaam.*

219.
Nigeria Refutes Tanzania's Charge before O.A.U.[1]

President Nyerere of Tanzania has circulated a pamphlet bearing his name as author entitled, the 'Nigeria-Biafra Crisis.' Since the imprint on the pamphlet indicates that it was printed by the Government Printer in Dar-es-Salaam, we are entitled to consider it as authentic.[2] I wish to take this opportunity to correct the fallacies and misconceptions, and rebut the deliberate distortions of established facts contained in the pamphlet.

By way of general observation, I must say that parts of the pamphlet do grave violence to the truth and throughout its pages, there is an evident effort to tailor the facts to suit the pre-conceived notions and the public position of President Nyerere which are so much at variance with his private protestations. I wish to add that the ordinary people of Nigeria do not accept the good faith or sincerity of President Nyerere in his protestation that he only wants to help. What kind of help is it to kick you violently and repeatedly in the groin in order to cure you of an ailment and what kind of friend is he who seeks your destruction?

President Nyerere has said at other times, that he only wants Nigerians to know how he feels about the methods which we have been compelled to employ in dealing with secession. It is time that he heard for a change how ordinary Nigerians feel about him.

The first glaring untruth in the pamphlet is that more than 29,000 Nigerians (the equivalent of the population of Gibraltar) died in the Nigerian riots in 1966. I need hardly remind you that the Federal Government has established and said repeatedly that the figure of the dead in those unfortunate and regrettable disturbances was less than 5,000 of all tribes. Why does President Nyerere repeatedly prefer the inflated figures given by the rebels for their own propaganda purposes?

The analogy drawn by President Nyerere between the Nigerian crisis and the Gibraltar dispute is obviously misconceived. It is totally incorrect to suggest that the Federation of Nigeria comprised two separate units—Nigeria and the so-called Biafra—which came together to form a Federation, from which one unit now wishes to withdraw. The position in Nigeria is in no way similar to the situation between Tanganyika and Zanzibar, nor did Nigeria acquire the so-called Biafra as Britain acquired Gibraltar.

The principle of self-determination for Gibraltar to which President Nyerere has referred, is not appropriate in the Nigerian case. We Nigerians, like most other Africans, consider that our national self-determination is collective and we do not concede to any part of Nigeria the right to secede. This is what the war is about.

President Nyerere suggests that the Federal Government threatens the Ibos with complete extermination through starvation. He knows, and the world knows, that this is a deliberate falsehood. The measures which the Federal Government has taken from time to time to facilitate relief, the agreement which the Government has reached with the International Committee of the Red Cross and other Relief Agencies for relief supplies to reach the secessionist enclave, all testify to the determination of the Federal Government that the innocent, the old and the infirm should not suffer needlessly. We have agreed that daylight relief flights should carry supplies to the secessionist area after due inspection by International Observers in Lagos. It is Ojukwu who has refused to accept these arrangements. Yet, President Nyerere claims that we threaten the Ibos with complete extermination through starvation.

President Nyerere points out that the remote causes of the American Civil War are not the same as those in Nigeria. I need only say that the immediate cause, namely secession, is the same in each case. Wherever there has been an attempt at secession, whether it be in the United States or the Republic of the Congo, or in the Soviet Union, or anywhere else, the answer of the Central Government has always been the same, namely, to deal with the threat by force when peaceful means have failed.

Indeed, the remote causes of secession cannot be the same in every instance. They may be due to economic separatism, to tribalism, to foreign intrigues, to political differences or to a host of other causes. In the final analysis, when an attempt to secede is accompanied by armed rebellion, the Central Government and the patriots of the country have no alternative but to quell the rebellion.

President Nyerere claims that during the riots of 1966 many people were killed with the assistance of the forces of law and order. This is another deliberate untruth. The facts are well established that the forces of law and order actively assisted the vast majority of refugees to proceed to their homes in Eastern Nigeria and that the forces of law and order brought the situation under control within a few days. How else could, to quote President Nyerere's figures, 2 million Ibo refugees have returned to the East alive?

President Nyerere pretends that he cannot see the analogy between Katanga and Biafra. He suggests that the comparison between Katanga and Biafra is superfluous and irrelevant because although the Central Government of the Congo objected to the attempted secession in Katanga, just as the Federal Government has objected to the attempted secession in Nigeria, the fact that war broke out for this reason is not important. But surely this is the very heart of the matter, and it cannot be treated as lightly as President Nyerere tried to do.

President Nyerere described Tshombe as a stooge of external economic interests but somewhat strangely refuses to see Ojukwu in the same light. Who does he suppose pays for Ojukwu's arms and propaganda machinery?

If President Nyerere considers that foreign interference in the Congo was generated by the Katanga's vast copper resources and similar interference in Nigeria arose from the oil resources in the so-called Biafra, it is clear that he does not even begin to understand that as far as the Federal Government is concerned, this is not a war over the control of mineral resources. As a matter of fact, over 85 per cent of Nigerian oil is well outside the Ibo area. Nigeria's oil resources are located mainly in the Mid-Western State and the Rivers State. At the outbreak of hostilities, the Oil Companies declared their open support for the secessionists, thus proving that the Oil Companies are prepared to deal with any one in control of the oil producing areas. But, I repeat, as far as the Federal Government is concerned, oil is not the central issue in Nigeria. The Foreign interference in the Nigerian Crisis has been mainly by certain European Powers interested in sustaining the secessionist regime at all costs in order to dismember our country. As regards the request of President Nyerere for a separate existence for the Ibos, at no time has any secessionist leader demanded a sovereign Ibo State. Their ambition has been to include the 5 million non-Ibos within their empire of the so-called Biafra. If by 'Biafra' President Nyerere understands a separate Ibo State, then he may know that such a State—the Central-Eastern State—does in fact exist today under the new 12-States structure in the country.

President Nyerere calls for peace 'before the Ibos are wiped out.' But nobody else of any repute believes that the Ibos are in danger of being wiped out. About 5 million Ibos out of a total of 7 million have returned to their homes in Federal areas. Over 50,000 Ibos live in Lagos. About 500,000 Ibos live in the Mid-West State. It is an odd argument, coming from a man who pretends to some understanding of logic, that the Federal Government has not sought to wipe out the millions of Ibos to whom it has access and who live in areas under Federal Authority, but that it wishes to wipe out those to whom it has no immediate access. If the Ibos are fighting for collective security and individual liberty, they are already assured of it within Nigeria.

It is an insult of the first order to suggest that 'the Nigerian people are not quite sure of what they are fighting for.' When President Nyerere speaks of the Nigerian people, he is obviously referring to the Government and people of Nigeria including the armed forces who are bearing the brunt of the civil war with resolution. I consider this an insult to our people and an ignorant statement from someone who pretends to some familiarity with the problems of Nigeria. Federal war aims are crystal clear. The Federal Government and people as a whole are fighting against secession, against the disintegration of their motherland, and against any threats of domination of the minority ethnic groups by the bigger ones.

President Nyerere suggests that the secessionists have no strong supporters. How would he then describe Portugal and South Africa, perhaps the greatest enemies of Africa today; to name only two, and others who supply the secessionists with arms and provide them with other services to sustain their secession?

President Nyerere says that 'it is estimated that more people have died in this war in the last 2 years than in Vietnam in the last 10 years.' Where did he get his estimate from? Here again, President Nyerere betrays himself as a rebel propagandist. We know for a fact that almost 5 million Ibos have returned to their homes in Federal areas. If it were true that another 2 million had died in the war, there would now be hardly anybody left in the secessionist enclave and the war would have been over, since there were only 7 million Ibos at the beginning of hostilities. President Nyerere described the Federal Government as 'an implacable enemy of the Ibos.' However, all the evidence of independent impartial International Observers, the recent testimony of Dr. Nnamdi Azikiwe—himself an Ibo leader—and the evidence on the ground in liberated areas which is there for all to see, falsify this assertion.

In the light of what has happened in the past 2 years, it is untenable to suggest that the rebel leaders are fighting for the survival or security of the Ibos. At the outbreak of hostilities in July, 1967, the rebels proclaimed that they were fighting for Southern-Nigeria solidarity, and they tried unsuccessfully to occupy the Western State and take over the Federal Government in Lagos. At that stage therefore, the rebel leaders were fighting an expansionist war. Now that the secessionist area has been reduced to a small enclave, the rebel leaders claim that they are fighting for the survival and security of the Ibos. These facts have been brought to the knowledge of President Nyerere, but it apparently serves his purposes to argue otherwise.

I admit that Nigeria is an accident of history, but so is Tanzania, so are most other African States, so is the United States of America or Canada, and so are the States of Southern America. Indeed, so are the vast majority of the countries of the world as they exist today. If we were to accept President Nyerere's arguments that these accidents of history should be permitted to disintegrate, we should have to rearrange the entire map of the world and hardly any country in Africa or outside it would survive.

President Nyerere suggests that if Nigeria disintegrates, there would be three resultant States. I am quite surprised by his lack of knowledge of the composition of Nigeria. Nigeria contains some 200 tribes and if the process of disintegration were once begun, the probabilities are that we would end up ultimately with 200 countries. Africa has some 2,000 linguistic communities. Would President Nyerere seriously suggest that there should be 2,000 member States of the OAU?

The Imperialist argument about India which President Nyerere has raised, cannot apply to Nigeria, because the late Sir Winston Churchill's statement referred to the relationship between an Imperialist Power and its colonies. Nevertheless, it will be recalled that when India did go, the other colonies including Nigeria and Tanganyika, followed and gained their independence from Great Britain.

President Nyerere pleads that 'Nigeria could decide to leave the Biafrans to go their own way.' One suspects that this is what Nyerere is really after. If so, he should have the courage to plead the cause openly and honestly, instead of pretending that his assistance to the rebels is only designed to bring us to the conference table. President Nyerere's argument can be used as a justification for breaking up any multi-lingual African country.

President Nyerere is entirely wrong in his judgment that Nigerians cannot live together in one country on the basis of equality of citizenship and mutual respect among the ethnic groups. If he allowed any tribal group in Tanzania to break away, he would soon find that the others would want to follow. President Nyerere says that he fully accepts the danger of tribalism in Africa, but his whole approach seems to be that in order to avoid this danger, we should permit armed tribalism to have its way. What a curious argument!

President Nyerere argues that each of the tribes of Nigeria has a better chance of forming a really viable and stable nation than many of the legal nations of Africa and other parts of the world. Again, this is an argument which could be applied to Tanzania and many other countries which are multi-ethnic in composition. Should we all therefore abandon our efforts at nation-building? President Nyerere says that 'no other political unit in our Continent has the same significance for Africa as Nigeria.' Can we then assume that this is the clue to his whole attitude towards Nigeria? If he asks what the different ethnic groups of Nigeria have in common, apart from territorial boundaries and a history of British rule, one would counter that by asking what he has in common with the Masais or the other groups in Tanzania different from his own except these same common factors. Would he advocate the disintegration of Tanganyika on that account?

President Nyerere claims that 'it was the refusal by Lagos to accept the necessity for a Constitution which recognizes both the unity of the country and the legitimate interest of the secessionists areas that finally led to secession.' This is another deliberate misrepresentation. It will be recalled that in September 1966, there was in progress a Constitutional Conference attended by leaders and civilian representatives of all parts of Nigeria, including the Ibos, and that substantial agreement had been reached at the Conference on a suitable Constitution for Nigeria when Ojukwu ordered his delegates out of the Conference. He never allowed them to return to that Conference.

Another deliberate untruth in the pamphlet is that Britain governed tribes of Nigeria separately 'for a few decades before independence.' I did not realize that President Nyerere was so ignorant of the history of Nigeria.

The truth is that Nigeria was governed as one integral unit for about half a century before the regional administrations were established. At no time in our history were the various ethnic groups in Nigeria governed as separate entities.

The single truth which President Nyerere permits himself to admit in the entire pamphlet is that the conflict in Nigeria is not a religious war. Yet

President Nyerere has been known in the recent past to have stated the very opposite. In the midst of this solitary statement of truth however, President Nyerere says that there have been attempts 'on both sides of the quarrel' to bring in religion. This is a fabrication. At no time has the Federal Governmen introduced the religious question into the conflict. Indeed, it has constantly been our claim and our position that the civil war in Nigeria is not a religious one. The probable consequences for Africa of the disintegration of Nigeria are not idle fears. We only have to look at the tribal composition of most African countries to realize that Africa cannot afford 'Biafranization.'

In an attempt to blame the OAU, President Nyerere writes: 'we African leaders had a golden opportunity at the OAU Summit Conference in Kinshasa, but we missed it because we were faced by the tribal domination theory. At that time, the Ibos had not declared their secession. At that time the whole of Africa including those countries which now recognize Biafra supported the territorial integrity of Nigeria.' This deliberate distortion of facts is the most glaring example in the pamphlet of the recurring attempts therein to make the facts suit the arguments, rather than the accepted practice of drawing conclusions from established facts. You may recall that the rebels declared secession on 30th May, 1967. Hostilities commenced on 6th July, after persistent rebel incursions into the Benue-Plateau and Kwara States. The OAU Summit in Kinshasa was held in September, 1967, long after the declaration of secession and the outbreak of hostilities. I need say no more on this.

President Nyerere suggests that the OAU should ask Nigeria to convince the Biafrans of their future within the Federation at a Conference table. What does he suppose we have been trying to do all the time in London, Kampala, Addis Ababa, Niamey and Monrovia? What does he think Dr. Azikiwe is now trying to do?

President Nyerere says 'We must ask Nigeria to stop more killing now.' The impression that this statement gives is not what people are doing on both sides as a result of fighting, but that the Federal Government is killing Ibos wantonly. This is a calculated attempt to further rebel propaganda and it is in direct contradiction to the evidence of independent International Observers.

In conclusion, let me say that no disrespect towards President Nyerere is intended in the remarks which I have made. If I have explained myself in plain terms, it is only in response to the demands of the situation created by President Nyerere's renewed attempt to sabotage the efforts of the OAU Consultative Committee. You will recall that it was after the establishment of the Committee in 1967 that President Nyerere recognized the rebel regime, and that from time to time, whenever it has appeared that we might be on the point of a break-through, President Nyerere has permitted himself some action of statement which served to revive the morale of the rebels.

It is unfortunate that President Nyerere seems to believe, like the soldier out of step with the rest of his unit, that all the members of the OAU are wrong. The older, wiser, more knowledgeable, more experienced Heads of State, the countries closer to Nigeria and better informed about Nigeria's problems, and all the Commonwealth countries, all these together are wrong.

Only President Nyerere has been pleased with divine inspiration to see the light.

I wish to say that the people of Nigeria will not permit President Nyerere or anybody else to destroy their heritage and undermine their common destiny.

President Nyerere does not like to be reminded of the role which Nigeria played in helping to save him in his hour of difficulty in 1964. Curiously enough, he has made no single acknowledgment, no single allusion to this fact since our crisis began. Africa will always remember how he has sought to repay us.

He says at the end of his pamphlet that African Leaders must not be like the French Monarch who said, 'I am the State.' I invite you to look at the pamphlet again and judge for yourselves how serious President Nyerere is on this point. If you notice the signature, you will see 'Julius K. Nyerere, United Republic of Tanzania.' Not Julius K. Nyerere, President of the United Republic of Tanzania or Julius K. Nyerere, Dar-es-Salaam, United Republic of Tanzania but plainly and simply, 'Julius K. Nyerere, United Republic of Tanzania', thus implying 'L'état c'est moi.'

[1] *Statement by Enahoro at a press conference held in Addis Ababa, September 1969. (Text from* That's False, Nyerere *(Lagos, 1969).)*

[2] *See* DOC *218.*

220.
O.A.U. Resolution on Civil War passed at Addis Ababa[1]

(*i*) Notes with satisfaction the progress report of the OAU Consultative Committee on Nigeria covering the past year;

(*ii*) Congratulates the Consultative Committee on the efforts it has exerted, and again expresses its full confidence in the committee's ability to carry out the important mission entrusted to it, within the shortest possible time;

(*iii*) Appeals solemnly and urgently to the two parties involved in the civil war to agree to preserve in the overriding interests of Africa, the unity of Nigeria and accept immediately the suspension of hostilities and the opening without delay of negotiations intended to preserve the unity of Nigeria and restore reconciliation and peace that will ensure for the population every form of security and every guarantee of equal rights, prerogatives and obligations;

(*iv*) Invites the Consultative Committee on Nigeria to offer its good offices to facilitate these negotiations; and

(*v*) Makes a solemn and urgent appeal to all governments, international organisations, humanitarian institutions as well as to all political, moral and religious bodies in the world to facilitate the implementation of the present resolution and to desist from any action, gesture and attitude likely to jeopardise the efforts of the OAU in finding an African solution to the Nigerian crisis.

[1] *Resolution on Nigeria adopted on 10 September 1969. (Text from news agency reports quoted in* Africa Research Bulletin, p. *1517.)*

221.
Gowon Speaks on Independence Day[1]

Fellow Nigerians:

On this occasion of the celebration of our National Day, I bring you greetings. I have directed that no formal celebrations be held but that you all, as individuals, groups of people or religious organizations should be asked to say prayers to God for the return of peace and understanding among our divers people and communities.

I ask you to rededicate yourselves on this ninth anniversary of our attainment of independence to the pursuance of only those things which will ensure the preservation of the unity of this country.

It is the inescapable duty of the Government of every sovereign nation to safeguard its territorial integrity. The policies of the Federal Military Government have been designed to enable it to carry out this duty. Some time ago, I told you that all our resources would be devoted to ensure that we achieve, as quickly as possible, complete victory over the rebellion which has plunged this nation into civil war. . . .

I have been asked now and again what is holding up the conclusion of the military operations. Let me answer this question by repeating once again that we are quelling a rebellion, not fighting an external enemy. We have conducted operations of the war in a very deliberate fashion, so that we can achieve national reconciliation on the cessation of hostilities.

Our detractors say that the reason for the delay is that we do not have the will or the capacity to achieve a military solution. This is not so. The responsibility for healing the nation's wounds in the future rests with us, not with any foreigner. So, let us not forget why we have gone to war—to keep Nigeria one.

Here, I wish to announce that in the spirit of forgiveness and reconciliation, I have instructed the Police to release from detention, as soon as practicable, all persons who have been detained during the current crisis and who are no longer considered to constitute grave security risk to the country. It is up to those affected to prove their loyalty and faith in the country and in our efforts to build a healthy society where no man is oppressed.

In the spirit of conciliation and with the paramount aim of preserving the unity of our country we have allowed our African brothers in the O.A.U. to help us to find ways and means of achieving a peaceful solution to our crisis. The recent meeting of the O.A.U. Assembly of Heads of State and Government at Addis Ababa passed a resolution which called on all Nigerians—including the secessionists—to agree to preserve in the over-riding interests of Africa, the unity of Nigeria and to accept immediately the suspension of hostilities and the opening without delay of negotiations intended to preserve the unity of this country and restore reconciliation and peace that will ensure for our people every form of security and every guarantee of equal rights, prerogatives and obligations.[2]

We accepted this resolution in its entirety and declared ourselves ready and prepared for negotiations which would be conducted in a spirit of realism in the interests of all our people.

We have offered several times in the past terms which guarantee to all the citizens of our country equality and full security of their persons and their property. We stand by these terms. In my speech at the O.A.U. Conference, I warned that unless the secessionist leadership accepted the opportunity offered by the O.A.U. to settle our crisis by peaceful negotiations, the Federal Military Government would have no choice but to carry on the military operation to its logical conclusion.[3]

There is still time for the secessionist leadership to retrace its steps, but time is fast running out. Developments in the war-affected areas have shown that the civilian victims in the areas still under the control of the secessionists are now beginning to appreciate that they are being used to satisfy the political ends of a few ambitious people. These misguided Nigerians thought that they saw in the temporary difficulties which have beset this nation the opportunity of creating an empire for themselves. It will not be long now before the sufferings of the innocent people are ended.

In the meantime, the Federal Military Government will continue to co-operate with genuine humanitarian organizations to enable food, medical supplies and other relief materials to reach the innocent people still under secessionist control.

I now wish to speak briefly about the recent wave of lawlessness and terror involving unprovoked attacks on innocent civilians and some law enforcement agencies in the Western State. It is the duty of Government not only to provide good and orderly administration but also to ensure that the legitimate grievances of the people, if any, are remedied without delay.

I am aware that the Government is taking the necessary steps to remove the causes of the grievances which are known to be genuine. But quite clearly, it is also the duty of the people to bring their grievances to the notice of the Government without resort to acts of lawlessness. It is, therefore, most regrettable that at this time of national emergency some people should allow themselves to be misguided into trying to obtain redress of their grievances through violence.

Why should our brothers in the Western State give the impression that they relish the taunts of those who disparagingly call the State 'Wild West'? Why must our Yoruba brothers, as it seems, choose to smear their tradition and reputation for progressiveness and enlightenment?

Honestly, I must advise our brothers in the Western State that it does them no credit to allow foreigners, and even some Nigerians, to say that the current Nigerian crisis originated from the West in 1962 and the people are yet not helping this country by not sinking their differences.

Every effort is being made urgently to determine the under-lying causes of the recent disturbances. I understand, however, that one reason may be the desire of some persons to have new States created in the country. The present 12-State Structure was designed to correct the structural imbalance of the former Federation and to remove the genuine fears of the domination of the country by any one section, or combination of sections of it, through size.

States were created to further political progress and stability and to ensure freedom and protection for all sections of the country. It should be obvious, therefore, that in the interest of continued stability, the present structure may, as I have indicated on previous occasions, have to be re-examined to determine whether there is need to have more than the present minimum of 12 States. But this is surely not the time for such re-examination.

Our nation is at war. All efforts must be directed towards the conclusion of the war. We cannot afford to dissipate our energies.

Once again, I must remind all the citizens of this country that this is not the time for partisan political activities at the local or national level. We must all strive to subdue personal ambition or sectional interests in the overall interest of the nation. Our legacy to future generations of Nigerians should be a united and stable country.

I appeal to the people of the Western State and the whole nation for that matter, not to do anything that will tarnish Nigeria's good name or provide support for the enemies of Africa who spread calumnies abroad about us.

Finally, I wish to assure you that the Federal Military Government remains as determined as ever to pursue relentlessly the search for an honourable and lasting solution to the Nigerian crisis. This can be achieved only with your continued co-operation and sacrifice. You have done extremely well but more is required of all in order to complete the task that God has called upon all of us to accomplish for the good of our beloved country and in the interest of the whole Africa. . . .

[1] *Address to the nation, 1 October 1969.*
[2] *See* DOC *220.*
[3] *See* DOC *217.*

222.
World Council of Churches Rethinks its Relief Rationale[1]

The Sub-Committee has reviewed the Division's present relationships and responsibilities regarding the conflict in Nigeria/Biafra, and makes the following recommendation:

1. The Division of Inter-Church Aid, Refugee and World Service welcomes wholeheartedly the action of the All Africa Conference of Churches (AACC) in appointing representatives to visit both Biafra and Nigeria, December 2nd–10th, 1969, not only to ascertain present conditions and human needs on both sides, but to re-enforce their relationships with the Christian communities there, and, hopefully, to exert an influence towards peace-making.

2. The Division strongly emphasizes the statement of the Central Committee of the World Council of Churches made in August 1969 that 'the only answer to this terrible situation is the ending of the fighting and the achievement of lasting peace'. We believe that the World Council of Churches, through its General Secretary, the Commission of the Churches on International Affairs (CCIA), and in co-operation with the AACC, the Roman Catholic Church and the governments concerned, should play an effective role in peace-making and must pursue any opportunity to do so. Meanwhile, we are concerned that the World Council of Churches should maintain its ability to act as a mediator by refusing to take a partisan political position with respect to the conflict.

3. The Division (which includes in its membership and consultants representatives of many of the agencies involved in the airlift being supported by the

consortium of agencies known as Joint Church Aid) expresses its gratitude that this humanitarian effort has saved the lives of many people. At the same time, the Division expresses its deep distress at the ambiguous position in which the tremendous effort has put Christian people, Churches and agencies because of its political side-effects. These side-effects include exposing the Churches to the charge of prolonging the war and adding to the suffering of the people.

4. The Division further recognizes that the agencies involved in Joint Church Aid face the issue as to whether, and by what means a short term emergency operation with unprecedented implications for the Churches, for the Division and for their relation to governments should be continued. Equally they face the implications for the people in Biafra if the operation is discontinued.

The Division raises the question whether the Churches and their agencies, especially through Joint Church Aid, should prolong the massive airlift in its present form. Likewise, should the Churches' major effort to meet this human need be the indirect means by which some governments are enabled to pursue their own ends and thereby achieve their own goals? The Division recommends therefore that Joint Church Aid at its upcoming meeting consider what ought to be the future of its operation in the light of:

a. the thinking of the people and the churches in Africa and especially in Nigeria and Biafra;

b. the continuing human needs and suffering in both Nigeria and Biafra and alternative ways of meeting them.

[1] *Statement made by the Deputy Director of the W.C.C. to the 5th Plenary Session of the Joint Church Aid meeting held in Norway, 8 December 1969 (Joint Church Aid Press Release No. 120).*

223.
Ojukwu's Message as He Flees Biafra[1]

Proud and heroic Biafrans, fellow countrymen and women, once again I salute you. My Government has been reviewing the progress of this war that has now raged for the past two and a half years with increasing fury. It is well that at each stage we remind ourselves of the purposes of this war, what we are fighting to safeguard, and why we are so determined to continue to defend ourselves.

You have borne the brunt of the strains of this fight. You have suffered unmentionable privations at the hands of an enemy that has used every conceivable weapon, particularly the weapon of starvation, against an innocent people whose only crime is that they choose to live in peace and security according to their own beliefs and away from a country that had condemned and rejected them.

Your heroism as a people has sustained our gallant armed forces in defending the territory of our fatherland and in giving you that protection that we all so ardently need and desire. You have had your villages and homes ravaged and plundered, your assets destroyed, millions of your sons and daughters murdered in cold blood, and your youth condemned to misery by the enemy's recent movements and indiscriminate shelling and bombing of hamlets, villages and refugees in their camps and on the roads.

All this sacrifice has been in the interest and with the sole purpose of achieving security which was the main motive forcing our taking up arms to defend ourselves. We had proclaimed ourselves a republic independent and sovereign because we were and are satisfied that only through it can we guarantee our security. Nevertheless we left the door open and [declared] on several occasions that we welcomed any other initiative that offers us the security we need. Each time we have said so our enemies and detractors have mischievously distorted our statements. We are entitled in the light of our recent experience to demand to know what measures are being proposed for our security.

The task of a leader of a people at war is to be responsive to the plight of his people, to determine what level of sacrifice can be accepted. Your patriotism has exceeded all expectations and earned worldwide admiration for your fortitude. Armed with your mandate I have striven to apply the forces at our disposal to the best of our ability against overwhelming odds. Throughout we have made strenuous efforts for peace, taking initiatives of our own to get peace talks going, made compromises in order to get our adversaries to settle our conflict at the conference table. Each time a callous world has imposed a new set of conditions. Each condition that we fulfil gives rise to an entirely new one.

More recently, some friends of both sides have made some proposals for an arrangement with Nigeria that in our view will offer to Biafrans the security to which we aspire. This has been referred to as certain forms of union, confederalties, association, or commonwealth arrangements with Nigeria.

Once more, to show our honesty, and in accord with my own frequent affirmations that I would personally go anywhere to secure peace and security for my people, I am now travelling out of Biafra to explore with our friends all these proposals further and fully and to be at hand to settle these issues to the best of my ability, always serving the interests of my people. Our detractors may see this move as a sign of collapse of our struggle, or an escape from my responsibilities.

If, God helping, we can by this latest show of earnestness secure for our people the end of destruction of your homes and property, I shall be satisfied that this venture on which I embark with your blessing has yielded fruit. I know that your prayers go with me as I go in search of peace and that, God willing, I shall soon be back among you.

In my short absence I have arranged for the Chief of General Staff, Maj-Gen. Philip Effiong, to administer the Government with the rest of the Cabinet to run the affairs of this Republic while I go on this mission, accompanied by my Political Adviser and my Chief Secretary.

I once more pay my tribute to the Biafra Armed Forces, and urge all ranks to maintain their positions while I seek an early and honourable end to this struggle and all the suffering it has brought on our people. Proud and courageous Biafrans, [noble] Biafrans, Biafra shall live. God bless you all.

---

[1] *Pre-recorded and broadcast over Biafran radio at 6.00 a.m., 11 January 1970. (Text from B.B.C. ME/3277/B1.)*

224.
Lt.-Col. Effiong Announces Surrender of Biafra[1]

Fellow Countrymen,

As you know, I was asked to be the officer administering the government of this republic on the 10th of January, 1970. Since then, I know that some of you have been waiting to hear a statement from me. I have had extensive consultations with the leaders of the community, both military and civil, and I am now encouraged and hasten to make this statement to you by the mandate of the Armed Forces and the people of this country. I have assumed the leadership of the government.

Throughout history, injured people have had to resort to arms in their self-defence where peaceful negotiations fail. We are no exception. We took up arms because of the sense of insecurity generated in our people by the events of 1966. We have fought in defence of that cause.

I take this opportunity to congratulate officers and men of our Armed Forces for their gallantry and bravery which have earned for them the admiration of the whole world. I thank the civil population for their steadfastness and courage in the face of overwhelming odds and starvation. I am convinced now that a stop must be put to the blood-shed which is going on as a result of the war. I am also convinced that the suffering of our people must be brought to an immediate end. Our people are now disillusioned, and those elements of the old government regime who have made negotiations and reconciliation impossible have voluntarily removed themselves from our midst.

I have, therefore, instructed an orderly disengagement of troops. I am despatching emissaries to make contact with Nigeria's field commanders in places like Onitsha, Owerri, Awka, Enugu and Calabar with a view to arranging armistice. I urge on General Gowon, in the name of humanity, to order his troops to pause while an armistice is negotiated in order to avoid the mass suffering caused by the movement of population.

We have always believed that our differences with Nigeria should be settled by peaceful negotiations. A delegation of our people is therefore ready to meet representatives of Nigeria Federal Government anywhere to negotiate a peace settlement on the basis of OAU resolutions. The delegation will consist of the Chief Justice Sir Louis Mbanefo as leader, Professor Eni Njoku, Mr. J. I. Emembolu, Chief A. E. Bassey, Mr. E. Agumah. The delegation will have full authority to negotiate on our behalf. I have appointed a council to advise me on the government of the country. It consists of the Chief Justice Sir Louis Mbanefo, Brigadier P. C. Amadi—Army, Brigadier C. A. Nwanwo—Army, Captain W. A. Anuku—Navy, Wing Commander J. I. Ezero—Air Force, Inspector-General of Police, Chief P. I. Okeke, Attorney-General Mr. J. I. Emembolu, Professor Eni Njoku, Dr. I. Eke, Chief A. E. Udoffia, Chief A. E. Bassey, Mr. M. T. Mbu, Mr. E. Agumah, Chief Frank Opuigo, Chief J. N. Echeruo. Any question of a government in exile is repudiated by our people.

Civilian population are hereby advised to remain calm and to co-operate with the Armed Forces and the Police in the maintenance of law and order. They should remain in their homes and stop mass movements which have increased suffering and loss of lives.

On behalf of our people, I thank those foreign governments and friends who have steadfastly given us support in our cause. We shall continue to count on their continued help and counsel. I also thank His Holiness the Pope, the Joint Church Aid and other relief organisations for the help they have given for the relief of suffering and starvation. I appeal to all governments to give urgent help for relief and to prevail on the Federal Military Government to order their troops to stop all military operations.

May God help us all.

¹ *Text taken from transcript of actual radio broadcast over the Biafran radio at 4.40 p.m. on Monday 12 January 1970. The version reproduced in the Federal Ministry of Information's* Victory for Unity *is a considerably edited one. That given in* The Times, *13 January 1970, is nearly verbatim, and marks the garbled passages.*

225.
General Gowon Welcomes Biafra's Surrender¹

My Dear Compatriots:

We have arrived at one of the greatest moments of the history in our nation. A great moment of victory for national unity and reconciliation. We have arrived at the end of a tragic and painful conflict.

Thirty months ago we were obliged to take up arms against our brothers who were deceived and misled into armed rebellion against their fatherland by the former Lieut.-Col. Ojukwu. Our objective was to crush the rebellion; to maintain the territorial integrity of our nation; to assert the ability of the blackman to build a strong, progressive and prosperous, modern state and to ensure respect, dignity and equality in the comity of nations for our posterity.

I salute you once again for the courage, loyalty and steadfastness of our fighting troops, and the loyal support and sacrifice of all Nigerians. I pay tribute to the courage and resourcefulness of those who have fought so long against lawful troops, as victims of Ojukwu's vicious propaganda and the machinations of certain foreign Governments.

You will have heard the broadcast of Lieut.-Col. Effiong asking the remnants of the secessionist troops to lay down their arms. This is in accord with our appeal. I accept in good faith Lieut.-Colonel Effiong's declaration accepting the OAU resolutions supporting the unity and territorial integrity of Nigeria. I urge all the secessionist troops to act honourably and lay down their arms in an orderly manner. Instructions have been issued to all field commanders of the Nigerian Army to put into immediate effect the contingency arrangements for the mass surrender of secessionist forces. The officers of the secessionist troops are urged to send emissaries to Federal field commanders at once to work out detailed arrangements for orderly surrender. All field commanders will take all necessary measures to give full protection to surrendering troops. Field commanders are instructed to push and establish effective Federal presence in all areas remaining under secessionist control. Federal troops in carrying out this directive will be accompanied by Police units and will exercise all care and shoot only if they encounter resistance. I appeal to all remaining secessionist forces to cooperate with Federal troops to avoid any further loss of life. All Federal troops must continue to observe the letter and spirit of the code of conduct issued at the beginning of the military operations.

We reiterate our promise of a general amnesty for all those misled into the futile attempt to disintegrate the country. Federal troops, East-Central State officials and authorized relief workers in the field will take adequate care of all civilians in the liberated areas. We must all demonstrate our will for honourable reconciliation within a united Nigeria.

Fellow countrymen, with your continued loyalty and dedication to the national cause, we shall succeed in healing the nation's wounds. We must all welcome, with open arms, the people now freed from the tyranny and deceit of Ojukwu and his gang.

Long live one united Nigeria.

We thank God for His mercies.

[1] *Broadcast at midnight on 12 January 1970 (Federal Ministry of Information Press Release No. 31/1970).*

226.
Ojukwu's Call from Exile[1]

Three days ago I left the Republic of Biafra with certain members of my Cabinet as a result of a decision taken by that Cabinet in the interest of our people's survival. Since my departure events have moved with such breathless speed that friends and foe alike have been left not only bewildered but confused.

It is therefore necessary for me to address these words to the international press in order to keep the records right, and in pursuit of the object of my leaving the Republic of Biafra.

It is necessary in order to understand events that have led to the drama of the past few days to look back at the origin of our conflict and conduct in this war. Biafra, once the eastern region of Nigeria, was one of the three sovereignties that banded together to form the Federal Republic of Nigeria. Three of the reasons which made the sovereignties bind themselves together were:
1. Mutual protection of life and property—hence the fundamental human rights entrenched in our constitution and the arrangements made for the joint control of the police.
2. Security against external and internal threats—hence the responsibility of the central Government for defence.
3. The promotion of international trade and good relations with foreign

2 G

countries—hence the assignment of exclusive responsibility to the central Government.

During the course of our first experiment in nationhood it was clear that the Federal organization had neither the will nor the desire to maintain that unity of purpose for which the Federation was founded.

In 1966 it became clear that the central authority was unable and unwilling to fulfil the terms for which it was established. Right under her nose the people of Eastern Nigeria, now Biafrans, were subjected to such acts of barbarism, such atrocities that gave clear indication of a genocide that was to come.

The people of Biafra, in full consultation and believing that the only guarantee for security lay in the resumption of their sovereignty, mandated me to proclaim their territory the sovereign and independent Republic of Biafra, and to take up arms if need be to protect the lives and property of our people and the independence thus proclaimed.

On July 6, 1967, the Federal forces crossed the boundaries of Biafra and attacked her defenceless populace. Our people, in the face of such aggression, had no alternative but to defend themselves as best as they could. The war that ensued has continued from that day with unabated fury until today when we find that, because of certain limitations, we are no longer able to offer formal military resistance to the Nigerian aggressors.

For three years we have fought against overwhelming odds. Our conduct of the war has contrasted sharply with that of the Nigerian hordes. We were always aware of our limitation, and therefore have never discontinued our efforts for peace and a negotiated settlement.

We had relied on the conscience of the world to respect the rights of our people to self-determination and security. We have been frustrated by an international conspiracy against the interest of the African.

Yet, believing in the justice of our cause and the ultimate triumph of truth over falsehood, outnumbered and outgunned, we have grimly held back the unrelenting enemy for three gruelling years with our bare hands.

Nigeria began her recent final offensive against Biafra in October, 1969, after months of preparations, which included the starvation of our entire populace to such sub-human level that the movement of enemy troops through our territory became a mere formality.

For months we cried to an unsympathetic world, pointing out the danger of a total blockade and siege warfare at this stage of world civilization. In answer to that cry our people were further subjected to more deprivation by the drastic reduction of relief supplies, not only to the menfolk but to our women and children, to the aged and the very young, to the old and the infirm.

By the end of November the Biafra armed forces were no longer able to feed themselves; our civil populace were neither able to feed themselves nor the army. Yet for over 30 grim days our gallant and heroic forces maintained their positions in the sheer hope of a miraculous respite.

In the first week of January, the Nigerian forces, by a fast military move, took control of the last areas from where we had any possibility of obtaining food. In quick succession demoralization set in, threatening national disintegration and bringing in its wake confusion and mass exodus.

I gathered together at Owerri during the night of January 8, 1970, those members of my cabinet who could be contacted to review the situation. At that meeting I presented in firm and clear terms the grim hopelessness of continued formal military resistance.

I informed the Cabinet that my primary duty in the circumstance was to seek the protection of our exhausted people and to save the leadership of our heroic republic. I therefore offered to go out of Biafra myself in search of peace.

I decided personally to lead any delegation in order to give it maximum effect and to speed up matters in order to save the lives of our people and preserve the concept of Biafra. I did this knowing that whilst I live Biafra lives. If I am no more it would be only a matter of time for the noble concept to be swept into oblivion.

I chose for the delegation the following persons: Dr. M. I. Okpara, my political adviser; Mr. N. U. Akpan, my Chief Secretary; Major-General Madiebo, the commander of my army.

In the fluid and uncertain military circumstances the Cabinet considered it advisable and reasonable that families of envoys in or going abroad should be sent out. My last hours in Biafra before my departure were spent in close consultation with Major-General Philip Effiong, whom I had appointed to administer the Government in my absence, and his last request to me was to take out his family and to maintain them under my protection. I agreed.

Since the departure of the delegation from Biafra we have remained faithful to our mandate. We have made contacts with friends and men of goodwill. We have spared no efforts to mobilize all forces in an effort to take food into Biafra on a gigantic scale. We have taken steps to alert the world to real fears of genocide at the hands of the Nigerians.

Nigeria's continuing efforts have always been directed at domesticizing the conflict in order to apply the final solution to the Biafran problem away from the glare of an inquisitive world.

From all indications it is clear that Nigeria will not feed our people. They have said so often enough, and their past records clearly underline this fact. There is no food whatsoever in Biafra and unless food can get into Biafran mouths in the next 72 hours it will be too late.

Nigeria's insistence to control the distribution of relief is both to ensure that Biafrans get no such relief, and also to shut out outsiders who might witness and expose the enormous crimes she plans to commit against our people.

Nigeria throughout this war has distinguished herself for a lack of control over her armed forces. It is therefore most unlikely that, flushed with intoxication of an unexpected military victory, she will be able to exercise any measure of control on her forces now on the rampage.

In any case Nigeria's aim is to destroy the elite of Biafra. The only possible way of preventing such a catastrophe is by interposing between the contesting forces some neutral force to prevent a genocide that would make 1939–45 Europe a mere child's play.

We have always believed in the futility of this war. We have always maintained that this war will solve no problems. If this carnage must stop, Nigerian leaders and their friends must borrow a leaf from the lessons of the last world war, where it was found that a permanent settlement could only emerge from an honourable peace.

Immediate efforts should therefore be directed towards early negotiations for peace without exacting full tribute of conquest. Only in this way can peace which the whole world desires have any chance.

I therefore appeal to all governments and international organizations, countries and churches of the world, men and women of goodwill, to both our friends and enemies, in the interest of humanity to come forward to assist and protect the lives and talents of Biafra, to relieve the starvation and wasteful death now the only companion of our exhausted people.

I implore the world to rise to this desperate need, to mount all possible pressures on Nigeria to ensure that food gets to my people.

I would like to conclude this statement with a solemn declaration, emphasizing again the point I have repeatedly made in this appeal to the governments of the world to save my people from extermination.

The sole motive behind Nigeria's determination to draw an iron curtain over Biafra and exclude international observers, relief agencies, journalists whom they have not carefully picked themselves, is to make sure that the atrocities they will certainly carry out in Biafra is unseen and unreported in the world press.

Once they have sealed off Biafra from the gaze of mankind, I hesitate to contemplate the fate of the Biafran leadership, the trained manpower, the scientists and professionals whom they would liquidate as planned before the world can interfere.

Genocide, I repeat, is not an internal affair of Nigeria, and it is the clear duty of those powers who have armed and helped Nigeria to gain victory over Biafra to step in and persuade Gowon to allow international agencies and observers to enter Biafra to feed the hungry, to heal the sick and to save a whole people from complete annihilation.

If they fail to persuade Nigeria to open her doors to these agencies then their declarations of humanitarian aid to Nigeria becomes mere propaganda. I repeat the aims of Nigeria are genocidal—the test that the contrary is the case is her willingness to admit humanitarian agencies whom Gowon has now openly declared he will exclude.

As a people we have endured as only giants endure. We have fought as heroes fight. We have dared as only gods dare. We are disillusioned by the world's insensitivity to the plight of our people. Yet because our cause is just we believe we have not lost the war, only that the battlefield has changed.

We are convinced that Biafra will survive. Biafra was born out of the blood of innocents slaughtered in Nigeria during the pogroms of 1966. Biafra will ever live, not as a dream but as the crystallization of the cherished hopes of a people who see in the establishment of this territory a last hope for peace and security. Biafra cannot be destroyed by mere force of arms.

May I take this opportunity to thank all those persons and organizations that have sacrificed that we might live—that we assure them that their sacrifice will not be in vain.

Biafra lives. The struggle continues. Long live the Republic of Biafra.

[1] *Statement issued through the Biafran Information agency in Geneva and reproduced verbatim in* The Times, *16 January 1970.*

227.

'The Dawn of National Reconciliation'—Gowon's Victory Message to the Nation, 15 January 1970[1]

Citizens of Nigeria,

It is with a heart full of gratitude to God that I announce to you that today marks the formal end of the civil war. This afternoon at Dodan Barracks, Lt. Col. Phillip Effiong, Lt. Col. David Ogunewe, Lt. Col. Patrick Anwunah, Lt. Col. Patrick Amadi and Commissioner of Police, Chief Patrick Okeke formally proclaimed the end of the attempt at secession and accepted the authority of the Federal Military Government of Nigeria. They also formally accepted the present political and administrative structure of the country. This ends thirty months of a grim struggle. Thirty months of sacrifice and national agony.

Exactly four years ago on January 15, 1966, a group of young army officers overthrew the Government of the country with violence. The country hoped, however, that the military regime which followed would quickly restore discipline and confidence in the army and introduce a just, honest, patriotic and progressive government. The country was disappointed in those hopes. There were further tragic incidents in the army leading to the death of many officers and men in July, 1966.

I then assumed the leadership of the Federal Military Government. I gave a solemn pledge to work to reduce tension in the army and the country, to restore the Federal Constitution and to prepare the country for an orderly return to civilian rule as early as possible. Despite my efforts and the co-operation of all other members of the Supreme Military Council, the former Lt. Col. Ojukwu pushed us from one crisis to another. This intransigent defiance of Federal Government authority heightened tension and led to the much regretted riots in September/October, 1966. He subsequently exploited the situation to plunge the former Eastern Region into secession and the nation into a tragic civil war.

The world knows how hard we strove to avoid the civil war. Our objectives in fighting the war to crush Ojukwu's rebellion were always clear. We desired to preserve the territorial integrity and unity of Nigeria. For as one country we would be able to maintain lasting peace amongst our various communities; achieve rapid economic development to improve the lot of our people; guarantee a dignified future and respect in the world for our posterity and contribute to African unity and modernisation. On the other hand, the small successor states in a disintegrated Nigeria would be victims of perpetual war and misery and neo-colonialism. Our duty was clear. And we are, today, vindicated.

The so-called 'Rising Sun of Biafra' is set for ever. It will be a great disservice for anyone to continue to use the word Biafra to refer to any part of the East Central State of Nigeria. The tragic chapter of violence is just ended. We are at the dawn of national reconciliation. Once again, we have an opportunity to build a new nation.

My dear compatriots, we must pay homage to the fallen. To the heroes, who have made the supreme sacrifice that we may be able to build a nation great in justice, fair play and industry. They will be mourned for ever by a grateful nation. There are also the innocent men, women and children who perished, not in battle but as a result of the conflict. We also honour their memory. We honour the fallen of both sides of this tragic fratricidal conflict. Let it be our resolution that all those dead shall have died not in vain. Let the greater nation we shall build be their proud monument for ever.

Now, my dear countrymen, we must recommence at once in greater earnest, the task of healing the nation's wounds. We have at various times repeated our desire for reconciliation in full equality, once the secessionist regime abandoned secession. I solemnly repeat our guarantees of a general amnesty for those misled into rebellion. We guarantee the personal safety of everyone, who submits to Federal authority. We guarantee the security of life and property of all citizens in every part of Nigeria and equality in political rights. We also guarantee the right of every Nigerian to reside and work wherever he chooses in the Federation, as equal citizens of one united country. It is only right that we should all henceforth respect each other. We should all exercise civic restraint and use our freedom, taking into full account the legitimate rights and needs of the other man. There is no question of second class citizenship in Nigeria.

On our side, we fought the war with great caution, not in anger or hatred, but always in the hope that common sense would prevail. Many times we sought a negotiated settlement, not out of weakness, but in order to minimise the problems of reintegration, reconciliation and reconstruction. We knew that however the war ended, in the battlefield or in the conference room, our brothers fighting under other colours must rejoin us and that we must together rebuild the nation anew.

Those now freed from the terror and misery of the secessionist enclave are therefore doubly welcome. The nation is relieved. All energies will now be bent to the task of reintegration and reconciliation. They will find, contrary to the civil [thus in press release; but probably 'evil'?] propaganda with which they were fed, that thousands and thousands of Ibos have lived and worked in peace with the other ethnic groups in Lagos and elsewhere in the Federation throughout the dark days of the civil war. There is, therefore, no cause for humiliation on the part of any group of the people of this country. The task of reconciliation is truly begun.

The nation will be proud of the fact that the ceremony today at Dodan Barracks of reunion under the banner of the Federal Republic of Nigeria was arranged and conducted by Nigerians amongst ourselves alone. No foreign good offices was involved. This is what we always prayed for. We always prayed that we should resolve our problems ourselves, free from foreign mentors and go-betweens however well intentioned. Thus, our nation is come of age. And the meaning of today's event must be enshrined in the nation's memory for ever.

There is an urgent task to be done. The Federal Government has mounted a massive relief operation to alleviate the suffering of the people in the newly liberated areas. I have as announced, assigned special responsibility for this to a member of the Federal Executive Council. We are mobilizing adequate resources from the Federal Government to provide food, shelter and medicines for the affected population. Rehabilitation and reconstruction will follow simultaneously to restore electricity, transport and communications.

We must, as a matter of urgency, resettle firms and reopen factories to ensure that normal economic life is resumed by everyone as soon as possible. Special attention will be given to the rehabilitation of women and children in particular, so long denied the comfort of homes, the blessing of education and the assurance of a future by Ojukwu's wicked tyranny and falsehood. We must restore at once to them hope and purpose in life.

Federal troops have a special charge to give emergency relief to the people in the areas they have liberated before civilian help can come. They must continue and intensify their splendid work in this regard. The state administrations are giving emergency relief the first priority. The Rehabilitation Commissions and the Voluntary Agencies are extending their efforts. The appropriate agencies of the Federal Government will soon make further announcements about additional relief measures.

My Government has directed that former civil servants and public corporation officials should be promptly reinstated as they come out of hiding. Detailed arrangements for this exercise have been published. Plans for the rehabilitation of self-employed people will also be announced shortly.

The problem of emergency relief is a challenge for the whole nation. We must prove ourselves equal to the task. Our resources, which have enabled us to prosecute the war successfully and without obligations to anyone, are considerable. I appeal to the nation for volunteers to help in the emergency relief operations in the newly liberated areas. Doctors, nurses, engineers, technicians, builders, plumbers, mechanics, administrators—all skilled hands willing to help are urgently required. The detailed arrangements for recruitment will soon be announced. I am sure that there will be a prompt and good response to this call.

You will have heard that my Government may seek the assistance of friendly foreign governments and bodies especially in the provision of equipment to supplement our national effort. There are, however, a number of foreign governments and organisations whose so-called assistance will not be welcome. These are the governments and organisations which sustained the rebellion. They are thus guilty of the blood of thousands who perished because of the prolongation of the futile rebel resistance. They did not act out of love for humanity. Their purpose was to disintegrate Nigeria and Africa and impose their will on us. They may still harbour their evil intentions. We shall therefore not allow them to divide and estrange us again from one another with their dubious and insulting gifts and their false humanitarianism.

Regarding the future, we shall maintain our purpose to work for stability with the existing political structure of a minimum of twelve states. The collision of three giant regions with pretensions to sovereignty created distrust and fear and led to the tragic conflict now ending. The multi-state structure will therefore be retained with the minimum of the present twelve states. Immediate post-war planning and reconstruction will continue on this basis. Any new constitution will be the result of discussion by the representatives of all the people of Nigeria.

I am happy that despite the war, Nigeria has maintained a strong and expanding economy. Plans are also far advanced for faster economic modernisation. Our enormous material resources and our large dynamic population will make this possible. We are pledged to ensure rapid development for the benefit of the Nigerian people themselves. It will be much easier to achieve reconciliation and reintegration in increasing prosperity.

Fellow countrymen, the civil war is truly over. We thank God. But the state of national emergency and emergency regulations remain. Discipline and sacrifice are essential if we are to achieve our goals in the immediate post-war period and lay sound foundations for the future. I demand of you patience, resolution and continued dedication. I demand of the workers and employers continued restraint in industrial relations in keeping with the recent decree. A decree on price control will soon be promulgated. We shall soon review wages and salaries to improve the lot of the ordinary man. The immediate economic problems are challenging and we must behave accordingly.

On this occasion, I wish to place on record the nation's gratitude to the Organisation of African Unity for its splendid diplomatic and moral support for the Federal cause. I thank particularly the Chairman of the Consultative Committee on Nigeria, His Imperial Majesty Haile Selassie 1 and the other members of the Committee. I also thank the President of the OAU General Assembly, Presidents Mobutu, Boumedienne and Ahidjo, who presided over OAU Summit discussions of the Nigerian crisis. The enemies of Africa were restrained by the demonstration of such solid support. I thank the Secretary-General of the United Nations, U Thant, for his understanding attitude towards our country's crisis and the specialised agencies for their assistance. I also thank the friendly governments who gave us moral and material support in the darkest hour of our need. The nation will remember them as true friends. It is the desire of my Government that our relations with them should grow stronger.

Consistent with our basic policy, we shall maintain correct relations with all foreign governments notwithstanding the anxieties they may have caused us. As we emerge from our greatest trial we shall endeavour to work for peace in the world and for a better economic deal for the less developed countries of the world.

The Armed Forces deserve the greatest praise for their valour in battle, their loyalty and dedication and for their resourcefulness in overcoming the formidable obstacles placed in our way. I praise them for observing strictly the code of conduct issued to them at the beginning of the operations. It is necessary now more than ever when the rebellion is ended, for them to maintain the high standard they have attained. The letter and spirit of the code must be obeyed. Their first duty is to protect the lives and property of all surrendering troops and civilians and to give them humane treatment. Stern disciplinary measures will be taken against any who violate the code. I know, however, that I can continue to count on your loyalty and discipline.

I also praise the civilian population everywhere in the country for their patience, sacrifice, loyalty and steadfast support for the fighting troops and for One Nigeria. We must all be justly proud.

All Nigerians share the victory of today. The victory for national unity, victory for hopes of Africans and black people everywhere. We must thank God for his mercies. We mourn the dead heroes. We thank God for sparing us to see this glorious dawn of national reconciliation. We have ordered that Friday, Saturday and Sunday be national days of prayer. We must seek his guidance to do our duty to contribute our quota to the building of a great nation, founded on the concerted efforts of all its people and on justice and equality. A nation never to return to the fractious, sterile and selfish debates that led to the tragic conflict just ending. We have overcome a lot over the past four years. I have therefore every confidence that ours will become a great nation. So help us God.

Long Live the Federal Republic of Nigeria.

[1] *Broadcast from Lagos, 15 January 1970. (Text from Nigeria House press release dated 19 January 1970.)*

Epilogue

So the Nigerian civil war was over—almost a thousand days after it started and exactly four years from that night of the long knives in January 1966 which proved to be the direct *casus belli* among so many indirect and interrelated ones. The war that in 1967 earned such derisive epithets as 'history's least reported war',[1] 'the war between blacks nobody cares about',[2] and 'the forgotten war',[3] had in 1968 given way to the description abroad of 'small but nasty',[4] an unwinnable 'vicious circle',[5] and 'just a dirty, lousy war',[6] and had by 1969 achieved the unwanted distinction of becoming the biggest, best-weaponed, and bloodiest war in the whole history of Black Africa. Indeed at times it gave the impression of being, far from forgotten, a matter of more urgent concern to the outside world than it was to those actually fighting it out in Nigeria. The one thing it was not was a senseless war. Nor was it, despite the faintly determinist history of independent Nigeria, a straightforward confrontation between North and South or the explosion of Hausa-Ibo rivalry. It was, finally, Ojukwu against Nigeria, 'a quarrel between one ambitious man and the rest of the country'.[7] Given the truism that every war is *per se* stupid, and none more so than the traumatic horror of a civil war, there are grounds to argue that a close examination of the passions and the principles of the participant leadership, set forth to a considerable extent in these pages, will eliminate the accusation of unadulterated futility. For all the enormity and tragedy of the Nigerian experience, independent Africa could, in the cathartic nature of a classical drama, emerge the 'better' from such a purification.

An epilogue to the chronicle of crisis and conflict compiled in these two volumes runs the risk, in the tradition of Nigeria's house-that-Jack-built political history, of becoming little more than a prologue to the next act. Yet some retrospective and prospective summary, however open the options must remain at this juncture [March 1970], is clearly in order.

The details of the factual aftermath of those few weeks following the cessation of the fighting[8] do not belong here, being beyond our im-

[1] *West Africa* (1968), p. 179. [2] *Jet* (Chicago), 27 July 1967, p. 14.
[3] *Scotsman*, 16 August 1967 and 26 March 1968; *Daily Mirror*, 4 February 1968; Lord Brockway in the House of Lords, 13 February 1968.
[4] *The Economist*, 28 July 1967. [5] *Guardian*, 15 April 1968.
[6] P. Trudeau, Canadian Prime Minister, quoted in *West Africa* (1968), p. 1301.
[7] See DOC 100.
[8] The Nigerian and overseas press, daily and weekly, for the six weeks from 10 January till the end of February 1970 offers extensive documentation. For other African reaction, see *Africa Research Bulletin*, pp. 1646–9.

mediate terms of historical reference; yet neither are they totally alien or superfluous, for some of the events and words of the moment have in them the seed of longer-term influence. If the story is not yet over as we write, at least its outline has been sketched, in however preliminary a fashion, for the four ineradicable years that preceded Nigeria's current reformation and renaissance. The cumulative minicrises that beset the Federal Government at the very moment of its hardwon victory gave a glimpse of the rocky course ahead even with the hazard of civil war safely negotiated. They may best be alluded to in a swift series of crisis cameos.

The two weeks that followed Biafra's formal surrender were packed with more high-voltage incidents than many a month of the seemingly inching war. At home, there came in quick succession the short-tempered but not entirely unprovoked rebuke to the more temerarious of the humanitarian agencies to 'keep their blood-money'[1] and pack their bags; the brief terminal communiqué as Joint Church Aid halted its relief operation and the I.C.R.C. closed down its Nigerian organization;[2] and the final report of the international team of observers,[3] whose qualification of the 'mass killings' of civilians by Federal troops from the notorious Third Division at Afikpo was confirmed by a statement from the Minister of Defence blaming the murders on 'a rebel terrorist gang, Biafran Organisation of Freedom Fighters'.[4] The handling of such incidents by a hard-pressed Federal Government was made no easier by other alarums. There was the arguable arrest and brusque sentencing of priests, who had flown into wartime Biafra on mercy missions, on a charge of illegal entry into Nigeria, seen at its worst as a Gilbert-and-Sullivan episode and at its best as a satisfying scapegoat or like punishing the fire brigade for not ringing the front door bell.[5] Governor Diete-Spiff's seeming indiscretion in ordering transport priorities of champagne and caviare over those of medical relief played straight into the hands of a press spoiling for a fight,[6] and Nigeria's apparent attachment to a symbol in refusing to use Uli airfield because of its resented association with outside intervention[7] (a move which might have hastened delivery of medical and food supplies but which more likely would have generated in its own right a transport free-for-all and snarl-up of appalling proportions), gave rise to scorn from a West that may not have fully understood the real situation.

[1] General Gowon's press conferences in Lagos, 13 and 22 January 1970.
[2] J.C.A. bulletin 127 of 23 January 1970, and I.C.R.C. bulletin of 20 February 1970. See also *Morning Post*, 7 February 1970.
[3] Released in Lagos on 14 February 1970.
[4] Quoted in *Sunday Post*, 15 February 1970. Cf. *The Times*, 2 and 16 February, and *Sunday Telegraph*, 15 February 1970.   [5] *Sunday Telegraph*, 1 February 1970.
[6] Cf. the headline 'Champagne at Wedding as Thousands Starve', *The Times*, 22 February 1970.
[7] 'Let us get Uli out of our minds, it has been used too much in international politics already'—General Gowon, quoted in the *Scotsman*, 23 January 1970.

Abroad there was the ill-judged public plea by the Pope for the protection of Biafrans against what His Holiness saw as 'a yet more cruel epilogue of horror . . . there are even those who fear a kind of genocide',[1] which brought a strongly worded rebuke from the Federal Government and was not entirely dissipated by the subsequent Papal backtracking praise for Nigeria's 'effective steps to banish the spirit of revenge . . . [and] advances towards that complete reconciliation which will make the Nigerian Federation truly great and prosperous'.[2] The fulsome thanks for Russia's quiet role accorded by Nigeria's Ambassador in Moscow, who simplistically described Soviet aid as being 'responsible for the Federal victory more than any other single thing, more than all other things put together,'[3] contrasted with Lagos Radio allusions to Britain, America, and Holland as 'fair weather friends'[4] or worse; and the impertinent wish by the British House of Commons to hold an emergency debate on sovereign Nigeria's post-war relief operations caused extreme and justifiable resentment in Lagos[5] with Gowon himself joining the hawks in a deservedly anti-European hard line.[6]

There were, too, more permanent and more genuine matters of uncertainly brought about by the final swiftness of the collapse of rebellion. There was the pitiful aftermath of suffering and starvation destined, in the view of the United Nations man-on-the-spot, to remain Nigeria's grim lot for some while longer—'the period of anxiety over bloodshed and violence will soon be ended but the question of malnutrition, poverty and death will remain a cause of alarm for many months'.[7] There were the areas of contradiction between Lord Hunt's assessment,[8] the international observers' report,[9] the optimistic opinion of U Thant,[10] and the copy filed by the world press (and described by Mr. Wilson as 'episodic and panoramic'[11]) as each recorded its own view of the plight of Biafra in the first weeks of would-be peace. There was speculation whether Ojukwu in the Ivory Coast would prove as ineffective in exile as Nkrumah had been in Guinea. There was, too, noticeable to those in Lagos at the time, no small anxiety among the Ibo intelligentsia as they sought to reconcile the reiterated wartime promises of having their jobs back with the not-unexpected peacetime caution of how 'we must not

[1] Quoted in *West Africa* (1970), p. 90.

[2] Quoted in *Morning Post*, 7 February 1970, under the headline 'Vatican is Now All Praise for Federal Government'.

[3] Quoted in *The Times* and *Daily Telegraph*, 21 January 1970.

[4] Quoted in *Daily Telegraph*, 28 January 1970.

[5] Parliamentary debate of 26 January 1970. Those in Lagos at the time, and the *Financial Times* of 24 January, alone appeared to be aware of this intensity of feeling.

[6] *The Times*, 30 January 1970.

[7] Report to U Thant by Said-Uddin Khan, released in Lagos and New York on 26 January 1970.

[8] Cmnd. 4275 of 1970.

[9] Released in Lagos on 14 February 1970.

[10] U.N. Press Release 36/T/284 of 19 January 1970.

[11] Speech in House of Commons, 22 January 1970.

forget those that have stuck to their posts', and with the careful procedures announced by the Federal Public Service Commission (subsequently stepped up to allow for a thorough screening in Enugu) for the
reabsorption of former civil servants from the East Central State.[1]
There were also the even more careful inquiries into the conduct of
former 'Biafran' army officers,[2] immeasurably relieved by Gowon's
promise that Nigeria would stage no Nuremberg trials. Above and
beyond and within it all could be discerned, on one of the few occasions
in the history of Nigeria's decolonization and independence, xenophobic
overtones in the repeated warnings to foreign do-gooders to keep out
and let Nigerians 'heal the wounds of civil war ourselves',[3] and in the
Black Power principles detected by some[4] in Gowon's identification
among his war aims of the intention 'to assert the ability of the Black
man to build a strong, progressive and prosperous modern state.' The
listing of potentially influencing events and verbatim remarks could be
extended to the very moment of publication. Here we have done no
more than mention selected highlights of the first few post-war weeks
as they obtruded on the eye and ear of the observer in Nigeria during
the immediate moments of the war ending. None may claim to be an
integral part of the story of this book, yet singly and signally each is
part of the future of Nigeria.

So much for the prologue to this epilogue. What of the epilogue proper?
Nigeria's civil war might be examined at a number of coexistent levels.
It can be described in a context of straightforward historical or political
narrative; it can be analysed for its internal influences or for its external results, for its impact on the minds of its participants or of its
observers; and it can be interpreted for its effect on and its meaning to
One Nigeria, or Africa, or the O.A.U., or the Western World. Only
those ignorant of the determinants of the past on the shaping of the
future, above all in the African context, would decry the historical
approach to the Nigeria of tomorrow. Slogans like 'the less we look at
the past, the better for us all' may satisfy glib politicians but they are too
naïve to appeal to the scholar; or to the thinking patriot, if he accepts
Santayana's dictum that nations which do not learn their lesson from
history are condemned to relive it. Finally, lifting our eyes in expectation
rather than looking back in anger, some attention may be given to the
political permutations that the 1970s could hold for *post-bellum* Nigeria.

Hypothesis apart, a number of certainties may be entered against
the alternatives and probabilities that will be subsequently postulated.
First, the history of the civil war and of its immediately prior political
episode has still to be written. The full story of the January and July

[1] P.S.C. circular issued on 6 January 1970. See also Mid-West P.S.C. circular of 14
February 1970.

[2] *Morning Post*, 7 February; *Daily Sketch*, 19 February 1970.

[3] Gowon's press conferences of 13 and 22 January, 1970.

[4] e.g., Michael Wolfers in *The Times*, 15 January 1970. Cf. pp. 21 and 39, fn. 1.

coups; the behind-the-scenes manoeuvring that accompanied the *ad hoc* constitutional conference, the Aburi meeting, and the downhill drift to secession; the conduct of the military operations, from the Benin blitzkrieg of August 1967 to the final break-through to Uli and the end of the road; and the real inside tale of the series of initiated or implored or imagined peace moves, of humanitarian relief operations, of lobbies and arms dealers, and international pressure groups—none of these aspects of the four years or crisis has in any way yet been fully documented, described, or discussed.[1] As we set out in the preface, these volumes are at the most a history towards a history of Nigeria, 1966–70. With much-needed modesty, they claim to have achieved little more than the chronological delineation of a framework of reference, the orderly presentation of the top leadership's *ipsissima verba*, and the pointing up of the abundance of material already available for specialist studies. The substance to this outline has still to be filled in as the records, from both sides, are gradually opened to and interpreted by those who, if they exist at present, can be said to have no axe to grind.

Secondly, for all the safety-valve exhortation to reduce the Biafran concept to nothingness and erase the sinister term from the Nigerian vocabulary, it is unlikely that *post mortem* 'Biafra' will be forgotten any more quickly than say the Confederates, the Jacobites, or the Bonapartists—the other losers of causes—have been. Memory does not respond thus to administrative decree; it is even less ready to do so when it has been blooded in sentiment. While Biafra must remain a dirty word in the future conceptualization of One Nigeria and its public use has been understandably banned in Nigeria save within the face-saving formula of quotation marks or where the academic context of historical accuracy demands it, so effective was the impact of Ojukwu's propaganda and so subtle the appeal of his would-be case for self-determination that, in the ambivalent West at least, the grim story may be remembered less as the Nigerian civil war and more as the Biafran war. For the man-in-the-street of Europe and America, the chances are that for many years to come the word 'Biafra' will at once conjure up pictures of starving, skeletal African children; wrongly, the imagery may be similar to that associated with reaction thirty years later to Belsen or Dachau instead of that associated with armed insurrection.

---

[1] It is too early to attempt the final analysis at this stage. When the time does come, historians may recall the judgement of Winston Churchill: 'Let us learn our lessons. Never, never, never believe any war will be smooth and easy, or that anyone who embarks on the strange voyage can measure the tides and hurricanes he will encounter. Once the signal is given, the statesman is no longer the master of policy but the slave of unforeseeable and uncontrollable events. . . . Antiquated War Offices, weak, incompetent or arrogant commanders, untrustworthy allies, hostile neutrals, malignant fortune, ugly surprises, awful miscalculations—all take their seats at the Council Board on the morrow of a declaration of war. Always remember, however sure you are that you can easily win, that there would not be a war if the other man did not think he also had a chance.' *My Early Life* (London, 1958).

With Rhodesia defiant on Britain's doorstep, the concepts of 'rebellion' and of defiance of lawfully constituted authority are less exciting and less emotive than they were among yesterday's Britons. Whatever opinion one has of Emeka Ojukwu, his story is willy-nilly here to stay for some time and, outside a totalitarian administration, no government can legislate it away. This being so, in a democratic society one must simply hope that the telling of that story will prefer the facts to the incipient legend and will carefully eschew any inclination to otiose hagiography.

Thirdly, the war—'Nigerian' or 'Biafran'—has been the graveyard of an unhappy number of reputations. The referential 'Old Guard' to describe the Ministers and M.P.s of the First Republic carries the stigma of corruption and failure, however unfair such a sweeping and uncompromising totality of opprobrium may be. The military *coup d'état* of 15 January 1966, culminating in the civilian coup of 27 May 1967, did far more than exterminate a national leadership cadre: it put paid to a whole political style and brought to an end an attitude and way of life that had come to be associated with everything that was, in the exuberant words of a highlife hit of 1960, 'Nigeria Independent'.

Britain's reputation ended the war as it had started it, in Biafran eyes, at an all-time nadir. At times it was not, for all Mr. Wilson's determined defence of his Government's policy to continue arms supplies to Lagos, much above this level in the opinion of many Nigerians, as the noisy reaction to her initial hesitancy over arms, and to the weary and on at least one occasion worthless debates of her House of Commons, testified.[1] America's reputation was even lower, as Secretary of State William Rogers was bluntly told when he visited Lagos a month after hostilities had ceased.[2] As for France, her tacit support (to put it at its diplomatic mildest) for the Biafran cause brought upon her name some of the virulence of Nigerian disgust and abuse. In all three countries, the success of pro-Biafran groups in marshalling public opinion was an added item of disrepute before Nigerian eyes. Scandinavia, the Netherlands, and Switzerland all received their share of verbal insult and condemnation. For too many, individuals and groups as well as governments, Biafra became a cause instead of a case. And the escalatory internationalization of a lost cause was, as Hungary, Cuba, Czechoslovakia, and Vietnam had already demonstrated, a peril at least equal to the original danger. Russia alone among the major powers emerged with public and unqualified credit.[3]

[1] See p. 464. The Editor of *The Times* was among those influential British people accused of living in the Victorian era and seeing 'Nigeria as a British territory and her people as Her Majesty's dark-skinned subjects'—*Daily Sketch* (Ibadan), 1 April 1970.

[2] e.g., *Daily Telegraph*, 20 February 1970, citing local reactions. 'We offer no welcome' —*Daily Express* (Ibadan), quoted in *West Africa* (1970), p. 246, along with hostile comment from the *New Nigerian* and *Nigerian Tribune*.

[3] See p. 464. Cf. *Spectator*, 31 January 1970, p. 135; *The Economist* 7 February 1970, p. 37.

The hostility was by no means reserved for European powers. African sister-states like Tanzania and Zambia, Ivory Coast and the Gabon, who had granted diplomatic recognition to Ojukwu's rebel republic, were exposed to such intense and on occasion indecent vituperation from the Nigerian government-inspired communications media that with the end of the war many were still left wondering how soon the breach could be honourably healed.[1] Sierra Leone, whose role has not been fully revealed, has yet to be cleared in some Nigerians' minds of what was looked on as her 'treachery' in seeking to pressurize Lagos into a cease-fire. Even Uganda was at one time suspect for daring to appear hesitant. Public arguments about who should make the first move in restoring diplomatic relations between Nigeria and those African States that recognized Biafra suggested that the process of reconciliation might be as uphill a task internationally as internally.[2] The O.A.U. had not emerged with as enhanced a reputation for unity or efficacy as many had hoped, despite the needed fillip that her endorsement of the Federal stand gave to a diplomatically hard-pressed Lagos in 1968. But the O.A.U.'s firm stand did more than strengthen the Nigerian case; it revealed that for all their anti-colonial clamour over imperialist-drawn boundaries, the opinion of Africa's statesmen would stomach coups and even political assassination, but never secession. The Nigerian civil war has lessons for all of Africa, the O.A.U., the Commonwealth, and the U.N.[3] As for most (but not all) of the international relief organizations, even the old adage about the less said the sooner mended may not be enough: certain of the rifts may never be repaired. For nations as much as individuals, the Pan-African political criterion was rigorously applied in its wartime context: those who are not seen to be with us are assumed to be against us. Neutrality, objectivity, even silence, at times became dispensable luxuries to a nation at war.

'Biafra' is dead; what of Nigeria? Nigeria has survived the war; how

---

[1] Reconciliation was discussed at the O.A.U. Ministerial Council meeting at Addis Ababa in February 1970. This medium alone gives cause for hope.

[2] For instance, March 1970 still found in existence such activist organizations as the Britain-Biafra Association, the Biafra Action Committee in France, and the American Committee to Keep Biafra Alive with its litany, still appearing in newspapers:

> It's over. Let us offer thanks
> To British planes and Russian tanks.
> The oil, so precious to the health
> Of Britain and the Commonwealth,
> Is safe again with British Shell.
> The Ibos may not fare so well,
> But Harold Wilson says he'll chide
> All victors bent on genocide. . . .

Within the African continent, the early reluctance for diplomatic détente was easy to detect in the Nigerian, Zambian, and Tanzanian press of the period. In Dar es Salaam, the support of Biafra went so far as the Ministry of Information's reprinting the Government's 1968 Statement on the recognition of Biafra and including it in the publicity materials handed out to visitors, reportedly even after the war was over.

[3] Cf. the editorial 'African Ponders Nigeria', *The Times*, 12 March 1970.

will she survive the peace?[1] A number of threads can be distinguished in the tapestry of *post bellum* Nigeria, even if it is, with the fighting over barely a month ago, too early to pick out the final pattern. The sampler itself is clearly defined: reconciliation and reintegration of the Ibo, rehabilitation and reconstruction of the Nigerian economy, and restoration of a democratic constitutional government once the military leadership judges the time right to lead its men back to barracks. The dominant strands include those of administrative structure, political or the shorter-term politico-military leadership, and the centre-state and intra-statal relationships, all set against a programmed constitutional handover. None of these can remain unaffected by the others; each is interwoven and interdependent. They may be briefly discussed in turn here.

National reconstruction takes priority. The spectre of dangerously hasty demobilization has been quieted by the decision not to run down the army for the present.[2] Of the reintegration of the Ibo, little can at this juncture be added to the programme set out by the Federal Government in a series of statements while the war was still on and cited in our text. The National Rehabilitation Committee had its guidelines laid well in advance, and with the shattered East-Central State's civil service put together again under the direction of the Administrator in Enugu and his staff, the immediate objectives of implementing relief operations and starting up a rudimentary civilian administration again were, in March 1970, already under way.[3] For what they are worth, however, personal impressions and conversations in Nigeria within those first weeks of peace prompted the tentative drawing of a distinction between reconciliation and reintegration and again between levels of reconciliation. The unhampered sincerity of 'welcome back' extended to the Ibo in the top echelons of Nigerian society—and nowhere was it quicker or warmer than in the officer corps[4]—was not automatically echoed by all those lower down where the Ibo shoe had pinched before: public protest along the lines of 'who are the guilty men?'[5] and Colonel Obasanjo's instruction to rebel officers that 'what is expected of you is a sign of remorse'[6] was more quietly echoed by private accounts of appar-

---

[1] Cf. *Daily Times* editorial, 14 January 1970.

[2] *West Africa* (1970), p. 305.

[3] In the immediate aftermath of peace, the distribution and planting of yam seedlings against the oncoming rains became as great a matter of urgency as the provision of medical supplies and famine relief. Both were bound up with the question of how to handle the useless Biafran currency, a problem on which the Federal government seemed initially uncertain on how best to proceed.

[4] M. J. Dent has recorded General Gowon's endorsement of the Federal Officers Association's wish to have no war medal struck or decoration awarded in a fight among brothers—*World Today*, March 1970, p. 103.

[5] e.g., 'It is time the rebel clique were clearly defined. . . . It could not have been Ojukwu and only half-a-dozen men who held the Federal forces at bay for nearly three year'—H. O. Davies, *Sunday Post*, 15 February 1970.

[6] Quoted in *Daily Times*, 16 February 1970.

2 H

ent intransigence among Ibo students readmitted to Ibadan University[1] and by Hausa and Middle Belt traders in the North recalling their traditional dislike of Ibo competitiveness. There were also disturbing undertones of the new-found anxiety among Northern intellectuals wondering whether, in the tight arena of employment opportunities for the educated, they might not have fallen out of the 1966 Ibo frying-pan into the 1970 Yoruba (Western State and Kwara) fire. More than one returning Ibo intellectual, too, recorded his view that the nature of the Federal victory—on the battlefield and not by popular mandate, a distinction with echoes of Germany's view of the hated symbol of Versailles—meant that a policy of wait-and-see must precede any final judgement of the value that could be attached to the letter of reinte-gration as it succeeded the genuine spirit of reconciliation.[2] Indeed, a wait-and-see attitude was, in March 1970, a common one; sadly, not everyone was waiting to see the same thing.

Of the economy, too, there is not much to say at this stage beyond emphasizing its remarkable buoyancy. The cost of N£300m.[3] is, of course, not the sort of war bill that can be ignored by any developing country. Nigeria is, however, in a far stronger position than most, the crucial factor being her oil potential. This promises to place her in the top dozen producers of the world, with an output in the mid-1970s of two million barrels a day, earning an annual £200m. in royalties.[4] As regards the process of demobilization, the economic considerations of how large a standing army can be afforded will have added to them the social problem how best to handle the run-down of 200,000 combat-geared troops. Many of them, as I wrote at the time of the national conference on post-war reconstruction held at Ibadan in March 1969,[5] are drawn from that vast reservoir of the partially educated and often unemployed whose ominous discontent frightened observers before the war. Will they gladly relinquish their new-found good and regular pay and free clothes, food, and accommodation? Can the swollen officer cadres, many of whom have earned rapid promotion or been commis-sioned from the ranks, be expected cheerfully to renounce their newly acquired élitist status and the rewards that go with it?[6] For the time being, however, it has been decided there will be no general demobiliza-

---

[1] More cases of this interpreted stiff-neckedness were cited to the author in Nigeria at the time, but they cannot be attributed here. There was also angry local reaction to the insensitive boycotting by Ibo students in the United Kingdom of the party held to welcome their return into the Nigerian Students' Union (*Scotsman*, 23 February 1970).

[2] A popular slogan in the Nigeria of February 1970 became 'Let's be our brothers' keepers'.

[3] The British National Export Council Mission was given the figure of £200m. annually to finance military expenditure—*Nigeria* (B.N.E.C. Report, 1970), p. 6.

[4] Cf. 'Now for the Reconstruction', *The Times* (Business Section), 19 January 1970.

[5] See 'Winning Nigeria's Peace', *West Africa* (1969), pp. 317–18.

[6] A mutiny on these very grounds was, in fact, reported by Colonel Olutoye to have been planned by certain field officers in the Second Division.

tion,[1] though other ranks recruited into the Biafran forces are not to be considered for absorption into the Nigerian army.[2] Former Federal officers who fought on the rebel side are having their cases examined by special military tribunal;[3] they seem unlikely to be reinstated.

Turning to the sensitive political side—the womb, after all, from which the tragedy of 1966 and 1967 was born—few would question that the multi-state structure has come to stay. Few, too, would today argue that it was not overdue or deny that it alone seems to offer the safest insurance against Nigeria's post-Independence history tragically repeating itself. My phrase is advisedly a multi-state, not necessarily twelve-state, structure. If there are to be more units, the present Western State, a focus of political tension throughout the crisis years,[4] looks likely to achieve the ambition held by many Yoruba of dividing into two states; it could even be three. Nor, as local feelings show, is a Yoruba regrouping to involve part of the Mid-West or Kwara State entirely academic. Few believe that the North-East State must retain its present boundaries, despite some sound reasons for doing so. Local anxieties over Tiv dominance in the Benue-Plateau, an odd-man-out attitude towards the Nupe in the North-Western State, or the pace-setting thrust from the southern areas of the North-Central State, are all potential points of friction of which, however parochial, the realist must at least be aware. And, though the Rivers and South-East States are building up a palpable sense of statehood, there is no reason to look on the present Ibo heartland of the East-Central State as an immutable unit. It may well remain so; equally, a division into two, rooted in an Onitsha and a Nnewi base, or a risorgimento link with kith and kin across the Niger have not been ruled out in at least exploratory terms. Clearly there is a limit beyond which the positive act of creating more states is in danger of deteriorating into negative and nihilistic balkanization. At its extreme, to open the Pandora's box too wide might result in direct rule from Lagos through a score or more provincial administrations instead of a dozen state governments—an outcome that, in national terms, need not spell total disappointment or disaster.

In the immediate future, grievances of this administrative nature have their outlet in the fulfilment of General Gowon's promise, made in May 1967 and reaffirmed in October 1969, that any divisions or towns not satisfied with the States in which they were initially grouped would obtain redress once the national emergency was over. This opportunity for adjustment granted—and it could well be postponed in the national

---

[1] Brigadier Hassan Katsina, quoted by Lagos Radio, 6 March. Cf. editorial in *New Nigerian*, 7 March 1970.

[2] General Gowon at a press conference in Lagos, 16 March 1970.

[3] See *Morning Post*, 7 February; *Daily Times*, 16 February; *Daily Sketch*, 19 February 1970.

[4] Cf. Paul Lewis, 'Test for the Federation's Future', *Financial Times*, 29 January 1970.

interest—the point remains that in the absence of another upheaval, the principle of smaller, weaker units has come to stay. Some of the States may indulge in micro-national tendencies, others perhaps seek to restore a golden age of bygone culturo-political hegemony. The facts that some have oil while others do not, that many are land-locked, and that there are at least three times as many administrations to link up, all indicate the need for an intensified economic interdependence rather than a revived politico-economic centrifugalism.

Whether there are twelve, or fifteen, or Awolowo's eighteen states based primarily on linguistic differences,[1] is for the time being of less importance than the indisputable fact that the multi-state structure alone furnishes a built-in warranty to cushion the strains and stresses inherited from what I have elsewhere identified as Nigeria's 'erstwhile politics of competitive ethnicity and involuted loyalties'.[2] Matters of state-centre relationships—of whether it is the 1st or 2nd XI that goes to the Federal bureaucracy and legislature; of the principles of revenue allocation and financial subventions; of integrated national development plans; of state or federal institutions of higher learning; of public service and corporation recruitment and career schedules of service; and of the many intra-statal relations—can only be adumbrated at this stage. It must suffice to say that, because of their integral association with the constitutional pattern, Nigeria may face the same chicken-or-the-egg problem that Ironsi encountered in 1966; which logically and legitimately comes first, constitutional reform or administrative reform? Indeed, unless Lagos begins to impose its authority quickly (in the event more likely at the level of economic control rather than of political confrontation) on the military governments, which have had time to establish themselves as fully-fledged bureaucracies during the three years when Lagos was too busy pursuing the war to lay down guidelines for proper statal relationships, Nigeria could relive the disastrous struggle between the components and the whole that marked the Regional era of 1954–65 and led to its destruction. In the process of returning to barracks, the Ghanaian experience may have lessons of commission or omission for other military regimes intent on handing back the country to a civilian government.

We are left, in March 1970, with the key question of political leadership. Assuming the absence of another civil war (a terrible postscript alluded to more by Nigerians than by outsiders) or a negotiated ethnic reformulation of present international boundaries—neither of which is likely, though both are theoretically possible and have been raised in discussions—there are two alternative procedures. Either the military government remains in power or it hands over to a civilian administration. If the latter, then the alternatives are of how soon or how late, and

[1] *Thoughts on the Nigerian Constitution* (Ibadan, 1966), pp. 181–7.
[2] 'The War of a Thousand Days', *Blackwood's*, March 1970, pp. 193–207.

of whether the handover is total or modified like, e.g., the N.L.C. transitional Presidential Commission troika in Ghana. A combination of Gowon's promises, of the 1966-limitations of the competence of the military in running a complex peacetime administration,[1] of the the current undertones of resentment against the quality of some of the army personnel and their *mores* (General Gowon boldly setting the pace as critic-in-chief[2]), and of the political ebullience that flows in every Nigerian's veins, suggests that at this stage a return to civilian rule is genuinely intended. It is on this premiss, qualified only by the widely shared Nigerian opinion that such a process must not be stampeded by political pressures, that our thumbnail discussion of political leadership is based.[3]

The war threw up no Grant or Lee. What successful leadership there was in the field was dour and dogged rather than daredevil or dazzling, Stonewall Jackson rather than Tecumseh Sherman.[4] The Patton-like, mayfly reputations of Adekunle and Murtala Mohammed were won and lost in a trice; they could be regained with equal speed. No Wellington or Eisenhower has so far emerged to carry his supreme military command into the arena of civil administration; Gowon is *sui generis*, and in any case he never held field command. If any Nigerian officers later play a prominent role in the country's political life, with one or two exceptions they may not be those who were senior commanders in the field. Among the politicians, many of the Old Guard have been swept away; some, like Zanna Bukar Dipcharima, have died since 1966. Though a number of familiar faces were seen among the Leaders of Thought assemblies in 1966 and 1967, especially in the North, there

---

[1] e.g., *The Times*, 5 May 1966.

[2] e.g., his warning delivered to the army in January 1969.

[3] Six months after this book went to press, General Gowon included, as expected, in his speech of 1 October 1970 marking Nigeria's tenth anniversary of independence, the Federal Military Government's new time-table for return to civilian rule. This programme, 'to guarantee peace, stability, and progress', lists nine 'major tasks which the Supreme Military Council must accomplish before the government of the country can be handed over with a full sense of responsibility'. These are:
(i) the reorganization of the armed forces;
(ii) the implementation of the National Development Plan and the repair of the damage and neglect of the war;
(iii) the eradication of corruption in Nigeria's national life;
(iv) the settlement of the question of the creation of more States;
(v) the preparation and adoption of a new Constitution;
(vi) the introduction of a new revenue allocation formula;
(vii) conducting a national population census;
(viii) the organization of genuinely national political parties;
(ix) the organization of elections and installations of popularly elected governments in the States and in the centre.
'The target year,' General Gowon solemnly concluded, 'for completing our political programme and returning the country to normal constitutional government is 1976.'

[4] An American Civil War parallel, in its *post bellum* context, is developed in *West Africa* (1969), p. 1020. Similarities were widely sought during the conflict, e.g., Vol. II, p. 59, and DOCS 218 and 219.

were many new ones too. Today men like Aminu Kano and J. S. Tarka have exchanged their out-group status under the First Republic for a popular and promising role in the future development of political Nigeria. Anthony Enahoro has made an even greater come-back and seems to some the best bet for accommodation with the far North,[1] where Inuwa Wada, Isa Kaita, and Yahaya Gusau remain a force and Maitama Sule continues to appeal to many new Northerners, in so far as it is legitimate if inaccurate to talk in 'Northern' terms. If popularity has any meaning, Asika and a handful of proven senior civil servants are more likely to play a prominent part in the rebirth of political leadership than some of the eleven military governors themselves, although it is to their Cabinets that one may helpfully and hopefully look for the emergence of many of the new political class of Nigeria. Dr. Azikiwe, Chief Awolowo, Sir Kashim Ibrahim, and the Emir of Kano can by no means be said to be men of the past alone; but talk of the emirs in the role of a political party does not impress. Yet, it is an axiom of African political study that those who command popular support to-day may by tomorrow have declined to nobodies. Perhaps just one certainty can be adduced here. It is that when political parties are re-suscitated the Federal Military Government is sure to insist that, eschewing the tragic lesson of Nigerian politics in the 1950s, they cut across statal and other boundaries and be founded on an inclusive, national basis.

Amid such inevitable speculation, one name stands unquestioned. Yakubu Gowon is the only new person to have emerged from the civil war with a reputation that has elevated him to a figure of inter-national stature. The transparent quality of his leadership, its adroit-ness, and its patent humanity have added a new dimension to the make-up of the typology of African Heads of State. He alone reminds one of Lincoln, he alone recalls the political style of the respected Abubakar Tafawa Balewa. Sincerity, magnanimity, and consensus are his political attributes. This is no place for flattery;[2] in any case, too much praise for what appeals to Western eyes as the hallmark of top-flight leadership may in Africa be the kiss of death. Rather let the lessons of history be learned so that none may have to write of Gowon, as was regretfully recorded of even the Lincoln and the Tafawa Balewa régimes, 'One can say that [he] was honest, but not that the country was free from corrup-tion during [his] administration.'[3] Few believe that the ending of the war spells the immediate ending of the ethnic factor as a determinant in the Nigeria of the 1970s. With Gowon at the helm during the months ahead, there is a greatly reduced likelihood of Nigeria's ship of state

[1] Thoughts in the Nigeria of February 1970 were beginning to crystallize on some sort of a far-North, far-South axis, perhaps motivated as much by a desire to keep certain political figures out as to draw others in.

[2] For a panegyric, see Samson Amali's praise-song in *Ibos and their Fellow Nigerians* (Ibadan, 1967), pp. 36–7.   [3] J. G. Randall, *Lincoln* (London, 1948), p. 40.

drifting towards disaster on another razor-edged reef of personal or political acrimony.

It is time for the curtain to come down: no final one, for the vitality of Nigeria makes it inevitable that there are other scenes to be played out, but simply one to signify the end of this act and announce the intermission between Biafra's war and Nigeria's peace. An optimistic 'how' or a pessimistic 'whether' Nigeria will lay what General Allenby once called the gaunt spectre of peace remains a study for another book. At the time of writing, the Federal leadership is riding high on its determination to avert such a bogey. Confounding the gloomiest of her prophets and convincing the staunchest of those who believed in her, Nigeria has survived the perilous 1960s. From the milestone date of 15 January she moves forward to face the challenge of the 1970s with goodwill to all and malice from few. It now remains for Nigeria, bereft of a million and more of her youth, to ensure that among those who have survived to live with the legacy of fratricide nobody shall unfairly gain nor unjustly lose more than his brother. Above all, there must be no more imbalance, no more fear of domination; in Gowon's own words, no more second-class citizenship. For many would feel that this is the real answer to the fundamental question posed at the end of Volume I: 'What was it all about?' Wole Soyinka's revision of the slogan that Nigeria had pursued throughout the war is as valid a watchword as any in the difficult days of reconstruction ahead: 'To keep Nigeria one justice must be done.'

Meanwhile one moral emerges incontrovertibly. As a Nigerian editorial commenting on 'Biafra's' surrender so responsibly reminded its readers: 'All of us must have learned the bitter lesson that in war there are no victors nor vanquished but only losers.'[1] Yet, despite this truism, the Federation could be identified as the winner if Nigeria remembers the dark fratricidal days of 1966–70 not as the 'Biafran War' but as 'the War of National Unity'. Nigeria's war could prove to have been Africa's lesson.

---

[1] *Nigerian Observer*, 13 January 1970. Cf. Asika's paraphrase of the well-known words on the American Civil War in the Afterword to Volume I of his collected speeches: 'As Nigerians, we may all claim a common share in the New Nigeria born out of this war. . . . Let me beseech you to lay aside all rancour, all bitter sectional feeling; and to make your place in the ranks of those who will bring about a consummation devoutly to be wished—a re-united country.'

NIGERIA 1966—1970
AN OUTLINE CALENDAR OF EVENTS

[Reference to the retrospective summaries and historical synopses of the events in the Nigerian civil war that appeared in the overseas press in the immediate aftermath of Biafra's surrender suggests a certain amount of confusion in the chronology of the story. The following framework calendar may be read in conjunction with the text and documentation contained in these two volumes.]

1966

15 Jan.	First Republic overthrown by military coup. Prime Minister, two Regional Premiers, and top army officers assassinated.
16	Acting President hands over power to Major-General Ironsi. Supreme Military Council established.
17	Decree No. 1, suspending constitution, takes effect (not promulgated till March). Major Nzeogwu negotiates conditional surrender with Ironsi.
18	Military Governors appointed: Hassan Katsina (N), Fajuyi (W), Ojukwu (E), Ejoor (MW).
22	Death of Sir Abubakar Tafawa Balewa officially announced.
21 Feb.	Ironsi announces his policy of reform.
25	Dr. Azikiwe returns privately to Nigeria.
7 Mar.	Former leading politicians in the Eastern Region detained.
31	Federal Executive Council enlarged to include the four Military Governors.
14 Apr.	N.A. councils and subordinate local government bodies in the North dissolved.
24 May	Ironsi announces abolition of the Regions and the unification of the civil services in a unitary government set up by Decree No. 34.
28–31	Serious riots in the Northern Group of Provinces.
8 June	Supreme Military Council restates its constitutional position.
26	Tribunal appointed to inquire into the May disturbances in the North.
29 July	Mutiny by Northern troops. Murder of Ironsi and Fajuyi.
31	Brigadier Ogundipe relinquishes his command and leaves Nigeria.

1 Aug. Lt.-Colonel Gowon assumes national leadership.

3   Awolowo and Enahoro released from prison.

4   Okpara released from detention. Gowon's first press conference.

9   Representatives of all Military governors meet in Lagos.

17   Tiv rioters [1964] released from prison.

29   Ojukwu declares a day of national mourning.

31   Gowon signs Decree No 59 to restore federal system of government in Nigeria.

12 Sept. Ad hoc constitutional conference assembles in Lagos.

30   Conference submits interim report.

1 Oct.   Weekend of severe violence and massacre in North following general breakdown of law and order and series of murders in East and North.

24   Constitutional conference resumes in Lagos, without Eastern Delegation.

16 Nov. Constitutional conference adjourned indefinitely.

30   Gowon announces plans for political future of Nigeria, for co-option of civilians to Federal Executive Council, and the principles for creation of new states.

22 Dec. Civilian advisers to the four Military Governors meet in Lagos.

1967

4–5 Jan. Gowon and Military Governors meet at Aburi, Ghana.

14   Federal Government officially announces death of Ironsi.

26   Gowon holds press conference on Aburi meeting.

25 Feb. Ojukwu threatens unilateral action before 31 March.

1 Mar.   Gowon addresses foreign diplomats in private on the situation.

10   Meetings of Supreme Military Council (without Ojukwu) to discuss draft 'Aburi' decree.

12   Meeting of all Law Officers in Benin.

17   Gowon promulgates Decree No. 8 to implement Aburi agreements.

23   Ghanaian mission flies to Enugu.

26   Ojukwu visits Accra. Civilian advisers to the four Military Governors meet in Benin.

30   Supreme Military Council meets, still without Ojukwu.

31   Ojukwu issues Revenue Collection edict.

22 Apr. Lagos replies with sanctions. Meeting of Supreme Military Council, Gowon announces programme for phased return to civilian rule by 1970.

4 May   National Reconciliation Committee sends delegation to Enugu.

17	Gowon announces plans for Nigeria's Military Governors to meet on neutral ground.
20	Gowon accepts recommendations of the National Conciliation Committee.
25	Lagos announces withdrawal of Northern troops from Ibadan and Abeokuta.
27	Gowon abolishes the Regions and replaces them with 12 states. Aburi Decree No. 8 repealed by Decree No. 13. Gowon declares a state of emergency.
30	Ojukwu takes Eastern Region out of the Federation and secedes under the name of the Republic of Biafra.
3 June	Gowon appoints 12 civilians to Executive Council. Ojukwu declares state of emergency in Biafra.
9	Lagos enacts decree establishing an Executive Council in each state.
12	11 civilians appointed Commissioners in Federal Executive Council.
6 July	Fighting breaks out between Federal and Biafran forces.
13	Gowon describes the fighting as a 'police action' in his first wartime press conference.
15	Nsukka captured by Federals.
25	Bonny captured.
9 Aug.	Biafra invades Mid-West and seizes Benin.
12	Awolowo calls on Yoruba to rally round Federal cause.
23	Biafran troops held at Ore, 100 miles from Lagos.
26	Federal Military Government forms a War Cabinet.
2 Sept.	Gowon announces 'total war'.
11	O.A.U. summit meeting at Kinshasa.
20	Okonkwo announces establishment of the Republic of Benin.
21	Benin recaptured by Federal forces.
23	Ojukwu executes four officers convicted of treason.
4 Oct.	Enugu captured by Federal forces.
9	Asaba captured.
14	Federal assault on Onitsha held.
19	Calabar captured.
27	Asika appointed Administrator of the East-Central State.
11 Dec.	Okpara leads Biafran delegation to East Africa.

1968

5 Jan.	Gowon names acceptable Ibo leaders to negotiate 'effective arrangements'.
11 Feb.	Commonwealth Secretariat reported to be exploring ways of solving the conflict.

19	Azikiwe visits East Africa and parts of francophone Africa on behalf of Biafra.
21	Joint appeal to the Federal Military Government by the World Council of Churches.
22	Onitsha finally captured by the Federal troops.
30	Azikiwe's press conference in Paris.
6 Apr.	Abakaliki captured by Federal troops.
13	Tanzania announces diplomatic recognition of Biafra.
21	Afikpo captured.
8 May	Gabon recognizes Biafra.
15	Agenda agreed by Nigerian and Biafran delegates in London for peace talks in Kampala.
	Ivory Coast recognizes Biafra.
19	Port Harcourt captured by Federal troops.
20	Zambia recognizes Biafra.
23	Peace talks open in Kampala.
31	Kampala peace talks broken off.
12 June	Debate in House of Commons on Nigerian arms supplies.
20	Lord Shepherd flies to Nigeria.
6 July	Lord Hunt flies to Nigeria to assess relief needs.
15	O.A.U. sponsors peace talks at Niamey, attended separately by Gowon and Ojukwu.
16	Lagos sends Arikpo to Moscow on a goodwill visit.
30	Adekunle claims to capture 'O.A.U.' towns in two weeks (Owerri, Aba, Umuahia).
1 Aug.	France declares support for Biafra's claim to 'self-determination'.
6	Peace talks open in Addis Ababa, attended by Ojukwu.
15	Gowon announces 'final offensive' to start on 24 August.
25	Federal army launches final offensive.
30	Lagos invites appointment of international observer teams.
4 Sept.	Aba captured by Federal troops.
9	Addis Ababa peace talks broken off.
	General de Gaulle issues statement in support of Biafra.
13	O.A.U. meeting in Algiers.
16	Owerri captured by Federal troops.
25	Lord Shepherd again flies to Lagos.
1 Oct.	Okigwi captured by Federal troops.
31	Indications crystallize that Federal 'final offensive' being held by Biafran troops reinforced by 'French' army supplies.
10 Dec.	Lord Shepherd again flies to Lagos.
13	Lord Brockway and James Griffiths make private visit to Biafra and Lagos.
15	Serious rioting in Western State.

1969

24 Jan.	Federal command launches a new major offensive.
10 Feb.	Azikiwe publicizes 14 point peace plan in Oxford speech.
6 Mar.	Russian warships pay first courtesy visit to Lagos.
13	Debate on Nigeria in House of Commons.
24	Haiti recognizes Biafra.
29	Prime Minister Wilson flies to Nigeria, returns via Addis Ababa.
17 Apr.	O.A.U. Consultative Committee meets in Monrovia.
22	Umuahia captured by Federal troops.
25	Owerri recaptured by Biafran troops.
9 May	Party of Italian oilmen held as hostages by Biafran patrol raiding Kwale.
12	Extensive redeployment of senior Nigerian field commanders announced.
22	Biafran air force resurrected by Count von Rosen.
1 June	Ojukwu issues Ahiara Declaration on the principles of the Biafran revolution.
5	International Red Cross relief plane shot down by Nigerian air force.
14	West African Co-ordinator of I.C.R.C. declared *persona non grata* by Lagos.
23	Federal army mounts another major offensive.
30	Lagos hands over to its own National Rehabilitation Committee co-ordinating role previously exercised by I.C.R.C.
1 July	Renewed disturbances in Western State.
12 Aug.	Gowon flies to Dahomey to discuss I.C.R.C. operations.
17	Azikiwe stops off at Lagos en route for Monrovia.
28	Azikiwe gives press conference in London on behalf of Federal Government.
6 Sept.	O.A.U. summit meeting at Addis Ababa.
13	Federal Government signs new agreement on relief flights with I.C.R.C.
22	More riots in Western State.
1 Oct.	Gowon declares amnesty for detainees.
10	National Rehabilitation Committee reorganized to include members from each state.
20	Biafra rejects I.C.R.C. proposal for daylight flights.
1 Nov.	Ojukwu repeats peace proposals.
16	Federal high command announces launching of another major assault.
8 Dec.	U.K. Under-Secretary of State flies to Lagos.
	World Council of Churches re-examines its role in relief supplies.

9	Lord Carrington visits Biafra and Nigeria.
	Debate in House of Commons on Nigeria.
15	Abortive peace talks, arranged for Addis Ababa.

1970

9 Jan.	Arochuku captured. Owerri falls to Federal troops.
10	Ojukwu flees Biafra after final Cabinet meeting.
12	Uli captured. First and Third Federal Divisions link up at Orlu.
	Effiong announces Biafra's surrender.
	Gowon accepts it.
14	Biafra armistice mission arrives in Lagos.
15	'The dawn of national reconciliation'; Gowon's victory message to the nation.

Bibliography

A Selective Note on Source Material

THE discussion of sources that comprises this bibliographical note is set within the context of a preliminary guide for research colleagues and has been constructed from the experience of the search for verbatim materials acquired in writing the present study. Such an outline bibliography of the Nigerian civil war complements the sources cited in the textual footnotes and identified in the documentary credits throughout both these volumes. It is inevitably and consciously selective and, together with the substance of the book, essentially sets out to be indicative of the location of most of the published materials so far available. In no way is the listing or the commentary below intended to be exhaustive. Because of the deliberately derived nature of this documentary record, published materials exceptionally take precedence over the unpublished in the following notes.

Material has been divided into the following categories: *Pamphlets and official documents; Public relations literature; Newspapers; Books and booklets; Journals, articles and reports;* and *Unpublished materials.*

PAMPHLETS AND OFFICIAL DOCUMENTS

The war of words was often noisier, and on occasions produced more immediately visible results, than the fighting on the front. To most observers it gave the impression of being fought more effectively by the Biafrans than by the Nigerians. If volume of the concurrent printed word is any criterion, the Nigerian war stands to be classified as one of the wordiest civil wars in history. It already shows signs of creating a literature comparable in scale to that generated by its frequent model, the American civil war.

Press releases are dealt with under the Section *Public Relations.* No attempt has been made to identify official publications, as usually understood, separately from propaganda pamphlets. In wartime conditions the line between the two becomes an understandably thin one— witness the Federal Government's document of October 1966, *The Current Nigerian Situation* and its official publication *Nigeria 1966,* or the Biafran Government's *Official Document No. 5 of 1967* and its whole series of *Nigerian Crisis 1966.* For the scholar, the latter may claim to stand in a class of its own within this Section, and because of the absence of complete sets in many university libraries (and the understandably general unavailability of Biafran pamphlets in many Nigerian institutions as at the end of the war), a listing of the full series is catalogued over and above the alphabetical inclusion of the individual titles. This whole section constitutes a major source of material.

Besides the pamphlet war[1]—in which activist organizations, pressure groups, and individual protagonists made their own contribution— waged by the competing Ministries of Information, a number of official reports were published by other governments. Attention may be invited to one major aspect, the legislative debates. In the United Kingdom, the Hansard volumes contain a lengthy record of the half-dozen full-scale debates on the Nigerian situation that the British Parliament indulged in between July 1967 and January 1970: they reflect attention to the affairs of a sovereign country far in excess of the interest ever bestowed by Westminster upon Nigeria in her colonial period. The debates of the legislatures in those anglophone African countries where the constitution had not been suspended also repay attention, for example, Tanzania, Zambia, Uganda, and Sierra Leone. This also applies to the parliamentary debates of a number of non-African countries where the issue became a matter of national concern, e.g., U.S.A., Ireland, Canada, Israel, and the Netherlands as well as in Scandinavia. In the United States of America, too, the Congressional Record contains a number of special reports on relief submitted to the legislature (for instance, the Diggs, Ferguson, and Goodell Reports, all submitted in early 1969), along with the major hearing on the Nigerian/ Biafran relief situation held before the subcommittee on African affairs of the Senate's Committee on Foreign Relations in October 1968.

Notable documentation is to hand in the continuing reports of the international observers teams from October 1968 to January 1970 and in the separate reports from the O.A.U. observer and from the personal representative of the Secretary-General of the United Nations.

Where a pamphlet or report has appeared under signed authorship, it has for ease of reference been placed in the Sections *Books and booklets* or *Journals, articles, and reports* according to its format.

Address by Dr. Nnamdi Azikiwe to 10th Battalion, Biafra Army (Enugu, 1968).[2]

Address by Lt.-Col. C. Odumegwu Ojukwu to the Second Meeting of the Consultative Assembly (Enugu, 1966).

Address by Lt.-Col. C. Odumegwu Ojukwu to the Joint Meeting of Chiefs and Elders and the Consultative Assembly (26 May) (Enugu, 1967).

---

[1] For a protest against their capacity for inciting bad feelings, see the letter in the *New Nigerian*, 8 August 1966.

[2] Though Enugu was captured by the Federal forces in October 1967, many Biafran publications continued to bear a spurious imprint. Similarly, Voice of Biafra broadcasts continued to announce that they were emitting from Enugu.

Address by Lt.-Col. C. Odumegwu Ojukwu to a Joint Meeting of the Consultative Assembly and Council of Chiefs (27 January) (Aba, 1968).

Address to a Joint Meeting of the Consultative Assembly and the Council of Chiefs (30 June) (Enugu, 1968).

Address by Lt.-Col. Odumegwu Ojukwu to the O.A.U. Addis Ababa (August 5) (Owerri, 1968).

The Ad Hoc Conference on the Nigerian Constitution (Enugu, 1966).

Administrative Structure of the South-Eastern State: pre-Akilu proposals (Calabar, 1968).

As We go to Kampala (Enugu, 1968).

Awolowo Tours West (Lagos, 1966).

Background Notes on the Events in the Federal Republic of Nigeria (Washington D.C., 1968).

Background Notes on the Nigerian Crisis (also available in French), (Lagos, 1967).

Biafra: Britain in the Dock (London, 1968).

Biafra Deserves Open World Support (Enugu, 1968).

Biafran Government Statement on Peace-talks with Nigeria (Enugu, 1968).

Birth of New Nigeria (Lagos, 1967).

Blueprint for Nigerian Unity (Lagos, 1967).

Blueprint for Post-War Reconstruction (Lagos, 1967).

British Involvement (Enugu, 1968).

Broadcast to the Nation by Major-General J. T. U. Aguiyi-Ironsi (24 May) (Lagos, 1966).

Budget Speech by Major-General J. T. U. Aguiyi-Ironsi (31 March) (Lagos, 1966).

Budget Statement by Col. M. O. Johnson (Lagos, 1969).

Call to Sacrifice (Ibadan, 1968).

The Case of Biafra (Enugu, 1967).

The Case for Biafra (Enugu, 1967).

The Case for Biafra (First Independence anniversary edition) (Enugu, 1968).

Causes of Instability and Tension in Nigeria (London, 1967).

Challenge of Unity (Lagos, 1967).

Civil Commissioners Join Military Government (Ibadan, 1967).

The Civil War in Nigeria—the Way Out (New York, 1968).

A Clarion Call for Action (Lagos, 1967).

The Collapse of a Rebellion and Prospects of Lasting Peace (also available in French) (Lagos, 1968).

The Collapse of Ojukwu's Rebellion and Prospects for Lasting Peace in Nigeria (Lagos, 1968).

The Coming of Age (also in Hausa, Kanuri, and Fulani) (Maiduguri, 1968).

Commission of Inquiry into the civil disturbances which occurred in certain parts of the Western state of Nigeria in December 1968 ([Ayoola] Ibadan, 1969).

The Concept of Territorial Integrity and the Right of Biafrans to Self-Determination (Enugu, ? 1967).

Conflict in Nigeria [C.I.I.R.] (London, 1968).

Conflict in Nigeria: the British View [C.O.I]. (London, 1969).

Convocation Address by Major-General Yakubu Gowon, Ahmadu Bello University (Lagos and Zaria, 1968).

Creation of States (Kaduna, 1967).

Crisis '66: Eastern Nigeria Viewpoint (Enugu, 1966).

The Current Nigerian Situation: Government Statement (Lagos, 1966).

The Curtain Rises: Lagos State 1968–1969 (Lagos, 1969).

The Dawn of Lasting Peace (Lagos and Washington, 1968).

18 Months of Stewardship (Benin, 1969).

Ending the Fighting (Lagos, 1968).

Enough is Enough (Lagos, 1967).

Exclusive Interview with Lt.-Col. Ojukwu [Britain-Biafra Association] (London, 1968).

Face-to-face with Brigadier Adebayo: 20 posers on the Western State (Ibadan, 1969).

The Fallacy of the Balkanization Theory (Enugu, ? 1967).

Federal Peace Efforts (Lagos, 1968).

First Hundred Days [*Daily Times*] (Lagos, 1966).

Forty-One Questions and Answers on the Mid-Western State (Benin, 1969).

Foreign Meddlers in the Nigerian Crisis (Lagos, 1968).

Four Decades of Useful Life [Brigadier Adebayo] (Ibadan, 1968).

Four Steps to National Stability (Lagos, 1968).

Framework for Settlement: the Federal Case in Kampala (also available in French) (Lagos, 1968).

Guide to the National Military Government (Lagos, 1966).

The Happy Warrior (Ibadan, 1967).

How Nigeria Broke up the Kampala Peacetalks (Enugu, 1968).

I believe in One Nigeria [Azikiwe] (London, 1969).

Ibos in a United Nigeria (Lagos, 1968).

The Ineffectiveness of Guarantees (Umuahia, 1968).

International Press Conference—by Lt.-Col. Odumegwu Ojukwu (28 January) (Enugu, 1968).

Introducing Biafra (Port Harcourt, 1967).

Introducing the North-Western State of Nigeria (Sokoto, 1968).

January 15: Before and After (also available in French) Enugu [1966] 1967.

Jawabi kan manufar gwamnatin jihar Kano [policy statement on Kano State] (Kano, 1968).

Kafa jihohi 12 a Nijeriya shi ne dauwamammen magani [12 State structure] (Apapa, 1969).

La Crise nigérienne—1967 (Lagos, 1967).

Latest Phase of the Nigerian Crisis [Foreign Press brief] (London, 1967).

L'Effondrement d'une rébellion (Lagos, 1968).

The Legality of the Government of Nigeria (Enugu, 1969).

Les Pourparlers de Kampala (Lagos, 1968).

Lieutenant-Colonel Adekunle Fajuyi (Ibadan, 1967).

Living Together (Benin, 1968).

Long Live African Unity (Lagos,1969).

Meeting of the Nigerian Military Leaders held at Peduase Lodge, Aburi, Ghana (Lagos, 1967).

Meeting of the Nigerian Military Leaders held at Aburi, Accra, Ghana (Official Document No. 5 of 1967) (Enugu, 1967).

The Meeting of the Supreme Military Council (Enugu, 1967).

Memoranda Submitted by the Delegations to the Ad Hoc Conference (Lagos, 1967).

Memorandum on Future Association between Biafra and the Rest of the Former Federation of Nigeria (Enugu, 1967).

Memorandum on the Deliberate and Continuous Contraventions of the U.N. Charter on Human Rights by Nigeria and her Practice of Genocide (Enugu, 1968).

Midwest State: One Year after Liberation (Benin, 1968).

Minorities Problem (Enugu, 1967).

Minorities, States and Nigerian Unity (Lagos, 1967).

Nigeria and Biafra: the Parting of the Ways (also available in French) (Enugu, 1967).

Nigeria Answers Questions (Lagos, 1968).

The Nigeria/Biafra Conflict: British Involvement (Enugu, 1968).

Nigeria-Biafra Crisis (Dar es Salaam, 1969).

Nigeria: A Communist Beach-head in Africa (Enugu, 1967).

Nigeria—The Dream Empire of a Rebel? (Lagos, 1968).

Nigéria et Biafra: au carrefour des options (Paris, 1968).

Nigeria: International Observers Team Reports (Lagos and London, 1968-1970):

  Interim report on visit to First Nigerian Division, 2 October 1968

  Interim report on visit to Third Nigerian Division, 15 October 1968

  Interim report on visit to Second Nigerian Division, 25 October 1968

  Report on activities of the representatives of Canada, Poland, Sweden and the U.K. during the period 24 November 1968 to 13 January 1969

  Report on activities of the representatives of Canada, Poland, Sweden and the U.K. during the period 1 May to 27 June 1969

  Final report of the international observers team, 1 October 1969 to 31 January 1970, Lagos, 14 February 1970

Report on circumstances of deaths at Okigwi 8 October 1968

Investigation into allegations of the massacre of civilians at Urua Inyang, 2 November 1968

Report on visit to prisoners of war at Kirikiri and Ikoyi, 1 November 1968

Final report of the first phase from 5 October to 10 December by the O.A.U. observers in Nigeria, Lagos and London, December 1968

First interim report by the representative of the U.N. Secretary-General to Nigeria on humanitarian activities, New York, 9 October 1968

Second interim report . . . New York, 30 October 1968

Third interim report . . . New York, 21 November 1968

Fourth interim report . . . Lagos and London, January 1969

Fifth interim report . . . New York, 21 January 1969

Report by the representative of the Secretary-General to Nigeria on humanitarian activities, New York, 27 January 1970

Report by the representative . . . New York, 4 February 1970

Nigeria Looks Ahead (Lagos, 1968).

Nigeria 1966 (Lagos, 1967).

Nigeria—Stop This War (London, 1968).

Nigeria's Experience Demonstrates Failure of One Man, One Vote Principle (Enugu, 1968).

Nigeria: Talking Points [Transport House] (London, 1968).

Nigeria Welcomes Zik (Lagos, 1969).

Nigerian Crisis [National Union of Nigerian Students] (Lagos, 1968).

Nigerian Crisis 1966 (Enugu/Aba, 1966–7). See note at end of section.

Nigerian Crisis: The Root Cause (Lagos, 1967).

Nigerian Crisis and the Midwest Decision (Benin, 1968).

Nigerian Leadership: A Disgrace to Africa and the World (? Owerri, 1968).

Nigerian Pogrom 1966 (London, 1967).

Nigerian Situation: Facts and Background (Zaria, 1966).

Nigeria's Targets for 1968 (Washington D.C., 1968).

Nigeria's 12-State Structure: The Only Way Out (also in Hausa), Lagos, 1968.

No Genocide (Lagos, 1968).

No Indiscriminate Bombing (Lagos, 1969).

North and Constitutional Developments (Enugu, 1966/Onitsha, 1967).

Notes de base sur la crise nigérienne (Lagos, 1967).

Notes on the Crisis in Nigeria (London, 1968).

Notes on the Management of Refugee Camps by the Biafran Rehabilitation Commission ([Enugu] Geneva, 1968).

Oil-Rich Rivers State (Lagos, 1967).

Ojukwu's Government is the People's Government (Enugu, ? 1968).

Ojukwu's New Type Democracy (Lagos, 1969).

Ojukwu's Rebellion and World Opinion (London, 1968).
Ojukwu's 'Self-Determination': A Reappraisal (Lagos, 1969).
On Aburi We Stand (Enugu, 1967).
100 Days of Liberated Mid-West (Benin, 1968).
Operational Code of Conduct for Nigerian Armed Forces (Lagos, 1967).
The Origins of the Nigerian Crisis of 1966–1967 (Enugu, 1967).
The Other Side of Nigeria's Civil War (Cambridge, Mass., 1969).
Our Case: Rivers (Lagos, 1969).
Our Stand in the War (Ibadan, 1967).
Our Stand—Survival and Unity of the Federation (Benin, 1966).
Peace and Solidarity (Ibadan, 1967).
Peace, Stability and Harmony in Post-War Nigeria (Lagos, 1968).
Pogrom (Enugu, 1966).
Present British Policy in Biafra: A Threat to British Investment Interests (Enugu, 1968).
Problem of Nigerian Unity: The Case of Eastern Nigeria (Aba, 1966).
Proclamation of the Republic of Biafra (Enugu, 1967).
Progress in the Northern States (Zaria, 1967).
Re-absorption of Former Civil Servants and the Appointment of Central-Eastern State Indigenes in the Public Service (Lagos, 1970).
The Real Face of the I.C.R.C. (Lagos, 1969).
The Realities of our Time (Kaduna, 1967).
Rebel Atrocities in South-Eastern State of Nigeria (Calabar, 1968).
Rebuilding the Mid-West (Benin, 1968).
The Recognition of the Republic of Biafra (Enugu, 1968).
Relief Problems in Nigeria (Washington D.C., 1968).
Report of the Tribunal of Inquiry into the Atrocities and Other Inhuman Acts Committed against Persons of Eastern Nigeria Origin in 1966 [Justice G. C. N. Onyiuke *et al.*] (Enugu, 1967).
Report on the O.A.U. Consultative Mission to Nigeria (Lagos, 1967).
The Rivers People's Golden Age (Lagos, 1967).
The Role of Federal Military Government of Nigeria today (Lagos, 1966).
Russians Now Hasten to Grab Nigeria (Enugu, 1967).
Sacrifice for Unity (Lagos, 1969).
Secessionist Régime and the Non-Ibo 'Minorities' in the East of Nigeria (Lagos, 1968).
Second Meeting of the O.A.U. Consultative Committee on Nigeria and the Preliminary Peace Talks in Niamey (Lagos, 1968).
70% Iboland under Federal Control (Lagos, 1969).
Soldier of Honour [General Gowon] (Lagos, 1968).
Sources of Wealth: the Rivers State (Lagos, 1968).
State of the Nation: Address by Lt.-Col. C. Odumegwu Ojukwu (30 May) (Enugu, 1968).
Statement by Chief Enahoro at Addis Ababa Peace Talks (7 August) (London, 1968).

Statement by Major-General Yakubu Gowon at a press conference (5 January) (Lagos, 1968).

Statement by Dr. Okoi Arikpo at the U.N., 11 October 1968 (New York, 1968).

Statements by Tanzania, Gabon, Ivory Coast and Zambia on their Recognition of Biafra (London, 1968).

The Struggle for One Nigeria (Lagos, 1967).

Support for Nigeria Challenges the Basis of Responsible Government (Enugu, 1967).

Survey of Nigeria: the economy and the war [*Financial Times*] (London, 1969).

A Testimony of Faith (Lagos, 1968).

That's False, Nyerere (Lagos, 1969).

Thirty-Nine Accusations Against Nigeria (Enugu, ?1968).

This is the North-Eastern State (Maiduguri, 1968).

A Time for Rededication (Lagos 1969).

Togetherness in Lagos State (Lagos, 1968).

Towards a new Nigeria [Committee of Ten] (Yaba, 1967).

Towards One Nigeria. Nos. 1–4 (No. 3 also available in French) (Lagos, 1967).

The Truth About Tax Riots (Ibadan, 1969).

Understanding the Nigerian Crisis (Benin, 1968).

United Nigeria in Anti-Imperialist Struggle (Lagos, 1968).

United We Stand (Aba, 1967).

Unity in Diversity (Lagos, 1967).

The Verbatim Report of the Proceedings of the Supreme Military Council Meeting (Aburi), (Enugu 1967).

Victory for Unity (Lagos, 1970).

Voices of Unity (Lagos, 1969).

War Chronicle (Kaduna, 1969).

The Way Out of the Civil War in Nigeria (London, 1968).

We are One in Biafra (Enugu, 1967).

Western State 1968: A Review of Achievements (Ibadan, 1969).

Winning the Peace ([Ogbemudia], Benin, 1970).

Yakubu Gowon: A Short Biography (Lagos, 1968).

Yoruba Central State: The Economic Case (London, 1969).

Yoruba Peace Recipes (Ibadan, 1967).

Zik in Lagos (Lagos, 1969).

Nigerian Crisis 1966 [Ministry of Information, Eastern Nigeria].

In all, seven volumes were issued. Published by the Eastern Region Ministry of Information, they were printed variously in Enugu, Aba, and Onitsha. In some cases, the pamphlets ran to a second impression. The colour of the cover may vary from first to second edition. The full set of titles is:

vol. 1. *Crisis '66: Eastern Nigeria Viewpoint*
2. *The Problem of Nigerian Unity*
3. *Pogrom*
4. *The Ad Hoc Conference on the Nigerian Constitution*
5. *The North and Constitutional Developments in Nigeria*
6. *The Meeting of the Supreme Military Council held at Aburi, Ghana*
7. *January 15: Before and After* (also published in a French edition)

PUBLIC RELATIONS LITERATURE

Excluding the materials classified under the Section *Pamphlets and official documents*, three main sources of material are treated here.

First and foremost, there is the material put out by the various Nigerian (and, after May 1967, Biafran) Ministries of Information. This took the form of: (*a*) press releases; (*b*) pamphlets; (*c*) lobbying handouts distributed to foreign delegations at the various peace talks and O.A.U. summit meetings. Items (*b*) and (*c*) have been included elsewhere; only (*a*) is dealt with here.

The press releases issued by the Federal Ministry of Information in Lagos and the four Regional Ministries in Kaduna, Enugu, Ibadan, and Benin retain a high degree of importance for 1966–7. This is in nearly every case the real source attached to the commonplace attribution 'A government spokesman has said that . . .'. No complete set has been located outside Nigeria.

From 1968 on, this home-based source was radically altered. In February that year, the H. Wm. Bernhardt public relations agency of the Markpress News Feature Service in Geneva took on the account of the Biafran Government and, under the title of the Biafran Overseas Press Division, issued over seven hundred press releases in the next two years. Their distribution was wide: for instance, British M.P.s and a number of editors, big-businessmen, and even academics received copies willy-nilly (some more 'willy' than others). In effect, this medium progressively became the Biafran Ministry of Information's link with the influential outside world of newspaper and radio editors.[1] Much of the same news made up the press releases issued from the offices of the Biafran representative in London (I. S. Kogbara) and in New York (Aggrey K. Oji): these then formed the bulk of the news put out by the Britain-Biafra Association in its *Biafra Bulletin*. This Association also published a *Newsletter* at irregular intervals from 1968. Selections of

---

[1] There has been a certain amount of documentation on the Markpress (the latest being in *The Times*, 14 January 1970). The most important is the letter sent out by Mr. H. Wm. Bernhardt to editors on 25 June 1968, in which he set forth his firms's attitude towards the Biafran cause.

these important (as far as the researcher is concerned) releases from Markpress have been published in three volumes of *Press Actions*, covering the periods 2 February–31 December 1968, 1 January–30 June, and 1 July–31 December 1969 respectively. The quality of the information contained in these releases is not at issue here.

The Nigerian Government had nothing to equal this propaganda abroad. In due course it awarded a small contract to a London public relations firm, Galitzine Chant Russell. From 30 July 1968 to 6 October 1969 they published on behalf of the Federal Government 12 issues of a broadsheet, *United Nigeria*. This was complemented by the publication in France of a much needed pro-Federal journal, *Nigéria demain*, but this did not start till as late as October 1969. At the same time an improvement was effected in the content and frequency of press releases issued by Nigeria House, London, although these were never numbered consecutively and their distribution was irregular. Standard Ministry of Information releases continued at home. Nigeria issued a few 'Briefing Notes for the Foreign Press' and Biafra issued an equally limited number of 'World Press Briefing Documents'.

Secondly, there are the radio broadcasts—and 'decree by radio' was a marked feature of government in 1966–7. It is unnecessary to suggest any independence of the Nigerian or Biafran Broadcasting Corporations from their respective governments: unusual in peacetime political Africa, it is unthinkable in any wartime situation. The home and overseas broadcasts, not only of news items (in most cases these were taken uncritically from the Ministry of Information press releases discussed above) but also of original radio talks, are again essential sources for unravelling and understanding governmental thinking on wartime topics. For the researcher outside Nigeria, the archives of the B.B.C. Monitoring Service provide an indispensable tool. Selective as their *Middle East and Africa* series [abbreviated in the footnote references as B.B.C. ME/ . . .] has to be, it does provide an extensive and unparalleled printed record of the spoken word from the various Nigerian radio stations over this period and, from mid-1967, from the Voice of Biafra (never, despite its claim, emitting from Enugu after October 1967) and the new Radio Benin. To a considerable extent, along with its verbatim press coverage, *Africa Research Bulletin* draws on radio reports, thereby reinforcing its deserved reputation as a major research tool. The B.B.C. archives also contain tapes and transcripts of hundreds of reports and interviews by their staff broadcast in such programmes as 'From our own Correspondent', 'The Week in Westminster', and 'The World at One'. Together with the I.T.A. companies and the leading American, French, and German TV companies, the B.B.C. possesses a great footage of telefilm, much of it shot by their cameramen in the battle area. For the hard-hitting radio talks from Lagos, four volumes of selected propaganda talks broadcast between June and September 1967 were published by the Federal Ministry of Information under the title *Towards One Nigeria*; at least one of these volumes is also available in French, *Vers l'unité de Nigéria*. There is no printed collection of the more vitriolic of the talks broadcast over Radio Kaduna and the Voice of Biafra.

Thirdly, there are the press releases and publicity literature put out by the different international relief agencies that became involved in the civil war. Joint Church Aid (International) issued 127 press releases between 24 October 1968 and its final communiqué of 23 January 1970. The International Committee of the Red Cross devoted a large amount of space in its regular press releases to its activities in Nigeria and Biafra. Caritas International published a number of individual reports and annexures on its Biafra relief programme and also issued a few press releases. Caritas, along with such humanitarian organizations as Oxfam and Africa Concern Ltd., also published annual progress and field reports of relevance. By way of illustration, the Caritas *Africa* for January 1969 carried articles on its Biafran airlift: the *Catholic Relief Services* devoted two special issues in 1968 to the Nigeria/Biafra relief operations; the first annual report of Africa Concern Ltd., was entirely given over to details of the implementation of its joint Biafra Famine appeal; *Oxfam's Year*, 1968–9, contained a report on 'The Agony of Nigeria and Biafra'; and a report by the Vice-Chairman of the Save the Children Fund on his first relief team visit to Nigeria was published in March 1969. These are useful sources for any study of the relief operations; moreover, the files contain a mass of information that will one day be of value to the researcher working on the role of the humanitarian agencies in the civil war.

NEWSPAPERS

From the standpoint of 'views behind the news', Nigerian and Biafran newspapers assume high priority among primary sources.

The Federal government-sponsored *Morning Post* (Lagos), the independent *Daily Times* (Lagos), and the important new-look Northern vehicle of public opinion, *New Nigerian* (Kaduna), are the principal national newspapers consulted. The Hausa vernacular *Gaskiya ta fi Kwabo* is of particular interest for 1966; so is the *West African Pilot* for the same period. After the war started, the *Morning Post* assumed further importance as the mouthpiece of Federal thinking, but the *New Nigerian* and *Daily Times* were generally of greater interest. From late 1968 onwards, when the war took a turn for the worse for the Federal side and the political situation in the Western State deteriorated into riots and continuing unrest, the *Nigerian Tribune* (Ibadan) and the *Daily Sketch* (Ibadan) became significant. For the Biafran material, newspapers were hard to come by outside the self-styled 'Republic' after 1967, and from the time they were reduced to publication on school exercise-books in 1968 they have become almost impossible to locate in any serial manner abroad. The *Eastern Outlook, Spotlight, Daily Flash, Daily Standard, The Mirror* and the *Biafran Sun* have been seen only in a spasmodic fashion after 1967.

Granted the significance attaching to this source, it is worth commenting on the availability of Nigerian newspapers to the researcher. The Ibadan University Library has an unequalled (though not complete) holding of Nigerian newspapers. In the U.S.A. certain university libraries have for some time entered subscriptions to the principal newspapers and their holdings are by and large good. In the U.K., on the other hand, the story is a sorry one. Not until August 1967 did the first academic institution (the Centre of West African Studies at Birmingham University) start taking the *New Nigerian.* Thus for the crucial eighteen months from the first *coup d'état* in January 1966, through the July coup and its aftermath, up to the secession of Biafra and the declaration of war there is, to the best of SCOLMA's and the British Museum's knowledge, no complete run of this very important newspaper in Great Britain. The *Morning Post* is not available in any British university, nor the *Daily Times* satisfactorily so. The only subscription copies traced were those of Africa Research Ltd.; but, despite the co-operation of its Director, these could not be considered as being 'kept' in any way acceptable to the researcher since they are heavily mutilated in order to provide the clippings for the organization's *Africa Research Bulletin.* The copies that might have been expected to be available in the Nigerian High Commission were, for internal reasons, in such scattered confusion and neglect in 1966 that they could not be consulted. Thanks to the good offices of the editor of *West Africa,* and to the editor of the *New Nigerian* through his U.K. agency of C. H. G. Nida, I was able to consult most Nigerian newspapers for 1966–7 and have managed to assemble a complete run of the *New Nigerian* for 1966–9. This will be deposited in the Bodleian Library.

It is for this reason of their virtual unavailability to the general researcher in the U.K. that in Volume I considerable prominence has been given to material from Nigerian newspapers. With the improvement of the U.K. holdings position from 1968, it has been possible in Volume II to give greater attention to the standard, and indexed, research tools of the leading British newspapers. In this connection, it may be noted that, besides the expected coverage in *The Times,* the *Guardian,* and the *Daily Telegraph,* and the serious Sunday newspapers, much reportage, editorial, and commentary of a no less important quality is to be found elsewhere, notably (and consistently) in the *Financial Times* and the *Scotsman;* while journalism prizes were awarded to the *Sun* for its reporting from Biafra.[1]

[1] For commentary on the opposing views held by journalists on the same newspaper,

The amount of copy filed has been prodigious. Of particular value to the researcher in this respect are the press cuttings kept (but not mounted, indexed, or filed apart from their loose retention in chronological folders) by Mr. R. J. Townsend, Librarian of the Institute of Commonwealth Studies, Oxford University, and his assistant. This is the most extensive collection yet located. Another major collection, assembled as the happy result of a long tradition of specialist staff, are the clippings of the Press Library of the Royal Institute of International Affairs, Chatham House. To both these institutions any newspaper researcher is likely to echo this writer's enormous debt of gratitude. In Nigeria, the librarian of the Institute of International Affairs, Lagos, Miss Irene Kluzek, has gathered an extensive collection of Nigerian, and some Biafran, clippings.

Because this documentary history is focused on Nigerian participation rather than external observation or commentary, no attempt has been made to comb the non-English speaking press of Western Europe. For those working on the pressurizing influence of public opinion on the governments of say Scandinavia, Switzerland, or France in their attitudes towards the Nigerian civil war, such a source would be of paramount importance. Again, for those engaged in the similarly attractive area of evaluating the attitudes of different African governments towards the argued rights and wrongs of the conflict, much material is at hand in the editorials and correspondence columns of the respective countries—anglophone, francophone, Arabic, and Amharic press. Here only the Tanzanian, Zambian, Sierra Leonean, and, because of the peace talks there, the Ugandan newspapers have been consulted. For the American press, the *New York Times* is *sui generis* in a country where national dailies as they are understood in England do not feature, but an extensive system of syndication offsets part of this and there has been some widely-read reporting by correspondents such as Lloyd Garrison, Albert Friendly, and Stanley Meiser.

Clearly the role of the press in the Biafran affair will attract close attention from scholars. Already researches have started. Morris Davis of the University of Illinois is analysing external communication in the war period; from the University of Ibadan, Ulf Himmelstrand and Bolaji Akinyemi have written papers on the attitudes of the world press, a topic that A. Bamisaiye and W. Ajibola are also working on and on which G. Zeiser of Salzburg University has completed a D.Phil. thesis with special reference to Biafra's *Propagandastrategie*. Objective evaluation of what William Norris of the Times once called 'the farrago of nonsense pumped out by the Biafran radio' and of the same newspaper's description of 'the cautious prevarications issued by the

---

see 'A House Divided: the *Guardian* in the Nigeria/Biafra war', *Peace News*, 21 November 1969. The latter paper devoted a lot of attention to the Biafran case, as did the weekly *Spectator*.

Federal Military Government' remains a challenge to researchers and is likely to feature among doctoral dissertations for some time to come.

In view of the grave inadequacy of Nigerian newspapers in the U.K., particularly for 1966–7, and of the alarming absence of any ordered files of Biafran newspapers from 1968 onwards, the hope may be expressed here that Africanist libraries, scholars, institutions, and associations will give the highest priority to the collection and preservation of such primary material before it is too late. In this connection, the appeal by the Librarian of the Royal Commonwealth Society (the assigned depository for Nigerian materials under the SCOLMA area specialization scheme) published in *The Times* on 26 January 1970, is of peculiar relevance and urgency. For what it is worth, the bulk of the materials on which this book has been based has been offered to this Library.

BOOKS AND BOOKLETS

At the time of writing [March 1970], the following books on the Nigerian civil war have either appeared or are announced as in press. It is noticeable that the preponderance of books published has been heavily in favour of presentation of the Biafran case; some adjustment of this imbalance in the record may be anticipated.

While it would be possible to identify a large number of published studies dealing with the politics of the First Republic as having an untrammelled relevance to the events of January 1966 and beyond, these are works standard enough among Nigerianist scholars to require no repetition here (e.g., Awa, Bretton, Coleman, Dudley, Ezera, Mackintosh, Post, Schwarz (F.A.O.), Sklar, and Whitaker). Thus only those pre-war general studies that have chapters directly describing and interpreting at least the first *coup d'état* have been included.

Pamphlets bearing an author's name are included in this section for ease of reference (see p. 483).

AGUOLO, Christian, *Biafra: the case for independence* (California, 1969).
AMALI, S. O. O., *Ibos and their fellow Nigerians* (Ibadan, 1967).
ANTENELLO, Paola, and others, *Nigeria gegen Biafra?* (Berlin, 1969).
ANYAOGU, Godwin N., *The Philosophy of the Biafran Revolution: a call for African originality* (New York, 1969).
ARIKPO, Okoi, *The Development of Modern Nigeria* (London, 1967).
ARMAND, Captain, *Biafra vaincra* (Paris, 1969).
ARMSTRONG, R. G., *The Issues at Stake—Nigeria 1967* (Ibadan, 1967).
ASANI, Olusola, *The Nigerian War Diary of all Events* (Ibadan, 1968).
ASIKA, Ukpabi, *No Victors, No Vanquished* (Lagos, 1968).
ASUHOA, R. I., *Pourquoi le Biafra?* (Paris, 1969).

ATEMENGUE, Joseph (ed.), *Nigéria : concilier l'inconciliable* (Paris, 1968). *Pourquoi le Nigéria* (Paris, 1968).

AWOLOWO, Obafemi, *Thoughts on Nigerian Constitution* (Ibadan, 1966). *The People's Republic* (Ibadan, 1968). *The Strategy and Tactics of the People's Republic of Nigeria* (London, 1970).

AZIKIWE, Nnamdi, *Peace Proposals for Ending the Nigerian Civil War* (London, 1969). *Military Revolution in Nigeria* (London, 1970). *My Odyssey* (London, 1970).

BIRCH, Geoffrey, and St. GEORGE, Dominic, *Biafra: the Case for Independence* (London, 1968).

BÜHLER, Jean, *Biafra: Tragödie eines begabten volkes* (also in French, under the title *Tuez-les tous!*) (Zurich, 1968).

CARON, G., and De BONNEVILLE, F., *La mort du Biafra* (Paris, 1968).

CHIMA, Alex, *The Future Lies in a Progressive Biafra* (London, 1968).

CHOMÉ, Jules, *Le drame du Nigéria* (Brussels, 1969).

[Christian Council of Nigeria], *Christian Concern in the Nigerian Civil War* (Ibadan, 1969).

COLLIS, R., *Nigeria in Conflict* (London, 1970).

CLARK, J. P., *Casualties* (London, 1970).

CRONJÉ, Suzanne (see Waugh).

DEBRÉ, François, *Biafra an II* (Paris, 1968).

DIAMOND, Stanley (ed.), *Nigeria: Model of a Colonial Failure* (New York, 1967).

EGBUNA, Obi B., *The Murder of Nigeria* (London, 1968).

ENAHORO, Anthony, *Nigeria's Struggle for Survival* (New York, 1967). *A Letter to British M.P.s* (London, 1968).

FIRST, Ruth, *The Barrel of a Gun: the politics of coups d'état in Africa* (London, 1970).

FORSYTH, Frederick, *The Biafra Story* (London, 1969).

GRAHAM-DOUBLAS, Nabo B., *Ojukwu's Rebellion and World Opinion* (Lagos, 1968).

GUTTERIDGE, W. F., *The Military in African Politics* (London, 1969).

HANBURY, H. G., *Biafra: A Challenge to the Conscience of Britain* (London, 1968).

HILTON, Bruce, *Highly Irregular: a Biafran relief story* (New Jersey, 1969).

HONORIN, M., *Les Chemins de la mort* (Paris, 1969).

JAKANDE, L. K., *The Case for a Lagos State* (Lagos, 1966). *Nigerian Revolution: the first coup* (Lagos, 1970).

JUNKER, Helmut, *Hinter den Fronten als Arzt in Biafra* (Würzburg, 1969).

KANO, Aminu, *Politics and Administration in post-war Nigeria* (Lagos, 1968).

KNAPP, George, *Aspects of the Biafran Affair* (London, 1968).

LEE, J. M., *African Armies and Civil Order* (London, 1969).

LETICHE, John M., *The Key Problems of Economic Reconstruction and Development in Nigeria* (Lagos, 1969).

MOCKLER, Anthony, *Mercenaries* (London, 1970).

MOK, Michael, *Biafra Journal* (New York, 1969).

[*Nigerian Opinion*], *Nigeria 1965: Crisis and Criticism* (Ibadan, 1966).

Nigeria 1966: Revolution and Reassessment (Ibadan, 1967).

[Northwestern University] *Problems of Integration and Disintegration in Nigeria* (Evanston, 1967).

NWANKWO, Arthur, and IFEJIKA, Samuel, *The Making of a Nation: Biafra* (London, 1969).

OHONBAMU, Obarogie, *Nigeria: The Army and the People's Cause* (Ibadan, 1966).

Whither Nigeria? (Lagos, 1967).

The Psychology of the Nigerian Revolution (Ilfracombe, 1968).

OJUKWU, Emeka, *The Ahiara Declaration* (Geneva, 1969).

Biafra: vol. i. Selected Speeches
vol. ii. Random Thoughts (New York, 1969).

OKEKE, Godfrey C., *The Biafra-Nigeria War: a human tragedy* (London, 1968).

OKIGBO, Christopher, *Labyrinths and Paths of Thunder* (London, 1970).

OKOH, Gim, *Nigeria: Its Politics and the Civil War* (Washington, 1968).

OKPAKU, J. (ed.), *Nigeria, Dilemma of Nationhood* (New York, 1970).

OTUBUSHIN, Christopher, *The Exodus and the Return of Chief Obafemi Awolowo* (Lagos, 1966).

Nigeria's Hour of Decision (Lagos, 1967).

PANTER-BRICK, S. K. (ed.), *Nigerian Politics and Military Rule: Prelude to Civil War* (London, 1970).

RENARD, Alain, *Biafra: naissance d'une nation?* (Paris, 1969).

SAMUELS, Michael A. (ed.), *The Nigeria-Biafra Conflict* (Washington, 1969).

SCHWARZ, Walter, *Nigeria* (London, 1968).

SEEBURG, G., *Die Wahrheit über Nigeria/Biafra* (Berne, 1970).

SOLODOVNIKOV, Vasily G., *Cessation of the Civil War in Nigeria and the Lessening of Sufferings of the Civil Population* (Moscow, 1969).

SOSNOWSKY, A., *Biafra: proximité de la mort, continuité de la vie* (Paris, 1969).

SOWANDE, Fela, *Come now, Nigeria* (Ibadan, 1968).

SOYINKA, Wole, *Idanre and Other Poems* (London, 1967).

Poems from Prison (London, 1969).

STOKKE, Olav, *Vär Idspolitikens dagsfrågor* (Stockholm, 1969).

STOLPER, Wolfgang F., *Economic Growth and Political Instability in Nigeria: on growing together again* (Ann Arbor, 1968).

SULLIVAN, John R., *Breadless Biafra* (Ohio, 1969).

TODD, D., *Des trous dans le jardin* (Paris, 1969).

TOYO, Eskor, *Nigerian Soldier, Peace and Future* (Ibadan, ?1968).

UWECHUE, Raph, *Reflections on the Nigerian Civil War* (London, 1969).

von ROSEN, Carl Gustav, *La ghetto biafrais tel que je l'ai vu* (translation from the Swedish, *Biafra: Sam jag ser det*) (Paris, 1969).

WOLF, J. and BROVELLI, C., *La guerre des rapaces: la vérité sur la guerre du Biafra* (Paris, 1969).

WAUGH, Auberon, and CRONJÉ, Suzanne, *Biafra: Britain's Shame* (London, 1969).

JOURNALS, ARTICLES, AND REPORTS

The literature under this heading is so extensive as to qualify as un-cataloguable *in toto* save by a team of specialist bibliographers.

In the selective list that follows, no account has been taken of any of the signed journalists' articles appearing in the daily and week-end press of Nigeria, Great Britain, or the United States, however noteworthy such contributions may have been: while many were subjectively off-beam, many were of a highly informed and informative nature. From Fleet Street alone, articles written by such journalists as Bridget Bloom, J. D. F. Jones, Norman Kirkham, Colin Legum, William Norris, John de St. Jorre, and Walter Schwarz invariably commanded respect; the Biafra-inclined group like Winston Churchill, Suzanne Cronjé, Stanley Diamond, Frederick Forsyth, Lloyd Garrison, Michael Leapman, and Conor Cruise O'Brien attracted equal attention. Roy Lewis and Patrick Keatley have also contributed, on a somewhat broader canvas, while later names include those of Michael Wolfers, Brian Silk, and Simon Dring. On the fighting front, local restrictions prevented the campaign from throwing up the customary 'dispatches from our war correspondent'. A number of the articulate, informed, and widely in-touch journalists may be expected to write books on the war.

Nor has any attempt been made to include a systematic listing of all the articles, signed or unsigned, appearing in the weekly press. Among these magazines *West Africa* must, on a number of counts, take pride of place as the outstanding medium of accurate information and authori-tative commentary on day-to-day events; articles by its editorial staff, David Williams and Kaye Whiteman (and earlier by Bridget Bloom), were notable contributions here and in other journals. The *Listener* in-cluded transcriptions of a number of broadcast talks; *The Economist* and the *New Statesman* carried frequent and influential articles; and in the *Spectator* Auberon Waugh so identified himself with the Biafran cause that he chose Biafra as his platform when announcing his in-tention to stand as an independent at the Bridgewater by-election. Across the Atlantic, *Time* and *Newsweek* gave constant coverage in their own vein to the civil war. For Nigeria, no comprehensive index has been attempted, either of articles appearing in the important *Nigerian Opinion* or in *Drum* and *Spear*, all of which contain much source material. Correspondents' exclusive interviews with the *dramatis personae* of the period have not been catalogued. In all cases, where one or two items from the serious weeklies have been included below, they serve simply as a representative reminder of the other articles that the researcher will find in those pages.

Turning from the daily newspapers and weekly magazines to the monthly or quarterly journals, the list below includes articles appearing in most of the standard scholarly Africanist periodicals as well as a number from the less specialized ones. *Africa Report, Venture, Round Table,* and the *World Today* have carried more articles than say the *Journal of Modern African Studies* or *African Affairs* so far. *Africa Confidential* and *Africa Digest* are informative rather than attributable in an index.

Beyond this, notice may be taken of the monthly listing of articles on Nigerian politics (by title where no author appears) prepared for a while in mimeographed form by Angela Baggott of the President Kennedy Library, Institute of Administration, Zaria; of the quarterly checklist *Nigerian Publications* produced by Ibadan University; of the bibliography on the Ibo being prepared by L. Maryagnes and Graham B. Kent of the Communication Center, Michigan State University, which expects to include articles and newspaper reports on the war; of the introductory bibliographic guide *Nigeria and the problem of Biafra, 1967–1968,* and the monthly *Current Bibliography on African Affairs* published by the African Bibliographic Center, Washington D.C.; and of the bibliographies compiled quarterly for *Africa* and *African Affairs* by Ruth Jones, and D. H. Simpson and R. J. Townsend respectively. I am particularly grateful to Bob Townsend of the Institute of Commonwealth Studies and Chris Allen of Nuffield College, Oxford, for drawing my attention to several articles not easily found in this country.

This leaves one kind of journal which could equally well be dealt with under propaganda or public relations literature. However, because of the undisputedly serial nature of these journals, they are mentioned here, though once again they have wittingly not been fully indexed in the bibliography below. Mention has already been made above of the twelve issues of the Federal Government's *United Nigeria*, appearing between 30 July 1968 and 6 October 1969. On the Biafran side, consistently more active, several items are noted. In London, the *African Monthly Review* (issues no. 1 and 2, August 1967; no. 3, September) was superseded by the *African Weekly Review*. This started on 20 October 1967 and continued at more or less regular intervals until no. 30 (two very different issues bear this number), which was dated 22 June 1968. In the United States, a bi-weekly newsletter, *Focus on Biafra*, was started in July 1967. The American Committee for Keeping Biafra

Alive published the first issue of what was planned to be a twice weekly *Current News from and about Biafra* in March 1969, edited by William Rogers in New York. In Ithaca, New York, Dr. Apia E. Okorafor announced the distribution under his management of *The Biafra Review* from January 1970, but events may have overtaken this intention. Also in circulation abroad was the *Biafra Newsletter*, printed and published in Biafra by the Biafran External Publicity Commission for Information. Volume 1 started on 27 October 1967 and closed with issue no. 12, dated 17 May 1968; volume 2 comprised at least 3 numbers, the last being dated 12 July 1968. There is evidence that the appearance of *United Nigeria* knocked the fringe circulation of both the *African Weekly Review* and the *Biafra Newsletter*. The Britain-Biafra Association sponsored an irregularly published newsheet *News from Biafra* in October 1968 and a *Biafra News Bulletin* was edited by Osita Agbim and published in London. At least two issues appeared of *Biafra Time* (Aba, 1968), and of *The Conch* (Paris, 1969), described as 'a Biafran journal of literary and cultural analysis' and edited by S. Anozie. There are also such ephemerides as the Nigerian army First Division's house magazine, the *Flying Horse*, and the Biafran army's magazine the *Leopard*, along with special State magazines like *South-Eastern State Today* and *One Nigeria*, 'a weekly news bulletin for our brothers in the Eastern States'.

Finally, mention may be made of some of the newspapers, magazines, and journals that devoted special issues or supplements to the Nigerian civil war. Apart from the Nigeria-dominated issues of mid-January 1966, June/July 1967, and mid-January 1970, where press copy is considerable, the following special issues are noted:

Administration (Ibadan), April 1968 and July 1969.
Africa Report (Washington), February 1968 and January 1970.
Daily Times (Lagos), April 1966, February 1967, and March 1970.
Federal Nigeria (Washington), April 1966.
Financial Times (London), 4 August 1969.
Help (London), April 1969.
History of the 20th Century, no. 100, 1970.
Jeune Afrique (Algiers), 27 January 1970.
Kroniek van Afrika (Leiden), Winter 1968.
Le nouvel observateur (Paris), 19 January 1970.
Revue française d'études politiques africaines (Paris), January 1970.
Spectator (London), 27 December 1968.
Sunday Times (colour supplement), 9 June 1968 and 1 June 1969.
Tam-tam (Paris), February 1969.
Transition (Kampala), no. 36, 1968.
Venture (London), July 1969.
War Chronicle (Kaduna), no. 1, 1969.

ACHEBE, Chinua, 'Biafra', *Transition* (Kampala), 36, 31–7.
   'The African Writer and the Biafran Cause', *The Conch* (Paris, 1969),
    8–14.
ADEBANJO, A., 'Beyond the Conflict', *Africa Report* (February 1968),
    12–15.
ADLER, Renata, 'Letter from Biafra', *New Yorker* (4 October 1969).
   'How the State Department Watched Biafra Starve', *Ripon Forum*
    (Boston, March 1970).
[Africa Concern] Joint Biafra Famine Appeal: First Annual Report
    (Dublin, 1969).
[Africa Research Group] The Other Side of Nigeria's Civil War (Boston,
    April 1970).
AGEDAN, Horatio, 'Envoys of the Rebel Regime', *Towards One Nigeria*,
    ii, 1–3.
   'Mercenaries and Collaborators', ibid., iii, 27–8.
AITKEN, William, 'On the Airstrip at Uli', *Venture* (July 1969), 13–16.
AJIBOLA, W. A., ' "The Wild, Wild West" ', *Nigerian Opinion* (Nov-
    ember 1969), 488–90.
AKINTUNDE, J. O., 'The Demise of Democracy in the First Republic of
    Nigeria', *Odu* (Ibadan, July 1967), 3–28.
AKINYEMI, O. I. A., 'Nigeria: Vision of Tomorrow', Commonwealth,
    4(1970), 127–36.
ALLAUN, Frank, 'Your Bullet?' *Help* (April 1969), 38–9.
ALEXANDER, H. F., 'The War in Nigeria', supplement to *United
    Nigeria* (9 December 1968).
   'Why the Civil War in Biafra Drags on', *Sunday Telegraph* (11 May
    1969).
ALUKO, S. A., 'Nigeria's Political System: The Future', *The New
    African* (May 1966), 79–81.
ANBER, Paul, 'Modernisation and Political Disintegration: Nigeria and
    the Ibos', *Journal of Modern African Studies* (1967), 163–79.
ANI, Felix M., 'The Assumptions of a Rebel', *Towards one Nigeria*, ii,
    4–6.
   'The Military Campaign to Preserve Nigeria', ibid., ii, 56–8.
   'The O.A.U. and the Nigerian Crisis', ibid., iv, 16–17.
   'The Price of Treachery', ibid., iv, 30–2.
   'The Real Face of the ICRC' (Lagos, 1969).
ANON., 'An Address to the Ibo nation', *Nigerian Opinion* (May 1967),
    207–12.
   'The Agony of Biafra', *Africa and the World* (June 1968), 3–6.
   'Biafra at Bay', *The Tablet* (9 March 1968), 221–2.
   'Biafra Hangs on', *Spotlight on Africa* (New York, November 1967),
    1–2.
   'The Case for Nigeria', *Nigerian Opinion* (August 1967), 230–2.
   'Coroner's Inquest', *Blackwood's Magazine* (March 1970), 277–81.
    2 K

'La faillite de la Fédération du Nigeria', *Revue française d'études politiques africaines* (June 1968), 47–64.

'The Fall of the Fulani Empire', *South Atlantic Quarterly* (Autumn 1968), 591–602.

'Is Biafra Ready for Peace?' *The Economist* (8 November 1969), 31.

'Is There a Basis for Peace in Nigeria?' *Africa and the World* (February 1968), 3–4 and 30–1.

'Lord Lugard is Dead', *Spectator* (27 December 1968), 897.

'Murder by proxy in Biafra', *Spotlight on Africa* (August 1968), 1–2.

'Nigeria's Civil War', *South Atlantic Quarterly*, 2 (1969), 143–51.

'Nigeria: Deadlock', *Commonwealth European and Overseas Review* (1 December 1968), 1–4.

'Nigeria: the War Continues', *Overseas Review* (December 1969), 3–6.

'Nigeria: the War Ends', ibid. (January 1970), 2–3.

'The Nigerian War: Some Assumptions Re-examined', *Africa Report* (February 1968), 20–5.

'Nigeria: What Now?' *Africa and the World* (February 1970), 3–4 and 29.

'Ojukwu has Made his Point', *The Economist* (30 August 1969), 13.

'The Politics of Relief', *Motive Magazine* (New York, February 1970).

'Prospects for Peace: Kampala and After', *Ibadan* (February 1969), 3–5.

'Reflections on the Nigerian Revolution', *South Atlantic Quarterly*, 4 (1966), 421–30.

'Relief Effort: Errors and Lessons', *Venture* (July 1969), 17–22.

'The War so far', *Biafra Time* (Aba, April 1968), 5–9.

'A War We Could Help to Stop', *The Economist* (13 December 1969), 17–18.

'Who Rules Biafra Now?' *New Statesman* (16 January 1970), 65–6.

ARMSTRONG, R. G., 'Nigeria 1965–67: Release from Old Prejudices', *Nigerian Opinion* (March 1967), 171–3.

ASIKA, A. Ukpabi, 'No Reason to Fail', *Drum* (July 1968).

'Why I am a Federalist', *Transition* (Kampala), 36, 39–44, and *Insight* (Lagos, October 1968), 7–14.

ASIODU, P. C., 'Challenge of Post-war Development and Reconstruction', *Management in Nigeria* (January 1970), 127–44.

ATIMOMO, Emiko (variously AFIMOMO and ATIMOKO), 'Political Conflicts and Economic Instability: The Nigerian Case', *Fume* (Benin, 1969), 21–6.

'The Problem of Integration in Post-war Nigeria', ibid., 51–6.

AUSPITZ, Lee, 'Biafra and the Bureaucrats', *Ripon Forum* (Boston, February 1969), 3–9.

AYANDELE, E. A., 'The "Humanitarian" Factor in Nigerian Affairs', *Nigerian Opinion* (November 1968), 357–64; January—May 1969 *passim*.

AYIDA, A. A., 'The Economic Consequences of the Nigerian Civil War', *Management in Nigeria* (March 1970), 171–6.

AZIKIWE, Nnamdi, 'Les Origines de la guerre civile au Nigéria', *Revue française d'études politiques africaines* (January 1970), 44–5.

BAKER, James K., 'The Nigerian Impasse', *African Forum* (Autumn 1966), 103–7.

BAKER, R. K., 'The Emergence of Biafra: Balkanisation or Nation Building?' *Orbis* (1968), 518–33.

BALOGUN, Ola, 'Le Dossier fédéral: la question de l'auto-détermination et la guerre civile au Nigéria', *Revue française d'études politiques africaines* (January 1970), 40–3.

BAPTISTE, F. A., 'Constitutional Conflict in Nigeria: Aburi and After', *World Today* (July 1967), 301–8.

BARRETT, Lindsay, 'The Nigerian Crisis: An Arena for Africa's Struggle for Self-determination', *Negro Digest* (Chicago, October 1969), 10–15.

BISCHMAN, Jim, 'Turmoil Hits Nigerian Campus', *Collage* (Michigan, 16 May 1968).

BLOOM, Bridget, 'The Last Interview', *West Africa* (22 January 1966), 113–14.

BOOTH, Alan, 'The Churches in the Nigerian War', *The Round Table* (April 1970), 121–8.

'Two Levels of Truth: The Case for Nigeria', *Help* (April 1969), 28–30.

BOURJAILLY, Vance, 'An Epitaph for Biafra', *New York Times Magazine* (25 January 1970), 32–3.

BROCKWAY, Fenner, 'Our Nigerian Peace Mission', *New Statesman* (3 January 1969), 7.

BROWN, Neville, 'Why Britain Didn't Stop the Nigerian War', *New Society* (18 July 1968), 85–6.

'Nigeria: The Arms Supply', *Venture* (July 1969), 8–10.

BROWN-PETERSIDE, Gally, 'Why Balewa Died', *Africa Report* (March 1966), 15–17.

BURNS, Tom, 'Nigerian Journey', *The Tablet* (7 and 14 December 1968).

BYRNE, Father Anthony, Extracts from diary, *Caritas Internationalis* (1968), *passim*.

CAROL, Hans, 'The Making of Nigeria's Political Regions', *Journal of Asian and African Studies* (Leiden, July 1968), 271–86.

CERVENKA, Zdenek, 'The O.A.U. and the Nigerian Crisis', in *The Organization of African Unity* (London 1968), 192–224.

CHESHIRE, Leonard, 'Why Peace Mission Failed', *Guardian Weekly* (22 November 1969).

CHICK, John D., 'Nigeria at War', *Current History* (February 1968), 65–71.

'The Nigerian Impasse', ibid. (May 1969), 292.

CHURCHILL, Winston S. [four contributed articles], *The Times* (3–6 March 1969).

CIROMA, Adamu, 'Lord Shepherd, the Communiqué and the Truth', *New Nigerian* (18 December 1968).

COHEN, Robin, 'The Army and Trade Unions in Nigerian Politics', *Civilisations* (1969), 226–30.

CONNETT, Paul, 'Life Behind the Battle', *Spectator* (9 May 1969), 609–10.

CORNEVIN, Robert, 'Ibo et non-Ibo; les chances d'une "nation biafraise"', *Revue de Psychologie des Peuples* (Autumn 1969), 157–67.

CRONJÉ, Suzanne, 'Sovereign State or Rebel Region?' *History of the 20th Century*, 100, 103–8.

'Two Levels of Truth: The Case for Biafra', *Help* (April 1969), 30–2.

D., O., 'The Military and Politics: Some Reflections from the Nigerian Case', *Nigerian Opinion* (October 1967), 245–52.

[*Daily Times*] Aburi Report, Lagos, 1967.

DAUDU, P. C. A., 'Administrative Stocktaking: The Cases of Three "Northern" States', *Administration* (Ibadan, July 1969), 301–12.

DEBRÉ, François, 'Le Conflit nigéro-biafrais: première guerre nationale africaine', *Revue française d'études politiques africaines* (March 1969), 29–47.

DE HEER-BOSWIJK, A. H., 'Eenheid en verdeeldheid in Nigeriaanse dagbladen voor de afscheiding', *Kroniek van Afrika* (Leiden, 1968), 44–64.

DENT, Martin J., 'The Gathering Storm', *History of the 20th Century*, 100, 91–4.

'Confession that set off the Slaughter', *Observer* (9 October 1966).

'Nigeria: The Task of Conflict Resolution', *World Today* (July 1968), 269–80.

'The Military and the Politics: A Study of the Relations between the Army and the Political Process in Nigeria', in K. Kirkwood (ed.), *African Affairs* (St. Antony's Papers), 3 (1969), 113–39.

'Nigeria, Ghana and the World', *Venture* (February 1969), 9–12.

'Nigeria After the War', *The World Today* (March 1970), 103–9.

'The Military and the Politicians', in S. K. Panter-Brick (ed.), *Nigerian Politics and Military Rule: Prelude to the Civil War* (London 1970), 78–93.

DIAMOND, Stanley, 'The Biafran Possibility', *Africa Report* (February 1968), 16–19.

'Who Killed Biafra?' *New York Review of Books* (26 February 1970). (Reprinted in *Kroniek van Afrika*, i, 1970.)

'Un Ethnocide', *Les Temps Modernes* (February 1970), 1194–1206.

'Reflections on the African Revolution: The Point of the Biafran Case', in P. Gutkind (ed.), *The Passing of Tribal Man in Africa* (Leiden, 1970).

DIGGS, Charles C., and BURKE, Herbert J., Report of Special fact-finding mission to Nigeria [Congress Committee Print, 12 March], Washington, 1969.

DIKE, Chijioke, 'Le Biafra et les grandes puissances', *Revue française d'études politiques africaines* (January 1970), 69–78.

DILLON, Wilton, 'Nigeria's Two Revolutions', *Africa Report* (March 1966), 8–14.

DUBULA, Sol, 'Nigeria in Turmoil', *The African Communist*, 36 (1968), 46–56.

DUDLEY, Billy, 'Nigeria Sinks into Chaos', *The Round Table* (January 1967), 42–7.

'Eastern Nigeria goes it Alone', *The Round Table* (July 1967), 319–24.

'Nigeria's Civil War: The Tragedy of the Ibo People', *The Round Table* (January 1968), 28–34.

'Whose Hands are Clean?' *Help* (April 1969), 36–7.

'Failures of the Political Class', *Venture* (July 1969), 25–9.

'Western Nigeria and the Nigerian Crisis', in S. K. Panter-Brick, op. cit., 94–110.

EFFIONG, Noah M., 'The Nigerian Civil War and the Gullibles', *Africa Today* (March 1970), 5–7.

EJINDU, Dennis D., 'Major Nzeogwu Speaks', *Africa and the World* (May 1967), 14–16.

'Report from Inside Biafra', *Africa and the World* (August 1967), 3 and 30–1.

EKPEBU, Lawrence, 'Background to the Nigerian Crisis', *Research Review* (Lagos, 1969), 2, 33–60.

ELIAS, T. O., 'Nigeria under Military Rule', in *Nigeria: The Development of its Laws and Constitution* (London, 1967).

ENAHORO, Peter, 'Why I left Nigeria', *Transition* (Kampala) 36, 27–30.

'Lagos Feels the Strain', *Spectator* (24 January 1969), 101–2.

'A Night of Deep Waters', *Help* (April 1969), 33–5.

'General Gowon Smells Trouble', *Spectator* (30 August 1969), 263–4.

ESSIEN-UDOM, E. U., 'Crisis and Opportunity', *Towards One Nigeria*, i, 23–5.

EZENWA, Vincent, 'Why Nigeria Burst up', *African Monthly Review* (August 1967), 6–9.

EZERA, Kalu, 'The Failure of Nigerian Federalism and Proposed Constitutional Changes', *African Forum* (Summer 1966), 17–30.

FEIT, E., 'Military Coups and Political Development: Some Lessons from Ghana and Nigeria', *World Politics* (January 1968), 179–93.

FERGUSON, C. Clyde, Report of the special co-ordinator for Nigerian relief [Congress, 24 April], Washington, 1969.

FERGUSSON, Sir Bernard, 'Tragic Facts of Nigeria Deny Genocide Story', Supplement to *United Nigeria* (6 January 1969).

'A British Observer's View of the Nigerian war', *The Times* (13 March 1969).

FORSYTH, Frederick, 'Remedies for Biafra', *Illustrated London News* (12 July 1969), 17–19.

'Report from the Battlefront', *Spectator* (20 December 1969), 863–4.

'Will the World Let Biafra Survive?' *Illustrated London News* (3 January 1970).

GANS, Bruno, 'A Biafran Relief Mission', *The Lancet* (20 March 1969), 660–5.

GARRISON, Lloyd, 'Biafra v. Nigeria: the Other Dirty Little War', *New York Times Magazine* (31 March 1968), 36–47 and 50–4.

GAVIN, R. J., 'A Time to Talk', *Nigerian Opinion* (October 1967), 252–4.

'History and Political Integration', *Nigerian Opinion* (December 1967), 274–9 (February 1968), 290–3.

GENTILI, A. M., 'Biafra, un' occasione per ripensare l'Africa', *Il Mulino* (April 1969), 370–81.

GOODELL, C., Report of the Biafra Study Mission [Congressional Record, 25 February], Washington, 1969.

GREEN, R. H. A., 'A Lament for Nigeria', *Mawazo* (Makerere, June 1967), 48–56.

GRUNDY, K. W., 'The Negative Image of Africa's Military', *Review of Politics* (October 1968), 428–39.

GUTTERIDGE, William, 'Military Élites in Ghana and Nigeria', *African Forum* (Summer 1966), 31–41.

HALL, Richard, 'The Biafran War', *History of the 20th Century*, 100, 95–101.

'Biafra's Cowboy Catholics', *Nova* (April 1970), 62–5.

HANNING, Hugh, 'Nigeria: A Lesson of the Arms Race', *World Today* (November 1967), 465–72.

'Lessons from the Arms Race', *Africa Report* (February 1968), 42–7.

'Queensberry Rules', *Help* (April 1969), 39–40.

'Britain's Part in the Nigerian War', *Round Table* (July 1969), 249–54.

'Nigerian Relief: The Lessons of Past Disasters', *The Times* (15 January 1970).

HATCH, John, 'Reuniting Nigeria', *New Statesman* (23 January 1970), 104–5.

'Nigeria, Biafra and Britain', ibid. (9 January 1970), 40–3.

HAWTIN, Guy, 'The Fight against Starvation', *History of the 20th Century*, 100, 109–12.

[*Help*] 'Nigeria/Biafra: The Years Ahead' (London, April 1969).

HOARE, Mike, 'Mercenaries Must Keep Out of Nigeria's Conflict', *The Times* (1 December 1967).

HOLT, George, 'The Value of the Lagos Talks', C.O.I. (April 1969).

HOUPHOUET-BOIGNY, Felix, 'Biafra: A Human Problem, a Human Tragedy', *African Scholar* (Washington, November 1968), 10–13.

HORNBY, R., 'The Search for Peace in Nigeria', *The Round Table* (January 1970), 34–8.

[HUNT, Lord] Nigeria: British Relief Advisory Mission, Cmnd. 3727, 1968.

The Problem of Relief in the Aftermath of the Nigerian Civil War, Cmnd. 4275, 1970.

[Her Majesty's Stationery Office] Nigeria: No. 1: Report of the Observer Team, Cmnd. 3878, 1969.

IGBOZUE, John, 'The Rise and Fall of Ojukwu', *Towards One Nigeria*, ii, 46–9.

'New Leadership in the Central Eastern State', ibid., iv, 5–7.

IJALAYE, D. A., 'Some Legal Implications of the Nigerian Civil War', *Proceedings of the First Annual Conference of the Nigerian Society of International Law* (Lagos, 1969), 70–114.

IKOKU, S. G., 'La Sécession biafraise: mythes et réalités', *Revue française d'études politiques africaines* (January 1970), 56–64.

ILORI, Remi, 'The Remaking of Nigeria', *Towards One Nigeria*, i, 5–6.

JACKSON, Edet, 'Nigeria's Final rejection of Ibo Domination', *Towards One Nigeria*, iii, 51–3.

JOWITT, David, 'The Nigerian Broadcasting Corporation presents "World in Action" ', *African Weekly Review*, ii (November 1967), 8–9.

KEAY, E. A., 'Legal and Constitutional Changes in Nigeria under the Military Government', *Journal of African Law*, 10, 2 (1966), 92–105.

KEMMIS, Patrick, 'Nigerian Experience', *United Nigeria* (9 July 1969).

KIRK-GREENE, A. H. M., 'The Cultural Background to the Nigerian Crisis', *African Affairs*, 262 (1967), 3–11.

'Nigeria Can Survive and still be One Country', *Commonwealth Journal* (February 1967), 3–10 and 49–50.

'The Politics of "Apart-hate" ', *Guardian* (21 June 1968).

'The War of a Thousand Days', *Blackwood's Magazine* (March 1970), 193–207.

'Biafra in Print', *African Affairs*, 275 (1970), 180–3.

KLINGHOFFER, Arthur J., 'Why the Soviets Chose Sides', *Africa Report* (February 1968), 47–9.

KOOYMANS, P. M., 'Biafra en het volkenrecht', *Kroniek van Afrika* (1968), 26–31.

KYLE, Keith, 'The Significance of Biafra', *Listener* (22 January 1970), 103–4.

LEAPMAN, Michael, 'Biafra: The Best Hope for Peace', *New Statesman* (6 December 1968), 775–6.

'The Moral of Biafra's Survival', *New Statesman* (7 March 1969), 317.

'Biafra: At the Front', *Venture* (July 1969), 11–13.

LEGUM, Colin, 'The Massacre of the Proud Ibos', *Observer* (16 October 1966).

'Can Nigeria Escape its Past?' *Africa Report* (November 1966), 19.

'The Tragedy in Nigeria', *Africa Report* (November 1966) 23-4.

'New Hope for Nigeria: the Search for National Unity', *The Round Table* (April 1968), 127–36.

'The Path to Peace', *Help* (April 1969), 41–3.

'The Civil War in Nigeria' (six articles), *Observer*, Foreign News Service (September 1969).

LEWIS, Roy, 'Britain and Biafra', *The Round Table* (July 1970), 241–8.

LINDSAY, Kennedy, 'Biafra and her Minorities', *African Studies Association of the West Indies* (April 1968).

'Traditions and Hunger in Biafra', *The Globe and Mail* (Toronto, 7 October 1968).

'How Biafra Pays for the War', *Venture* (March 1969), 26–8.

'Nigeria's Colonel Adekunle', University of the West Indies reprint (April 1969).

'Guerilla Warfare in Biafra', *Venture* (September 1969), 14–16.

'Can There Be a Peace Settlement in Nigeria?' *Africa Report* (January 1970), 14–15.

'Political Factors in Biafran Relief', *Venture* (February 1970), 7–10.

LLOYD, P. C., 'The Ethnic Background to the Nigerian Crisis', in Panter-Brick, op. cit., 1–13.

LUCKHAM, A. R., 'The Nigerian Military Disintegration or Integration?' ibid., 58–77.

MAFO, Adeola, 'The Ojukwu Phenomenon', *Nigerian Opinion* (March 1967), 173–5.

MANUE, G., 'La Dislocation du Nigéria', *Revue des deux mondes*, 13 (1967), 38–42.

MARIENSTRAS, R., 'Biafra: la fin d'une nation', *Les Temps Modernes* (February 1970), 1169–73.

MARSHALL, Randolph L., 'L'administration en période de crise: l'exemple du Nigéria entre 1966 et 1967', *Bull. Inst. Int. Adm. Pub.* (Paris, October 1968), 77–86.

MARTIN, Kingsley, 'Unsettled State', *New Statesman* (9 August 1968), 172–3.

MATTHEWS, R. O., 'Domestic and Inter-State Conflict in Africa', *International Journal* (Summer 1970), 459-85.

MAYO-SMITH, I., 'A New Administrative Structure for the New States?' *Administration* (Ibadan, April 1968), 169–79.

McKENNA, J. C., 'Elements of a Nigerian Peace', *Foreign Affairs* (July 1969), 668–80.

MEISLER, Stanley, 'The Nigeria Which Is Not at War', *Africa Report* (January 1970), 16–17.

[Mid-West Government] 'Understanding the Nigerian Crisis', *The Economist* (20 July 1968), 82–8.

[MOORE, C. Robert], Nigerian/Biafran relief situation [Hearing Before the U.S. Senate Committee on Foreign Relations. 4 October], Washington, 1968.

MEZU, S. O., 'Du Nigéria oriental à la république du Biafra', *Esprit* (Paris, December 1969), 787–806.

MOREL, Y., 'La Guerre du Nigéria vue par les pays enrichis', *Tam-tam* (Paris, February 1969), 15–23.

MUFFETT, D. J. M., 'The Failure of Mass-élite Communications: Some Problems Confronting the Military Régimes and Civil Services of Nigeria', *South Atlantic Quarterly*, 1 (1968), 125–40.

MURCIER, Alain, 'Pétrole et guerre au Nigéria', *Revue française d'études politiques africaines* (November 1969), 51–60.

MURRAY, D. J., 'Nigeria After Biafra', *Current History* (March 1970), 135–41.

NAGEL, R. and RATHBONE, Richard, 'The O.A.U. at Kinshasa', *World Today* (November 1967), 473–83.

NEWBURY, C. W., 'Military Intervention and Political Change in West Africa', *African Quarterly* (Delhi, October 1967), 215–21.

NIENHAUS, Michael, 'Die Verwaltungsreformen in Nord-nigeria', *Int. Afrikaforum* (Munich, June 1969), 439–40.

NYERERE, Julius, 'Why We Recognised Biafra', *Observer*, 28 April and *Los Angeles Times*, 5 May 1968.

NZEGWU, Henry, 'Hidden Facts about January Coup', *African Monthly Review* (September 1967), 12–13.

'Genocide or War? A Biafran Accuses', *New African*, 51 (1968), 8–9.

OBILADE, A. O., 'Reform of Customary Court Systems in Nigeria under the Military Government', *Journal of African Law* (Spring 1969), 28–44.

O'BRIEN, Conor Cruise, 'Inside Biafra', *Observer* (8 October 1967).

'The Tragedy of Biafra: A Condemned People', *New York Review of Books* (21 December 1967), 14–20.

'A Critical Analysis of the Nigerian Crisis', *Pan–African Journal* (New York), 1, 1(1968), 34–40 [see above entry].

'Biafra: Genocide and Discretion', *Listener* (30 January 1969), 129–31.

'What More Must Biafrans Do?' *Observer* (11 May 1969).

'Biafra Revisited', *New York Review of Books* (22 May 1969), 15–27.

O'CONNELL, James, 'Political Integration: The Nigerian Case', in Arthur Hazlewood (ed.), *African Integration and Disintegration* (1967), 129–84.

'The Anatomy of a Pogrom: An Outline Model with Special Reference to the Ibo in Northern Nigeria', *Peace* (July 1967), 95–100.

'The Scope of the Tragedy', *Africa Report* (February 1968) 8–12.

'The Ibo Massacres and Secession', *Venture* (July 1969), 22–5.

OFONAGORO, Walter, 'The Anglo-Nigerian Harassment of Biafra', *Pan-African Journal* (Spring 1968), 120–4.

OHONBAMU, Obarogie, 'Solving the Nigerian Problems', *Towards One Nigeria*, i, 20–2.

OHAZURIKE, F. I., 'The Economic Causes of Nigeria-Biafra War', *African Weekly Review* (26 January 1968), 13.

OKORO, Innocent, 'The Division and Disintegration of the Nigerian Federation', *African Weekly Review*, 23 December 1967, 10–11; 19 January 1968, 14; 3 February 1968, 6; 30 March 1969, 8–9, 14.

OKERE, T., 'La Fédération du Nigéria: un défi', *Tam-Tam* (February 1969), 27–30.

OKPAKU, Joseph, 'The Writer in Politics: Okigbo, Soyinka and the Nigerian Crisis', *Journal of the New African Literature and the Arts* (Stanford, Autumn 1967), 1–13.

OKUNNU, Femi, 'Legal Implications of Secession', *Towards One Nigeria*, i, 7–9.

OLSEN, C., 'Les Pays scandinaves et le Biafra', *Revue française d'études politiques africaines*, 52 (1970), 77–111.

OLUONUGORUWA, G., 'The Nigerian Crisis', *The Nigerian* (London, 1970), 1, 2-10.

ONWU, Chukwu A., 'Nigeria at the Crossroads', *The New African* (March 1967), 5–6.

ONYIA, E. I., 'Un Drama ignorato: la guerra Nigeria-Biafra', *Il Mulino*, (April 1968), 293–310.

OTEGBEYE, Tunji, 'Nigeria and the National Question', *Peace Freedom, and Socialism* (London, October 1969), 24-6.

OUDES, Bruce, 'The Other Nigerian War', *Africa Report* (February 1970), 15–17.

OYEBOLA, Areoye, 'Ten Years of High Hopes, Errors and Triumphs', *Daily Times*, special end of war supplement (March 1970), 10ff.

PANTER-BRICK, S. K., 'The Right to Self-Determination: Its Application to Nigeria', *International Affairs* (April 1968), 254–66.

'From Military Coup to Civil War', in S. K. Panter-Brick, (ed.), *Nigerian Politics and Military Rule: Prelude to the Civil War*, 14–57, and DAWSON, P. F., 'The Creation of New States in the North', ibid., 128–38.

PARKER, Franklin, 'Biafra and the Nigerian Civil War', *Negro History Bulletin* (December 1969), 7–11.

PASKOV, David, 'White Men in a Black War', three articles in Gemini News Service, March 1970.

PERHAM, Margery, 'The Nigerian Crisis and After', *Listener* (27 January 1966), 121–3.

'Why Biafran Leaders Should Surrender', *The Times* (12 September 1968).

'The War in Nigeria', *Listener* (19 September 1968), 353–5.

'A Letter to General Gowon', *Spectator* (31 January 1969), 132–3.

'Nigeria's Civil War', *Africa Contemporary Record* (ed.), Colin Legum and John Drysdale (1969), 1–12.

Letters and articles reprinted in *Colonial Sequence*, ii (London, 1970), *passim.*

'Reflections on the Nigerian Civil War', *International Affairs* (April 1970), 231–46.

PERSON, Y., 'Genocide et unité nationale: la tragédie du Biafra', *Les Temps Modernes* (December 1968), 1055–71.

POST, K. W. J., 'The Crisis in Nigeria', *World Today* (February 1966), 43–7.

'Revolt in Nigeria', *The Round Table* (July 1966), 269–73.

'Is There a Case for Biafra?' *International Affairs* (January 1968), 26–39.

RAKE, Alan and FARRELL, J. D., 'Nigeria's Economy: No Longer a Model', *Africa Report* (October 1967), 19–22.

REED, David, 'A Nation is Dying!' *Reader's Digest* (March 1969), 75–80. (also published in European edition as 'Must Biafra die?' ibid. (April 1969), 157–62.)

SAIDU, M., 'La crise nigérianne', *Tam-tam* (February 1969), 24–6.

SANDERS, Charles L., 'The War between Blacks that Nobody Cares about', *Jet* (Chicago, 27 July 1967), 14–18.

SANNI, Muhammed, 'The Inhumanity of the Rebel High Command', *Towards One Nigeria*, iii, 17–20.

SARGOS, P., 'Médecin au Biafra', *Esprit* (February 1970), 371-80.

SCHATZ, Sayre P., 'Nigeria: A Look at the Balance Sheet', *Africa Report* (January 1970), 18–21.

SCHNEYDER, P., 'Le Martyre du Biafra', *Esprit* (October 1968), 414–19.

SCHWARZ, Walter, 'Tribalism and Politics in Nigeria', *World Today* (November 1966), 460–7.

'Nigeria and Biafra: The Mythology of Nationalism', *New Society* (19 December 1968), 913–14.

'Civil War in Nigeria', *Venture* (December 1968), 5–6.

'A Troubled People', *Help* (April 1969), 20–7.

'The Next Escalation', *Venture* (July 1969), 5–7.

'Foreign Powers and the Nigerian War,' *Africa Report* (February 1970), 12–14.

[SCOTT, Robert], An appreciation of the Nigerian conflict (verbatim excerpts), *Sunday Telegraph* (9 January 1970).

SEIBEL, H. D., 'Interethnische Beziehungen in Nigeria', *Soziale Welt*, 4 (1967), 331–40.

SENGHOR, Leopold S., 'Si on veut la paix du Nigéria', *Jeune Afrique* (Paris, December 1968), 24–5.

SIMONDS-GOODING, H., 'Biafra's Ghastly Plight', *New Outlook* (May 1968), 31–3.

SIRCAR, Parbarti K., 'The Crisis of Nationhood in Nigeria', *International Studies* (Delhi, January 1969), 245–69.

SKLAR, Richard L., 'Nigerian Politics in Perspective', *Government and Opposition* (July 1967), 524–39.

'Dialog: The United States and the Biafran War', *Africa Report* (November 1969).

SKURNIK, W. A. E., 'Nigeria in Crisis', *Current History* (March 1967).

SMITH, J. H., 'The Creation of State Administrations in the Former Northern Region of Nigeria', *Administration* (Ibadan, April 1968), 121–9.

SMOCK, Audrey C., 'The N.C.N.C. and Ethnic Unions in Biafra', *Journal of Modern African Studies* (January 1969), 21–34.

'The Politics of Relief', *Africa Report* (January 1970), 24–6.

'The Nigerian Misunderstanding', offprint (Munich, 1967).

STEPHAN, Klaus W., 'Der Krieg in Nigeria: seine Hintergründe und seine möglichen Folgen', *Europa-Archiv* (1968), 124–32.

'Der nigerianische Sezessionskrieg: Verlauf der Kämpfe und Verhandlungen', *Europa-Archiv* (1969), 387–98.

TORRES, A., 'La Guerre au Nigéria', *Esprit* (Paris, December 1969), 807–16.

UDOH, E. A., 'The Creation of the Administration for the South-eastern State of Nigeria', *Administration* (Ibadan, April 1968), 140–7.

UGWU, Omeke, 'Why Nigeria bust up', *African Weekly Review* (10 February 1968), 6–7.

UGOKWE, J. B. C., 'The Politics and Consequences of the Nigerian Biafra war', *African Scholar* (August 1968), 17–21.

UNONGU, Paul, 'The Genesis of the Nigerian Civil War', *Nigerian Journal*, 1 (New York, 1 December 1968).

UPHOFF, N. T., and OTTEMOELLER, H., 'After the Nigerian Civil War: With Malice Toward Whom?' *Africa Today* (March 1970), 1–40.

UWECHUE, Raph, 'Des Concessions réciproques pour une paix juste et durable', *Revue française d'études politiques africaines* (January 1970), 24–39.

van der MEULEN, J., 'Biafra en Afrika', *Kroniek van Afrika* (1968), 32–8.

VICKERS, M., 'Competition and Control in Modern Nigeria: Origins of the war with Biafra', *International Journal* (Summer 1970), 603–33.

VINCENT, Stephen, 'Should Biafra Survive?' *Transition* (Kampala, August 1967), 53–7.

WARREN, B., 'Des Causes de la guerre', *Les Temps Modernes* (February 1970), 1174–93.

WAUGH, Auberon, 'Britain and Biafra: The Case for Genocide Examined', *Spectator* (27 December 1968), 906–11.

'New Hope for Biafra?' ibid. (30 May 1969), 711–12.

WELCH, Claude E., 'Soldier and State in Africa', *Journal of Modern African Studies* (November 1967), 305–22.

WEST, Richard, 'Biafra and the Left', *Spectator* (16 May 1969), 644.

WHITEMAN, Kaye, 'The O.A.U. and the Nigerian Issue', *The World Today* (November 1968), 449–53.

'The Passionate Whites', *Venture* (July 1969), 37–9.

'Enugu: The Psychology of Secession', in Panter-Brick, op. cit., 111–27.

WILLIAMS, David, 'Nigeria: Economic Prospects after the War', *Venture* (July 1969), 32–5.

'Nigeria: One or Many?' *African Affairs* (July 1969), 245–9.

'Nigeria's Next Task', *New Society* (22 January 1970), 125–6.

WRIGLEY, C. C., 'Nigeria: The Colonial Imprint', *History of the 20th Century*, 100, 87–9.

'Prospects for the Ibos', *Venture* (July 1969), 29–32.

'Biafra in Print', *African Affairs*, 275 (1970), 183-4.

WYNDHAM, Francis, 'Conversations in Biafra', *Sunday Times*, 27 July 1969.

YANNOPOULOS, T., 'Luttes de classe et guerre nationale au Nigéria', *Rev. française de sci. pol.* (June 1968), 508–23.

ZANZOLO, Albert, 'The National Question and Nigeria', *The African Communist*, 36 (1969), 18–24.

ZUKERMAN, Morris E., 'Nigerian Crisis: Economic Impact on the North', *Journal of Modern African Studies* (April 1970), 38–54.

UNPUBLISHED MATERIALS

This material divides into five parts.

Supplementary to the books already published or advertised (which are listed in the Section *Books*), research leading to a likely book-length publication has risen to a new peak now that the war is finished and a total survey can be made of what might otherwise have been a partial or partisan study. To give some idea of research currently in progress, M. J. Dent's analysis of 'The military and the political process in Nigeria' is now well advanced; A. R. Luckham's doctoral thesis on the Nigerian officer corps is completed; and N. Miners' study of the Nigerian army 1956–1966 is now ready for publication. There have been press announcements that Bridget Bloom of the *Financial Times* and John de St. Jorre of the *Observer* are both writing books on the Nigerian conflict; two other close observers of the Nigerian scene, Billy J. Dudley and James O'Connell, have been mentioned as working on their various writings on Nigeria in crisis. While the war was on Sir Rex Niven was working on a book-length presentation of the Federal case, and there were reports of a study by three or four Nigerian academics designed overduly to correcting the Biafran viewpoint so ceaselessly propounded, but with the cessation of hostilities the argument has been advanced by at least one of the joint authors that the impetus for the project may have run out of steam; knowing the importance of some of the classified material to which they have been given access, one may be allowed to hope that something will emerge from the scheme. By and large, university supervisors have been rightly chary of encouraging graduate students to undertake research towards a thesis on any local aspect of the war while the war was still on; this situation could now alter, depending on the co-operation of the Nigerian Government and the observance of the proprieties in handling an understandably delicate subject. D. J. M. Muffett has almost completed his thesis on the Nigerian *coups d'état* and P. Martens is working on 'les modalités de l'intervention humanitaire dans le cadre du conflit Nigéria-Biafra'. From among the participants, Brigadier Ogundipe is reportedly writing an autobiographical account; there has been in restricted circulation a manuscript by one of the five original plotters, Major Ifeajuna, written in gaol; Count von Rosen is said to have written his memoirs; N. U. Akpan and Okechukwu Mezu, both senior Biafran officials (though the former has returned to Nigeria), are working on their manuscripts, and the odds must be on Ojukwu writing further apologia.

Secondly, the pressure groups and *engagé* individuals have circulated a large number of memoranda giving their interpretations of and solutions to the constitutional crises and the civil war. This authorship has included Nigerian, 'Biafran', and expatriate lecturers, at home and abroad; numerous seminar papers in the U.K. and U.S.A.; former missionaries and administrators, notably those dedicated to the old Eastern Region; activist organizations like the Committee for Peace in Nigeria, Britain-Biafra Association, Co-ordinating Committee for Action on Nigeria/Biafra, and the United Nigeria Group; proliferated *ad bellum* student organizations; and many independent agitation movements for separate states, in Nigeria and overseas. Once more, the volume of this exceptionally fugitive material is daunting; while its quality is no less varied than might be expected, its importance as primary material is often high.

A third group of unpublished material, in the sense that it is not always in print, deserves mention because of its research potential. This is the songs inspired by the war and its political prelude. For instance, there are the poems of Wole Soyinka and Christopher Okigbo, and J. P. Clark's *Casualties*; there are the frequent *wak'ok'in yabon sojoji* appearing in *Gaskiya ta fi Kwabo*, including the final entries in a competition won by Akilu Aliyu and Hassan Idris, and the chauvinistic songs of Dam Maraya Mai Kutigi; there is verse in the *West African Pilot* and more poems in *The Conch* and in the March 1968 issue of *Transition*; there are privately printed poems such as that composed by E. Efiom to signal the liberation of Calabar or by Samson O. Amali in his *Ibos and their fellow Nigerians*; there are Hausa poems collected by A. V. King and Ibrahim Mukoshy; and there is unpublished poetry, often by Nigerians abroad or Biafrans in exile. Related to these songs are those that have been composed for highlife or *juju* music. Notable examples now obtainable as discs include 'To keep Nigeria one' (Ebenezer Obey and his International Bros.) and a series of personal praise-songs such as 'Major General Gowon/Col. Benji Adekunle Special' (Haruna Ishole), 'Lt.-Col. Ojukwu/Major Chukwuma Nzeogwu' (Grant 500), 'Major Boro' (Cardinal Rex Jim Lawson), 'Lt.-Col. Fajuyi' (I. K. Dairo), and the notorious 'Machine-Gun' that was banned in mid-1966. Players like the Ogunde troupe have dramatized the crisis and the war in such plays as 'Keep Nigeria One' and 'Ogun Pari'. There are, too, as political historians are well aware, contributive deductions to be made from cartoons: once again, the Nigerian civil war has inspired a lot of this satirical art in the press at home and especially overseas.

A fourth group of materials for the researcher consists of the private papers of those who were living in or visited Nigeria and Biafra during the four years of constitutional crisis or armed conflict. For example, a surprising number of 'diaries of events' were kept by perceptive residents during that uncertain week-end of mid-January 1966; the personal exchange of letters between Northern students in Nigeria and their 'brothers' or friends outside the country affords an added dimension to a grasp of much of the resentful undercurrent swirling around the North between January and July 1966; no less revealing are letters sent by 'Biafrans' from inside the besieged enclave during the expectant months of 1967–9; and reports sent back from those working in Biafra, the ravished Mid-West, and the liberated areas round Calabar and Port Harcourt, as the tide of war ebbed and sometimes flowed across the lesser towns, make compelling if gruesome reading. Together with such private papers may go the oral history record obtainable from interviews with those who participated in the events of this period. Samples of taped interviews and personal testimony so far recorded have proved exceptionally rewarding, though their use here has perforce and properly been circumscribed by considerations of non-attribution and diplomatic sensitivity at this unripe stage. Developed under local Nigerian aegis, it could furnish a major and unique contribution towards recording the ultimate truth.

The fifth category has no place in this book, and is included in this bibliographical note only as another source for other researchers at another time. It covers the top-secret official papers. None has been quoted in this collection of documents, where the scope of inquiry has been purposely restricted to 'public' documentation (the two one-time classified entries have now been made public, one by a deliberate Biafran leak and the other through the advertised intention of an activist organization to publish it *in toto*—here it is reproduced only in part and with studied anonymity of those who may still be alive). Yet, as those following the Nigerian cause intimately in Europe and the U.S.A. will be aware, during these four years several restricted memoranda and reports have been made available, for one reason or another, in the strictest confidence to selected individuals. To have quoted any of these so revealed would have been a breach of personal trust. With the war behind us, however, researchers will legitimately turn their investigation to such unpublished documents as, for 1966, the Nwokedi report, the inquiry and draft White Paper on the January and July *coups d'état*, or the emirs' letter to Ironsi after the May riots; for 1967, the details of the plot to overthrow Ojukwu in August-September, or the findings of the Biafra Historical Research Centre in Paris; and, for 1968–9, the minutes of the O.A.U. Consultative Committee on Nigeria, or the diplomatic involvement in pressing for peace negotiations. The archives of Nigeria and erstwhile 'Biafra' may, when the time and the research atmosphere are appropriate and inoffensive, put a lot of so far *faute de mieux* 'facts' in a truer perspective. Such is the challenge of historical research.

ADEDEJI, Adebayo, 'Federation, economic planning and plan administration in national reconstruction and development in Nigeria', seminar paper (Ibadan, 1969).

ANON., 'The anatomy of a pogrom: an outline model' (California, 1966).
'The politics of power and unity in Nigeria' (California, 1967).
'Relief politics', memorandum (1968).
'The Biafran illusion', memorandum (1968).

ARIKPO, Okoi, 'The Nigerian situation', address (London, 1968).
'A testimony of faith', address (New York, 1968).

ASIKA, A. Ukpabi, 'Reflections on the political evolution of one Nigeria' (Enugu, 1969).
'Rehabilitation and resettlement', seminar paper (Ibadan, 1969).

AYIDA, A. A., 'Development objectives in national reconstruction and development in Nigeria', seminar paper (Ibadan, 1969).

AZIKIWE, Nnamdi, 'Origins of the Nigerian civil war', address (1969).
'Impression of my visit to Nigeria and Liberia', address (London, 1969).
'Fact-finding mission to Nigeria', address (London, 1969).

BAMGBOYE, Bolaji, 'Unfruitful propaganda', memorandum (California, 1967).

BARRETT, Lindsay, 'A message to black activists on the Nigerian crisis', memorandum (Enugu, 1969).

[Biafran Association in the Americas] 'Biafra still suffers', memorandum (California, 1968).

[BIAGEN] 'Genocide in Nigeria', memorandum (Boston, 1967).

BOOTH-CLIBBORN, S., 'Some reflections on the Nigerian war and the role of the Churches of Britain', memorandum (London, 1969).

BYRNE, Father Anthony, 'History of the relief programme to Biafra', memorandum (New York, 1968).

[Co-ordinating Committee for Action on Nigeria/Biafra] 'The Nigerian civil war: the background and the economic and political consequences', memorandum (London, 1968).

'Military rebellion of 15 January 1966', memorandum (London, 1969).

DINA, I. O., 'Fiscal measures in national reconstruction and development in Nigeria', seminar paper (Ibadan, 1969).

EMEKWUE, E. C., [Background history to Biafra's secession], address (London, 1968).

ENAHORO, Anthony, Speeches delivered to the Commonwealth Club, San Francisco, and the World Affairs Council, Boston (New York, 1969).

FERGUSON, W., 'The Nigerian civil war', memorandum (London, 1968).

GEORGE, H., 'The struggle for states in Eastern Nigeria', memorandum (London, 1968).

GUSAU, Yahaya, Opening address to conference on national reconstruction and development in Nigeria (Ibadan, 1969).

HAWKINS, E. F. C., 'Notes on the Nigerian civil war', address (London, 1968).

HORTON, Robin, 'Eastern Nigeria: five million non-Ibo lives at risk' (letter to editor of *The Times*).

[Ibadan University] Papers prepared for the conference on national reconstruction and development in Nigeria (Ibadan, March 1969).

JAMES, E. S., 'Minorities in Biafra', memorandum (London, 1968).

KENDALL, R. Elliott, 'Background paper on Nigeria', memorandum (London, 1967).

LAST, D. Murray, 'Continuity in bureaucracy and dissent', seminar paper (Zaria, 1969).

[London School of Economics] Papers prepared for a seminar on the Nigeria-Biafra war (London, May-June 1968).

[Michigan State University] Papers prepared for a seminar on the background and prospects of the Nigerian crisis (1967).

MUFFETT, D. J. M., 'The nationalization of tribalism: some problems confronting the military régime in Nigeria', seminar paper (Pittsburg, 1970).

MURRAY, D. J., 'The Western Nigerian civil service through political crises and military coups', seminar paper (London University, 1969).

NDEM, Eyo, 'Tribalism in Biafra: sympton and cures', paper (Owerri (?), 1969).

NIVEN, Sir Rex, Letter addressed to British M.P.s, 26 April 1968.

[Northwestern University] Papers prepared for a seminar on problems of integration and disintegration in Nigeria, March 1967 (Evanston, 1967).

2 L

NWOKOLO, C., 'Biafran refugees: problems of disease', seminar paper (Owerri (?), 1969).

O'CONNELL, James, 'The fragility of stability: the fall of the Nigerian Federal Government 1966', address (Zaria, 1968).
   'Reconciliation and reconstruction in Nigeria', seminar paper (October 1969).

OGUNSHEYE, Ayo, 'Education and manpower [in] national reconstruction and development in Nigeria', seminar paper (Ibadan, 1969).

[Operation Outrage] 'Perspectives: Biafra', conference papers (Washington, 1969).

PARKER, Franklin, 'The Nigerian civil war', address (West Virginia, 1968).

PERKINS, N. C., and JAMES, E. S., 'The Nigeria-Biafra war', memorandum (London, 1969).

SMITH, John, 'The impact of the creation of states upon the public service of Northern Nigeria', seminar paper (London University, 1969).

[University of the West Indies] 'Symposium on Nigeria-Biafra crisis', (Jamaica, 1969).

UNONGO, Paul I., 'American intervention in Nigeria will be resisted', seminar paper (Lagos n.d.).

LIST OF DOCUMENTS